ISBN 978-1-331-68532-6
PIBN 10221224

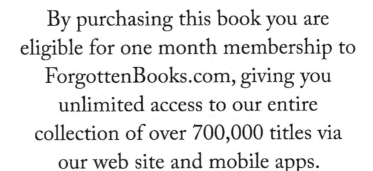

English
Français
Deutsche
Italiano
Español
Português

www.forgottenbooks.com

Mythology Photography **Fiction**
Fishing Christianity **Art** Cooking
Essays Buddhism Freemasonry
Medicine **Biology** Music **Ancient**
Egypt Evolution Carpentry Physics
Dance Geology **Mathematics** Fitness
Shakespeare **Folklore** Yoga Marketing
Confidence Immortality Biographies
Poetry **Psychology** Witchcraft
Electronics Chemistry History **Law**
Accounting **Philosophy** Anthropology
Alchemy Drama Quantum Mechanics
Atheism Sexual Health **Ancient History**
Entrepreneurship Languages Sport
Paleontology Needlework Islam
Metaphysics Investment Archaeology
Parenting Statistics Criminology
Motivational

A STANDARD HISTORY

OF

CHAMPAIGN COUNTY
ILLINOIS

An Authentic Narrative of the Past, with Particular
Attention to the Modern Era in the Commercial,
Industrial, Civic and Social Development.
A Chronicle of the People, with
Family Lineage and Memoirs

J. R. STEWART
Supervising Editor

Assisted by a Board of Advisory Editors

VOLUME I

ILLUSTRATED

PREFACE

Champaign County is representative of all that is best in American life. To the state and the country at large it is chiefly known for its extraordinary agricultural capacity and for the great University which has been planted in its midst, and which has drawn to its territory thousands of able and inspiring men and women. Many have remained to become a part of its higher life, both in intellectual and moral endeavors. Those who know Champaign County more intimately, natives or old-time residents, also appreciate the solidity of its material wealth and the sturdy fiber of its sons and daughters. There is no county in the United States which has been more faithfully cultivated and the richness of whose soil has been conserved in a more intelligent and scientific manner. The grains, the fruits and the live stock of the county, the artificial drainage, and the various auxiliaries to wholesome and prosperous living, are of the same high grade as its men and women.

All that is best in American life, as we find it illustrated in Champaign County, has been set forth in this work, as far as the strength, the industry and the ability of the editor, with the invaluable assistance of his associates, could realize the high and broad aim of the history. In this connection we cannot but refer in sorrow to the death of Judge J. O. Cunningham, who, though feeble in health as the work progressed, freely gave of his time and advice. Had he not been called away, he would have made several special contributions to this history. It has been thought both wise and expedient, therefore, to make generous extracts from the history which he had already published.

In taking farewell of Judge Cunningham and this history of Champaign County, it is appropriate to call special attention to the prospectus which was issued by the company of publication, a paper which was a promise to those interested in the progress of the county, to cover a multitude of topics relating to its past and present activities; and, as the history goes forth, to assert that all the promises therein contained have been fulfilled, as far as is humanly possible.

J. R. STEWART.

TABLE OF CONTENTS

CHAPTER X

INDEX

CHAPTER I

PHYSICAL FEATURES

TIMBER AND PRAIRIE LANDS—BEAUTIFUL AND HISTORIC GROVES—WHY "DEAD MAN'S GROVE"—FORDS—OLD "NEIGHBORHOODS"—ALTITUDE OF CITIES AND VILLAGES—ACTION OF GLACIERS—SOIL—ORIGIN OF THE PRAIRIES—WATER SUPPLY—SWAMP LANDS RECLAIMED—STANDARD CHAMPAIGN COUNTY CEREALS—DAIRY PRODUCTS AND LIVE STOCK—BIRDS AS INSECT DESTROYERS—CEREALS SUPPLANT FRUITS—HISTORY OF HORTICULTURE IN COUNTY—AGRICULTURAL AND HORTICULTURAL SOCIETIES—AGRICULTURAL, HORTICULTURAL AND MECHANICAL ASSOCIATION—THE FARMERS' CLUE AND FAIR ASSOCIATION—CHAMPAIGN COUNTY FARMERS' INSTITUTE—THE FARM BUREAU.

One of the richest, most prosperous and progressive counties in southern Illinois, Champaign also represents a nucleus of mental activity and culture, national, even international, in its scope. The cities of Champaign and Urbana, virtually one municipal community, although separately incorporated, are of unique character in that their prosperity has been largely stimulated by the activities of what has become a great university; that their material growth still is invigorated by its membership; that they are practically without industries, and yet that they thrive and expand and possess a vigorous and developing life seldom enjoyed by a university town, and certainly by no other like municipality in the United States.

Champaign County has two cities and seventeen incorporated villages within its limits. It is divided into twenty-eight townships, is bisected by the fortieth degree of north latitude, which crosses it about four miles south of the courthouse at Urbana, and is about thirty-six miles from north to south and twenty-eight east and west.

1

TIMBER AND PRAIRIE LANDS

There are no bold features of the landscape to be recorded, its contour being usually rolling and pleasing, and particularly conducive to the cultivation of the grains. Champaign is the banner corn county of the United States, and there is no farming community in the country which is more contented or prosperous. The county is situated entirely within what the early French explorers denominated the Grand Prairie of the West, which they described as extending from the headwaters of the Mississippi to the Wabash River. Originally the timber lands extended pretty generally along the courses of the streams, and embraced such groves as Linn, Mink, Sadorus, Hickory, Burr and Cherry. As the pioneers were disinclined to get far away from the timber strips, the more fertile easily cultivated prairie stretches were long neglected; as the wooded lands received the more attention, it is believed that their quantity was not as great as has been supposed and that the old estimate that one-fifth the surface of Champaign County was originally covered with native forests is too high.

There is a distinct watershed running through the western part of the county. The Kaskaskia, emptying into the Mississippi and the Sangamon, flowing into the Illinois, also a part of the system embraced by the Father of Waters, drain the western third, while the Salt Fork of the Vermilion, the Middle Fork of that stream and the Little Vermilion, and the Embarrass, are portions of the Wabash system and drain the remainder of the county. Generally speaking, the Sangamon River and its branches, Wild Cat, Big and Tree Creek, Water Mahomet, Condit, Newcomb, East Bend and Brown townships, and the Kaskaskia, with its tributaries, Scott, Champaign, Tolono, Colfax, Sadorus and Pesotum. The Embarrass rises south of Urbana on the University farm, and drains the southwestern part of Urbana Township, and Philo, Crittenden, Raymond and Ayers townships. North of the Embarrass, the Vermilion system spreads over such eastern townships as South Homer, Sidney, St. Joseph, Ogden, Stanton, Compromise, Rantoul, Kerr and Harwood.

BEAUTIFUL AND HISTORIC GROVES

Before the county was divided into townships, many of the localities outside the villages and other distinct centers of population were designated by groves and fords and other natural features. "The Big Grove," says Judge J. O. Cunningham, "was the large grove of natural timber just north of the city of Urbana, lying partly in Town 19 and partly in Town 20. The Salt Fork was a general term used to designate not only the lands covered by the timber along that stream, but the neighboring farms, from its northern extremity to the point where it leaves the county. Homer and Sidney were villages along the stream and the names were used to specialize neighborhoods. So, 'On the Sangamon' was understood to refer to the neighborhoods on both sides of the river

OLD SUGAR CAMP, SADORUS GROVE

from its headwaters to the Piatt County line. There were the Okaw and the Ambraw settlements, by which was understood the neighborhoods about and in the timber belts along those streams, so far as they lay in this county. Middle Fork (of Salt Fork) was understood to mean the timber sometimes called Sugar Grove in the northeast corner of the county. Sadorus Grove was the designation of the isolated grove of timber at the head of the Kaskaskia River in which Henry Sadorus and his family settled when they came to the county. Bowse's Grove referred to a small grove of natural timber on the east side of the Embarrass River. Linn Grove, as a name, early became attached to the beautiful eminence crowned with trees of Nature's planting in the southwest corner of Sidney Township, which name it yet retains. Lost Grove, at the northwest corner of Ayers Township, is supposed to have received its name from its remoteness from everywhere else. Hickory Grove, in St. Joseph and Ogden townships; Burr Oak Grove, in Ogden; Mink Grove, in Rantoul, and Dead Man's Grove, in St. Joseph Township, like those above named, had a definite meaning and referred to certain localities, though, like some of them, these names now mean nothing, having passed from use. The last name has not been in use for many years, the grove referred to having long been called Corray's, taking its later name from a nearby dweller. It received its first name from the circumstance of finding there the body of a man who had died alone.

WHY "DEAD MAN'S GROVE"

"The tradition is that many years since and before the settlement of the prairies, a band of regulators from an Indiana settlement, having found the trail of a horsethief, who had successfully carried his stolen animal as far as the Tow-Head, overtook the thief there, finding him fast asleep under the shade of this little grove. Without the form of a trial the offender was promptly executed by being hung by the neck to one of the trees until he was dead, where his body was found by the next passerby. This grove of timber was near the road which led from Salt Fork timber westward to Sadorus Grove and the Okaw.

"About one mile north of the village of Philo, in the early times, was a tuft or small patch of timber and brush—along the margin of a small pond, which protected it from the annual prairie fires—of less than one acre, which, from the earliest settlement of the country, was a noted landmark for travelers, and which was known far and wide as the Tow-Head from its supposed resemblance to something bearing that name. Its position upon a very high piece of prairie made it visible for many miles around. It has long since yielded to the march of improvement, and its foster guardian, the pond, has likewise given way to the same enemy of the picturesque, and now yields each year fine crops of corn.

"A little distance north of the village of Ivesdale is a grove of small timber, formerly known as Cherry Grove by early settlers. Its name, perhaps now obsolete, was probably derived from the kind of timber growing in the grove, or most prevalent, as was the case with other groves heretofore named. These groves and belts of timber served the early comers here as landmarks, so conspicuous were they on the horizon, and, in the absence of trails to guide the traveler, they served an excellent purpose as such.

"Adkins Point referred to a point of timber reaching to the north from the northwest corner of the Big Grove in Somer Township, and got its name from the residence there of the family of Lewis Adkins.

"Nox's Point meant the locality of the village of Sidney, and received its name from the first settler in the point made by the Salt Fork timber in its eastward trend. The settler was William Nox.

"Pancake's Point called to mind a point of timber reaching westward from the Sangamon timber in Newcomb Township, and owes its name to Jesse W. Pancake, who lived there more than fifty years since.

"There was Sodom, a neighborhood above the village of Fisher, which was afterward used as the name of a postoffice established there. Why the location got this name so suggestive of evil reputation is not known.

"So, Wantwood was applied to a treeless expanse of prairie reaching north from the head of Sangamon timber, the early settler knew not how far.

FORDS

"There were also fords across the streams where early roads, in default of bridges, led the traveler through deep waters. Of these there were Strong's Ford and Prather's Ford, both across the Salt Fork, one about a mile north and the other the same distance south of the village of St. Joseph. The former was where the iron bridge on the State road spans the stream, and was later called Kelley's Ford. Both fords received their distinctive names from nearby dwellers A ferry was maintained by Joseph T. Kelley at the former. The latter, or Prather's Ford, was at the crossing of the Salt Fork by the Danville and Fort Clark road.

"On the Sangamon were two well known fords with distinctive names. One at the village of Mahomet (or Middletown, as the village was known fifty years since) was called Bryan's Ford, from John Bryan, a contiguous land-owner, who maintained a ferry there. The iron bridge a few rods away has, for many years, furnished a better means of crossing the stream. The other, of historic fame, was known as Newcom's Ford, from Ethan Newcom, a pioneer who came to the county in the early '30s. It was at the crossing of the Sangamon River by the Danville and Fort Clark road, and, besides being a ford of the river, was a place where travelers camped in great numbers. It was near the line which divides Township 21 and 22, Range 8, and in later years it gave the name of Newcomb to another township, although the final "b" of the name, as thus used, is in addition to the spelling in use by the owner. Mr. Newcom spelled his name 'Ethan Newcom' where signed to a deed.

OLD "NEIGHBORHOODS"

"Then there were neighborhoods in the county which, from some peculiarity or other in their early settlement, took upon themselves peculiar names, most of which have been forgotten or fallen into disuse. Among these may be recalled the Kentucky Settlement, now in Rantoul Township. This was on account of the coming there prior to 1860 of B. C. Bradley and many other thrifty farmers from Kentucky. The settlement was a compact gathering of good families upon a hitherto unbroken prairie, so arranged that the social and school advantages enjoyed elsewhere were not suspended. In like manner the location about the ridge in Philo Township, which divides the waters of the Salt Fork from those flowing into the Ambraw (Embarrass), about 1856 became the home of a colony from Massachusetts and other Eastern states, among whom may be named E. W. Parker and his brother, G. W. Parker, Lucius, David and T. C. Eaton, and others of New England origin—which gave the neighborhood the name Yankee Ridge, which it bears to this day. So, the gathering upon the flat lands bordering the headwaters of the Salt Fork in Compromise Township, of a large number of Germans, who distinguished themselves as good farmers and good citizens, has given their neighborhood the name of Dutch Flats, which it is likely to maintain."

Thus have the water courses of Champaign County had a large share in fixing local nomenclature upon many sections which have not been officially named either by the postoffice department of the general Government or the Legislature of the State.

ALTITUDES OF CITIES AND VILLAGES

The topography of the county has been thoroughly delineated by the State Geological and the United States Geological surveys, as well as by experts connected with the University of Illinois, especially by Prof. C. W. Rolfe of the Illinois State Laboratory of Natural History. Based upon such authorities, it is found that the altitudes of the incorporated cities and villages in the county are as follows: Ludlow, 770; Champaign, 741; Rantoul, 756; Urbana, 718; Philo, 737; Tolono, 733; Thomasboro, 731; Fisher, 721; Pesotum, 715; Mahomet, 709; Sadorus, 691; Ivesdale, 679; Longview, 678; St. Joseph, 676; Sidney, 673; Homer, 661.

ACTION OF GLACIERS

A consideration of these elevations and others in other portions of the county indicates a general inclination of the land surface from northwest to southeast, although, as stated, there is a distinct watershed which divides the Wabash system from that of the Illinois and the Mississippi. This general trend was determined by glacial action, the great ice sheet moving down from the north, scouring off the land, its successive onward stages being indicated by ridges or, geologically speaking, moraines, which rise above the surface of the surrounding country to heights varying from twenty to a hundred feet. The glaciers which moved across what is now Champaign County were portions of what have become known as the Bloomington and the Champaign systems, the former, which plowed across the northeast corner, being bold and aggressive in character and leaving behind ridges from fifty to a hundred feet high. The streams have cut these into knolls or hills, creating the most considerable heights in the county—near Ludlow, from 820 to 830 feet above sea level; near Dillsburg, from 810 to 820 feet, and just east of Gifford and Flatville, 820 feet. The second moraine enters from Piatt County in a series of ridges which join the Bloomington system when well within Champaign County. The main ridge enters near Mahomet, is broken by the Sangamon River, its heights ranging from 750 to 670 feet, and after reaching out into the central parts of the county, breaks into three distinct ridges and passes over into Vermilion County. At Rising, where an altitude of 810 feet is reached, the large branch which connects the Bloomington and Champaign systems, is given off to the northeast. These moraines are the watersheds of the Wabash and Mississippi basins.

No other single agent has been so potent in the modification of the surface of the earth as have glaciers and ice sheets; and this statement applies with particular significance to central Illinois and Champaign County. When it is remembered that these ice sheets were hundreds and possibly thousands of feet thick, and were hundreds of miles in width and length, some adequate idea may be formed of their power to plow up and completely change the surface structure of the earth.

The debris which they brought from the Laurential mountains of Canada was distributed over Illinois generally, greatly to the enrichment of its soils. This material, which eventually became the wonderfully productive soil in all the glacial areas, was transported in several ways. Much of it was pushed along mechanically in front of the advancing ice-sheet, so that when the forward movement began to be retarded, this material was left scattered along the edges of the advancing body. Much material was carried along under the ice-sheet and was ground and distributed over the glacial area. Other material, again, was carried to the surface of the ice-sheet, and often deeply imbedded in it. When the movement was finally checked, the superimposed material becoming heated by the sun, worked its way through the ice and rested on the ground, the whole body of ice eventually melting.

Vast quantities of material were also carried by the streams which continually flowed from the melting ice. Much of the detritus was left on the broad, flat prairies, but much was carried into the streams which overflowed their banks, where it was deposited as alluvium.

The material which these glaciers brought into the State of Illinois, as the basis of her vast material wealth, goes under the general name of Drift. Its composition varies, but its main constituents are clay, sand and boulders. This drift is sometimes found stratified, but more generally is without definite layer formation.

Without going into details as to authorities, it may be stated that, in North America, there seems to have been three great centers of glacial movement—one known as the Labrador ice sheet; a second called the Kewatin ice sheet, and the third, the Cordilleran ice sheet. The first sheet had its center of movement near the central point of the peninsula of Labrador; the second, near the western shore of Hudson Bay, and the third moved from the Canadian Rockies.

The ice sheet, the center of which rested on the Labrador peninsula, moved northeast, northwest, south and southwest, the movement in the direction last named starting a large section of the vast body toward what is now the State of Illinois. The Labradorean sheet reached its extreme southern limit in southern Illinois, some 1,600 miles from the point of departure. The advancing front in Illinois took the form of a gigantic crescent, and its extreme southern reach, according to the most recent geological surveys, may be traced from Randolph County southeast, through the southern side of Jackson eastward through southern Williamson, east and northeast through southeastern Saline, northeastward to the Wabash through the northwest corner of Gallatin and southeastern White. That line also marks the southern limit of the prairie areas, and is coincident with the northern foothills of the Ozark Mountains, which trend east and west across the State through Union, Johnson, Pope and Hardin.

According to the more recent investigations, Illinois was subject to at least four ice-sheet invasions. In the order of time, these were (a) the Illinois sheet, which covered nearly the entire State; (b) the Iowan sheet, moving over the area bounded by the Rock River on the west, Wisconsin on the north, Lake Michigan on the east, and on the south by a parallel extended from the southerly bend of that body of water; (c) the Earlier Wisconsin, covering the northeastern fourth of Illinois, and (d) the Later Wisconsin, plowing out the western borders of Lake Michigan and extending some fifty or sixty miles westward. The Illinois ice-sheet is the one, obviously, which included Champaign County in its operations. The details of its work, in this more limited area, have already been given.

Soil

The surface of Champaign County, as a general thing, is composed of black prairie soil, from one to five feet in thickness. This prairie soil is underlaid by a yellow clay subsoil. Below this clay subsoil occur alternate beds of clay, gravel and quicksand of the drift formation to the depth of from 120 to 250 feet, below which there are other alternations of shale, slate, soapstone and limestone, with one or more beds of coal.

Much of the loose materials found above the rocky beds of Champaign County are composed of what is called "drift," which consists of clay, sand, rounded and water-worn masses of granite and porphyry, together with the red sandstone of the Lake Superior region, all of which have been swept southward from their native beds with a force sufficient to obliterate the angles from the hardest fragments; and these have been rudely intermingled with the surface materials of the formations over which they were transported. This drift, as it was deposited, filled up the beds of the ancient valleys and covered much of the remaining surface to a greater or lesser depth. The transportation of this "drift" for such a long distance is probably due to the slow but powerful movement of immense glaciers from the frozen regions of the north, in the same manner as the glaciers of the mountain regions of Europe are now slowly melting and sliding and dragging with them huge masses of mountain rock, wrenched off with Titantic force by the departing ice.

Origin of the Prairies

Nothing in the New World was more interesting to the European than the broad prairies between the Mississippi and the Ohio. In 1817 Governor Edward Coles, then a young man returning from a diplomatic mission to Russia, stopped in France and England. He was a Virginian, but had traveled through the West and had himself been greatly charmed by the rich grandeur of the prairie lands. The French and the English never tired of his graphic descriptions of them, and among his charmed auditors was Morris Birkbeck, a prosperous tenant farmer of England, who was thereby induced to come to America and settle in Edwards County, southeastern Illinois. In later years Dickens went into raptures over his first sight of a "western" prairie, revealing his sentiments in his "Notes on America."

·When the first French explorers reached the Mississippi Valley, they were amazed at the great sweep of timberless areas, although they originally applied their word, "prairie," to describe the flat bottom lands of the river valleys. Nor is the application of the word to such tracts inappropriate, as it has been shown by geologists that the formation of the prairies of central Illinois is identical in character with the formation of the bottom lands along the Mississippi, the Ohio and other smaller rivers.

When the first settlers came to the Illinois country they are said to have found about one-fourth of it timbered and the remainder timberless, or prairie lands. They designated the largest timberless area the Grand Prairie, and it was virtually limited by the great watershed which divides the basins of the Mississippi and the Ohio. It extends from the northwestern part of Jackson County through Perry, part of Williamson, Washington, Jefferson, Marion, Fayette, Effingham, Coles, Champaign and Iroquois, crosses the Kankakee River and extends to the southern end of Lake Michigan. Champaign County is therefore almost in the center of the Grand Prairie of Illinois.

The origin of the prairies has been a debatable question for many decades. Three general theories have been advanced to account for their existence at the time of the coming of the earliest settlers into the limits of Illinois. One explanation is that the great prairie fires which annually swept over the Grand Prairie effectually kept the trees from making any headway. But there are two scientific explanations which seem to go more to the bedrock of the matter.

Says a late writer on this subject: "Professor Whitney holds to the theory that the treeless prairies have had their origin in the character of the original deposits, or soil formation. He does not deny, in fact admits, the submersion of all prairie lands formerly as lakes or swamps; but he holds that while the lands were so submerged there was deposited a very fine soil, which he attributes, in part, to the underlying rocks, and in part to the accumulation in the bottom of immense lakes, of a sediment of almost impalpable fineness. This soil in its physical, and probably in its chemical, composition prevents the trees from naturally getting a foothold in the prairies.

"Professor Lesquereux holds to the theory simply stated that all areas properly called prairies were formed by the redemption of what was once lake regions and later swamp territory. He points out that trees grow abundantly in moving water, but that when water is dammed the trees always die. His theory is that standing water kills trees by preventing the oxygen of the air from reaching their roots. He further shows that the nature of the soil in redeemed lake regions is such that without the help of man trees will not grow in it. But he further shows that by proper planting the entire prairie area may be covered with forest trees.

"As rich as was the soil of our prairies, the first emigrants seldom settled far out on these treeless tracts. Most of the early comers were from the timbered regions of the older states and felt they could not make a living very far from the woods. Coal had not come into use and wood was the universal fuel. There was a wealth of mast in the timber upon which hogs could live a large part of the year. Again, our forefathers had been used to the springs of New England, Kentucky, Tennessee and Virginia, and they did not think they could live where they could not have access to springs. The early comer, back in the '30s, therefore, rode over the prairies of central Illinois, and then entered 160 in the timber, where he cleared his land and opened his farm."

After a careful investigation of the subject, some of the most eminent geologists of Illinois have arrived at the conclusion that the extensive prairies of the West, with their peculiar soil, have been formed in the past pretty much as prairies on a smaller scale are being formed at the present day. The black, friable mold, of which the prairie soil is composed, is due to the growth and decay of successive crops of coarse swamp grasses, submerged in spring, and growing luxuriantly in summer, only to be submerged again, and returned, in a rotten condition, to the annual accumulations before made. It is not difficult to believe that in a few hundred years, more or less, as the great sheet of water that once covered the entire valley of the Mississippi and tributaries, gradually receded to the present water courses, and left the prairies in the condition of alternate wet and dry swails, that a black, mucky soil was produced to the depth now found upon the prairies. In process of time, by more complete recession of the waters, the surface of the prairies became dry, and adapted to the wants of animals and men. The fact of there being no trees on the prairies is accounted for on the ground that such a condition of the soil as is here described is not favorable to their growth, as may be often noticed in the marshy spots of timbered regions.

Water Supply

The splendid water supply of Champaign County is accounted for by the presence of the glacial drift, which forms the striking feature of the surface geology of Champaign County. Miss DeEtte Rolfe, who has written much and well on this subject, explains the matter thus: "Irregularly interspersed in this drift are long strips and beds of gravel which have their outcrops on the flanks of the moraines. These, being surrounded by the dense clay, form pockets which become reservoirs for the storage of water. It is on these reservoirs that the county must rely for its water supply. The water obtained from them is of good quality, except in the somewhat rare instances where the outcrop of the gravel bed is so situated as to be exposed to contaminating influences, or in those cases, which should never occur, where the wells themselves are contaminated. As these gravel beds are distributed through the drift at different depths, the well, even on adjoining lots, may vary in depth. The quantity of water furnished by a well is governed by the size of the gravel bed from which it draws its supply. The deep wells of the county generally draw from the beds deposited between the two sheets of drift; their difference in depth depends on the irregularities of the first drift surface."

What is termed the "Artesian Water Region of Illinois" extends a short distance into the northeastern portion of Champaign County. It is simply a stratum of water-bearing sandstone, overlaid by a thick stratum of tough clay, which confines the water to the sandstone level. Wherever holes are drilled through this overlying clay, the confined waters of the sandstone rise to the surface through the outlets, furnishing an economical and valuable supply of water for agricultural purposes. This stratum of sandstone is called the St. Peter's, and is supposed to be the same stratum that supplies artesian water to the counties of LaSalle, Grundy, Will and Cook.

Clay and sand are the only elements underlying the Champaign prairie-sod that can be used for building purposes. Of the clay, a fair quality of brick and drain tile are being made in several places. The fire-clay, soapstone and limestone are covered too deeply with "drift" to admit of their being economically brought to the surface. Our chief sources of building stone and lime must continue to be the quarries of Kankakee.

Swamp Lands Reclaimed

Until about forty years ago a class of Champaign County lands was as carefully avoided as the prairies of an earlier period; like the prairie lands, they also proved of unusual value. For years the swamps and lowlands were considered as tracts which were worse than valueless; as so many pestilential breeders of malaria and other diseases. But in the early '50s much Federal and State legislation was directed toward the policy of donating such overflowed lands to the various counties. The result was to direct the attention of the county authorities more particularly to the subject, and cause them to consider whether after all they should not attempt to reclaim the swamp lands to conditions of productiveness. In 1853 Benjamin Thrasher was appointed to examine all the unsold lands in the county coming within the definition of the Federal Act as "swamp and overflowed lands," and to submit a report thereof to the County Court. He reported that 85,000 acres in Champaign County answered to that description, and nearly 36,000 acres of such land was subsequently confirmed to the county. These lands were sold and the funds used, in part, for the erection of a courthouse in 1860 and to increase the school fund.

It was upon these lands that the great work of drainage was accomplished nearly twenty years thereafter. In 1878 the State Constitution was amended by the addition of the drainage section, which authorized the formation of drainage companies, the digging and tiling of ditches, and for purposes of regulation and systematic work it divided the submerged lands into districts, with supervising officials. Soon after the year 1880 the system and the work were in operation. Since then the cost of these improvements has been great, having been estimated at considerable over $1,000,000. This embraces expenditures made by private individuals, by local districts organized by township authorities, and by the authority and direction of the County Court. The lands thus reclaimed now embrace some of the most productive and valuable tracts in the State. Some of the most important of these drainage districts are known as the East Lake Fork, Two-Mile Slough, Beaver Lake, Big Slough, Kankakee, Embarrass River, Wild Cat, Hillsbury Slough, Spoon River and Little Vermilion River.

Standard Champaign County Cereals

The soils of Champaign County seem to be especially formed to raise corn and oats. The elements were what they should be, as furnished by Nature, and the husbandman has not allowed the necessary ingredients to be exhausted. The result is that year after year corn and oats are bumper crops, and grain dealers throughout the country have long considered the Champaign County cereals as standard. In the production of corn the county not only leads the State but the United States. The figures vary considerably, as in other sections of the State, one of the most productive years being that of 1915, in which the county raised 13,742,000 bushels of corn and 11,928,000 bushels of oats, valued together at $11,219,924. In 1916, the yield dropped to 8,131,644 bushels of corn and 9,124,920 bushels of oats, the total value of which was $9,699,037—$6,505,315 for corn and $3,193,722 for oats.

Modern Sanitary Dairy Barn

In that year, also Champaign County led all the counties of the State in the yield and value of its oats, and, on the whole, has but one serious competitor in Illinois, McLean County. The county has a large acreage in winter wheat—nearly 30,000 acres, and has made a good start in alfalfa and timothy seed.

DAIRY PRODUCTS AND LIVE STOCK

Its dairy products comprise milk, cream and butter in the following quantities (1916) : 70,884 gallons of milk and 69,866 gallons of cream, valued respectively at $19,139 and $69,886, and 98,876 pounds of butter, at $36,584. In the central division of counties, to which the State Board of Agriculture assigns Champaign, the county ranks fifth in the annual sale of butter, which brought, on an average, 37 cents in 1916.

For the raising of live stock Champaign County possesses unusual advantages, on account of its abundant and pure water supply, its equable temperature and the adaptability of its soils to the production of nutritious grasses. Its horses, especially, are hard to beat, either in quality or quantity. In this regard it stands second among the central counties of Illinois, and fifth in the entire State. In the raising of horses McLean is the star county of the State, having 49,757 in 1916, as compared to 25,424 in Champaign. In May, 1916, the latter had, also, 13,339 beef cattle, valued at $233,551, 6,719 dairy cows, at $537,520, and 25,115 hogs, valued at $375,210.

BIRDS AS INSECT DESTROYERS

The farmer has no greater enemy to his crops and to his consequent well-being than the obnoxious insect, and there is seldom one which does not retard some form of vegetable life if allowed to flourish unchecked. Consequently certain varieties of the feathered tribe are the farmers' most useful friends; which they are, and what kind of obnoxious insects are their specially favored diets are thus told by O. M. Schantz, president of the Illinois Audubon Society:

"It is with very mixed feelings that I come to this meeting of the State Farmers' Institute to talk to the people of southern Illinois about birds. I am not a farmer and do not belong to this part of the country, but my wife was born in Carbondale and my mother-in-law in Metropolis, and I have heard of southern Illinois ever since I married into this interesting family of which I am a member. [Applause.]

"The State of Illinois is 378 miles long in its greatest length and

210 miles wide. Owing to its length and its peculiar position, it has almost as great a range of climatic influences, geographical influences, and so on, as any State in the Union. Therefore, its flora and fauna, its animal and vegetable life are extremely varied. The northern part is entirely different in its geography and its animal life from the southern part. By its location, part of it touching Lake Michigan and the rest of it being tributary to the great Mississippi Valley, except for the water fowl of the Atlantic and Pacific coasts, more migratory birds pass through the Mississippi Valley than through any other part of the United States.

"In the consideration of a question of so great importance to the Illinois farmer as the relation of birds to farm economy, it is very necessary to make clear in the most direct manner possible, just how and why the farmer is to be benefited.

"The proper time to plant, seasonable weather during the growing season and also for the harvesting of crops, are, naturally, the most evident factors in successful farming.

"The old-fashioned, unprogressive farmer gave little thought to other and less noticeable handicaps, such as plant diseases and the myriads of insects that were the natural enemies of both his fruit and cereal crops. With the rapid increase in the value of farm lands, the competition for markets, and so forth, it has become absolutely necessary for a farmer to know every factor that may enter farm economy, or he fails to win out.

"The lax use of powers of observation is rapidly disappearing, and today our farmers are growing more and more alive to the fact that a knowledge of scientific farming is the only way to make 150 to 250 acres yield a profit.

"The agricultural colleges of many states, and the Federal Department of Agriculture, have for many years past conducted most exhaustive research as to the losses due to noxious insects, and the most effective means of curtailing these losses.

"We have, by cultivation and removal of forests, disturbed the natural balance of nature. Some of the changes have been beneficial, others very harmful. We have made conditions extremely favorable for the rapid increase of certain noxious insects. Insect life increases at such an incredible rate that with no check of any kind everything green would soon disappear, and in a short time the land would be uninhabitable.

"On the other hand, it is a well known fact that certain of our most useful birds increase as a result of the settlement of land.

"Many birds are very tolerant of man, if reasonably protected and allowed to rear their young undisturbed.

"In the earlier years of the settlement of the country there did not exist the same need for watchfulness that is necessary today.

"The problem of adequate food supply for the world is a part of the problem of the United States. One hundred years ago, very few men devoted even a small portion of their time to the study of insects in their relation to the food supply, or to the careful study of birds as the most effective check on the spreading of injurious insects. Today thousands of men and women are preparing earnestly for these very important studies, and the biological departments of our colleges and universities are of the most importance and popular in all parts of the United States.

"The Illinois Audubon Society was organized less than twenty years ago by a few very earnest bird lovers in Chicago. Their primary object was no doubt a humane desire to protect from destruction the many beautiful birds that came in such great numbers to the woodlands and parks in and around Chicago. The time has come when a much greater field is open for it and similar societies, for intelligent work for the protection of birds, not only for their beauty and wonderful songs, but as a vital factor in the economics of the country's food supply.

"The problem of the city bird lover is largely different from that of the farmer and the people of the smaller cities and villages.

"The larger cities, particularly Chicago, are flooded with thousands of immigrants, to whom the United States means all sorts of liberty. License to kill birds, we understand, is in some parts of southern Europe held out as a great inducement to prospective emigrants in connection with cheaper living. Cheap firearms are sold everywhere, and Sundays and holidays during the summer months see each day a veritable 'armed host' scouring the prairies and woodlands ready to kill anything that flies.

"Where transportation is cheap, these irresponsible shooters reach the farms, and not only trespass on the fields of growing grain, but shoot thousands of the farmers' best friends, the birds, or if no birds can be found, his domestic chickens, ducks or turkeys.

"The problems of Illinois are those of Iowa and the other adjoining prairie states.

"No crop raised by the farmer is immune from insect foes. Many of these insects are so minute that they ordinarily escape the notice of the casual observer, yet the damage annually done on a single farm by these inconspicuous insects may run into large sums of money.

"The different aphides or plant lice, whose life cycle is only a few days, increase with such astounding rapidity that the figures startle.

1—2

FARMERS' FRIENDS
(Insect Destroyers)

"These soft small insects, of which thousands could be held in one's hand, frequently cover the stems of their host plants completely.

"The greatest enemy of the different aphides is the warbler family, which numbers among the twenty-five or thirty varieties that visit us many of our smallest birds. The number of insects that a pair of these little birds will consume for a single meal is almost beyond comprehension.

"To better understand the ability of birds to check insects, it is necessary to know something of their marvelous powers of digestion. Birds fill themselves to running over with either weed seeds or insects so that frequently they are replete up to the bill. The process of digestion is so powerful and rapid that they can eat almost without stopping, many birds consuming an amount of food each day equal to about one-third of their own weight.

"The temperature of birds and their circulation is much greater than that of other animals, consequently it is largely a matter of fuel enough to keep the machinery going properly.

"Much painstaking work has been done recently in the State of Massachusetts in order to ascertain the effect that wild birds have on the awful insect pests which have become so serious a problem in that State.

"While the conditions in Illinois are vastly different from those in Massachusetts, the results of the investigation should be of great interest to Illinois farmers.

"It has been proven that almost without exception all birds have a good balance to their credit over and above the damage they do; that even such conspicuously aggressive birds as the bluejay, grackle and crow have a large credit in assisting to destroy both larvæ and adults of the gypsy and brown-tailed moths. Such birds as feed on fruits—robins, catbirds, cedar birds and others—also devour enough insect pests to have the balance in their favor.

"Many birds are peculiarly adapted to attend certain insects, and the birds have been very happily alluded to by one writer as the police of the orchard and garden.

"The seed-eating birds, which include the sparrows and finches, destroy weeds by the million. Three mourning doves' stomachs contained by actual count a total of 23,100 weed seeds, consumed at one meal.

"All of the thrush family, of which the robin and bluebird are the best known members, are valuable insect destroyers. The flycatchers, headed by the kingbird and phoebe, and containing about eighty nearly related species, the swallows, martins, night hawks and chimneyswifts, are policemen of the air.

"The towhee and many sparrows forage on the ground; the nut-hatches, woodpeckers and brown creepers take care of the trunk and branches; and the warblers and vireos examine the leaves and buds. The entire tree or shrub is thoroughly guarded. Out in the open, the meadow lark, bobolink, bobwhite, prairie chicken and many others keep tab on grasshoppers, crickets and myriads of other insects. No insect family escapes; it has an ardent, relentless foe in some bird.

"Now, what is your duty to your bird friends? Make your premises attractive. Furnish bird boxes or nests; feed the birds in winter; exterminate stray cats; plant vines and shrubbery bearing fruits agreeable to birds; help to legislate against shooting; train the small boy to respect and love the birds and not to collect birds' eggs; teach him also to shoot with a field or opera glass. If a bird helps itself to a little of your fruit, before destroying the bird look up its record and see what insects he preys upon.

"Observe closely the birds at nesting time and note the tireless energy with which the young birds eat, and then do a little calculating by multiplying the number of times fed by the insects fed at a meal.

"Read literature on the subject of bird conservation. Result: Sure and lasting conversion to the side of the birds.

"Scientific men look with alarm at the rapidly decreasing bird population. The rapid increase of population, encroaching more and more on the nesting places, lessens the available woodland and prairie where the birds may nest and not be disturbed.

"Intelligent planting of shrubbery and vines along roadsides, as is contemplated by the Lincoln Highway movement, will in part overcome this condition.

"Concerted efforts by states and at Washington for better bird protection, the education of all classes as to the beneficial part the bird has in our daily life, vigorous prosecution for violation of our present game laws, the taxing of cats, the encouragement of organizations for bird study—all these are necessary and important features of the growing intelligent effort for bird conservation.

"See that some one attends to the purchasing of good bird books for your public library; offer prizes to your children for best observations or well written papers about birds, their habits and usefulness—these papers, or the best of them, to be published in your local paper.

"There is no reason why, in this tremendous State, a powerful and concerted effort should not be made for bird conservation and protection which would place the State of Illinois in the first rank in the Union for such work.

"Nowhere in the entire United States is there a greater and more interesting bird' migration, both spring and fall, than in this State. The State's length gives it a wonderfully interesting plant life and variety of climate. This, in part, explains its variety of bird life.

"A very small sum as an individual contribution, if given by enough people, would maintain a paid expert whose duty might be that of State ornithologist.

"There is a man in Massachusetts who gives his entire time and energy to this very important work, and whose book, 'Useful Birds and Their Protection,' is the last word in bird conservation."

CEREALS SUPPLANT FRUITS

The friable soil and the equable climate of Champaign County are adapted to the raising of fruits, and its horticultural society has been maintained for many years. Despite the advantages of soil and climate and the best efforts of the birds, however, the insect pest has been most aggressive of late years, and the cereals have almost superseded the fruits. In early times that great drawback was little known in the county or the State, and before the year 1853 the planting of orchards in the county had become quite common. Apples were the favorite fruit and the Milam the favorite variety. Peaches were also abundantly grown, while the smaller fruits flourished in their wild state. Thickets of plums grew along the margins of the timber belts and in some of the groves, and wild blackberries and strawberries in the denser woods. But these conditions are now almost things of the past, although there still remain striking evidences of what may be done in horticulture with extreme care and large means in the wonderful Dunlap orchards at Savoy. As early as 1858 M. L. Dunlap settled at Rural Home, planted his first orchards, set out his nurseries and protected all by belts of forest trees, and now sends out his luscious apples by the ton, and resides in a country palace which is world-famed. But his is the notable exception to the general rule that other branches of agriculture have supplanted horticulture in Champaign County.

HISTORY OF HORTICULTURE IN THE COUNTY

In 1870 the most complete account of the development of the horticultural interests of the county was written by H. J. Dunlap, now of Kankakee, Illinois, but for many years secretary of the County Agricultural, Horticultural and Mechanical Association. It is as follows:

"The first orchard planting of which I have been able to obtain any information was done about the year 1838 by William Sadorus, in the timber near the southwest corner of the county, now called Sadorus' Grove. It was made of fifty Milam sprouts obtained near Terre Haute, Indiana, eighty miles distant, and afterwards extended by planting 150 more of the same sort. These trees commenced to bear in 1842, four years after planting, and continued to produce large annual crops until 1854 or 1855, since which time there have been several failures, and many of these trees are now dead or dying. Several years after the orchard was planted some of the trees were grafted over to Vandevere Pippin, Yellow Bellflower, Roxbury Russet, etc. Some of these varieties have very good quality. The Roxbury Russet does not bear large crops, and is not a very good keeper. This orchard is in a cove in the timber, protected on the south, west and north. Mr. Sadorus is still living, and takes quite an interest in horticulture.

"Many other orchards were set out in this neighborhood from the sprouts produced from these Milams. The only valuable apple that was planted seems to have been the Milam.

"Several years after Mr. Sadorus' planting, orchards were set at or near Big Grove, near Urbana, by James T. Roe, Robert Brownfield, —— Fielding, Martin Rhinehart, James Clemens, William Robert and others. James T. Roe had a small nursery which consisted principally of Milams. Mr. Brownfield procured 100 trees from Kentucky, most Milam, Winter Wine and Yellow Bellflower, which continue healthy and bear good crops.

"Martin Rhinehart's orchard consisted of Bellflowers, Vandevere Pippin, Seek-no-farther, Winter Wine, Fall Pippin, Pound Sweet and Pumpkin Sweet. Mr. Brownfield now owns this orchard, also the one of 100 trees originally planted by him. Four years ago the first 100 trees yielded 400 bushels. This season both orchards had only 600 bushels. There had been no insects to diminish the yield of fruit until two years ago, when the coddling moth first made its appearance in numbers sufficient to destroy nearly the entire crop. Mr. Brownfield turned in his hogs to eat the fallen fruit, and thinks, had they been kept in it all the season, that he would have headed the moth, but as soon as the fruit was large enough to sell the hogs were removed. The fruit was not picked up every day, so that a sufficient number of worms escaped to injure the past season's crop, but not to as great an extent as the preceding one.

"Josh Trickle planted twelve seedling trees at an early day, some of which are now dead, others remaining thrifty and fruitful.

"Mr. Brownfield thinks the Green Winter Pippin his most valuable winter apple. The Rawles' Janet is one of the best keepers. Large Romanite was also planted quite extensively by the early settlers. The principal varieties brought to market from the old orchards are Milam, Pennock, Vandevere Pippin, Yellow Bellflower, Rawles' Janet and Winesap.

"It is almost impossible to find a good eating apple in either Champaign or Urbana during fall or early winter except Milams; but Snow, Rambo, Porter and some others of the newer varieties begin to make their appearance from the later planted orchards. Of these there are quite a large number commencing to bear. Prominent among these are the orchards of M. L. and M. Dunlap, J. B. Phinney, C. F. Columbia, R. Allen and others.

"Until 1856 there had been no established nursery in the county, but several parties had kept small stocks sent from abroad to be sold here. Nearly all the trees prior to that time came from the Rochester nurseries, and were mostly Baldwins, Northern Spys, Russets, Greenings, etc., nearly all of which are valueless on the prairie, although isolated instances occur where individual trees of these varieties, from some local cause, have done well.

"The Messrs. Curtis of Paris, Edgar County, L. Ellsworth & Co. of Naperville, DuPage County, and other Western nurserymen, furnished more or less trees. To their credit be it said more of them are better adapted to our climate and soil than those brought from the East. I suspect this to be more the result of accident than design, for fifteen or twenty years ago the subject of what varieties were best adapted to the West was but little understood, owing to the limited experience of the orchardists in the West. Now the thing is different, and there is no valid excuse for a man to plant trees that are not hardy, productive and valuable.

"In April, 1856, M. L. Dunlap established the first nursery for growing and selling trees, commencing by planting 120,000 grafts, comprising nearly 150 varieties. Owing to the extreme dryness of the season, nearly all the grafts failed to grow. Doubtless this was a blessing to the future purchasers of these trees, had they lived and grown, for in this list of varieties were nearly 100 that are unsuitable for Western orchards; but at that time they were untried, and, therefore, it was not possible to know their value. The writer has often sold 100 trees for an orchard in which were from sixty to seventy varieties, the purchaser wanting as many varieties as possible. Now the desire of most planters has been narrowed down to ten or fifteen well-known sorts, and a disposition manifested to let some one else experiment.

"Mr. Dunlap, intending to make fruit-growing a part of his business, planted an orchard of 1,500 trees, 500 of these being seedling, into which it was the intention to top-graft new and untried varieties. Some

Samples of Home-Grown Corn

of these have been grafted, others still remain. The first orchard was more of an experimental one than anything else, many varieties being then planted that the proprietor would not now allow to be set on his grounds, while others, new and untried, have proved valuable.

"Other nurseries soon sprung up, and tree planting was stimulated to a great extent; and had all the trees lived that have been planted in the county we should now be supplied with an abundance of fruit; but, as is usual (so far as my observation goes), not one in ten has even brought forth fruit.

"In the early planting of fruit trees, I have been unable to find that any pears, quinces, cherries or plums were planted, except the common Morello cherry; but of late years they have been extensively set out. The first cherry trees sold were, of course, from Rochester, and consisted of many thousands. I doubt if one tree ever bore a full crop, or else did it once and died. The principal variety now planted is the Early May (Richmond), of which hundreds of bushels are sent to the Chicago market from this station annually.

"Pear culture is yet in its infancy, but there is no good reason why it should not be as successful here as elsewhere. In the spring of 1865 the writer planted the first acre of strawberries in the county for market. The next season Mr. G. M. Rice set out five acres, Platt, Fuller & Earle twenty, G. D. Wicks three and several other parties smaller quantities. From that beginning of one acre five years ago has sprung up a large trade in this fruit, several thousand bushels being shipped from the country every season.

"In raising other small fruits not much is done, although the culture of raspberries, blackberries and grapes is extending, so that in two or three years the products from the present plantations will begin to make a perceptible impression on the markets.

"In my conversations with the old settlers I have often inquired if seedling appear to retain their vigor longer than grafted varieties, and have been told that out of a given number of trees by far the largest number of seedling give up the ghost first.

"It also appears strange that there should not be some old pear trees, but I can not hear of one more than twenty years old.

"The first May cherries of which I have any knowledge were planted fourteen years ago. They were on Mazzard, Mahaleb and Morello stocks. Those on Mazzard are years since dead and forgotten; some of the Morellos are still alive and bear good crops, although the annual cuttings they received in their early days when scions were scarce have sadly marred their beauty and thrifty look.

"Peaches were extensively grown, while the county was new and before railroads brought in the curculio; but the winters of 1855-56 destroyed many trees, since which time, owing to the unfavorable seasons and curculio, not enough of this fruit has been raised for home use."

In 1877, or seven years after Mr. Dunlap's article was written, another authority in the county reviewed the horticultural situation which at that time was quite bright. He said: "We cannot close this article without at least a glance at the horticultural progress made during the past twenty years. Then there was not sufficient fruit grown in the county for home use. Great numbers of wagons came from the Wabash country every fall, laden with apples, mostly Milams, Vandivere Pippins and Pennsylvania Redstreaks. Now one seldom sees a specimen of either of the above-named, their places having been filled with varieties of Eastern and Northern origin. There are now thousands of barrels of apples and carloads of small fruit shipped from this county every year, and this industry may be said to rank next to wheat in its importance and value. In selecting a site for an orchard it is necessary to have all dry ground. Underdraining in an orchard is so much money thrown away. In two or three years the tree roots will fill the largest tile and entirely obstruct the flow of water. We should prefer to have a belt of some forest-trees on the south, west and north sides of an orchard, in order to break the force of the wind. A good hedge is also almost indispensable.

"For varieties for home use, where early bearing is required, we would recommend for summer, Red Astracan, Red June, Sweet Bough and Benoni; for autumn, Snow, Stanard, Rambo, Lowell and American Pearmain, which is not an early bearer, but is one of the most delicious apples on the list. For winter, Jonathan, Smith's Cider, Minkler, Wagoner, Ben Davis, Winesap, Rawles' Janet and Willow Twig.

"For market purposes we should plant not to exceed four varieties and they of winter fruit, viz.: Ben Davis, Winesap, Rawles' Janet and Willow Twig.

"There are a great many other good varieties, much better in quality than those named, but all possess some defect.

"Of pears, peaches, plums, cherries, etc., the nurserymen keep an assortment of well-known varieties, all of which are more or less profitable."

AGRICULTURAL AND HORTICULTURAL SOCIETIES

Since the early '50s Champaign County has strongly supported every organization and interest which tended to develop its great agricultural resources and the abilities and enterprise of its farmers and horticul-

CLEANLY LIFE OF MODERN SWINE (CONCRETE WALLOWS)

turists. From the first there was a deep realization of the desirability of cooperation and education along these lines, both as a guarantee of future growth and a safeguard for continuous livelihood and prosperity. The result was that even during the early '50s, when Prof. Jonathan B. Turner of Jacksonville and others were urging the establishment of a State university, its basic idea was recognized as the encouragement of the broad and intelligent development of agriculture, and the farmers' clubs were solidly behind the movement. Some fifteen years afterward, when the Illinois Industrial University was incorporated and located at Urbana, that object was still uppermost. The president of the State Agricultural Society was perhaps its most influential trustee, and of its departments the agricultural was first in its publications.

AGRICULTURAL, HORTICULTURAL AND MECHANICAL ASSOCIATION

The oldest of these organizations in this section was the Champaign County Agricultural, Horticultural and Mechanical Association, which was organized in 1870. Its constitution, as adopted October 8 of that year, reads thus:

Article I. The name of this association shall be "The Champaign County Agricultural, Horticultural and Mechanical Association."

Art. II. The capital stock of this association shall not be less than fifteen thousand ($15,000) dollars, and shall be divided into shares of fifty ($50) dollars each.

Art. III. The owner of one or more shares shall be a member of the association, but no member owning two or more shares shall be entitled to more than two votes.

Art. IV. The officers of this association shall consist of a president, one vice-president for each township in the county, secretary, treasurer and an executive committee made up of seven (7) stockholders, and such others as may be necessary.

Art. V. The term for which the officers of the association shall be elected shall be one year from the 1st day of January next ensuing after their election.

Art. VI. The annual election of officers shall be held each year at the October quarterly meeting.

Art. VII. At all elections the holder of one share shall be entitled to one vote; the holder of two or more shares to two votes.

Art. VIII. This association shall have a seal, which shall be circular in form, and bear the following superscription on its face: "The Champaign County Agricultural, Horticultural and Mechanical Association."

Art. IX. This Constitution and By-Laws may be altered or suspended by a majority vote of all the capital stock.

Art. X. Quorum—At all meetings one-third of the stock taken shall be represented to constitute a quorum.

THE FARMERS' CLUB AND FAIR ASSOCIATION

The Farmers' Club was also an early organization which did a good work, and the first farmers' institute was organized about 1873, but was a short-lived affair. The so-called Fair Association had charge of the agricultural and live stock exhibits, originally held in and near the courthouse square. The first regular fair grounds were four blocks south of the courthouse. H. J. Dunlap, now of Kankakee, who was prominently connected with these organizations in the early days, says that the Fair Association went out of existence about 1900, and adds: "The first fair was held in courthouse square in 1852, the first one which I attended being in 1856. In a year or so ground was purchased for the fair north of the city, near the new cemetery. I think that fairs were held there until about 1870 when the old association disbanded, and a new company purchased forty acres of what is now known as Fairview, or then ground west of the university."

`After the disbandment of the old Fair Association, as just stated, the Champaign County Fair and Driving Association was incorporated on March 3, 1905. The former fair grounds in Champaign were sold and platted into a city addition known as Fairland Place, one of the most desirable residence sections of the city. The new organization procured commodious grounds just north of Urbana, on which the county fair is held annually. The officers of the association for 1917 are: Fred Rising, president; H. D. Oldham, secretary; Lewis Prather, treasurer.

CHAMPAIGN COUNTY FARMERS' INSTITUTE

The present Champaign County Farmers' Institute was organized in January, 1891, more than four years before the creation of the Illinois Farmers'·Institute. The State body came into being through a legislative Act approved June 24, 1895. The original Act, with its several amendments, provides that the body shall consist of three delegates from each county of the State, elected annually, and that its affairs shall be managed by a board of directors, consisting of the state superintendent of public instruction, the professor of agriculture of the State of Illinois, president of the State Board of Agriculture, president of the State Horticultural Society and president of the State

Dairymen's Association. Its superintendent of institutes "shall devote his entire time to the organization, promotion and general supervision of the farmers' institute work in the State, under the direction of the board of directors and the executive committee. He shall organize a bureau of speakers, the same to include farmers, dairymen, horticulturists, live stock breeders, feeders anl others who have adopted scientific and practical methods—secured beneficial results, and are able to tell about them, together with such instructors from the College of Agriculture and Experiment Station as may be assigned to the institute

A CANNING CLUB IN ACTION

work and whose allotment of time shall be under his direction. These speakers shall be assigned work as far as possible, in accordance with the wishes of the district directors, officers of the Department of. Household Science (where their interests may appear) and the county institute officers. He shall make recommendations as to lines of work which he believes will prove profitable for the ensuing year, together with general plans for their execution and estimates of expense."

The State body cooperates closely with the county farmers' institufes, delegates being called together for conference who comprise one general representative from each county institute and one delegate from the Department of Household Science, when organized, as well as the county superintendent of schools. The purpose of these conferences is to arrange the times and places for holding the next county institutes and to cooperate in securing speakers. If the officers of a county farmers' institute fail to arrange for the holding of meetings as provided for in the act of incorporation, the Board of Directors of the Illinois Farmers' Institute may furnish instructors for, and hold such meetings as may be beneficial to the agricultural interest of said county. The sum of $75 is provided for the purpose of holding one or more annual meetings of the county institute, and in 1911 the Legislature

MODERN DUMP CRIB AND FEED MILL

passed an Act authorizing a county board to appropriate $300 (no more) "for use of county farmers' institutes in their efforts to promote the adoption of the latest approved methods of crop production, the improvement of live stock, the conservation of soil fertility and the improvement of agricultural conditions generally."

The membership of the farmers' institute is unlimited. There are no initiation or membership fees, and the meetings are open to the public free of charge; anyone who wishes may be present and take part in the discussions, in the administration of the business and in the election of its officers.

Through the courtesy of Mrs. H. A. McKeene, secretary of the Illinois Farmers' Institute, the following information is furnished regarding the Champaign County Farmers' Institute, comprising, as will be seen, the time and places of meeting of the different institutes, and the years of service of its principal elective officers:

Meetings—January 7-8, 1891, Champaign; January 19-20, 1892, Homer; February 4-5-6, 1893, Rantoul; February 23-24, 1894, Fisher; January 2-3, 1895, Champaign; January 2-3, 1896, St. Joseph; February 25-26, 1896, Urbana; January 21-22, 1897, Champaign; December 14-15, 1897, Urbana; January 18-19, 1899, Sidney; January 18-19, 1900, Philo; January 17-18, 1901, Rantoul; February 13-14, 1901, Tolono; January 7-8-9, 1902, Champaign; February 13-14, 1902, Mahomet; September 23-24, 1902, Philo; January 13-14, 1903, Fisher; October 7-8, 1903, Pesotum; January 13-14, 1904, St. Joseph; October 12-13, 1904, Sadorus; February 14-15, 1905, Urbana; January 16-17, 1906, Philo; October 11-12, 1906, Tolono; January 16-17, 1908, Pesotum; December 10-11, 1908, Homer; January 14-15, 1909, Ludlow; December 16-17, 1909, Fisher; January 13-14, 1910, Sidney; December 15-16, 1910, Mahomet; February 8-9, 1911, Rantoul; October 10-11, 1911, Sadorus; December 12-13, 1911, Ogden; October 15, 1912, Seymour; October 16, 1912, Tolono; October 17-18, 1912, Ivesdale; October 14, 1913, Ludlow; October 15, 1913, Gifford; October 16, 1913, Foosland; October 6, 1914, Pesotum; October 7, 1914, Sidney; October 8, 1914, Seymour; October 9, 1914, Newcomb; March 4-5, 1915, Homer; October 5-6, 1915, South Raymond; October 7-8, 1915, Newcomb Center; September 26-27, 1916, South Raymond; September 28-29, 1916, Fisher; October 3-4, 1916, St. Joseph.

Presidents—C. Dyer, Mahomet, January, 1891-97; J. M. Love, Philo, December, 1897-99; Isaac S. Raymond, Philo, 1899-1911; M. O. Stover, Mahomet, 1911-13; W. B. O'Neal, Sadorus, 1914; Wilson P. Jones, Champaign, 1914-17.

Secretaries—Z. R. Genung, Rantoul, 1891-97; J. A. Hossack, Champaign, 1897-1914; J. Ray Stanner, Urbana, 1915-17.

Treasurers—Z. R. Genung, Rantoul, 1891-97; M. A. Dewey, Urbana, 1897-99; Z. R. Genung, 1899-1915; W. B. O'Neal, Sadorus, 1915-16; J. Ray Stanner, Urbana, 1917.

The Department of Household Science, to which several references have been made, was organized in 1898 as a distinct division of the Illinois Farmers' Institute and the county organizations. Its objects are well set forth in the following paragraphs published in the year books of the State body for 1914 and 1915: "The conservation of the home is woman's chief business, and scientific home management is the only executive plan for us to follow. Let us give to the world our

THRESHING SCENE

STEAM TRACTOR IN ORCHARD

experiences. History and records of home-making are as valuable to humanity and civilization as the history of any other phase of life."

"No community can rise higher than the standard of its homes. We believe the home can reconstruct better than school, better than church and better than state, but all must stand together, for whatever affects the home affects the state. To interest women in all that pertains to home-making, their highest known profession, is the object of this organization."

Another, and perhaps even a more definite conception of the scope of the Department of Household Science, may be gained by a mention of the titles of some of the addresses presented and discussed at its meetings. They follow: "A Four Course Vegetable Luncheon;" "Comfort and Beauty in the Home;" "Common Sense in Dress;" "Cooperation in the Business of the Home;" "Foods for Health;" "Millinery;" "Neighborhood Cooperation;" "The Underaveraged Child in the Home;" "The Farm Woman's Birthright;" "Home Canning of Fruits and Vegetables;" "Boys' and Girls' Clubs;" "Quick Breads;" "Salads and Sandwiches;" "The Building of a Country Home;" "The Planning of Meals."

The Farm Bureau

The Farm Bureau, which is doing work somewhat similar to that of the institute, is an outgrowth of the Farmers' League, and was incorporated in September, 1913. Its annual expenses of over $5,000 are met by the subscriptions of its 435 members, amounting to about $3,000; a $1,000 appropriation from the board of county commissioners; $900 contributed by the University of Illinois and $300 by the National Department of Agriculture. The subscriptions are graduated according to the size of the farms, and the active lecturer and adviser, known as the "farm expert," is C. H. Oathout. The president of the bureau is W. P. Jones, and the secretary James A. Hossack, who held the position so long with the Champaign County Farmers' Institute.

CHAPTER II

HISTORIC RULE OF THE WHITES

Progress of the French Through Great Interior Waterways—
Marquette and Joliet on Illinois Soil—Indian Paintings on
the Bluffs—Slaying of the Monster—Outlined in Death—
The So-Called "Piasa" Bird—The Return Journey—Up the
Illinois River—Joliet Loses Data in the St. Lawrence—
Death of Marquette—Triumphs of La Salle—His Brave Lieu-
tenant, Tonti—La Salle Starts for the Illinois Country—
Tonti Joins La Salle at Fort Miami—In the Illinois Country
—Deserted Kaskaskia Village with Supplies—Interviews the
Kaskaskias—Builds Fort Crevecoeur Below Peoria—Sends
Expedition to Upper Mississippi—Departs for Fort Frontenac,
Leaving Tonti Behind—Iroquois Ravages at Starved Rock and
Fort Crevecoeur—La Salle Assassinated—Death of Tonti—
Permanent Pioneer Settlements of Illinois—Fort Chartres,
Center of Illinois District—First Land Grant in District—
Prairie du Rocher—Life at the Pioneer French-Illinois
Settlements—Illinois Comes Directly Under Royal Control
—Illinois Spiritually Assigned to the Jesuits—Failures
Result in Good—Fortunate and Progressive Illinois—French-
English Contests for the Ohio Valley—Fort Chartres
Rebuilt by the French—Illinois Triumphs Over Virginia—
Fort Duquesne Abandoned—New Fort Chartres Passes into
British Hands—St. Louis Founded Under a Misapprehension
—Last French Stronghold Falls—English Judges Sit at Fort
Chartres—Pontiac Buried at St. Louis—Last of Fort Chartres
—Kaskaskia Taken by Americans Under Clark—Bloodless
Capture of Vincennes—Virginia Creates County of Illinois—
Condition of Illinois When Todd Arrived—Military and Civil
Personnel—American Civil Government Northwest of the
Ohio—Old St. Clair County—The County Divided—Legisla-
ture of Northwest Territory—Division into Two Territories—
Illinois Territory Created—First Illinois Preemption Law—
First State Constitutional Convention—State Machinery in
Motion—Illinois Black Code—Illinois Counties in 1818—New

35

CAPITAL, VANDALIA—EARLY PERIOD OF WILD-CAT BANKING—THE
SLAVERY ISSUE (1822-24)—THE FAMOUS SANGAMON COUNTRY—
FUNDAMENTAL SCHOOL LEGISLATION—STATE BANK IN LIQUIDATION
—SYSTEM OF INTERNAL IMPROVEMENTS—CAPITAL MOVED TO SPRING-
FIELD—REMAINS OF INTERNAL IMPROVEMENTS SYSTEM—REVISING
THE OLD CONSTITUTION—THE CONSTITUTION OF 1848—BANKING
LEGISLATION—REAL WILD-CAT BANKS—THE NATIONAL BANKING
SYSTEM—THE CONSTITUTION OF 1870—BUILDING AND LOAN
ASSOCIATIONS AUTHORIZED.

What was the old Northwest Territory, between the Ohio and the
Mississippi Rivers, and what are now the State of Illinois and Champaign
County remained under French dominion for nearly a century—from
the historic voyages of Marquette and Joliet, in 1672-73, to the surrender of Fort Chartres to the English in 1765. These pioneers of
French discovery revealed to the world two great waterways from their
northern domain to the portentious Father of Waters, which was
discovered to cleave a new continent in twain, instead of being either
diverted to the South Seas or the Atlantic Ocean. Their ascent of
the Illinois, on their return voyage, as a shorter and easier route
between the Great Lakes and the Great River, was significant of the
commencement of an era which marked the trend of the most wonderful
development in North America of every material and intellectual force
which advances the civilization of the white man of the western
hemisphere.

PROGRESS OF THE FRENCH THROUGH GREAT INTERIOR WATERWAYS

The grand march of French exploration and discovery up the valley
of the St Lawrence, through Cartier and Champlain; around the fringes
of the upper Great Lakes and gradually into the outlying country by
the same far-seeing, brave and patriotic Champlain; the wonderful
combination of Church and State, which penetrated the wilderness,
subdued its savages both by the mysteries of Catholicism, gentle and
brotherly offices and the pageantry of a gorgeous government—all these
successive steps leading to the voyages of Marquette and Joliet which
drove the wedge into the very center of the American continent and
commenced to let in the light of the world, have been so often told that
they comprise the common knowledge of the reading universe.

MARQUETTE AND JOLIET ON ILLINOIS SOIL

A landing on Illinois soil was effected on their trip down the

Mississippi, in June, 1673. On the 17th of that month their canoes, containing Joliet, Marquette, five French boatmen, or voyageurs, and two Indian guides, shot from the mouth of the Wisconsin into the broad Mississippi. The voyagers were filled with a joy unspeakable. The journey now began down the stream without any ceremony. Marquette made accurate observations of the lay of the land, the vegetation and the animals. Among the animals he mentions are deer, moose, and all sorts of fish, turkeys, wild cattle, and small game.

Somewhere, probably below Rock Island, the voyagers discovered footprints and they knew that the Illinois were not far away. Marquette and Joliet left their boats in the keeping of the five Frenchmen and after prayers they departed into the interior, following the tracks of the Indians. They soon came to an Indian village. The chiefs received the two whites with very great ceremony. The peace pipe was smoked and Joliet, who was trained in all the Indian languages, told them of the purpose of their visit to this Illinois country. A chief responded and after giving the two whites some presents among which were a calumet and an Indian slave boy, the chief warned them not to go further down the river for great dangers awaited them. Marquette replied that they did not fear death and nothing would please them more than to lose their lives in God's service.

After promising the Indians they would come again, they retired to their boats, accompanied by six hundred warriors from the village. They departed from these Indians about the last of June and were soon on their journey down the river.

INDIAN PAINTINGS ON THE BLUFFS

As they moved southward the bluffs became quite a marked feature of the general landscape. After passing the mouth of the Illinois River, they came to unusually high bluffs on the Illinois side of the Mississippi. At a point about six miles above the present city of Alton, they discovered on the high smooth-faced bluffs a very strange object, which Marquette describes as follows: "As we coasted along the rocks, frightful for their height and length, we saw two monsters painted on these rocks, which startled us at first, and on which the boldest Indian dare not gaze long. They are as large as a calf, with horns on the head like a deer, a frightful look, red eyes, bearded like a tiger, the face somewhat like a man's, the body covered with scales and the tail so long that it twice makes the turn of the body, passing over the head and down between the legs, and ending at last in a fish's tail. Green, red, and a kind of black are the colors employed. On the whole, these two monsters are so well painted that we could not believe any Indian to have been the designer, as good painters in France would find it hard to do as well; besides this, they are so high upon the rock that it is hard to get conveniently at them to paint them."

SLAYING OF THE MONSTER

In an early day in Illinois, the description of these monsters was quite current in the western part of the state. So also was a tradition that these monsters actually inhabited a great cave near. It described, however, but a single monster and but a single picture. The tradition said that this monster was a hideous creature with wings, and great claws, and great teeth. It was accustomed to devour every living thing which came within its reach; men, women, and children, and animals of all kinds. The Indians had suffered great loss of their people from its ravages and a council of war was held to devise some means by which its career might be ended. Among other schemes for its extermination was a proposition by a certain young warrior to the effect that, upon the departure of the beast on one of his long flights for food, he would volunteer to be securely tied to stakes on the ledge in front of the mouth of the cave, and that a sufficient number of other warriors of the tribe should be stationed near with their poisoned arrows so that when the bird should return from its flight they might slay it.

This proposition was accepted and on a certain day the bird took its accustomed flight. The young warrior who offered to sacrifice his life was securely bound to strong stakes in front of the mouth of the cave. The warriors who were to slay the beast were all safely hidden in the rocks and debris near. In the afternoon the monster was seen returning from its long journey. Upon lighting near its cave, it discovered the young warrior and immediately attacked him, fastening its claws and teeth in his body. The thongs held him securely and the more it strove to escape with its prey the more its claws became entangled in the thongs.

At a concerted moment the warriors all about opened upon the monster with their poisoned arrows, and before the beast could extricate itself, its life blood was ebbing away. Its death had been compassed.

OUTLINED IN DEATH

The warriors took the body and, stretching it out so as to get a good picture of it, marked the form and painted it as it was seen by Marquette. Because the tribes of Indians had suffered such destruction of life by this monster, an edict went forth that every warrior who went by this bluff should discharge at least one arrow at the painting. This the Indians continued religiously to do. In later years when guns displaced arrows among the Indians, they continued to shoot at the painting as they passed and thus it is said the face of the painting was greatly marred.

The So-Called "Piasa" Bird

Judge Joseph Gillespie, of Edwardsville, Illinois, a prolific writer and a man of unimpeachable character wrote in 1883 as follows: "I saw what was called the picture sixty years since, long before it was marred by quarrymen or the tooth of time, and I never saw anything which would have impressed my mind that it was intended to represent a bird. I saw daubs of coloring matter that I supposed exuded from the rocks that might, to very impressible people, bear some resemblance to a bird or a dragon, after they were told to look at it in that light, just as we fancy in certain arrangements of the stars we see animals, etc., in the constellations. I did see the marks of the bullets shot by the Indians against the rocks in the vicinity of the so-called picture. Their object in shooting at this I never could comprehend. I do not think the story had its origin among the Indians or was one of their superstitions, but was introduced to the literary world by John Russell, of Bluff Dale, Illinois, who wrote a beautiful story about it."

The bluff has long since disappeared through the use of the stone for building purposes.

As Marquette and Joliet proceeded down the river they passed the mouth of the Missouri, which at that time was probably subject to a great flood. When considerably below the mouth of the Kaskaskia River they came to a very noted object—at least the Indians had many stories about it. This is what is known today as the Grand Tower. This great rock in the Mississippi causes a great commotion in the water of the river and probably was destructive of canoes in those days.

On they went down the river past the mouth of the Ohio, into the region of semi-tropical sun and vegetation. The cane-brakes lined the banks, and the mosquitoes became plentiful and very annoying. Here also, probably in the region of Memphis, they stopped and held councils with the Indians. They found the Indians using guns, axes, hoes, knives, beads, etc., and when questioned as to where they got these articles, they said to the eastward. These Indians told the travelers that it was not more than ten days' travel to the mouth of the river. They proceeded on down the river till they reached Choctaw Bend, in latitude 33 degrees and 40 minutes. Here they stopped, held a conference, and decided to go no further.

The Return Journey

They justified their return in the following manner: First, they were satisfied that the Mississippi emptied into the Gulf of Mexico, and not into the Gulf of California, nor into the Atlantic Ocean in Virginia. Second, they feared a conflict with the Spaniards, who occupied and claimed the Gulf coast. Third, they feared the Indians of the lower Mississippi, for they used firearms and might oppose their further progress south. Fourth, they had acquired all the information they started out to obtain.

Up the Illinois River

And so, on the 17th of July, 1674, they turned their faces homeward. They had been just two months, from May 17th to July 17th, on their journey. They had traveled more than a thousand miles. They had faced all forms of danger and had undergone all manner of hardships. Their provisions had been obtained en route. France owes them a debt of gratitude which will never be fully paid. Indeed not only France, but the world is their debtor.

Nothing of interest occurred on their return journey until they reached the mouth of the Illinois River. Here they were told by some Indians that there was a much shorter route to Green Bay than by way of the upper Mississippi and the Wisconsin and Fox portage. This shorter route was up the Illinois River to the Chicago portage and thence along Lake Michigan to Green Bay.

Marquette and Joliet proceeded up the Illinois River. When passing by Peoria Lake they halted for three days. While here Marquette preached the gospel to the natives. Just as Marquette was leaving they brought him a dying child which he baptized. When in the vicinity of Ottawa, they came to a village of the Kaskaskia Indians. Marquette says there were seventy-four cabins in the village and that the Indians received them kindly. They tarried but a short time and were escorted from this point up the Illinois and over the Chicago portage by one of the Kaskaskia chiefs and several young warriors.

Joliet Loses Data in the St. Lawrence

While in the village of the Kaskaskias, Marquette told the story of the Cross to the natives, and they were so well pleased with it that they made him promise to return to teach them more about Jesus. Marquette and Joliet reached Green Bay in the month of September, 1673. Probably they both remained here during the ensuing winter. In the summer of 1674, Joliet returned to Quebec to make his report to the governor. On his way down the St. Lawrence, his boat upset and he came near losing his life. He lost all his maps, papers, etc., and was obliged to make a verbal report to the governor.

DEATH OF MARQUETTE

Father Marquette remained in the mission of St. Francois Xavier through the summer of 1674, and late in the fall started on his journey back to Kaskaskia. The escort consisted of two Frenchmen and some Indians. They reached the Chicago portage in the midst of discouraging circumstances. The weather was severe and Father Marquette, sick unto death, was unable to proceed further. On the banks of the Chicago River they built some huts and here the party remained till spring. During the winter Father Marquette did not suffer for want of attention, for he was visited by a number of Indians and by at least two prominent Frenchmen.

By the last of March he was able to travel. He reached the Kaskaskia village Monday, April 8, 1675. He was received with great joy by the Indians. He established the mission of the Immaculate Conception of the Blessed Virgin. Seeing he could not possibly live long, he returned to St. Ignace by way of the Kankakee portage. He never lived to reach Mackinaw. He died the 18th of May, 1675.

This expedition by Marquette and Joliet had carried the lilies of France nearly to the Gulf of Mexico. The Indians in the great plains between the Great Lakes and the Gulf had been visited and the resources of the country noted. There remained but a slight strip of territory over which the banner of France had not floated, from the Gulf of St. Lawrence to the Gulf of Mexico. If this short distance were explored, then the French government would have completely surrounded the English colonies in North America.

THE TRIUMPHS OF LA SALLE

Chevalier de La Salle came to America in the year 1667. Shortly after arriving in this country he established himself as a fur trader at a trading post called La Chine, on the Island of Montreal. Here he came in contact with the Indians from the far west. Within two years he had departed on an exploration. For the next two or three years he had probably visited the Ohio River and had become quite familiar with the country to the south and west of the Great Lakes.

Count Frontenac built a fort on the shore of Lake Ontario where the lake sends its waters into the St. Lawrence River. La Salle was put in charge of this fort. He named it Fort Frontenac. The purpose of this fort was to control the fur trade, especially that from up the Ottawa, and prevent it from going to New York. In 1674 La Salle went to France and while there was raised to the rank of a noble. The king was greatly pleased with the plans of La Salle and readily granted him the seigniory of Fort Frontenac, together with a large quantity of land. For all this La Salle promised to keep the fort in repair, to maintain a garrison equal to that of Montreal, to clear the land, put it in a state of cultivation, and continually to keep arms, ammunition, and artillery in the fort. He further agreed to pay Count Frontenac for the erection of the fort, to build a church, attract Indians, make grants of land to settlers, and to do all for the ultimate purpose of furthering the interest of the French government.

La Salle returned from France and was perhaps at Fort Frontenac when Joliet passed down the lakes in the summer of 1674. The next year he began the improvement of his fort. For two years he prosecuted a thriving trade with the Indians and also engaged in farming, ship-building, cattle-raising, and study.

The fall of 1678 found him in France with a request that the king grant him permission to explore the western part of New France and if possible find the mouth of the Mississippi River. La Salle had matured plans by which New France was to be connected with the western country by a line of strong fortifications. Fort Frontenac was the first step in this plan. He there explained how easy it would be to reach the region of the Great Lakes by the St. Lawrence route or by the Mississippi. There is no doubt that both Frontenac and La Salle wished to transfer the emphasis from the converting of the Indians to that of the conquest of territory for France. and to the more profitable business, as they saw it, of commerce. Frontenac had therefore strongly endorsed La Salle and his plans. Through Colbert and his son, La Salle succeeded in getting his patent from the king.

HIS BRAVE LIEUTENANT, TONTI

While in France La Salle met Henri de Tonti, an Italian who had just won distinction in the French army. His father had been engaged in an insurrection in Italy and had taken refuge in France where he became a great financier, having originated the Tontine system of life insurance. Henri de Tonti had lost a hand in one of the campaigns, but he was nevertheless a man of great energy, and destined to win for himself an honored name in the New World.

La Salle returned to New France in 1678, bringing with him about thirty craftsmen and mariners, together with a large supply of military and naval stores. It can readily be seen that La Salle would be opposed by the merchants and politicians in the region of Quebec and Montreal. He had risen rapidly and was now ready to make one of the most pretentious efforts at discovery and exploration that had been undertaken in New France.

Late in the fall of 1678, probably in December, he sent Captain La Motte and sixteen men to select a suitable site for the building of a vessel with which to navigate the upper lakes. Captain La Motte stopped at the rapids below Niagara Falls and seems to have been indifferent to his mission. La Salle and Tonti arrived the 8th of January, 1679. The next day La Salle went above the falls, probably at Tonawanda Creek, and selected a place to construct the vessel.

Tonti was charged with building the vessel. It was launched in May, 1679, and was christened the Griffin (Griffon). It was of forty-five to fifty tons burden and carried a complement of five cannon, and is supposed to have cost about $10,000.

An expedition of traders had been dispatched into the Illinois country for the purpose of traffic, in the fall of 1678. Tonti and a small party went up Lake Erie and were to await the coming of the Griffin at the head of the lake. The Griffin weighed anchor August 7, 1679, amid the booming of cannon and the chanting of the Te Deum. It arrived at what is now Detroit on the 10th, and there found Tonti and his party. The vessel reached Mackinaw on the 27th of August. Here La Salle found the men whom he had dispatched the year before to traffic with the Indians. He found they had been dissuaded from proceeding to the Illinois country by the report that La Salle was visionary and that his ship would never reach Mackinaw. Tonti was given the task of getting these men together, and while he was thus engaged, La Salle sailed in the Griffin for Green Bay.

Green Bay had been for several years a meeting place between white traders and explorers, and the Indians. When La Salle reached the point, he found some of the traders whom he had sent ahead the year before. These traders had collected from the Pottawattamies large quantities of furs. For these furs La Salle exchanged a large stock of European goods with which the Griffin was loaded. It is said that he made a large sum of money in this transaction. The Griffin was loaded with these furs and made ready to return to the warehouses at Niagara.

La Salle Starts for the Illinois Country

On September 18th, the Griffin, in charge of a trusted pilot, a super-cargo and five sailors, started on the return voyage. La Salle on the 19th of September, 1679, with a company of fourteen persons in four birch bark canoes, loaded with a blacksmith's forge, carpenter's tools, merchandise, arms, provisions, etc., started on his journey for the Illinois country. He coasted along the western shore of Lake Michigan. Their provisions were exhausted before they reached the present site of Milwaukee. They had been forced ashore three times to save their boats and their lives. They now went in search of food and fortunately found a deserted Indian village with plenty of corn. They appropriated the corn, but left some articles as pay. The next day the Indians returned and followed the whites to their boats and it was only by presenting the calumet that La Salle was able to appease them.

From Milwaukee they coasted south past the mouth of the Chicago River and following the southerly bend of the lake reached the mouth of the St. Joseph River November 1, 1679. This had been appointed as the meeting place of the two expeditions—the one under La Salle and the one under Tonti. La Salle was anxious to get to the Illinois country, but he also desired the help of Tonti and as the latter had not yet arrived, La Salle occupied the time of his men in building a palisade fort which he named Fort Miami. Near by, he erected a bark chapel for the use of the priests, and also a storehouse for the goods which the Griffin was to bring from Niagara on its return.

Tonti Joins La Salle at Fort Miami

Tonti arrived at Fort Miami on the 12th of November with only a portion of his company, the rest remaining behind to bring word of the Griffin. La Salle was now impatient to proceed, and dispatching Tonti for the rest of his crew waited for his return. The ice began to form and fearing the freezing over of the river, La Salle ascended the St. Joseph in search of the portage between the Kankakee and the St. Joseph. He went up the St. Joseph beyond the portage and while searching for it was overtaken by a courier who told him Tonti and his party were at the portage farther down the river. This point is supposed to have been near the present city of South Bend, Indiana. Here was now assembled the party which was to become a very historic one. There were in all twenty-nine Frenchmen and one Indian. Among them were La Salle, De Tonti, Fathers Louis Hennepin, Zenobe Membre, Gabriel de La Ribourde, La Metairie (a notary) and De Loup, the Indian guide.

They crossed the portage of three or four miles under great difficulties, dragging their canoes and their burdens on sledges. The ice was getting thick and a heavy snow storm was raging.

IN THE ILLINOIS COUNTRY

By the 6th of December, 1679, the expedition was afloat on the Kankakee. For many miles the country was so marshy that scarcely a camping place could be found, but soon its members emerged into an open region of the country with tall grass and then they knew they were in the Illinois country. They suffered from lack of food, having killed only two deer, one buffalo, two geese, and a few swans. As they journeyed on they passed the mouths of the Iroquois, the Des Plaines, and the Fox. They passed the present site of Ottawa and a few miles below they came to the Kaskaskia village where Marquette had planted the mission of the Immaculate Conception in the summer of 1675. Father Allouez had succeeded Marquette and had spent some time at the Kaskaskia village in 1676, and in 1677 he returned. But on the approach of La Salle, Allouez had departed, for it was understood that almost all of the Jesuit priests were opposed to La Salle's plans of commercializing the interior of North America. The Kaskaskia Indians were themselves absent from the village on an expedition to the southland, as was their winter custom.

DESERTED KASKASKIA VILLAGE WITH SUPPLIES

This Kaskaskia village of four hundred lodges was uninhabited. The huts were built by covering a long arbor-like frame work with mats of woven rushes. In each lodge there was room for as many as ten families. In their hiding places, the Indians had secreted large quantities of corn for the spring planting and for sustenance until another crop could be raised. La Salle's party was so sorely in need of this corn that he decided to appropriate as much as they needed. This he did, taking 30 minots. On January 1, 1680, after mass by Father Hennepin, they departed down the Illinois River. On the morning of the 5th they had arrived at the outlet of what we call Peoria Lake. Here they saw large numbers of boats and on the banks wigwams and large numbers of Indians. The Indians were much disconcerted upon seeing La Salle's party land, and many fled while a few held communication with the new comers. La Salle held a consultation with the chiefs and told them of his taking their corn. He offered to pay for the corn and said that if he were compelled to give up the corn he would take his blacksmith

and his tools to the next tribe, the Osages, whereupon the Indians gladly
accepted pay for the corn taken and offered more.

INTERVIEWS THE KASKASKIAS

La Salle told them he wished to be on friendly terms with them,
but that they must not expect him to engage in conflicts with the
Iroquois whom his king regarded as his children. But if they would
allow him to build a fort near, that he would defend them, the Kaskaskias, against the Iroquois if they were attacked. He also told them
he wished to know whether he could navigate a large boat from that
point to the mouth of the Mississippi River, since it was very difficult
as well as dangerous to bring such European goods as the Indians would
like to have from New France by way of the Great Lakes, and that it
could not well be done by coming across the Iroquois country as they
would object, since the Illinois Indians and the Iroquois were enemies.

The Kaskaskia chiefs told La Salle that the mouth of the Mississippi
was only twenty days' travel away and that there were no obstructions
to navigation. Certain Indian slaves taken in battle said that they had
been at the mouth of the river and that they had seen ships at sea that
made noises like thunder. This made La Salle the more anxious to
reach the mouth of the river and take possession of the country. The
chiefs gave consent to the construction of the fort and La Salle had
a bright vision before him. This vision was sadly clouded on the
morrow when an Indian revealed to him the visit to the chiefs, on the
night before, of a Miami chief by the name of Monso who tried to
undermine the influence of La Salle. He said La Salle was deceiving
them. In a council that day he revealed his knowledge of the visit of
Monso and by great diplomacy won the Kaskaskia chief to his cause
the second time. It was supposed this chief Monso was sent at the
suggestion of Father Allouez. Four of La Salle's men deserted him and
returned to the region of Lake Michigan.

BUILDS FORT CREVECOEUR BELOW PEORIA

La Salle, fearing the influence of the stories among the Indians,
upon his men, decided to separate from them and go further down the
river where he could construct his fort and built his boat. On the
evening of the 15th of January, 1680, La Salle moved to a point on
the east side of the river three miles below the present site of Peoria.
There on a projection from the bluffs he built with considerable labor
a fort which received the name of Crevecoeur. This was the fourth of

the great chain of forts which La Salle had constructed, namely: Fort Frontenac at the outlet of Lake Ontario; Fort Tonti on the Niagara River; Fort Miami at the mouth of St. Joseph River, and Crevecoeur below Lake Peoria on the Illinois River.

Fort Crevecoeur is currently believed to have been so named because of the disheartened frame of mind of La Salle, but this would not be complimentary to the character of the man. It is now rather believed to have been so named in honor of Tonti, since as a soldier in the Netherlands he took part in the destruction of Fort Crevecoeur near the village of Bois le Duc in the year 1672.

In addition to the building of the fort, La Salle began the construction of a vessel with which to complete his journey to the mouth of the river. The lumber was sawed from the timber and rapid progress was made. The keel was 42 feet long, and the beam was 12 feet. While this work was in progress and during the month of February, several representatives of tribes from up the Mississippi and down the Mississippi, as well as from the Miamis to the northeast, came to consult with La Salle. His presence in the Illinois country was known near and far. The Indians from the upper Mississippi brought tempting descriptions of routes to the western sea and also of the wealth of beaver with which their country abounded.

Sends Expedition to Upper Mississippi

La Salle desired to make a visit to Fort Frontenac for sails, cordage, iron, and other material for his boat, besides he was very anxious to hear something definite about the Griffin, and its valuable cargo. But before embarking on his long journey, he fitted out an expedition consisting of Michael Ako, Antony Auguel, and Father Hennepin, to explore the upper Mississippi. Michael Ako was the leader. They started February the 29th, passed down the Illinois River and thence up the Mississippi. They carried goods worth a thousand livres, which were to be exchanged for furs. Father Hennepin took St. Anthony for his patron saint and when near the falls which we know by that name, he set up a post upon which he engraved the cross and the coat of arms of France. He was shortly captured by the Indians and was later released by a French trader, De Lhut. He then returned to France.

Departs for Fort Frontenac, Leaving Tonti Behind

Before starting for Frontenac, La Salle commissioned Tonti to have charge of the Crevecoeur fort, and also to build a fort at Starved Rock.

On March 1st, the day following the departure of Ako and Hennepin for the upper Mississippi, La Salle departed, with three companions, for Fort Frontenac. This was a long, dangerous, and discouraging journey. Every venture which he had engaged in seems to have failed. After finally getting together supplies such as were needed, he started on his return journey. He was continually hearing stories from the travelers of the desertion of Crevecoeur. When he came within a few miles of the Kaskaskia village he began to see signs of destruction. On arriving at the village nothing but a few blackened posts remained. The Iroquois Indians had made a campaign against the Illinois Indians and their trail could be traced by death and destruction.

Iroquois Ravages at Starved Rock and Fort Crevecoeur

When La Salle left the locality of Starved Rock for Fort Crevecoeur, on his way from Canada, he passed the Iroquois on one side of the river and the Illinois on the other. He searched everywhere for Tonti but could find no trace of him. He came to Crevecoeur about the first of December, 1680, and found the fort deserted and the storehouse plundered; the boat, however, was without damage. La Salle went to the mouth of the Illinois River in search of Tonti but without success. He returned to Fort Miami in the spring of 1681. Here he began the organization of all the Indian tribes into a sort of confederation.

Upon the approach of the Iroquois shortly after the departure of La Salle from Fort Crevecoeur, in March, 1680, Tonti and his party were scattered far and near. Tonti and Father Membre made their way to Green Bay and from there to Mackinaw. La Salle heard of them here and went immediately to them. Another expedition was organized. La Salle, Father Membre and Tonti visited Fort Frontenac, where supplies were procured, and late in December, 1681, the expedition had crossed the Chicago portage. There were in this company fifty-four people—twenty-three Frenchmen and thirty-one Indians.

They passed the Kaskaskia village near Starved Rock, but it was in ruins. On January 25, 1682, they reached Fort Crevecoeur. The fort was in fair condition. Here they halted six days, while the Indians made some elm bark canoes. They reached the Mississippi the 6th of February. After a little delay they proceeded down the river, passed the mouth of the Missouri, and shortly after that a village of the Tamaroa Indians. The village contained one hundred and twenty cabins, but they were all deserted. La Salle left presents on the posts for the villagers when they returned. Grand Tower was passed, later the Ohio. The trip to the mouth of the Mississippi was without special interest.

They reached the mouth of the river in April, and on the ninth of that month erected a post upon which they nailed the arms of France wrought from a copper kettle. A proclamation was prepared by the notary, Jacques de la Metairie, and read. It recited briefly their journey to the country drained by the Mississippi and its tributaries.

On the 10th of April the party began the return journey. La Salle was stricken with a severe illness and was obliged to remain at Fort Prudhomme, which had been erected on the Chickasaw bluffs just above Vicksburg. Tonti was sent forward to look after his leader's interests. He went by Fort Miami, but found everything in order. He reached Mackinaw the 22d of July.

La Salle reached Crevecoeur on his way north. He left eight Frenchmen here to hold this position. He reached Fort Miami, and thence passed on to Mackinaw. He then sent Father Membre to France to report his discovery to the king, while he himself set about the building of Fort St. Louis, at Starved Rock, on the Illinois. The detachment left by La Salle at Crevecoeur was ordered north to Fort St. Louis, and he began to grant his followers small areas of land in recognition of their services with him in the past few years. The fort was completed and in March, 1683, the ensign of France floated to the breeze. The tribes for miles in circuit came to the valley about the fort and encamped. La Salle patiently looked for French settlers from New France but they did not come.

During the absence of La Salle at the mouth of the Mississippi, Count Frontenac had been superseded by Sieur de la Barre, who had assumed the duties of his office October 9, 1682. He was not friendly to La Salle's schemes of extending the possessions of France in the New World. La Salle suspected, in the summer of 1683, that the new governor was not in sympathy with him. After a great deal of fruitless correspondence with the new governor, La Salle repaired to France to lay before the king his new discoveries as well as plans for the future.

LA SALLE ASSASSINATED

Tonti was displaced as commander at Fort St. Louis and ordered to Quebec. La Salle not only secured a fleet for the trip to the mouth of the Mississippi, but also had Tonti restored to command at Fort St. Louis. La Salle sailed to the Gulf in the spring of 1685. He failed to find the mouth of the river and landed in what is now Texas. After hardships and discouragement almost beyond belief, he was murdered by some of his own men the latter part of March, 1687.

1—4

La Salle went to France in the summer of 1683 and left Tonti in charge of his interests in the Illinois country. Tonti was active in the defense of his superior's interests. In this duty he was forced to defend the Illinois country against the Iroquois, and to struggle against La Salle's enemies in New France. He made expeditions of trade and exploration throughout all the western country, took part in a great campaign against the Iroquois, and was the life of a growing community around Fort St. Louis.

Death of Tonti

The death of La Salle occurred in the spring of 1687. Just one year previous to this Tonti had made a trip to the Gulf in search of La Salle, but failing to find him returned sorrowfully to Fort St. Louis. In September, 1688, Tonti heard definitely of the death of La Salle. In December of that year he organized an expedition to rescue the colonists whom La Salle had left on the coast of the Gulf. This expedition also proved a failure. For the next ten years Tonti remained in the region of the Lakes, but when Bienville began planting new settlements near the mouth of the Mississippi River, Tonti abandoned Fort St. Louis and joined the new settlements. He died near Mobile in 1704.

Permanent Pioneer Settlements of Illinois

The death of La Salle in 1688 and of Tonti in 1704, concluded the most romantic chapter of the early French explorations which prepared the way for permanent settlement and the solid satisfaction of home-building. Without going into the rather intricate claims as to the priority of the pioneer settlements of Illinois which assumed permanence, it will be conceded that Kaskaskia was for several generations the most notable. The mission of the Immaculate Conception founded there by Father Marquette, with the fertile lands in that region, eventuated in drawing thither not only the soldiers of the cross, but French traders and agriculturists. The Indians and Frenchmen who came to Kaskaskia in the eighteenth century built their huts by weaving grasses and reeds into frameworks of upright poles set in rectangular form. The roofs were thatched. The ground was very rich and a sort of rude agriculture was begun. In those days the French were just taking possession of the mouth of the Mississippi; and Kaskaskia became quite an important intermediate port of call for fresh supplies. The trading with the Indians was also a large factor in the building up of the place, which was located on the west bank of the Kaskaskia, six miles from the Mississippi.

Cahokia, its rival, situated a short distance below the present city of East St. Louis, was also a mission and a trading post, but it met with a setback quite early in its history. The village was first built on the east bank of the Mississippi on a little creek which flowed across the rich alluvial bottoms, but by 1721 the river had carved a new channel westward leaving the village half a league from free water communication. The little creek also took another course, and Cahokia was left decidedly inland.

The Mississippi River has swept away even the site of Kaskaskia, and Cahokia is little more than a name.

FORT CHARTRES, CENTER OF ILLINOIS DISTRICT

Fort Chartres, which was situated sixteen miles northwest of Kaskaskia, was founded in 1718 and became the military and the civil center of the Illinois district of Louisiana, and so continued for nearly half a century. As completed, its outer structure consisted of two rows of parallel logs filled between with earth and limestone, the latter quarried from an adjacent cliff. It was surrounded on three sides by this two-foot wall, and on the fourth by a ravine, which during the springtime was full of water.

The fort was barely completed when there arrived one Renault, a representative of the Company of the West (a creation of the famous John Law), the director general of the mining operations of that concern which were designed to re-enforce the uncertain finances of France. He had left France in the spring of 1719 with two hundred miners, laborers and a full complement of mining utensils. Among his force were also several hundred St. Domingo negroes, whom he had bought on his way to Louisiana to work the mines and plantations of the province. Those whom he brought to the Illinois district were the original slaves of the State of Illinois.

Renault made Fort Chartres his headquarters for a short time, and from here he sent his expert miners and skilled workmen in every direction hunting for the precious metals. The bluffs skirting the American Bottoms on the east were diligently searched for minerals, but nothing encouraging was found. In what is now Jackson, Randolph, and St. Clair counties the ancient traces of furnaces were visible as late as 1850. Silver Creek, which runs south and through Madison and St. Clair counties, was so named on the supposition that silver metal was plentiful along that stream.

Failing to discover any metals or precious stones, Renault turned his attention to the cultivation of the land in order to support his miners.

FIRST LAND GRANT IN DISTRICT

On May 10, 1722, the military commandant, Lieutenant Bois-briant, representing the king, and Des Usins representing the Royal Indies Company (the Company of the West), granted to Charles Davie a tract of land five arpents wide (58.35 rods) and reaching from the Kaskaskia on the east to the Mississippi on the west. This is said to have been the first grant of land made in the Illinois district in Louisiana.

The next year, June 14th, the same officials made a grant to Renault of a tract of land abutting or facing on the Mississippi, more than three miles. This tract contained more than 13,000 acres. It reached back to the bluffs, probably four to five miles. It is said the grant was made in consideration of the labor of Renault's slaves, probably upon some work belonging to the Company of the West. This grant was up the Mississippi three and a half miles above Fort Chartres. The village of St. Phillipe was probably started before the grant was made, at least the village was on the grant.

PRAIRIE DU ROCHER

As soon as Fort Chartres was complete there grew up a village near by, which usually went by the name of New Chartres. About the year 1722 the village of Prairie du Rocher was begun. It was located near the bluffs due east from Fort Chartres about three and a half miles. It is said that some of the houses were built of stone, there being an abundance of that material in the bluffs just back of the village. To this village there was granted a very large "common" which it holds to this day. The common is about three miles square and lies back of the village upon the upland.

There were, probably, as early as 1725, five permanent French villages in the American Bottom, namely: Cahokia, settled not earlier than 1698, and not later than 1700; Kaskaskia, settled in the latter part of the year 1700, or in the beginning of the year 1701; New Chartres, the village about Fort Chartres, commenced about the same time the fort was erected, 1720; Prairie du Rocher, settled about 1722, or possibly as late as the grant to Boisbriant, which was in 1733; St. Phillipe, settled very soon after Renault received the grant from the Western Company, which was 1723.

The villages were all much alike. They were a straggling lot of crude cabins, built with little if any reference to streets, and constructed with no pretension to architectural beauty. The inhabitants were French and Indians and negroes.

Life at the Pioneer French-Illinois Settlements

The industrial life of these people consisted of fishing and hunting, cultivation of the soil, commercial transactions, some manufacturing, and mining. The fishing and hunting were partly a pastime, but the table was often liberally supplied from these sources. The soil was fertile and yielded abundantly to a very indifferent cultivation. Wheat was grown and the grain ground in crude water mills usually situated at the mouths of the streams as they emerge from the bluffs. And it is said one windmill was erected in the bottom. They had swine and black cattle, says Father Charlevoix, in 1721. The Indians raised poultry, spun the wool of the buffalo and wove a cloth which they dyed black, yellow or red.

In the first thirty or forty years of the eighteenth century, there was considerable commerce carried on between these villages and the mouth of the river. New Orleans was established in 1718 and came to be, in a very early day, an important shipping point. The gristmills ground the wheat which the Illinois farmers raised on the bottom lands, and the flour was shipped in keel boats and flatboats. Fifteen thousand deer skins were sent in one year to New Orleans. Buffalo meat and other products of the forest, as well as the produce of the farms, made up the cargoes. Considerable lead was early shipped to the mother country. The return vessel brought the colonists rice, sugar, coffee, manufactured articles of all kinds, tools, implements, and munitions of war.

Illinois Comes Directly Under Royal Control

In 1720 a financial panic struck France and John Law was forced to flee from the country. The Company of the Indies kept up a pretense of carrying on its business, but in 1732 upon petition by the company the king issued a proclamation declaring the company dissolved and Louisiana to be free to all subjects of the king. There were at this time (1732) about 7,000 whites and 2,000 negro slaves within the limits of the Louisiana territory. The rules of the Western Company had been so exacting that many of the activities of the people had been repressed. Every one seems to have been held in a sort of vassalage to the company. Now the territory was to come directly under the crown.

In 1721 the whole of the Mississippi Valley had been divided into nine civil jurisdictions, as follows: New Orleans, Biloxi, Mobile, Alabama, Natchez, Yazoo, Natchitoches, Arkansas and Illinois. "There shall be at the headquarters in each district a commandant and a judge, from whose decisions appeals may be had to the superior council established at New Biloxi." Breese's History of Illinois gives a copy of an appeal of the inhabitants of Kaskaskia to the Provincial commandant and judge relative to the grants of lands to individuals and to the inhabitants as a whole.

ILLINOIS SPIRITUALLY ASSIGNED TO THE JESUITS

The religious life of Kaskaskia, Cahokia, and other French villages was quite free from outside influence. By the third article of the ordinance issued by Louis XV in 1724, all religious beliefs other than the Catholic faith were forbidden. The article reads as follows: "We prohibit any other religious rites than those of the Apostolic Roman Catholic church; requiring that those who violate this shall be punished as rebels, disobedient to our commands." This ordinance also made it an offense to set over any slaves any overseers who should in any way prevent the slaves from professing the Roman Catholic religion.

By an ordinance issued in 1722, by the council for the company, and with the consent of the bishop of Quebec, the province of Louisiana was divided into three spiritual jurisdictions. The first comprised the banks of the Mississippi from the gulf to the mouth of the Ohio, and including the region to the west. The Capuchins were to officiate in the churches, and their superior was to reside in New Orleans. The second spiritual district comprised all the territory north of the Ohio, and was assigned to the charge of the Jesuits whose superior should reside in the Illinois, presumably at Kaskaskia. The third district lay south of the Ohio and east of the Mississippi River and was assigned to the Carmelites, the residence of the superior being at Mobile. Each of the three superiors was to be a grand vicar of the bishop of Quebec. The Carmelites remained in charge of their territory south of the Ohio only till the following fall, December, 1722, when they turned over their work to the Capuchins and returned to France.

As evidence of the activity of the Jesuits in the territory which was assigned to them, we are told they had already, in 1721, established a monastery in Kaskaskia. It is stated in Monette's Mississippi Valley, that a college was also established there about the year 1721. Charlevoix, quoted by Davidson and Stuve, says: "I passed the night with the missionaries (at Cahokia), who are two ecclesiastics from the seminary at Quebec, formerly my disciples, but they must now be my masters. * * * Yesterday I arrived at Kaskaskia about nine o'clock. The Jesuits have a very flourishing mission, which has lately been divided into two." All descriptions which have come down to us of the conditions in the Illinois country in the first part of the eighteenth century represent the church as most aggressive and prosperous. Civil government certainly must have passed into "Innocuous desuetude" by 1732.

The government was very simple, at least until about 1730. From the settlement in 1700 up to the coming of Crozat there was virtually no civil government. Controversies were few and the priest's influence was such that all disputes which arose were settled by that personage. Recently documents have been recovered from the courthouse in Chester which throw considerable light upon the question of government in the French villages, but as yet they have not been thoroughly sorted and interpreted.

The Company of the West realized that its task of developing the territory of Louisiana was an unprofitable one, and they surrendered their charter to the king, and Louisiana became, as we are accustomed to say, a royal province by proclamation of the king, April 10, 1732.

FAILURES RESULT IN GOOD

The two efforts, the one by Crozat and the other by the Company of the West, had both resulted in failure so far as profit to either was concerned. Crozat had spent 425,000 livres and realized in return only 300,000 livres. And although a rich man, the venture ruined him financially. The Company of the West put thousands of dollars into the attempt to develop the territory for which no money in return was ever received. But the efforts of both were a lasting good to the territory itself. Possibly the knowledge of the geography of the country which resulted from the explorations in search of precious metals, was not the least valuable. Among other things, these two efforts brought an adventurous and energetic class of people into Illinois.

FORTUNATE AND PROGRESSIVE ILLINOIS

For many years after 1732, when Louisiana became a royal province, the Illinois country, or district, was spared many of the hardships of war which so distressed and retarded the French domain both north and south of it. The massacre at Natchez, and the campaigns against the Natchez and Chickasaw Indians which ravaged the southern country for a decade, were events of this character. The French and the Indians north of the Ohio were on very good terms and the settlements in the Illinois country grew rapidly, especially after 1739, with the subjugation of the turbulent Indians who had so interfered with the free navigation of the Mississippi. Neither did King George's war, which broke out between France and England in 1744, disturb the even progress of the western country. In the fall of 1745 the rice crop of lower Louisiana was almost ruined by storms and inundation, which misfortune worked to the advantage of Illinois by creating an unusual demand for its wheat and flour.

FRENCH-ENGLISH CONTESTS FOR THE OHIO VALLEY

King George's war, which had its origin in European political complications, closed in 1748. The treaty which closed the war provided for the return of Louisburg to the French, and all other possessions of England and France in America to remain as they were prior to the war. It could easily be seen that the next struggle between the French and the English would be for the permanent control of the Ohio Valley and the adjacent territory east of the Mississippi River. The English had never relaxed in their determination to possess the Ohio Valley. In 1738 a treaty was made at Lancaster, Pennsylvania, between English commissioners and three Indian chiefs representing twelve towns in the vicinity of the Wabash. The purpose of the treaty was to attach the Indians north of the Ohio to the English cause. The Ohio Land Company was formed in 1738. It contained residents of England and Virginia. It received from King George II a grant of a half million acres of land on and about the Ohio River. They were given the exclusive right of trading with the Indians in that region.

In 1749 the governor general of Canada sent Louis Celeron, a knight of the Military Order of St. Louis, to plant lead plates along the valley of the Ohio which might eventually prove French priority of occupation of this territory. Several of the plates were afterward unearthed. In 1750 Celeron wrote a letter to the governor of Pennsylvania warning him of the danger of his people who might trespass upon the French possessions along the Ohio. In 1752 agents of the Ohio Company established a trading post within a few miles of the present site of Piqua, Ohio. In the same year the French and Indian allies destroyed this post, killing fourteen Twightwees Indians, who were under a treaty with the English. Logstown, about eighteen miles below the forks of the Ohio, was settled in 1748 by the English, and in 1752 a treaty was made there in which the Indians ceded certain rights and privileges to the English.

The French began in 1753 to build a line of forts from the lakes to the Mississippi by way of the Ohio and its tributaries from the north. The first fort was located at Presque Isle (now Erie, Pennsylvania); the second one was Fort Le Boeuf on French Creek, a branch of the Alleghany. The third was called Venango, at the mouth of the French Creek. From here they pushed south and found some Englishmen building a fort at the junction of the Alleghany and Monongahela. The French drove the Englishmen from the place and finished the fort and named it Fort Duquesne. This was the fourth fortification in the line of forts reaching from the lakes to the Mississippi River. The French and Indian war was now fairly begun and we shall return to the Illinois to see what part this region was to play in this final contest for supremacy between the two great powers of the Old World.

We have called attention to the activity of the French in building forts on the upper Ohio to secure that region from the English. The same activity marked their preparations in the west for the impending struggle. Fort Chartres had been originally of wood. There never were many soldiers stationed there at any time—only a few score soldiers and officers, but following King George's war it was decided to rebuild Fort Chartres on a large scale.

Fort Chartres Rebuilt by the French

The old fort had been hastily constructed of wood. The new fort was to be of stone. It was planned and constructed by Lieutenant Jean B. Saussier, a French engineer, whose descendants lived in Cahokia many years, one of whom, Dr. John Snyder, now lives in Virginia, Cass County, Illinois. When complete it was the finest and most costly fort in America. The cost of its construction was about $1,500,000, and it seriously embarrassed the French exchequer. The stones were hewn, squared and numbered in the quarries in the bluff just opposite, about four miles distant, and conveyed across the lake to the fort in boats. The massive stone walls enclosed about four acres. They were eighteen feet high and about two feet thick. The gateway was arched, and fifteen feet high; a cut-stone platform was above the gate with a stair of nineteen steps and balustrade leading to it; there were four bastions, each with forty-eight loopholes, eight embrasures, and a sentry box, all in cut stone. Within the walls stood the storehouse, ninety feet long, thirty feet wide, two stories high; the guard house with two rooms above for chapel and missionary quarters; the government house, eighty-four by thirty-two feet, with iron gates and a stone porch; a coach house, pigeon house, and large well walled up with the finest of dressed rock; the intendant's house; two rows of barracks, each 128 feet long; the magazine, which is still standing and well preserved, thirty-five by thirty-eight and thirteen feet high; bake ovens; four prison cells of cut stone; one large relief gate on the north. Such was the pride of the French empire, and the capital of New France.

Illinois Triumphs Over Virginia

The fort was scarcely completed when the French and Indian war broke out. In May of 1754 George Washington and his Virginia riflemen surprised the French at Great Meadows, where Jumonville, the French commander, was killed. A brother of the slain French commander, who was stationed at Fort Chartres, secured leave from Makarty, in command there, to avenge his death. Taking his company with him they proceeded to Fort Duquesne, and there gathering some friendly Indians they attacked Washington at Fort Necessity, which was surrendered on July 4th. This was the real beginning of the old French war. Flushed with victory, the little detachment returned to Fort Chartres, and celebrated the triumph of Illinois over Virginia.

Fort Duquesne Abandoned

In the French and Indian war the demand upon Makarty at Fort Chartres for men and provisions became incessant. In fact, Fort Chartres became the principal base of supplies in the West. In 1755, Captain Aubry was sent to re-enforce Fort Duquesne with 400 men. The fort held out for some time, but later Colonel Washington compelled its abandonment.

New Fort Chartres Passes into British Hands

The power of the French began to wane. They maintained the struggle gallantly, however, and made one more desperate effort to raise the siege of Fort Niagara. . They failed. The flower of Fort Chartres went down at Niagara. The surrender of Canada soon followed, but Fort Chartres, now called New Fort Chartres, still held out for the

French king. They hoped that they would still be considered with Louisiana, and remain in French territory.

Their disappointment was bitter when they learned that on February 10, 1763, Louis XV had ratified the treaty transferring them to Great Britain.

St. Louis Founded Under a Misapprehension

While the French at Fort Chartres were waiting for a British force to take possession, Pierre Laclede arrived from New Orleans to settle at the Illinois, bringing with him a company representing merchants engaged in the fur trade. Learning of the treaty of cession he decided to establish his post on the west side of the Mississippi, which he still believed to be French soil. He selected a fine bluff sixty miles north of Fort Chartres for the site of his post, and returned for the winter. In the spring he began his colony, and was enthusiastic over its prospects. Many of the French families followed him, wishing to remain under the French flag. Their disappointment was still more bitter when they learned that all the French possessions west of the Mississippi had been ceded to Spain. This is now St. Louis.

Last French Stronghold Falls

The elder St. Ange, who had been at Vincennes, returned to take part in the last act. Though the territory had been transferred to King George, the white flag of the Bourbons continued to fly at Fort Chartres, the last place in America. The Indian chief Pontiac was another power not taken into confidence at the treaty. Pontiac loved the French, but detested the English. When the English companies, under Loftus, Pitman and Morris, respectively, came to take possession, each was balked by the wily red man. Chief Pontiac gathered an army of red men and proceeded to Fort Chartres where he met St. Ange, and boldly proposed to assist him in repelling the English. St. Ange plainly told him that all was over, and advised him to make peace with the English. Fort Chartres was finally surrendered to Captain Stirling on October 10, 1765. The red cross of St. George replaced the lilies of France. St. Ange and his men took a boat for St. Louis, and there enrolled in the garrison under the Spanish, which St. Ange was appointed to command.

English Judges Sit at Fort Chartres

The first court of law was established at Fort Chartres in December, 1768, Fort Chartres becoming the capital of the British province west of the Alleghanies. Colonel Wilkins had assumed command under a proclamation from General Gage, and with seven judges sat at Fort Chartres to administer the law of England. After the surrender by the French the church records were removed to Kaskaskia. The records of the old French court were also removed there.

Pontiac Buried at St. Louis

A constant warfare had been kept up by the Indians, until Pontiac was killed near Cahokia by an Illinois Indian. Pontiac's warriors pursued the Illinois tribe to the walls of Fort Chartres, where many of them were slain, the British refusing to assist them. St. Ange recovered the body of Pontiac, and it was buried on the spot now occupied by the Southern Hotel in St. Louis, a memorial plate marking the place.

Last of Fort Chartres

In 1772 high water swept away one of the bastions, and a part of the western wall of Fort Chartres. The British took refuge at Kaskaskia, and the fort was never occupied again. Congress, in 1778, reserved to the government a tract one mile square, of which the fort was the center. But this reservation was opened to entry in 1849, no provision being made for the fort.

Kaskaskia Taken by Americans Under Clark

What manner of military rule and civil government the English established over the Illinois country has been described in general; their dominion lasted but thirteen years. During the progress of the Revolutionary War it became evident to the American Colonies that the capture of the British military posts northwest of the Ohio River was a step which could not long be delayed, and Governor Patrick Henry, in behalf of Virginia, authorized Lieutenant Colonel George Rogers Clark to organize an expedition for that purpose in January, 1778. In May, with seven companies of fifty men each recruited in western Virginia and Kentucky, he commenced his journey down the Monongahela and Ohio, and in the following month disembarked at old Fort Massac, ten miles below the mouth of the Tennessee River on the north side of the Ohio. He hid his boats in the mouth of a small stream which enters the Ohio from Massac County a short distance above the fort. The expedition now made preparations to march overland to Kaskaskia, about a hundred miles distant. Because of the inefficiency or treachery of the guides, the expedition did not reach Kaskaskia until the fourth day of their departure from Fort Massac, at ten or eleven o'clock at night. Clark divided his army into two divisions, one of which was to scatter throughout the town and keep the people in their houses, and the other, which Clark himself commanded, was to capture the fort in which the commander, Chevalier de Rocheblave, was asleep. In a very short time the task was finished and the people disarmed. The soldiers were instructed to pass up and down the streets, and those who could speak French were to inform the inhabitants to remain within their houses. The Virginians and Kentuckians were in the meantime keeping up an unearthly yelling, for the people of Kaskaskia had understood that Virginians were more savage than the Indians had ever been, and Clark was desirous that they should retain this impression. The French of Kaskaskia called the Virginians "Long Knives."

On the morning of the 5th, the principal citizens were put in irons. Shortly after this Father Gibault and a few aged men came to Clark and begged the privilege of holding services in the church, that they might bid one another goodbye before they were separated. Clark gave his permission in a very crabbed way. The church bell rang out over the quiet but sad village, and immediately every one who could get to church did so. At the close of the service Father Gibault came again with some old men to beg that families might not be separated and that · they might be privileged to take some of their personal effects with them for their support. Clark then explained to the priest that Americans did not make war on women and children, but that it was only to protect their own wives and children that they had come to this stronghold of British and Indian barbarity. He went further and told them that the French king and the Americans had just made a treaty of alliance and that it was the desire of their French father that they should join their interests with the Americans. This had a wonderfully conciliatory effect upon the French. And now Clark told them they were at perfect liberty to conduct themselves as usual. His influence had been so powerful that they were all induced to take the oath of allegiance to the state of Virginia. Their arms were given back to them and a volunteer company of French militiamen was formed.

Kaskaskia was captured on July 4, 1778. On the morning of the

5th occurred the incident previously referred to, relative to the conduct of the priest. Evidently very early in the day, quiet was restored and better relations were established between captors and captives. The treaty of alliance between France and the United States was explained, and immediately the oath of allegiance to Virginia was taken by the people. On the same 5th of July an expedition was planned for the capture of Cahokia. Captain Bowman with his company, or probably a portion of it, and a detachment of the French militia under French officers, together with a number of Kaskaskia citizens, made up the army. Reynolds says they rode French ponies. The distance was sixty miles and the trip was made by the afternoon of the 6th. At first the people of Cahokia were greatly agitated and cried "Long Knives!" "Long Knives!" But the Kaskaskia citizens soon quieted them and explained what had happened at Kaskaskia only two days before. The fort at Cahokia may have contained a few British soldiers or some French militia. In either case they quietly surrendered. The oath of allegiance was administered to the people and the citizens returned to Kaskaskia.

Bloodless Capture of Vincennes

For the first few days of Clark's stay in Kaskaskia he and his men talked about the fort at the falls of Ohio and of a detachment of soldiers they were expecting from there every day. This was done for the purpose of making an impression upon the people of Kaskaskia. Clark was a shrewd diplomatist, as well as a good soldier, and he suspected that Father Gibault was at heart on the side of the Americans. By conversation Clark learned that the priest was the regular shepherd of the flock at Vincennes, and evidently had very great influence with the people there. Clark therefore talked of his expedition against Vincennes from the fort at the falls of the Ohio. Father Gibault then told Clark that while the post at Vincennes was a very strong one and that there were usually many Indians about that place, just at this time, the lieutenant governor or commandant, Edward Abbot, was not at Vincennes but was in Detroit. He also told Clark that there were no soldiers there except probably a few citizen-officers and that he had no doubt, if the people there knew the real nature of the conflict between England and the colonies and that France had joined against the hated British, there would be no opposition to Clark and his purposes. The priest further suggested that he himself would head an embassy to Post Vincennes for the purpose of attempting to secure the allegiance of the people there to the American cause.

This was the most cheering word that had come to Clark in all his first days at Kaskaskia. An expedition was immediately planned. The priest should be accompanied by a citizen of Kaskaskia, Doctor John Baptiste Lafont. The two gentlemen were accompanied by several attendants, among whom was a spy who had secret instructions from Clark.

They departed the 14th of July, and reached Vincennes safely. The priest had no difficulty in making it clear to the people that France was on the side of the Americans. The commander, Governor Abbot, had recently gone to Detroit, and there was no one in military command. They all took the oath of allegiance to Virginia. They also organized a militia company and took possession of the fort, over which the flag of Virginia floated, much to the wonder of the Indians. The Indians were told that the old French king, their father, had come to life, and if they did not want the land to be bloody with war they must make peace with the Americans.

August 1st Father Gibault and his companions returned to Kaskaskia and reported the success of their mission.

Clark was busy just then reorganizing his little army. The term of enlistment of the soldiers was drawing to a close, and he saw that unless he could re-enlist his men, all the good that had been accomplished would go for naught. Clark succeeded in re-enlisting about a hundred of his little army while the rest were to be mustered out at the falls of the Ohio, their places being filled with enlistments from the French militia. Captain Bowman was made military commandant at Cahokia, Captain Williams had charge at Kaskaskia, Captain Helm was sent to Vincennes to take charge, Captain Linn was sent with the soldiers who did not re-enlist to the falls of the Ohio, and Captain Montgomery was sent with Chevalier de Rocheblave and dispatches, to Williamsburg. It had been Colonel Clark's intention to treat with great consideration his distinguished captive, but M. Rocheblave behaved so rudely that he was sent a prisoner to Virginia, his slaves were confiscated and sold for 500 pounds sterling and the money distributed among the soldiers.

Colonel Clark by early fall restored order and obedience in all the Illinois country. He soon found the need of civil courts. The courts established by Wilkins under the British occupation had not been put in operation. Rocheblave had given little if any attention to civil administration. Colonel Clark made inquiry as to the customs and usages of the people and decided to organize courts for the adjustment of claims and disputes. Accordingly Captain Bowman held an election in Cahokia at which the citizens voted and elected judges, one of whom was Captain Bowman. Later, judges were elected at Kaskaskia and at Vincennes. Colonel Clark himself constituted the appellate court, and from a letter afterward written to Jefferson he must have been quite busy in this line of work, for he says, referring to this matter of being relieved from civil duties: "The civil department of the Illinois had heretofore robbed me of too much of my time that ought to be spent in military reflection. I was now likely to be relieved by Col. John Todd. I was anxious for his arrival and happy in his appointment, as the greatest intimacy and friendship has subsisted between us. I now saw myself rid of a piece of trouble that I had no delight in." This extract is from a letter written by Clark to Jefferson when he heard that Col. John Todd had been selected to administer civil government in the Illinois country.

VIRGINIA CREATES COUNTY OF ILLINOIS

The people of Virginia were soon aware of the success of the Clark expedition. The common people were, of course, greatly surprised, and the officials who had stood back of the enterprise were greatly relieved and delighted. The legislature in session in October took steps to extend civil government over the newly conquered country.

In October, 1778, the legislature of Virginia took the following action creating the county of Illinois: "All the citizens of the commonwealth of Virginia who are already settled or shall hereafter settle on the western side of the Ohio shall be included in a distinct county, which shall be called Illinois County; and the governor of this commonwealth with the advice of the council may appoint a county lieutenant or commander-in-chief, during pleasure, who shall appoint and commission as many deputy commandants, militia officers, and commissaries, as he shall think proper in the different districts, during pleasure; all of whom, before they enter into office shall take the oath of fidelity to this commonwealth and the oath of office, according to the form of their own religion.

"And all civil officers to which the inhabitants have been accustomed necessary for the preservation of the peace, and the administration of justice, shall be chosen by a majority of the citizens in their respective districts to be convened for that purpose by the county lieutenant or commandant, or his deputy, and shall be commissioned by the said county lieutenant or commander-in-chief."

In accordance with the provisions of the law creating the county of Illinois west of the Ohio River, the governor of Virginia, Patrick Henry, appointed John Todd, Esq., a judge of the Kentucky court, as county lieutenant or commander-in-chief of the newly created county.

His commission bears date of December 12, 1778, but he did not arrive in Illinois County until May, 1779. Clark had returned from his campaign, and capture of Vincennes. It is stated that Colonel Todd was received with great joy by the citizens of Kaskaskia. He was no stranger to many about the village, for he had come with Clark in the campaign of 1778, when the Illinois country was captured from the British. He is said to have been a soldier with Clark and to have been the first to enter the fort which Rocheblave surrendered. Be that as it may, he arrived now with the authority of the commonwealth of Virginia behind him. On June 15, 1779, he issued a proclamation which provided that no more settlements should be made in the bottom lands, and further that each person to whom grants had been made must report his claim to the proper officer and have his land recorded. If his land had come to him through transfers, then all such transfers must be recorded and certified to. This was done to prevent those adventurers who would shortly come into the country from dispossessing the rightful owners of those lands.

CONDITION OF ILLINOIS WHEN TODD ARRIVED

The country to which Colonel John Todd came as county-lieutenant was in a very discouraging condition. It had reached the maximum of prosperity about the time the French turned it over to the English in 1765. Very many of the French went to New Orleans or to St. Louis during the British regime. The English king had attempted to keep out the immigrant. The cultivation of the soil was sadly neglected. The few French who remained were engaged in trading with the Indians. Many came to be expert boatmen. Trade was brisk between the French settlements in the Illinois country and New Orleans.

Previous to the coming of Clark and the French gentlemen, Chevalier de Rocheblave, who was holding the country in the name of the British government, had been not only neglectful but really very obstinate and self-willed about carrying on civil affairs. He allowed the courts, organized by Colonel Wilkins, to fall into disuse. The merchants and others who had need for courts found little satisfaction in attempts to secure justice. During the time between the coming of Clark and of Todd, there were courts organized, but the military operations were so overshadowing that probably little use was made of them.

Military and Civil Personnel

It appears from the records of Colonel Todd that on the 14th of May, 1779, he organized the military department of his work, by appointing the officers of the militia at Kaskaskia, Prairie du Rocher, and Cahokia. Richard Winston, Jean B. Barbeau, and Francois Trotier were made commandants and captains in the three villages respectively.

The next step was to elect judges provided for in the act creating the county of Illinois. Judges were elected at Cahokia, Kaskaskia, and at Vincennes, and court was held monthly. There seems to have been a scarcity of properly qualified men for the places as in many instances militia officers were elected judges, and in one case the "deputy-commandant at Kaskaskia filled also the office of sheriff."

Todd issued permits or charters of trade and encouraged those about him to engage in business. He also gave attention to the subject of land-claims. No new claims were to be recognized except such as were made according to the custom of the French and inhabitants.

Colonel Todd found enough work to keep him busy and it is doubtful if it was all as pleasant as he might have wished. The records which he kept, and which are now in the possession of the Chicago Historical Society, show that severe penalties were inflicted in those days.

Colonel Todd held this position of county-lieutenant for about three years. During that time he established courts, held popular elections, and executed the law with vigor.

There was a deputy county-lieutenant or deputy-commandant in each village, and when Colonel Todd was absent, the reins of government were in the hands of one of these deputies. On the occasion of his absence at the time of his death he had left, it seems, Timothy Demountbrun as county lieutenant. This man seems to have been the only one authorized to rule, until the coming of St. Clair in 1790.

American Civil Government Northwest of the Ohio

Virginia ceded her western lands in 1783, in the following year Congress passed an ordinance which established a preliminary form of civil government north of the Ohio; in 1785 a national system of surveys was adopted, and in 1787 was passed the famous Ordinance of 1787 by which the territory northwest of the Ohio was "made one district for temporary government and provision made for a definite form of government." The first county created by Governor St. Clair, in July of that year, was Washington, with Marietta the seat of government. In

January, 1788, the governor and the newly appointed judges visited Losantiville (Cincinnati) and created the county of Hamilton, with that place as the seat of government. Then the governor and secretary proceeded westward and, reaching Kaskaskia on March 5, 1790, erected the county of St. Clair, with Cahokia as the county seat. On their return to Marietta, Knox County was organized, with Vincennes as the county seat.

OLD ST. CLAIR COUNTY

The St. Clair County thus established included all the territory north and east of the Ohio and the Mississippi and Illinois rivers, and west of a line running from Fort Massac through the mouth of the Mackinaw Creek a short distance below the city of Peoria. The county was divided into three districts, with Kaskaskia, Prairie du Rocher and Cahokia as centers of administration. Before leaving, Governor St. Clair created the offices of sheriff, judges of the court, probate judge, justice of the peace, coroner, notary, clerk and recorder, surveyor and various military officers, and named the appointees.

THE COUNTY DIVIDED

In 1795, Judge Turner, one of the three Federal judges, came to hold court, and from a contention which he had with the governor, St. Clair County was divided by a line running east and west through New Design. Cahokia was established as the county seat of the north half, or St. Clair County, and Kaskaskia, the seat of government of the south half, Randolph County.

LEGISLATURE OF NORTHWEST TERRITORY

The Ordinance of 1787 provided that when there should be 5,000 free male whites of the age of twenty-one years in the Northwest Territory they might organize a legislature on the basis of one representative for each 500 whites of the age of twenty-one. This was done in the year 1798. Shadrach Bond was elected to represent St. Clair County and John Edgar, Randolph County. The legislature met at Cincinnati on the 4th of February, 1799. There were twenty-two members in the lower house, representing eleven counties. William H. Harrison, who had succeeded Sargent as secretary of the Northwest Territory, was elected a delegate to congress.

THE UNITED STATES IN 1798

DIVISION INTO TWO TERRITORIES

In the session of congress in the winter of 1799-1800, the proposition to divide the Northwest Territory into two territories was referred to a committee of which Harrison was chairman. The report was favorably received by congress and on the 7th of May, 1800, an act was passed dividing the Northwest Territory by a line runing from the Ohio to Fort Recovery and thence to the line separating the territory from Canada.

The western part was to be known as the Indiana Territory and its government was to be of the first class. Its capital was located at Vincennes and the governor was William Henry Harrison. The eastern division was called the Northwest Territory, its capital was Chillicothe, and Governor St. Clair was still the chief executive. The east division was admitted as a state February 19, 1802. Illinois, Indiana, Wisconsin, and Michigan now became the Indiana Territory.

ILLINOIS TERRITORY CREATED

Illinois remained a portion of Indiana Territory from February, 1802, until February, 1809. During that period Vincennes was the capital. The congressional act of February 3, 1809, set off the territory of Illinois from Indiana by a dividing line running north from Vincennes to Canada. A prominent argument in favor of the division was that the people in the Illinois region were favorable to slavery, while the Indiana people were indifferent to the subject. Several efforts had been made to either strike out the clause in the Ordinance of 1787 forbidding slavery within the Northwest Territory, or suspend its operation for a stated period.

By the creative act, Illinois was made a territory of the first class, and thus remained until May, 1812, when, under authority of the Ordinance of 1787, it entered the second class, thus enfranchising all males over twenty-one years of age instead of allowing only freeholders to vote. Ninian Edwards, formerly a Kentucky judge, was appointed governor of the new territory, and Nathaniel Pope secretary, on April 24, 1809. Mr. Pope was a resident of St. Genevieve, Missouri, but practiced law in Illinois.

Illinois as a territory did not participate in the battle of Tippecanoe, or the War of 1812, but Governor Edwards left nothing undone to protect its soil against Indian depredations or British expeditions. Not a few soldiers and officers, however, went from the "American bottom," and it is estimated that fully two thousand Illinoisans participated in this border warfare. The apprehension of the settlers in the valleys of the Mississippi and Illinois were intensified by the Fort Dearborn massacre.

In September, 1812, following the advancement of Illinois to a territory of the second class, Governor Edwards and the judges, acting as a legislative body, created three new counties. The two old ones were St. Clair and Randolph, and the three new ones were Madison, Gallatin, and Johnson. On the same day an election was ordered in these five counties for five members of the legislative council, and for seven members of the house of representatives, and for a delegate in congress. The election was held October 8, 9 and 10. Those chosen were, for the lower house: from Madison, William Jones; St. Clair, Jacob Short and Joshua Oglesby; Randolph, George Fisher; Johnson, John Grammar; Gallatin, Philip Trammel and Alexander Wilson. Those chosen for the council were: from Madison, Samuel Judy; St. Clair, William Biggs; Randolph, Pierre Menard; Johnson, Thomas Ferguson; Gallatin, Benjamin Talbot.

Under the second-class form of government the legislature met biennially. In the summer of 1814 Col. Benjamin Stephenson was elected delegate in congress, and in 1816 Nathaniel Pope, who served till the admission of the state in 1818. Two new counties were added in 1815, White and Edwards, making seven in all. In 1816 four more were added—Monroe, Jackson, Pope and Crawford. In 1817 Bond was added, and in 1818 Franklin, Union and Washington were created, these making fifteen counties at the admission of the state in 1818.

The general assembly of 1812 met at Kaskaskia November 25th, and proceeded to organize by choosing Pierre Menard president of the Council and George Fisher, speaker of the House. It is said the whole of the assembly boarded at one house and slept in one room. The work before this first session was to re-enact the laws for the territory which served while the territory was of the first class, to adopt military measures for the defense of the people against the Indians, and to provide revenue for the maintenance of the Territorial Government. The legislature was in session from the 25th of November to the 26th of December, following.

First Illinois Preemption Law

This legislature elected Shadrach Bond as delegate to congress. He took his seat in the fall of 1812. During his term of office in congress Bond secured the passage of the first preemption law of Illinois. This law provided that a man who settled upon a piece of land and made an improvement while it was still government land, should have the right to buy the tract so improved in preference to anyone else. The law prevented persons from buying land which someone else had improved to the detriment of the one who made the improvement.

The wave of immigration often traveled westward faster than the surveyors did. In such cases the settler never knew just where his land would fall when the region was platted. And again, after the surveyor had done his work, it often happened that the surveyed land was not placed on the market for a number of years. The settler usually selected his lands and made improvements with the expectation that he would buy the land when it came on the market. Unprincipled men would watch and would often step in ahead of the settler at the land office and buy the improved land at government prices. This often resulted in violence and bloodshed. So the Bond law was a real peacemaker.

There was a rapid increase in the population of the territory of Illinois from the day it became a territory of the second grade. New counties were added to the five previously named. The new ones were Edwards and White in 1815; Monroe, Crawford, Jackson, Pope, Bond, in 1816; Union, Franklin and Washington in 1818.

First State Constitutional Convention

The Enabling Act became a law the 18th of April, 1818. The election of delegates to the constitutional convention was fixed for the first Monday in July, and that body was to convene the first Monday in August. But the first thing to do was to take the census of the territory, and if it did not have the forty thousand then there would be no need for the convention. It was soon evident that the territory did not have the required number. The story is told that the marshal stationed his enumerators on the public highways and counted the travelers and immigrants, regardless of their destination. Not only this, but it is asserted that often the same traveller or immigrant was counted twice or even thrice. At last the enumerators returned forty thousand inhabitants, but as the returns were afterward footed up there were really only thirty-four thousand six hundred and twenty people in the proposed state. The delegates were duly elected and assembled at Kaskaskia on the first Monday in August.

The convention met August 3, 1818, and finished its labors and adjourned August 26th. Jesse B. Thomas from St. Clair County was elected chairman, and William C. Greenup was made secretary.

STATE MACHINERY IN MOTION

The constitution was not submitted to the people for ratification and the only officers whom the people might elect were: Governor, lieutenant governor, members of the general assembly, sheriffs and coroners. The offices which were filled by appointment of either the governor or the general assembly were: Judges of the supreme, circuit and probate courts; prosecuting attorney, county clerk, circuit clerk, recorder, justice of the peace, auditor of public accounts, attorney general and secretary of state.

The day fixed by the constitution for the election of state officers was the third Thursday (17th) of September, 1818, when Shadrach Bond was chosen governor, Pierre Menard, lieutenant governor, and John McLean, representative in Congress. There were also elected fourteen senators and twenty-nine representatives.

The legislature was called to meet at Kaskaskia the first Monday in October (the 5th). The first thing for this legislature was the canvass of the votes, and on Tuesday (the 6th), Governor Bond was inaugurated. The legislature proceeded to the election of two United States senators. The choice fell upon Ninian Edwards and Jesse B. Thomas. The Legislature chose the following state officers: state treasurer, John Thomas; auditor, Elijah C. Berry; attorney general, Daniel P. Clark; supreme judges, Joseph Phillips, chief justice, William P. Foster, Thomas C. Brown, and John Reynolds. The governor appointed Elias Kent Kane secretary of state.

Under the Constitution of 1818 the governor did not have the veto power as a sole prerogative. It was exercised by him in conjunction with the Supreme Court, the joint body being known as the Council of Revision. It abolished imprisonment for debt; declared against the introduction of slavery and the indenture of anybody except on condition of a bona fide consideration. The constitution did not affect the slaves held by the French and their descendants. Provision was, however, made that slaves hired in slave states could be brought into the salt works at Shawneetown and held for one year; then hired again for a like period; but even this traffic must cease by 1825. Of course, the constitution provided for the regular division of the government into legislative, executive and judicial departments, and the election or appointment of the officials designed to fulfill their functions.

Governor Bond was elected without opposition, largely on the strength of his authorship of the Preemption Act while serving as a territorial delegate to Congress.

Following the announcement of the acceptance of the constitution by Congress, Governor Bond called the Legislature in special session for January 4, 1819. The machinery of the first state government was thus set in motion. In his short and unassuming message the governor recommended the early completion of the canal connecting the head waters of the Illinois River with Lake Michigan; the passage of measures to relieve the state treasury, and a modification of the criminal laws in force during the territorial period. But the Legislature went ahead, in its own way, and passed such measures as a code of laws based on the Virginia and Kentucky statutes; levying taxes on lands owned by non-residents, and on slaves and indentured servants, and moving the capital from Kaskaskia to a point on the Kaskaskia River, east of the third principal meridian, as well as asking Congress to donate lands for the purpose.

ILLINOIS BLACK CODE

The Legislature of 1819 also passed the Illinois Black Code, entitled "An Act Respecting Free Negroes, Mulattoes, Servants and Slaves." The Black Laws, as they were generally called, remained upon the statute books of Illinois until February 12, 1853, and were therefore in force throughout Champaign County for about twenty years from its organization. They comprised twenty-five sections, and were copied from old laws in force during the territorial period and originating in the old slave states.

ILLINOIS COUNTIES IN 1818

When Illinois became a State in 1818, it was only the southernmost counties which were fully organized. Substantially they embraced the territory between the Mississippi and the Ohio rivers south of a line drawn east and west bounding St. Clair and Washington on the north, cutting off a northern tier of sections in Marion County of today, passing through nearly the center of Clay County and the upper third of Richland and east and southeast through Lawrence County to the Ohio. That area was then divided into St. Clair, Washington, Edwards, Randolph, Monroe, Jackson, Franklin, Gallatin, Union, Johnson and Pope. The remainder, and by far the larger portion of Illinois, was divided into Madison, Bond and Crawford counties. · The last named embraced more than thirty of the counties now included in eastern, northeastern and central Illinois, and stretching from Crawford, Jasper, Effingham and Fayette counties on the south to the Wisconsin state line. The present county of Champaign was just southeast of the center of this vast unorganized country.

New Capital, Vandalia

The Legislature of 1819 appointed five commissioners to locate the gift of lands made by Congress as the site of a new capital. They selected four sections immediately west of the Kaskaskia River, and completed a two-story frame building as a capitol so that it was ready for the Legislature in the summer of 1820. When that body convened in December, of that year, it met in the new capital city of Vandalia.

Early Period of Wild-Cat Banking

The second General Assembly, which met at Vandalia, attempted to relieve the hard times prevalent in the state, especially caused by the matured debts of land owners who had bought recklessly in years past, by chartering the Illinois State Bank, with headquarters at Vandalia and branches at Edwardsville, Brownsville, Shawneetown and Albion. Bills of various denominations were issued on personal and real estate securities, and the State Senate passed a resolution asking the secretary of the treasury to accept the bills in payment of land. But its recommendation was not followed by the state treasury. Notwithstanding which, the State Branch and all its branches withered, and at the expiration of its charter in 1831 the commonwealth borrowed $100,000 in order to close up its business in an honorable way. It is fitting to remark that Governor Bond and the State Supreme Court, acting as the Board of Revision, had vetoed the original measure, and that the Legislature passed it over their earnest objections.

This season of wild-cat banking, which so disturbed every legitimate business and agricultural interest in Illinois, had but an indirect effect upon the development of Champaign County, as permanent settlement had only fairly commenced during the later period of its operations.

At the second session of the State Legislature, and the first held at Vandalia, several new counties were created—Lawrence, Greene, Sangamon, Pike, Hamilton, Montgomery and Fayette. Chicago was then in Pike County.

The Slavery Issue (1822-24)

The slavery issue in Illinois was a burning question in the Coles administration in 1822-24, but it culminated in the fall of the latter year in a decided popular vote against reopening the matter by calling a convention to consider a revision of the state constitution in regards to its pronunciamento against the continuation of the institution. With the exception of Union and Johnson, all the southern counties, where black labor was most in demand, favored the calling of the convention.

The stronghold of the anti-slavery sentiment was that wonderfully fertile and charming Sangamon region, which lay along the valley of that river and stretched from the southern rim of the valley of the Illinois toward the central regions of the state. It was rapidly settling up, and a few of the more adventurous had even "squatted" on choice timber tracts along the headwaters of the Sangamon.

The Famous Sangamon Country

The Sangamon region was settled by immigrants from all the older states but probably those from the northern states predominated. More than two hundred families had settled in the Sangamon country before the land was surveyed. In the vote on the convention question, Sangamon County cast 875 votes—153 for and 722 against, the convention, This would show a population of over 4,000 in 1824. It also means that these settlers were from the free states chiefly.

By the spring of 1825, the result of the slavery contest was known in all the older states, and as if people were waiting for a favorable report, the movement of immigration began.

The fame of the "Sangamon country" had spread into all the older settled portions of the United States and the migrations were largely toward that region. In the summer of 1825, the road leading into the "Sangamon country" was literally lined with movers seeking new homes. In Vandalia alone it is said 250 wagons were counted going north in three weeks.

The first to systematically explore the Sangamon region was Ferdinand Ernst, a German traveler, to whom had been carried even to Europe, marvelous stories of that country; and he wished to "see for himself." He reached the site of Vandalia before the sale of lots took place, which occurred the 6th of September, 1819. From here he visited the Sangamon country. There was a very good road leading from Edwardsville into the Sangamon country. As nearly as this road can be now traced, it ran in almost a straight line from Edwardsville to the present city of Carlinville, passing on the way the site of the present flourishing city of Bunker Hill. From Carlinville the road bent to the east-of-north, passing out of the present county of Macoupin at the northeast corner, three miles east of the present city of Virden; from this point east-of-north to a point very near Rochester, and thence to a point near the junction of the south branch and north fork of the Sangamon River, leaving the site of the present capital some four or five miles to the west. From here the road continued the same general direction to the present city of Lincoln. The road continued this general direction till it left the present county of Logan at the old Kickapoo capital. Here it struck Tazewell County and thence turned northwest to Lake Peoria. This was the route taken by Governor Edwards in his campaign in 1812.

Mr. Ernst, the traveler, took this road in 1819. He started from Vandalia and went northwest, crossed Shoal Creek, left the headwaters of Silver and Sugar Creek to the southwest, passed not far from Mt. Olive and Gillespie, and came into the road described above, a few miles north of Bunker Hill. He describes the big prairie which separates the headwaters of the Macoupin and the Sangamon. He says the moment one passes over the divide into the drainage basin of the Sangamon he sees a marked difference in the character of the soil. The second night out the traveler stayed with a family on Sugar Creek, about two miles west of Pawnee. Sixty farms had been opened on this stream since the spring of 1819. The sod-corn was from ten to fifteen feet high. The land was not yet surveyed and could not be for some three years. This was called "the beautiful land of the Sangamon." From this point Mr. Ernst traveled west in a circuit around the present site of Springfield to Elkhart Grove. Here lived a Mr. Latham who had thirty acres in cultivation. This farm was the farthest north of any east of the Illinois river. However, there were some farms laid out at the old Kickapoo capital just in the edge of Tazewell County, but no settlements made. Mr. Ernst went north to Salt Creek, but not being able to get across he retraced his steps.

Mr. Ernst says: "In the vicinity of this town (Vandalia) is a large amount of fine land; but every one is full of praise of those sixty or eighty miles northward upon the River Sangamon. The expression the 'Sangamon country,' applied to all that country through which the Sangamon river and its branches flow. Peck's Gazetteer, page 131, says: 'This country contains a larger quantity of rich land than any other in the state. The Sangamon, in particular, is an Arcadian region, in which nature has delighted to bring together her happiest combinations of landscape. It is generally a level country. There is a happy proportion of timbered and prairied lands. The soil is of great fertility. All who have visited this fine tract of country admire the beauty of the landscape, which nature has here painted in primeval freshness.'"

It was most fitting that this beautiful, fertile and invigorating region of Illinois should be first settled by an energetic, enterprising class of freemen and women, constitutionally opposed to the introduction of any form of slavery into their virgin land.

FUNDAMENTAL SCHOOL LEGISLATION

Joseph Duncan of Jacksonville, afterward congressman and governor, secured the passage of the free school law of 1825, which was the basis of the system of today. For its support, taxes were to be collected on the property of the people in the district, and provision was made for a board of directors who were to have control of the schools and buildings, examine the teachers and have general local oversight of all educational matters of a public nature.

In 1826-27 the Legislature provided for better securities from those who were borrowing the money for which the school lands had been sold. But in 1829 the Legislature repealed the part of the Duncan law of 1825 which gave 2 per cent of the net revenue of the State to the schools. Every commendable feature of the Duncan law was now repealed and the schools lay prostrate till 1855.

The Legislature of 1828-29 also adopted the plan of selling the school and seminary lands. The law provided that the sixteenth section of each township might be sold whenever nine-tenths of the inhabitants (evidently voters) were in favor of the sale. Later the law allowed the sale if three-fourths were in favor of it.

The immigrants coming into an unsettled township were always eager to dispose of the sixteenth section, as it made a fund with which the authorities might assist the schools. But this section when sold for $1.25 per acre, the regular Government price, would bring only $800, and this at 10 per cent interest would bring only $80 per year. This would not be of much service when distributed among the schools of the township.

STATE BANK IN LIQUIDATION

Joseph Duncan stepped from Congress into the governorship, in 1834, and during his administration was chiefly engaged in wrestling with banking and internal improvement problems, which were so intimately connected. In 1837 the State Bank, with other similar institutions of the country, suspended specie payments, and in 1843 the Legislature passed a law "to diminish the State debt and put the State Bank into liquidation." The bank was given four years in which to wind up its business.

SYSTEM OF INTERNAL IMPROVEMENTS

While the affairs of the State Bank and its branches were in chaos, an ambitious system of internal improvements was assumed by the State, despite the opposition of Governor Duncan and the Council of Revision. The bill as prepared by the Vandalia convention to consider internal improvements became a law. It appropriated $10,200,000 for the following objects: Improvement of the Wabash, the Illinois, Rock, Kaskaskia and Little Wabash rivers, and the Western Mail Route $9,350,000; for railroads—Cairo to Galena, $3,500,000; Alton to Mount Carmel, $1,600,000; Quincy to Indiana line, $1,800,000; Shelbyville to Terre Haute, $650,000; Peoria to Warsaw, $700,000; Alton to Central Railroad, $600,000; Belleville to Mount Carmel, $150,000; Bloomington to Pekin, $350,000, and Vincennes to St. Louis, $250,000; $200,000 "to pacify disappointed counties" which had failed to be promised any improvement whatsoever by the State. In addition, the sale of $1,000,000 worth of canal lands and the issuance of $500,000 in canal bonds were authorized, the proceeds to be used in the construction of the Illinois & Michigan Canal, $500,000 of this amount to be expended in 1838. A competent historian graphically tells what happened: "Work began at once. Routes were surveyed and contracts for construction let, and an era of reckless speculation began. Large sums were rapidly expended and nearly $6,500,000 quickly added to the State debt. The system was soon demonstrated to be a failure and was abandoned for lack of funds, some of the 'improvements' already made being sold to private parties at a heavy loss. This scheme furnished the basis of the State debt under which Illinois labored for many years and which, at its maximum, reached nearly $17,000,000."

Although as a whole the internal improvements scheme was a disaster to the State as a promoter of public works, it was the means of furthering the project of a great railroad to be projected through central Illinois from north to south, it eventually materialized into one of the splendid railroad systems of the country, being kept alive through private promotion and management.

CAPITAL MOVED TO SPRINGFIELD

It was at the same session which originated the internal improvements scheme that the Legislature voted to move the State capital from Vandalia to Springfield, Sangamon County. Jacksonville, Peoria and Alton were also competitors. Lincoln led the Sangamon County delegation to victory, its solid support of internal improvements hinging largely on the outside backing received as a candidate for the State capital. The legislative act by which the removal was accomplished went into effect July 4, 1839, and the Legislature convened at the new capitol in December of that year.

REMAINS OF INTERNAL IMPROVEMENTS SYSTEM

In 1840 the Legislature abolished the board of fund commissioners and the board of public works which had in charge the internal improvements of the State and that loose-jointed system collapsed. One fund commissioner was then appointed who was authorized to act, but was without power to sell bonds or to borrow money on the credit of the State. Another board of public works was also created, which, with the fund commissioner, was to wind up pending business without delay, to operate any roads which were near completion, complete the work on the Illinois & Michigan Canal and burn all bonds remaining unsold.

The Great Northern Cross Railroad, which was planned to be constructed from Springfield to Quincy, half way across the State to the Mississippi River, had actually been built from the State capital to Meredosia, Morgan County, on the eastern bank of the Illinois River, fifty-eight miles distant. This road, which became a part of the Wabash system, was sold in 1847 to Nicholas H. Ridgly of Springfield for about $21,000. Thus a commencement had been made in at least two rail-roads which now traverse the territory of Champaign County.

REVISING THE OLD CONSTITUTION

After the defeat of the convention in 1824 nothing was done toward revising or amending the State Constitution until 1840-41. In the Legislature of that year a resolution was adopted calling on the voters to express themselves relative to a convention at the coming State election in August. The Democrats favored such a convention, but when a bill passed the Legislature abolishing the Circuit Court judges and creating five new judges on the Supreme bench, all of which places were filled by Democrats, the need of a convention did not seem so apparent.

The Democrats now controlled the Legislature, the executive and the courts. When the election was held in August the Democrats generally voted against the proposition to hold a convention; but the Whigs later passed another act calling on the people to vote on the question of a convention at the general election in August, 1846. The proposition was strongly urged upon the people by the Democratic press and it was not very generally opposed, and so it carried.

The act providing for the constitutional convention determined the number of delegates which should sit therein, the date of their election, which was fixed for the third Monday in April, 1847, and the date of the meeting of the delegates in the convention, the first Monday in June, 1847. There was no special argument against a convention, but several were urged in its favor.

There were a number of other changes which were considered during the canvass preceding the election in April. When the members came together June 7, 1847, it was found that the Whigs and Democrats were about evenly divided. The convention organized by electing Newton Cloud president and Henry W. Moore secretary. There were 162 delegates in this body.

In the legislative department the following features may be noted in the constitution of 1848: No member of the General Assembly shall be elected to any other office during his term as a legislator. The Senate shall consist of twenty-five members and the House of seventy-five members till the State shall contain 1,000,000 people. After that an addition of five in each House shall be made for every increase of 500,000 till there shall be 50 senators and 100 representatives, when the number shall remain stationary.

The governor must be a citizen of the United States and thirty-five years of age, and shall be a citizen of the United States fourteen years and have resided in the State ten years. The governor must reside at the seat of government. He shall have the veto power. His salary was $1,500—no more. The secretary of state, auditor and treasurer shall be elected at the same time as the governor and lieutenant-governor are chosen. . The governor shall issue all commissions.

THE CONSTITUTION OF 1848

The constitution was completed on August 31, 1847. On March 6, 1848, it was submitted to the people for ratification. The vote on the constitution stood nearly 60,000 for and nearly 16,000 against. It was declared in force April 1, 1848. By the terms of the document itself an election should be held on Tuesday after the first Monday in November, 1848, for governor and other executive officers, as well as for members of the Legislature. In compliance therewith, in November, 1848, Governor French was re-elected governor for four years from January 1, 1849.

The new constitution authorized the Legislature to provide for township organization. In pursuance thereof a law was passed in 1849 which allowed counties, when authorized by a vote of the people, to organize under this new system. This new system of county organization is distinctly a New England product, and was therefore championed by the northern counties, which had been largely settled by immigrants from New England and the Middle States. The Legislature on February 12, 1849, passed a general law governing all counties under township organization. This first law was somewhat imperfect, and has therefore been subject to amendments up till the present time.

BANKING LEGISLATION

In the thirty years which had passed since the adoption of its first constitution, the State of Illinois had learned several lessons through the impressive process of distressing experience. Perhaps the most important thus instilled were those connected with reckless expansion of the financial institutions and the public utilities within her borders. Under the constitution of 1818 the credit of the State might be used to foster such enterprises as banks, railroads and canals. But the constitution of 1848 says: "No State bank shall hereafter be created, nor shall the State own or be liable for any stock in any corporation or joint stock association for banking purposes to be hereafter created." It was not possible, therefore, for the State to engage in any banking business or improvement schemes, but it might grant charters, or pass laws, in the encouragement of such enterprises. Further safeguards are thrown around the State, as witness this provision: "No act of the General Assembly, authorizing corporations or associations with banking powers, shall go into effect or in any manner be enforced, unless the same shall be submitted to the people at the general election next succeeding the passage of the same, and be approved by a majority of the votes cast at such election for and against such law." Another section of the same article (X) provides that all stockholders in banking associations issuing bank notes should be individually responsible proportionately to the stock held by each for all liabilities of the corporation or association. Since the winding up of the affairs of the old State Bank and the Bank of Illinois there were no banks of issue in the State. The money in circulation comprised gold and silver and paper money issued by banks in other states.

Following the ratification of the constitution of 1848, there began, almost immediately, an agitation for banks of issue in Illinois. The New York free banking law had been in operation for a decade. The

1—6

bank bills were secured by bonds of the United States or State, or mortgages approved by the state comptroller, in whose hands the securities were placed. That official issued the bills put in circulation, which were countersigned by the bank officers. The bank bills were to be redeemed when presented by the holders within a reasonable time and, if necessary, the comptroller was authorized to sell the bonds deposited with him for that purpose, or if the State were required to wind up the affairs of the bank.

In the session of 1851 the Legislature passed a law founded on the New York system, and it was ratified at the general election in November. Under it, also, no bank could be organized with a smaller issue of bills than $50,000. It was also provided that if any bank refused to redeem its issue, it was liable to a fine of 12½ per cent on the amount presented for redemption.·   ·

On the face of it, the law seemed fairly to protect both the bank-note holder and the State; but various schemes were worked to keep the people from presenting their bills for redemption. One of the most ingenious was the interchanging of bills between banks in widely separated sections of the country. A bank, say, in Springfield, Illinois, would send $25,000 of its own issue to a bank in Massachusetts, say, in Boston; the Boston bank returning a like amount to the Springfield bank. Each bank would then pay out this money over its counter in small quantities and in this way the Springfield bank issue would become scattered all over New England and no person holding but a few dollars would think of coming to Springfield to get his bills redeemed. The issue of the Boston bank would be scattered through the West. In this way, and in other ways, the money of Illinois became scattered in other states, while in the ordinary business transaction in this State one would handle a large number of bills daily which had been issued in other states.

REAL WILD-CAT BANKS

No doubt many corporations went into the banking business under this law with clean hands and carried on a properly conducted banking business, but there were ways by which irresponsible and dishonest men might go into the banking business and make large sums of money without very much capital invested.

These banks were known as wild-cat banks. The name is said to have originated from the picture of a wild cat engraved on the bills of one of these irresponsible banks in Michigan. However, they may have been named from the fact that the words "wild cat" were often applied to any irresponsible venture or scheme.

There were, in Illinois, organized under this law, 115 banks of issue. Up to 1860 the "ultimate security" was sufficient at any time to redeem all outstanding bills, but when the Civil War came on the securities of the Southern States, on deposit in the auditor's office, depreciated greatly in value. The banks were going into liquidation rapidly. They redeemed their bills at all prices from par down to forty-nine cents on the dollar. It is estimated that the bill-holders lost about $400,000, but that it came in such a way that it was not felt seriously. This system of banking was followed by the national banking system with which we are acquainted today.

The 115 banks of issue which were in operation in Illinois just prior to the Civil War issued nearly 1,000 different kinds of bank bills. Because of the large number of kinds of bills counterfeiting was easy, and it is said that much of the money in circulation was counterfeit. Banks received reports as to the condition of financial institutions over the State daily. One never knew when he presented a bill in payment of a debt whether it was of any value. Often the merchant would accept this paper money only when heavily discounted.

The agitation of the slavery question, which had centered around the debates on the Missouri Compromise and the efforts of the Free Soilers at least to restrict the spread of the institution, swept through Illinois and was violent in Champaign County, where both Lincoln and Douglas were not unfamiliar figures. In 1858 they also electioneered in their famous contest for the United States Senate.

THE NATIONAL BANKING SYSTEM

In February, 1863, Congress passed an act creating a national banking system, and in that year several of the free banks of Illinois changed accordingly. All free banks which had their notes secured by bonds of the seceding states were obliged to furnish additional security, or redeem their notes and suspend. Thus the free banks began to disappear. In March, 1865, Congress passed a law which placed a tax on all bills issued by the State banks, which had the effect of forcing the remainder of the free banks out of business, or inducing them to join the ranks of the National banks. The National Banking Law of 1863 is the basis of the system of today. It has been greatly reinforced of late years by the statutes by which banks are chartered and regulated by the State, and by the National enactments of even later date by which the National banks cooperate and protect the entire financial system of the country and especially promote and conserve the vast agricultural interests of the nation.

The Constitution of 1870

The coming and progress of the Civil War, and how Champaign County participated in it, is told in another chapter. Perhaps the next broad event affecting Champaign County at many points was the adoption of the State Constitution of 1870. It is divided into twenty sections. Briefly, it provides for minority representation and for free schools; prohibits the paying of money by any civil corporate body in aid of any church or parochial school; creates fifty-one senatorial districts, each of which is entitled to one senator and three representatives; declares the inviolability of the Illinois Central Railroad tax; lays the basis of the present railroad and warehouse laws; prohibits the sale or lease of the Illinois & Michigan Canal without a vote of the people; prohibits municipalities from subscribing for any stock in any railroad or private corporation; limits the rate of taxation and amount of indebtedness that may be incurred; prohibits special legislation; authorizes the creation of appellate courts, and fixes the salaries of State officers by legislative enactment.

Building and Loan Associations Authorized

A word as to the origin and workings of the building and loan associations of Illinois and Champaign County. They were authorized by the General Assembly of 1879. They are cooperative associations, having for their aim the creation of a fund through small monthly payments by investors, which, when sufficiently large, may be loaned to borrowers. The borrower, in turn, becomes an investor, and when his investment amounts to a sum equal to the amount he borrowed, the interest having been paid monthly, the debt is cancelled. This plan enables those who have small savings each month to invest in building and loan stock. The earnings are usually better than other forms of investment, as the borrower pays his interest monthly. This interest is immediately loaned and is compounded several times by the end of the year. The borrower finds it easy to pay his interest monthly, and his investment also, and so, in a sense, profits much from this plan of paying for a home.

It will readily be understood that this chapter is presented as a background for the more detailed delineation of Champaign County. Much of it deals with events which transpired long before it had a name or a political existence, but they have all had a bearing on the history and development of this section of the State, and now and then direct reference has been made to such connection. When the white civilization of the region first commenced to develop, the red man still occupied many choice spots in eastern and central Illinois. Their habitats, as indistinctly defined, are noted in the following chapter, as well as the facts of their final departure from the territory now known as Champaign County.

CHAPTER III

FLEETING GLIMPSES OF THE RED MAN

The Illinois Confederacy—The Kaskaskias—The Peorias—
Miamis and Pottawattamies—The Kickapoos—Famous Indian
Camps at Urbana—Favorite Resort Near Sadorus—Shemauger,
the Friendly Pottawattamie Chief—Told to "Git"—Indian
Scares—Pleased with the White Man's Coffin—Indian
Sepultures—Miamis Passing to the West—En Route for
Washington—Last of the Champaign County Indians.

The Indians found in Illinois by Marquette and Joliet belonged to
the Algonquin family; and there was undying hatred between the Iroquois of the East and the Algonquins of the Northwest.

The Illinois Confederacy

The Illinois Indians formed a loose confederacy of about half a
dozen tribes, the chief of which were the Metchigamis, the Kaskaskias,
the Peorias, the Cahokias and the Tamaroas. In addition, there were
the Piankashaws, the Weas, the Kickapoos, the Shawnees and probably
other tribes, or remnants, who occupied Illinois soil for longer or
shorter periods. The first five tribes are probably all who should be
included in the Illinois Confederacy.

The Metchigamis were found along the Mississippi River. Their
principal settlement was near Fort Chartres. They also lived in the
vicinity of Lake Michigan, to which they gave their name. They were
allies of Pontiac in the war of 1764, and perished with other members
of the Illinois Confederacy on Starved Rock, in 1769.

The Kaskaskias

The Kaskaskias were originally found along the upper courses of
the Illinois River, and it was among the members of this tribe that
Marquette planted the first mission in Illinois. They moved from
the upper Illinois to the mouth of the Kaskaskia River in 1700, and
founded there the old city of Kaskaskia, which eventually became the

86

center of French life in the interior of the continent. During the following century the Kaskaskias occupied the region at and about their
city, but in 1802 were almost exterminated by the Shawnees at the
battle near the Big Muddy, Saline County. The Kaskaskias afterward
moved to a reservation on the lower Big Muddy, and eventually to the
Indian Territory. The Cahokia and Tamaroa tribes were merged with
the Kaskaskias under one chief.

The Peorias

The Peorias made their home in the region of Lake Peoria and were
always quiet and peaceable. The Piankashaws, a small tribe of the
Miami confederation, first resided in southeastern Wisconsin, and after
the misadventure at Starved Rock moved to the Wabash River, and
eventually to a Kansas reservation and to the Indian Territory. They
were always very friendly to the white settlers.

Miamis and Pottawattamies

Although the Miamis and the Pottawattamies were familiar to the
early settlers of central Illinois and Champaign County, they were not
settled representatives of the red men in those sections of the State, but
rather made their appearance as warriors or hunters.

The Kickapoos

The Kickapoos seemed to have been intimately associated with the
Miamis and Pottawattamies in the Indian campaigns against St. Clair,
Wayne and Taylor. They were bold marauders and warriors, and were
in special force at the battle of Tippecanoe. They were scattered
throughout the Illinois country, but for fifty years before the Edwardsville treaty of 1819 held strong sway over the eastern part of what is now
the State, and in the late '20s and early '30s, when the first permanent
white settlers were arriving in the present Champaign County, still occupied the soil of that region with undisputed title to its possession among
the people of their own race.

The Kickapoos, as a tribe, first acknowledged the authority of the
United States at the treaty mentioned, which was signed July 30, 1819.
A month later, the Government concluded a treaty at Vincennes with
a smaller division of the Kickapoos, known as the tribes of the Vermilion
River, who claimed territory embracing the county by that name and
the eastern part of Champaign. Thus relinquishing all title to their

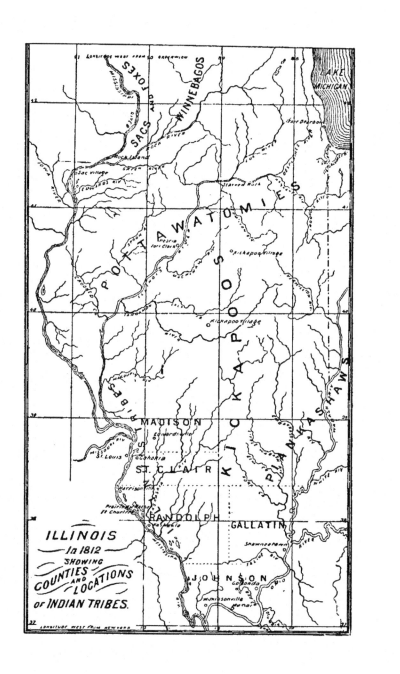

lands in Illinois, the Kickapoos honorably observed their contracts and moved as a body to their western lands, although weak remnants of the tribe lingered until the early '30s on several favorite camping grounds, near the scenes of their old centers of power in Champaign and McLean counties. The Pottawattamies of the Kankakee, in their annual hunts, also visited the region after the white pioneers had commenced to take up land for themselves and their children. As the timbered tracts of Champaign County and contiguous territory abounded in game, the climate was less rigorous than that of the more northern sections, and as the soil yielded plentifully of cereals and vegetables, the region was naturally a favorite to the Kickapoos and the more migratory Pottawattamies. The latter especially adopted as favorite camping places the immediate site of Urbana and wooded haunts along the Okaw, Sangamon and the Salt Fork.

FAMOUS INDIAN CAMPS AT URBANA

The late Judge Cunningham, writing more than a decade ago, says: "But a few years since, and plainly to be seen until the white man's plow had turned up the sod and effaced the evidences of their occupation, were many Indian trails across the prairies; and it is within the memory of many now living, as well as attested by the well remembered statements heard from the early settlers, that the corn-hills of the Indian occupants were found not far from the site of the Public Square in Urbana, as late as 1832. Many yet remember a fine spring of water which came from the bluff two or three rods south of the stone bridge on Main Street, which was obliterated by being covered with earth only a few years since. This spring afforded an abundance of water to the campers in the edge of the timber; as it did to the families of William Tompkins and Isaac Busey, who afterwards took possession of the site for their homes, though they frequently shared it with their returning Indian visitors. This was a point having great attractions for the latter. Indian trinkets and ornaments of bone and metal were often picked up in the neighborhood of this spring by the whites after settlements were established here, and the bones of game animals strewn over the ground showed a long and extensive occupancy of the locality for camping purposes before the white occupancy.

FAVORITE RESORT NEAR SADORUS

"A favorite resort of the Indians upon the Okaw was a place near that stream about half a mile north of the village of Sadorus, and upon the east bank of the stream. There they often encamped in the autumn and awaited the coming of deer and other game when driven by the prairie fires from the open country into the timber. To this day the plow upon that ground turns up stone-axes and arrow heads, left there by these long-ago tenants of the .prairies. The cabinet of Capt. G. W. B. Sadorus contains many of these and other relies. Even after the settlement of the country, the Indians followed the practice of here awaiting the annual coming of their prey. Many were the incidents told by the settlers about the Big Grove—few of whom yet remain —in connection with the visits made here by the Pottawattamies, which continued for many years after the first occupancy by the whites. The prairies and groves of this county, as well as the neighboring counties of Illinois, were favorite hunting grounds of the people of this tribe, whose own country was along the shores of Lake Michigan, as they had been of the former occupants and claimants, the Kickapoos, who had relinquished their rights. Not only was this region esteemed by those people on account of the game with which it abounded, but it yielded to their cultivation abundant returns in cereals and vegetables. Its winters were not so long and much less rigorous than were those of the lake regions, so that the red visitors of the pioneers of Champaign and Vermilion counties were not rarities. No complaint has come down to the inquirers of later years of any hostile or unfriendly acts from these people, but on the contrary, from all accounts they avoided doing any harm and were frequently helpful to the new comers.

Shemauger, the Friendly Pottawattamie Chief

"Our early settlers around and in these timber belts and groves well remember many of their Indian visitors by name, and the writer has listened with great interest to many enthusiastically told stories from them of personal contact with these people. Particular mention was made by many of a Pottawattamie chief named Shemauger, who was also known by the name of Old Soldier. Shemauger often visited the site of Urbana after the whites came, and for some years after 1824. He claimed it as his birthplace, and told the early settlers that the family home at the time of his birth was near a large hickory tree then growing upon a spot north of Main Street and a few rods west of Market Street. He professed great love for this location as his birthplace, and the camping ground of his people for many years. At the time of the later visits of Shemauger there was not only the hickory tree, but a large wild cherry tree standing about where the hall of the Knights of Pythias is now situated. Besides these trees there were others in the neighborhood of the creek, which made this a favorite and most convenient and comfortable camping place for the Indians; and, from what is known of the habits of these people, it is not improbable that the chief was correct in the claim made upon Urbana as his birth-place. It is remembered of Shemauger that he would sometimes come in company with a large retinue of his tribe and sometimes with his family only, when he would remain for months in camp at points along the creek. In the winter of 1831-32, these Indians to the number of fifteen or twenty remained in their camp near the big spring on what, of late years, has been known as the Stewart farm in the neighborhood of Henry Dobson's, about two miles north of Urbana.

A BIT OF THE SITE OF THE POTTAWATTAMIE VILLAGE

"Another favorite camping ground of Shemauger was at a point known as the Clay Bank on the northwest quarter of Section 2, Urbana Township, sometimes called Clement's Ford, towards the north end of the Big Grove. One early settler. (Amos Johnson, who died twenty years since) related to the writer his observations of these people while there in camp. His father occupied a cabin not far away, and the family paid frequent visits to the camp out of curiosity, fearing nothing. Some of the braves amused themselves by cutting with their tomahawks mor-tices into contiguous trees, into which mortices they inserted poles cut the proper lengths. These poles, so placed horizontally at convenient distances from each other, made a huge living ladder reaching from the ground to a great height. Up this ladder the Indians would climb when the weather was warm and sultry to catch the breezes and to escape the annoyances of the mosquitoes. He saw the bucks thus comfortably situated upon a scaffold in the tops of the trees, while their squaws were engaged in the domestic duties of the camp on the ground below. Thirty-five or more years ago, trees from near the Clay Bank were cut and sawed into lumber at the nearby mill of John Smith, when these mortices, overgrown by many years' growth of the trees, were uncovered, showing the work of these Indians forty years before, and corroborating the story as related to the writer.

"Shemauger told another early settler (James W. Boyd, who died many years since), or in his hearing, that many years before, there came in this country a heavy fall of snow, the depth of which he indicated by holding his ramrod horizontally above his head, and said that many wild beasts, elk, deer and buffalo perished under the snow. To this fact, within his knowledge, he attributed the presence of many bones of animals then seen on the prairies.

"Shemauger was remembered by those who knew him personally as a very large, bony man, always kind and helpful to the white settlers. It was also said that, upon being asked to do so, he would, with a company of followers, attend the cabin raisings of the early settlers and assist them in the completion of their cabin homes. All accounts of Shemauger represent him as kind to the whites and ambitious for the elevation of his people. One early settler (Jesse B. Webber) at the Big Grove, who came here in 1830 and remained all of that winter before making himself a home, spent much of his time in the company of the chief and formed for him a high esteem. In 1830 Shemauger was about seventy-five years of age and had, in his time, participated in many of the Indian wars with the whites and, with his experience, would gladly remain at peace with them. The Kankakee Valley was the home of the chief during the last years of his stay in Illinois, and he was seen there by those who made trips to Chicago. Following the Black Hawk War his tribe—or the remnant of it remaining east of the Mississippi River—went West and its members were seen here no more.

Told to "Git"

"In the summer of 1832, before the organization of the county and the fixing of its county seat—when the site of Urbana was perhaps only what it had been for generations before, an Indian camping ground— a large number of Indians came and camped around the spring above alluded to as situated near the stone bridge. It happened to be at the time of the excitement caused by the Black Hawk War, and caused not a little apprehension among the few inhabitants around the Big Grove, although the presence in the company of many women and children of the Indians should have been an assurance of no hostile errand. A meeting of the white settlers was had, and the removal of the strange visitors determined upon as a measure of safety. A committee consisting of Stephen Boyd, Jacob Smith, Gabe Rice and Elias Stamey was appointed by the white settlers charged with the duty of having a talk with the red men. The committee went to the camp and, mustering their little knowledge of their language, announced to the Indians that they must 'puck-a-chee,' which they understood to be a command to them to leave the country. The order was at once obeyed. The Indians gathered up their ponies, pappooses and squaws and left, greatly to the relief of the settlers.

INDIAN SCARES

"During the Black Hawk War, and before the passage through the country of the volunteers from Indiana and the Wabash country, many wild reports of Indian depredations nearby, and the reports that hostiles were encamped as near as on the Sangamon River and at the Mink Grove, spread from cabin to cabin through the country, made a general stampede imminent. Like reports of threatened danger were rife among the Sangamon settlers, but in their case the supposed hostiles were encamped lower down the river near the Piatt settlement. So great was the alarm in the latter case that all gathered at the cabin of Jonathan Maxwell, where the men made defensive preparations against the apprehended attack. It was soon ascertained in all the settlements that the reports were false, the supposed hostiles being, in fact, fugitive bands of friendly Indians who were running away from danger in the northern part of the State, as unwilling as the white inhabitants for the happening of hostilities. Men who were then children in the settlements have related to the writer how these wild reports, told from cabin to cabin, made their hair stand on end, and of the hasty preparations of the heads of families for flight to the eastern settlements, in view of the possible danger to their families.

PLEASED WITH THE WHITE MAN'S COFFIN

"The Nox family settled near where the village of Sidney is situated about 1828, and then, and for some years thereafter, the Pottawattamies frequently camped near their house and at other places along the Salt Fork. While thus encamped on one occasion, on the north side of the creek near the residence of William Peters, one of their chief men died.

The tribe was about to emigrate to the West and, wishing to transport the body of their dead chief thither, they applied to William Nox and Mr. Hendricks, who were somewhat skilled in the use of tools, to manufacture for the deceased a white man's coffin. This they did by splitting from a log some thin puncheons and working them into suitable shape. The finished coffin so well pleased the braves that they gave to each workman a nicely tanned buckskin. Upon their removal soon after to the West, the coffined body was taken with them.

INDIAN SEPULTURES

"Early white settlers were induced to observe the mode of sepulture practiced by some of the Indian sojourners here. In the timber at what was called Adkins Point, at the north extremity of the Big Grove, was a place of deposit for the bodies of their dead. Instead of burying the bodies in the ground, they first wrapped them in blankets around which bark stripped from a tree was placed, tying the whole tightly together with thongs cut from rawhide. The bodies were then bound with withes to horizontal limbs of large trees. Fifteen or twenty might have been seen thus suspended at one time. As the encasing blankets and bark coffins rotted away, the corpses would drop to the ground. It was the custom to deposit the ornaments of the dead Indian with him, and rings, bells and brooches of silver were sometimes found there.

MIAMIS PASSING TO THE WEST

"About 1832 a large body of Indians (believed to have been Miamis), 900 in number, in moving from their Indiana reservation to the western territories, passed through Champaign County, crossing the Salt Fork at Prather's Ford a mile or so above St. Joseph, thence by the north side of Big Grove to Newcom's Ford and by Cheney's Grove. It is said the caravan extended from Prather's Ford to Adkins' Point, as the northern extremity of Big Grove was then called. These Indians were entirely friendly to the whites and encamped two days at the Point for rest, where the settlers gathered around for trade and to enjoy their sports.

EN ROUTE FOR WASHINGTON

"In the winter of 1852-53 came a company of braves from the West through Urbana, on their way to Washington to have a talk with the President. While stopping here one of their number died, and was buried in the old cemetery at Urbana. His comrades greatly mourned him, and planted at the head of his grave a board, upon which were divers cabalistic decorations. After committing his body to the grave, his comrades blazed a road with their tomahawks to the Bone Yard branch, to guide the dead man's thirsty spirit to the water."

LAST OF THE CHAMPAIGN COUNTY INDIANS

As stated, as late as the Black Hawk War scattered bands of Kickapoos, Pottawattamies and Delawares were still roaming through the woods and over the prairies of central and eastern Illinois, killing squirrels, wild turkeys, grouse and deer. About the 1st of March they usually returned in a body toward the Kankakee for the purpose of making maple sugar. But at the close of the war, the whites of Indiana and Illinois made a general demand upon the Government to see that all Indians were moved to their reservations west of the Mississippi, according to treaty stipulations.

The Kickapoos of the Vermilion were the last of the Illinois Indians to emigrate. Finally, in 1833, the last of them joined the main body of the tribe in their reservation west of Fort Leavenworth, Kansas, and were afterward moved to the Indian Territory.

CHAPTER IV

PIONEER SETTLERS AND EVENTS

Two years after the Indian treaty at Edwardsville, by which the Kickapoos of the Vermilion ceded their lands in Champaign County to the general Government, the surveyors of the United States commenced their work in the southeastern sections. In 1821, Jacob Judy, James Thompson and James Messenger made surveys in the region now embraced by the townships of Raymond, Ayers, Sidney, Homer, St. Joseph, Ogden and Stanton and parts of Rantoul and Compromise. In the following year the territory included in the rest of the county was surveyed by Richard P. Holliday, David Anderson, Patrick O. Lee, Benjamin F. Messenger, Enoch Moore and E. Starr.

A Pioneer Couple in the Old Home

Work of the United States Surveyors

Writing in 1905, the late Judge J. O. Cunningham thus describes the nature and importance of the work as performed by the Government surveyors, shortly before the first white settlers came to Champaign County: "It will thus be seen that shortly following the treaty with the Indians which extinguished forever their claim upon the territory now known as Champaign County, came the United States surveyors, those pioneers of civilization whose work was to last through all time and be law to all future dwellers. The lines as then fixed and marked by these surveyors are the lines which now divide the townships, school districts and farms of the county, and which determine its boundaries and the locations of most of its public roads.

"When the treaty already referred to was made and when the work of the United States surveyors was performed, the territory later organized into the county of Champaign was within the bounds of the county of Crawford. The section corners, then marked by the throwing up of mounds of earth around stakes charred in their camp fires, were easily found by other surveyors many years after they were established.

The County's Original Survey Record

"In the office of the county clerk may be found a book commonly called the Original Survey Record, which contains transcripts of all of these surveys carefully copied from the reports and plats made by the General Land Office by these original surveyors. Upon the left hand pages of this very interesting and important record may be found directions for locating every section corner, as marked and left by these men eighty years ago, while upon the opposite pages are found very carefully prepared plats in colors showing every grove of timber and hazel brush, every stream or considerable branch, and every pond, as well as the courses and location with reference to section lines. The number of acres in each section is also marked thereon, and where the section is fractional—that is, the section contains more or less than one square mile—the number of acres in each one-eighth of a section is also shown.

"This record, besides being important as a factor in determining the lines and titles to the lands within the county, is of interest to one inquiring into the early history of the county. These plats and notes were made by the men of the white race who first minutely examined these landscapes. They show the county with reference to the space occupied by timber and open prairie, just as they appeared to Runnel

Fielder, Henry Sadorus and William Tompkins when they came here a few years thereafter.

"The question has no doubt often been, mentally if not audibly, asked by the dwellers in these groves and upon these premises: 'Who surveyed these lands into the sections and townships which now divide the country into farms, neighborhoods and sections and townships? Who piled up the mounds at the corners of the sections, in the absence of better monuments? Whose eyes first minutely examined these landscapes, and who, in their day-dreams, heard the tramp of our coming?' These questions have often been asked by me, and I presume by others. I am able to answer from official intelligence.

"It is well here to speak briefly of the Rector family, who were famous in Illinois in early days.

"The Rector family came to Kaskaskia in 1806, when the lands of the United States were to be surveyed. This was a numerous family, consisting of nine brothers and four daughters. They were natives of Virginia. All were remarkable for fearlessness.

"William Rector had, before the War of 1812, been a deputy surveyor. During that war he commanded a regiment as its colonel, in the campaign against the Indians, at the head of Peoria Lake. In 1816, Colonel Rector was appointed surveyor-general of Illinois, Missouri and Arkansas. Some of his brothers were deputies under him. Colonel Rector took up his residence in St. Louis on receiving his appointment, as likewise did the rest of the family.

"Townships from 17 to 20, in ranges 7 to 8, including the towns of Sadorus, Colfax, Scott, Mahomet, Pesotum, Tolono, Champaign and Hensley, were surveyed into sections by Richard T. Holliday, for Elias Rector, deputy surveyor, in 1812.

"Townships 21 and 22, in ranges 7 and 8, including the towns of Newcomb, Brown, Condit and East Bend, were surveyed by David Anderson and Patrick Oscar Lee, deputy surveyors, in 1823.

"Townships 17, 18, 19, 20 and 21, range 9, including the towns of Crittenden, Philo, Urbana, Somers and a part of Rantoul, were surveyed by Benjamin Franklin Messenger, deputy surveyor, in 1821.

"Township 22, in ranges 9 and 10, including the towns of Ludlow and Harwood, were surveyed in 1822, by Enoch Moore, deputy surveyor.

"Townships 17, 18, 19, 20 and 21, range 10, including the towns of Raymond, Sidney, St. Joseph, Stanton and parts of Rantoul and Compromise, were surveyed in 1821, by Jacob Judy, deputy surveyor.

"Townships 17, 18, 19 and 20, range 14 west, including the towns of Homer and Ogden, were surveyed in 1821, by James Thompson, deputy surveyor.

"Township 21, range 14 west, including part of Compromise Township, was surveyed in 1821, by James Messenger, deputy surveyor.

"Township 22, range 14, including part of Kerr Township, was surveyed in 1822, by E. Starr, deputy surveyor.

"These facts in relation to the regular townships will settle the question in relation to the narrow, irregular strips running through the eastern part of the county, known as range 11, for the fixing of the corners of sections in the regular townships at the same time operated to divide this strip into townships and sections.

A PIONEER FAMILY

"The surveyors went heavily armed for defense against the cunning red man, and not unfrequently were ambushed and killed. It required not only a knowledge of instruments and mathematics, but familiarity with weapons and the modes of Indian warfare.

"Nelson Rector, a brother of Elias and Colonel Rector, nearly lost his life while engaged in surveying. He had a 'company of surveyors out on the waters of the Saline Creek, in Gallatin County, where, on the 1st of March, 1814, he was fired on by the Indians and severely wounded. His left arm was broken, a ball entered his left side and another touched his face. His horse carried him off, and he recovered from his wounds.' "

PIONEERS SETTLED IN GROVES AND TIMBER BELTS

As has been noted, the pioneers of the county chose for their homesteads locations in the beautiful groves and timber belts. Among the most noted of these was Big Grove, comprising a body of heavily timbered rich land, on a branch of the Salt Fork and nearly in the center of the county, twelve miles long and averaging three miles in width. The prairie country around was also most delightful, with an abundance of good water everywhere. Such advantages, with the added fact that the well known Fort Clark Road, which runs from near Danville on the Vermilion River, in the eastern part of the State, to the Illinois River, skirted its northern borders, naturally directed the attention of potential home-makers to the desirability of Big Grove as a place of residence. Even before generally traveled by white men, it was a favorite route for the Kickapoos journeying between the Vermilion and their chief interior village in what is now McLean County.

ROUTE OF FORT CLARK ROAD THROUGH COUNTY

The earliest comers to Champaign County followed this convenient thoroughfare from a point about two miles northeast of the present site of Homer northwest through Hickory Grove and a short distance north of the present village of St. Joseph, where it crossed the east branch of the South Fork at Prather's Ford, thence followed the western branch of that creek past Hays Grove to the northern point of the Big Grove, thence crossing what was afterward Adkins Point and Beaver Dam, and thence it bore to the northwest, crossing the Sangamon at Newcom's Ford, and from that point up the west bank of the river through Cheney's Grove (Saybrook) to Bloomington and Peoria—the latter then called Fort Clark.

RUNNEL FIELDER, FIRST SETTLER

It was in the Big Grove, a short distance south of the Fort Clark Road and about four miles northeast of the present site of Urbana, that Runnel Fielder, the county's first settler, squatted with his family upon a bluff near Salt Creek, in 1822. He built his cabin near the northwest corner of Section 12, but a few rods from what is known as the Blackberry Schoolhouse. This was the first residence erected in Champaign County by a white man, and its builder also broke the first land in that section, thereby representing the pioneer farmer of the white race. Charles Fielder, the son of Runnel, taught school near Big

Grove in the winter of 1827-28, and was, in all probability, the first teacher of the county.

The pioneer settler of Champaign County was never more than a squatter upon his original homestead. Another eventually obtained a title to his land, although he did enter the eighty-acre tract east of his home place in June, 1828, which was the first entry of public lands in the Big Grove neighborhood. In the following September, Runnel Fielder was appointed, by the Board of Commissioners of Vermilion County, supervisor of the Fort Clark Road from Prather's Ford on the Salt Fork to the western line of Vermilion County. Soon afterward he emigrated from the county, and about 1831 settled in Tazewell County; that is, the records show that in March, 1832, he executed a deed in that county for his eighty acres in Big Grove to Isaac Busey.

TOMPKINS SQUATS ON SITE OF URBANA

Soon after the coming of the Fielders to Big Grove, William Tompkins settled on the site of Urbana. He built a cabin of unhewn logs twenty feet square near the southwest corner of the southwest quarter of Section 8, which was known, after the platting of Urbana, as Lot No. 7 of Hooper & Parks' Addition. The site of the Tompkins home was a patch of hazel brush and small timber, also upon the bank of Salt Creek. The cabin was standing as late as 1855, in the heart of Urbana, and was then pointed out as the oldest house in town. The locality was of special historic interest also, because it marked a well known camping ground of the Kickapoos and Pottawattamies, and the remains of old corn fields were plainly visible for several years after the locality commenced to be well settled.

"Tompkins," says Judge Cunningham, "like other early settlers of the county, must have occupied this land as a squatter, for the records show no entry of lands by him until February 5, 1830, when he entered the eighty-acre tract where he lived, which embraced all the territory in Urbana bounded on the north by the city limits, east by Vine Street, south by the alley north of Main Street and west by a line running north from the stone bridge. On November 1, 1830, he also entered the eighty-acre tract lying immediately south of that tract, bounded on the north by the first entry, east by Vine Street, south by the city limits and west by the alley next west of Race Street. Before this last entry Tompkins had improved and fenced about twenty acres which lay mostly south of Main Street."

Henry Sadorus

After the Fielders and Tompkinses, the next family to settle in Champaign County with any degree of permanence was that headed by Henry Sadorus, who continued to reside on the Okaw, in the southwestern part of the county, for a period of fifty-four years. He gave his name to the grove and the township, as well as the village in the extreme northeastern part of the latter. Mr. Sadorus had served as a soldier in the War of 1812, and about 1818, then thirty-five years of age, immigrated with his family to Indiana. He was a natural tradesman and money-maker, and had amassed quite a capital for the times, when he started for the Vermilion country, with his wife and six children, in 1824. The eldest of the children was a lad of fourteen, who assisted his father in managing the five yoke of steers which drew the prairie wagon toward the Okaw. It was in the fall of the year, and when he discovered an abandoned cabin on the southeast quarter of Section 1, Township 17, Range 7, he took possession of it and the family commenced housekeeping. He remained a squatter until December 11, 1834, when he entered the quarter section at the Vandalia land office. His son William, at the same time, entered the eighty-acre tract adjoining on the north, which were the first entries of land in Sadorus Township.

At the time of Mr. Sadorus' death on July 18, 1878, the Champaign County Gazette published a complete and appreciative sketch of the deceased, in which occurred the following: "The State Road from Kaskaskia having been opened and passing near his residence, Mr. Sadorus decided to erect a building for a tavern. The nearest saw mill was at Covington, Indiana, sixty miles away, but the lumber (some 50,000 feet) was hauled through unbridged sloughs and streams, and the house was built. For many years Mr. Sadorus did a thriving business. His corn was disposed of to drovers who passed his place with herds of cattle for the East, besides being fed to great numbers of hogs on his farms. His first orchard, now mostly dead, consisted of fifty Milams, procured somewhere near Terre Haute, Indiana. From them were taken innumerable sprouts, and that apple became very common in this section.

"In common with nearly all the pioneers, Mr. Sadorus grew his own cotton, at least enough for clothing and bedding. A half-fare sufficed for this, and the custom was kept up until it became no longer profitable, the time of the mother and three daughters being so much occupied in cooking for and waiting upon the travelers that they could not weave; besides goods began to get cheaper and nearly every immigrant had some kind of cloth to dispose of. About the year 1846 Mrs. Sadorus died, and seven years later he again married, this time a Mrs. Eliza Canterbury of Charleston.

"Some years ago, becoming tired of attending to so much business, Mr. Sadorus divided his property among his descendants, retaining, however, an interest which enabled him to pass his declining years in ease. He died full of years, respected by all who knew him, and beloved by a large circle of friends. He was kind and hospitable to strangers, and never turned a needy man away empty-handed from his door."

Judge Cunningham adds, speaking of the old Sadorus home and Grove: "The home thus set up far from other human habitations was the abode of contentment, hospitality and reasonable thrift, in the first rude cabin which sheltered the family, as well as in the more pretentious home to which the cabin gave place in due time. The Grove was a landmark for many miles around, and the weary traveler well knew that welcome and rest always awaited him at the Sadorus home. Here Mr. Sadorus entertained his neighbors—the Buseys, Webbers and others, from Big Grove; the Fiatts, Boyers and others, from down on the Sangamon; Coffeen, the enterprising general merchant, from down on the Salt Fork; the Johnsons, from Linn Grove, and the dwellers upon the Ambraw and the Okaw. He was also the counsellor and adviser of all settlers along the upper Okaw in matters pertaining to their welfare, and his judgment was implicitly relied upon."

THE COMING OF SADORUS AND SMITH

The circumstances surrounding the coming of Henry Sadorus to the grove which bears his name, with the main facts of his journey thither, are thus told by Judge Cunningham: "Henry Sadorus, lovingly known by the whole country to the day of his death as Grandpap Sadorus, was born in Bedford County, Pennsylvania, July 26, 1783, four years before the adoption of the Federal Constitution. The spring of 1817 found him living with his little family—of whom William Sadorus (until of late also a venerable resident of the county), then about five years old, having been born July 4, 1812, was the eldest—on Oil Creek, Crawford County, in the same State. The Western fever, which has prevailed among Americans since the landing of the Pilgrims, attacked the elder Sadorus and, from the native timbers of that region, he constructed a raft or flat boat, upon which he loaded his worldly goods and family, and, after the manner of that time, set out by water upon a long journey westward.

"The flat boat was built upon the waters of Oil Creek, and down the adventurers set forth in pursuit of a home in the West, they knew not where. Following the creek to its junction with the Allegheny River, that stream soon bore them to Pittsburgh and the Ohio River, by which means their frail bark in time landed them in Cincinnati, then the emporium of the Far West. One shipwreck alone, at the head of Blennerhasset Island, befell the travelers. The flat boat, having served its purpose, was sold in Cincinnati for $1,700 in James Piatt's shinplaster money, making the travelers rich for the time being, but in six months it shared the fate of its kind and was worthless, Mr. Sadorus again being a poor man.

"The family remained in Cincinnati two years, when Mr. Sadorus again drifted westward, stopping successively at Connersville, Flat Rock and Raccoon, in the State of Indiana, where they found themselves in the spring of 1824, still with a desire to go West. Early in that year, Mr. Sadorus and a neighbor—one Joe Smith—fitted themselves out, each with a team of two yokes of oxen and a covered wagon, suitable for moving their families and goods. Thus accoutred, they again set their faces westward, intending to go to the Illinois country, possibly as far as Fort Clark, since called Peoria.

"An almost trackless forest lay between them and their destination. They passed the site of the city of Indianapolis, then but recently selected as the State capital, where the foundations of the old capitol buildings had but just been laid. Crossing the Wabash River by a ferry at Clinton, Indiana, the party soon encountered the Grand Prairie. After entering Illinois, they met with only one house between the State line and the Okaw River, and that was the home of Hezekiah Cunningham, on or near the Vermilion River, where he kept a small trading post for traffic with the Indians. On April 9, 1824, the party reached the isolated grove at the head of the Okaw River, since known as Sadorus Grove, and, as usual, encamped for the night near the place which eventually became the permanent home of the Sadorus family.

DISCOVER AND DIVIDE THE GROVE

"A brief survey of their surroundings satisfied the party that a point had been reached which fully met all their demands for a home. So far as they knew they were thirty or forty miles from neighbors, but were surrounded by as fruitful a country as was to be found, in which wild game abounded and where every want might easily be supplied. Accordingly, they determined here to remain and to set about making themselves comfortable. They found the grove whose shelter they had accepted was three or four miles long and nearly equally divided by a narrow place in the timber, through which the Wabash Railroad now crosses the stream. So the two heads of families partitioned the tract covered by this grove between themselves, Smith taking the south end and Sadorus the north end—the Narrows, as the line was called, being the boundary.

First Smith and Sadorus Cabins

"Having so divided the beautiful grove of timber between them, the two pioneers proceeded to make arrangements for a permanent stay in the place chosen for a home by building for each a cabin. Smith erected his cabin upon the site of the first encampment, and near where the old Sadorus home now stands, in the southeast quarter of Section 1. It was built of split linn logs, sixteen by sixteen feet, covered with split oaken boards, with linn puncheons for a floor. The roof, after the manner of cabin building, was laid upon logs or poles laid lengthwise of the cabin, each succeeding pole being a little higher than the last and converging toward the apex. These boards, for the want of nails, which were not to be had, were held in place by weight poles laid lengthwise over the butts of each course. The door was made of split boards held in place by wooden pins. The window was only a hole cut in the log wall to let in the light, subsequently covered with greased muslin to keep out the cold.

"The Sadorus home, which was built two miles north on Section 36, in what is now Colfax Township but within the grove, was less pretentious. It was built of the same material, ten by twenty feet, but entirely open upon one side—what is called a 'half-faced camp.' In this cabin windows and doors were entirely dispensed with.

"Settled in these crude homes, the pioneers set about preparing for their future. The summer was spent in the cultivation of little patches of corn and garden by means of a crude prairie plow and other tools which they had brought with them, and in hunting the wild game for their meat and peltries, the result being that, as the autumn approached, the larders of the families were well supplied with the best the country afforded. The wolves, however, ate and destroyed much of their sod corn.

Sadorus Sole Proprietor of the Grove

"In the fall the heads of the two families, having well laid in table supplies, concluded to know what lay to the west of them. Filling their packs with small supplies of provisions, with their rifles upon their shoulders, they again set out on foot together for the West, leaving their families housed as we have seen. They traveled as far as Peoria, where Smith determined to remove his family. Their course led them by the way of Mackinaw and Kickapoo Creek, through Indian country. Returning as they went, after an absence of two week, they found at their homes everything quiet and in order.

"Smith at once sold his cabin and improvements to Sadorus, the consideration being the hauling by the latter of a load of goods from the Okaw timber to the Illinois River, which was paid according to agreement, and the south end of the grove, with all the improvements, passed to Mr. Sadorus, who thus became the only inhabitant of the south end of the county.

Occupation and Improvement of the Smith Cabin

"The Sadorus family lost no time in taking possession of the Smith cabin, which became its home then, and, with the land upon which it was erected, is still the home of a member of the household, Mr. Allen Sadorus. Its comforts were exchanged in place of the 'half-faced camp,' and all claim to the upper half of the grove was abandoned. The land, thus occupied for a few months by the family, many years afterward became the home of James Miller.

"The Smith cabin was daubed that fall, which means that the interstices between the logs were filled with chinks and mud to prevent the cold from intruding, and its foundations were banked with earth for a like purpose. A mud chimney was built outside with a fireplace opening inside the cabin, and carried up above the cabin roof with sticks and mud. A companion cabin, built subsequently a few feet away, in like manner supplied with a mud and stick chimney and daubed as was the first, added to the comforts and conveniences of the family. A single sash window was bought in Eugene, Indiana, a few years thereafter and that, glazed with glass, gave the family one glass window—the first in Champaign County—and in time other openings, answering for windows, were likewise supplied.

"These cabins did duty as the Sadorus domicile until 1838, about fourteen years, when the permanent home was erected."

Matthias and Martin Rhinehart

The Rhinehart family was prominently identified with the early period of the county's development. Matthias, the ancestor in these parts, brought his family from Chester County, Pennsylvania, in 1828 or 1829, and made a settlement in the west half of the southwest quarter of Section 26, Somer Township. In association with his son-in-law,

Walter Rhoades, he entered that tract in February, 1830. The first postoffice in what is now Champaign County, called Van Buren, was established thereon. Mr. Rhoades lived upon that tract until about 1857, when he sold to A. M. Pauley. There the son, Martin Rhinehart, reached manhood. When he was twenty years of age he enlisted in the Black Hawk War for service in Captain Brown's company of Mounted Rangers. He furnished his own horse, gun and clothing, and received for his services $1 per day. For many years he shared with Thomas L. Butler, who had settled near Homer at about the same time as the Rhinehart family farther to the northwest, the honor of being the only survivor who participated in that campaign from what is now Champaign County. Martin Rhinehart became a prominent and a wealthy citizen.

A HOUSEHOLD TREASURE

When he came as a youth to the central part of the county there were but thirty-five families living within its borders.

INCIDENTS RELATED BY RHINEHART

"The year 1831," he once related, "was almost without a summer; the cold weather continued until late in the spring and a hard frost set in on September 20th, it being so severe that it froze the corn, cob and all. In consequence of the loss of the crop, times got close and money was extremely scarce. The following year settlers were compelled to send to Kentucky for their seed corn. In December, 1836, a deep snow lay upon the ground. It began to rain and continued all day, when suddenly it turned intensely cold, making ice over the ground and freezing very hard. The sudden change caught many persons unprepared and they were frozen to death. Two men named Hildreth and Frame were crossing Four Mile Prairie on that day; they became bewildered, lost their way and were out when the change came. They killed their horses and Frame crawled inside the body of his horse for protection against the cold. But it proved his tomb, as he was found there frozen to death. Hildreth wandered around all night, and when found in the morning was so badly frozen that he lost his toes and fingers."

Mr. Rhinehart also spoke of the early doctors of that day. Dr. Saddler was one of the first physicians of the county and was accounted a good one. It is related of him that he attended a family east of Urbana. This family had a large patch of fine, ripe and juicy watermelons. The doctor continued his visits long after the patient was convalescent, and the family dropped upon the idea that the watermelon patch was the chief attraction and the cause of his repeated visits. They gently broke the news to him that his patient was entirely well, and hinted that further visits were entirely superfluous. The doctor went home and sent in a bill that covered all the visits. The family refused payment. Suit was brought to recover the amount, when the family rendered an account for watermelons devoured by the doctor as an offset, and obtained a small judgment against him. All the neighbors declared that the decision was a most just one."

TRIPS TO CHICAGO

When the Sadorus family first came to the Grove their nearest post-office and county seat was Paris, Edgar County, fifty-two miles to the southeast. Their chief trading point for fifteen years, where they marketed their hogs and bought some of their supplies, was Eugene, Indiana, sixty miles away, with occasional trips to Chicago. The first trip made by Mr. Sadorus to that growing trading post on Lake Michigan was in the fall of 1834. Besides himself and his son, Henry, were Uncle Matthew Busey and his son, Fountain J.; Captain Nox, of Sidney, father of Solomon Nox; Pete Bailey, of Salt Fork, and Hiram Jackson. There were four wagons, each drawn by five yoke of oxen. The Sadorus outfit had oats for sale. The company assembled at Poage's, north of Homer, journeyed northward by way of Pilot Grove and Bourbonnais Grove, forded the Kankakee River and swam creeks and streams to the number of eleven, before they reached Fort Dearborn, after three weeks of almost continuous rain.   The Sadorus oats had sprouted from one to two inches when the caravan arrived at its destination, but the garrison at the Fort was glad to get them at that, for fifty cents a bushel.   Mr. Sadorus purchased of the widely known trader, Gurdon S. Hubbard, for his return trip, salt, sugar, coffee and other family supplies.

These trips to Chicago became quite frequent.   In 1830 the Conkey family had come from Massachusetts and settled in Edgar County, and two years afterward William A., then a boy of twelve, made his first visit to Ford Dearborn and the trading post at that point.   His elder brother "geed" and "hawed" the ox-team.   The wagon was loaded with flour, meat, butter, eggs and other produce, and the trip was made by way of Danville.   Nothing disagreeable occurred until the Calumet River was reached, when the precious freight was, for a time, threatened by the soft mud of its bottom.   But the cargo and wagon were finally rescued, and Gurdon Hubbard was none the wiser.   The Conkeys laid in a good supply of salt and other family provisions for the return journey.

One Thousand Mile Trip of the Conkey Family

The same younger Conkey brother settled at Homer in 1843 as one of the pioneer physicians of the county, and years afterwards read a paper before the Champaign Historical Society describing the one thousand mile journey of the family, made in 1830, from their old Massachusetts home to their new home in Edgar County, Illinois.   It reads thus: "At the earnest solicitation of my friend, Judge Cunningham, one of the promoters of this society, I consented to present a paper setting forth a few incidents of the trip (as I now remember them) of the immigration of my father and his family from Massachusetts to Illinois in the year 1830.   Some few years previous to that time a brother of my mother's from the adjoining town to our residence, against the wishes and entreaties of his friends, relatives and neighbors, started west to see if he could find a country presenting better facilities for a permanent home than he had among the hills and rocks of the East. He had a distant relative of his wife living in Vigo County, Indiana, and to that point they drifted; and after examining the country around there went west to the prairies of Illinois, which presented such an inviting appearance to him that he at once decided to stop there and make it his future home, being near Paris, the county seat of Edgar County. The glowing description he gave his old associates of the country he had found induced my father to join him in Illinois.   My oldest brother having preceded the rest of the family a year or so before, and having purchased a forty-acre tract of land adjoining his uncle's for the use of the family on which to make a new start in life. Some time about the first of May, 1830, we bade goodbye to the old homestead in Charlemont, Franklin County, Massachusetts, and the old friends and neighbors, which to them seemed more like a funeral than a temporary separation, and started with such household goods, clothing, etc., as loaded two wagons and teams, hired for the purpose of conveying them to Troy, N. Y., a distance of about fifty miles; at which place we were joined by a brother and sister of my mother's with a span of horses and a light wagon which accompanied our family the entire trip. Remaining in Troy two or three days, we got passage on a canal boat for the entire family (save the uncle, who drove his team to Buffalo), the family then being my father, mother, aunt and a sister aged thirteen and myself—five in all. After a slow and tedious trip we joined my uncle and team again at Buffalo—a distance of about 250 miles from Troy.

"The trip while on the canal was a slow and tedious one. Not having any record of the time and after an absence of nearly seventy years, I will not attempt to say how long it took us. It was on this part of our journey that I first heard boys scientifically swear; it seemed that at every change of horses and drivers the new driver endeavored to show us that he could do more hard swearing than any of our former ones, and I think if such a thing were possible our last one was entitled to the plum.

"On our arrival at Buffalo we had to wait two or three days before we were able to get passage to Perrysburg, situated on the lake at the mouth of the Maumee River, at or near where Toledo is now situated. Having succeeded in getting passage on a popular schooner, commanded by Captain Wilkinson, an old lake captain, we loaded our goods, horses and wagon on board, and with a few other men going west and with two additional ladies, took possession of the cabin, located in the 'hole' of the craft and quite a cozy, neat apartment. When supper was announced, a majority of the passengers asked to be excused from participating, the rolling of the boat having relieved them from all feeling of hunger, besides occupying their time in attending to the duties required to keep their stomachs from getting in their mouths; but fortunately I had not yet taken the disease and was able to do justice to the good things we had for supper, awaiting my time until later. Sometime after midnight a heavy storm came up; the waters became very angry, and occasionally a wave would wash over our boat so that the most of those who did not want any supper forgot their sickness and fully expected to go where sickness never comes. Before morning and to cap the climax, a very strong gale of wind broke the mainmast of our craft and all below at the crash expected to find themselves at the bottom of the lake; but about this time, the fury of the storm began to abate and, with the smaller mast, the sailors kept the boat in an upright position until day-break when at about 10 or 11 o'clock they landed at Dunkirk and rigged another mainmast so that by dark they were in condition to proceed, but waited until the latter part of the night before they left. Before start-ing from Buffalo they had erected a good strong fence or pen around our horses which were on top of the boat and fortunately when the mast broke it fell in such a direction as not to strike them. Well, when morn-ing came and breakfast was ready, and the tender-footed found they were alive, the most of them partook of such diet as they thought their stom-achs would stand. Now, in all seriousness, this was no pleasant trip so far, and in after years the recollection of that night brought up memo-ries in the minds of most of those present that were far from pleasant.

"The next night after leaving Dunkirk the lake again became very rough, accompanied by high winds that drove our boat and stranded it in shallow water near Long Point, which extends into the lake from the Canada side, and not to exceed one-fourth of a mile from the mainland; and on getting up in the morning we found ourselves fast on the sand, and all that could be done was to remain there until we could attract the attention of some passing boat for our relief by coming to our assist-ance and lightening our boat so it would again float. As soon as it became light enough, our captain had his flag of distress run up to the highest point of our mainmast, but having by the wind been driven so far north and out of the usual track, we remained in our then-present position for five days and nights before our distress signal was seen, when a passing schooner discovered it, came to our relief, and after taking enough of our cargo to allow our boat to again float, we got into deeper water, and reloading our freight again proceeded on our voyage. Having been delayed there so long, our provisions were getting short, but got a supply from our rescuer to relieve us until we landed at Cleve-land without any suffering, except food for our horses which, while stranded, had eaten all we had provided for them, and the Canada shore having no show of vegetation we unpacked several crates of queensware on board and fed them the dirty, musty straw which they ate with avidity, and which kept them alive until we reached Cleveland. Before getting to the pier we sailed along close to the land for quite a distance where stock was grazing on the green grass, which our starved horses aboard discovered, and they became perfectly frantic and so cross that the sailors passing them on deck dared not go near them. When we got to where we could take them off and where they could get something to eat they soon got all right.

"Here we also took our wagon off the boat and my uncle drove them to Perrysburg, getting there a few days after the boat arrived, and where we waited until he joined us. Here we saw many Indians, and in fact hardly a day passed until we got to Logansport, Indiana, that we did not encounter more or less of them. While awaiting the arrival of uncle with the team, at Perrysburg, we contracted to be conveyed by keel boat up the Maumee River to Fort Wayne, Indiana, a distance of about ninety miles on a straight line, but how far by that tortuous river I don't know; it seemed a long way. Our crew was composed of a captain who steered the boat and six men, three of which worked on each side of the boat and propelled the craft by long poles, the lower end of each pole covered with a sheath of iron drawn to a point and by walking from stern to bow dragging the poles thus equipped, and then facing the stern of the boat, placing the lower end on the bottom of the river and the upper end against their shoulders, pushing the boat the length of it and getting up a speed to carry it along until they walked again to the bow and repeated their trip to stern as before stated, walking on a wide board with slats nailed across the top to prevent their slipping, and when the boat is loaded is but a few inches above the water.

"At Perrysburg we again put our wagon on board the boat, and either uncle or father rode one of the horses and led the other; there was no wagon road the most of the way, only a trail traveled by the mail carrier on horseback and marked by cutting three notches in each side of a tree occasionally as a guide. After arriving at Fort Wayne (an old town from the appearance of the buildings, and I think a population not exceeding 200 or 300) we were compelled to remain there until our men folks went across a low flat timbered country some twelve or fifteen miles to the Wabash River to see what the chance was, if any, to get transportation down said stream to a point about seven miles above Terre Haute. They were gone three or four days, and on their return reported that the only chance to get down said stream that they could find or hear about was to purchase a pirogue and float down. They accordingly found one made of a large poplar tree, about fifty feet in length, holding its size pretty well its entire length, the inside measure at the large end nearly three feet and the small end twenty-eight inches. This they purchased, the party agreeing to have it at a certain place where it could be reached by wagon from Fort Wayne, and returned.

"We then engaged a couple of wagons and teams to haul us to the

1—8

river in a day, but owing to the condition of the roads and no wagons having passed over them since the fall before, trees had been blown down and across the track, some of which were where we could not get around, and consequently had to spend so much time in removing them that dark overtook us some four miles from the river. We consequently halted, and after building a big fire interested the female portion of our party in preparing supper. We then changed the position of the load in one wagon so as to get a sleeping place for my mother and her sister, while my sister and I stowed ourselves away; and there we all spent the first night of our lives in a wagon, while the older males of the party put in the time until morning keeping up the fire and spinning yarns, after having satisfied some six or eight Indians who visited them (having been attracted by the fire) that we had no whisky.

"The next morning, after getting breakfast, we struck out and found our boat, in which we proceeded to place our freight, having plenty of room for sleeping quarters. Here again we loaded on our boat our wagon and, as on part of our voyage previously spoken of, one of the older ones traveled with the horses, saluting our craft occasionally through the day, and if convenient, staying with us at night. The weather was warm and comfortable, and by this time (it being June) we leisurely floated along for several days without anything unusual occurring. Almost any one of us could steer our craft until one night, when all together and all asleep, the moon having gone down and hardly a ripple on the water, our craft tipped to one side, and before we could get it righted up was at least one-third full of water; and, attracted by a noise on shore like the cracking of brush, we were fully satisfied that someone had stepped upon the edge of our craft, as we always thought, for the purpose of purloining something, and having tipped our boat and at the same time awakened its occupants, left in a hurry; and on the next morning we found footsteps to and also going in the direction of the cracking heard the night before. After righting up our boat we went to work and dipped all the water out we could get, and where our clothes were wet replaced them by dry ones, but we did no more sleeping that night.

"The next day was bright and warm and again we started on our journey, and as luck would have it, my uncle, who was with the horses, found another pirogue nearly as large as the first one, only about thirty-five feet long, which he bought, and when we got along he hailed us in good time to land, when they lashed the two boats together and made a very safe and commodious craft. The only thing missed from our boat was my mother's willow work basket in which she had her knit-

The Old Cabin, Within and Without

ting and other work, which we found the next morning in a drift about a mile below where it was tipped out the night before.

"The balance of our trip was free from any other mishaps worthy of note, drifting with the current by day and tying up at night, making stops only at towns occasionally to replenish our larder, until we arrived at Durkee's Ferry, seven miles above Terre Haute, where we found my oldest brother, who had come to meet us, and a representative of the distant relative of my uncle and wife, spoken of in the fore part of this paper, tendering us the hospitality of their home until we could get moved to our destination, which invitation was thankfully received, and on the same day had our goods conveyed there and remained until everything was unpacked and such as had got wet from the tipping over of our craft, thoroughly dried.

First Sight of the Grand Prairie

"After a day or two my father and uncle, with our own conveyance, drove to the place of our destination, about fifteen miles west, where father procured a couple of yoke of oxen and a wagon and returned to where he had left us. After reloading a portion of our goods, he returned to where he had procured a log cabin in the neighborhood, and in which we remained until he built a house on the land heretofore spoken of. My father permitted me to accompany him with the first load. The first nine miles of the road was through timber, when we struck the Grand Prairie as it was then called. The grass waving in the beautiful sunlight of June and all the wild flowers indigenous to the prairies bowing their heads to the breeze, presented a sight that I thought the most beautiful I had ever beheld, the remembrance of which, notwithstanding seventy years have passed and gone since then, is still as vivid to my mind, it seems, as the day when I first viewed the beauties of the grand old prairies of Illinois.

"This brings us to the end of our trip, a distance of 820 miles in straight lines, as follows: from Charlemont to Troy, fifty; thence to Buffalo, 250; thence to Perrysburg, 240; thence to Fort Wayne, ninety; thence to Durkee's Ferry, 180; thence to destination, fifteen; said computations being from points named derived from the scale of miles marked on the map of each state traveled. Taking into account the tortuous course of the streams navigated, and land traveled, the distance was at least 1,000 miles."

Colonel Matthew W. Busey

The pioneer of the Busey families, who have been so prominent in all fields of development in Champaign County, was Colonel Matthew W., who came to the Urbana region in the early part of 1828 with his wife and eight children, and purchasing the claims of one, Sample Cole, a squatter on the north end of the west half of the northeast quarter of Section 15 for $100, established there his homestead, which he occupied until his death in 1852. Born in Shelby County, Kentucky, May 15, 1798, the Colonel was blessed with the typical hospitality and geniality of his southern forefathers, although the paternal family moved to Washington County, Indiana, at an early date. In the matter of friendliness and neighborliness the Buseys certainly lost none of these traits by moving from Kentucky to Indiana. In the Hoosier State young Busey learned the trade of brick mason, which he at first followed and, for one of his enterprising temperament, naturally developed into the business of a builder and contractor. He was also a lover of fine livestock and a natural farmer; so that he was well fitted to become useful and prominent in the newer country of Illinois. Before settling in Champaign County he had been commissioned colonel in the Indiana State militia, and a few years after his arrival here was similarly honored by the governor of Illinois. So that his "colonel" was no empty title. It is said that on general muster day there was no more resplendent and imposing figure than the hearty and able Colonel Busey. [See more extended biography elsewhere.]

Simeon H. Busey

The most prominent of Colonel Busey's sons were Hon. Simeon H. and General Samuel T. Busey, and they were leaders in business, finance and public activities. S. H. Busey, the elder, and the first son born to the Colonel, moved with the family from his native place—Greencastle, Indiana—to Urbana, when he was twelve years of age. He became a wealthy farmer and stock-raiser, but invested in outside business interests and assisted in the organization of the First National Bank of Champaign. In 1867, several years after his brother, S. T., had made his fine military record in the Civil War, he sold his interest in the Champaign institution, and the two brothers founded Busey's Bank in Urbana. S. H. Busey also was interested in Chicago and Peoria banks and other large enterprises, which proved the value of his business judgment. He represented his district in the thirtieth General Assembly (1876-78), having previously been active and influential in the location of the University of Illinois at Urbana, and the building of what was afterward known as the Peoria & Eastern Railroad, a part of the Big Four system. He was a Democrat and a prominent Mason. His death occurred June 3, 1901.. Of his sons, Matthew W. Busey is president of Busey's Bank, Urbana; George W. Busey is president of the Commercial Bank of that place. [See more detailed biography elsewhere.]

GENERAL SAMUEL T. BUSEY

General Samuel T. Busey was also born in Greencastle, Indiana, in 1835, and was eleven years younger than Simeon H. He engaged in mercantile pursuits at Urbana from 1856 to 1862, when he sold his business and was commissioned by Governor Yates to recruit a company, with which he went into camp at Kankakee August 6, 1862. At its organization as Company B, Seventy-sixth Regiment, Illinois Volunteers, he was elected its captain and subsequently was chosen lieutenant-colonel of the regiment. The details of his efficient and gallant service are given in the chapter on military matters; for the present purpose it is sufficient to say, that he reached the rank of brevet brigadier-general. After the war General Busey engaged in farming, and was thus employed when, with his brother, he organized Busey's Bank in 1867. General Busey afterward bought the interest of Simeon H., and associated himself in its management with his nephew, Matthew W. General Busey's prominence in public life is briefly indicated by the facts that he served as mayor of Urbana for five terms and was a member of the Fifty-second Congress, his opponent in the campaign having been Joseph G. Cannon. General Busey, who was a very active man up to the end of his life, was drowned in a Minnesota lake August 22, 1909, while he was away with his family on a summer outing. His more extended biography appears elsewhere.

SETTLERS IN 1828

At the time that the Colonel established his household in the Cole cabin, only five families lived in what was known as the Big Grove settlement—those of Runnel Fielder, Sample Cole, William Tompkins, Philip Stanford (who lived north of the Grove) and Thomas Rowland, who resided on Section 1, Urbana. No one had settled on the Sangamon. Henry Sadorus was already at Sadorus Grove, the squatter Straley at Linn Grove, and William Nox at Sidney.

In 1840, Colonel Busey was elected to represent his district in the State Legislature and was reelected in 1842. He was very active in the movements against the Mormons, which were at their height during his last term in the Legislature. His extensive acquaintance throughout the state, acquired while a member of the Legislature, made his services valuable in securing the charter of the Illinois Central Railroad, and during the fights for the location of the county seat Colonel Busey was mainly instrumental in securing it for Urbana. For many years he served as assessor for the county and township. In the meantime he had given much of his attention to farming and livestock operations, and was especially known as a breeder of fine stock. In fact, he was a leading representative in everything which most vitally concerned the well-being of his section of the state and of Illinois at large.

While yet a resident of Washington County, Indiana, Colonel Matthew W. Busey was married to Miss Elizabeth Bush, who survived him until 1880, when she died at the home of her son, Colonel S. T. Busey. By that union there were six children, who all arrived at maturity: Simeon H., John S., Mary C. (Mrs. John C. Kirkpatrick), Louisa J. (Mrs. W. H. Romine), Colonel Samuel T., Sarah (Mrs. J. W. Sim), Elizabeth (Mrs. Allen McClain) and Matthew.

As early as May, 1831, Colonel Busey entered 160 acres in Section 8, whereon is now built a considerable portion of the city of Urbana, and upon which stands the home built by his son, General S. T. Busey. This step was taken presumably with a view of making this land the site of his homestead, although he did not move his family thither until 1836. Before his death December 18, 1852, he became the owner of most of the land now included in western Urbana and eastern Champaign.

ISAAC BUSEY AND ISAAC G. BECKLEY

About 1831, Isaac Busey came with his son-in-law, Isaac G. Beckley, and bought out William Tompkins who, on February 4, 1830, had entered the lands in Sections 8 and 17, Urbana, where he had lived for some time as a squatter. Beckley settled on the southwest quarter of Section 5, Urbana.

EARLIEST LAND ENTRIES

The earliest actual entries of land in the county were made in what was known as the Salt Fork Timber, in the northeast quarter of Section 12, Sidney Township. Jesse Williams made the first in the east half of that quarter on February 7, 1827. The tract appears to have been actually occupied by Thomas L. Butler. In October of the same year, John Hendricks entered the other half, the quarter section. In

November, 1827, Josiah Conger entered land about two miles east of the Williams piece.

Big Grove Pioneers

Big Grove appears, as has been noted, to have the honor of attracting most of the pioneer settlers, nearly all of whom were "squatters." Besides Fielder and Tompkins, there were Elias Kirby and family, who came in August, 1829. Early settlers who entered their lands in that locality were John Brownfield, who entered his claim in Section 35, Somer Township, at the Palestine land office, September 2, 1830, and Levi Moore, who entered 240 acres in Section 21, Somer Township, which he sold some years later to Lewis Adkins, who in turn gave his name to Adkins Point. Matthias Rhinehart entered land in the southwest quarter of Section 26, same township, in February, 1830, and he had already resided in that locality since 1828.

Northern Sections Settled Later

The timber lands in the southern and central portions of the county were first to be settled, as being more convenient of access to trading points in Edgar County, and other settled districts in eastern Illinois and western Indiana. When Danville got to be of more importance as a basis of supplies, the favorable attention of the pioneers was directed to more northern points in what is now Champaign County, especially to the Sangamon region. The first entry of lands in the Sangamon Timber was made by Isaac Busey, October 22, 1832, at the Vandalia land office. His claims covered 120 acres in Section 14, 80 acres in Section 15 and 160 acres in Section 23, now in Mahomet Township. Later in that year he entered other lands in Sections 22 and 23, and on October 27, Jonathan Maxwell who, it is claimed, was the first to make his home in the township, entered 40 acres in Section 22. Within the following four years Sangamon timber lands were all the rage.

The far northeastern part of the county also commenced to get a large accession of settlers. The first of them was Samuel Kerr who, in 1833, entered land in what has since been known as Sugar Grove, Section 9. He gave his name to the township in the northeastern corner of the county.

A rapid review has thus been taken of the pioneer period in Champaign County, inclusive of the year 1833, when it attained civil and political entity and was organized as a self-governing body.

Judge Cunningham's Pioneer Epitome

Our late advisory editor, the lamented and honored Judge J. O. Cunningham, was the best authority on all these early matters and pioneer characters. From the records of his pen, now at rest, the following is extracted as the most complete epitome of this period, being a portion of his paper read before the Old Settlers' Reunion of July 29, 1886, on "Urbana and Somer Townships": "The local history of these two townships and, in fact, the early history of the county during the period to which I shall refer, which will be anterior to the period of history of others given here today, are practically one; for around the Big Grove, and upon territory embraced in both townships, were made the first settlements of the county.

Indian Occupation

"Our earliest historic accounts accord the territory in this part of Illinois to the ownership of the Kickapoo Indians, as Indian titles were then regarded. In the year 1819, at Edwardsville, Illinois, at a treaty between the Kickapoo nation and the United States government, represented by Ninian Edwards, a treaty was concluded by which that people relinquished their rights here, and then passed west of the Mississippi. The Indian occupation spoken of today was subsequent to this date, and by bands of the Pottawattamies, who hunted and, at time, abode here. Tradition, supported by the testimony of many old settlers, some of whom are here today, says that the site of Urbana and along the Bone Yard branch, was an Indian village of the Pottawattamies. The presence there of good water, fuel and an abundance of game, made it a favorite camping ground with them. They also frequently camped at the Clements or Clay Bank ford farther down the creek. They buried their dead at Adkins Point near where John Thornburn now lives.

First White Occupancy

"So far as I am informed, the first white men to see this country were the United States surveyors who. divided it into townships and sections. These townships were surveyed in the summer of 1821 by Benjamin Franklin Messenger under the authority of the Federal Government. There doubtless were hunters, trappers, and traders, and perhaps squatters here before that date, but they left no name. The earliest squatters known to us were Runnel Fielder, said to have been the first white inhabitant of the county, who settled in 1822 near the northeast corner of Section 11, Urbana, and built a cabin there, which I have often seen. Fielder entered no land until June 21, 1828, when he entered the west half of the northwest quarter of Section 12—a part of the Roe farm now owned by Bate Smith—on which he planted an orchard, the first in either town, if not in the county. Some of the trees may be seen yet. Then there were John Light, who had a cabin where Tom Brownfield now lives; Gabriel Rice, who had his cabin on Sol Nox's place; Phillip Stanford, who lived near where William Roberts now resides and afterward entered part of that farm, and David Gabbert, who built his cabin just north of this park. This cabin was the first home of the family of Colonel M. W. Busey, who came here in 1836. The Colonel had been here before, for he entered the eighty where we now are in 1830. Besides these, there were Daggett, who settled on the west side of the Grove, and William Tompkins, who built his cabin near the creek near where Halberstadt's mill is, afterwards in 1828 entering the land which he sold to Isaac Busey in 1830. Tompkins had a son near the Harvey Cemetery, who was also a squatter, for he never owned any land. In his cabin, it is said, was born the first white child in the county. Soon after 1828 permanent settlers began to come in—Thomas Rolland in 1828; Matthew Busey in 1829; Isham Cook in 1830; and soon thereafter and, in some cases before, came James T. Roe, John Brownfield, T. R. Webber, W. T. Webber, Jacob Smith, Jacob Heater, John G. Robertson, Isaac G. Beckley, Sample Cole and James Clements. Before many of these, perhaps, were Phillip M. Stanford, Sarah Coe, Robert and William Trickle, Elias Kirby, and Mijamin Byers, the latter of whom was a justice of the peace for this part of Vermilion County. They all settled about the Big Grove in these two townships and soon began to enter the lands. These names I love to recall, as being the names of those who laid the foundation of our present greatness.

First Land Entries

"The first entry in Urbana was made by Fielder, as before stated, in 1828, and the first in Somer by Sarah Coe, who, in 1829 entered the west one-half of the southeast quarter of Section 27, now in William Roberts' farm. During the three years following entries of land, now lying in both townships, were made by Mijamin Byers, Isaac Busey, John Whitaker, William Tompkins, Phillip Stanford, Charles Busey, Martin Rhinehardt, Walter Rhodes, John Light, John Brownfield, Robert Trickle and others.

DISEASES AND PIONEER PHYSICIANS

"Like all new countries blessed with a soil holding the elements of wealth, this country when first settled, and until by cultivation and artificial drainage facilities were afforded for the surface water to pass rapidly away, was the home and nursery of malarial diseases. They appeared in the form of ague, chills and fever, flux and other bowel complaints, and were a great hindrance to the rapid settlement of the country. These diseases were universal and the later part of every summer and every fall people looked for a visitation from these diseases as much as they looked for the ripening of their crops. It was understood that unless the work of the season was completed before the sickly season came on, it had to go over, for during that period all would be sick, or if some were spared, their time would be monopolized in the care of their sick. Many times there were not well persons enough in a family or neighborhood to care for the sick. Physicians were few, or entirely wanting. Dr. Fithian, the veteran physician of Danville, was often called to this county, while Dr. Stevens, of Homer, and Dr. Somers, of Urbana, who were early on the ground, had a wide range of practice in these diseases. The effect of these annual recurrences of miasmatic diseases upon the individual was to weaken and sap the constitution of the strongest. The death roll of the first thirty years of our history, if it could be called, would startle us even at this distance of time. Strong men and women gradually weakened and finally fell before the unseen foe, while little children, ague-ridden from their birth, endured a dwarfish growth for a few years and went shaking to their graves. While this is true of many, we yet have monuments of the olden time in many whitened heads all around us, which have reached or long since passed the allotted three score years and ten, and still linger as good specimens of well preserved manhood and womanhood, equal in healthful appearance to any found in our most favored localities—men and women who have spent their thirty, forty, fifty, or even near sixty years. We may now congratulate ourselves that, drainage accomplished, we can compare favorably with any country for healthfulness.

EARLY DEATHS

"So far as I can ascertain, the first death among the white inhabitants of the county was Isham Cook. In 1830 he entered land in Section 5, north of Urbana. In the fall of that year he died and was buried there. The farm is known as the Dean farm. In 1831 a woman named Pugh, a member of a family traveling through, died at Rhinehart's, and was the first death in Somer Township. The wife of Isaac Busey died in 1834, and was the first to be buried in the old cemetery in Urbana. In 1833 several members of the Moss family and others died of cholera, north of the grove. The deaths were startling and spread consternation among the people. I mention also others who died within a few years after coming here, as follows: James Brownfield, brother of John and father of Robert; Thomas Rolland, father of Mrs. William I. Moore, of Danville; Isaiah Corray, father of Elisha; John Truman, ancestor of those remaining of that name; William Boyd, the grandfather of James Boyd; Isaac Busey, his son John and his grandson Isaac: David Shepard, father of Parris; William T. Webber, father of T. R. and W. H. Webber; James Brownfield, grandfather of William and Thomas; Jesse Tompkins, a squatter on the government lands; Samuel Brumley, father of Mrs. T. L. Truman; Jacob Bradshaw, Stephen Gulick, Charles Busey—and the list might be extended, but space forbids.

Deceased Revolutionary Soldiers

"Two of the earlier deaths were of men who were veterans of the Revolutionary War. One was Robert Brownfield, above noted, who died in 1841. The other was William Hays, who died afterward. Both are buried in Somer, and in unmarked graves. It would redound to the credit of the people to erect lasting monuments to mark the last resting place of these patriots, and to keep these spots in remembrance upon each recurring Decoration Day.

Schools

"John Light, the squatter, probably taught the first school within the territory of these townships in a cabin near where Frank Apperson now lives. James Boyd, who is with us today, was a pupil of Light's, and believes this to be the first. It was taught in the winter of 1832-33. Charles Fielder and John B. Thomas, afterwards a lawyer and judge of the county court, also taught school in the settlement in the north part of the grove. Asahel Brauer, a veteran of the War of 1812, who died five years since, also taught early in the '30s, in the grove.

Mills of Early Date

"The first mill for grinding corn was brought by Robert Trickle from Butler's Point in 1826. It consisted of a hollow log or 'gum,' in which were inserted the upper and the nether mill stones. These stones were worked out from rough bowlders and, with the appliances for making the upper stone revolve, served a very good purpose. Fielder in 1828 and John Brownfield in 1836, built horse mills, which were improvements on the hand mill. Brownfield's mill was quite pretentious and was built by James Holmes, a preacher of the Methodist Episcopal Church. The frame of the building used still stands. The stones were subsequently built into a water mill in the creek in 1842 by Mr. Brownfield, which superseded the horse mill. The stones are still preserved by Tom Brownfield as mementoes of other days. John Hap-

OLD TIMER OF A SAWMILL

tenstall built a saw mill on the creek below the town about 1840, and Jacob Mootz in 1842 built another on a site here in the park of Colonel Busey. These mills were not attended with success and were superseded by the first steam saw and grist mill built in the county, erected in Urbana in 1850 by William Park.

PIONEER PHYSICIANS

"The first physician who located here was Dr. Fulkerson, who came in 1830 and boarded with Mrs. Coe, a widow who had improved land in Section 27, Somer. He did not remain long, but moved on. Dr. Lyons stopped at John Shepherd's in Urbana Township for a time, before locating permanently at Sidney. He subsequently represented the county in the Legislature. Dr. John Saddler located in Urbana in 1839, leaving not long after, and was followed by Drs. Winston and W. D. Somers in 1840 and 1843. The former honored his profession until his death in 1871; the latter soon entered the law practice as the first lawyer of the county.

Religious Pathfinders

"One Mahurin, a Baptist, was the first minister to proclaim the Gospel here. He became chaplain of a regiment in the Black Hawk War and never returned. Alexander Holbrook, who lived where Captain Howell now resides, was a Methodist exhorter and often made the woods ring with his wild eloquence. William Phillips, known to the settlers as 'Bub Phillips,' and Rev. J. Holmes, who was a transient millwright, were local preachers of the same persuasion and materially aided the moral work. Father John G. Robertson, who in 1830 entered land in Section 10, Urbana, and who, as a Baptist layman, was ever a zealous Christian worker, is said to have held the first religious meetings in the then village of Urbana. He died at Mahomet a few years ago. The first Methodist class, and the germ of the present society in Urbana, was organized in 1836 at the house of Walter Rhodes, the first leader. The Baptist Church of Urbana was organized in 1841, at the Brumley schoolhouse, two miles east. The Roes, Brumleys, Trumans, Cooks, Coxes and Nancy Webber were among the constituent members. The officiating clergyman was Rev. Newell."

More About the Preachers

As stated, one of the first ministers to hold religious services in the county was Rev. John Dunham, of the United Brethren Church, who, at a very early day, came among the scattered settlements of Big Grove and Salt Fork. He lived in McLean County, and often, as late as 1835, passed through the settlements on his ministerial tours. Alexander Holbrook, the Methodist exhorter, lived on Howell's farm and often held meetings in the neighborhood, sometimes riding a steer to his appointments. Rev. William Phillips, who settled the Meyers farm, north of Champaign, sometimes preached about the Grove. Rev. Mr. Holmes organized the first Methodist class in the county, of which Walter Rhodes was made leader. Another eccentric pioneer preacher was Rev. Samuel Mapes. He rode also on a steer, but his steer was ornamented, usually, with a bell. He rode barefoot and carried a gun.

Rev. William I. Peters, of Salt Fork, used to preach much over the country. He bought whisky by the barrel on the Wabash at twenty cents per gallon, and retailed so as to clear thirty cents a gallon. The people not only regarded his practice as unobjectionable, but thought it a religious duty to buy their whisky of "Uncle Billy," as he was called, thereby assisting to spread the gospel and securing a good article of whisky at the same time.

A PROFESSIONAL LAND-GRABBER

David Gabbert, a widely known county pioneer, was honest and red-headed, unprepossessing in appearance and eccentric in manner. He never owned any land himself, but was often employed by others to enter land for them at Palestine or Vandalia and secure the receiver's certificate of entry. At any hour of the day or night he would set out, usually on foot, and never stop until his errand was accomplished. Gabbert lived on an eighty-acre farm in Section 15. Matthew Busey wanted to annex it to his farm; so one afternoon he started for Palestine, with the specie, to enter the farm.

It chanced that Anderson Rice, also, wanted the same land; so Gabbert was placed upon a horse after dark and started for Palestine. "Uncle Mat" had ridden leisurely forward until evening, when he stopped for the night. Gabbert, however, rode all night, passed Mr. Busey, and by the time the latter reached the land office, Gabbert had the receiver's certificate in his pocket, and Anderson was owner of the land. In this way did the pioneer settle once and forever many land titles.

WINTER OF THE DEEP SNOW

In the winter of 1830 and '31 came the deep snow. The weather during the fall had been dry, and continued mild until late in the winter. The snow came in the latter part of December and a great snow it was. The settlers were blockaded in their cabins and could do very little but pound their corn, cut their wood and keep their fires blazing. A great deal of stock was frozen to death. The deer and wild turkeys, which had been very numerous, suffered greatly and were nearly exterminated. The wolves became very bold and impudent. The stories of this deep snow would fill a volume. The depth of the snow was certainly over three feet, and many estimates place it at four. Fences were hidden. The summer following was celebrated for fever and ague, one of the severest scourges that afflicted the settlers. It was a disease that induced a feeling of despondency and took away that strong will and spirit of enterprise which enabled the settlers to endure the hardships of their lot.

First Marriage and Marrying Ministers

It is said that the first marriage in the county was that of Melinda Busey, daughter of Isaac Busey, to John Bryan, a young man lately from Kentucky, and that soon after, in 1834, Miss Nancy Drusilla Busey, daughter of Matthew Busey, wedded Elias Stamey, a settler who had entered land two miles north of Urbana.

The first ministers of the Gospel to perform marriage ceremonies were Cyrus Strong, an elder of the Christian Church, and William S. Crissey and James Holmes, Methodists, the latter the first organizer of Methodism in the county.

A Circular Hunt

Every new western county has had its famous hunts, by which its citizens aimed to round up such obnoxious animals as wolves, foxes and skunks, with such good food animals thrown in as wild turkeys, deer and various game in season. Champaign County had some successes and some failures in that line. The following is a notice to the hunters of that region, published in the Urbana Union of January 11, 1855: "Those who love the sports of the chase will have an opportunity of enjoying a rare hunt on Saturday next. By a well-matured plan the citizens of the county intend to have a Circular Hunt. The perimeter of the circle touches at Urbana, Robert Dean's, the old Boyer farm, Sadorus Grove and Sidney. The center is about nine miles south of this place."

The same paper of a week later has this pathetic account of the results of the Circular Hunt, so well-matured: "Instead of returning laden with the trophies of the chase, and for weeks fattening on good venison, our hunters came in early in the afternoon with jaded horses, empty stomachs and frozen fingers; in short, with everything but plenty of game. It appears that detachments from other settlements not so venturous as our hunters did not venture to brave the cold winds of the prairies that day, and the circle was not completed until they arrived upon the ground near the center; therefore the game was comparatively scarce. A few deer and wolves were headed, but from the few hunters on the ground, all escaped but one wolf."

Lancaster and Bloomville Strictly Paper Towns

The records of Vermilion County show that on July 16, 1832, Noah Baxter filed a plat of the town of Lancaster, laid out on what is now the northeast quarter of Section 6, Urbana Township, about two miles north of the city on an extension of Lincoln Avenue. It was near Salt Fork, adjoining the Big Grove and in the vicinity of one of the finest springs in the county. There was an ample public square in the center of the Lancaster plat, and a number of regular, carefully bisected streets. The tract was originally in possession of Sample Cole. Champaign County was organized the year after Lancaster was platted, but it nowhere appears as a competitor for the county seat—or, in fact, anywhere else but in the Vermilion County records.

The records of the county show that J. Q. Thomas, in September, 1855, laid out the town of Bloomville, comprising thirty-two lots on the northwest quarter of the northeast quarter of Section 8, about two miles northwest of Mahomet. The filing of the plat seems to have put a period to the enterprise.

Early Roads

Judge Cunningham in 1905: "The roads now, and for many years, running from Urbana northeasterly, known as the Heater Road and the Brownfield Road, were not in use after the location of the county seat. A trail, and perhaps wagon road, affording communication from the settlements north of the Big Grove with those on the south, led from the Clements farm south, crossing the creek at what was known as the Clay Bank ford running to the neighborhood of Samuel Brumley and of Matthew Busey. Now a county road and upon a section line, follows nearly the same route. The former road afforded pupils on the north side of the grove a road to the Brumley schoolhouse in later times.

"Until farms were occupied and enclosed, and travel confined to the legal roads, little work was done upon prairie roads. Here and there a culvert was put in at a slough crossing. No grades were thrown up and little pains were taken to close up the inevitable ruts made by passing vehicles. When a rut became too large for comfort, all the traveler had to do was to travel elsewhere in parallel lines, where mud had not been made. By the repetition of this process roads often attained great width. The liberty to go elsewhere always afforded comparatively good roads, at least in ordinary seasons, and it need hardly be said that the age of good roads in Illinois, for a time at least, passed with the fencing up of the roads so as to confine travel to one line.

1—9

"It was a common practice for the early settlers, for the purpose of marking the best line of travel between two places or between two timber points, to mark the route with a furrow, to be followed until the track became plain. It was in this manner that the road from Urbana to Middletown, now known as the State road, was at first marked and traveled, the furrow, in this case, being made by Fielding L. Scott. The road, as thus laid out by Mr. Scott as early as 1836 between Urbana and Mahomet, is still in use. So Henry Sadorus ran a furrow from his cabin to the Ambraw, for his own use and that of the traveling public. R. R. Busey tells of the work of his father who, in like manner, ran a furrow from

AN EARLY STAGE COACH

his house to Linn Grove, and again from the present site of Sidney to Sadorus Grove. These lines were, of course, run without regard to section lines."

WHITE MAN SHAMED BY RED "SAVAGE"

Peculiarly painful and pathetic circumstances attended the death of Mr. Cook (the first white to die in Champaign County), as told by Judge Cunningham, who says: "Isham Cook came early in the year 1830, and having bought out a squatter named Bullard, on July 1st of that year, entered the west half of the northwest quarter of Section 5 and, after erecting a cabin thereon, returned to Kentucky for his family. In the dead of winter, the family, on their way to their new home, arrived at Linn Grove, where Mr. Cook sickened and died. The bereaved family, with the body of their dead uncoffined, were in sore straits; for the members thereof consisted of the widow and four small children. One of the daughters, then a young girl, informed Judge Cunningham, in after years, that Joseph Davis took the remains of Mr. Cook and, with the grief-stricken and bewildered family, drove across country to Big Grove, in the western edge of which the dead father had partly prepared a cabin for his household the autumn before. The party was late and Davis was anxious to return home and, without ceremony, dumped the dead body of Cook upon the ground near the cabin, and set out on his journey home. This heartless proceeding, together with the helpless and unprotected condition of the family, caused the mother and her little children to cry aloud, with, as they supposed, no one near enough to hear them. It was otherwise, however, for a company of wild Indians, who were encamped a short distance east of the cabin across the creek, heard the cries of distress and at once came to the cabin. They were able to speak the language of the family and were informed of the action of the heartless Davis. Pagans as they were, they were indignant, and offered to pursue the hard-hearted Davis and take his scalp; but Mrs. Cook persuaded them otherwise, when they set about making the family comfortable in their cheerless camp. A fire was made, provisions furnished and cooked, and all cared for as best might be done. The next day these same wild men returned and again ministered to the needs of the family. The remains of the dead father, coffined in a roll of bark found near by, and which it must be supposed he himself had taken from some tree used in the building or roofing of his cabin, were placed in a grave made by them, and everything that the knowledge of the wild men could suggest was done to make the family comfortable. This place remained the home of the Cook family until broken up by the death of the mother and the marriage of the daughters, which took place ten years or more after they came here.

"James Madison Cook, the youngest of Isham Cook's family, and the only son, was drowned in Spring Creek, Iroquois County, about 1843, when on his way by wagon to Chicago.

"The land entered by Cook was subsequently owned by Samuel G. Bickley and became the home of James Dean, about 1850, where he resided until his death in 1870. Mr. Dean always respected the burial place of the Cooks, and though the graves remained unmarked, the ground was never broken or used in any manner. A small bunch of young timber and bushes covered the site for many years."

Tax-Payers at the Creation of the County

At the time the county was created there were 111 tax-payers in the county. They were mainly grouped in three settlements: The Salt Fork, the Big Grove and the Sangamon.

In the first was George Akers, the Baileys, and the Bartleys; Sarah and William Coe, whose descendants are yet here; William Copeland, who also has descendants. There, too, also lived the following, who have descendants now in the county: John Coddington Larkin and Thomas Dier, Jefferson Huss, James Freeman, John W. Leird, William Nox, Sr., and William Nox, Jr., William I. Peters, Abraham and William Peters, Hiram Rankins, David and John Swearingen, Cyrus Strong, Adam and Joseph Thomas, and Jacob Thomas, Sr., and Jacob, Jr., Henry and Moses Thomas; Adam Zeazel and John Zormes. There too lived others: Moses Argo, Levi Moore, Robert Prater, Joseph Stayton, and a few other families.

At Big Grove were the Buseys, Matthew and Isaac and Charles, Samuel Beckley and William Boyd, Mijamin Byers, Samuel Bromley, Asahel Bruer, yet living in Urbana, honored and revered by all, John Brown, Noah Bixler, the Broomfields, James, John, Jr., and Benjamin, whose numerous descendants are citizens of this county; Nancy Cook, William Curry, David Gabbard, the pioneer, Jacob Heater, Alexander Holebrooks and Lackland Howard, James and Amos Johnson, William, Elijah and John Jackson, Elias Kirby, James Mass, George Powell, Daniel T. Porter and Thomas Rowland, Gabriel G. Rice, James T. Roe, John G. Robertson, Matthias Rhinehart, Walter Rhodes, John Salisbury, Philip Stanford, Andrew Stevenson, John Truman, Joshua Taylor, Martin Tompkins, Joshua and Robert Trickles, the Webbers, William T. and Thompson R., and John Whitaker.

On the Sangamon were Ethan Newcom and family, the Osborns, James, Henry, William and Jonathan and Henry Hannahs. Frederick Bouse was at Linn Grove, and Henry Sadorus was on his farm on the banks of the Okaw or Kaskaskia.

An Inside Story Relating to the County Seat

On February 20, 1833, John Reynolds, governor of Illinois, signed the act of the Legislature creating the county of Champaign from the lands attached to Vermilion. The act appointed John F. Richardson, of Clark County, James P. Jones, of Coles County, and Stephen B. Shelledy, of Edgar County, commissioners to locate Urbana, which it was declared should be the county seat. These men met, as required by law, at the house of Phillip M. Stanford and found various points contesting for the honor of being the capital of the new county. Stanford wanted it at his house north of the grove, where the principal part of the population of the settlement was then located; in which his neighbors all joined him. At that time the only postoffice in this part of the county was known as Van Buren and was kept on the adjoining farm of Matthias Rhinehart. Isaac Busey and William T. Webber, owners respectively of the west one half of the northwest quarter and the east half of the northeast quarter of Section 17, in Urbana, and Colonel M. W. Busey, who owned contiguous lands, were making liberal offers of land for county purposes. The Stanford location was on the Fort Clark road and was surrounded by a considerable population, while the latter site was covered by hazel brush and decidedly in the backwoods. It was thought that the commissioners had decided in favor of Stanford's, when Isaac Busey prevailed upon them to go home with him to stay all night before driving the stake that was to settle the controversy. They went, and before another sun arose, tradition informs us that the stake was driven in a patch of hazel brush where the courthouse now stands. The driving of that stake, although an unimportant circumstance at that time, has proved an eventful one upon many things happening since. There are those who indulged in dark hints at the time of undue influences, the echo of which may be yet heard, but no doubt the commissioners acted from honest motives. Had Stanford's been accepted, Somer would have been the site of the county seat, instead of Urbana. The circumstances soon began to work necessary changes. Population began to gather on the south side of the grove; stores, limited, however, to a few articles only, were opened in Urbana. Courts were held here, and roads were opened leading to other parts of the county. The postoffice had its name changed from Van Buren to Urbana, and T. R. Webber, in addition to the office of clerk of the Circuit Court, and perhaps other offices, became postmaster.

This fixing of the county seat at Urbana, which also marked the birth of Champaign County as a civil organization, is carried over into the following chapter as the commencement of a distinct era and subject. Although some of the sub-topics of the preceding pioneer period have overlapped the year 1833, the main treatment of the subject has been consistent.

OLD SETTLERS SOCIETY

A number of old settlers of Champaign County effected an organization at the courthouse in Urbana, May 16, 1870, with Henry Sadorus as president. The members comprised those who were twenty years of age in 1840 and resided in the county at the time, and included the following: Henry Sadorus, William Sadorus, J. S. Wright, T. R. Webber, John G. Robinson, Fielding Scott, Stephen Boyd, John Maxfield, Asahel Bruer, James Clements, Joseph Maxwell, Paris Shepherd, William Rock, Robert Brownfield, John Corray, James Myers, D. O. Brumley, T. L. Truman, James Kirby, Abraham Leazel, H. W. Drullinger, James Bartley, B. F. Argo, John K. Patterson, Hiram Rankin, David Swearingen, Samuel Mapes, Thomas Richards, Michael Firebaugh, J. J. Swearingen, F. J. Busey, Harrison Heater, John R. Brownfield, Thomas Swearingen, William Romine, David Argo, B. F. Harris, Mrs. Elizabeth Busey, Mrs. Stephen Boyd, Mrs. Bryant, Mrs. William Harvey, Mrs. John Maxwell, Mrs. Sarah Robertson, Mrs. Fielding Scott and Mrs. William Rock. A point was stretched, however, and Archa Campbell, C. F. Columbia and J. T. Everett were admitted to membership. T. R. Webber was chosen first secretary and treasurer. There is a long hiatus in the records, as the next meeting noted was held in August, 1882. A new constitution and by-laws were adopted and J. O. Cunningham was elected president. Irregular meetings have been held since, but have become less and less frequent with the falling asleep of the old settlers until a regular organization has virtually been nonexistent for a number of years. It may be added, as a fitting conclusion, that L. A. McLean was long its secretary.

CHAPTER V

COUNTY MATTERS AND INSTITUTIONS

UNDER VERMILION COUNTY—JOHN W. VANCE, FATHER OF CHAM-
PAIGN COUNTY—THE CREATIVE ACT—JUDGE THOMAS ISSUES FIRST
ELECTION CERTIFICATES—THOMAS R. WEBBER—BALANCE OF FIRST
COUNTY OFFICERS—COUNTY DIVIDED INTO ELECTION DISTRICTS—
CONTESTANTS FOR THE COUNTY SEAT—REPORT OF LOCATING COM-
MISSIONERS—SOURCES OF REVENUE IN 1833—OFFICIAL HAPPENINGS
OF 1834, 1835 AND 1836—TEMPORARY COURTHOUSE—FINANCES IN
1837—MILL SEATS AND BRIDGES—FIRST COUNTY JAIL—PIONEER
CHURCHES AND SCHOOL—MATTERS IN 1844 AND 1845—COUNTY
FUNDS IN 1846—NEW COURTHOUSE COMPLETED—PUBLIC SQUARE
FENCED—ONLY WEBBER AGAINST INCORPORATION—FIRST TERM
OF CIRCUIT COURT OPENED—THE COURTHOUSE OF 1848—SCENE OF
FAMOUS SPEECHES AND MEETINGS—COURTHOUSE TOO SMALL—
TREASURED WORDS OF LINCOLN—RESULT OF 1856 AND 1860 CAM-
PAIGNS—LINCOLN-DOUGLAS SENATORIAL CONTEST—MAIN SPEECHES
AT THE FAIR GROUNDS—TWO POINTS OF VIEW—ONE COURTHOUSE
SOLD; ANOTHER BUILT—TOWNSHIP ORGANIZATION ADOPTED—
OTHER CHANGES IN OFFICERS—THE COURTHOUSE OF 1901—MUR-
DERER ESCAPES FROM OLD COUNTY JAIL—LINCOLN CALLS UPON SON
OF FOSTER BROTHER—THE SECOND AND THIRD JAILS—THE COUNTY
POORFARM—ROSTER OF COUNTY OFFICERS—STATISTICS—FIRST
ASSESSMENT IN CHAMPAIGN COUNTY (1833)—INCREASE OF COUNTY
REVENUES—PROPERTY VALUATION AND TAXES (1916)—POPULA-
TION (1833-1917)—BY TOWNSHIPS, CITIES AND VILLAGES.

If a Book of Chronicles were to be written for Champaign County,
its introduction would be something in this order: And St. Clair
County begat Knox, and Knox begat Gallatin, and Gallatin begat
Edwards, and Edwards begat Crawford, and Crawford begat Clark,
and Clark begat Edgar, and Edgar begat Vermilion, and from Vermilion
was born the special land of which this book is a record.

UNDER VERMILION COUNTY

Vermilion County, as created in 1826, embraced much of the state east of its central districts, including not only the present county by that name, but Iroquois, Ford and Champaign. At that time the few people in the western part of the county had mostly settled at Big Grove, and the Vermilion County Commissioners divided it into two voting precincts. All the territory north of a line running through the center of Town 18 was named as the Township of Ripley, with its voting place at the house of James Butler, at Butler's Point (now Catlin, Vermilion County), and "accommodated" the Big Grove Colony; south of that line was the Township of Carroll, and Henry Sadorus, the sole voter in the precinct within the bounds of what is now Champaign County, had to go to the Little Vermilion, if he desired to exercise his right of suffrage. John Light, one of the Big Grove squatters, was appointed constable for Ripley Township, and was the first settler to hold office in what is now Champaign County.

While still a portion of Vermilion County, the election districts embracing the present territory of Champaign County were changed in area, and various voting places named, more convenient of access. Such settlers as Runnel Fielder, John Powell, James Osborn, John Light and Thomas Rowland were named as judges of election. In 1828 the so-called Big Grove district embraced the territory west of the line between St. Joseph and Sidney, and Urbana and Philo extended to the northern and southern boundaries of the county. The records also show that the citizens along the upper Salt Fork and Big Grove were called to serve upon various juries of the Circuit Court sitting at Danville.

In 1830-31 Mijamin Byers, living on Section 10, Urbana, and Moses Thomas, whose home was on Section 30, a few miles northwest of the present village of Homer, were chosen justices of the peace.

But the settlers of Big Grove were impatient to get the civil machinery in motion, and could not wait for the results of the April election, and at the March term petitioned the Board of County Commissioners of Vermilion to appoint John Whitaker and Thomas R. Webber, of their number, acting constables. In the case, at least, of Mr. Webber this was done, as the record states that he "at once entered into bond with Philip M. Stanford and Moses Thomas as his sureties, which bond was by the court approved."

John W. Vance, Father of Champaign County

In the meantime John W. Vance, who resided at the Salt Works, a few miles west of Danville, the county seat of Vermilion County, had entered land in the Big Grove District and was evidently convinced that the section was destined to flourish. He had been sent to the State Senate several terms previous to his election to that body in August, 1832, and he is said to have fathered and perhaps prepared the act approved by Governor Reynolds, February 20, 1833, which created the county of Champaign with its bounds of today. Several attempts have been made to dismember it, and, although the acts tending thereto passed the Legislature, they were finally rejected by popular vote.

The Creative Act

The text of the act is as follows:

"Section 1. Be it enacted by the People of the State of Illinois represented in the General Assembly, That all the tract of country west of Vermilion County and east of Macon and McLean counties, to-wit: beginning at the southwest corner of Section 34, on the line dividing Townships 16 and 17 North, in Range 14 West of the Second Principal Meridian, thence west on said line to the east line of Macon County, thence north with said line to the line dividing 22 and 23, thence east with said line to the northwest corner of Section 3, Township 22 North, in Range 14 West, thence south on section line to the place of beginning, shall form a new county to be called Champaign.

"Section 2. For the purpose of fixing the seat of justice of said county, John F. Richardson, of Clark County, James P. Jones, of Coles County, and Stephen B. Shelledy, of Edgar County, are hereby appointed commissioners, who, or a majority of them, shall meet at the house of Philip Stanford in said county, on the third Monday of June next, or in six days thereafter, and, being duly sworn before some justice of the peace of the state, faithfully and impartially to take into view the conveniences of the people, the situation of the present settlements, with a strict view to the population and settlements which will hereafter be made, and the eligibility of the place, shall proceed to explore and carefully examine the country, determine on and designate the place for the permanent seat of justice of the same; Provided, the proprietor, or proprietors of the land shall give and convey by deed of general warranty for the purpose of erecting public buildings, a quantity of land in a square form, or not more than twice as long as wide, not less than twenty acres; but should the proprietor neglect to make the donation, then and in that case said commissioners shall fix said county seat, having in view the interests of the county, upon the land of some other person who will make the donation aforesaid. If the commissioners shall be of the opinion and decide that the proper place for the seat of justice is, or ought to be, on lands belonging to the Government, they shall so report, and the County Commissioners shall purchase one-half quarter section of the tract set forth in their name, for the use of the county. The commissioners appointed to locate the seat of justice shall, as soon as they decide on the place, make a clear report to the Commissioners' Court of the county, and the same shall be recorded at length in their record book. The land donated or purchased shall be laid out into lots and sold by the commissioners of the county to the best advantage, and the proceeds applied to the erection of public buildings, and such other purposes as the commissioners shall direct, and good and sufficient deeds shall be made for lots sold.

"Section 3. An election shall be held at the place of holding as now laid off by Vermilion County in the said county of Champaign on the second Monday of April next, for one sheriff, one coroner and three county commissioners, who shall hold their offices until the next general election and until they be qualified; and the Justices of the Peace and the constables who are now in office and residing within the limits of the said county of Champaign, shall continue in office until the next quadrennial election for Justices of the Peace and constable, and until their successors be qualified. It shall be the duty of the clerk of the Circuit Court of said county to give public notice, at least ten days previous to the election to be held on the second Monday in April next, and in case there shall be no clerk in said county, it shall be the duty of the recorder, or judge of probate, to give at least fifteen days' notice previous to said election, who shall be legal voters, and the returns of the election shall be made to the Clerk, Recorder or Judge of Probate, as the case may be, who gave the notice aforesaid, and by him, in the presence of one or more Justices of the Peace, shall be opened and examined, and they jointly shall give to the persons elected commissioners' certificates of their election, and like certificates to the persons elected sheriff and coroner, to forward to the governor, which election shall in all respects be conformable to law.

"Section 4. The commissioners appointed to locate the county seat shall be allowed two dollars per day for each day they may be necessarily employed in making said location, to be paid by said county.

"Section 6. The seat of justice of said county shall be called and known, by the name of Urbana.

"Approved February 20, 1833, by

"John Reynolds, Governor."

JUDGE THOMAS ISSUES FIRST ELECTION CERTIFICATES

Moses Thomas, mentioned as one of the sureties of Mr. Webber on his bond as constable, was a friend of Senator Vance, author of the Champaign County Bill. He was also one of the justices of the peace while the territory was under the jurisdiction of Vermilion County and, previous to the April election of 1833, ordered in the creative act, had been appointed probate judge by the General Assembly. At the election on the second Monday in April, held at the house of John Light, Isaac Busey, Jacob Bartley and George Akers were chosen commissioners of Champaign County and John Salisbury, sheriff. It is probable that the first official act of Probate Judge Thomas was to canvass the returns of the election and issue certificates to the successful candidates. Such procedure was authorized by the organic act, and the record shows that Judge Thomas issued such certificates of election.

THOMAS R. WEBBER

On the 6th of May, 1833, these first commissioners of Champaign County met at the cabin of Philip Stanford, on Section 28, Somer Township, and appointed Thomas R. Webber clerk of the Board. He held that position, either by appointment of the board or by popular election, for more than twenty years, and served as clerk of the Circuit Court for twenty-three years, from 1835 to 1857, inclusive. He was also the first postmaster at Urbana and in the county, and was, altogether, of such unusual capacity that his subsequent public career is here noted. He was a Kentuckian of German extraction and one of the pioneers and shining lights of the Big Grove contingent. In addition to his long service as county and circuit clerks, he acted as master in chancery for a period of forty years, being succeeded by M. W. Mathews in 1873. In 1847 he was elected to represent Vermilion, Champaign, Piatt and Coles counties in the constitutional convention of that year, and in 1862 he represented in a similar convention, the counties of Champaign, Piatt, DeWitt and Macon. The constitution prepared by the latter convention was rejected by the people, and hence the names of its framers were not so impressed upon the history of the state as if it had been incorporated into the fundamental laws. Mr. Webber was a man of high personal character, as well as ability, and widely beloved. He died at his residence south of Urbana on December 14, 1881, in the seventy-fifth year of his age.

BALANCE OF FIRST COUNTY OFFICERS

After the appointment of Mr. Webber as the first county clerk, the new commissioners chose Garrett Moore as constable and Moses Thomas as assessor and treasurer.

The next meeting of the Board, or Court (as it was originally called), was held June 3, 1833, when Mr. Webber was recommended to the governor for recorder. The appointment promptly followed, his commission dating from July 2. At the same meeting Garrett Moore the constable, was appointed surveyor, and Assessor Thomas reported the revenue of the county to be $71.37.

COUNTY DIVIDED INTO ELECTION DISTRICTS

The Court also divided the county into two election districts, calling one the Salt Fork precinct and appointing Moses Thomas, Robert Prather and Captain William Nox, Jr., judges, and the second, the Big Grove precinct, with Matthew Busey, Joshua Trickle and John Whitaker as judges. The meeting then adjourned to assemble at the call of the clerk at such time as the commissioners appointed by legislative act to locate the county seat should be ready to report.

CONTESTANTS FOR THE COUNTY SEAT

The late Judge Cunningham thus sizes up the situation at the time the locating commissioners were endeavoring to decide upon the site of the county seat, which was to be called Urbana: "It will be remembered that at this time there was no established town or village to claim the boon of the seat of justice, nor was there any densely settled district with influence. The law under which these gentlemen were to act only required them to 'take into view the conveniences of the people, the situation of the present settlements, with a strict view to the population and settlements which shall hereafter be made, and the eligibility of the place.' The 'settlements' and the 'people' whose conveniences were to be consulted as then located, were found in three groups: one upon the Salt Fork, another at the Big Grove mostly upon the Fort Clark road at the north side, and the third upon the Sangamon—the largest settlement of the three being the first, and the smallest, the last named.

"The positions occupied by the first and last named settlements, and opposite sides of the county, excluded both from the consideration of the commissioners, leaving the Big Grove settlement at the center of the county alone to be considered. On the north side were most of the inhabitants, including Stanford (at whose house the Commission was required to meet), John Whitaker, the Brownfields, John Light, Thomas Rowland (the friend of Senator Vance), and many others who had influence. On the south side were Isaac Busey, then the largest land owner in the county; Matthew Busey, his brother, and Thomas R. Webber, all on the ground with land to give, besides Colonel Matthew W. Busey, then a resident of Greencastle, Indiana, but a large land owner, who was then on the ground seeking, with others with like interests, the location of the new county seat. So, also, William T. Webber, who had made valuable selections of lands on the south side, then a resident of Kentucky, represented by his son, T. R. Webber, threw his influence into the arena of contest. Those on the north side wished the new town of Urbana to be located there, where was then established Van Buren postoffice, the only office in the county.

"The commissioners looked at the location about two miles east of Urbana in Section 15, where Matthew Busey then lived and, admiring the lay of the land, solicited from him an offer of land for public purposes. The suggestion was repelled by Mr. Busey, upon whose vision the thought of profits from the sale of corner lots and town sites, does not seem to have made any impression. He declared that he had purchased this land for a farm and a home, and was determined to use it as such, which he did to the day of his death, thirty years afterwards. The commissioners also looked at a very pretty town-site upon the land of John Brownfield near the creek in the Big Grove, believed to have been the geographical center of the county. So, also, the town of 'Lancaster,' laid out but a year before, was a candidate for the favor, and not without friends. Noah Bixler, the proprietor, was not a man to remain silent when such an opportunity offered to aid his town. It had many things to recommend its claims. The land there and near by was entirely suitable for a town, and the location was not more than two miles from the geographic center of the new county. Possibly its name was against it, for the law said 'the seat of justice of said county shall be called and known by the name of Urbana.'

"The controversy narrowed down to the two points—north of the grove and south of the grove. The former was championed by Stanford, Heater, Brownfield, Rhinehart, Light, and many other dwellers along the Fort Clark road, who could claim for their settlement age, numbers, the postoffice, and the only public road through the county, and as being at the front; while the south side was without any of these advantages, and was an out-of-the-way place with no advantages whatever. In fact, the south side had nothing to recommend as a county seat. It had no roads, but bridle paths and Indian trails. It had no population except the families of Isaac Busey, Jacob Smith, and the Webbers; and it is still told by those who then noted the controversy, that it had no vegetation but the hazel brush, which grew in great abundance and to a wondrous height."

The secret of the unexpected decision in favor of the "hazel brush site" on the south side of the Big Grove was never divulged; only the fact that Commissioners Richardson and Shelledy adjourned from Mr. Stanford's house on June 20, 1833, to the residence of Isaac Busey, with the general understanding that they favored the "north-siders," and that on the following day they reported for the south side site.

REPORT OF THE LOCATING COMMISSIONERS

At the meeting of the county commissioners on the 21st, Clerk Webber made this record:

"This day came Stephen B. Shelledy and John F. Richardson, a majority of the commissioners appointed to locate the permanent seat of justice for the county of Champaign, appeared in court and made the following report, which is ordered to be committed to record and filed in the Clerk's office:

"We, the undersigned commissioners appointed to locate the seat in and for Champaign County, do certify that agreeably to 'An act creating Champaign County,' approved January 20, 1833, we met at the house of Philip Stanford in said county, and after being duly sworn, faithfully and impartially to take into view the conveniences of the people, the situation of the present settlement, with a strict view to the population and settlement which will hereafter be made, and eligibility of the place, proceeded to explore and carefully examine the country and have selected a site and obtained donation of forty-three acres of land, titles to thirty acres of which we have procured to be executed to the County Commissioners' Court of Champaign County, 19 50-100 of which lies in the northeast quarter of Section 17, Town 19 North, Range 9 East, and ten and a half acres in the west half of the southeast quarter of Section 8, Town 19 North, Range 9 East; the metes and bounds of which are particularly described in the deed executed by Isaac Busey and wife; also ten acres in the east half of the southeast quarter of Section 8 and the east half of the northeast quarter of Section 17, Town 19 North, Range 9 East; the metes and bounds of which are particularly described in a bond for a deed, under penalty of $10,000, executed by T. R. Webber and M. W. Busey; also three acres described in a bond for a deed executed by M. W. Busey and T. R. Webber.

"Given under our hands and seals at the house of Isaac Busey, in said county, this 21st day of June A. D. 1833.

"John F. Richardson, (Seal)

"S. B. Shelledy.   (Seal)."

For twenty years the official affairs of Champaign County were made matters of detailed record by T. R. Webber, and from his methodical and neat books are extracted most of the following items of interest, which illustrate its material development in so many ways.

Sources of Revenue in 1833

The meetings of the court had been heretofore held at the house of Philip Stanford, but at the September meeting (1833) it was ordered that hereafter they be held at the house of Matthew Busey. John Salisbury was appointed sheriff soon after the organization, and September 2, 1833, he was ordered to proceed and collect the revenue, amounting to $71.37. As it was necessary to have a source of revenue, on November 7, 1833, a license was granted to Isaac H. Alexander to retail goods, wares and merchandise until the end of the next term of court—the license being $5. Afterwards, the time was extended $3.00 worth. Soon after this the commissioners fixed the following rates of prices to be charged the public, viz.: For keeping a man and horse one night, including supper, bed and horse feed, 75 cents; single meal, 18¾ cents; horse feed, 12½ cents; one-half pint whisky, 6¼ cents; one-half pint French brandy, 18¾ cents; one-half pint wine, 18¾ cents; one-half pint gin, 12½ cents; one-half pint rum, 18¾ cents; one-half pint domestic brandy, 18¾ cents.

The first fiscal statement was made by T. R. Webber, and showed county orders unpaid, $85.25; fees for surveying 84 lots in the town of Urbana, $21; recording plat, $3.36; fees of commissioners and for stationery, $17.55; making a total indebtedness of $127.36; deducting the revenue, $71.37, left $55.99; then deducting license of Alexander, $5.00, left the indebtedness of the county December 2, 1833, at $50.99.

March 3, 1834, the county was divided into road districts and William Peters, Daniel T. Porter, John G. Robertson, Mijamin Byers, Philip M. Stanford, Wm. Nox, Jr., John Whitaker, were appointed road supervisors.

OFFICIAL HAPPENINGS OF 1834, 1835 AND 1836

March 4, 1834, the first grand and petit juries were appointed, as follows: Grand jury—Thomas Deer, Jefferson Huss, Wm. Nox, Sr., Joseph Thomas, Henry Thomas, Robert Trickle, James Brownfield, Walter Rhodes, James Johnson, Samuel G. Beckley, John W. Swearingen, John B. Swearingen, John Zanes, Robert Prather, Valentine Iliff, Gabriel G. Rice, Matthew Busey, John Tineman, Samuel Bromley, Arthur Beaird, Harris Wilson, William Corray and James Osborne. Petit jury—James Moss, Matthew W. Busey, Elias Stamey, David Gabbert, William T. Webber, Augustine M. Webber, Larkin Deer, Stephen Boyd, Elijah Jackson, Andrew Wilson, Adam Yeazle, James Freeman, Jacob T. Hobbs, John Coddington, Jacob Heater, Moses Kirby, Elias Kirby, John Brownfield, Sr., William Coddington, Elias Thomas, Moses Argo, William I. Peters and Hiram Rankin.

At a meeting of the county commissioners, held December 1, 1834, it was ordered that hereafter they meet at the house of Isaac Busey. The court appointed T. R. Webber agent in July, 1835, to sell the lots in Urbana at following prices: Corner lots on Main Street, on public square, at $30 each; corner lots elsewhere, $20; back lots, $10.

TEMPORARY COURTHOUSE

January, 1836, a temporary court house was ordered to be built on lot 25, to be of hewn logs, good size. The building was to be 24x20 feet, one and one-half story, shingle roof, hewn joists and sleepers, one door and two windows on each side. The contract was let to John Craig, but the building was never finished to the satisfaction of the commissioners and court continued to be held in private houses until 1837, when a frame courthouse 22x30 feet, with two rooms, was built by Moses and William Harvey. This building was replaced in 1841 by a brick building 30x40 feet, two stories, with offices below and court and jury above.

The revenue increased in 1836 to $258.85. On December 3, 1836, Jonathan Osborne and Isaac Busey were appointed a committee to locate a state road from Urbana to Bloomington, to run by the house of John Bryan. Joseph Stayton and Elias Thomas, on same date were appointed to locate a road from Urbana to Paris. At the December term, 1836, a license was granted Wm. Osborn to keep a ferry on the Sangamon River at a point where the state road crosses it, leading from Moses Thomas' to Bloomington—Osborn to pay $2 license. The following ferry rates were established at the same meeting, viz.: Ferrying one man, 6¼ cents; one horse, 6¼ cents; one-horse wagon, 25 cents; two-horse wagon, 37½ cents; cattle, per head, 6¼ cents; sheep and hogs, per head, 3 cents.

At the March meeting, 1837, it was ordered that the office of assessor and treasurer be let to the lowest bidder; and Thomas L. Freeman having bid the sum of $12.50, was appointed to that office and qualified as such.

FINANCES IN 1837

In 1837, the liabilities of the county were $216.34½; and the revenue being $258.85, the county had money in the treasury for the first time, amounting to $32.56½, to which add $431.50 in notes on sale of town lots in Urbana, and cash donations unpaid $45, made the cash and resources of the county $476.50.

March, 1837, it was ordered that the following property be taxed one-half per cent, viz.: Horses, mares, mules, asses and neat cattle over the age of three years, clocks and watches with their appendages, and pleasure carriages.

In 1837, licenses to retail goods were granted and license charges as follows: A. Bruer, $5; James T. Roe, $5; T. R. Webber, $15; James H. Lyons, $25; Daniel T. Porter, $5; Noah Bixler, $5.

June, 1837, ordered that Matthew W. Busey have a writ of ad quod damnum for condemning a mill seat on north end of E½ SW¼ Sections 8, 10, 9. The same year Green Atwood was allowed a license to keep a tavern at Homer; also a license was granted to Isaac A. Brown to keep a tavern at Sidney, each to pay a license of $4.

MILL SEATS AND BRIDGES

September, 1837, a writ of ad quod damnum was granted to Charles Haptonstall to build a mill. A like writ was granted at same meeting to A. H. Jose for a mill seat on Sangamon River, on lot 15, Sec. 16, T. 20, R. 7. At same meeting it was ordered that a bridge be constructed over the Salt Fork at Cyrus Strong's ferry, and that Major Nox attend to advertising for bids and to insert an advertisement in the Danville Enquirer. The building of this bridge was let in October,

1837, to Wm. I. Peters for the sum of $426, and he to have one year to build it.

FIRST COUNTY JAIL

The first county jail, to be completed by March, 1839, was arranged for January, 1838; it was to be 18 feet square, the lower story to have two windows, one foot square each. The building was to have a brick and log foundation and to be built of logs, and to be two stories. It was struck off to Col. M. W. Busey at the sum of $850.

FIRST COUNTY JAIL (1838-39)

Judge Cunningham speaks of the old jail: "This building was standing and in use by the sheriff for the detention of prisoners in 1853, when the writer came to the county. An outside stairway afforded the means of reaching the second story where, by the only door of the building, access and egress were had. Through it prisoners were taken for confinement, and from the second story a trap door in the floor gave access to the lower story, where the worst prisoners were placed. The prisoner was sent down the ladder which, being removed, he was considered safe. The only light was admitted through narrow grated windows in the lower story. No means of heating either story existed. The writer, when acting as justice of the peace in 1855, in the case of a person charged with horse stealing, found in the evidence probable guilt and, as required by the letter of the law, committed the unfortunate to this bastile in the dead of winter, with no means furnished but an abundance of bed-clothing to keep him from freezing. The law would have been more honored in the breach than in the observance in that case. The prisoner did not die of cold, however, but met his fate in another manner."

On March 19, 1838, it was ordered that an election precinct be established on the Middlefork and that elections be held at the house of John Manning, near the town of Brotherton in said precinct.

In June, 1838, a license was granted Groenendyke & Coffeen to retail goods at Homer, and that they pay for same $15. At the same meeting a county road was ordered from the south end of Market Street, in Urbana, to Sidney. December, 1838, A. Bruer was granted a license to keep a tavern in Urbana and that he pay $2 for the same.

PIONEER CHURCHES AND SCHOOL

At the December term, 1839, it was ordered the clerk convey to the officers of the Methodist Episcopal Church a lot to be selected by them if they shall have erected a house of worship thereon in twelve months. And "we also make to the Baptist society the same offer in all respects." The Methodist people raised the money and built a church, which was afterwards known as Renner's livery stable. The Baptist people, however, did not comply at that time.

Col. M. W. Busey having donated a three-acre tract to the county, permission was given to erect a schoolhouse on the same. December, 1839, Colonel Busey, Jacob Bradshaw and Elias Stamey were appointed a committee to select a suitable spot for said house.

June term, 1840, it was "ordered that we sell to Rev. A. Bradshaw lot 51 (where Hubbard's hardware store now stands) for the sum of $3, the same to be deeded to the Methodist society, which has a legal right to receive a deed. Also that we sell to David Cox, for Baptist Church, with same restriction, lot 76, east of Kerr's Tavern, for $2."

The salary of T. R. Webber as clerk was not very heavy; he was allowed $77.98 in full for his services as clerk for year ending June 7, 1841.

At the June term, 1842, M. D. Coffeen represented that it was too far for the people of Homer to go to the house of James Copeland, in the Salt Fork precinct, to vote. He therefore presented a petition that the name of the precinct be changed to Homer precinct and the voting be done at the schoolhouse in Homer, which was ordered done.

October 2, 1843, the contract for building a bridge across the Sangamon at Mahomet was awarded William Harvey of Urbana.

MATTERS IN 1844 AND 1845

June, 1844, on petition of citizens, an election precinct known as the Middlefork precinct, was ordered, and that the voting place be at the house of Samuel Swinford, and Samuel Swinford, Samuel Kerr and James Kellor were appointed judges. At the same meeting, James Orr, Sr., Henry Swearingen and Elias Thomas were appointed judges of Homer, Marshall Cloyd, John Crabb and James Myers, of Urbana, and Jonathan Maxwell, Benjamin F. Harris and Joseph T. Everett of Sangamon precincts.

The tax books for the year.1844 show that the taxable property was increasing, the amount returned being $334,373. The levy was as follows: 20 cents on the $100 for state purposes, making $668.75; 20 cents for county, $668.75; and 10 cents for road making, $334.37.

William D. Somers seems to have been the county physician in 1844. At the December meeting of the County Court it was "ordered that Dr. William D. Somers have an order on the treasury for the sum of $2 in full for medical charge for attending Robert H. Newlon."

At the June meeting, 1845, William D. Somers was appointed to take the census of the county.

COUNTY FUNDS IN 1846

Col. M. W. Busey, county treasurer, made his report July, 1846. He reports a balance on hand of $561.37, as follows: $332 in paper money; $155.52 in gold, and $73.85 in silver. The county seems to have been in good condition, as Colonel Busey was ordered to loan the county funds at 6 per cent interest, reserving a sufficient sum to pay outstanding orders, and that he take ample security in all cases, and that he collect the interest in advance; that the notes be so drawn that additional security may be required if it is deemed necessary by the treasurer or commissioners.

At the July term, 1848, Col. M. W. Busey was appointed a messenger to carry the vote of this county for senator to Danville, for the purpose of being canvassed, and William Harvey was appointed a like messenger to Decatur, to carry the vote for representative.

New Courthouse Completed

May 2, 1849, the new courthouse having been completed, the old one was sold to the Urbana school district for $105 on a credit of twelve months. At the June meeting a bridge was ordered to be constructed at Homer, provided the cost did not exceed $400. June 20, the contract was struck off to M. D. Coffeen, James S. Wright, Harmon Stevens, John B. Thomas, Solomon Dill, Samuel A. Harvey and W. S. Coe for $600, $400 to be paid by the county and the balance by private donations—the bridge to be completed by the following December.

October, 1849, it was ordered that Clapp & Russell have leave to renew their license to retail goods on the same terms as before. March term, 1850, Henry M. Russell having bought out A. O. Clapp, was granted license for one year by paying $25.

The County Court cut and carved the bills, in the olden times, very much as is done in later days. March, 1850, Benjamin C. Morris presented a bill of $22.25 for services, board, medical attendance and funeral expenses of Daniel Wheat, a poor person. The court, after examining into the matter, decided that said Morris is justly entitled to pay for the coffin and shroud and therefore allowed him $7.25 and rejected the rest of his claim.

Public Square Fenced

At the March term, 1851, it was decided to enclose the public square with a fence, which contract was let to Wm. Park and John Cantner for $80. At the July term, 1851, on petition of Samuel Dean and David Cantner, permission was granted them to establish a ferry on the Sangamon River at the crossing of the state road leading from Urbana to Bloomington. The following rates were fixed as ferry charges: For man and horse, 10 cents; footman, 5 cents; wagon and one horse, 15 cents; wagon and two horses or oxen, 20 cents; each additional horse or ox, 5 cents; each head of cattle, 4 cents; each hog or sheep, 2 cents.

Only Webber Against Incorporation

At the October term, 1851, J. W. Jaquith, John Gere, Calvin Higgins, president and trustees of the town of Urbana, and William D. Somers, clerk, presented to the court a poll book of an election, whereby it appears that at an election held in the town of Urbana, September 8,

1851, for the purpose of voting for or against the incorporation of said town the following votes were cast in favor of same, viz.: W. D. Somers, Geo. O. Potter, Wilson Lewis, W. S. Garman, Joseph M. Harry, Elisha Harkness, Wm. Park, John Cantner, Calvin C. Higgins, Wm. Abel, Robert Logan, Wm. Waters, Lewis Higgins, John Black, Edward Ater, Asa Gere, Wm. Gill, Samuel M. Logan, Thomas J. Newport, Silas Chadwick, John C. Hankins, David M. Ireland, J. W. Jaquith, Samuel Waters, George W. Toy; total, 25. Against: Thomson R. Webber. At the election, Joseph M. Harry was the judge and John Ireland clerk.

The foregoing is a synopsis of the business transacted in the county from 1833 to and including February term, 1852. While some of the business might seem insignificant, yet it was entered of record by the clerk, T. R. Webber, in detail, and there was no mistaking the meaning of the persons doing the business for the people.

First Term of Circuit Court Opened

On March 2, 1833, a legislative act was approved by the governor providing that "when the counties of Iroquois and Champaign shall be organized under the provisions of the acts of this Legislature, then the judge of the Fourth Judicial Circuit shall have power to change the time of holding courts in the county of Coles so as to suit the time of holding courts in the said counties of Champaign and Iroquois." Until 1835, however, no Circuit Court was convened in Champaign County. Legally, there was no circuit judge during that period, although one of the judges of the State Supreme Court was authorized to hold court therein. But a more specific law was passed in 1834, and on January 19, 1835, under its provisions Justin Harlan of Clark County was commissioned judge of the Fourth Circuit. On April 6 of that year he opened the first term of the Circuit Court of Champaign County, at the house of Isaac H. Alexander.

With Judge Harlan (uncle of the late United States Senator James Harlan of Iowa) appeared Andrew Stevenson, sheriff, who had succeeded the first incumbent of that office, John Salisbury. The court appointed Thomas R. Webber clerk; by like appointment, Mr. Webber continued as clerk of the Circuit Court until the adoption of the constitution of 1848, and after that, by popular election until 1857.

The Courthouse of 1848

The third courthouse for the accommodation of the established courts and the officials of Champaign County was completed during the constitutional year of 1848 by E. O. Smith of Decatur, at a cost of $2,744, and was pronounced a "very pretty building of brick and wood, with a bell tower on the center of the roof, stone floor, window sills and caps."

Scene of Famous Speeches and Meetings

In that building were delivered several of Lincoln's great speeches, notably his third speech in his famous debates with Douglas on the Nebraska Bill. An eye-witness of that historic oration of October 24, 1854, who had just called on Lincoln and Judge Davis at the old Pennsylvania House, across the street, says: "After some further conversation and a few preliminary arrangements, the old court room opposite shone resplendent in the coruscation of eleven tallow candles, glued on the top of the nether sashes of the windows, to which place we adjourned and where, with no preliminaries Mr. Lincoln delivered to a full house the third speech on the mighty issue of slavery in our nation."

Two years later it was the courthouse which was the center of the political maelstrom which surged through Champaign County and the country, and resulted in the birth of the Republican party, and the election of Lincoln four years later. One of the early calls for a meeting to discuss the issues of that day appears in the Urbana Union of May 8, 1856. It reads: "The citizens of Champaign County, without regard to past political differences or divisions, who are opposed to the repeal of the Missouri Compromise, to the policy of the present administration, to the extension of slavery over territory now free, in favor of the admission of free Kansas, and of restoring the government to the principles of Washington and Jefferson, are requested to meet in convention at the court house in Urbana on Thursday, the 18th day of May, to deliberate on the great political measures that now agitate the public mind, and to appoint a delegate to the State Anti-Nebraska Convention. The undersigned would join in the call, hoping that all who can will be present.

"Signed: A. Campbell, W. W. Beasley, J. W. Sim, James Dean, Winston Somers, H. M. Russell, S. S. Cunningham, David O. Quick, James Core, James D. Jaquith, Chalmers M. Sherfy, W. C.

Cassell, James W. Somers, W. H. Talbutt, Henry Robinson, J. O. Cunningham, John M. Dunlap, J. Ingersol, A. M. Ayers, Sol. Bernstein, Henry Fitzgerald, A. O. Howell, E. Harkness, James Curtiss, W. C. Beck, J. H. Thomas, William H. Somers, J. C. Sheldon, Arthur Bradshaw, F. B. Sale, James Yeazle, William Park and F. M. Owens."

Two weeks later the Union reports that the meeting was duly held. It was called to order by J. D. Jaquith; Rev. Arthur Bradshaw was chosen chairman and J. O. Cunningham secretary. Resolutions were adopted that the meeting was opposed to any interference with slavery in the states where it existed; also to its extension to free territory; that Congress had the constitutional power to thus limit its operations; that Kansas ought to be admitted as a free state; that William H. Bissell was the choice of the meeting for governor of Illinois, and that, regardless of party, all should co-operate against the extension of slavery.

COURTHOUSE TOO SMALL

In the fall of 1856, at the height of the Fremont campaign, the crowds which gathered at the county seat were so large that they overtaxed the little brick courthouse and had to be held in the open; as witness the following from the Urbana Union of September 25: "Early in the morning (of the 18th) the people from every direction commenced flowing into town with banners, badges and mottoes, and the loudest 'shrieks for freedom.' Some came with processions, with delegations from their neighborhoods, and some came singly, while others came in wagons, carriages, on horseback, on mules and on foot—none forgetting that they were assembled as a free people for the purpose of 'securing the blessings of liberty to themselves and to their posterity.'

"After raising the flag of our Union to the top of a pole 150 feet high, which had been previously raised, and giving three hearty cheers for Fremont, the throng moved, not to the courthouse (as it was claimed was done by the other party a few days before), but to Webber's Grove. The procession was headed by the Urbana band and Reynold's band of Danville, both of which, during the day, acquitted themselves with credit in discoursing music for the occasion.

"The dinner, although consisting of large quantities of provisions— over two whole beeves, several muttons, thirty dozens of chickens, turkeys, pigs, etc., with huge quantities of bread, besides piles of cakes and pies contributed by the ladies of the county—was insufficient to supply the wants of the vast throng."

HOTEL WHERE LINCOLN STOPPED IN URBANA (WINDOW
OF HIS ROOM IN UPPER LEFT CORNER)

UNDER BIG ELM TREE (EAST OF BIG FOUR SHOPS) LINCOLN
MADE FAMOUS SPEECH

Treasured Words of Lincoln

It came out incidentally that Abraham Lincoln was one of the speakers and reviewed the procession. One of the attractions of the parade was a "float" loaded with pretty girls representing the states of the Union which then existed. In passing upon that feature of the procession, Lincoln remarked that it reminded him of "a large basket full of roses." When those pretty girls became the grandmothers of Champaign County, and the homely, unassuming Lincoln of 1856 had gone into history as the great emancipator and martyred President of the United States, that remark was recalled by the old ladies with unfeigned pride and tenderness.

Result of 1856 and 1860 Campaigns

The result of the 1856 campaign, which centered in the courthouse, was to give Fremont 722 votes in the county, Buchanan 556, and Fillmore 236. Four years later Lincoln received 1,720, Douglas 1,251, Bell 99 and Breckenridge 12.

Lincoln-Douglas Senatorial Contest (1858)

In the fall of 1858, the courthouse was also the scene of an enthusiastic meeting during the Lincoln-Douglas campaign for the United States Senate. In reply to a speech delivered by the Little Giant, Lincoln had spoken at the fair grounds in Urbana—although the exhibition had closed the day before—notwithstanding which, he had met with a rousing reception, and in the evening, with William Bross, editor of the Chicago Tribune, and Judge Terry of Danville, spoke at the courthouse. Although the lank son of Illinois seems to have carried most of the meetings with him, he lost the senatorial election, but progressed far toward the presidency.

Main Speeches at the Fair Grounds

The fair grounds at Urbana will always be remembered by the pioneers of the county as the scene of two famous speeches delivered by Lincoln and Douglas in their historic campaign for a seat in the United States Senate. But the Little Giant was too firmly seated to be displaced by his already popular but then less prominent opponent. Douglas spoke on the closing day of the fair, September 23, 1858, and Lincoln on the day after, when "the show was over and the people had all gone home." But to the surprise of all, Lincoln drew nearly as large a crowd as Douglas. They had already met in joint debate at various Illinois towns, the last time before the Urbana appointment, at Charleston, on the 18th. Their speeches had been widely and earnestly discussed—there were no neutrals in those days—and all were anxious to weigh the arguments as they came from the lips of the distinguished orators.

At the time of the Urbana clash, the fair grounds of the Agricultural Association lay upon both sides of what is now Lincoln Avenue, about a mile north of Springfield Avenue and within the bounds of Crystal Lake Park. From all accounts, Judge Douglas was a fine "mixer" and made hosts of friends by appearing at the grounds on the afternoon of the day before his speech. On the afternoon of the speaking the usual procession formed, near the head of which was a wagon bearing a platform of hickory poles loaded with cheering Democrats (Hickory Boys), among whom was the Senator himself. The correspondent of the Chicago Democrat, who heard his speech, criticized his delivery rather severely, concluding: "As an orator he is no more to be compared to Lovejoy, Farnsworth, Arnold, Palmer or Herndon than the merest tyro at debating. I venture the assertion that twenty men can be found in every county in Illinois who, before an impartial audience, would receive the palm over him for declamatory skill."

Two Points of View

The Chicago Democrat was one of Lincoln's warm supporters; what we would call Republican newspapers, in some cases, retained their old political designation.

By reading the following it is evident that the Urbana Constitution, from which the extract is taken, was a Douglas paper: "The announcement that Senator Douglas would speak here last Thursday—the closing day of the county fair—called together by far the largest crowd ever assembled in the county of Champaign. A delegation of ladies and gentlemen on horseback, and a string of wheeled vehicles loaded down with citizens, the whole delegation being near a mile in length, escorted the Senator from West Urbana to the fair grounds, arriving there at about two o'clock. His arrival at the grounds was greeted by the masses there with deafening shouts and applause.

"After he was escorted to the stand, a very neat and appropriate reception speech was delivered by A. E. Harmon, Esq., of West Urbana, introducing him to the audience. He spoke about an hour and a half in a calm and dignified review of the great issues before the people, and was listened to with the profoundest attention by the thousands who were fortunate enough to obtain positions where they could hear. The extent of the crowd may be judged by the fact that the Senator's voice, heavy and sonorous as it was, was insufficient to reach many hundreds on the outer edge of the crowd. The demonstrations of applause with which he was greeted by the old line Whigs and Americans, as well as by the Democratic masses assembled there, show that his speech is producing a good effect in favor of Democratic principles. The Urbana Saxehorn and Military Band added much to the occasion by their spirited music.

"We cannot forbear acknowledging the marked courtesy with which the Senator and his friends were treated by the Republicans generally, and especially by those who hold influential positions in the Agricultural Association."

But, according to the Constitution, the Lincoln meetings were of quite another type. "The Republicans had a fine meeting here on Friday," it remarks, with apparent candor, "and were addressed by Mr. Lincoln." Then: "Mr. Lincoln's speech was a complete backdown from every position he assumed in his opening speech at Springfield, except in one respect—that he insisted on the right and duty of Congress to prohibit slavery in the territories. This dogma, as Lincoln well knows, however, is the merest humbug, because it cannot be carried out while the decision of the Supreme Court upon that subject remains.

"Mr. Lincoln was probably not very well satisfied with his day's work, as in the evening he again assembled at the courthouse, where he delivered a discourse on that passage of the Scripture which declares that 'a house divided against itself cannot stand,' and the necessity of 'the perseverance of the saints' to the 'ultimate extinction of slavery in all the states.' Also, he gave his views on the cranberry and hoop-pole laws of Indiana; after which, Deacon Bross spoke. The deacon made a magnificent speech. He referred to the letter Washington had written to Henry Clay and to the fact that Lafayette was one of the fathers of the constitution. He said that the Republican party held that the negroes are not the equals of the whites in respect to social and political rights, but that they are the equals of the whites in the sense of the Declaration of Independence, which declares that 'all men are created equal.' This distinction was so clear and satisfactory that the deacon was vociferously cheered. The deacon also made several beautiful appeals to heaven, which were applauded in the most lively manner."

The afore-mentioned Chicago Democrat gives its version of the chief Lincoln meeting at the fair grounds: "Lincoln has been with us, and the occasion has been one to be long remembered in eastern and central Illinois. It is no new thing for us to greet the honest face of Mr. Lincoln in our streets that it should stir up commotion, for half-yearly for many years he has been in the habit of spending a week here in the practice of his profession upon the most familiar and easy terms with all; so that a desire to see a man who grapples with and overcomes the Little Giant could not have induced a single person to leave his home and come here through the dust, all having seen him frequently and heard him speak, and very many being intimately acquainted with him; nothing but the respect and love for the cause of which he is the exponent in Illinois, could have brought together such a throng.

"The time was perhaps the most unfavorable one in all the year for getting together a crowd coming, as it did, one day after an exciting county fair of three days, in an unusually sickly season when there is scarcely a family in the county more than able to take care of its own sick, and upon a day when the least stir in any of the roads was sufficient to raise a suffocating cloud of dust; yet the affair has been a most successful one in every way. The number present was very nearly, if not quite, as large as those in attendance at the Douglas demonstration of yesterday—the enthusiasm ten times as great—and the effect never exceeded by that resulting from any speech ever delivered in the county before.

"At an early hour the people began to flock into town, and by the time designated for forming the procession, the streets were so blocked up that it was almost impossible for a vehicle of any kind to pass. At ten o'clock a procession led by the Urbana brass band, German band, and Danville band, and over sixty young ladies on horseback with their attendants, thirty-two of whom represented the states of the Union, marched to the Doane House for the purpose of escorting Mr. Lincoln to the fair grounds, where the speaking was to take place. When returning, the procession was augmented by a large delegation from the western part of the county; also a large delegation from Piatt County—so that the entire procession reached more than one and a half miles.

"In this form the grounds were reached when, it being the hour of midday, the throng marched in good order to the dinner tables, where the ladies of the two Urbanas had spread out a sumptuous and bountiful dinner. All had enough and to spare. The people then repaired to the stand and, after being seated, listened to an eloquent reception speech made by Hon. M. L. Dunlap, formerly of Cook County, who then introduced Mr. Lincoln. Cheer after cheer, lustily and heartily given, greeted his appearance. His speech was commenced by acknowledging his gratitude at seeing so lively an interest taken in the great issue of the day. After a few other introductory allusions, he took up the various questions at issue in the campaign, meeting and refuting the common dogmas of Democracy, and probing to the bottom every subject touched. Throughout his remarks were terse, eloquent and witty, frequently eliciting loud demonstrations of merriment and applause. At the close of his remarks, loud cheers rang through the forest, in which the larger part of the audience took part.

"One thing is worthy of notice in contrast with yesterday's proceedings. On that occasion the audience sat under the thunderings of the Little Giant as still as if attending a funeral discourse, while this audience of Mr. Lincoln's was most enthusiastic and attentive, continuing as large at the enunciation of the last word as at the beginning.

"The meeting broke up, formed in procession, and escorted Mr. Lincoln to his lodging, at the residence of Mayor Boyden, where his lady attendants and all parted from him with rapturous cheers."

In all of these rapturous cheers and generally hot enthusiasm, the Republican Wide-Awakes bore the same prominent part taken by the Hickory Boys in Democratic demonstrations; and the same was true throughout the country, the Republicans and Democrats having organized their big boys and young men into clubs of Wide-Awakes and Hickory Boys.

ONE COURTHOUSE SOLD; ANOTHER BUILT

In 1859, the year before the election of Lincoln, the second frame courthouse, which had been twice moved and occupied for several years as a schoolhouse, was sold at auction and torn down. It then stood at the corner of Elm and Vine.

The 1848 courthouse of historic fame was also ordered to be replaced in 1859 by the fourth temple of justice which graced the square at Urbana. It is generally called the third permanent courthouse. It was built of brick, stone and iron by B. V. Enos, an Indianapolis contractor, at a cost of $30,000, and was not ready for complete occupancy, both by the county officers and the Circuit Court, until the autumn of 1861. During a period of forty years this courthouse well served its purposes.

Township Organization Adopted

The fall of 1859 was the commencement, further, of a new epoch in the county government. From the organization of the county in 1833 until 1849, when it came under the provisions of the constitution of 1848, its governing board of three members was known as the Court of County Commissioners. Although declared to be "a court of record," it possessed no real judicial authority. Under the constitution of 1848 that body was superseded by the County Court, comprising the county judge and his two associates—Edward Ater, of Urbana, and John P. Tenbrook, of Sadorus, and Lewis Jones of Salt Fork. The County Court managed the affairs of the county until the November election of 1859, which resulted in the adoption of the system of township organization and the inauguration of a Board of Supervisors.

Other Changes in Officers

As to the other county officers, it has already been stated that under the 1818 constitution the judge of the Circuit Court appointed his clerk, and by the early statutes the clerk of the County Commissioners' Court was chosen by that body. The county treasurer and assessor was also appointed by the Commissioners' Court, leaving only the sheriff and the coroner to be chosen by the people. The constitution of 1848 made these offices elective.

The foregoing are the chief changes in the forms of the county government and its officials, which have not been noted in previous pages.

The Courthouse of 1901

The courthouse now occupied, which is modern and elegant within and attractive without, was fully completed in the fall of 1901, the September term of the Circuit Court for that year being opened in the new building by Judge Francis M. Wright. Forty years previously, in the preceding month, Hon. Oliver L. Davis, then judge of the Twenty-seventh circuit, opened the term of court in the courthouse of 1859-60,

Answering the demands for more space, consequent on greatly increased population and wealth, the building which had done service almost half a century, underwent an elaborate process of remodeling and enlargement which converted it into an imposing public edifice covering an area of 108 by 116 feet and three stories in height, with ample rooms for the courts and all the county offices. It is in the

COURTHOUSE, JAIL AND SHERIFF'S RESIDENCE (1901)

UPON THIS SPOT
ABRAHAM LINCOLN
ON OCT. 24, 1854
DELIVERED HIS THIRD
SPEECH IN OPPOSITION TO
SENATOR DOUGLAS
AND THE NEBRASKA BILL

FACSIMILE OF COURTHOUSE TABLET

Romanesque style of architecture, and its exterior is done in red sand-stone and mottled brick, and its tower stands 135 feet high. The building thus remodeled and enlarged was dedicated August 22, 1901.

The courthouse of 1901 was completed at a cost of $150,000, and no feature of it attracts more attention than a large marble tablet near the entrance to the county clerk's office, on the second story, which reads: "Upon this spot Abraham Lincoln, on October 24, 1854, delivered his third speech in opposition to Senator Douglas and the Nebraska bill."

MURDERER ESCAPES FROM OLD COUNTY JAIL

The building of the first county jail by Colonel M. W. Busey in 1840 has been briefly told. No special interest seems to have attached to this log jail eighteen feet square except that in 1845 Bill Weaver, the convicted murderer of David Hiltibran, escaped from it with the aid of an auger and little difficulty, and it was once visited by Lincoln. Weaver was to have been hanged on the 27th of June. Years afterward tidings of him were received from Wisconsin, but the murderer was never recovered.

Other escapes from the jail followed, of offenders great and small, until in January, 1855, after a specially aggravating break-away, the Urbana Union bursts forth with the prevailing public sentiment, thus: "It (the jail) might answer for the imprisonment of infants, or of men who are badly crippled, but will not do for the detention of rascals."

1—11

LINCOLN CALLS UPON SON OF FOSTER BROTHER

The decrepit old jail becomes somewhat famous in our day from a bit of Lincolnia attached to it by Major Whitney in his "Life on the Circuit with Lincoln." The story, as he tells it, is as follows: "In the summer of 1856, when he was one of the electors-at-large on the Fremont ticket, a crippled boy was aiding a drover to drive some horses to the northern part of the state. They stopped over night at Champaign and, while there, this boy went to a small watchmaker's shop kept by an old decrepit man named Green upon an errand, and stole a watch. The theft was discovered in time to cause the boy's arrest at the noon stopping place. He was brought before my father as a justice of the peace. The case being made out, he was committed, but the boy had requested that the case be left open until he could send for his uncle, Abraham Lincoln, to defend him. That being denied him, he wanted it continued until I should return home. But the case seeming too clear to be aided by lawyers, my father committed him to jail to await the action of the grand jury. Upon my return home, I was informed of the circumstances, but paid no attention to it at all, and forgot all about it at once.

"Not long thereafter, a mass meeting was held at Urbana, our county seat, to which Mr. Lincoln came as one of the speakers, and as soon as he saw me he said: 'I want to see you all to yourself.' When we had got beyond the hearing of others he said: 'There is a boy in your jail I want to see, and I don't want anybody to know it except us. I wish you would arrange with the jailor to go there, on the sly, after the meeting, and let us in.' I then recollected this crippled boy, and Lincoln explained to me that when his father married his second wife she had a boy about his own age (John D. Johnston) ; that they were raised together, slept together and loved each other like brothers. This crippled boy was a son of that foster brother, and he was tending to the bad rapidly. 'He is already under the charge of stealing a gun at Charleston,' said Lincoln sadly. 'I shall do for him what I can in these two cases, but that's the last. After that, if he wants to be a thief, I sha'n't help him any more.'

"The jail was a rude log-cabin structure, in which prisoners were put through a trap door in the second story, there being no other entrance. So Lincoln and I were secretly admitted into the small enclosure surrounding the jail, and as we approached the one-foot square hole through which we could converse with the prisoner, he heard us and set up a hypocritical wailing, and thrust out toward us a very dirty Bible, which Lincoln took and turned over the leaves mechanically. He then said: 'Where were you going, Tom?' The boy attempted to reply, but his wailing made his answer incoherent, so Lincoln cut him short by saying: 'Now, you do just what they tell you—behave yourself—don't talk to anyone, and when court comes I will be here and see what I can do. Now stop crying and behave yourself.' With a few more words we left, Lincoln being very sad; in fact, I never saw him more so."

THE SECOND AND THIRD JAILS

About a year after this incident occurred, the county built a jail of brick and iron in the public square, at a cost of $7,000. Many additions and improvements were made, both to the jail and the jailor's residence, but these were not sufficient to meet the requirements of a wealthy and advanced county, with the result that in 1906 the massive, attractive and commodious structure, east of the courthouse, was erected.

One execution took place in the 1857 jail—that of Richard Collier, convicted of the murder of Charles Freebriant, which took place December 16, 1898.

THE COUNTY POOR FARM

The County Poor Farm, with suitable buildings for the care of the indigent and insane, is located about a mile east of the courthouse. The original property at that site was purchased in 1865, although seven years before eighty acres for the purpose had been bought in Section 7, St. Joseph Township. The latter location, however, was found to be too far from the county seat, as well as from the center of population.

ROSTER OF COUNTY OFFICERS

With the exception of the judges of the different courts who have presided in Champaign County, and the prosecuting attorneys of the circuit and county, whose records will be found in the chapter on the "Bench and Bar," the county officials include the following:

Court of County Commissioners: 1833, Isaac Busey, Jacob Bartley and George Akers; 1834, John Brownfield, William Nox and Daniel T. Porter; 1836, Cyrus Strong, Hiram Johnson and William Nox; 1838, under a change in the law, James Clements was elected for one year; Daniel T. Porter for two years and Jefferson Huss, for three years. Afterwards until the adoption of the constitution of 1848, the following were elected each year: James Clements, 1839; Daniel T. Porter, 1840; Jefferson Huss, 1841; James Clements, 1842; William Taylor,

1843; John W. Swearingen, 1844; Archa Campbell, 1845; B. F. Harris, 1846; William Nox, 1847; James Clements, 1848.

As stated, under the constitution of 1848 the county was placed under the government of the county judge and his two associates (See Bench and Bar). The system was again changed in 1860, when the county adopted township organization, thereby creating the cooperative Board of Supervisors.

County Treasurers: Moses Thomas, 1833; Green Atwood, 1837; Jacob Bradshaw, 1839; M. W. Busey, 1843; Elisha Harkness, 1851; William H. Pearce, 1853; Chalmers F. Sherfy, 1855; William Munhall, 1857; Pleasant M. Parks, 1859; Robert T. Miller, 1861; George W. Kennard, 1865; James M. Davies, 1869; John W. Hill, 1871; Thomas A. Lewis, 1873; James W. Davidson, 1886; Paul W. Woody, 1890; E. A. Kratz, 1894; Ellis M. Burr, 1898; Daniel P. McIntyre, 1902; John A. Scott, 1906; Lou N. Bear, 1910; Edward Rogers, 1914—

Sheriffs: John Salisbury, 1833; A. H. Stevenson, 1834; David Cox, 1838; Wilson Lewis, 1844; Edward Ater, 1850; F. M. Owens, 1854; Penrose Stidham, 1856; N. M. Clark, 1858; Randolph C. Wright, 1860; Nathan Towle, 1862; John D. Johnson, 1864; Thomas J. Scott, 1866; Peter Myers, 1868; Henry C. Core, 1870; John D. Johnson, 1874; James E. Oldham, 1878; James C. Ware, 1882; P. B. Burke, 1886; Samuel C. Fox, 1890; Daniel D. Cannon, 1894; Ernest Lorenz, 1898; Cyrus S. Clark, 1902; Jonathan M. Peters, 1906; George W. Davis, 1910; Augustus M. Evans, 1914—

Clerks of the County Commissioners and County Courts: Thomas R. Webber, clerk of the County Commissioners' Court, 1833 to 1849, when he was elected county clerk; Thomas A. McLaurie, 1853; Solomon J. Toy, 1857; Nathan M. Clark, 1865; John W. Shuck, 1869; James S. McCullough, 1873; Thomas A. Burt, 1896; Charles W. Webber, 1906; Fred Hess, 1910—

Prosecuting Attorneys: Under the first state constitution the attorney general was also prosecuting attorney of the circuit. After the adoption of the 1848 constitution, until 1856, T. H. Campbell, of Springfield, and Amzi McWilliams, of Bloomingon, served in that capacity. In the year named, Ward H. Lamon was elected prosecuting attorney of the Eighth circuit, holding office until 1861. After the creation of the twenty-seventh circuit in 1861, Joseph G. Cannon was elected for two terms: Martin B. Thompson then served from 1868 to 1876, and, under the new law providing for the election of a prosecuting attorney for each county, Milton W. Mathews held the office from 1876 to 1884; Lewis A. Smyres commenced his service in 1884; Randolph C. Wright,

1892; Andrew J. Miller, 1896; Fielding A. Coggeshall, 1904; Louis A. Busch, 1912—

County Surveyors: Garrett Moore, 1833; James S. Wright, 1838; John L. Somers, 1850; John Thrasher, 1857; R. C. Wright, 1859; L. T. Eads, 1861; John Thrasher, 1865; T. B. Kyle, 1869; F. M. Price, 1875; T. B. Kyle, 1879; Joseph O'Brien, 1900; E. V. Burton, 1912; R. T. Fisher, 1916—

County Coroners—James Myers, 1847; A. M. Kerr, 1854; B. Thrasher, 1858; W. S. Garman, 1860; A. M. Kerr, 1862; W. J. Foote, 1864; H. Miner, 1866; W. J. Foote, 1868; J. M. Tracy, 1870; S. K. Reed, 1872; George W. Burr, 1876; Jacob Buch, 1880; W. B. Sims, 1892; Henry S. Penny, 1896; John V. Swearingen, 1908; J. J. Hanmore, 1912; John V. Swearingen, 1916—

STATISTICS

In the matter of statistics, as of all else, the '30s in the history of Champaign County constituted the days of small things; therefore, of special interest—easy to grasp and analyze in all their details.

It has been seen how in June, 1833, Moses Thomas, the assessor, reported the total revenue of the county to be $71.37. Of that amount, $61.61 was assessed on the personal property of the 111 tax payers; upon their horses and cattle, clocks and watches and pleasure carriages. The item last named yielded but 62½ cents, as only three citizens allowed that they possessed such luxuries as "pleasure carriages." Asahel Bruer reported one carriage valued at forty dollars, for which he was taxed twenty cents; Mason S. Martin, another which he returned as a fifty-dollar luxury and for which he was assessed twenty-five cents, and James T. Roe, the third pleasure carriage, valued at thirty-five dollars, and yielding the county thirty-seven and a half cents in revenue. But while the Buseys, the Boyds, the Byers, the Rhineharts, the Trickles and others had a number of horses, they appear to have been shy on pleasure vehicles.

FIRST ASSESSMENT IN CHAMPAIGN COUNTY (1833)

The details presented by Assessor Thomas in 1833 were as follows:

	Horses.		Cattle.		Clocks and Watches.		Value of	Taxes
Owners' Names.	No.	Value.	No.	Value.	No.	Value.	Property.	Assessed.
Westley Arrasmith	1	$10	2	$20	..	....	$30	$0.15
Moses Argo	1	40	1	8	1	$6	54	.27

Owners' Names	Horses. No.	Value.	Cattle. No.	Value.	Clocks and Watches. No.	Value.	Value of Property.	Taxes Assessed.
George Akers	..	....	2	$20	..	....	$20	$0.10
Isaac Burris	..	....	3	40	..	....	40	.20
Arthur Baird	2	$80	1	10	..	....	90	.45
John Bailey, Sr.	2	100	9	114	1	$30	244	1.22
John Bailey, Jr.	2	80	2	20	..	....	100	.50
Jacob Bartley	1	50	4	32	..	....	82	.41
George Bartley	3	120	2	16	2	13	149	.47½
Matthew Busey	3	150	15	181	1	17	348	1.74
William Boyd	4	160	2	18	1	20	198	.99
Mijamin Byers	5	200	14	190	1	20	410	2.05
Samuel Bromley	3	120	3	30	1	20	170	.85
Asahel Bruer	2	70	5	40	1	10	160	.80
Isaac Busey	4	300	9	100	1	60	460	2.30
Samuel Beckley	2	100	7	76	..	....	176	.88
John Brown	..	....	2	20	..	....	20	.10
Noah Bixler	..	....	1	10	..	....	10	.05
Charles Busey	3	90	11	124	1	20	234	1.17
James Brownfield	5	250	2	20	1	20	290	1.45
John Brownfield, Jr.	2	50	1	10	..	....	60	.30
John Brownfield, Sr.	6	300	3	50	1	16	366	1.83
Benjamin Brownfield	1	30	...	.....	1	6	36	.18
Frederick Bouse	2	80	11	124	1	20	224	1.12
Reuben S. Bullard	2	130	1	10	..	....	140	.70
Joshua Chapman	3	130	2	20	..	....	150	.75
Nancy Cook	1	30	1	10	..	....	40	.20
Sarah Coe	1	20	2	16	1	20	56	.28
William Curry	2	60	6	60	1	20	140	.70
William Coe	1	40	1	8	..	....	48	.24
James Copeland	1	40	4	46	1	18	104	.52
Curtis Carmean	1	50	1	10	1	9	69	.34½
John Coddington	2	100	7	84	1	16	200	1.00
Larken Dier	1	50	1	8	..	....	58	.29
Thomas Dier	2	100	1	8	1	10	118	.59
Benjamin Delaney	1	50	3	24	..	....	74	.37
James Freeman	2	80	1	10	..	....	90	.45
Robert French	1	50	...	.....	..	....	50	.25
Abner Fuller	..	....	3	27	..	....	27	.13½
David Gabbard	3	60	3	24	..	....	84	.42
Jacob Heator	..	....	1	8	1	16	24	.12
Alexander Holebrooks	1	50	5	70	..	....	120	.60
Lackland Howard	1	30	2	16	1	20	66	.33
Jefferson Huss	2	60	3	24	..	....	84	.42
Enoch Humphries	1	75	...	.....	..	....	75	.37½
Thomas Hobbs	..	....	3	38	..	....	38	.19
William Harris	1	10	..	.....	..	....	10	.05
Henry Hannahs	1	50	1	10	..	....	60	.30
Valentine Iliff	1	30	3	40	1	6	76	.38
John Jayne	1	10	2	16	..	....	26	.13
James Johnson	..	....	1	10	1	5	15	.07½
Amos Johnson	1	40	...	.....	..	....	40	.20
William Jackson	2	70	2	16	..	....	86	.43
Elijah Jackson	1	30	1	8	..	....	38	.19
John Jackson	..	....	6	75	..	....	75	.37½
Elias Kirby	2	70	1	10	..	....	80	.40
John W. Leird	..	....	1	8	..	....	8	.04
Garret Moore	..	....	3	38	..	....	....	....
Mason S. Martin	1	50	...	....	2	16	116	.58
Levi Moore	3	100	2	16	1	20	136	.68
James Moss	3	90	5	40	..	....	130	.65

Owners' Names	Horses. No.	Value.	Cattle. No.	Value.	Clocks and Watches. No.	Value.	Value of Property.	Taxes Assessed.
William Nox, Sr	2	$75	10	$122	..	....	$197	$0.98½
Ethan Newcomb	1	50	6	75	..	....	125	.62½
William Nox, Jr.	1	50	1	8	..	....	58	.29
James Osborn	1	40	10	116	1	$20	176	.88
Henry Osborn	..	....	5	64	..	....	64	.32
William Osborn	1	50	2	18	..	....	68	.34
Jonathan Osborn	1	30	5	50	..	....	80	.40
George Powell	1	50	2	40	..	....	90	.45
William I. Peters	2	70	2	16	..	....	86	.43
Abraham Peters	..	....	1	8	..	....	8	.04
William Peters	2	80	3	24	..	....	104	.52
Robert Prather	2	40	5	60	..	....	100	.50
Daniel T. Porter	..	....	1	10	1	15	25	.12½
Thomas Rowland	2	60	5	65	1	16	141	.70½
Gabriel G. Rice	1	40	2	20	..	....	60	.30
James T. Roe	2	100	1	8	..	....	143	.71½
John G. Robertson	2	50	3	30	..	....	80	.40
Mathias Rhinehart	4	200	8	94	1	25	319	1.59½
Hiram Rankins	2	80	7	100	..	....	180	.90
Walter Rhodes	1	100	2	16	1	25	141	.70½
Robert Russel	1	20	...	....	..	....	20	.10
John Salisbury	1	40	3	100	..	....	140	.70
John W. Swearingen	2	75	5	58	..	....	133	.66½
Joseph Stayton	3	120	3	30	..	....	150	.75
David Swearingen	1	25	1	8	..	....	33	.16½
John Swearingen	..	....	1	10	..	....	10	.05
Cyrus Strong	2	100	6	57	1	16	173	.86½
Andrew Stevenson	1	70	...	....	..	....	70	.35
Philip Stanford	2	100	5	40	1	20	160	.80
Henry Sadorus	2	80	13	160	1	20	260	1.30
John Trueman	2	40	1	10	..	....	50	.25
Joshua Taylor	1	50	1	10	..	....	60	.30
Martin Tompkins	..	....	4	50	..	....	50	.25
Joshua Trickle	3	120	4	32	1	20	172	.86
Robert Trickle	2	100	3	21	1	28	149	.74½
Jacob Thomas, Sr	2	100	4	36	1	20	156	.78
Henry Thomas	1	35	5	62	1	20	117	.58½
Adam Thomas	..	....	..	....	..	....	35	.17½
Joseph Thomas	..	....	8	87	..	....	87	.43½
Jacob Thomas, Jr.	1	30	1	10	..	....	40	.20
Moses Thomas	4	150	14	182	1	16	348	1.74
William T. Webber	1	65	2	30	..	....	95	.47½
T. R. Webber	1	60	3	40	1	5	105	.52½
John Whiteaker	3	125	14	188	1	20	333	1.66½
Andrew Wilson	1	40	1	8	..	....	48	.24
Harris Wilson	2	80	2	18	1	20	118	.59
Henry Wilson	..	....	2	30	..	....	30	.15
Samuel Wilson	1	45	2	16	..	....	61	.30½
Adam Yeazel	2	80	1	8	1	16	104	.52
John Zornes	..	....	1	10	..	....	10	.05
Total	171	$87,085	387	$4,336	45	$776	$12,322	$61.61

INCREASE OF COUNTY REVENUES

By 1836 the revenue of the county had increased to $258.85, and by 1844 to $1,672.87. This represented taxable property valued at over

$334,373, as compared with $12,322 in 1833—quite an increase in a decade. After that the figures increased by leaps and bounds, and it will serve no useful purpose to present them; those who are interested in such comparative details, year by year and decade by decade, have free access to the assessors' books at the county seat. A very striking and interesting comparison, however, is that between the first assessor's report of 1833 and the last, of 1916; the first showing property valued at $12,322 and assessed as $61.61 and the last, a valuation of $33,824,061 and an assessment of $1,275,276.12.

Property Valuation and Taxes

The material stability of Champaign County is well illustrated by the returns of the assessors in 1916, which, as stated, indicate that the real estate, comprising both country lands and village and city lots, and the personal and corporation property, are valued for purposes of taxation at $33,824,061, and that the taxes levied for all purposes amounted to $1,275,276.12. The assessed value of railroad property within the county was $1,926,251, and of telegraph and telephone companies, $82,800. The largest items among the tax levies were: For roads and bridges, $187,919; school, $473,455; state, $270,592; county, $148,963, and cities and villages, $149,796.

The showing by townships is as follows:

Townships.	Value of Property.	Taxes Levied.
Ayers	$ 662,746	$ 19,586.57
Brown	1,100,360	35,857.42
Champaign	5,273,764	309,567.42
Colfax	809,295	21,498.71
Compromise	1,333,984	37,757.79
Condit	851,185	23,752.78
Crittenden	832,301	28,271.84
East Bend	881,156	24,013.30
Harwood	876,583	21,706.09
Hensley	825,372	19,811.97
Kerr	397,840	13,282.52
Ludlow	954,496	27,800.99
Mahomet	779,371	27,289.55
Newcomb	753,555	24,100.68
Ogden	1,202,782	33,309.63
Pesotum	879,580	29,396.78
Philo	1,098,216	28,554.65
Rantoul	1,556,917	48,020.11
Raymond	1,005,611	33,327.99

Township	Value of Property	Taxes Levied
Sadorus	$1,110,050	$34,410.27
Scott	991,354	27,401.48
Sidney	1,146,985	32,111.85
Somer	831,708	22,050.85
South Homer	945,271	34,916.94
Stanton	811,705	21,406.94
St. Joseph	1,118,509	36,047.04
Tolono	1,058,336	34,772.31
Urbana	3,735,039	225,251.94
Total	$33,824,061	$1,275,276.12

POPULATION (1833-1917)

The statistics of population relating to Champaign County, according to the returns of the state and federal census takers, are as follows, the deduction being that when the county was organized in 1833 it contained about eight hundred people: 1835, 1,038; 1840, 1,475; 1845, 2,041; 1850, 2,649; 1855, 6,565; 1860, 14,629; 1865, 21,124; 1870, 32,737; 1880, 40,863; 1890, 42,159; 1900, 47,622; 1910, 51,829; 1917 (estimated), 60,000.

BY TOWNSHIPS, CITIES AND VILLAGES

According to the Federal census returns for the last three decadal years the population of the townships, cities and villages of Champaign County was as follows:

	1910.	1900.	1890.
CHAMPAIGN COUNTY	51,829	47,622	42,159
Ayers Township, including Broadlands Village and part of Allerton Village...................	929	865	719
Allerton Village (part of).....................	15	....	....
Total for Allerton Village in Ayers Township,. Champaign County, and Sidell Township, Vermilion County	379	....	....
Broadlands Village	480	....	....
Brown Township, including Fisher Village..........	1,396	1,544	1,312
Fisher Village	850	614	....
Champaign Township, including Champaign City....	13,353	9,966	6,619
Champaign City	12,421	9,098	5,839
Ward 1..................................	1,805	....	....
Ward 2..................................	1,964	....	....
Ward 3..................................	1,990	....	....
Ward 4..................................	1,524	....	....
Ward 5..................................	1,423	....	....
Ward 6..................................	1,997	....	....
Ward 7..................................	1,718	....	....
Colfax Township	800	901	914

	1910.	1900.	1890.
CHAMPAIGN COUNTY	51,829	47,622	42,159
Compromise Township	1,557	1,576	1,650
Condit Township	689	777	750
Crittenden Township	683	820	932
East Bend Township	879	1,113	1,122
Hardwood Township	737	750	761
Hensley Township	596	610	642
Kerr Township	418	427	366
Ludlow Township, including Ludlow Village and part of Rantoul Village	1,530	1.060	1,152
Ludlow Village	305	306	298
Rantoul Village (part of)...................	523	....	....
Total for Rantoul Village in Ludlow and Rantoul townships	1,384	1,207	1,074
Mahomet Township, including Mahomet Village.....	1,329	1,277	1,247
Mahomet Village	565	515	473
Newcomb Township	744	854	959
Ogden Township, including Ogden Village..........	1,389	1,392	1,433
Ogden Village	428	419	334
Pesotum Township, including Pesotum Village......	1,096	1,094	1,038
Pesotum Village	376	....	....
Philo Township, including Philo Village...........	1,239	1,175	1,240
Philo Village	562	502	491
Rantoul Township, including Thomasboro Village and part of Rantoul Village....................	1,995	2,365	2,391
Thomasboro Village	321	....	....
Rantoul Village (part of)...................	861	1,207	1,074
Raymond Township, including Longview Village.....	1,052	1,093	1,204
Longview Village	257	....	....
Sadorus Township, including parts of Ivesdale and Sadorus villages	1,688	1,757	1,655
Ivesdale Village (part of)....................	429	476	323
Total for Ivesdale Village in Sadorus Township, Champaign County, and Bennent Township, Piatt County	436	476	323
Sadorus Village (part of)...................	299	284	277
Total for Sadorus Village in Sadorus and Tolono townships	336	340	277
St. Joseph Township, including St. Joseph Village...	1,406	1,491	1,599
St. Joseph Village	681	637	552
Scott Township	984	1,026	978
Sidney Township, including Sidney Village.........	1,303	1,452	1,623
Sidney Village	481	564	581
Somer Township	866	940	1.072
South Homer Township, including Homer Village....	1,655	1,821	1,669
Homer Village	1,086	1,080	917
Stanton Township	759	865	847
Tolono Township, including Tolono Village and part of Sadorus Village......................	1,379	1,663	1,777
Sadorus Village (part of)...................	37	56	....
Tolono Village	760	845	902
Urbana Township, including Urbana City...........	9,378	6,948	4,488
Urbana City	8,245	5,728	3,511
Ward 1..............................	1,800	....	....
Ward 2	1,962	....	....
Ward 3..............................	1,066	....	....
Ward 4	1,815	....	....
Ward 5	1,602	....	....

In explanation of the figures relating to the population of the incorporated cities and villages of the county the government reports give the following facts: Thomasboro Village was incorporated in 1900. In 1900 Rantoul Village was returned as in Rantoul Township only, and Ivesdale as in Champaign County alone. Longview Village was incorporated in 1903 and Pesotum Village in 1906. In 1907 the part of Champaign City in Urbana Township was annexed to the corporation.

CHAPTER VI

LEGAL AND MEDICAL

SUPREME COURT AND CIRCUIT JUDGES—WILLIAM WILSON, FIRST
CIRCUIT JUDGE—FIRST PROBATE JUDGE—JUSTIN HARLAN—SECOND
TERM OF CIRCUIT COURT—FIRST CRIMINAL INDICTMENT—POPULAR
RESORT FOR BENCH AND BAR—AS EFFECTIVE AS BOLTS AND BARS—
AUGUSTUS C. FRENCH—AARON SHAW AND O. B. FICKLIN—CIRCUIT
DUTIES AGAIN IMPOSED ON SUPREME COURT—THE COUNTY IN THE
EIGHTH CIRCUIT—FIRST MURDER TRIAL IN THE COUNTY—UNDER
THE 1848 CONSTITUTION—DAVID DAVIS—JOSEPH G. CANNON'S
MAIDEN PROSECUTION—OLIVER L. DAVIS—UNDER THE CONSTITU-
TION OF 1870—C. B. SMITH—FRANCIS M. WRIGHT—SOLON PHIL-
BRICK—FRANKLIN H. BOGGS—HOME JUDICIAL TIMBER—WHAT THE
CIRCUIT COURT RECORDS SHOW—JUDGE HARLAN'S LAST WORK—PRO-
BATE JUDGES—JOHN BROWNFIELD—SETTLED OUT OF COURT—ARCHA
CAMPBELL, LAST PROBATE JUDGE—COUNTY JUDGES—JUDGE J. O.
CUNNINGHAM—WILLIAM D. SOMERS, FIRST RESIDENT LAWYER—
COL. W. N. COLER, SECOND LAWYER—JUSTICE JAMES S. GERE—
JAMES W. SOMERS—HENRY C. WHITNEY—JAMES B. MCKINLEY—
S. B. RADEBAUGH—GEORGE W. GERE—JOHN C. BLACK—MILTON W.
MATHEWS—ROBERT C. WRIGHT—WILLIAM B. WEBBER—THE MEDI-
CAL PROFESSION—CHOLERA EPIDEMIC OF 1834—DR. T. FULKERSON,
FIRST RESIDENT PHYSICIAN—DR. JAMES H. LYON—VICTIMS OF
MIASMA—DRS. HARMAN STEVENS AND JOHN S. SADDLER—DR.
WINSTON SOMERS—DR. WILLIAM A. CONKEY—DR. PHILIP C.
MOSIER—PIONEERS AT URBANA AND WEST URBANA—READY FOR
THE CHOLERA EPIDEMIC OF 1854—THE WIPING OUT OF A FAMILY—
DR. CHARLES A. HUNT—DR. SAMUEL W. KINCAID—DR. HERMAN
CHAFFEE—OTHER MEMBERS OF THE PROFESSION.

The word professional is very broadly applied in these days—to the
activities of lawyers and judges, to the work of the medical fraternity,
to the labors of civil enginers, and the many and complex duties of the
litterateur. This chapter confines itself to dealings with those men and
women, the efficient performance of whose life work is based upon a preliminary education and training prescribed by institutions and individual
authorities, and which earns for those who have completed them the

official right to pursue their careers in the communities which they may select. The chapter is also limited to professions which operate either through the machinery of the county government, and the members of which depend chiefly upon their individual exertions, rather than upon business operations, for their success. Such a definition would include teachers and clergymen, but the former have a chapter solely devoted to them, and the clergymen, with their churches, are spoken of at length in the histories of the various communities to which they have contributed their best in the field of Christianity and spiritual progress. The same may be said of the press and the newspaper men and women of the county, who represent powers in the interest of enlightenment and progress not easily to be gauged. The legal and medical fields are therefore those left open for the consideration of this chapter.

SUPREME COURT AND CIRCUIT JUDGES

As a rule, justice in Champaign County has been faithfully conserved and wisely administered through the Circuit, Probate and County Courts. Under the constitution of 1818 the judicial power of the state was vested in the Supreme Court, comprising a chief justice and three associates, with such inferior courts as the Legislature might establish. The operations of the five Circuit Courts, which were in existence when Champaign was set off from Vermilion County, in 1833, were conducted by four associate justices of the State Supreme Court (act of 1829), and the special circuit judge assigned to duty for the territory northwest of the Illinois River. Champaign County was in the fourth circuit and, by law, Judge William Wilson, of Carmi, White County, was assigned to its courts; but he never appeared at Urbana to administer justice in that capacity.

WILLIAM WILSON, FIRST CIRCUIT JUDGE

Under the statutes, William Wilson was the first circuit judge of Champaign County, and is therefore entitled to a short sketch. In early life he came to Kaskaskia, Illinois. His character was above reproach. He had not enjoyed a collegiate education, but his legal attainments were good. It is said by a friend that "he was social in disposition, candid and artless by nature, with a manner pleasant and winning." For nearly thirty years he was one of the supreme judges of our state. His home for many years was about two miles from Carmi, the capital of White County, and here he exercised genuine old Virginian hospitality. Mr. Wilson was circuit judge for a short time, and on the 7th of August, 1819, was appointed to fill the vacancy on the Supreme Bench of the state created by the resignation of the gentlemanly swindler, William P. Foster, who had never gone near his circuit, but had drawn his salary with the regularity of a modern member of Congress. When the constitution of 1848 went into effect Mr. Wilson retired to private life. He died at his home April 29, 1857, at the age of sixty-three years, and met death with the serenity that accompanies the consciousness of a well-spent life.

FIRST PROBATE JUDGE

As has been noted, while the few settlers in what is now Champaign County were still under the jurisdiction of Vermilion, a number of justices of the peace had been appointed to settle any legal difficulties which might arise, and not long before the first election in April, 1833, one of their number, Moses Thomas, was elected by the Legislature to the probate judgeship, the first to occupy that bench for Champaign County. He canvassed the election returns, issued certificates of election to the successful candidates, and commenced at once to perform the other authorized duties of his office. The Probate Court was the pioneer body to actually administer justice in Champaign County.

It was a new era in the judicial history of the county which commenced in 1835. In that year the state was divided into six judicial circuits, and five additional circuit judges having been elected, the supreme judges were again relieved from Circuit Court duties. Champaign County was still in the fourth circuit, and on January 19, 1835, Justin Harlan, an uncle of the late United States Senator James Harlan, of Iowa, was commissioned its judge. On the following 6th of April he opened the first term of the Circuit Court of Champaign County at the store of Isaac H. Alexander, a resident of Danville, whose local interests were managed by County Clerk Webber.

JUSTIN HARLAN

Justin Harlan was an Ohio man, who, when a young man, had settled in Clark County, Illinois, and had served in the Black Hawk War from that section of the state before assuming his official duties. He served as circuit judge until 1841, was a delegate to the constitutional convention of 1847, was elected to the Circuit Bench under the constitution of 1848 and reelected in 1855, held the office of Indian agent from 1862 to 1865, was chosen county judge of Clark County in 1872, and died while on a visit to Kentucky, in March, 1879.

With Judge Harlan appeared Sheriff-elect Andrew Stevenson, ready to enforce any decrees of the court, and Thomson R. Webber was appointed circuit clerk. The grand jury impaneled and sworn comprised Jacob Bartley (foreman), Samuel Wilson, James Copeland, Jonathan Maxwell, William Jackson, James Osborn, John Bryan, Benjamin Dulemy, John Baily, Sr., John Jayne, Larkin Deer, George Bartley, Isaac Busey, Charles Busey, Charles Hapstonstall, Joshua Trickle, Matthew Busey and Joshua Taylor.

The official bonds of the sheriff, clerk and Coroner Adam Yeazel, were approved, and the two cases on the calendar were continued. The latter were two actions for slander, McDonald Osborn vs. William Phillips and the same plaintiff against Nathaniel Hanline.

Before the end of the day the Grand Jury reported that there were no indictments to be made; whereupon that body was discharged and the court adjourned.

Second Term of Circuit Court

The second term of the Circuit Court was held at the house and store of Israel Knapp, the successor, in occupancy and proprietorship, of Mr. Alexander, in October, 1835. It was held by Judge Alexander F. Grant of Shawneetown and occupied two days. It was one of his last appearances on the bench, or in life. He was a lawyer and a judge of marked ability. In February, 1835, he had been appointed by the Legislature as judge of the third circuit to succeed Henry Eddy, the pioneer lawyer and editor of Shawneetown, under whom he had studied his profession. Soon after holding court at Urbana, Judge Grant died in Vandalia, Fayette County.

The petit jurors sworn to try the slander suit of Osborn against Phillips were Jacob Heater, John Jayne, Nelson Powell, William Corray, James Copeland, John Baily, Sr., Hiram Rankin, Frederick Bouse, Garret Moore, Isaac Burris, William Galliher and Hiram Johnson. The record shows that the jury returned a verdict in favor of Phillips, and evidently the second suit was not pressed. Samuel McRoberts, Osborn's attorney, who appeared at this October term as the first lawyer to try a case in the Circuit Court of Champaign County, was then the receiver at the Danville Land Office and stood high in his profession. While a resident of Monroe County, in the late '20s, he had served as one of the circuit judges of the state. In 1841 he was elected to the

United States Senate and served in that body until his death in 1842.
But despite his ability and standing he lost the slander cases brought
before Judge Grant.

FIRST CRIMINAL INDICTMENT

There was no April term in 1836, but at the October term of that
year Justin Harlan again opened court. It convened in the temporary
courthouse. The court rendered a judgment by default against Isaiah
Corray in favor of Mr. Chestnut for $265. The grand jury, of which
Colonel M. W. Busey was foreman, returned the first criminal indictment in the legal history of the county. Aaron Shaw, the state's

OLD KELLY TAVERN, ST. JOSEPH
(One of Lincoln's stopping places)

attorney, charged John H. Busey with having disturbed the peace. The
indictment was quashed at the April term, which also convened in the
make-shift courthouse. It appears that both bench and bar were more
comfortable in private houses than in official quarters, for the September term of 1837 was held at the residence of Isaac Busey.

POPULAR RESORT FOR BENCH AND BAR

Although this temporary courthouse was notably unpopular with the
pioneer judiciary and legal practitioners of Champaign County, it
proved to be the seed of something very dear to the old-time members
of the profession. The lot upon which it was originally built, with an
adjoining tract, was sold to Asahel Brauer in 1841. He moved the log
house to the consolidated site, clapboarded it, added to it, and opened

the Urbana House. The hotel was long the best stopping place afforded by the county seat, a favorite headquarters of professional life, and provided shelter and food to such judges as Treat and the Davises, and such lawyers as Lincoln, Linder, Leonard Swett, Kirby Benedict, D. B. Campbell, Josiah Lamborn, J. A. McDougall, J. N. Roberts, Amzi McWilliams and John Pearson. In time, the Urbana House became the Pennsylvania House, with which the names of John H. Thomas, C. M. Vanderveer and Samuel Waters are associated as proprietors and hosts.

As Effective as Bolts and Bars

Until 1841 the bench and bar of Champaign County, at their headquarters in Urbana, were shifted around from pillar to post. The temporary courthouse of 1836, as well as the little frame building of 1837, was abandoned, and the court and lawyers were accommodated in the log houses of various residents. Until 1840 there was not even an excuse for a jail, although several petty criminals had been convicted. It is related that on one occasion a prisoner, having been tried, and while awaiting the verdict of the jury deliberating in a nearby thicket of hazel brush, was detained by the sheriff thus: His hands were tied behind him and his feet were bound together; a sapling was bent down and fastened to his feet, which, being left free, raised the legs of the prisoner their length from the ground. He was about as secure as bolts and bars would have made him.

Augustus C. French

Among the practitioners of these primitive days before the Circuit Court, Judge Cunningham mentions Aaron Shaw, then of Clark County; O. B. Ficklin, of Charleston, Coles County; John J. Brown, of Danville; Matthew Van Deveer, of Champaign County, and Augustus C. French, of Crawford County. Three of those mentioned earned national reputations. After serving in the Legislature several terms, and as presidential elector in 1844, Mr. French was elected by the Democrats as the ninth governor of Illinois and thus served in 1846-52. He was afterward appointed state bank commissioner, was a member of the constitutional convention of 1862, and died at Lebanon, where he had held the chair of law at McKendree College, in September, 1864.

Aaron Shaw and O. B. Ficklin

Both Aaron Shaw and O. B. Ficklin served several terms in Congress. Mr. Shaw was a member of the first Internal Improvements

1—12

convention of Illinois, was states attorney of Lawrence County and a member of the Legislature; judge of the twenty-fifth circuit for four years and served in the thirty-fifth and forty-eighth Congresses, 1856 and 1882, respectively.

Orlando B. Ficklin served in the Legislature and as state's attorney, while a resident of Wabash County; three terms in the Legislature, after he had moved to Charleston (1838); was a congressman from Coles County, in 1843-49 and 1851-53, and subsequently presidential elector; delegate to national Democratic convention and a member of the state constitutional convention of 1862. He died at Charleston May 5, 1886.

CIRCUIT DUTIES AGAIN IMPOSED ON SUPREME COURT

The foregoing sketches should convey an idea of the large caliber of the early judges and lawyers who graced the profession in Champaign County during the earlier period of its history. Among the occupants of the Circuit bench none stood higher than Justin Harlan, who continued to preside in Champaign County until he was legislated out of office by the act of February 10, 1841. That measure repealed all acts authorizing the election of circuit judges by the Legislature; provided for the appointment of five additional associate judges of the Supreme Court, making nine in all; reimposed the circuit duties on the members of the State Supreme Court, and divided the state into nine circuits.

THE COUNTY IN THE EIGHTH CIRCUIT

Under the law of 1841 Champaign County was included in the eighth circuit which embraced the fifteen counties between the Illinois River and the Indiana line, with Livingston on the north and Sangamon on the south. Judge Samuel H. Treat was assigned to that circuit, thus succeeding Justin Harlan.

Judge Treat, who had been a resident of Springfield for a number of years and appointed to the Circuit Court in 1839, at the reorganization of the Supreme Court in 1841, became one of the leading members of that body, and at the time of the adoption of the constitution of 1848 was acting chief justice. He continued to preside over the court in Champaign County until that year, remaining on the Supreme bench under the new constitution until 1855, when he resigned to assume the judgeship of the United States District Court for the Southern District of Illinois. He was filling that position at the time of his death, which occurred at Springfield, March 27, 1887, and concluded one of the longest judicial careers in the history of the state.

First Murder Trial in the County

The name of the first murderer and his victim are alike unknown. A tradition, however, informs us that in early times, before the settlement of this county, a thief who had stolen a horse in Indiana, fled with his booty westward. A band of "regulators" pursued and overtook him at a point known as Tow Head, an isolated clump of trees on the ridge a mile north of the present village of Philo. Overcome by fatigue, he was sleeping beneath a tree, with the stolen horse tethered near. The avengers sent a rifle-ball crashing through his brain, and he passed without a struggle from the repose of sleep to the repose of death. His body was left to rot unburied, and the bleached skeleton was seen by early settlers who passed the lonely grove.

The first murder in this county for which there was a trial and conviction, was that known as the Weaver-Hiltibran murder. On the 10th day of October, 1844, William Weaver, of Urbana, a miserable, drunken, reckless wretch, shot David Hiltibran in the right side with a rifle, without any apparent motive, except the fiendish recklessness that often attends men who have become besotted. He was arrested and indicted at the May term of 1845 by a grand jury, of which William D. Somers was foreman. Judge Treat was on the bench; J. A. McDougall, attorney for the State, T. R. Webber, clerk, and Wilson Lewis, sheriff.

The following jurors tried the case: Joseph White, Harrison W. Drellinger, Alexander Walter, Henry Sadorus, W. H. Brobst, Charles W. Pitchan, David Hammer, John Hammer, John Mead, Winston Somers, Michael Finebaugh, and Wells Edgerton.

On the opening of the trial, Abraham Lincoln, who became before his death "the foremost man of all the world," and Asahel Gridley, were appointed by the court to defend the prisoner, but his guilt was too well established during the trial to admit of any verdict but "guilty," and William Weaver was accordingly sentenced to be hung on Friday, June 27, 1845. A few days, however, before the day of execution, he made his escape from jail, fled to Wisconsin, and was never recaptured. He subsequently changed his name, reformed, and lived a decent life. His near view of the gallows seems to have somewhat revolutionized him and put him on his good behavior.

Under the 1848 Constitution

The constitution of 1848 made all judicial officers elective by the people, and provided for a Supreme Court of three judges, Circuit,

County and Justices' Courts; also conferred upon the Legislature power to create inferior municipal courts. Appeals lay from the Circuit courts to the Supreme Court for the particular division in which the county might be located. The term of office for Supreme Court judges was nine years and for Circuit judges, six. Vacancies were to be filled by popular election, unless the unexpired term of the deceased or retiring incumbent was less than one year, in which case the governor was authorized to appoint. Circuit courts were vested with appellate jurisdiction from inferior tribunals, and each was required to hold at least two terms annually in each county, as might be fixed by statute.

DAVID DAVIS

Judge David Davis, who succeeded Judge Samuel H. Treat as the first Circuit judge for this circuit, under the constitution of 1848, attained perhaps the highest national rank of any one who has appeared upon any Champaign County bench. His service extended from the May term of 1849 until the end of the April term of 1861, when Champaign County was set off from the Eighth and attached to the Twenty-seventh circuit. Previous to his election as judge of the Eighth circuit, Judge David had practiced law at Bloomington for a number of years and served a term in the lower house of the Legislature. He was reelected to the bench in 1855 and 1861, resigning in the following year to ascend the bench of the United States Supreme Court, under appointment of his close friend, Lincoln. Resigning from the national Supreme Court to become United States senator in 1887, he served until the end of his term in 1885, and died in June of the following year, at his home in Bloomington.

JOSEPH G. CANNON'S MAIDEN PROSECUTION

The last term held by Judge Davis in Urbana, that of April, 1861, was notable in many ways. Not only did it mark the severing of strongly cemented relations which had been formed by his honorable and able course as a circuit judge, and his warm and attractive personal character, but the birth-pangs of the Civil War were well advanced; and the second murder trial in the history of the county was tried during that period, under the maiden prosecution of the newly elected attorney of the circuit, Joseph G. Cannon. John Murphy had been indicted for the murder of S. S. Rankin, and while Mr. Cannon was making his closing address, as prosecuting attorney of the circuit, Beauregard opened fire upon Fort Sumter. Mr. Cannon was then a struggling young lawyer of Danville, and held the position of state's attorney until 1868. A few years afterward he commenced his phenomenal career as a congressman.

OLIVER L. DAVIS

Oliver L. Davis was elected judge of the new Twenty-seventh circuit in March, 1861, at which time Mr. Cannon was chosen prosecuting attorney. He was also from Danville and had served several terms in the General Assembly before being elected to the bench. He resigned in 1866, but served a second term in 1873-79, having been assigned to the Appellate bench in 1877. He died January 12, 1892.

In 1866 Judge Oliver L. Davis was succeeded by James Steele, of Paris, Edgar County, who held court but one term before the county was taken from the Twenty-seventh circuit and attached to the Seventeenth, over which Charles Emmerson then presided. He had already been serving on the Circuit bench for fourteen years. Judge Emmerson's home was in Decatur. In 1867 he was defeated for a justiceship of the State Supreme Court; was elected a delegate to the constitutional convention of 1870, but died in April of that year before that body had concluded its deliberations.

UNDER THE CONSTITUTION OF 1870

The constitution of 1870 retained the popular elective feature of the judiciary and the terms of office of the Supreme and Circuit Court judges as fixed by the constitution of 1848. The number of Supreme Court judges was increased to seven, as at present. In 1873 the state was divided into twenty-seven circuits and in 1877, into thirteen. Under the provisions of the latter year, while the twenty-six judges already in office were retained, an additional judge was authorized for each district to serve two years, making the entire Circuit judiciary to consist of thirty-nine judges. In all this legislation Cook County was in a class by itself, constituting one circuit; the same is true regarding the act of 1897, which increased the number of circuits to seventeen (exclusive of Cook County), while the number of judges in each circuit remained the same.

The constitution of 1870 provided for the organization of Appellate Courts after 1874. The Legislature established four of these tribunals, Champaign County being in what was denominated the Central Grand Division. Each Appellate Court is held by three Circuit Court judges named by the State Supreme Court, each assignment covering three years, and no judge is allowed to receive extra compensation or sit in review of his own rulings or decisions. Two terms are held in each district yearly. The Appellate Courts have no original jurisdiction.

C. B. SMITH

Arthur J. Gallagher, who succeeded Judge Emmerson as circuit judge of the court held in Champaign County, in 1867, held over during the judicial reorganization brought about by the constitution of 1870, and was succeeded in 1873 by Judge C. B. Smith. Judge Smith served the people and the profession so acceptably that he was retained on the Circuit bench for three terms, or eighteen years, and the period of his incumbency was a remarkably busy and important one.

FRANCIS M. WRIGHT

Francis M. Wright, his successor in 1891, had been a resident of Urbana since 1868, much of the time as junior member of the well known law firm of Somers & Wright. Judge Wright was reelected to the Circuit bench in 1897, serving altogether nearly twelve years, during nine of which he was a member of the Appellate judiciary. He resigned in January, 1903, to accept appointment as judge of the United States Court of Claims, moving to Washington, D. C., to assume that position. There he served until his appointment by President Roosevelt, in 1908, as judge of the Federal Court for the Eastern District of Illinois. Judge Wright died at his home in Urbana, July 15, 1917.

Judge Wright's term of office as Circuit judge was signalized by the completion of the present massive and attractive courthouse, and on the fourth Monday of September, 1901, he opened the fall term of court in the elegant and commodious quarters provided for the accommodation of the judiciary, the juries, officials connected with the legal department and members of the profession. It was certainly a large step from the temporary courthouse of 1836 to the fine structure of 1901.

SOLON PHILBRICK

Solon Philbrick, a lawyer of Champaign City and member of the firm of Gere & Philbrick, succeeded Judge Wright in the Circuit judgship by appointment January 20, 1903, and in the following June was elected to that bench, and again elected in June, 1909. Previous to ascending the bench he had been city attorney of Champaign and master in chancery of Champaign County.

Judge Philbrick died in Springfield, April 13, 1914.

Franklin H. Boggs

In September, 1914, Franklin H. Boggs, the present incumbent of the bench, was elected to succeed Judge Philbrick. He had been engaged in a leading practice at Urbana, during most of the period as junior member of the firm of Cunningham & Boggs.

Home Judicial Timber

So that the ever increasing importance of Champaign County in the affairs of the Sixth circuit has been recognized for the past twenty-five years by the selection of local professional ability in the construction of judicial timber.

What the Circuit Court Records Show

The late Judge Cunningham, whose death cut off much interesting material, which would otherwise have appeared in this history, has already recorded the following, in connection with the early formative period of the Circuit Court system in Champaign County: "The records were originally written, not in a book, but, as it would seem, upon loose sheets of paper such as were in use generally at that date. No ruling appears upon the sheets as manufactured, the lines followed having been made by a ruler and lead plummet. The paper is rough and coarse, and has apparently been since bound into book form, with subsequent records.

"The record of the first term is in the handwriting of Judge Harlan, briefly written, but generally in the approved forms of judicial records. The record of the second term is largely in the handwriting of Judge Grant. Subsequent records are partly in the handwriting of the clerk, Mr. Webber, and partly the work of others, presumably of the judges or lawyers for some years, but finally wholly the work of the clerk. Judge Treat wrote much of the record of terms held by him in his well known strong hand. With this judge, in 1841, came a bound book of a better quality of paper ruled in the manufacture. There came also the use of forms in the record which more nearly conform to those in use in later years.

"During the first twenty years of the life of the county, a singular repetition of the same names in the juries called, appears—being mostly the names of those who came early to the county. New names keep dropping in every year. Each day's record is duly signed by the presiding judge, and as the terms usually lasted but two days, the record must have been actually written up as the business of the court proceeded.

JUDGE HARLAN'S LAST WORK

"The last work done by Judge Harlan in finishing up his long term of service in the county, was the writing of a decree of divorce of nine lines, whereby he forever divorced Robert Prather, the owner of Prather's Ford, from his wife, Letitia. According to modern lights on the divorce question, the merest tyro in law forms would hold that, for all of this decree, Robert and Letitia, long since dead, died in the bonds of holy wedlock.

"Another feature of interest in the record is the small number of indictments found by the grand juries. Not until more than three years of the life of the county was the first indictment returned into court, and only twenty bills were found during the first ten years. These were for offenses most likely to occur in a new country. The offenses charged were: Disturbance of the peace; obstructing a road; passing counterfeit money; assaults of various kinds; selling whisky without license; kidnapping; larceny, and carrying deadly weapons. Only two convictions followed."

PROBATE JUDGES

The continuity of the county judiciary inferior to the Circuit Court, is carried along through the Probate and County systems, with the justices of the peace as useful and, at times, very busy auxiliaries; in fact, under the constitution of 1818 and for thirty years thereafter, matters usually classed as probate and those now assigned to justices of the peace, were under the jurisdiction of what were denominated probate justices of the peace, or as they were more generally known probate judges. Moses Thomas, the first probate judge, served from 1833 to 1837, when John B. Thomas was elected. He was followed by M. W. Busey in 1839, John Brownfield in 1841, Daniel T. Porter in 1843 and Archa Campbell, in 1848.

JOHN BROWNFIELD

Among the best known of these officials were John Brownfield and Archa Campbell. The Brownfield family had moved from Kentucky in October, 1832, and settled near the old Fort Clark road in the Big Grove section. John Brownfield, the head of the family, was then a man about forty-seven years of age, and a blacksmith. He at once built a horse grist mill near his home, which became a most popular institution with the neighborhood settlers. A few years afterward he erected a saw and a grist mill, operated by the creek about three miles below Urbana. Mr. Brownfield was very useful and popular, both by virtue of his sound abilities and his personal relations. He had married a sister of James Clements, another leading settler, and he himself raised thirteen children, some of whom married into leading families of the county.

SETTLED OUT OF COURT

Mr. Brownfield died in July, 1863, and the following is told as to his native shrewdness, and his aptitude for settling cases out of court: "Born and reared at a time and in a section of the country, when and where educational facilities were out of the question, he was conspicuous for his lack of book learning, and as conspicuous for his strong common sense, which never deserted him in any emergency. Although without a knowledge of the world beyond his limited line of observation, he was too shrewd and alert to be overreached by the most casuistic of sharpers. He would have proven himself equal to the ingenuousness of any of the modern confidence men, had they visited him in that day. His shrewdness in settling by the most peaceable of measures a threatened lawsuit well illustrates his aptness in dealing with men. In his water mill above spoken of, he made use of a wheel fashioned after one which somebody had patented, without thinking of infringing on any one's rights, others of the same pattern being in use in the neighborhood. An agent of the patentee came through the country looking after infringers upon his patent. He came to Urbana one day, put up his team and enquired for Mr. Brownfield's mill and residence, and was told he was in town. The two soon met and the stranger made known his business. He said he was informed that Mr. B. had in use one of his patent wheels—that he had already settled like infringements on his letters-patent with so-and-so, and was disposed to settle with him without suit. Mr. Brownfield said if he had infringed upon the rights of anyone he was willing to pay, but from the stranger's description of his wheel he doubted if his own wheel was any infringement. He invited the claimant to go with him to his mill and examine for himself. It was then near noon, and it was agreed that the two should meet soon after dinner and together go to the mill, three miles away. After his dinner the stranger drove out with a spirited team for Mr. Brownfield to pilot him to the mill, but he could not be found. After some further search he concluded to go alone and inspect the wheel. He soon reached the mill, but found no wheel in it. The smoking embers of a bonfire near by plainly showed that the wheel and all evidence of its character, had been reduced to ashes. The evidence from which to base a suit was gone, and the suit thus settled by peaceable means."

ARCHA CAMPBELL, LAST PROBATE JUDGE

Archa Campbell, the last of the probate justices, was also self-educated and a practical man, but of broader character than Mr. Brownfield. He was a New Yorker, one of those traveling merchants, whose store was his wagon, and in the course of his business wanderings through Indiana and Illinois, in 1839, stopped overnight at Urbana. In 1842 he returned to that locality to make it his home. He not only held the office of probate justice, but was one of the three commissioners who managed the county affairs. It was during his term as commissioner that the second courthouse, the frame building, was moved from the public square and the three thousand dollar brick courthouse was completed. With his associates, he had to weather a somewhat violent uprising on the part of some "thrifty" taxpayers who rebelled at such reckless extravagance. Mr. Campbell was the first mayor of Urbana, president of the Urbana Railroad Company which did the preliminary work on its first street railway, and one of the first to join the new Republican party. Although specifically a Methodist, he was a friend and practical helper to other religious denominations and many charities, as well as a constant promoter of kindliness in his private relationships.

COUNTY JUDGES

In 1848 the new constitution authorized the organization of a County Court, comprising a judge and two associates, which constituted the governing body of the county. Under that law, in 1849 John B. Thomas was elected county judge; Jesse W. Jaquith and Matthew Johnson, associates. In 1853 Elisha Harkness was chosen judge, with M. D. Coffeen and William Stewart, associates. Edward Ater was elected judge in 1857; Lewis Jones and John P. Tenbrook, associates. Fielding L. Scott was elected in place of Mr. Jones, in 1859. Of the foregoing, Judge Tenbrook was widely known in the western part of the county, coming from Piatt County in 1850 and locating at Sadorus. He resided in that village for many years, his being the first house erected there. After the county adopted township organization, he served several times as a member of its Board of Supervisors and was widely honored and popular.

Fielding L. Scott was a much earlier settler, coming from Vermilion County in 1830. He settled on a farm near the present village of Mahomet, where he resided until his death in 1877. He was a stanch Union man, and one of his sons was killed and another repeatedly wounded in the Civil War.

JUDGE J. O. CUNNINGHAM

Under township organization, J. O. Cunningham was elected the first county judge in 1861. During the four years that he held the judgeship he saw the necessity for some well considered work on probate law, and some years afterwards assisted in editing and publishing the standard book entitled "County and Probate Court Practice," by Jones and Cunningham. Judge Cunningham was a versatile and graceful writer, especially on political and historic topics; was for several years after coming to Urbana editor and part proprietor of the Urbana Union, and was afterwards connected with the Union and Gazette. He was also identified with the early building of the State University; but his main business in life was the practice of the law. He was able, generous, sympathetic and philanthropic, and the "Cunningham Deaconess Home and Orphanage" will long stand as a tribute to such qualities. As a Methodist, a Mason and a man of ability and practical spirituality, the Judge rooted himself into the hearts of the people of Champaign County for sixty-four years, and his death in April, 1917, caused keen and widespread sorrow. The details forming the life of this sound and good man will be found in a more extended biography elsewhere.

Judge Cunningham was succeeded by Alexander M. Ayers, who came to Urbana in 1855 and resided there until his death in 1900. He had served during the last three years of the Civil War in the quartermaster's department, and was elected county judge upon his discharge from the Union service in June, 1865. He served continuously in that office until 1873; in the following year was appointed postmaster of Urbana, holding that office until 1878, and thereafter practicing law during the remainder of his active life.

The successor on the County bench of Judge Ayers was Joseph W. Sim, who served from 1873 until the conclusion of his term of four years. When he was a young man of twenty-three the Sim family had settled on a farm about a mile east of Urbana, and after serving as principal of the village school for a time commenced the study of law with the pioneer lawyer and newspaper man, Colonel William N. Coler. Upon examination he was admitted to practice, and at once formed a partnership with his preceptor, as Coler & Sim. He afterward formed a professional connection with J. O. Cunningham. In 1864-66 he served as mayor of Urbana. In the late '60s he withdrew from practice, because of ill health, and engaged in farming and stock-raising. He was thus employed when he was selected judge of the County Court, in the fall of 1873. His death occurred on April 16, 1890.

Judge Sim continued on the County bench until 1877, and his successors have been elected as follows: James W. Langley, in 1877; Calvin C. Staley, 1890; Thomas J. Roth, 1906; William G. Spurgin, 1910; Roy C. Freeman, 1914.

In the foregoing pages a rapid survey has been taken of the courts identified with Champaign County as institutions, and the personnel of the judges which have given them so enviable a standing. Some of the early leaders of the bar have also been noticed and a few connected with the history of the later times. Among the practitioners of note whose names have not fallen naturally into the course of the narrative are the following:

WILLIAM D. SOMERS, FIRST RESIDENT LAWYER

William D. Somers, of Urbana, was the first resident lawyer to practice in Champaign County, and because of his practical ability, eloquence, scholarship and his genius for imparting his knowledge to others, was the honored preceptor of most of the members of the bar who received their preliminary training in the county. No member of the profession had more fast friends than Mr. Somers throughout the long period of his active and honorable life. Although he had the misfortune to lose his mother during his youth, resulting in the dispersal of the family, Mr. Sómers had the good fortune to be received into the household of Major Joe Williams, of the prominent and highly educated North Carolina family of that name. During that period of seven years he studied medicine, and practiced that profession in partnership with his brother Winston for two years in the state named. In 1840-46 they continued together, as practicing physicians at Urbana, but in the spring of the latter year William D. Somers commenced the study of the law under Judge David Davis of Bloomington.

In November, 1846, Mr. Somers was licensed to practice law, and at once commenced active work in that field. In 1855 he was appointed local attorney for the Illinois Central Railroad, a position he held for many years. During the Civil War he served the township of Urbana as supervisor and faithfully cared for many dependent families of soldiers at the front. He acted with the Whig party until 1859, and thereafter supported the Democracy, although some of his most steadfast friends were Republicans. In the days of his legal activity, his power with a jury was acknowledged by even the great masters in that field. He was associated with such as Abraham Lincoln, Leonard Swett, O. B. Ficklin and other distinguished lawyers, and often crossed swords with them in the legal arena with results not to his discredit. His deep knowledge of the law enabled him also to maintain his supremacy before the judges as well as before the juries. Mr. Somers introduced Lincoln to the first audience he addressed in Champaign County, and was on intimate terms with him for many years. During the later years of his life the Nestor of the county bar retired from active practice to the charms and rest of his host of friends, both human and literary.

COL. W. N. COLER, SECOND LAWYER

Colonel William N. Coler was the second lawyer to locate in the county. He was also one of the founders of the Urbana Union, the first number of which pioneer newspaper was issued in September, 1852, and he started the Grand Prairie Bank, the first institution of the kind in the county, and which failed as a result of Secession. Colonel Coler earned his title in the Civil War, and about seven years afterward moved to New York City, where, with his son, the well-known Bird N. Coler, he established a successful bond-brokerage business. He died in 1914. Colonel Coler was a native of Ohio, and when nineteen years of age became a member of the Second Ohio Regiment of Volunteers for service in the Mexican War, returning after the full term of enlistment, three years. He studied law in the office of his old commanding officer, Colonel G. W. Morgan, of Mount Vernon, and under Amzi McWilliams, the prominent Bloomington lawyer. He came to Urbana in 1852, the year after his admission to the bar, and on the 23d of September of that year, with H. K. Davis, issued the first number of the Urbana Union. Soon afterward he commenced the active practice of the law, in connection largely with real estate transactions. A leading Democrat, in the summer of 1861 he recruited from Champaign and adjoining counties the Twenty-fifth Illinois Volunteer Infantry, of which he was colonel until the fall of 1862, when he resigned and resumed business, with headquarters in Champaign. There he continued, largely engaged in the real estate and loan business, until he moved to New York City in 1872.

JUSTICE JAMES S. GERE

James S. Gere, who came to Urbana from New York in the fall of 1836, was one of the early justices of the peace, holding the position for many years. He kept the old Champaign House and a general store in the Big Grove and later became quite an extensive contractor in furnishing ties and wood to the Illinois Central and other railroads. Mr. Gere died in 1858.

JAMES W. SOMERS

James W. Somers, son of Dr. Winston Somers, was ten years of age when his father and uncle moved from North Carolina to Urbana to engage in the practice of medicine. He was a pupil of the eccentric Samuel C. Crane, the pioneer teacher of that place, and in his youth attended what is now De Pauw University at Greencastle, Indiana. About 1854 he began the study of law in the office of his uncle, Judge William D. Somers, continuing his classical and literary studies under the direction of Rev. Dr. Janes, a local educator. After a course at the Union College of Law, Chicago, he was admitted to the bar in 1856 and became the junior partner in the firm W. D. & J. W. Somers. Judge Somers gave it a solid standing from the first and the younger attorney soon increased its reputation. He was a ready and forceful writer, as is attested by the early issues of the Urbana Union, and was one of the most enthusiastic founders of the Republican party in Champaign County. He filled the position of corresponding secretary of the county central committee of the young party for several years, and his services were often utilized in the various campaigns which agitated the county and the state. A growing deafness, however, blocked many of his ambitions, and in 1861 he accepted an appointment from President Lincoln in the Department of the Interior. He afterward occupied a position as a member of the Board of Review in the Pension Office, and for more than thirty years was in continuous official service at Washington. In view of such length of service, his scholarly attainments and engaging personality, he became a well known figure in the national capital. Neither did he ever forget Champaign County and his many friends therein, and during the lifetime of his parents his visits to his old home were frequent. For a few years preceding his death he resided in California. His life was cut off by an accident at Hollywood, a suburb of Los Angeles. As he was returning to his home in that city, June 6, 1904, he was run over and killed by an electric car.

Henry C. Whitney, author of "Life on the Circuit with Lincoln," thus refers to Mr. Somers: "The most promising orator on our circuit of the young men was James W. Somers of Urbana. Of an engaging personality, debonair and suaviter in modo, and bold and trenchant in debate, he joined to accurate and exhaustive knowledge of current politics an exuberant imagination, which rendered him one of the most captivating political speakers in the ranks of the young men. Originally designed for the law, he would have taken rank with the foremost jury advocates, but for an impairment of hearing, which led him to accept a position under his friend Lincoln's administration; and he has continued in the public service since, a credit to himself and his highly influential family—his legal education peculiarly fitting him for his duties, which are of a high and quasi-judicial character."

HENRY C. WHITNEY

The first lawyer to locate at West Urbana was Henry C. Whitney, who moved thither from Urbana in 1855. His father, Alfred M. Whitney, built a residence at the southwest corner of Market and Main streets, and upon the same lot built an office, which was occupied by the two. Major Whitney is widely known as the author of that graphically written and valuable book, "Life on the Circuit with Lincoln," his relations with that great man being especially friendly.

JAMES B. McKINLEY

James B. McKinley and James S. Jones were the next of the profession to locate in that place, and they spent the remainder of their lives there as active and leading lawyers and business men. Mr. McKinley, who was an uncle of the Illinois Congressman, W. B. McKinley, and a relative of the famous Ohio family which has given a President and other distinguished citizens to the nation, spent his earlier years in his native county of Ross, Ohio. While teaching in the neighborhood of Hennepin, Illinois, he began reading law and finished his professional studies at Petersburg, where Lincoln was at that time well known. He practiced at Clinton for several years, and during his earlier life had frequently associated with him, David Davis and other noted members of the state bar. For some years he was in partnership with the late Judge Lawrence Weldon, afterward a member of the United

States Court of Claims in Washington. Mr. McKinley was in general practice at Champaign in 1857-60, but afterward, until his death, October 23, 1903, engaged in the loaning of money to Illinois farmers and in general banking business during the later portion of that period in partnership with his nephew, William B. McKinley. He was one of the founders of the Champaign National Bank, at one time mayor of the city, and an honorable citizen of fine financial and executive ability.

S. B. RADEBAUGH

S. Barclay Radebaugh was another of Judge Somers' "boys." He came to Urbana with his parents in 1861, during the Civil War was connected with the office of Capt. William Fithian, provost marshal of Danville, and did not resume his law studies until 1864. He then studied in the office of William D. Somers until his admission to the bar in 1865. Mr. Radebaugh practiced successfully for twenty years, during which he served as city attorney of Urbana for five terms, and was appointed postmaster in August, 1885. He was a Democrat and continued in office during the Cleveland administration.

GEORGE W. GERE

George W. Gere, son of one of the pioneer merchants of Urbana, was a lawyer of a comparatively late period. Five years after his graduation from the University of Chicago Law School, in 1870, he formed a partnership with General John C. Black, under the firm name of Black & Gere, and opened an office at Champaign. Five years later General Black moved to Danville, and Mr. Gere was afterward associated with Henry M. Beardsley and Solon Philbrick. He died June 15, 1911.

JOHN C. BLACK

General Black, who had been admitted to the bar in his nineteenth year and reached the rank of brevet brigadier-general at the age of twenty-six, practiced in Vermilion and Champaign counties for twenty years. In 1885 he was appointed commissioner of pensions, serving until 1889, when he moved to Chicago. He became head of the Grand Army of the Republic, was president of the United States Civil Service Commission, and one of the strong characters of the nation. He died

August 17, 1915, and it is with pride that this history claims even a short identification with the life lines of General John C. Black.

MILTON W. MATHEWS

Milton W. Mathews made a fine record as a lawyer, a state legislator and an editor. While studying law at Champaign he taught school for a time, and in 1867 located in Urbana, where he continued his professional training and was admitted to the bar in August of that year. G. W. Gere was his preceptor, with whom he formed a partnership which lasted for two years. Thereafter Mr. Mathews practiced alone and became a leader of the central Illinois bar. Besides gaining distinction in his private work, he made a signal official record by his service of nine years as master in chancery of the Circuit Court and eight years as state's attorney of Champaign County. In 1888 he was elected a member of the state Senate, and during the session of 1891 was president pro tem. of that body. As a presiding officer and legislator he was vigorous, decisive and eloquent. During this period of his career Governor Fifer appointed him a member of his military staff, with the rank of colonel. In 1879, Colonel Mathews purchased the Champaign County Herald, of which he continued as owner and editor until his death May 10, 1892. He was twice president of the Illinois State Press Association, and for many years was a Republican leader. He was identified with the banking interests of Urbana, for many years was a leading fraternalist, and in every way an inspiring influence.

ROBERT C. WRIGHT

Robert C. Wright came from Indiana with his parents when he was an infant, in 1830, the family settling northeast of Homer in the edge of Vermilion County. When a boy he made his home with his uncle, David C. Wright, in Champaign County. While obtaining his education he taught school, and had acquired considerable political standing in the county before he was admitted to practice. The Republicans elected him sheriff in 1860; he held the office for the term of two years; was admitted to the bar in 1863; in 1870 was chosen to represent his district in the Legislature, and thereafter, for twenty years, was a leader both at the bar and in politics. Mr. Wright was elected state's attorney of Champaign County in 1892, and his four years' tenure of office was marked by a vigorous and successful prosecution of criminals, and general efficiency in his department of the county government.

Colonel John S. Wolfe

One of the most original and noteworthy men who ever practiced law in Champaign County was Colonel John S. Wolfe, who came from Carlinville in 1860, and took up his residence in Champaign. He had been admitted to the bar in 1859, and he practiced in the courts of Champaign County continuously, except for the time spent in the military service during the Civil War, until his death at his home in Champaign, June 23, 1904. Colonel Wolfe was a man of excellent literary taste and studious habit. He was a wise counselor, an able advocate, a good speaker, and a first-class citizen.

William B. Werber

During the active years of his practice and his service as a public man, William B. Webber was of particular prominence as a direct link of connection between the founders of the county and the early formation of its bar, with the government and the profession of the present. His father, Thomson R. Webber, whose official duties in county service were, as a whole, of more importance and covered a longer period than those of any other one man and, as a member of two constitutional conventions, also was a real force in the consolidation of the state government, died at his home in Urbana, as a most honored citizen, in 1881. Nearly twenty years before, the son had been admitted to the bar, after having enjoyed the professional guidance of Judge William D. Somers, and was associated both with his preceptor and with the late Judge J. O. Cunningham. In 1884, he was elected to the Thirty-fourth General Assembly and attained much prominence in connection with the drainage laws of the state, which he initiated and formed into a system of vast importance to the farmers of Illinois. He served as chairman of the House Drainage Committee and was also at the head of the committee which directed the legislation through both houses of the Legislature. Mr. Webber revised what was known as the Drainage and Levee Act, drafted the new bill and secured its passage; also reported to the House and secured the passage of the Farm Drainage Act, which originated in the Senate. He was also an influential friend of the University of Illinois, securing for that institution a large appropriation and being instrumental in eliminating its old name—Illinois Industrial University—which no longer described the grandeur of its scope. He died at his home in Urbana, September 8, 1916.

THE MEDICAL PROFESSION

The physicians and surgeons of Champaign County have always maintained high rank; those of the early days faithful and cheerful in the midst of their long and difficult journeys and crude appliances, and those of later period well educated, ethical and progressive. As an illustration of what was often required of the old-time country doctor, it is related that Winston Somers, the pioneer physician, was compelled to amputate a limb at once to save the life of a patient, and that in lieu of the proper surgical instrument, used a common hand saw; yet the operation was a success.

CHOLERA EPIDEMIC OF 1834

But the first physicians of the county appeared almost simultaneously with the Asiatic cholera at Big Grove, in 1834. The scourge, which had broken out among the soldiers at Fort Dearborn two years before, had spread terror in the minds of settlers in the interior, especially those who had been in the habit of visiting the Chicago district for family supplies. The pioneers of Champaign County were therefore panic-stricken when cholera appeared in the family of James Moss, near the north end of the Big Grove, and within a few days took the father and three of his children. Mary Heater, the mother of Jacob, and the wife of James Johnson, with two of her children, also were victims. Others fell before the plague, although its ravages were not as severe as in more settled districts.

DR. T. FULKERSON, FIRST RESIDENT PHYSICIAN

At the time of the first visitation of cholera to Champaign County, the only resident physicians within its limits were Dr. T. Fulkerson and Dr. James H. Lyon. Dr. Fulkerson, rather an irresponsible unmarried man who boarded at the Widow Coe's not far from the Moss family, had been practicing in the Big Grove region since 1830, and is generally recorded as the first of his profession to appear in the county. He remained but a short time, and is chiefly known to fame and authentic history as defendant in a suit brought by the county authorities to collect $2 in default of work upon the public road. He paid the judgment obtained, as the records show, and is believed to have left the county soon after.

Dr. James H. Lyon

Dr. Lyon, who came a little later than Dr. Fulkerson, made his home with Mijamin Byers, the justice of the peace, who lived two miles east of Urbana. He remained at the Big Grove but a short time, but made his permanent home at what was then known as Nox's Point. In 1837, he became one of the proprietors of the town of Sidney, where he raised a family and reached prominence, both as a physician and a public man.

Victims of Miasma

But the permanent scourge of the pioneers of Champaign County, which mowed down its victims, young and old, for a period of fifty years, was represented by the miasmatic diseases, caused largely by undrained sloughs and swamp lands. These troubles largely disappeared with systematic drainage and greater care as to public sanitation and personal hygiene. Among the early settlers who died of this class of diseases were James Brownfield, father of Robert and Samuel; Mrs. Isaac Busey and her son John; Nicholas Smith, father of Jacob; William Boyd, father of Stephen; David Shepherd, father of Paris; John Brownfield, father of John, and William T. Webber, father of the old-time County and Circuit Court clerk, and ancestor of the large family by that name.

Drs. Harmon Stevens and John G. Saddler

The next physicians to locate in Champaign County, after Drs. Fulkerson and Lyon, were Dr. Harmon Stevens, who settled near the present village of Homer in 1835, and Dr. John G. Saddler, who was the first of his profession to become a resident of Urbana, which he did in 1839. Dr. Saddler remained at the county seat but a few years, while Dr. Stevens, after the establishment of the village of Homer, moved to that place and practiced for many years. When quite aged and virtually retired, he moved to Saline County, Illinois, where he passed the last years of his useful life.

Dr. Winston Somers

The Somers brothers, Drs. Winston and William D., as has been noted, settled in Urbana the year following Dr. Saddler's coming, and were well established before he departed. About 1846 Dr. William D.

Somers abandoned medicine for the law, and became the leader of the Champaign County bar, as Dr. Winston stood at the head of his profession for many years. His clientele was scattered over much of Champaign County, extending to the Sangamon, Okaw, Ambraw and Salt Fork timbers, and even as far as the Middle Fork. His long journeys, through swamps and forests, in all kinds of weather, were made on horseback when his trips were through sections which were virtually roadless. In such cases his saddle bags were thrown across his wise and faithful horse, and contained the most commonly used medicines and surgical instruments, never forgetting what was then considered the indispensable blood-letting lancet. In the bags were also stowed a generous supply of quinine and calomel.

DR. WILLIAM A. CONKEY

Dr. William A. Conkey became a resident physician of Old Homer in 1843. His journey from Massachusetts with other members of the family, when a boy, has been narrated. The Conkey family was reared on the Edgar County farm, and William A. graduated from a medical college at Louisville, Kentucky, a short time previous to locating at Homer. There he practiced for a number of years, as well as at Eugene, Indiana, but finally abandoned the profession for merchandising and farming. He was engaged in agricultural pursuits for the balance of his active life, and about 1900 turned his farm over to one of his sons, moving to the village of Homer. Dr. Conkey was a leading Republican of the county, and served for many terms as a member of the board of supervisors. He was also a prominent Mason. There were seven children in his family who were reared to maturity, of whom Frank M. adopted the near relative of the profession of the father, and is a leading dentist and citizen of Homer.

DR. PHILIP C. MOSIER

Dr. Philip C. Mosier was a pioneer physician of Homer, who had a large practice in the eastern part of the county and over the line into Vermilion. He was an Indiana man. Dr. Mosier worked hard for his education, and after studying under private tutors and taking several side courses at the Western Agricultural College, he taught school for some time in order to complete the purchase of his doctor's outfit. He was paid a dollar a day for his pedagogic services, out of which he might board himself or "board 'round." The prices of books and medi-

cines were then high. Quinine was $5 an ounce and opium $8 a pound.
But the young man finally supplied himself with a workable outfit, and
after practicing for a time in Indiana came to Old Homer in April,
1851. At that time the section of which that place was the center was
regarded as one of the most sickly portions of the state. Fever and
ague and other malarial diseases generally prevailed, and from the time
of his coming Dr. Mosier was busy night and day in fighting them. In
the course of a few years his own health was so seriously undermined
that he was obliged to abandon practice and retire to the farm which
he had purchased about two miles south of Homer. There, engaged in
farming, land dealings and other work more healthful and less arduous,
and devoting a portion of his time to the public affairs of the county,
Dr. Mosier regained his health, accumulated much valuable property,
and covered the span of life fairly due to one of his natural vigor and
vitality.

DR. JOSEPH T. MILLER

Pioneers at Urbana and West Urbana

The early '50s also witnessed quite an accession to the ranks of the profession at Urbana and Champaign (West Urbana), although the latter was not incorporated as a village until 1857. Dr. Joseph T. Miller arrived in Urbana in 1853, and practiced there for more than half a century, being long its veteran physician and surgeon; also with no rival in the county in length of continuous service. Dr. James Hollister also located at the county seat in 1853, but remained only a few years. Dr. Hartwell C. Howard and Dr. Shoemaker were the pioneer physicians of West Urbana, settling there in 1854. In that year Dr. C. H. Mills came to Urbana, but in 1856 joined the little professional colony at West Urbana.

Dr. Howard was a very enterprising man outside his profession, being one of the founders of a steam flouring mill at Champaign, the only structure of the kind ever erected in the township. His first professional card appears in a local paper of April 10, 1856, about a year before West Urbana was incorporated as a village. He retired from regular practice about 1906.

Ready for the Cholera Epidemic of 1854

By 1854, therefore, when cholera again made its appearance in Champaign County, there were a number of capable physicians to combat the plague and compose the minds of residents who would otherwise be thrown into a condition of terror considered most favorable for the planting of its seeds. As was the case twenty years before, the epidemic was imported from Chicago, and ran like wildfire along the lines of railroad laborers then laying the rails for the Illinois Central road. Most of the fatalities were in the Urbana neighborhood, but although more died in the county than at the first visitation, because the population was far greater, the panic was not so great, since the medical fraternity and intelligent people everywhere had been learning more of the nature of the disease and of the fairly efficacious measures for its prevention and cure.

The Wiping Out of a Family

Most of the deaths which occurred in 1854 were of foreign laborers, exposed to the inclemencies of a late fall, unable to obtain medical assistance, and doubly racked with terror and the natural agonies of the disease. An illustration of the havoc not infrequently caused among this class of unfortunates is given by a county paper of that period. "A family of Prussians," it says, "consisting of the father, mother, several children and an aged woman, the mother of the wife, came down from Chicago on a passenger train as far as it then ran, and were set out on the open prairie, about where the village of Ludlow now stands. No shelter was afforded them. Their destination was Danville, where they hoped to find friends in the family of a brother of the husband. A hack, from the termination of the run of the passenger trains, was then making trips to Urbana, but did not afford facilities for the transportation of the family and their belongings. Money was sent by the father to Urbana by the driver to employ a wagon to carry them forward. The next day it was returned with the information that no wagon could be had for that purpose. In the meantime, several members of the family, including the aged mother, were attacked by the cholera then prevailing along the line of the railroad and among the men employed in its construction. The father, in default of aid from Urbana, from information received of the direction of Danville, with two of his little boys, set out for that place, hoping to reach Pilot Grove, the nearest settlement in the direction of Danville, the first night. In this he was disappointed, and stayed upon the prairie all night. The youngest boy with him was attacked during the night and died of cholera. The surviving boy was left in charge of the corpse, while the father proceeded to the settlement for assistance. All day he watched at the side of his dead brother and for the return of his father. Near nightfall, getting no tidings from his absent father, the boy went in search of assistance and found the house of a solitary farmer to whom by the aid of signs and the little of the English he had learned, he told of the misfortunes of the family. The good people into whose hands the lad had fallen, after having given sepulchre as best they could to the body of the little brother who had died on the prairie, sent a messenger to Danville to inform the friends of the family of their misfortunes and need of assistance, set about finding the missing father. Soon all—the sick and dying —were loaded into the wagon and started for Danville, across the great stretch of prairie intervening. On the road the aged mother died and one child—a little girl—and were informally buried out on the prairie, as had been the other members of the family. Upon reaching Danville the mother also died, as did the brother who had rescued them."

DR. CHARLES A. HUNT

Dr. Charles A. Hunt, who was educated both under private tutorship and at the Ohio College of Medicine, Cincinnati, completed his medical course in 1845, and practiced his profession in Indiana and Illinois until he settled at Urbana in 1855. There he continued in the drug business until the opening of the Civil War, although during that period he was incessantly reading and writing upon medical, surgical, scientific and political topics. After the firing upon Fort Sumter, as soon as he could arrange his business and personal affairs, he joined the Union service as surgeon of the 126th Regiment, Illinois Volunteer Infantry, and was a faithful and able officer. At the siege of Vicksburg the regimental hospital in his charge was located at Haines Bluff, on the Yazoo, a renowned breeder of miasmic disorders, and where he spent the summer of 1863 in the discharge of his medical and surgical duties. He broke under the strain and unhealthful conditions and was taken north to the general hospital at Mound City, where he expired August 2, 1863, only a few hours after the arrival of his wife who, upon hearing of his illness, had hurried to his side. The widow survived him for about fifty years.

DR. SAMUEL W. KINCAID

Dr. Samuel W. Kincaid, of an Ohio family widely known in the profession and in politics, was graduated from the Medical College of Ohio in 1853, practiced for the succeeding two years at Tolono, and in 1855 established himself at Champaign, then West Urbana. Dr. Kincaid was accomplished and genial, public-spirited and popular. He was an early member of the American Medical Association and of the Illinois State Medical Society, and one of the founders of the Champaign County Medical Society. After many years of active practice at Champaign he returned to Adams County, Ohio, and died near his birthplace in West Union.

DR. HERMAN CHAFFEE

Dr. Herman Chaffee, who was educated at Albany Medical College and at Paris, France, entered upon his long and honorable practice at Tolono in April, 1857. He was the first physician, as well as the first postmaster of the village, and was a leader in all public improvements. Dr. Chaffee's death occurred May 22, 1890, and his widow survived him for some twenty years.

OTHER MEMBERS OF THE PROFESSION

Then there were Dr. Myron S. Brown, who settled permanently at Urbana in 1858, in 1860 attended his first course of lectures in Chicago, entered the Union army as assistant surgeon and concluded his service as a division surgeon, was then a practicing physician at Urbana for several years, as well as at Danville, where he died in 1900; Dr. James M. Bartholow, who settled at Philo in 1869 and afterward moved to Urbana, and Dr. Thomas N. Burwash, who, in 1878, commenced the practice at Plainview and afterward settled at Champaign.

MEN OF A LATER DATE

Among these may be named Drs. J. T. Fugate, S. H. Birney, M. S. Brown, M. Lindley of Urbana; Drs. J. T. Pearman, E. A. Kratz, S. K. Page, J. W. Scroggs of Champaign; and Drs. J. G. Chambers, T. M. Hess, Homer Shaw, A. T. Darran, James Core, A. Catron, G. W. Hartman, David Jennings and S. S. Salisbury, all in various parts of the county.

Later still came Drs. A. M. Lindley, W. F. Burress, J. M. Bartholow. J. S. Mason, E. J. Davis, C. D. Gulick, J. J. Hanmore, H. W. Miller, O. O. Stanley, E. S. Smith, D. E. Yantis, C. L. Vandorn and others of Urbana; Drs. C. Bennett, C. M. Craig, G. E. Cogswell, C. S. Davis, J. H. Finch, W. L. Gray, W. M. Honn, C. B. Johnson, A. D. Kirby, H. C. Kariher, Jennie Lyons, J. D. Mandeville, T. J. McKinney, Ellen Miner, L. C. Miller, W. K. Newcomb, C. F. Newcomb, J. W. Osborne, P. S. Replogle, W. F. Secker, S. W. Shurtz, C. H. Spears, J. L. Polk, A. S. Wall, H. D. Wilson, L. S. Wilcox, A. L. Zorger, W. H. Zorger, etc.

Among prominent physicians located in other Champaign County towns may be named J. Brayshaw, E. M. Brewer, K. W. Bundy, A. J. Dalton, T. A. Dicks, F. S. Diller, R. P. Dowd, T. J. Exton, J. M. Hadden, L. E. Hartrick, J. F. Harris, S. J. Hicks, J. M. Lawson, J. E. Lowry, John Marten, J. T. Miller, J. O. Pearman, G. A. Potter, R. P. Ratts, C. F. Ryan, L. O. Sale and A. L. Volborn.

CHAMPAIGN COUNTY MEDICAL SOCIETY

The Champaign County Medical Society was organized in March, 1859, and has been a continuous and prosperous organization ever since. Today it is one of the largest and best associations of its kind in Illinois. Save in July and August, this society holds monthly meetings throughout the year. At the sessions the latest discoveries in medicine are reported and the best approved means and methods for handling diseased conditions reviewed and discussed.

Among those present at the first meeting, held March 4, 1859, according to our advisory editor, Dr. Charles B. Johnson of Champaign (to whom we are indebted for most of the information which follows), were Drs. H. C. Howard and C. H. Mills of that city, and Dr. Joseph T. Miller of Urbana. In 1860 the society published in pamphlet form its constitution, with the code of ethics of the American Medical Association, which is still the law and gospel of the profession. Dr. A. E. Kratz has a copy of that precious publication. It is therein stated that the objects of the new organization are: (a) "The establishment and maintenance of union, harmony and good government among its members, thereby promoting the character, interest, honor and usefulness of the profession," and (b) "the cultivation and advancement of medical science and literature by the collection, diffusion, interchange, preservation and general circulation of medical knowledge among its members."

The pioneer members of the society (names first published in 1860) were: S. L. Bearse, Robert H. Brown, A. Jackson Crane, William M. Goodwin, H. C. Howard, John F. Isom, S. W. Kincaid, J. T. Miller, C. H. Mills, Samuel K. Page, Winston Somers, John Swain, M. B. Thompson, C. A. Thompson.

Dr. Johnson, so long its secretary, gives the following history of the society:

"With the history of the Champaign County Medical Society during the first fifteen years of its existence the writer knows nothing only what he has gleaned from its records and conversation with the pioneer members. But of its work since he can speak with some authority; for more than forty years he has had the privilege of being one of its members, and for about ten years served as its secretary. Some one has said that the secretary of a medical society is the society. This is strong language, nevertheless a secretary has very much to do in making a medical society a success or the reverse.

"In 1874, Dr. M. S. Brown was secretary of the society and did his work especially well. In a year or two he was succeeded by Dr. L. S. Wilcox, who filled the place acceptably for several years. The last half of the '70s was a most prosperous period for the society and the men who at that time might be referred to as its pillars were Drs. William M. Goodwin, M. S. Brown and S. H. Birney of Urbana; Drs. H. C. Howard and J. T. Pearman of Champaign; Dr. A. T. Darrah of Tolono; Drs. James Core and T. M. Hess of Homer; Dr. G. W. Hartman of Sidney and Dr. David Jennings of St. Joseph. The meetings occurred monthly and the society was 'on wheels,' as one of the members expressed it; that is, meetings were held at various towns in the county. Besides Champaign and Urbana, it met in Tolono, Philo, Sidney, Homer, Rantoul, etc. At most of these meetings some hospitable member threw open his doors, especially the one that led to the dining room, where would be found a table literally groaning under its weight of good things from which every doctor was expected to feast heartily. The social features of these meetings added not a little to the attendance and interest. Frequently three sessions were held, namely, a forenoon, an afternoon and an evening session. The papers read were carefully prepared and never failed to call out full and animated discussions. Almost to a man the older members of the society were at this time good off-hand talkers, and what the younger members may have lacked in this direction they sought to, in a measure, make up by preparing carefully written papers.

"An edition of the constitution and by-laws published at this period shows a list of twenty-three members. And as an illustration of the mutations of time it is interesting to note that of these twenty-three doctors thirteen are dead, three have moved out of the county, and one, strange to say, has grown rich, but not in the practice of medicine, as many years ago he changed his calling. He is today a farmer and stock raiser on an extensive scale and can count his cattle on a thousand hills— corn hills. And only six of the above named twenty-three members are left in Champaign County to practice medicine.

"With the advent of the '80s, the society passed into a period when not much interest was taken in its meetings. Several causes conduced to this state of relative apathy. One was the fact that several of the old 'wheel horses,' so to speak, were lost to the society by death or removal from the county. But the organization was faithfully kept up and not long after the advent of the '90s the society received a new impetus and entered upon the highly prosperous career that for about twenty years past it has been enjoying. One reason for this renewed life is the fact that a great many bright, active, new men have come into the county. The meetings of the Champaign County Medical Society occur near the middle of each month, are well attended and much interest is manifested in them by those in attendance. Two or three papers are presented at each session and these unfailingly draw out free discussions."

The presidents, vice-presidents and secretary-treasurers of the society have been as follows:

Presidents—Dr. A. T. Darrah, 1874; Dr. J. T. Pearman, 1875; T. M. Hess, 1876; William Goodwin, 1877; C. B. Johnson, 1878; H. C. Howard, 1879; Lyman Hall, 1880; L. S. Wilcox, 1881; D. R. McKinney, 1882; S. H. Birney, 1883; J. D. Mandeville, 1884; A. L. Whitcomb, 1885-87; J. C. Harmon, 1888-89; William Dillon, 1890; W. K. Newcomb,

1891; H. E. Cushing, 1892; W. J. Fernald, 1893-94; C. B. Johnson, 1895; J. E. White, 1896; J. A. Hoffman, 1897; W. L. Gray, 1898; W. F. Burres, 1899; T. J. McKinney, 1900; John Laughlin, 1901; A. S. Wall, 1902; J. T. Purcell, 1903; S. S. Salisbury, 1904; J. M. Bartholow, 1905; C. M. Craig, 1906; J. C. Dodds, 1907; J. S. Mason, 1908; W. E. Schoengerdt, 1909; John Marten, 1910; William Rees, 1911; T. E. Walker, 1912; C. D. Gulick, 1913; T. J. Exton, 1914; F. S. Diller, 1915; J. H. Finch, 1916; O. O. Stanley, 1917.

Vice-Presidents—J. T. Pearman, 1874; B. D. Keater, 1875; C. B. Johnson, 1877; C. W. Allen, 1878; J. T. Purcell, 1879; J. D. Mandeville, 1880; C. T. Pope, 1881; F. W. Prentice, 1882-83; J. B. Clark, 1884; J. T. Pearman, 1885-88; W. K. Newcomb, 1890; H. E. Cushing, 1891; C. N. White, 1892; Z. L. Whitmire, 1893-94; J. A. Hoffman, 1895; S. W. Shurtz, 1896; C. M. Craig, 1897; W. F. Burres, 1898; J. C. Dodds, 1899; John Laughlin, 1900; John Marten, 1901; Z. E. Matheney, 1902; S. W. Shurtz, 1903; W. L. Gray, 1904; C. M. Craig, 1905; John Marten, 1906; J. S. Mason, 1907; W. E. Schoengerdt, 1908; F. H. Powers, 1909; Ellen Miner, 1910; Lucy Exton, 1911; G. W. Rice, 1912; T. J. Exton, 1913; H. W. Bundy, 1914; D. A. Kirby, 1915; L. O. Sale, 1916; H. W. Bundy, 1917.

Secretary-Treasurers—M. S. Brown and J. D. Mandeville, 1874; S. H. Birney, 1875; L. S. Wilcox, 1876; L. S. Wilcox and J. D. Mandeville, 1877; M. S. Brown and J. T. Pearman, 1878; M. S. Brown, 1880-82; C. B. Johnson, 1883-89; C. N. White, 1890-91; J. E. White, 1892; C. B. Johnson, 1893-94; W. L. Gray, 1895-96; Ellen Miner, 1897; John Laughlin, 1898; J. C. Dodds, 1899; John Laughlin, 1900; A. S. Wall, 1901; H. E. Cushing, 1902; J. S. Mason, 1903-04; C. D. Gulick, 1905-07; C..F. Newcomb, 1908-09; N. M. Baker, 1910; Jennie Lyons, 1911-12; Jennie Lyons and W. V. Secker, 1913; W. V. Secker, 1914-16; J. C. Dallenbach, 1917.

PIONEER PHYSICIANS BY LOCALITIES

In 1909 Dr. Johnson published a remarkably interesting history, in commemoration of the fiftieth anniversary of the founding of the society, entitled "Medicine in Champaign County." At that time Dr. Joseph T. Miller of Urbana and Dr. Hartwell C. Howard of Champaign were the only living representatives of those who organized the Champaign County Medical Society fifty years before. Dr. Miller located at the county seat in 1853 and Dr. Howard at Champaign in 1855.

Among other complete and interesting data collected by the author is that which covers the dates when the pioneer physicians of the county settled at the various towns, villages and cities. The localities are arranged alphabetically, and speak for themselves:

Bondville—This village had its origin about 1870 and was named in honor of L. J. Bond of Monticello, an officer in the early history of the railway that goes through the town. The first physician to locate in Bondville was Dr. O. B. Simmons, who came there in the '70s and remained until 1896.

Broadlands—This village was laid out in 1883, but in 1881 Dr. W. F. Burres practiced medicine in that locality and had his office at the Old Head Quarters House. Dr. Burres moved to Sidney in 1882.

Champaign—The first physician to locate in Champaign was Dr. R. W. Schumacher, brother-in-law to Judge Calvin C. Staley. November 9, 1854, Dr. Schumacher published a card in the Urbana Union announcing his new location. Dr. H. C. Howard came in 1855; also Dr. S. W. Kincaid, who remained but a few years. A little later came Drs. J. Hollister, S. K. Page, Joseph Hagar, C. L. Swain and A. J. Crane. Dr. Page continued in practice till advancing years compelled his retirement late in the '70s. Dr. C. H. Mills came in 1856 and remained until his death in 1907. Dr. J. T. Pearman located in Champaign in 1864 and remained in active practice till about a year and a half before his death in May, 1896.

Fisher—Dr. James G. Elder was the first physician in this place. Dr. Joseph Carr was the next, but did not remain long. About 1880 Dr. A. L. Elder practiced there for a time, when he removed to Nebraska. Dr. W. K. Newcomb located in Fisher and continued in active practice there till 1896, when he removed to Champaign.

Foosland—The first physician in this village was one Dr. Stephens, who, about 1870, was succeeded by Dr. H. L. Harris, who practiced there for a number of years, when he in turn was followed by Dr. A. C. Albright. In 1892 Dr. J. E. Lowry became the successor to Dr. Albright.

Gifford—This village was laid out in 1876 and was named in honor of Benjamin Gifford. The first doctor in the place was Dr. Salmons, who remained but a short time. He was followed by Dr. T. J. Berry. Later came Dr. W. Van Camp, and in 1877 Dr. D. R. McKinney, who practiced medicine there for about twenty years and then went to Indiana.

Homer—Old Homer, situated on the creek about a mile north of the Homer of today, was first settled in 1835. Dr. Harmon Stevens was one of the earliest physicians to locate in Champaign County.

When the Wabash Railway was built through the southern part of Champaign County in 1857, New Homer came into existence at the railway station, a mile south of Old Homer, and the last named village soon passed out of existence. Dr. Stevens at once removed to the new village and practiced medicine there a good many years till his removal to Newton, Illinois. In 1840 Dr. W. A. Conkey located in Old Homer and continued in practice there till 1850, when he retired permanently. In 1851 Dr. C. P. Mosier came to Homer, and five years later removed to the new town site, but all the while he continued in active practice till his retirement in 1859 to engage in farming and other pursuits. In 1853 Dr. James Core arrived in Old Homer, engaged in practice, removed to the new village at its beginning and continued the practice until his death in 1888.

Ivesdale—This village, just within the borders of Champaign County, dates its origin from about 1864, and is named for a Mr. Ives, who owned a tract of land in its vicinity. The writer has not been able to ascertain much of its early medical history, but among the physicians who have practiced there may be named Drs. W. F. Benefield, C. M. Craig, M. A. Morgan, C. M. Bailey, H. P. Mack and L. H. Smith.

Longview—This village was laid out in 1883 and the first physician to locate there was Dr. R. P. Ratts.

Ludlow—This village, at first called Pera, had its origin in the '50s. The first physician to locate there was one Dr. Emmons.

Mahomet—The first physician to locate in Mahomet was Dr. N. H. Adams, who opened an office there in 1843. He remained there ten to fifteen years, when he died. About 1846 Dr. C. C. Hawes came to Mahomet and continued practice there until his death in 1872. Early in the '50s, Dr. C. L. Crane located in Mahomet, where he remained till his death in 1856, the result of injuries received by the bursting of an anvil that was fired on the Fourth of July. Dr. J. D. Culver came to this village about 1857 and remained in practice there till his death in 1890. Dr. John D. Gardner located and practiced medicine there during the latter part of the '50s and the early '60s. His son, Dr. John H. Gardner, came to Mahomet in the early '70s and practiced till his death, August 22, 1902.

Ogden—This village was laid out in 1870 and took its name from a family in the neighborhood. The first physician to locate there was Dr. Edward Tourtellotte, who came in 1870, but a year later he died. In 1871 Dr. Job S. Coggeshall located there and engaged in practice till his death, September 14, 1902.

Pesotum—Dr. E. I. Birdsell was the first physician to locate in this village, arriving there late in 1869.

Penfield—Penfield was laid out in 1876 and takes its name from John Penfield of Rantoul, Illinois. The first doctor to locate in the village was Dr. M. M. Hazel; and his near successors Dr. W. S. Higgins, Dr. W. Van Camp and Dr. P. E. Cole.

Philo—The village of Philo was laid out in 1864 by E. B. Hall, son of Philo Hall, from whose Christian name both the village and township are named. The first physician to locate in Philo was Dr. B. C. Morris; the next one was Dr. Hall, whom Dr. James M. Bartholow succeeded in 1869. Dr. Bartholow remained in Philo till 1895.

Rantoul—The village of Rantoul, as well as the township in which it is located, takes its name from Robert Rantoul, one of the original stockholders and charter members of the Illinois Central Railroad corporation. Rantoul was first settled in 1855-56. The first physician to locate there was Dr. D. M. Marshall, who came in 1856 and remained till 1860. Dr. J. Sweat located in Rantoul in 1857 and continued in practice there till his death ten years later.

Sadorus—This village was laid off about 1856 and in that year came its first physician. Dr. A. Catron. In 1869 Dr. J. G. Chambers located there and practiced a number of years, when he removed to his farm in Sadorus Township, where he yet lives.

Seymour—The first doctors to locate there were Dr. J. M. Hadden and one Dr. Clark, about 1870.

Sidney—Excluding the "medicine men" of the Indian tribes, who were no doubt frequent visitors to this spot, and possibly a doctor in the employ of the Government, the first physician to practice his profession in the eastern part of Champaign County was Dr. Lyon, who was an Eastern gentleman of some ability and refined tastes. He evidently had great hopes for the future of his location, for it was he, in connection with a Mr. Davis, who laid off the original village of Sidney, the name being given in honor of Miss Sidney Davis, the eldest daughter of one of the founders of the village. He also designed a very large park, a part of which is now the public school grounds, the remainder long ago having been sold in town lots. He devoted some time at least to training horses, as he had built for his use a training track and barn. The old track was one-half mile southeast of Sidney. The doctor sold all his interests later to J. R. C. Jones and then moved to Texas, where he was visited by friends in 1865, who found that he had been elected to the Legislature in that State. For some years after the departure of Dr. Lyon the practice in the locality was done by Drs. Conkey and

Mosier of Old Homer. Dr. H. S. Hickman came to Sidney about 1859 and practiced with Dr. Hartman. In the beginning of the War of the Rebellion, he was among the first to enlist, being a private in Company I, Second Illinois Cavalry. He served to the close of the war, and, on his return, finding the field of medicine well filled at the place, went to Newman, Illinois, where he practiced for twenty years, then moving to the new town of Longview, remained but a short time, when he moved to Wichita, Kansas. Dr. S. D. Jerauld came to Sidney in the spring of 1858, having a good practice when the war broke out. Three sons enlisted, William, Walter Hall and T. D. Jerauld. William was killed at Vicksburg, Walter Hall was a prisoner at Andersonville, Georgia, and died while a prisoner. T. D. Jerauld, the youngest, returned after the close of the war and was discharged January 6, 1866. Dr. S. L. Jerauld contracted quick consumption going South after his son William, who was killed. He died April 5, 1865.

St. Joseph—The first physician to locate at Old St. Joseph was Dr. James Gillespie and the next Dr. Anthony Doyle, and a little later Dr. George Doyle. Dr. William Goodwin was also there for a time. Later came Dr. David Jennings.

It was about 1870 that old things in this region passed away and new things came about when Old St. Joseph gave away to New St. Joseph. In the latter village Dr. David Jennings was the first physician to locate, and Dr. W. B. Sims the next, both of whom came about 1870.

Tolono—This village dates its origin from about 1856. The first physician to locate there was Dr. Herman Chaffee, who built the fourth frame house erected in the place. Dr. Chaffee remained there until his death in 1900. About 1857 Dr. B. D. Keator came to Tolono and continued in active practice till 1878, when he moved to Missouri. In 1861 Dr. S. S. Salisbury arrived in Tolono and practiced until death overtook him in old age. In 1865 Dr. A. T. Darrah came to Tolono and began the practice of medicine and continued it until his removal to Bloomington in 1883. In 1874 Dr. C. B. Johnson removed to Tolono from Crittenden Township, where he had practiced three years, and answered professional calls until his removal to Champaign in April, 1879.

Urbana—Dr. John S. Saddler located in Urbana in 1839 and was the first doctor to make his home there, but he remained only a few years. Dr. Winston Somers came in 1840 and continued to practice medicine until his death in 1871. Dr. William D. Somers, brother of Dr. Winston Somers, located in Urbana about the same time and the brothers were partners till Dr. W. D., in 1847, abandoned medicine for the law. In the '50s came Drs. J. F. Snyder, J. T. Miller, James Hol-

1—14

lister, C. H. Mills. C. A. Thompson, M. B. Thompson, Joseph Hager, M. Lindley and W. M. Goodwin. Drs. Hollister and Mills removed to Champaign in 1856.

PATRIOTISM AND POLITICS

Dr. Johnson notes with keen interest what a large part the physicians of the county have taken in patriotic service and in politics. Among those who served as surgeons in the Civil War may be mentioned the names of Dr. S. H. Birney, One Hundred and Thirty-fifth Illinois Infantry; Dr. J. G. Chambers, One Hundred and Ninetieth Pennsylvania Infantry; J. S. Coggeshall, Second Indiana Cavalry; A. Jackson Crane, Second Illinois Cavalry; Jacob Culver, Seventy-first Illinois Infantry; W. S. Franklin (went from Champaign County as surgeon in an Ohio regiment, but what regiment is not known) ; Dr. M. Garst, Seventy-first Illinois Infantry; Dr. Lyman Hall, Sixty-third Illinois Infantry; Dr. William H. Hess, One Hundred and Forty-fifth Illinois Infantry; Dr. D. P. McClure, Sixty-fourth Ohio Infantry; Dr. J. T. Miller, Sixtieth Illinois Infantry; Dr. C. H. Mills, One Hundred and Twenty-fifth Illinois Infantry; Dr. C. A. Thompson, One Hundred and Twenty-fifth Illinois Infantry, Thirteenth Illinois Infantry and Ninetieth Illinois Infantry; Dr. C. A. Hunt, One Hundred and Twenty-sixth Illinois Infantry.

In addition to the above list of medical men who gave their professional service and one of them his life to the country, there is a goodly number of doctors in Champaign County who served in the ranks when mere boys. Among these may be named Dr. E. C. Bartholow, Dr. J. M. Bartholow, Dr. John M. Gardiner, Dr. Goodman, Dr. J. M. Hadden, Dr. Apollis Hess, Dr. J. C. Harmon, Dr. H. S. Hickman, Dr. R. H. Huddleston, Dr. David Jennings, Dr. Charles B. Johnson, Dr. E. A. Kratz, Dr. Wesley Lawson, Dr. J. D. Mandeville, Dr. D. R. McKinney, Dr. John North, Dr. J. T. Purcell and Dr. W. B. Simms.

Of the physicians who became prominent in politics were Dr. E. C. Bartholow of Mahomet, who was elected to the Legislature in 1876 and was instrumental in having the Illinois Medical Practice Act placed on the statute books; Dr. James Core of Homer, a member of the lower House of the Legislature in 1878; Dr. James H. Lyon of Sidney, who was elected to the Illinois Legislature in 1836 and served with Abraham Lincoln, Stephen A. Douglas, E. D. Baker, General Shields, Col. John Hardin, U. F. Linder and other able and famous men; Dr. J. W. Scroggs of Champaign, a member of the Legislature of 1868 and active in locating the Industrial University at Urbana, and Dr. L. S. Wilcox, also of Champaign, who served as revenue collector for the Springfield district 1889 to 1893 and as consul to Hankow, China, at a later date.

ILLINOIS MEDICAL PRACTICE ACT

This measure had its inception in Champaign County. In 1876, centennial year, the Illinois State Medical Society met in the Twin Cities May 16, 17 and 18. The sessions of the society were held in the chapel of the main university building.

The propriety of a medical practice act regulating the practice of medicine and the organization of a State Board of Health came up for consideration the last day of the meeting. And after being fully discussed, Dr. S. H. Birney of Urbana moved that a committee, consisting of a medical man from each congressional district, be appointed to memorialize the Illinois Legislature upon the urgent need of the proposed medical legislation.

Dr. William M. Chambers of Charleston offered a substitute that, after receiving some modifications, read as follows:

"Resolved, That a committee be appointed to memorialize the next Legislature on the subject of the appointment of a State Board of Health, and that, with proper modifications, the act by which the Board of Health of Massachusetts was inaugurated be submitted to the same as a basis for the Illinois State board.

"Resolved, That as members of the State Medical Society, each one shall consider himself bound to urge the propriety of a State Board of Health upon the representatives of his district."

The memorializing committee was appointed and consisted of the following physicians: E. W. Gray of Bloomington, William M. Chambers of Charleston, S. H. Birney of Urbana, William Massey of Paris, F. B. Haller of Vandalia.

The committee did its work well, and at the session of the Legislature of 1876-77 the original Illinois Medical Practice Act passed both houses, was signed by Governor Cullom and speedily became the law of the commonwealth.

Champaign County was fortunate in having in the Legislature at that time Dr. E. C. Bartholow of Mahomet and Hon. R. A. Bower of Tolono, both of whom worked assiduously for the bill. In due time Governor Cullom appointed the members of the first board of health and upon this Champaign County was represented by J. M. Gregory, LL. D., regent of the university, and one of the leading educators of the West. Dr. Gregory did most excellent work in organizing and putting the new board on its feet. With his well known versatility, he prepared several excellent papers on medical education and sanitation. During his term of service he was honored with the presidency of the board for two years.

CHAPTER VII

SCHOOLS AND TEACHERS

Only scraps of information come down to us regarding efforts of the Jesuit missionaries, and later settlers in the Illinois country of British and American connections, to plant the seeds of learning in this western region amid the unfavorable conditions of wilderness life. It is said that the Jesuits even founded what was called a College at Kaskaskia and which lingered for some thirty years. When the order was suppressed in France in 1764, its Kaskaskia property was confiscated, as elsewhere in the world. The college buildings, a brewery and a well-stocked farm at that place, were all sold to the highest bidder.

212

Pioneer American Teachers in Illinois

There was virtually no educational activity in Illinois during the British rule, in 1765-78, but among the soldiers of George Rogers Clark, the American officer, were some educated men, with families, who taught school in such settlements of Illinois as New Design, Monroe County, Kaskaskia, and a few places in Randolph, Madison and St. Clair counties. Although some of these teachers were college-bred, the description applied to one of them would lay down the rule, "faithful, but not learned." All these schools, and scores of others, of which there is no record, were subscription concerns. The teachers charged a small fee for each pupil per month or quarter, and it was generally planned that they should board in the homes of the patrons.

Territorial School Legislation

The first General Assembly of Indiana Territory passed an act in 1806 which laid the foundation for the University of Vincennes, and when the territory of Illinois was set off in 1809 that institution was outside its limits. The Illinois Territorial Legislature passed an act locating the township which the general government had agreed to give the state to support a seminary of learning. It proved to be partly in the Kaskaskia Valley and as it was then thought to be of little value, at the request of the territorial authorities, Congress agreed to another selection, comprising thirty-six sections scattered throughout the territory.

Educational Provisions in the Enabling Act

When Nathaniel Pope, the Illinois delegate to Congress, drew the act enabling the territory to become a state, he formulated as the Sixth section thereof four clauses referring to the offer of the general government to donate lands to the state of Illinois for the use of public schools. The first clause provided that Section 16, in each township was to be given to the state of Illinois to the inhabitants of such township for the use of schools; the second, refers to the gift of the salt lands; the third, provides that five per cent of the amount realized from the sale of the public lands in Illinois should be reserved for the state— two per cent for the improvement of roads leading into the state and three per cent for school purposes, of which latter one-half per cent was to be applied to a college or university; the fourth sets aside an entire township of land for the use of a seminary of learning to be vested in the State Legislature. The first provision gave the state nearly a million acres of land, the proceeds of which passed into a permanent township school fund and is the financial basis of the public school system of Illinois.

The State's Initial School Legislation

In Governor Bond's first message to the Legislature, in 1819, he recommended to that body a revision of the territorial laws and called special attention to education in these words: "It is our imperious duty, for the faithful performance of which we are answerable to God and our country, to watch over this interesting subject." In response to this call of duty by the governor, the Legislature passed laws making it an offense to cut timber from any school lands, the rents resulting therefrom to be applied to the cause of education. The same General Assembly passed laws chartering academies at Edwardsville, Carlyle and Belleville, and at the second session, in 1820, the Legislature incorporated the Belleville Debating and Library Society, and took steps toward advancing the cause of education at Alton, and in Monroe and White counties; but it does not appear that any practical results evolved from this legislation.

First Step Toward a State-Wide Public School System

But the time was at hand when a measure was to become fundamental law which should prove the first step toward a free-school system for the entire state. Its author was Joseph Duncan, state senator from Jackson County, and destined for seats in Congress and the gubernatorial chair. On the face of it the law was a good one. It provided for schools in every county, created the proper officers and the means of electing them. School sites and tax levies for the support of the system. were to be fixed by the legal voters in mass meetings. The taxes, which could be paid in money or merchantable produce, must not be more than one half of one per cent on the assessed value of property in the county, and in no case more than ten dollars for any one person. School houses were to be built and kept in repair by a poll tax payable in labor. The local taxes were to be increased by the distribution of a general state fund derived from one fiftieth of the entire state tax and five-sixths of the interest due on the school fund which the state had borrowed.

Still-Birth of the Duncan Law

The Duncan law nominally appropriated two dollars out of each hundred dollars received by the state treasury, to be distributed to those who had paid taxes or subscriptions for the support of schools. But as the aggregate revenue of the state at that time was only about $60,000, the sum realized from the Duncan law would have been but little more than $1,000 per annum. It practically remained a dead letter, and in the sessions of 1826-27 the taxing power authorized by it was nullified, and a return and a retrogression taken to the popular subscription plan, or no system at all. No provision was made for the examination of the teacher, who was usually selected by the subscribers to the local school.

Conditions in Champaign County

This was the condition of affairs when the first schools were established in Champaign County, and so remained, without radical change, until the foundation of the present system was laid in 1855. For many years the schoolhouses of Champaign County, especially those outside the larger centers of population, were of the most primitive character. They were usually built of logs, about sixteen or eighteen by twenty-four feet. The men of the neighborhood would go into the timber, cut the logs, haul them to the designated site and on a certain day would meet and carry up the walls. The structure was perhaps covered with clapboards, which were riven out of the oak trees by some patron of the school who had been trained to such work. The boards were seldom nailed on, but were held in position by straight poles resting on the lower ends of each layer. These weights were secured by pins at each end of the pole set into the ribs of the roof, or by flat rocks resting on the roof just below the weight poles. The doors were frequently of sawn boards, but now and then they were constructed of clapboards. The hinges were often of wood, home-made. Windows were openings in the side of the room made by removing a log or two. In the very early schoolhouses the openings were filled with oiled paper, glass being substituted later. The seats for the scholars might be made of split logs with pins in the rounding sides for legs. The split surface was made smooth with broadaxe and plane. Desks were arranged around the side of the room, made of sawn boards or hewn slabs, and were used for writing purposes only. The pupil often stood when writing. Paper was scarce and costly and slates were more often than not brought into use for that purpose. The pens in early use were made of quills and the ink was of home manufacture, soot being the basis of its make. The fireplace occupied one end of the building, and was often lined with flat rocks set edgewise and held in place by mortar made of clay, or lime and sand. Often the wooden fireplace was protected against the fire by a liberal coating of clay plastered upon the inner side of the structure. The fuel was wood from the timber near by. It was furnished by the patrons of the school and was brought in the form of long poles or logs. The task of preparing it fell to the teacher and the larger boys. And this was the form of fuel long after stoves became common in the schoolhouses. The wood lay exposed to the snows of winter and the rains of early spring, and often great difficulty was experienced in burning it as fuel. Blackboards were at first very few and very crude, one or two wide planks planed and painted serving the purpose. The carpenter's chalk served as crayon. The blackboard was not, however, considered a necessary adjunct of the schoolroom. Books were indeed scarce, Webster's speller and McGuffey's readers being the most popular; although in some schools the Bible was the text book in reading. It was nothing uncommon to find about the home a board shaped like a paddle, upon the smooth sides of which was written the multiplication table. A leather thong passing through a hole in the handle secured the device to the wrist, or to the plow handle, and thus was always handy for the use of the learner.

The schools of the earlier days in Champaign County were often conducted at the homes of settlers, or in abandoned cabins, and at a later period, when the settlers became more affluent and commenced to build separate buildings for educational purposes, the structures were often used by struggling churches as well.

CHARLES FIELDER, FIRST TEACHER IN COUNTY

It is probable that the first school in the county was taught by Charles Fielder, son of Runnel Fielder, the pioneer settler who, in 1822, established his home near Saline Creek near the northwest corner of Section 12, about two miles east of Urbana. He is said to have opened the school in his father's cabin in the winter of 1827-28, after a number of families had settled in the north end of the Big Grove, in the neighborhood of the old Fort Clark Road.

OTHER PIONEER TEACHERS AND SCHOOLS

Chiefly on the good authority of Thomas R. Leal, who served as county superintendent of schools from 1857 to 1873, the following were the best known of the early successors to Mr. Fielding.

In 1832 Claudie Tompkins, a son of the first inhabitant of Urbana, taught a school in what is now known as Stewart neighborhood. two

First Schoolhouse Built Near Urbana (1832)

miles north of Urbana, and at the same time Asahel Brewer (or Bruer) taught in the Brumley neighborhood, two miles east.

Thomas Freeman taught in Ogden Township as early as 1839, and was succeeded in the same neighborhood by Sarah Laird and William Jeremiah.

First School in South Homer Township

The first school taught in South Homer Township was by Abram Johnson in 1829. Its location was in the neighborhood where Moses Thomas first made his home, about three miles northwest of the village, near which were also settled Thomas Freeman, Isaac Burres, John Bailey and others heretofore named. The school was taught in a log house which had only greased paper windows. It was a pay school, and was patronized by fifteen pupils at $2.50 per term.

In 1831, when the territory of Champaign County was part of Vermilion County, the late James S. Wright of Champaign—twice elected a member of the General Assembly, once to each house—helped in the organization of the first Sunday School in the county. It must have been near where the first day school was taught. The next year the same neighborhood organized and maintained a singing school.

The first school taught in Sidney was by Andrew Stevenson (probably the same who was the second sheriff of the county), in the winter of 1833, at the home of William Nox. George Acres and George Nox were also early teachers in the neighborhood.

UNION OF CHURCH AND SCHOOL

Some three miles southeast of Urbana was the home of John Brownfield and a school was established in the early '30s for the children of settlers on the Salt Fork in that vicinity. Rev. James Holmes, a Methodist missionary and a millwright, came to the neighborhood in 1835, chiefly to build a gristmill for Mr. Brownfield. He built the mill and then looked around to consider the feasibility of organizing a Methodist class. The schoolhouse, which took his eye, is described by Martin Rhinehart, one of the interested settlers, as follows: "Built of split logs, with puncheon floors, basswood bark loft, greased paper windows, half-log benches (flat side up), and cost, furniture and all, not to exceed $25." In this schoolhouse Elder Holmes organized the first class in Methodism in Champaign County, probably in the winter of 1836.

FIRST SCHOOL ON THE SANGAMON RIVER

Charles Cooper taught the first school on the Sangamon River in Champaign County, in 1835. The scene of his labors was a log cabin, sixteen by eighteen feet, located about a mile south of the village of Mahomet, and his scholars included the children of the Robertson, Maxwell, Scott, Osborn and Lindsay families.

Levi Asher taught a school at Lewis Kuders' house, in Kerr Township, during the fall and winter of 1837. Another school was opened on the other side of the Middle Fork at Sugar Grove. C. W. Gulick, afterward of Champaign, was a pioneer teacher in that part of the county.

In 1838 Henry Sadorus employed James F. Outten, afterward county clerk of Piatt County, to teach a school in his own house for the benefit of his own children and those of the neighborhood. The Piatt children attended that school. Not long afterward a daughter of Dr. Lyon, who laid out the village of Sidney, taught in a log schoolhouse north of the village of Sadorus. Thomas Hunter and

Miss Julia Coil, afterward Mrs. Dr. Leal, were similarly employed in that neighborhood. About 1843 Miss Margaret Patterson taught in a log schoolhouse built by William Rock, about four miles south of Sadorus.

Jeptha Truman, who became a citizen of Kansas, but who came to Champaign County with the family (his father was John Truman), in 1830, about 1837 attended a school at the town of Byron taught by Billy Phillips, which he often described in his mature years. The schoolhouse had been used for a country store. The classes were made up mainly of the young members of the Jacob Heater, Lewis Adkins and Charles Heptonstall families and were drawn from the Big Grove region.

Besides those already named as teachers in Urbana, may be mentioned Messrs. Parmenter, Standish and Samuel C. Crane, and Moses Argo, John B. Swearingen and Mrs. Joseph Peters were early teachers in St. Joseph.

Old Courthouse as a Schoolhouse

The first exclusive schoolhouse to be occupied in Urbana was the old courthouse of 1841. In 1848, to make room for a new courthouse, it was moved to the lot subsequently occupied by the First M. E. Church. In it, for several years, the juveniles of Urbana had the advantage of instruction from such men as John Wilson, R. P. Carson, John Campbell, Samuel C. Crane, Noah Levering, William Sim and Joseph W. Sim.

John B. Thomas was one of the pioneer schoolteachers in the eastern part of the county. He entered land in Ogden and South Homer as early as 1834 and taught about that time. Afterward he served as probate justice, county judge and school commissioner. At the time of his death in 1861 he was a practicing lawyer at Homer.

Pioneer Schools and Teachers of the Townships

The townships of the county have always taken a laudable pride in the fact that the pioneers established schools for their children as soon as their means would allow, and supported them to the limit of their purses. So that although everything connected with the old-time subscription school was crude, "they did what they could." A chronological record of other early schools established in the different townships would read in this wise, some of the facts perhaps overlapping those furnished by the old superintendent of schools, Thomas R. Leal.

St. Joseph Township

The first school in this township was conducted on the farm of Squire William Peters, the father of John M. Peters, and was opened by John Laird, who continued· through its first term in 1833. The class was mustered in the Squire's kitchen.

The next school at Hickory Grove had as its teacher Moses Argo, and was held in a log hut, also on the William Peters place in Section 26. The school continued at that locality for three years, when the building was moved to the Rankin place, Section 23.

Mahomet Township

George Cooper taught the first school in Mahomet Township, although a house for that special purpose was not built until 1837. It was erected that year on Section 14 and called District No. 1. The district named was formed by Jonathan Maxwell, T. S. Scott and John G. Robertson.

South Homer Township

Moses Thomas was the leader in having the first schoolhouse of the township erected on his farm. The next building solely for school purposes was completed in Old Homer during 1838 and R. C. Wright opened it as such.

·Kerr Township

In 1838 Levi Asher had charge of the first school in Kerr Township; but the pioneer schoolhouse was built on James Skinner's farm, Section 21. William Y. Courtney, Samuel Tarves and Richard Bryan also taught in this first exclusive schoolhouse. About 1845 an old barn at Sugar Grove was transformed into a schoolhouse, and it is known that Stephen Ireland taught in it.

Sadorus Township

The first school in this section of the county was opened by James Outen in a log cabin during 1838. In 1842 William Rock, Mr. Beaver and others built a log schoolhouse, with greased paper for window glass, and hired Margaret Patterson as a teacher, at the rate of one dollar per week and "board 'round." Besides the children of the subscribers named, the Earlys and Munns attended the school. The cabin thus erected for educational purposes stood near Mr. Rock's house, and was not abandoned until more than forty years had passed.

COLFAX TOWNSHIP

The first school in the township was taught in a log building erected for the purpose in 1848. It is said that most of its subscribers lived in Tolono and Sadorus townships. Religious meetings were also held there. Jane Lyon, of Sidney, was the first teacher, and the Millers, Hamiltons, Sadoruses and Cooks subscribed twelve dollars per month for her benefit and the future of their children.

CONDIT TOWNSHIP

The first school in Condit Township was taught by C. Taylor in an old log house near what was afterward the residence of John Phillips in 1848.

CRITTENDEN TOWNSHIP

As soon as there was a sufficient number of children to justify them in so doing, a teacher was engaged and a subscription school opened in a cabin in Bouse Grove, Obadiah Johnson being the teacher. The first term was taught in 1852-53. A man by the name of Tompkins and a Miss Merry were also among the pioneer teachers. A schoolhouse was erected in 1857 by Alfred Bocock on Section 14 and Martha Chapin (subsequently Mrs. Cristy) was employed to teach.

NEWCOMB TOWNSHIP

The first schoolhouse built in Newcomb Township was located on Section 27 and was opened in the fall of 1852. It was a log cabin sixteen by eighteen feet, and its presiding genius, R. Banes, taught two terms. But a sort of a school had preceded it in Jesse Pancake's old log house, which he had abandoned for a better residence; for in 1851 Miss Martha Newel taught a term therein.

HENSLEY TOWNSHIP

In the winter of 1853 the first schoolhouse was built in this township, the class which gathered there being conducted by John Thrasher at twelve dollars per month. The second school was taught in 1854 by Dicy Ann Newel (afterward Mrs. Ragin).

Champaign Township

Dr. Shumacher (Shoemaker) taught the first school in the township during the winter of 1854 in a small one-story frame building. It was a subscription school of about a dozen pupils. During the Civil War Dr. Shumacher held a commission in the Confederate service and died in the South.

In the summer of 1855 a young man named Howard Pixley taught a private school west of the Illinois Central tracks, in a little one-story frame between Hickory and Tremont streets, Champaign.

The first public, or free school in the township, was taught by Mrs. M. A. Fletcher, assisted by her son, in the winter of 1855-56. It was held in the old Goose Pond Church.

Ogden Township

The children of Ogden Township, in the earlier days, attended school in St. Joseph and Homer townships, adjoining Ogden. Eleazer Freeman once stated that the first school in the township was taught in his kitchen, in the immediate vicinity of Ogden, by Tiffin Donaldson, in 1855.

Philo Township

The first schoolhouse credited to Philo Township was built on Section 9 in 1857 near the residence of L. Eaton, and was called Yankee Ridge schoolhouse. The pioneer school was opened in February of that year by Miss Emeline Keeble (afterward Mrs. Collor).

Pesotum Township

The first schoolhouse erected in Pesotum Township was what was long known as the Nelson School, erected in 1857. Mr. Brown was its teacher. About this time Miss Sarah Pennington taught a class in the freighthouse at Pesotum, and Misses Carrie Kelly and Mary Walling also conducted pioneer enterprises of the same nature.

Scott Township

The first schoolhouse was erected in 1857 near Samuel Koogler's place, the children of the locality, previous to that year, having been sent to a school in the Harris district, Mahomet Township.

RANTOUL TOWNSHIP

The first teacher in the township was J. A. Benedict, who taught four months in the winter of 1857-58. In the fall of 1859 the first public schoolhouse was built by Archa Campbell, a few rods west of his log cabin at the Grove. John Penfield, John A. Benedict and John Roughton were the first school directors of the township.

RAYMOND TOWNSHIP

.Perhaps the pioneer school in this township was taught by Addie Kuble in 1857, and the house was an old log cabin which stood near what became the homestead of William Martinie. Miss Annie Southworth was also a pioneer schoolma'am. In 1859 J. R. Southworth erected the first schoolhouse in the township. It was considered quite imposing—octagonal in shape, with the roof terminating in a central point, from which arose the chimney, and containing three windows. Miss Sarah Mulligan had the honor of being the first teacher in this temple of education.

HARWOOD TOWNSHIP

Augustus Crawford taught the first school in the township on Section 11, opening it in 1860. The building was a log cabin about ten by twelve feet and stood on John S. Webber's place. It appears that the log building was first erected for a house on Solomon Kuder's place in Kerr Township, and was moved by Jacob Huffman to the locality where he settled, on Section .1, Harwood Township. William Hughes then changed the location of the building to the Webber place on Section 11, in order to preempt the land there. As a structure, in fact, previous to its occupancy as a schoolhouse, it became quite noted as a wanderer.

TOLONO TOWNSHIP

A young man named Christian taught the first school in this township, holding forth in a small frame house which long stood in the southern part of the village. The first schoolhouse was built in 1863.

ASAHEL SMOKING OUT THE BOYS

Asahel Bruer (or Brewer), who reached a venerable age as a resident of Urbana, has been mentioned as having taught school two miles east of Urbana as early as 1832. There were few in Champaign County who taught earlier than he, and the clap-board roofed log house in which he gathered his classes was one of the first schoolhouses to be erected. His service as a teacher was quite long for those times, covering fully eighteen months. Mr. Bruer was a Kentuckian, as will become evident further along in this story, and was said to be nicely adaptable to the rough ways of the Illinois country in which he had settled rather late in life.

The tale runs, as told both by the heroes of it and some of the victims, that on the first Christmas he taught Schoolmaster Bruer treated the scholars, according to custom, to one gallon of whiskey and a bushel of apples, and everything passed off harmoniously. When the next Christmas came around, he found the door of the schoolhouse barred against him and, in answer to his request for admittance, a note was handed him through a crack between the logs asking not only that he treat to a bushel of apples and a gallon of whiskey, but that he give the scholars a vacation of one week. He answered that he could not and would not, and then mounted the roof of the house. The clapboards being held on the roof by weight poles, he had no difficulty in taking out enough to cover the top of the chimney. As there was a large fire made from green wood in the fireplace below, the room was soon filled with smoke. James Kirby, one of the older scholars, took the poker, a piece of a pole, and by throwing it up the chimney knocked the boards off. They were soon replaced by Mr. Bruer and on a second attempt to knock them off Mr. Bruer caught the poker, threw it on the outside and re-covered the chimney. The house was soon filled with smoke, almost to suffocation. The smaller children began to cry and everyone seemed to wish there was an end to the matter. About this time William Trickle crawled into the garret, pulled aside the boards and jumped out and down to the ground, with Mr. Bruer after him. The boys, seeing Mr. Bruer after Trickle, threw open the door and everyone piled out, smoke and all.

The boys soon caught Mr. Bruer and began rolling him in the snow, and he said, pulled his hair. He protested that they had no right to do this, when the boys submitted the matter to Stephen Boyd and Mr. Bromley, who decided that they had a right to bar him out of the schoolhouse, but not to pull his hair or roll him in the snow.

As soon as Mr. Bruer was released, he made a run for the schoolhouse, closely followed by James Kirby and the rest, but the old gentleman was first in the schoolhouse, where he was master of the situation for a short time. But the boys finally surrounded him and he surrendered, saying: "I just wanted to see whether you had any Kentucky blood in you." He then told the boys where to find a gallon of whiskey and a bushel of apples, hidden a short distance from the schoolhouse, which were soon produced and the afternoon spent in roasting apples and drinking apply toddy. James Kirby, William and Ashford Trickle, James W. Boyd, Moses Deer, Mrs. Mary Ann Moore (of Danville), Fount Busey, Sol Nox, James Roland, Susan Trickle (afterward Mr. Kirby's wife) were present, and, as men and women, often described the circumstance with gusto. It remained especially vivid in the mind of James Kirby, who always insisted that he was the hero of the tale, rather than Mr. Bruer.

But gradually order, under the control of the constituted authorities, got the upper hand, although a consistent county system of schools was not developed until the passage of the legislative acts of 1854 and 1855, the former creating a state superintendent of public instruction and the latter a uniform state system, including a more compact county organization.

INADEQUATE REVENUES

Under the previous law no township could sell its sixteenth, or school section, until it had fifty inhabitants, which provision for many years barred out many townships in Champaign County from taking advantage of even that small revenue. Again, the law permitted the people of any school district, by the affirmative vote of two-thirds of the legal voters, to levy a tax equal to 15 cents on each $100 of taxable property for the support of the public schools. In view of the comparative poverty of the people in the early times, when considered as owners of taxable property, this also was an insignificant source of revenue. Each county was also entitled to a certain quota, based on population, of the State interest on the school, college and seminary funds. But how small the public revenues of the county were previous to the '50s is well illustrated by the figures for the decade ending 1851, as compiled by Mr. Leal. The total for that decade was $2.064, or a yearly average of $206.40.

Under the old law the secretary of state was ex-officio state superintendent of common schools, and each county elected a commissioner, to whom was committed the care and sale of the school lands and the examination of teachers, but he was in nowise authorized to superintend the schools. There was therefore neither a public system or public support, each locality depending on the intelligence and generosity of resident subscribers for the quality of the education supplied to the com-

1—15

munity. When a young man or woman became especially anxious to secure a higher grade of education than the locality afforded, the nearest centers where such ambition could be partially gratified were Danville and Georgetown, Vermilion County, both seats of seminaries.

PRESENT COUNTY SYSTEM

But, commencing with the movement inaugurated by Prof. Jonathan B. Turner of Jacksonville, which eventuated in the founding of the University of Illinois, and culminated in the passage of the 1854-55 laws, which, in turn, laid the foundation of a solid system of free schools headed by the State which threw out tentacles into all the counties and townships of the commonwealth, the present-day era of popular education was born. Now each county elects a superintendent of schools, whose duty it is to visit the schools not controlled by city or village boards, conduct teachers' institutes, advise with teachers and school officers and instruct them in their respective duties, conduct teachers' examinations, and exercise general supervision over the public educational affairs of the county. The subordinate officers are township trustees, a township treasurer, a board of district directors, or (in cities and villages) boards of education. The superintendent of schools is responsible to the county board of education, of which he is an ex-officio member; that body is to consist of not less than five nor more than eight persons, of whom the chairman of the county board is also an ex-officio member. A compulsory educational law is in force and women are eligible to any office created by the general or special school laws of the State.

Under the old dispensation of county education, the following served as school commissioners: John Meade, elected in 1838; Moses Thomas, 1840; John B. Thomas, 1846 and 1848; William Peters, 1850 to 1853; Paris Shepherd, 1853, resigned, and John B. Thomas served until 1857.

SCHOOL COMMISSIONERS AND SUPERINTENDENTS

Under the old dispensation of county education, in March, 1836, John Meade was appointed school commissioner by the County Commissioners' Court and served seven years. Moses Thomas was appointed in March, 1843, and served three years; John B. Thomas, April 20, 1846, four years; William Peters, elected in March, 1850, and served until December, 1853; Paris Shepherd, elected at date mentioned and resigned in March, 1854; J. W. Jaquith appointed at the latter time and resigned in the following month; John B. Thomas, appointed in April, 1854, and served until the November election of 1857. Mr. Thomas, therefore, was in office during the period of transformation from the old to the new system. His successor, Thomas R. Leal, was elected county school commissioner in November, 1857, and served until December 3, 1873, or a period of sixteen years and one month.

Thomas R. Leal

No individual ever did so much for the Champaign County system of education as Commissioner Leal; and he was faithful, thorough and prominent in whatever he undertook. He was of New York nativity and in his youth a schoolmate of the noted Jay Gould, but, unlike his comrade of the early days, never acquired wealth. As he quaintly expressed it, "I was poor then and I have held my own with wonderful success." Mr. Leal came to Champaign County in 1852, when twenty-three years of age, and settled in Urbana, and after teaching in this and adjoining counties for several years was elected school commissioner, as noted. He not only served in that capacity for sixteen years, but was a member of the State Board of Education for six years of that period. He organized the first teachers' institutes in Champaign, Macon, Coles, Douglas, Effingham, Ford, Piatt, Vermilion and Iroquois counties, and took a prominent part in the educational affairs of the entire State.

County Teachers' Institutes

The first teachers' institute in Champaign County met in the spring of 1857 with seventeen teachers in attendance; Dr. L. M. Cutcheon, Dr. Hunt, Judge J. O. Cunningham and others assisted in organizing and conducting the exercises. For several years after its organization the Champaign County Teachers' Institute held only two sessions annually of one week each. The meetings gradually increased in length, interest and instructive value until they covered three weeks, and even more, with fine programs and unflagging zeal on the part of both lecturers and teachers. Originally, also, the expenses of the institute were paid by the teachers and their entertainment undertaken by the people of the localities where the meetings were held, but of late years, under the provisions of the constitution of 1870, the county institute and the normal schools have been under the supervision of the county board of education and supported by it as an integral part of the county system.

PROGRESS DURING MR. LEAL'S ADMINISTRATION

The foundation of the present system had only fairly been laid when Superintendent Leal went out of office in 1873, and, as stated, he more than any other individual is credited with founding it on an enduring and yet an elastic basis. In 1857, when he assumed the commissionership, there were forty-six schools in the county, twenty-six of which were kept in log schoolhouses and the remainder in small frame schools or dwelling-houses, with the exception of those occupied in Homer, Urbana and Champaign. These places contained comfortable brick buildings for the accommodation of the regular grades. Estimating the value of the forty-three houses outside these population centers at $200 each—which is pronounced a liberal estimate—and the graded school buildings at $20,000, the total value of the schoolhouses in the county in 1857 was $28,600. The houses, for the most part, were low, open and unsightly; seats usually made of slabs, or of boards or puncheons, with long sticks thrust in them for legs. The desks were so high that an average-sized pupil could not more than reach the top with his chin when seated on the bench, or touch his toes on the floor. Not a school-yard in the entire county was fenced, unless it happened to be in the same enclosure with the field in which it was located. The schoolhouses were heated with cook stoves, often so broken that they seemed to stick together simply from force of habit. Within the following two decades, largely covered by Mr. Leal's incumbency, there was a marked improvement in the buildings occupied for school purposes throughout the county. The old log houses, with their puncheon and slab seats, entirely disappeared, and only one of the old ramshackle frame schoolhouses remained. Buildings, furniture, apparatus and outbuildings had virtually reached the grade adopted by the advanced communities of the old Middle West or the East, and an estimate made by the authorities of the early '70s placed the value of the county school buildings at $310,000, of which sum the graded buildings were placed at $150,000.

The conclusion of Superintendent Leal's last term in December, 1873, marked the end of a noteworthy educational career. When he commenced visiting the county schools in 1857, there were only two bridges in the county, and, as noted, forty-six schoolhouses; when he retired there were over 200 good houses. When he assumed the commissionership there were no maps, globes or other apparatus except at Urbana. He had hard work even to introduce blackboards into the schools, frequently putting them in at his own expense in order to induce the boards of directors to try them as "experimental frills."

About two years after retiring as superintendent of schools, Mr. Leal commenced farming on land he had bought near Sidney, and thus continued for many years. He was also appointed drainage commissioner by the county board, and during his term collected about $27,000 on swamp land account that many had charged was sunk in building the courthouse. He held the receipts for that sum until his successor was appointed, and much of it would never have been collected but for his honorable persistency. In 1885 his report as sanitary inspector of Urbana was published in all the metropolitan papers by the State Board of Health as a model document of its kind, showing the thorough manner in which Mr. Leal always responded to a call for the public good. But it is, of course, as the father of Champaign County's system of popular education that he will be the highest honored and the longest remembered.

George R. Shawhan, Later-Day Builder

Mr. Leal was succeeded in the superintendency by S. L. Wilson, who was elected to the office in November, 1873, and served until 1877. Mrs. Calesta E. Larned served from 1877 to 1881, and was succeeded by George R. Shawhan, whose service extended from 1881 to 1902, twenty-one years. He shares the honors with Mr. Leal in developing the county system of free schools, and made a special mark for the zeal and efficiency by which he raised the grade of qualifications required of country teachers, and expanded the practical work of the teachers' institutes and the county normals. He also introduced many features into the schools, in line with modern thought and practice, tending to make them and their surroundings more pleasant and artistic. Like Mr. Leal, he was always so strong a leader of public sentiment in regard to the development of the system as to keep the general interest alive and retain the loyalty of the brightest and most thoughtful of the pupils.

Mr. Shawhan was of an old Kentucky family, his father, William M., having become prominent as a farmer and public-spirited citizen of Rush County, Indiana, before locating in Raymond Township in the spring of 1856. He was a leader in the Christian Church and died in the Sidney house of worship of that denomination in 1875. Superintendent Shawhan taught school in that place for several years; then took a course in literature and science at the University of Illinois, from which he graduated with high honors in 1875, and was principal of the Homer schools for four years previous to 1881, when he was appointed county superintendent of schools to fill the vacancy caused by the legislative change in the time of holding the election. In 1882 he was elected to the position by the Republicans, receiving the largest majority of any man on the ticket. During his long period of service as county superintendent he evinced the deepest interest in the welfare of the Illinois Industrial University, and in 1885 was chairman of the committee of the alumni that was so instrumental in changing the name of the institution to that of the University of Illinois.

PRESENT STATUS OF THE SCHOOLS

Mr. Shawhan was succeeded by the present superintendent of schools, Charles·H. Watts, in 1906. Under Superintendent Watts the progress of the schools has continued, and Champaign County does not suffer in comparison with any other section of the State of virtually equal population and financial resources. The status of the system as it exists today is best told in the report of Superintendent Watts covering the year 1917. The statistics indicate the enrollment of pupils, number of teachers, value of school property and tax levy by school districts.

Districts.	Enrollment.	Teachers.	Value of Property.	Tax Levy.
Sadorus	426	11	$16,205	$7,540
Colfax	205	9	9,650	4,500
Scott	267	9	12,450	5,400
Mahomet	352	12	22,245	8,850
Newcomb	258	7	9,978	4,350
Brown	386	18	45,890	17,150
Pesotum	417	11	17,440	7,350
Tolono	416	14	18,345	8,427
Champaign	2,290	94	673,979	141,850
Hensley	173	6	7,300	3,650
Condit	178	8	8,525	5,450
East Bend	249	10	10,360	5,750
Crittenden	212	9	8,440	4,700
Philo	357	11	16,800	6,400
Urbana	2,104	68	342,735	93,775
Somer	230	10	9,550	6,550
Rantoul	630	22	40,550	14,650
Ludlow	250	9	14,000	5,150
Raymond	436	12	12,792	6,825
Sidney	374	12	22,060	8,371
St. Joseph	381	14	34,160	11,975
Stanton	216	9	8,500	4,875
West Compromise	337	12	9,650	5,300
Harwood	164	9	9,225	4,700
Ayers	139	6	8,100	3,800
Homer	373	14	20,388	10,375
South Ogden	249	7	11,650	4,600
North Ogden	115	5	4,950	2,075
East Compromise	251	7 ·	18,375	6,625
Kerr	68	3	1,900	1,650
Township 20, Range 11	48	1	500	600
Township 21, Range 11	10	1	375	250
Township 22, Range 11	44 ·	2	1,325	850
Totals	16,101	452	$1,448,392	$424,363

From the annual report of the superintendent for the year ending June 30, 1916, it is learned that the total current expenses incurred by all the schools under his control amount to $414,223.48. The average salary of men teachers is $740.90 per annum and of women teachers $522.83.

STATE EXAMINING BOARD

The last biennial report of the state superintendent of public instruction contains much interesting and valuable matter, especially covering the legislation relating to the State and county, systems for the past decade. Cullings from that report, issued by Francis G. Blair in the fall of 1914, are especially instructive and encouraging as showing the advancement made in the qualifications required of teachers and the specialization in the supervision of the rural schools.

"When the public school system of Illinois was in its infancy," says Superintendent Blair, "boards of directors examined their own teachers. Later on, the law placed this function in the hands of the township trustees. It soon became apparent that if standards of education were to be established, some greater uniformity in the qualification of teachers was necessary. No such uniformity in teaching qualification was possible, unless the certificating authorities were more uniform in their requirements. This led to giving the county superintendent the power to examine any certificate teachers within his county. At the same time, the superintendent of public instruction was empowered to grant certificates of State-wide validity. The number of certificates granted by the superintendent of public instruction from 1855 down to 1914 has been a very small number of all the certificates issued in the State. The great mass of the teachers taught on county certificates. For the last twenty-five years it has been generally known that standards of qualifications for county certificates differed widely in the different counties of the State, as teachers were passing from one part of the State to the other, carrying certificates and asking that they be recognized wherever they went. Some of the county superintendents in the State began also to feel the burden of the preparation of questions and the grading of the manuscripts of the candidates examined. It was such a function as usurped much of the valuable time of a county superintendent which should have been spent on the supervision of his schools. Finally, after many years, a bill was drafted which received the support of the State Teachers' Association and the county superintendents. It passed the Forty-eighth General Assembly, and became effective on July 1, 1914. It provided for a State examining board which should make such rules as were necessary to carry into effect the provisions of the law. The superintendent of public instruction was made ex-officio a member and chairman of this examining board. The law required that three of the four appointed members should be nominated by the county superintendents' section of the State Teachers' Association and appointed by the superintendent of public instruction. The other member of the board was to be appointed by the same authority.

"In order that the three county superintendents upon the examining board might represent, in a general way, the three large sections of the State, the superintendent of public instruction asked that the county superintendents from each one of these sections should nominate a candidate. At the meeting of the State Teachers' Association in December, 1913, the county superintendents' section nominated Cyrus S. Grove, county superintendent of Stephenson County, for the northern portion of the State; Ben C. Moore, county superintendent of McLean County, for the central section, and Elmer Van Arsdall, county superintendent of Richland County, for the southern section. They were subsequently appointed. The superintendent of public instruction appointed as the other member of the examining board Hugh S. Magill, Jr., superintendent of the city schools of Springfield, Illinois, who, as a State senator, had had more to do with the enactment of the law than any other one member of the General Assembly.

"The examining board met and organized by electing Superintendent Magill secretary of the board.

"Very few boards have faced as large a task as lay before this examining board. It had to deal with 30,000 teachers in service and provide means for making the transfer of their old certificates for those under the new law; it had to arrange for examinations to accommodate those who wished to secure certificates before the opening of the school year. The law was, necessarily, extended and detailed. Few laws, covering such broad field and such complicated interests, have been freer from perplexing inconsistencies in provision and language. However, it has been found necessary to interpret some of the language of the law so as to make it consistent with certain other provisions. It has been necessary to issue circulars of instruction to county superintendents and teachers, and to provide blanks covering every detail of the inauguration of the law.

"The examining board has held fifteen meetings up to the 1st of November, 1914. The first examination was held on July 16 and 17, 1914.

GROWTH OF WORK OF SUPERINTENDENT OF PUBLIC INSTRUCTION

"The history of the movement to establish the office of superintendent of public instruction has been told in detail many times. The need of such an office had been felt long before the State took the first step toward its permanent establishment. Three lines of work were assigned to it by the Legislature:

"The first one of these related to gathering and tabulating statistics and data relating to public education.

"The second one related to the giving of legal and educational advice and counsel to all the school officers of the State.

"The third related to the supervision of the State common school system.

"The first one of these functions occupied the time and energy of the superintendent of public instruction for the first ten or fifteen years, along with some advice and counsel to school officers. The superintendent of public instruction was given no assistance and practically no expense fund. One stenographer helped him in the preparation of all the reports and in the getting out of all his circulars. This statistical work has grown rather than diminished, but the Legislature has, in recent years, been more liberal and has provided the officer of superintendent of public instruction with two clerks, who give practically all their time to the collection of this data and the preparation of the statistical reports.

"Advice on legal matters is now given by one assistant, who is a trained lawyer, and who has made a special study of the School Law of the State. The advice on educational matters is divided up amongst the heads of the various departments—the persons in charge of rural schools giving advice to rural school officers; those in charge of elementary schools, advice to elementary school officers; those in charge of the high schools, to high school officers. Thus it will be seen that the advisory function of the Superintendent of Public Instruction has become more effective through the enlargement of the office force and the placing of special men in charge of special fields of work.

"This last result, however, has been made possible, mainly, through the enlargement of the office force for the performance of the third legal duty—that of supervision.

"From the very beginning of the office, the Superintendent of Public Instruction did whatever supervising he could in the little time which was left over from his other burdensome duties. At the very best, he could do nothing which merited the name of supervision.

SUPERVISION AND STANDARDIZATION OF RURAL SCHOOLS

"In 1906 the work of building up the office for the performance of this duty was begun. A supervisor of rural schools was appointed, who was to go into the field, work with and through the county superintendents for the supervision and improvement of rural schools. Two years later, another assistant was allowed whose duties were to supervise rural and village schools.

"In 1913 the Legislature provided for a high school supervisor, with an annual salary of $4,000. With these three men, it was possible for the Superintendent of Public Instruction to arrange for a systematic supervision of the country schools, the elementary schools, and the high schools. As high school supervisor, the Superintendent of Public Instruction appointed Principal John Calvin Hanna, of the Oak Park High School. It is believed that the office of Public Instruction can serve the cause of public education in no more effective way than through giving advice and counsel in directing the growth of secondary education. The last twenty years has seen a tremendous development in high schools. In no other field has there been such a demand and such a need for careful, competent advice and counsel. The work of recognizing the high schools, as required by the certificating law, is proceeding with thoroughness and care.

"Mention has been made of the appointment of rural school supervisors.

"In 1909, a system of standardization for the improvement of rural and graded schools was adopted by this office. In brief, it provides for the visitation by a supervisor from the Department of Public Instruction, who, with the county superintendent visits the schools. If these schools meet the minimum requirements in physical equipment, in course of study and in teaching, a diploma, signed by the supervisor and by the Superintendent of Public Instruction, is granted to the school. A door plate is also given by the Department of Public Instruction to be placed on the front door of the schoolhouse. It was found, in a very short time, that school officers wanted something to work for above the minimum standards already set. It was decided to offer a superior diploma for a one-room country school which should furnish superior equipment, course of study and teaching, and a superior school plate was made.

"Under this movement schools have been standardized as follows: In 1909, 84; in 1910, 142; in 1911, 277; in 1912, 469; in 1913, 641; in 1914, 629. In 1912 twelve schools were standardized in Champaign County, and eleven in 1914.

High School Tuition Act

"In 1909, the Legislature passed an act requiring districts which did not maintain a high school to pay the tuition of their eighth grade graduates in some four-year high school, selected by the parents upon the approval of the directors of the local district. This law, however, in its passage through the Senate, was amended by the insertion of the clause which said, that the tuition should be paid by the district, provided the parents or guardian were unable to pay. It was known by those who were interested in the measure, that this amendment weakened greatly, if it did not destroy the law. Very shortly after it went into effect, it was attacked in various courts on various grounds. Finally, a decision was given by the Supreme Court that it was unconstitutional, inasmuch as a Board of Education was not competent to decide who was able and who was not able to pay the tuition. The State Teachers' Association, which had taken up this matter, again went before the Legislature with a demand for an enactment of a law without this unconstitutional provision. Such a law was passed by the Forty-eighth General Assembly and went into effect July 1, 1913.

"It is difficult to over-estimate the far-reaching consequences of such a law. Immediately upon its going into effect, every square foot of territory within the State became high school territory. Before that time over 300,000 boys and girls were living in districts where no high schools were established. When they completed their eighth grade work, all free high school opportunity for them ended. If they attended any high school, their parents had to pay the tuition. Here arose that old and ugly distinction where society was divided by a money consideration. With the going into effect of this new law, every graduate of the eighth grade in every district in the State had this free high school opportunity open for him. He was not compelled to accept it, but it was open if he desired it.

"In the first year under this law it has been tested and tried in practice as well as in the courts. Many of the decisions based on this law are of great interest. Two of them are printed in this biennial report. It is sufficient here to say that the law has been held constitutional by the Supreme Court. Under its provisions, at least 5,000 boys and girls, who would not otherwise have been in high school, have gone. In the year closing June 30, 1913, there were enrolled in the high schools of the State 78,942; in the year closing June 30, 1914, there were 85,301 pupils enrolled, a gain of over 8 per cent, whereas the gain in the enrollment in the elementary schools is only 2.6 per cent. While the enrollment in the high schools, as compared with the enrollment in the elementary schools, has been gradually increasing, this rapid and unprecedented growth must be attributed to the free high school tuition law. Some difficulties have appeared. It has been found that some school districts cannot raise enough money under the limit set by the law to maintain a good elementary school and, at the same time, pay the tuition of their high school pupils. Wherever such a condition exists, the directors have had to do one of two things—cut down the character of their elementary school, or refuse to pay the high school tuition. The courts have held that the directors in such districts are under no compulsion to pay high school tuition, unless they have money remaining after paying for the maintenance of a good elementary school. It is believed that some provision will have to be made for meeting these peculiar cases. One proposal is to have the Legislature appropriate a special amount which shall be used to aid these needy districts. This has the objection of making it appear that the fault somehow lies in these particular districts, whereas the fault generally lies in unwise methods of taxation and distribution of the revenues. A second proposal is, that when the distributive fund is sent to each of the counties, the county superintendent shall be required to distribute to all the high school districts upon the school census basis, as now provided by law; that he shall withhold out of the other portion a sufficient amount to pay the tuition of all the pupils from the non-high school districts and then distribute the balance to those districts on the school census basis.

STATE EDUCATIONAL SURVEY

"The last ten years has witnessed the development of a new tendency in public education—that of the school survey. It has arisen out of the desire of taxpayers, as well as school officers, to have some sort of an appraisement of the quantity and quality of the work which is being done in public education. Unfortunately, for the success of this movement, these surveys took the form, in the beginning, of private ventures. Certain clubs, organizations or individuals provided money to employ experts to conduct these investigations or surveys. In several notable instances, the experts thus employed seemed to be more interested in getting out a startling, sensational report, rather than in arriving at conclusions which would assist school officers in making the work of the public school system more effective. In many parts of the country, school officers and school teachers were beginning to think that these experts were like some surgeons, who were reputed to care very little whether the patient survived or not, so long as the operation could be pronounced successful. No one could deny, however, that the desire for these surveys and appraisements represented a distinct and worthy demand on the part of the public. It became necessary, therefore, for school officers and school teachers to devise methods whereby the public might be informed in some tangible sort of a way concerning the work of public education. In the State of Illinois, the State Teachers' Association has undertaken a State-wide survey of public instruction. The State Association and its various sections appropriated money out of their treasury. A number of the normal schools, colleges and the State University added to this amount. A committee was appointed to take direct control of this survey. A plan was formulated. The various lines of investigation were placed under the immediate direction of men and women especially fitted to carry them out. Professor Lotus D. Coffman, of the School of Education of the University of Illinois, was made secretary of the State Association and director of the State Survey. It may take two years, three years, or four years to carry out this survey to a conclusion. When it is done, however, it will have the distinction of having been thorough-going and complete, but at the same time, sympathetic and considerate. The taxpayer will have no reason to question the genuine, *bona fide* character of the survey, and the friends of public education cannot quarrel with this conclusion on account of any lacking of sympathy on the part of the investigators."

GREGORY
1867-80

PEABODY
1880-91

JAMES
1904-

BURRILL
ACTING PRESIDENT
1891-4

DRAPER
1894-1904

PRESIDENTS OF THE UNIVERSITY OF ILLINOIS

CHAPTER VIII

THE UNIVERSITY OF ILLINOIS

239

BUILDINGS—SCHOOLS AND COLLEGES REORGANIZED, 1906-1915—
SCHOOLS AND DEPARTMENTS ADDED, 1905-1916—DR. GREGORY'S
PREDICTION—GROWTH OF UNIVERSITY BY YEARS, 1867-1917—
ANNALS OF THE UNIVERSITY—FIRST MEETING OF THE BOARD (1867)
—UNIVERSITY OPEN TO STUDENTS (1868)—1870—1871—1872,
1873, 1874—1876, 1877—1881, 1882—1884, 1885, 1886, 1887—
1891, 1892, 1893, 1894—1896, 1897—1899, 1900—1901-1904—
EDMUND J. JAMES BECOMES PRESIDENT—1905-1910—NEW AUDI-
TORIUM DEDICATED—1911-1916—DEATH OF DR. T. J. BURRILL—
ADMINISTRATION—DEPARTMENTS AND COURSES—THE COUNCIL OF
ADMINISTRATION—GENERAL ADMINISTRATIVE OFFICERS—THE COL-
LEGES AND SCHOOLS—THE UNIVERSITY SENATE—NUMERICAL
STRENGTH OF THE FACULTY—EXPERIMENT STATIONS AND SCIEN-
TIFIC BUREAUS—AGRICULTURAL EXPERIMENT STATION—ENGINEER-
ING EXPERIMENT STATION—STATE LABORATORY OF NATURAL HIS-
TORY—THE STATE ENTOMOLOGIST'S OFFICE—STATE WATER SURVEY
—STATE GEOLOGICAL SURVEY—BOARD OF EXAMINERS IN ACCOUNT-
ANCY—INVESTIGATION OF ILLINOIS COAL PROBLEMS—ACCREDITED
HIGH SCHOOLS—UNIVERSITY HONORS—PRIZES AND MEDALS—
SCHOLARSHIPS AND FELLOWSHIPS—LOAN FUNDS—UNIVERSITY
EXTENSION WORK—AGRICULTURE—CERAMIC ENGINEERING—HOME
ECONOMICS—UNIVERSITY FINANCES—TOTAL VALUATION OF UNIVER-
SITY PROPERTY.

A survey of the University of Illinois seems at first sight to be an
undertaking almost appalling in the multitude of the details which
arise for consideration. Before getting deep into the work, it may be
well to note briefly how the great educational institution of the state
and the nation stands with reference to other noble monuments of a
similar character. Two years ago, it passed permanently beyond the
attendance mark of 6,000 students, and in that regard it is exceeded by
the universities of Columbia, California and Michigan. When the
strength of its faculty is taken into consideration, in connection with
the attendance, the records show that it ranks with the University of
California in all that goes to make up a complete machine for the
instruction of men and women in the practical, professional and scientific matters of life, and as a wonderful force of inspiration in the high
realms of investigation and reflection.

Fortunately the story of how the University of Illinois has developed
from a small school devoted to a modest teaching of the fundamentals
of literature, agriculture and the industrial arts, to an institution which

is a veritable city of intellectual, moral, artistic, spiritual and life activities, has been often told in detail, but never so well as by the official publication of the University itself. The Historical Sketch, as edited by Dr. Vergil V. Phelps, executive secretary of the University, and endorsed by President Edmund J. James, was published in the 1916 Directory. As finally revised by Dr. Phelps it follows:[1]

Germs of the Public School System

The germ from which the University of Illinois has developed may be found in the clause of the famous Ordinance of 1787, "Religion, morality and knowledge, being necessary to good government and the happiness of mankind, schools and the means of education shall forever be encouraged."

This provision, a half century before the appearance of our public school system and seventy-five years before the Land Grant Act of 1862 providing for state universities, was merely the ideal from which ideas might continually arise until suddenly a complete state educational system emerged in our national life. It was well into the fifties before public schools began to spread in Illinois, and even in the eighties high schools were regarded as questionable necessities. President James relates that when he was principal of the high school at Evanston, Illinois, in 1878, that the question was presented annually to the voters of this period, not whether the principal or superintendent of schools should leave, but whether the people of a given locality desired to continue their high school.

However, higher education was provided for as early as 1804, when Congress made three districts in Indiana Territory and directed the Secretary of the Treasury to locate one township of land in each district for the use of a seminary of learning. At this time Illinois belonged to Indiana Territory. Later, in 1818, when Illinois became a state, a second township was given for the endowment of a seminary, and also one-sixth of three per cent of the net proceeds of government lands sold after January 1, 1819.[2] This latter donation to the state was to be "exclusively bestowed upon a college or university."

---

[1] In June 1917, appeared the History of the University of Illinois by Allen Nevins in the Oxford University Series. It is the first comprehensive history of the University of Illinois in one volume.

[2] See Papers of the Amer. Hist. Soc. Vol. 1, No. 3, W. L. Pillsbury, p. 36; Ill. School Report, 1887-88, p. CXVII.

The people of Illinois, however, made no attempt to establish an institution of learning with these funds as a foundation until 1833. In that year a bill was introduced to incorporate an institution to be called "Illinois University." The bill met with strong opposition, as Springfield was named for the location. Through jealousy, Vandalia stirred up the opposition of other neighboring cities. Friends of the infant colleges of McKendree, Shurtleff, and Illinois looked with alarm upon the establishment of such a state-endowed university; and, in addition, the men in control of state affairs, in order to avoid taxation, had already used all moneys received for the college fund and from the sale of the seminary lands for the current expenses of the government. And any proposition to cut off the use, in a similar way, of further receipts from the same source was decidedly unpopular. Furthermore, they would have had to resort to taxation in order to restore the trust funds already misappropriated. Fortunately perhaps for them, the bill met with defeat, and for several years after this the efforts made to establish a state institution of higher learning were wholly unorganized. The people took little interest in the matter and attempts were even made from time to time to divide up the college and seminary funds among the colleges of the state.[1]

Again, in 1851, the Senate passed "An Act to Establish a State University," but upon reconsideration the bill was laid upon the table. An examination of this bill shows that the proposed university was to be a board of men to distribute the income of the college and seminary funds to the several colleges of the state, upon conditions named, for the purpose of educating teachers for the common schools.

PROPOSED AGRICULTURAL AND INDUSTRIAL UNIVERSITY

After this failure, however, a movement arose to establish an institution of a rather different character. The Buel Institute, an agricultural society of Putnam County, at its fair in September, determined to hold a farmers' convention at Granville in November "to take into consideration such measures as might be deemed expedient to further the interests of the agricultural community, and particularly to take steps toward the establishment of an agricultural university." Prof. Jonathan Baldwin Turner of Jacksonville was invited to be present and address

---

[1] See Ill School Rep., 1887-88, p. CXIX.

the convention. The attitude of the leaders of this convention toward higher education and what they sought to obtain through their proposed university may be shown by quoting the resolutions presented by a committee, of which Professor Turner was chairman.

"*Resolved,* That we greatly rejoice in the degree of perfection to which our various institutions for the education of our brethren engaged in professional, scientific, and literary pursuits, have already attained, and in the mental and moral elevation which those institutions have given them, and in their consequent preparation and capacity for the great duties in the spheres of life in which they are engaged; and that we will aid, in all ways consistent, for the still greater perfection of such institutions.

"*Resolved,* That, as the representatives of the industrial classes, including all cultivators of the soil, artisans, mechanics and merchants, we desire the same privileges and advantages for ourselves, our fellows and our posterity in each of the several callings, as our professional brethren enjoy in theirs; and we admit that it is our own fault that we do not also enjoy them.

"*Resolved,* That, in our opinion, the institutions originally and primarily designed to meet the wants of the professional classes, as such, cannot, in the nature of things, meet ours, no more than the institutions we desire to establish for ourselves could meet theirs. Therefore,

"*Resolved,* That we take immediate measures for the establishment of a university in the State of Illinois expressly to meet those felt wants of each and all the industrial classes of our state; that we recommend the foundation of high schools, lyceums, institutes, etc., in each of our counties, on similar principles, so soon as they may find it practicable so to do.

"*Resolved,* That, in our opinion, such institutions can never impede, but must greatly promote, the best interests of all those existing institutions."

PROFESSOR TURNER'S LEADERSHIP

The prominence which this convention holds may be attributed largely to the bold and vigorous way in which Professor Turner discussed the questions, "What do the industrial classes want?" and "How can that want be supplied?" His answer to the first question was, "They want, and they ought to have, the same facilities for understanding the true philosophy—the science and the art of their several pursuits, their life business—and of efficiently applying existing knowledge thereto and widening its domain, which the professional classes have long enjoyed in their pursuits." Replying to the second question, his belief was that the want neither could, nor should, be supplied by existing institutions which were designed to educate the professional classes, and whose spirit was literary and intellectual as distinguished from industrial and practical. He said the need was for a "university for the industrial classes in each of the states" and presented his "plan for the state university."

This plan was quite elaborate. It was insisted upon that such a university would, of right, receive the college or university fund which the state held from the general government, and it was doubtless intended to claim also the seminary fund, though this is not stated distinctly.

The address greatly aroused the convention, a report of which, including the address in full, was published and widely circulated. The report of the Illinois State Board of Agriculture and the United States Patent Office report of 1851 reproduced it; the New York Tribune and the New York Horticulturist noticed it with approval; the attention of the National Agricultural Association was called to it; the Philadelphia North American gave it editorial approval, etc., etc.[1] Acceding to the request of the convention, the governor, in summoning an extra session of the Legislature to meet June 7, 1852, laid before that body the subject of industrial education as presented at the Granville meeting.

At a second convention, held at Springfield, June 8, 1852, representatives and friends of some of the colleges attended and claimed that their institutions, rather than the proposed new university, legitimately should receive the college fund. They made a bid for the seminary fund, agreeing to establish teachers' departments if it were bestowed upon them. A discussion, sharp and angry, took place and the quarrel was transferred to the Legislature. The convention presented its land grant memorial and enlarged the plan for a university by adding a normal school, to be co-ordinate with the industrial department,[2] in order to meet the demand that the seminary fund be used in training teachers for the common schools. The convention also urged in its memorial that a beginning be made at once to carry into effect either the original plan or some modification of it which the General Assembly might think preferable, "and if possible, on a sufficiently extensive scale honorably to justify a successful appeal to Congress in conjunction with eminent citizens and statesmen in other states, who have expressed their readiness to co-operate with us for an appropriation of public lands in each state

[1] Univ. Studies, Vol. IV, No. 1, November, 1910, The Origin of the Land Grant Act of 1862, by Edmund J. James, p. 21.
[2] Ill. School Rep. 1887-88, p. CXXI.

in the Union for the appropriate endowment of universities for the liberal education of the industrial classes in their several pursuits in each state in the Union."

In the Legislature, the House referred the whole subject to its committee on education, and the college men won at first by securing from it a bill to divide both funds among the existing colleges. But the result was a drawn battle; for the bill was laid upon the table, and as if to be rid of a troublesome contest, both Houses joined in a resolution asking authority from Congress to add both the college and seminary funds to the common school fund, so that the income from them might be forever given to the support of the public schools.

Illinois Industrial League Organized

A third convention was held in Chicago in November, 1852, at which the Industrial League of the State of Illinois, with Professor Turner for chief director, was organized—the purpose being to promote the interests of the industrial classes. This convention published an address to the people of the state, prepared a memorial to the Legislature, and arranged for petitions both to the Legislature and to Congress.

At a fourth convention held in Springfield, January 4, 1853, again the request for an industrial university was set forth, and the Legislature was urged to memorialize Congress, asking for each state an appropriation of public lands, of a value not less than $500,000 for the liberal endowment of an industrial university.

In 1854, Governor Matteson proposed the subject of industrial education to the Legislature for consideration at its special session. In the following January, 1855, the Industrial League held a fifth convention in Springfield and a bill was introduced in the Legislature for "An Act to Incorporate the Trustees of the Illinois University." The trustees were to locate the university and to receive from the state the college and seminary funds for its endowment, on condition that they raised a like amount from other sources. They were also to receive any grants which Congress might make for industrial education. The plan of the proposed institution was broad and liberal as it appears in the bill, which did not, however, obtain any definite action from either House.

There was little apparent sympathy in Congress with this subject, which was arousing such widespread interest, perhaps due to the fact that in 1854 President Pierce had vetoed a bill proposing land grants to the states for establishing asylums for the indigent insane, and in this veto had used language which showed clearly that his action would be the same toward a bill providing land grants to the states for colleges of agriculture and science.

With the coming of a new President in 1857, friends of industrial education again bestirred themselves, and their measure was House Bill No. 2, introduced by Justin S. Morrill of Vermont, a man from one of the older states that had not thus far benefited by the land grant of the federal government. It met with strong opposition, and the bill was finally defeated at the hands of President Buchanan who interposed his veto, largely upon constitutional grounds,[1] and it was considered useless to seek for further action by Congress while Buchanan was President. The bill provided for a grant to the several states of 20,000 acres for each member of Congress from the state, according to the apportionment to be made after the census of 1860. The states were to establish within five years not less than one college, where the leading object should be to teach agriculture and the mechanic arts, without the exclusion of other scientific and classical studies.

MORRILL BILL PASSED

Again, early in December, 1861, Mr. Morrill renewed the agitation in favor of a national grant of land to each state in the Union for the promotion of education in agriculture and the mechanic arts, and secured the passage of the so-called Morrill bill by both houses. It was approved by President Lincoln, July 2, 1862. The act was substantially the same as the previous bill. The chief differences were a grant of 30,000 acres of land for each member of Congress instead of 20,000; the exclusion of states in rebellion; and the requirements of acceptance by the states within two years instead of five, and that instruction be given in military science. The grant was to constitute a perpetual fund, the income of which was to be "inviolably appropriated" by the state "to the endowment, support, and maintenance of at least one college, where the leading object shall be, without excluding other scientific and classical studies, and including military tactics, to teach such branches of learning as are related to agriculture and the mechanic arts, in such manner as the Legislatures of the states may respectively prescribe in order to promote the liberal and practical education of the industrial classes in the several pursuits and professions of life."[2]

---

[1] Cong. Gl., First Session, Thirty-fifth Cong. 1412.

[2] Text in Laws of the U. S. and the State of Illinois Concerning the Univ. of Ill.

The Honor Due Professor Turner

The results of this movement may reasonably be looked upon with satisfaction and pride, and great honor is surely due to Professor Turner. In a study by President James entitled, "The Origin of the Land Grant Act of 1862," may be found conclusive evidence that to "Jonathan B. Turner, the Illinois professor and farmer, belongs the credit of having first formulated clearly the plan of a national grant of land to each state in the Union for the promotion of education in agriculture and mechanic arts, and of having inaugurated the agitation that made possible the passage of the so-called Morrill Act. To his memory should be raised a monument in each of the sixty-eight institutions which have grown out of his effort or whose power and usefulness have been increased by these appropriations."

It is well within the rules of propriety that Illinoisans congratulate themselves that the movement so full of good to the nation, to labor, and to youth everywhere, had its inception here in Illinois; that from Illinois came the demand upon the federal government; that to an Illinois senator is due the first movement in its favor in Congress; and that an Illinois President gave it life by affixing his signature.

On February 14, 1863, the Legislature formally accepted the provisions made by Congress, and in due time the land scrip for the 480,000 acres, to which Illinois was entitled, was sent to the governor.

But even after the passage of the bill, there was much controversy over the funds thus made available for educational purposes. Some wished to divide the fund among several agricultural colleges; while others preferred one college and favored having it made a part of an already existing institution. Questions of this nature caused much bitter strife. Those who had struggled for the passage of this bill had sought to establish one institution and to make it unlike the existing colleges of the state, and entirely separate from them. Naturally, they deprecated any attempt to divide the fund or to use it in establishing departments in existing colleges. The views of this party were embodied in a bill drafted by a committee of which Jonathan B. Turner was chairman and substantially similar to the charter finally granted in 1867. Resolutions were adopted by the State Agricultural and the State Horticultural Societies insisting upon one institution, and opposing an effort to divide the fund, or to use it in establishing departments in existing colleges. They proposed that the location should be made, after the consideration of bids, at that place which seemed to offer the greatest facilities.

University Hall

The General Assembly of 1867 passed a bill giving any county, city, township, or incorporated town power to vote bonds and to make proposals for securing the location of the University. The people of Champaign were early alert to the idea of securing the institution, and put forth every effort to obtain the prize. Nor were the opposing counties by any means idle. In their efforts to defeat this county, the latter sent out warnings and appeals through circulars and newspaper articles to the people of the state, in which ridicule and derision of the claims of Champaign County formed the burden. The seminary property—a large brick building which formed a part of the offer of Champaign County, received the label "The Champaign Elephant,"[1] and this epithet was well kept before the people of the state; certain Chicago papers lending ready and nimble hands in the propagation of this and other like derogatory attacks. Champaign County, on the other hand, lost no opportunity to gain' influence and to make friends for its cause. After a not altogether creditable contest among the several competing counties— Champaign, Logan, McLean and Morgan—the Legislature accepted the offer of Champaign County, and, subject to certain conditions, located the University at Urbana.

ILLINOIS INDUSTRIAL UNIVERSITY FULLY INCORPORATED

Governor Oglesby approved the act incorporating the Illinois Industrial University, February 28, 1867. This act provided that five trustees were to be appointed from each of the three grand judicial districts of the state, and one trustee from each of the thirteen congressional districts who, with the governor, superintendent of public instruction, president of the State Agricultural Society, and the regent, when elected, as *ex-officio* members, should constitute the board of trustees. In pursuance of the law, the board met for the first time in the Representatives Hall in Springfield on March 12, 1867. Governor Oglesby, the temporary president of the board, prescribed the oath to each member, according to the constitution of 1848, then in force. This oath,

---

[1] Jonathan Stoughton had promoted the erection of this building which was financed by the sale of adjoining lots. The building was to be used for a higher institution of learning. The Civil War interfered with the scheme, but there is little doubt that if the building had not been already in existence that the Legislature would never have voted to locate the institution in Urbana-Champaign. Clark R. Griggs was largely instrumental in securing the University, since he traveled over the entire State before the Legislature met and sacrificed the speakership of the House for the chairmanship of the committee on the location of the university. He skillfully manoeuvered the vote for the rival communities first and then when all were voted down there was nothing left but to locate the institution in Urbana.

among other things, solemnly pledged each man not to engage in dueling during his term of office, and declared that each had not been guilty of dueling since the adoption of that constitution.

Dr. John M. Gregory Chosen Regent

Under the law, the first business to be transacted was the election of the regent, or president of the University. The board chose Rev. John Milton Gregory, LL. D., a man of broad and enlightened views, who at the time was president of Kalamazoo College, Michigan.

Therefore, as the act provided that one-third should serve for a term of two years, one-third for a term of four years, and one-third for a terms of six years,[1] the trustees drew for their terms of office. At the first meeting, the board also passed the following resolution:

"*Resolved,* That, sensible of our dependence on the Divine blessing in the great work in which we are engaged, it should be a standing order of this board to commence each day's proceedings by the Word of God and Prayer." The motion carried unanimously.[2]

The new board of trustees, including Regent Gregory, was largely chosen from the laity and clergy of the Baptist Church, and for some time fear was entertained that the new university would become largely a denominational school; or, on the other hand, an irreligious institution. However, the first fear was groundless, as the bias in the actions of the board, which many looked for, did not appear, and in Dr. Gregory's long administration it would be difficult to point out anything in his action tending in that direction, and the second fear was refuted by the daily compulsory chapel service and Sunday afternoon vesper services at which Dr. Gregory preached.

His acceptance of the position as regent of the University did not occur until after he had made a trip to Chicago and Champaign. He said that in both these places only one opinion was expressed to him, and that was, that this new institution was to be "the grandest university on the American continent." He accepted the election and became the first regent of what was then the Illinois Industrial University, serving as its executive head from April 1, 1867, a year before the institution was formally opened, until 1880.

---

[1] Rep. of Univ. of Ill., 1868, pp. 16, 19.

[2] The popular accusations brought against the university in these early days were paradoxical charges that it was (1) a Baptist nursery, and (2) a school for infidelity.

BIOGRAPHY OF JOHN MILTON GREGORY

John Milton Gregory was born at Sand Lake, New York, July 6, 1822. He was a graduate of Union College, and a pupil of Eliphalet Nott, one of the greatest educators of his day. He studied law from 1836 to 1848, and later, after some time spent in the study of theology, he entered the Baptist ministry. For a time he taught in a secondary school in Michigan, and in 1858 was elected State Superintendent of Public Instruction of that state. He held this position until 1863, when he was elected to the presidency of Kalamazoo College. He received his degree of LL. D. from the University of Michigan in 1866. After serving this college for four years, he entered upon the duties of regent of the University.

Dr. Gregory was a man of high ideals and broad sympathies, of great vigor and considerable oratorical ability, and his general plan of university organization has continued to the present day. His personal influence upon the student body was marked. His vision of what a State University should be was far-reaching.

During the year following his election to the regency, and previous to the opening of the University, not only were the plans for the institution pushed forward at the seat of the proposed university, but Dr. Gregory also traveled over the state, seeking to interest young men everywhere in securing a higher education. Many of the addresses which he made were delivered from the rear end of a farmer's wagon at a county fair. To many young men who afterwards came to the University and who have since been of great value to their state, the appeal came from the lips of this college president on some such occasion.[1]

One of the first great tasks of Dr. Gregory was to prepare an outline of the general aims of the new university, and a course of study. This he did, as chairman of a committee appointed by the board. The following departments and courses of study were suggested to be developed as soon as practicable.

PROPOSED DEPARTMENTS AND COURSES

I. The Agricultural Department, embracing—
   1. The course in Agriculture proper
   2. The course in Horticulture and Landscape Gardening

---

[1] Alumni Quarterly, Vol. IV, Makers of the University, by Henry Mahan Beardsley, '79, p. 5.

II. The Polytechnic Department, embracing—
    1. The course in Mechanical Science and Art
    2. The course in Civil Engineering
    3. The course in Mining and Metallurgy
    4. The course in Architecture and Fine Arts
III. The Military Department, embracing—
    1. The course in Military Engineering
    2. The course in Tactics
IV. The Department of Chemistry and Natural Science
V. The Department of Trade and Commerce
VI. The Department of General Science and Literature, embracing—
    1. The course in Mathematics
    2. The course in Natural History, Chemistry, etc.
    3. The course in English Language and Literature
    4. The course in Modern Language and Literature
    5. The course in Ancient Language and Literature
    6. The course in History and Social Science
    7. The course in Philosophy, Intellectual and Moral [1]

The report of this course of study committee caused considerable excitement among the people. The idea of teaching "English Literature" and "Ancient and Modern Languages and Literatures" proved as the red flag to the infuriated bull of the story. The institution was denounced as no more than one of the "old colleges" and the question was derisively asked, "Why add, by a public grant of lands, to these old institutions, of which the people already have too many?" It is probably due to the warfare aroused by this course of study that only fifty-seven were enrolled at the opening of the University on March 11, 1868, and of these, forty-five were from Champaign County. Untrue and sensational tales were told and believed, greatly to the discredit of the new University. Many demanded that the classics should be excluded from the course of study; others that they should be tolerated, but not cherished. By some it was claimed that the students of belles-lettres would constitute an aristocratic class in that institution and that the students of agriculture and mechanic arts would be looked upon as inferiors. The dissatisfaction showed itself in newspaper articles and in public addresses. Dissensions took place in the board of trustees. Finally, in 1870, a convention of delegates from the several county agricultural societies met at Bloomington to consider the past, present and future condition of the Illinois Industrial University. Dr. Gregory attended this convention and delivered an address. He explained at

---

[1] Rep. of Univ. of Ill., 1868, p. 50.

length the act creating the University and the course of study, answered some reasonable questions, and as a result very much improved the existing feeling. They appointed a committee to visit and investigate the institution and report thereon. This committee's report served greatly to strengthen the University as, for instance: "We found 196 male students in attendance; . . . fourteen young ladies. . . . About fifty of the students present were in the agricultural and horticultural departments, fifty-four in mechanical and civil engineering, sixty-five in chemistry, fifteen in comparative anatomy, 138 in mathematics, twenty-three in military tactics, fifty in the commercial department, ninety-two in English, sixty-three in German, twenty-six in French and twenty in Latin; none in Greek. From this statement it appears that only one-tenth of the students are studying the classics at all; and inasmuch as each student pursues three studies, only one-thirtieth of the working force of the institution is expended upon the ancient languages, whereas in an ordinary college, from half to two-thirds of the working force would be so expended.

"We were further assured by the acting regent that it is the full purpose of the faculty to fulfill all laws enacted for the government of the institution, and to meet the requirements of the industrial classes by making it, in the true sense of the word, an industrial school in contradistinction to the ordinary colleges and professional schools of the country." [1]

The subjects actually taught at the opening of the University were algebra, geometry, natural philosophy, history, rhetoric and Latin, and the work was carried on in the brick building which was the donation of Champaign County. This building also served as a dormitory and came to be known as the Old Dormitory building.

Owing to the belief that it is the separation of the theoretical and practical which renders so much education mere "book learning," the board of trustees decided that a manual labor system should be thoroughly tried, and all students not excused for physical disability were required to labor from one to three hours a day. The students went out in squads, under their military officers, and under the general supervision of members of the faculty. The maximum compensation of such labor was 8 cents an hour. Many students worked voluntarily over hours, and received for such over-work 12½ cents an hour. In a short time, however, labor was made wholly voluntary, except as it was a part of some course of study, as the shop practice in the course of mechanical science and art.

---

[1] Rep. of Univ. of Ill., 1869, p. 62.

STUDENT'S GOVERNMENT SYSTEM

In matters of discipline Dr. Gregory believed in treating the students as men, and in appealing to their manhood for the maintenance of good order. His love of freedom showed itself in the establishment of the Students' Government System, first tried in 1870. By permission of the faculty, the general assembly of the students was organized, and a constitution adopted providing for the election of a president, vice-president, secretary and marshal. There was also a senate of twenty-one members, and a court consisting of a chief justice and two associate judges. Under this constitution, the senate enacted laws, which became valid only when approved by the regent of the University. All offenses against these laws were tried before the students' court, and punished by fines according to the claims of offense. Cases requiring the severer penalties of suspension or expulsion from the University were referred to the faculty, and students refusing to pay the fines·imposed by the students' government were suspended from University privileges. For a time this system of government worked admirably, but later politics crept in and perverted justice, and the system was abandoned in 1883.

The faculty for the first term consisted of the regent, two instructors, a head farmer and two non-resident lecturers. A decided contrast in numbers with our faculty of today! The two towns likewise presented a very different appearance. Street pavements were not laid until some twenty years later; the buildings, for the most part, were of the cheaper grade of scantling frames; and the streets themselves were more often adorned by wood piles than by sidewalks. Stock of all ·kinds ran at large in both towns and in the country, so that all houses were securely fenced to keep out the predatory cows and hogs.

WOMEN FIRST ADMITTED

Women were not at first admitted to the University. In 1869 the question of their admission was raised,. and after a lengthy discussion, upon the motion of Mr. John S. Johnson,[1] it was settled in the affirmative in March, 1870. The story is told that a group of boys, much interested in the outcome of the discussion, listened to the deliberations of the trustees through a friendly stove-pipe hole, and when the vote was finally taken, and announced as favorable to the young women, an approving shout was heard from the gallant fellows above.[2] Girls

[1] Rep. of Univ. of Ill., 1870, p. 84.
[2] Facts for Freshmen Concerning the Univ. of Ill., by T. A. Clarke, p. 7.

THE PRESENT WOMAN'S BUILDING

ever since have been thus kindly received, and their presence has come to be viewed as a matter of course. In the first year, twenty-two were registered; while during the year 1916-17, their attendance has increased to 1,641, out of the total number of 6,828, or nearly one-fifth of the whole enrollment of the University of Illinois. Thus their early kindly reception seems to have been appreciated.

In spite of the prominence of agriculture in the state and the important part which the farmers took in the industrial movement, the agricultural department languished. The proportion of agricultural students during the first decade was insignificant.

COLLEGE OF ENGINEERING FOUNDED

Meanwhile the engineering courses developed rapidly. Stillman W. Robinson, elected to the professorship of Mechanical Engineering in 1869, may be regarded as the real founder of the College of Engineering. He appreciated the educational possibilities of shop work and made it a part of the engineering instruction. In January, 1870, a mechanical shop was fitted up with tools and machinery. Dr. Peabody, in speaking of it, says, "It is probable that tool or machine instruction was first given in America at the Worcester Free Institute, which was formally inaugurated in November, 1868, six months after the inauguration of this University. I have not been able to find that Professor Robinson's practice shop had any other predecessor in this country." In the summer of 1871 the mechanical building and drill hall (burned on June 9, 1909) were erected and equipped for students' shop work in both wood and iron, and for military drill.

MAIN UNIVERSITY BUILDING COMPLETED

The Legislature, in its session the same year, authorized the construction of the main University building, according to the plans and estimates, laid before it, at a cost of $150,000. They appropriated $75,000, and provided that the $75,000 additional should be appropriated at the next meeting. Work on the building was commenced, but the Legislature failed to make the expected additional appropriation. A broad, white streak on the west wall remains the indelible record of the time when the work could go no further. It was deemed advisable to provide temporarily for the continuance of the work by the sale of the Champaign County bonds. This was done, and the work was resumed. Every effort was made that this money should be repaid by the State, but such efforts were unavailing. The building was finished and dedicated December 10, 1873.[1]

The other of the larger buildings erected during this period was the Chemical Laboratory, which was authorized by the Legislature of 1877 and dedicated at the commencement in 1878. Its cost, when fitted and furnished, was $40,000. There were other smaller appropriations made during the period, which were used in the construction of a house and barn on the horticultural grounds, a gardener's house, a greenhouse, and a barn for the agricultural department.

A re-organization of the Board of Trustees occurred in 1873. The number of members was reduced from 31 to 11—The Governor and the President of the State Board of Agriculture, *ex officio,* and nine others, who were still appointed by the Governor.[2] Beginning at this time also, the President of the Board was chosen by the members from among their own number for a term of one year. At the meeting held July 10, 1873, Emory Cobb was elected the new president. He gave much time and attention to the affairs of the University for more than a quarter of a century.

The Four Pioneer Colleges

At the end of the first five years the organization of the University consisted of four colleges—the College of Agriculture, of Engineering, of Natural Science, and of Literature and Science. These were subdivided as follows:

The College of Agriculture embraced the Schools of Agriculture and Horticulture.

The College of Engineering included the four Schools of Mechanical, Civil, and Mining Engineering and Architecture.

The College of Natural Science included the School of Chemistry and the School of Natural History.

The College of Literature and Arts and Science embraced the School of Modern Language and Literature and the School of Ancient Language and Literature.

Besides these, there were the Schools of Commercial Science, the School of Military Science, and a School of Domestic Economy. The instruction in the last named school began with the college year 1872-'73. The full course in the beginning embraced general literary work while in the second and third years lectures on topics of domestic

---

[1] Rep. of Univ. of Ill. 1888, Hist. Address by Selim H. Peabody, p. 207.
[2] Laws of the U. S. and State of Ill. Concerning the Univ. of Ill., p. 37.

1—17

economy took the place of the mathematical studies. This was the first School of Domestic Economy of high grade, and with a complete course, organized in the United States, if not the first in the world.

Admission requirements at first were very low in all departments; but fewer than half the students of the earlier years were able to meet them, and members of the faculty found themselves overloaded with elementary work to the detriment of higher instruction. In accordance with Dr. Gregory's views, the entrance requirements were gradually advanced, and in 1875 a preparatory year was instituted which later developed into the Academy. Candidates in the preparatory classes had to be fifteen years of age and be able to pass satisfactory examinations in arithmetic, geography, English grammar, and United States history. Like other institutions of the Middle West, Illinois, after some experiments, adopted the "accredited school" system. The first school so accredited was the Princeton High School, and by 1880 the number had increased to twenty-two.[1]

In the early days of the institution, the elective system predominated. Although liberty had its risks, it was "not thought useful or right to attempt to urge every student, without regard to his capacity, tastes, or practical wants, to take entire some lengthened curriculum."[2] But gradually this system of complete freedom was modified, and students who desired to "graduate," were required to complete some one of the courses outlined in the catalog. The introduction of academic degrees at the commencement 'of 1878 strengthened this tendency. Distinct courses were then defined, to each of which a degree was given.

According to the original state law, the usual diplomas and degrees could not be given by the University. Certificates showing the studies pursued and the attainments in each were given instead. But this was a new dispensation which the great world was unwilling to accept. The graduates found their paper not current in the market. The name of the institution was persistently misinterpreted. The regent had to be at all times prepared to show that he was not only a trustee of the people but also their servant. It is a matter of record that when the earlier professors went to the State Teachers' Association and sought admission to the college section, it was denied them because an institution that gave no degrees had no rightful claim to call itself a college.[3]

---

[1] Rep. of the Univ. of Ill., 1880, p. 44.
[2] Fourth Annual Circular, pp. 25-27.
[3] Rep. of Univ. of Ill., 1888, Hist. Address by Selim H. Peabody, p. 207.

Authorized to Grant Degrees

In 1877 the alumni petitioned the Legislature to give the University authority to grant degrees. The authority was given, and a fee of $5.00 required for each diploma.[1] Graduation with a certificate was still permitted to those who had obtained the requisite number of term credits, but not in subjects prescribed for any particular degree.

Earliest Literary Societies

The social life during this period, was, in the main, simple and democratic. A number of student organizations were formed, many of which are still in existence. The earliest literary societies were the Adelphic and Philomathean organized in March, 1869. Two years later the women of the University organized the Alethenai. In the same year (1871) the University band furnished its first music for commencement. The first student publication appeared in November, 1871, and was known as *The Student* and published monthly. The paper two years later changed its name to *The Illini*. The Young Men's Christian Association and the Agricultural Society date back to the same year. In 1874, there was organized an association for the advancement of telegraph, known as the Illinois Industrial University Telegraphic Association. Instruments on the line numbered twenty-five, and the central offices were open for practice all hours of the day.

Professor S. W. Shattuck

In the fall of 1868 Professor Samuel Walter Shattuck came to the University as Assistant Professor of Mathematics and Instructor in Military Tactics. Three years later, he became Professor of Mathematics and continued to serve the University in this department to Sept. 1, 1912. He also filled various other positions. He was Professor of Civil Engineering for the year 1869-70. He was Acting President for six months in 1873, and served as the first Vice President from 1889 to 1894. He became the financial manager in 1873. A high sense of honor and true loyalty in service have been embodied in his career, and the University very appropriately showed its appreciation of him by conferring upon him in June, 1912, the highest honor it can bestow, the degree of LL. D. He died Feb. 13, 1915.

---

[1] Rep. of Univ. of Ill., 1878, p. 86.

No sketch of the University would be complete without the mention of Edward Snyder, who was appointed at the same November meeting in 1868 as Professor Shattuck. His primary interest was in modern languages, but the exigencies of the time compelled him to teach a great variety of subjects as remote as bookkeeping and military tactics. He was a most sympathetic adviser and friend of the students. He continually gave or lent them money; and in 1890, three years after his retirement from active service, he gave to the University $12,000, to be loaned to needy students. He died in 1903.

Professor Nathan Clifford Ricker began his work as Instructor in Architecture in the University in March, 1873. He has twice acted as Dean of the College of Engineering. Many of the University buildings have been constructed after plans drawn by him. Professor Ira Osborn Baker came to the University as Assistant in Civil Engineering and Physics in September, 1874, after having graduated the spring before. Thus two of the present faculty have been connected with the institution approximately forty years.

Dr. Gregory's Administration

The period of Dr. Gregory's administration is not marked as one of great prosperity financially. The University was the owner of 480,000 acres of land scrip. The Board of Trustees proposed at first to locate 50,000 acres of its land scrip, and to sell the rest; but the pressure for funds was so great that it located but 25,000 acres, about 9,000 being in the state of Nebraska and 16,000 in the state of Minnesota. The large amount of land scrip thrown upon the market by this and other land grant universities had greatly depreciated its value,[1] and the 455,000 acres sold brought but $319,178.87, or seventy cents an acre.

As fast as the cash was received it was invested in such securities as the law demanded, and the rate of interest then current in the state, eight to ten per cent, yielded from $25,000 to $30,000 per annum and was utilized for the payment of current expenses of instruction. The money panic of 1873 did not seriously affect the finances of the University until about 1877, when debtors began to refund their loans at lower rates of interest. In this way, the income of the University was largely diminished. During the year 1878 the expenditures were found to be $3,500 in excess of the income. No surplus funds were on hand

---

[1] Ill. School Rep., 1887-88, p. CXLIII.

and there was no prospect of increasing the interest on the endowment fund. Something had to be done. So it seemed best to reduce somewhat the salaries of the teaching force. Dr. Gregory suggested that the reduction should begin with himself, not because his salary was the largest, but rather because he would prefer to see his own compensation reduced 20 to 25 per cent than the already too meager salaries of his associates lessened. The reduction of $3,500 was made by taking small amounts from the various salaries and departments, and at the request of the regent, $400 from his own salary. Places which became vacant were left so. Certain departments were cut off—those of mining commerce, and domestic economy. The fees of students were raised. Economy in its most rigid form was practiced everywhere.

Meanwhile the internal condition of affairs became gloomy. The cordial agreement which had existed between the students and the regent and faculty became strained, and finally open rebellion occurred.

Under these discouraging circumstances Dr. Gregory submitted his resignation at the June commencement 1880 and it was immediately accepted by the Board. He spent the remainder of his life in Washington, D. C., where he served on the commission of education, for a time, and from 1895-7 was acting president of Pennsylvania State College. He died in Washington October 19, 1898. On Sunday, the 23d of October of that year, a memorial convocation was held in the old University Chapel, and his body was laid to rest in ground just west of University Hall. In speaking of him, the alumni of the University, gathered in Chicago, expressed themselves as follows:

"Full of years and honor, like a shock of ripened corn in an abundant year, our beloved instructor and friend, Dr. John M. Gregory, the founder and first regent (president) of our Alma Mater, has been gathered to his fathers."[1]

Dr. Gregory served the University for thirteen long and hard years, at a time when wisdom, foresight, promptness, enthusiasm, and courage —all the characteristics of a competent leader—were in most urgent demand, and in none of these respects was he found wanting.

BIOGRAPHY OF DR. S. H. PEABODY

Upon his resignation the Board appointed Dr. Selim Hobart Peabody, formerly Professor of Physics and Mechanical Engineering, Regent *pro tempore*. Dr. Peabody was born at Rockingham, Vermont,

---

[1] Alumni Quarterly, Vol. IV, January, 1910, p. 11.

August 20, 1829. He spent one year in the Public Latin School of Boston, but owing to his father's death, circumstances compelled him to leave school and help earn a livelihood for himself and others. After working five years he entered the University of Vermont at the age of nineteen and graduated in 1852. The next two years were spent, first, as principal of the high school at Burlington, Vt., and then as teacher in the Collegiate Institute at Fairfax, Vt. In 1854 he became Professor of Mathematics and Physics in the Polytechnic College of Philadelphia. Three years later he accepted the position of Chief Clerk in the United States land office at Eau Claire, Wisconsin. In 1859 he took charge of the city school at Fond du Lac, and in 1862 he became superintendent of schools at Racine, Wis. Three years later he became an instructor in the City high school. On March 11, 1868—Inauguration Day—he was offered the professorship of mechanical science and engineering in the Illinois Industrial University. This he declined, but in 1871 he went to the Massachusetts Agricultural College at Amherst as Professor of Physics and Civil Engineering, where he remained three years, and then returned to his old position in Chicago. In 1877 he received the degree of doctor of philosophy from the University of Vermont. On the 10th of October, 1878, he accepted the appointment of Professor of Mechanical Engineering and Physics in Illinois Industrial University and served in this capacity until the close of March, 1880, when he resigned to accept the work of editor-in-chief of what later became the International Cyclopedia. On July 27th, of this year, he was reappointed to the same professorship and made regent *pro tempore,* assuming the new duties on August 15th. The following March, 1881, he was elected regent of the University and continued as such until he presented his resignation June 10, 1891.[1]

Almost all of his adult life, to the time of his election to the regency, had been spent in teaching and accompanying activities. It is said that at the time of his appointment he could have taught successfully any subject offered in the curriculum of the institution.

The Peabody Administration

Dr. Peabody encountered numerous annoyances and difficulties during his regime. In the beginning, many of the students assumed a questioning attitude toward him. The seniors were said to have held a meeting to determine whether they would return or not, but kindly con-

---

[1] Alumni Quarterly, Vol. V, July, 1910, Makers of the Univ., by Thomas J. Burrill, p. 203ff.

sented to give the new man a trial.[1] The first serious hitch came from
a clash between certain secret fraternities and the court of the organized
students' government. As a result, the regent recommended, and the
trustees approved, a ruling that no student could enter the University
until he had pledged himself not to join a fraternity, and that no
student should be graduated until he certified that he had not belonged
to any fraternity while in the University. The adoption of these rules
disclosed the existence of four such organizations. Their members
petitioned the faculty to repeal the rules, but the faculty only turned
their petitions over to the Board, which recommended that their requests
be refused. The rule was strenuous, and was not repealed until September, 1891.[2] From the time of the passage of the rule, more or less
antagonism existed, directed chiefly toward the regent, whose duty it
was to execute the mandate. Unfortunately for him, he was a man
sufficiently sensitive to criticism to find it discomforting.

Another occurrence, trivial in itself, also inflicted no little injury.
One of the cadet captains in the military organization failed to receive
an examination grade sufficient to permit him to continue in his official
position. His brother officers undertook to compel his re-instatement
by entering upon what we would call a strike. Dissatisfied students
were allowed to take their grievances to the Board of Trustees, and it
in turn sat as a sort of high court, and in effect, put the faculty upon
trial. In this case, a matter which should have been adjusted without
great difficulty, became unnecessarily burdensome.

President Peabody systematized administrative affairs, instituted
improved book-keeping and gathered up loose ends everywhere. He
personally attended to numerous details. Dr. T. J. Burrill, in writing
of his work, said that "throughout his administration he had no
stenographer. The University did not own during his time a type-
writing machine. The official correspondence was mainly conducted in
his own handwriting. There was no registrar. At the beginning of
each term he personally issued class permits and at the close recorded
class grades. Aside from his headship in the department of Mechanical
Engineering and Physics, he taught classes (during different terms) in
Mechanics and Hydraulics and Mental Science, the latter subject being
required of all seniors. It is little wonder that there was not much
time for effective campaigning outside or for dreaming of future greatness."

But in spite of many obstacles, and in spite of the fact that these

---
[1] Rep. of Univ. of Ill., 1888, Hist. Address by President Peabody, p. 210.
[2] Rep. of Univ. of Ill., 1892, p. 151.

were days of small things educationally, progress was made during his administration. In 1879-80 there were 434 students (reduced in 1880-81 to 379), and 26 teachers of all grades, of whom 15 were of professional rank; in 1890-91, there were 519 students and 40 instructors, 24 of whom were of professional rank. Thus there was a gain in students of 19.6 per cent and in the corps of instruction of 53.9 per cent, and for those having professional rank, 60 per cent. For the first named year the total income from all sources was about $60,650; for the last named, $124,600, or 146 per cent gain. The total legislative appropriation for the session of 1879 was $25,500; that for the session of 1891 was $147,200. This latter figure included $70,000 for the Natural History Building, but excluding this, the gain was $51,700, or 203 per cent.[1]

Before President Peabody's administration, all state appropriations had been clearly for specified purposes and exclusive salaries for instruction. At the legislative session of 1881, the trustees resolved to ask in addition to the usual sums, for an appropriation for the current expenses of instruction. The Legislature granted the sum of $11,400 to help cover the amount of the loss suffered by the University because of the reduction in the interest on its investments.[2] The next Legislature was asked for $14,000, for the same purpose, and the grant was made. During the biennial periods which followed, the sums of $24,000, $32,000,[3] and $40,000 were allowed, respectively.

Appropriations for buildings were small, and were slow in coming. After much persuasion and political wire pulling on the part of the regent and his local aids, $10,000 was secured for a Drill Hall in 1889. This caused great rejoicing. During the year the students purchased and placed in the Drill Hall $125 worth of gymnastic apparatus, the money being for the most part the proceeds of an athletic entertainment given the year before in Champaign. Those who at that time wished to practice in the gymnasium paid 50 cts. a term for a ticket, and with the money so secured, instructors were employed from among the students. At the next General Assembly, Regent Peabody, almost unaided by others connected with the University, succeeded in winning sufficiently the good will of the legislators to cause the passage of a bill carrying $70,000 for a new Natural History building.

[1] Alumni Quarterly, Vol. V, No. 3, July, 1910, Makers of the Univ., by T. J. Burrill, p. 211.

[2] Rep. of Univ. of Ill., 1882, p. 182.

[3] Rep. of Univ. of Ill., 1888, p. 211.

Trustees Made Elective

In 1887, a law was passed making membership in the Board of Trustees elective, at a general state election, and restoring the Superintendent of Public Instruction as an *ex officio* member, thus there are today three *ex officio* and nine elective members of the Board. The change in the manner of election helped materially to bring the institution before the people of the state. It also made it possible for women to serve on the Board. None became members, however, until November, 1904, when Mrs. Lucy L. Flower was elected. It is interesting to note that she received many times the number of votes that have been cast for any other woman as a candidate for office in this state.[1] While she was the first woman regularly elected a member of the Board, Mrs. Julia Holmes Smith served a short time before her, having been appointed by the Governor to fill an unexpired term.

Sale of Nebraska Lands

In 1884 the opportunity seemed favorable to begin the sale of the 9,000 acres of land located in Nebraska, and by judicious management the endowment fund was thus raised from about $320,000 to upwards of $450,000.[2] The sale of this land stretched out over a period of twenty-five years, the last being sold only in 1909. The sale of the land in Minnesota began at a somewhat later date, and all is now sold. The total endowment fund received by the University up to June 1, 1916, from the sale of its land scrip amounted to $649,012.91. The pressing need for funds and the dislike for paying taxes upon this land caused much of it to be sold at a very low price.

· Agricultural Experiment Station Founded

In 1887 the federal government again took up the work it had begun in 1862. By the passage of the Hatch Act, approved March 12 of that year, the national government appropriated $15,000 per annum to each state for the purpose of establishing and maintaining, in connection with the colleges founded upon the congressional act of 1862, agricultural experiment stations "to aid in acquiring and diffusing among the people of the United States useful and practical information to subjects connected with agriculture, and to promote scientific investi-

[1] Minutes of Board of Education of Chicago, June 28, 1911.
[2] Rep. of Univ. of Ill., 1888, p. 211.

South Campus and South Farm Today

gation and experiment respecting the principles and application of agricultural science." President Peabody took a prominent part in the discussion of the convention which led to the passage of this act. Under its provision, the Agricultural Experiment Station of Illinois was founded in 1888 and placed under the direction of the trustees of the university, and a part of the university farm, with buildings, was assigned for its use. State appropriations have been added to the federal grants to the Station, until its revenues have become the largest of those of similar institutions throughout the world.[1]

In 1890, by another measure known as the Morrill College Aid Act,[2] the Congress of the United States made further appropriations for the land grant colleges. Under this enactment each such college or university received the first year $15,000, the second $16,000, and thereafter $1,000 a year additional to the amount of the preceding year, until the amount reached $25,000, which sum was to be paid yearly. The use of this fund, although restricted, made possible indirectly a considerable development in the humanities as well as in the natural sciences.

Present Name Adopted

As the institution developed, the name "Illinois Industrial University" was felt to be a serious handicap. It was never understood in the sense originally intended. The promoters had meant to establish an institution in which a liberal education should be offered, and one which should be particularly suited to those engaged in Industrial pursuits, in distinction to the profession as they were then recognized. But the prevailing impression gained for the name was that manual labor was a prominent feature. The name came to be considered a serious obstacle to the institution, and a bill was introduced in the Legislature of 1885 for its change. The application for a change of name met with bitter opposition, especially in the senate, many of the opponents contending that the change would be detrimental to the "industrial ideas of the early advocates." But on June 19, 1885, Governor Oglesby approved the bill changing the name to "The University of Illinois."

In this same year the State Laboratory of Natural History was transferred to the University from Normal. This laboratory was created for the purpose of making a natural history survey of the state, publishing the results, and furnishing specimens to the public schools and to the

---

[1] Univ. of Register, 1911-12, p. 449.

[2] Act approved August 30, 1890, in Laws of U. S. and State of Ill., Concerning the Univ. of Ill.

state museums. These collections amounted to 75,000 specimens, in round numbers, besides 15,000 bottles, vials, and other packages, the contents of which were largely unclassified. The apparatus transferred with this material consisted chiefly of a very full outfit of collecting apparatus for both terrestrial and aquatic work and a considerable amount of microscopic materials and apparatus.

During the régime of Dr. Peabody, knowledge of the University was spread among the people of the state principally by means of addresses and exhibits. It has been estimated that during 1888 alone over 100 gatherings were attended by members of the faculty and more than 200 addresses were delivered. The most notable of the technical exhibitions were kept on display, as follows: six months at the State House in Springfield; sixteen months at the expositions at New Orleans; at the great educational displays at Madison, Wisconsin, and Chicago; and at the state fairs.[1]

Resignation of Dr. Peabody

Many things conspired to make Dr. Peabody's office a hard one to administer. Matters of discipline, disturbances in the cadet battalion and a radical change in the personnel of the Board were circumstances which so strengthened the opposition to the regent as to defeat his re-election in 1891 for the next biennial period. In June he offered his resignation, which was at once accepted. That he succeeded as well as he did is evidence of great personal and professional power among men and of exalted devotion to the cause he espoused.

Dr. Thomas J. Burrill

Upon his resignation the Board temporarily appointed a man who had made his life a part of the University and who through the varying fortunes of the institution had filled many important and critical gaps, Dr. Thomas Jonathan Burrill. He first came to the University as a special assistant to teach algebra, on the agreement that as soon as botany could be provided for, he should have charge of it. Three months after his first connection with the institution, T. J. Burrill became Assistant Professor of Natural History, which at that time included botany. He became full Professor of Botany and Horticulture in 1871. His professorship began at "sun up" and lasted indefinitely and included anything that needed doing. He taught most of the day,

---

[1] Rep. of Univ. of Ill., 1888, p. 221.

planted with his own hands or saw to the planting of most of the trees on the campus, wrote reports, lectured here and there, served on innumerable committees, collected specimens up and down the state, and was even charged at one time by the Board with the sale of a pair of mules, whose labors on the South Farm showed that they were not so able to stand the strenuous life as he was. After the founding of the Agricultural Experiment Station in 1888, Professor Burrill became its horticulturist.

In 1875 Dr. Burrill became the corresponding secretary of the Board of Trustees, a position he held for thirteen years. In 1878 he was appointed Dean of the College of Science, and for a brief time was acting regent. When the regency changed in 1880, he filled the place temporarily. Four years later when the head of the University was absent for a brief time on University business he was made presiding officer. Upon the resignation of Dr. Peabody in 1891, Dr. Burrill began an indefinite interregnum. Almost his first undertaking was to organize the military department, which had caused a great deal of trouble in preceding years. He effected such an organization that it has never caused any trouble since.

Students were allowed greater freedom and responded with greater sanity of conduct. Everywhere a better spirit grew up. The old fixed courses of study were abolished and substantially our present system evolved. In September, 1891, the Board passed the following resolution with regard to fraternities:

"Resolved, That the pledge hitherto required for candidates for entry to the University in regard to college fraternities be omitted, and that the subject of these fraternities be referred to the committee on rules."

DR. BURRILL'S ADMINISTRATION

During Dr. Burrill's administration,. the attendance rapidly increased. Student organizations were stimulated. We find the first University Glee Club organized in October, 1891. The first annual concert of the Illinois Military Band was given in February, 1892. Besides there were organized the Mandolin Club, Chemistry Club, Art Club, Students' Assembly for "Social and Intellectual Purposes," etc.

But perhaps the point of greatest triumph in his administration was the finances. The Board had been accustomed to ask support for the University in a most modest way, and the result was that it had been doled out to them in 50-cent pieces. Dr. Burrill advocated asking for everything wanted, leaving the Legislature to cut down the request if it saw fit. From the appeal to the Legislature in 1893 came the appropriation for the engineering building, and greatly increased sums for other expenses. The total appropriation rose from $147,000 to $295,000.[1]

NEW COURSES OF STUDY CREATED

Several new courses of study had their origin in this period, such as the Graduate School, as well as the School of Philosophy and Pedagogy, included in the College of Literature and Arts; the department of Municipal and Sanitary Engineering and Architectural Engineering were likewise created. In January, 1893, the agricultural short course was offered. The office of Registrar was created August 16th. of the same year, and the appointment of W. L. Pillsbury was made. In 1894 an appropriation of $1,800 was made for a biological station at Havana and $1,200 for a summer school at the University. The first summer session began the following June and continued four weeks; thirty-eight persons were enrolled, twenty-six of whom were teachers from over the state. Members of the regular faculty gave the instruction and the full resources of the University, laboratories, libraries, and apparatus made available for the work.

Although the preparatory class served as an important feeder for the university it was not the intention of the governing boards that this class should be largely increased. In March, 1894, however, the Board established a two years' course in the preparatory school. Preparatory classes had been taught almost from the beginning of the institution, but with the anticipation that the time would soon come when such instruction might be wholly left to the high schools. If it had seemed possible, the University authorities would gladly have abandoned the preparatory work, but if, as it appeared, it must be continued, better provision had to be made for it. Hence, a principal was appointed, teachers were employed, and a course of instruction mapped out.

While the faculty confined itself in the main to undergraduate instruction, the graduate department was slowly taking shape. The first fellowships were instituted in 1892, and in 1894 the faculty was authorized to define the requirements for doctors' degrees.

The University gradually extended its relations with the public school system of the state through its accredited schools, and also by the aid of the county superintendents who conducted examinations for scholarships, and by its course of University extension lectures. A

[1] Alumni Quarterly, Vol. II, October, 1908, Makers of the Univ., by C. M. Moss, p. 229.

great change came over the state in its attitude toward the University. Dr. Burrill's policy was one of open discussion, friendly co-operation with all educational and other interests of the state, and had much to do with allaying opposition on all sides.

HIGHEST HONOR TO DR. BURRILL

Forty-four years is a long time to serve an institution, and when that service has been rendered with faithfulness, kindly benevolence, and utter unselfishness, the institution should certainly honor the man. Accordingly, at the 41st commencement, the University conferred upon Dr. Burrill the highest honor that it can give—the honorary degree of doctor of laws. Although Dr. Burrill retired from active duty Sept. 1, 1912, he retained his office in the Natural History Building to the time of his death, the institution having still the benefit of the counsel of this superior man whose visions were not even then of the past University, but of the future.

PRESIDENT ANDREW S. DRAPER

Various causes delayed action in electing a new Regent after the departure of President Peabody, but it was felt that the important thing was to find the right man, no matter how much time it might require. Finally after three years of inquiry and discussion, the Board tendered the appointment, April 13, 1894, to Andrew Sloan Draper of New York. The title of regent as applied to the chief executive of a collegiate institution was found to be confusing, since the term was generally used for a member of the board of control—a trustee. The legislative enactment founding the University designated the executive by this name and it was so used from that time up to the appointment of Dr. Draper. With his appointment the Board of Trustees gave authority for the title "President" to be used instead of the title "Regent" as given in the University charter. The time fixed for the beginning of Dr. Draper's services was August 1, 1894, and upon that date he assumed the duties of this office.

The third president of the University was of sturdy New England stock. He was born June 21, 1848, at Westford, New York. He was educated for the profession of law in the Albany Law School of Union College, graduating in 1871. For nearly a dozen years after his graduation in law, he practiced his profession. He was a member of the New York State Legislature in 1881, a judge of the United States

Court of Alabama Claims from 1884 to 1886, and State Superintendent of Public Instruction from 1886 to 1892. He received the honorary degree of laws from Colgate in 1889, from Columbia in 1903, and from the University of Illinois in 1905.[1] For two years previous to his coming to the University he .was superintendent of the public schools of Cleveland, Ohio.

President Draper did not aspire to the presidency of the University. He was sought out by the Board. He says, "I had serious misgivings about the advisability of accepting the post. I doubted my adaptability to it." The fact that he was not a university man caused him to ' hesitate. While for a long time he had followed educational thought, he had not concerned himself much about college and university work. But his wide experience with men, in politics and educational work, and his ability as an organizer, aided greatly in his management of University affairs.

President Draper early sided with the many friends of the University who felt that, while the institution was organized primarily to educate people for industrial vocations, it was not doing its whole duty as long as its efforts were confined within these limits. Conferences were held with the trustees and faculties as to the best means of beginning departments of law, medicine, and teaching. The result of this activity was that during his administration the University organized and established a number of new schools and departments.

SCHOOLS OF PHARMACY AND MEDICINE, CHICAGO

The first new school was that of Pharmacy. The Chicago College of Pharmacy made a proposition to turn over and donate its school and property to the University on the provision that it be maintained as a part of the University of Illinois. The Board accepted the proposition at its April meeting, 1896,[2] and on May 1, this College became the School of Pharmacy.

Negotiations looking toward the affiliation of the College of Physicians and Surgeons of Chicago with the University, which had been going on for several years, were concluded by the Board of Trustees March 9, 1897.[3]

On April 21, 1897, it became the School of Medicine of the University of Illinois. It had been one of the foremost of such schools of

---

[1] Who's Who in America, 1908-09, Vol. V, p. 530.

[2] Rep. of Univ. of Ill., 1898, p. 238.

[3] Rep. of Univ. of Ill., 1898, p. 74.

the Middle West. Its buildings were substantially constructed and its location directly opposite the Cook County Hospital, and in the very center of opportunities for medical research, gave the students unusual clinical privileges. The first year there were 409 registered at this medical college.

School of Law and State Library School

The organization of a School of Law was a matter which had long been in the minds of the authorities, and nearly two years previous to the opening of the School, the Board of Trustees had determined that the step should be taken. Pursuant to their action of Dec. 8, 1896,[1] the School of Law was organized and instruction began September 13, 1897. The formal opening was through a public meeting held in the chapel of the University, which was addressed by Justice Jacob W. Wilkin of the Supreme Court of the state. The faculty of the School of Law has been composed from the beginning of professors devoting their entire time to instruction, and of other professors who taught related subjects in the University, such as constitutional law, the history of jurisprudence, and non-resident lecturers. The course of study at first covered two years, but a very short time later it was rearranged on the three-year basis. On February 9, 1900, the School of Law became the College of Law; and on the same date the School of Medicine became the College of Medicine.[2]

In 1897, the School of Library Economy which had been established in 1893 at the Armour Institute of Technology in Chicago was transferred to the University; the director of that school was appointed librarian of the University Library; and the State Library School was opened. There were but three other such schools in the country and no other west of the Allegheny Mountains. In 1897 admission to the school was made requisite upon two years of college work.

From time to time some slight provision had been made for musical instruction and in 1895 the work had been reorganized and enlarged. By vote of the trustees on June 9, 1897, the department became the School of Music with a separate faculty and organization.[3] Instruction was given in violin, piano, and voice, and a course was offered leading to the degree of bachelor of music.

---

[1] Rep. of Univ. of Ill., 1898, p. 44.
[2] Rep. of Univ. of Ill., 1900, p.. 254.
[3] Rep. of Univ. of Ill., 1898, pp. 124, 125.

1—18·

DEAN OF WOMEN'S DEPARTMENT

The adequate supervision of social interests was felt to require distinct administrative attention, and at the March meeting, 1897, the Board of Trustees created a Dean of Women's Department and appointed a dean in the person of Dr. Violet D. Jayne of Minneapolis, Minnesota.[1] Events proved the selection to be a wise one. In 1901, a similar measure was adopted with reference to male students, by the appointment of Professor Thomas Arkle Clark, Dean of Undergraduates, who served in this capacity until 1909, when he became Dean of Men.

In 1899 some additional courses were offered in railway engineering. Two years before this the Big Four Railway Company had built a dynamometer car for the use of the University upon its system, and in 1900 the Illinois Central Railroad did the same thing, and decided improvements were made upon the first car offered.

SUMMER SESSION ESTABLISHED

In the summer of 1899 the University made an earnest effort to establish the summer session. Some such efforts had been made years before, but without much success. It secured the attendance of 148 students during a term of nine weeks. The work was satisfactorily initiated and the results were considered quite substantial. The work offered was largely of a character which would appeal to teachers in the high schools of the state, and persons of this class responded in considerable numbers. Students were allowed to do work which might count towards a University degree, and many availed themselves of the privilege.

The work of the State Entomologist's office had been done at the University of Illinois since January, 1885. By legislative enactment in 1899 it became permanently established at the University, the trustees of which are required by that act to provide for the Entomologist and his assistants such office and laboratory rooms as may be necessary to the performance of their duties.

COLLEGE OF DENTISTRY ORGANIZED

On March 12, 1901,[2] a College of Dentistry was organized as a department in the College of Medicine. In the following fall the school opened with an enrollment of 134 students.

---

[1] Rep. of Univ. of Ill., 1898, p. 65.
[2] Rep. of Univ. of Ill., 1902, p. 54ff.

School of Commerce and Engineering Experiment Station

The General Assembly in 1900 made an appropriation for the establishment of courses of training for business, and, in accordance with that action, the trustees approved the organization of the Courses in Business Administration (frequently given elsewhere under the name of School of Commerce). The department opened in 1902 with two new professors, one called from Yale, and the other from Tome Institute.

One year later the special appropriation by Congress to the state made possible the founding of the Engineering Experiment Station. Within its scope were embraced several problems connected with architecture, and civil, electrical, mechanical, and sanitary engineering. The quarters were in the University buildings and shops.

President Draper's Administration

President Draper managed in a large degree to put the University in a more favorable light before the people of the state, who in many cases had looked upon it with disfavor or with indifference. One of the menaces of the University's power to do good was the claim often made through the secular newspapers of the state that there was little religious spirit in the University. President Draper early began placing the facts before the people to show that this was untrue. Statistics from the Young Men's and Young Women's Christian Associations refuted these charges; greater efforts were made by the several church denominations; and near the end of his administration the percentage of men and women who were parties to the great Student Volunteer Movement for Christian Missions was shown to be greater than in any other state institution.

President Draper overcame much of the opposition which had existed in a measure between the University and other colleges of the state by showing in addresses and papers that all of these colleges and the state's big school were needed to do the work which should be done.

The increase in attendance at the University during the decade from 1894 to 1904 was marvelous. The attendance at Urbana increased from 750 in 1893-4 to 3,100 in 1902-3, and during the latter year there were about 900 in the Chicago departments. The number of instructors increased proportionately. Especially striking was the growth of the College of Agriculture. In the early nineties the attendance of regularly matriculated students had almost reached the vanishing point, a result due partly to defective equipment and partly to the prevailing skepticism among the farmers themselves with regard to the possibilities of scientific instruction in agriculture. During this period new interest sprang up, the appropriations increased, and in 1903, for the first time, there came to the University a substantial number of agricultural students.

Not only were the appropriations increased for the College of Agriculture, but there was also a general increase throughout the University. For the biennium commencing July 1, 1895, the appropriation for the general current expense was $180,000, and for the following two-year periods, respectively, $220,000; $270,000; $350,000; and $500,000; making a total in ten years of $1,520,000.[1] In addition to these increased appropriations for current expenses, there were large appropriations for buildings.

Library and Agricultural Buildings Completed

The Library building, dedicated at commencement in 1897, was occupied in the September following. It was both designed and constructed by graduates of the University of Illinois. The interior decorations were made by Newton A. Wells, and it is said that they present the best example of a pure Byzantine style to be found in the United States. The architects were Professors N. Clifford Ricker and James M. White. A new Astronomical Observatory was completed, equipped, and occupied. Under the dome a fine twelve-inch telescope was erected by the foremost telescope builders in the United States. Another important addition to the group of University buildings was the Electrical Engineering building located just north of Engineering Hall; and the Central Heating Plant located to the east of the Electrical building—both designed by professors in the department of Architecture. All the University buildings are heated by the Central Heating Plant. The pipes are carried in brick tunnels a third of a mile in length and large enough to enable a person walking erectly to pass through them.

At the close of the year 1900, the main group of agricultural buildings was completed on the South Campus, from an appropriation of $150,000. This was the first time the state had expended any considerable amount of money to provide an agricultural plant.

Other buildings erected during President Draper's administration were a new wood shop on the site of the old one which had been burned, a president's house, a splendid gymnasium, an excellent building for applied mechanics, a testing laboratory, and University water station.

[1] Alumni Quarterly, Vol. IV, April, 1910, p. 99.

The Library of the University

South of the Science building a substantial and capacious chemical laboratory was constructed. The old chemical laboratory was remodeled and given over to the College of Law. The building of the College of Medicine in Chicago was largely reconstructed, and the West Division high school property was also acquired and put into excellent condition. In 1897 a new gymnasium was installed on the upper floor of the old mechanical building. It was not ideal in appearance, but was adequately equipped and well suited for practical use. It was provided with a very satisfactory equipment of lockers, and also with reasonable toilet and bathing accommodations. Illinois field was considerably enlarged and much improved in appearance. The unsightly board fence was removed and a handsome iron one put in its place. The running track was enlarged so as to be a full third of a mile in length.

The Legislature of 1903 made provision for the establishment of the Woman's building, three agricultural buildings, a foundry, and a steam laboratory.

A new greenhouse was constructed and occupied opposite the new electrical building, and added an attractive feature to the University grounds. In connection with the Electrical building and the Central Heating Plant there was installed and put into operation an electric lighting plant. It supplied arc lights upon the campus and also incandescent lights in the buildings which are wired for the purpose.

Two Buildings Struck by Lightning

Lightning struck the chemical building in August, 1896. The roof and practically the whole of the interior of the building were destroyed. Nothing remained but the four walls. Steps were at once taken to renew the roof and the interior was replaced in a very hasty, rough and unsubstantial manner because of lack of time and funds to do the work properly. A year later, in June, 1897, the Natural History building was struck by lightning. The results were not so serious as with the chemical laboratory, but fire followed and not only the roof but also the upper portions of the interior, and the building and its contents, were seriously injured by water. The damage to the latter building was repaired in time to prevent any interruption of University work.

On June 9, 1900, the oldest building on the campus, which accommodated the wood shops, testing laboratory, hydraulic laboratory, repair shops, and gymnasium was totally destroyed by fire. The building was an old one, yet substantial and exceedingly useful, and housed important interests.

Perhaps the event which caused the most concern on the part of the administration was the defalcation of the treasurer in February, 1897. All the cash balances of the several funds were involved. All the appropriations had been collected from the State Treasurer to the end of the year, and there were no means which could be applied to salaries and other expenses. Fortunately the Legislature was in session and official notice was brought to the attention of that body, which came to the relief of the University by assuming charge of the whole matter and restoring the funds completely.

President Draper showed the keenest personal interest in students and student activities. The united action of the students in all important measures to be advanced, the kindly and frank treatment of each other in their personal and class relations, and the hearty and loyal support of all University interests were immense factors in the control and enlargement of the institution. The adoption of orange and blue as the University colors by the general assembly of students within a month after the beginning of the administration was a step in this direction. Encouragement was given to athletics by the employment of coaches and instructors in the department, and were made more popular by the president's attendance upon the games. The grounds were beautified and made attractive by making open spaces for sward, the paving of walks and drives, and the planting of a colony of squirrels upon the campus.

While President Draper stood for what furnished students social and physical enjoyment, at the same time he was a rigid disciplinarian. The enforcement of authority has been made easier down to the present time because of President Draper's successful stand in administering justice after a certain class riot, which occasioned considerable difficulty.

Dr. Draper resigned in March, 1904, his resignation taking effect after two months' leave of absence, thus practically rounding out ten years of service. They were a splendid ten years for the University of Illinois. Things were favorable when he began. The excellent opportunity for the chief executive was turned to the best account. He quickly appreciated the situation and with abundant forcefulness and admirable generalship, carried the institution forward in its remarkable career. Having been elected to the newly created office of Commissioner of Education in the state of New York, he gave up his work in Illinois with abundantly demonstrated evidences of its success during the ten years of his presidency.

Dr. Edmund J. James Succeeds President Draper

On November 5, 1904, Dr. Edmund Janes James, the fourth president of the University, assumed the duties of that office. His formal installation took place in October of the following year. On this occasion delegates were present from a large number of American and foreign universities, making the exercises of unusual interest. Perhaps one of the most striking features was a series of conferences on various questions of educational policy.

President James is the first native of Illinois to be elected to the presidency of its state university. Moreover, he has served the two other great universities of the state, having presided over Northwestern for a time and having been for six years a professor in the University of Chicago. He was born May 24, 1855, at Jacksonville, Ill., and is a descendant of a pioneer Methodist minister. He prepared for college in the Model Department of the Illinois State Normal School and in the fall following his graduation there, became a student at Northwestern University. After spending one year at this institution and one year at Harvard, he entered the University of Halle in 1875, where two years later, at the age of twenty-two, he received his doctor's degree. He first taught as principal of the high school at Evanston, going from there to accept a similar position in the High School Department of the Illinois Normal University. In 1883 he became Professor of Public Administration in the University of Pennsylvania. While there he was for a time secretary of the graduate faculty and organized the instruction in this department. He was also Director of the Wharton School of Finance and Economy.

In 1896 he accepted a position as Professor of Public Administration and Director of the University Extension Division in the University of Chicago. Six years later he resigned this position to become President of Northwestern University, and in 1904 he again resigned his position in order to accept a similar one at the University of Illinois.

He received the honorary degree LL. D. from Cornell College (Iowa) in 1902, from Wesleyan, 1903, Queen's College, 1903, Harvard, 1909, and Michigan and Northwestern in 1914.

The progress of the University during the last few years has been rapid and uninterrupted. Opportunities for advanced work in nearly every department of the University have been materially increased. Perhaps the organization of the Graduate School as a separate administrative body was a step which aided most greatly along this line. The Legislatures of 1907 and 1909 appropriated for the work of the school

EDMUND J. JAMES

a sum of $50,000 a year. This was a step unprecedented in the history of state universities and the act was warmly welcomed by educational authorities.

Hand in hand with graduate work goes the necessity for a strong library. While not yet all that can be desired, the University library has grown rapidly. The number of volumes in 1904 was 63,724, and the number of pamphlets, 14,512; while on June 1, 1917, the general University library, including Chicago departments with 21,389 books, 4,195 pamphlets and 8 maps, contained 397,710 volumes, and 102,029 pamphlets, 4,123 pieces of sheet music, 3,188 maps, and a file of photographs.

School of Commerce Building

The courses in Business Administration were established in a modest way in 1900. Five years later an effort was made to put the work on a better basis, and the legislature gave the School an annual income of $25,000. Since that time it has become one of the strongest in the country. The legislature recognized the importance to the state of this department in the substantial way of making an appropriation for a commerce building, the cornerstone of which was laid March 21, 1912.

The department of Household Science assumed a notable position when in 1910, for the first time in any university, it offered a complete four-year course in household management, as distinguished from Household Science.

The College of Literature and Arts and the College of Science were consolidated July 1, 1913, thus eliminating unnecessary duplications and increasing exceedingly the efficiency of these departments. The new college is making a definite effort not only for the promotion of research, but also toward the uplifting of secondary education by giving to prospective teachers opportunities for higher work and better preparation.

School of Education Created

During the year 1905, the trustees created a School of Education. In some respects this was a grouping of the courses in the University which pertained most directly to the future work of the teacher. All instructors who offer courses primarily for prospective teachers are on the faculty of this school. In framing its organization, the presidents of the normal schools of the state were consulted, and their advice has proved most helpful on many important points.

School of Ceramics

The Legislature in 1905 made the small appropriation of $5,000 for the establishment of courses in ceramics, in response to a request from the various ceramic societies of the state, who asked that the University give thorough and reliable instruction in the geology of clay working materials, their origin, classification, physical and chemical properties, and their behavior under such influences as are met with during the processes of manufacture. Courses in ceramics and ceramic engineering, supplemented by a course in cement making, were organized and have become regular four-year courses in the College of Science. It is a School which has proved itself of much benefit to the people of the state in a number of ways. It has found a method of making high grade brick and tile from material before regarded as worthless. It has shown, in the manufacture of enamel brick, that Illinois clays may be used more profitably than those of other states. It has compounded a white and cheaper grade of stoneware. It has given to the people formulæ for compounding crystalline and fritted glazes which rereto fore had been kept secret.

State Geological and Water Surveys

In the same year the State Geological Survey and the State Water Survey became scientific departments connected with the University. The Legislature created the State Geological Survey as a bureau of the University, with the objects and duties usual to such surveys. The University has furnished suitable quarters for the offices of this survey, and it has found in the laboratories of the University a most valuable assistance in the prosecution of its work. The presence in the University of men of the scientific standing of those engaged in the Survey has been of very substantial, though indirect value to the scientific advance in these various subjects. The State Water Survey had for its purpose the study of the water supply of the state in all its aspects. Its work has been both in the field and in the laboratories.

The College of Agriculture and the Experiment Station have produced a profound influence upon the farming practice of the state in the last ten years.

The main contribution of the College of Engineering, in the same period, as distinguished from what it has done hitherto, probably lies in the stimulus given to industrial research through the Engineering Experiment Station. As the work and purposes of the Station have become better understood in the state, the officers in charge have been flooded with applications for help.

School of Railway Engineering

On January 30, 1906, the Board of Trustees created a department of Railway Engineering. One year later, supplementing that action, the School of Railway Engineering and Administration was established. This School offers courses in railway, civil, electrical, and mechanical engineering as well as in management.

A Mine Rescue Station was established at the University in 1909. It is in cooperation with the State Geological Survey and the College of Engineering of the University. Its purpose is to demonstrate to mine operators and others the value of oxygen helmets and resuscitation apparatus in connection with rescue work in mines, as an aid to fighting mine fires, and in the opening of mines which have been sealed on account of fires. The Station not only gives demonstration but also undertakes to train men in the use of such apparatus, the service being given gratuitously.

General Property Tax for University

June 13, 1911, a bill was passed providing for a one mill tax on each dollar of the assessed valuation of all the property of the state for the support of the University. On the present taxing basis, the law should yield about two and one-quarter million dollars a year. This sum is not automatically appropriated to University uses, although it can be used for no other purpose. This means that the ambitious interests within the University will reach an agreement on the campus; the budget will be made here; and the united requests, within the sum available, can be presented as a unit to the legislative committee. The one mill tax puts the regular support of the University upon a safer foundation, and assures a regular income. No other event in the history of the institution is more important than the passage of this bill.

Improvement in Chicago Departments

The Chicago departments of the University have undergone a considerable improvement and reorganization in the past few years. Because of failure to receive appropriations for the operation of its medical department, the University was compelled to close it June 30, 1912. The College of Physicians and Surgeons again opened a school on the same site. This caused such consternation among medical alumni and friends of medical education in Illinois that they proceeded to secure the capital stock of the College of Physicians and Surgeons and then presented it to the trustees of the University. The College of Medicine was then re-opened March 6, 1913. A vigorous policy of expansion and development followed. The equipment has been perfected and brought down to date, and the entrance requirements have been raised to a par with those of the best medical schools of the United States. The College of Medicine has graduated 3,206 students and enrolled a total of 10,824. The dental department, which was closed at the same time as the medical department and for the same reasons, was reopened October 1, 1913. The College of Dentistry has also undergone considerable development within the last few years, as well as the School of Pharmacy.

The College of Agriculture is now organized with the following departments: Agronomy, Animal Husbandry, Dairy Husbandry, Horticulture, Veterinary Science and Household Science.

GROWTH OF COLLEGE OF AGRICULTURE, 1890-1917

The following table gives the registration of students and the size of the faculty since 1890.

Year.	Students Registered.	Faculty.	Year.	Students Registered.	Faculty.
1890-91	7	3	1904-05	406	37
1891-92	6	3	1905-06	430	44
1892-93	13	3	1906-07	462	50
1893-94	5	3	1907-08	528	61
1894-95	9	3	1908-09	531	63
1895-96	14	3	1909-10	660	74
1896-97	17	6	1910-11	720	74
1897-98	19	8	1911-12	829	100
1898-99	25	9	1912-13	905	120
1899-00	90	16	1913-14	1,014	137
1900-01	159	17	1914-15	1,184	149
1901-02	232	23	1915-16	1,255	153
1902-03	284	27	1916-17	1,202	153
1903-04	339	37			

THE MILITARY DEPARTMENT

The military department of the University has developed in harmony with the spirit of the Land Grant Act of 1862 until today the University has the largest student enrollment in military of any college in the United States and probably in the world. October 30, 1915, the trustees authorized the creation of a battery of field artillery, which has already become well organized. All freshmen and sophomores are required to take the work. The Cadet Brigade consists of two regiments of infantry (24 companies), a foot battery of field artillery, signal corps, engineer company and hospital company (consisting of sopho- mores). There are 2,279 cadets including the band of 165 men and 113 commissioned officers. By virtue of his position the president of the University is the Colonel of the Cadet Brigade. A School of Mili- tary Aeronautics was opened at the University May 21, 1917, in co- operation with the United States government and in the summer of 1917 enrolled about 200 cadets.

LIBRARY SCHOOL

The Library School was transferred to the University of Illinois from Armour Institute, Chicago, in September, 1897, two years of col- lege work being required for entrance; in 1903 this requirement was raised to three years, and in 1911, to four years of college work. The school draws graduates from colleges and universities in all parts of the United States, and its graduates receive appointments to libraries in all sections of the United States.

Two hundred and sixty-eight students have completed the two years of work and have received the degree of Bachelor of Library Science; two hundred and eighty-seven others have completed the first year's work. About four hundred are now engaged in library work.

THE GRADUATE SCHOOL

Although for many years the University of Illinois has offered advanced students facilities for study and research in various lines, graduate work was undertaken under the name of the Graduate School for the first time in 1892. In 1894 the administration of the school was vested in the council of administration, and the vice-president of the university became dean of the school. In 1906 the Graduate School was organized as a separate faculty, consisting of a dean and members of the university faculty assigned to this duty by the president. No means of support were provided, however, separate from those provided for undergraduate work. In the winter of 1906-07 the Forty-fifth Gen- eral Assembly of the State passed an act appropriating $50,000 per year for the support of a Graduate School of Fine Arts and Sciences in the State University. This is the first time in history when a State Legislature has made a specified appropriation for such a purpose, and the act is noteworthy as committing a democratic government definitely to the promotion of advanced scholarship and research in lines which are not primarily practical. This appropriation has been continued by succeeding Legislatures, and has enabled the university to carry on valuable investigations for the State and promote the world's knowledge, thereby bettering the quality of instruction and establishing the reputation of the university in the world of scholarship. One of the strongest evidences of educational progress of any university lies in the increased estimation in which she is held by her sister institutions throughout the country. Dean Kinley, in writing of this, said, "Our admission to the Association of American Universities and the consequent recognition of our graduate work by foreign universities, expressions of opinion in the newspapers and magazines and personally by distinguished educators, are all cumulative evidence that we have advanced to a higher educational plane in the opinion of those most able to judge."

At the present time the School of Pharmacy is the only department of the university which does not require full standard high school preparation for admission to the university. After September 1, 1916, by action of the board of trustees, the College of Pharmacy required the usual fifteen high school units.

General Progress in Teaching and Student Strength

With the increased appropriations and the increased attendance has also come a material strengthening of the teaching force. Salaries of men of professional rank have been increased 50 per cent, and distinguished scholars have been brought to the university from all over the world. The standing today consequently of the faculty of the University of Illinois is indicated by the fact that in the 1903 edition of Who's Who in America there were thirty-four names of members of the faculty of the University of Illinois, while the edition of 1916-17 gives a list of 105, a gain of about 200 per cent. Similarly in the 1906 edition of the American Men of Science there were six members of the faculty of the University of Illinois among the 1,000 greatest scholars of the country, while in 1910 the number had increased to seventeen.

With the growth and variety of university interests, the problem of administration became more and more complicated. While in the early days matters of discipline were settled by the faculty, and if unsatisfactory, carried to the board of trustees, at the present time the council of administration, which is made up of the president, vice-president and the deans, has complete control of discipline. The general faculty has given way to the University Senate, consisting of the members of the council and all full professors; although each college maintains its separate faculty, whose action in important matters requires the ratification of the senate or the council.

Naturally the increased attendance has meant increased activity in all kinds of student life. Fraternities and sororities have almost doubled in number. The installation of a chapter of Phi Beta Kappa, Sigma Xi, Tau Beta Pi, and other honorary organizations, is a tribute of the esteem which sister institutions in the country hold for Illinois. Interest has developed in debate and oratory and at the same time a record has been maintained in athletics of which Illinoisans may be proud. One of the most comprehensive organizations within the university perhaps is the Illinois Union. It came into existence at a mass meeting of the students on March 3, 1909. The union is an organization of all Illinois men, whether graduate, undergraduate or faculty, whose purpose is to develop good fellowship among the students and to promote the Illinois spirit by all possible means. It is hoped that a club building may be erected at an early date and greater co-operation established between the alumni and outgoing students.

One of the sources of strength to any institution is the good will and co-operation of its former students. The interest and pride of the alumni of the University of Illinois in its work seem steadily and plainly to increase. The Alumni Record made its first appearance in 1906 and contained an account of the life and work of each graduate of the institution up to that time, as well as similar accounts of the faculty and trustees. The 1913 publication was an attempt to continue the work, expanding and correcting the biographies. The University of Illinois Directory of 1916 is the first attempt to locate all persons who have ever been connected with the Urbana-Champaign departments, the 35,000 names being arranged both alphabetically and geographically.

The university has grown from 3 teachers and 77 students in 1868 to 840 teachers, 55 administrative officers, a library staff of 50, and 6,828 students in 1917. The most striking development has occurred within the last twenty years. More degrees were conferred annually by the Chicago departments, from the time of their addition to the university up to the year 1907, than by the Urbana departments. In 1903 there were 301 degrees conferred by the Chicago departments, but only 181 in 1904, because of the raising of the standards of the school, while the Urbana departments have increased from 183 in 1902 to 989 in 1917, in spite of the increase of entrance requirements. More degrees were conferred by the Urbana departments of the university in 1917 than were conferred in all the years from 1868 to 1898, twelve times as many as in 1899, and over twice as many as in 1908. Altogether since its foundation the university has conferred 10,440 degrees in the Urbana departments and in all its departments 14,847 degrees. On June 15, 1917, the university conferred 1,166 degrees. The total number of degrees conferred by the university in 1917 represents a larger number than the total attendance at the University of Illinois in any single year prior to 1898, and the number of degrees conferred since 1910 exceeds the number of degrees conferred in the entire previous history of the University of Illinois.

Today the University of Illinois has one of the largest undergraduate departments in America and also has one of the largest enrollments of men students. There are 5,017 undergraduates, of whom 3,812 are men. The total attendance in all departments of the university is 5,187 men and 1,641 women. All of these except about 500 are nine-month students and this fact should be emphasized in all comparative college statistics, where night and Saturday and three-month students are included in the college enrollment.

SUMMARY OF GROWTH, 1903-17

The rapid growth of the University of Illinois, especially during the past decade, is seen especially in the size of its student body and faculty, which have more than doubled, by its land holdings, value of buildings and size of the library, which have nearly trebled. The following table will perhaps present a useful summary:

	Faculty.	Attendance, Urbana.	Attendance, Chicago.	Land, Acres.	Buildings.
1903-04	351	2,674	1,042	641	$1,127,500
1916-17	840[1]	6,757	558	2,483[2]	3,180,635

	Biennial Income.	Library Volumes.	Important Buildings.
1903-04	$1,814,863.78	67,040	12
1916-17	5,622,928.87[3]	397,718[4]	52

IMPORTANT BUILDINGS ERECTED SINCE 1914

Addition to Chemical Laboratory (to May, 1916)	$358,755.00
Stock Judging Pavilion (1914)	110,355.00
Administration Building (1915)	154,715.01
New Armory (1915)	229,119.17

[1] With a total of 868 as at February 21, 1917, omitting all duplicates and including the Chicago departments and administrative officers.

[2] Seven hundred and sixty-nine acres were given by Capt. T. G. Smith on condition that the university would erect a building for the School of Music costing at least $215,000. The figures cited do not include leased land.

[3] Estimated at $6,200,000 for 1915-17.

[4] Excluding pamphlets, etc.

Ceramics (1916) $129,880.50
Vivarium (1916) 55,204.93
Genetics (1916) 11,100.00

From 1908-14

Auditorium	$143,143.58	Physics	$191,300.00
Commerce	97,375.00	Horticultural Glass House..	85,390.00
Lincoln Hall	224,875.00	Transportation.	80,500.00
Natural History	184,200.00	Woman's	194,000.00

Chief Buildings Before 1908

University.Hall (1873).   Agriculture (1900).
Law (1878).   Library (1897).
Engineering (1894).   Gymnasium (1901).

Proposed Buildings

Woman's Residence Hall	$110,000.00	Addition to Natural History	$75,000.00
School of Education	140,000.00	Addition to Transportation.	30,000.00
Smith Music Building	215,000.00	Agricultural buildings	76,000.00
Medicine and Pharmacy	100,000.00		
			$746,000.00

The Smith Music Building is the gift of Capt. Thomas J. Smith in honor of his wife and will supply a great need. It is the first large private gift made to the university. Mr. Homer A. Stillwell (la 1878-80) has made an offer of $25,000 towards the Gregory Memorial Art Building to be erected in honor of the first president, and it is hoped to make this an alumni gift to the university.

Schools and Colleges Reorganized 1906-16

Graduate School (1906).   Colleges of Literature and Arts and
College of Medicine and College of   Sciences consolidated (1913).
   Dentistry (1913).   College of Commerce (1915).

Schools and Departments Added 1905-16

Railway Engineering and Administra-   Mining Engineering (1909).
   tion (1907).   School of Education (1905).
Department of Ceramics (1916).   Mine Rescue Station (1909).
State Geological Survey (1905).   Summer School for Coaches (1914).
Genetics (1912).   Aeronautics (1916).

Dr. Gregory's Prediction

At the time ex-President Gregory came to the University of Illinois, he states in an address at the dedication of University Hall that when he was considering accepting the presidency of the institution and was interviewing friends in Champaign and Chicago, the trustees residing in or near Champaign expressed the generally prevalent faith in the institution, that it was to be "the grandest university on the American continent," and in his concluding remarks at this dedication he says, "Some of those who are here today—the youngest of you, perhaps, that hear my words—shall come here on other anniversary occasions and attend dedications of yet other halls that a great and liberal State, mindful of its own civilization, its own grand central, commanding position—the keystone of the continent—shall consecrate to this great work. Gray-haired and sage, you will recall the memories of this day—you will look still in fancy on this meeting and think on the prediction this day made, in your hearing."

With a State such as Illinois, rich in resources and central in location, realizing its opportunities in its State university, there is every reason to believe that the prediction of its founders will be realized at no distant date.

GROWTH OF UNIVERSITY BY YEARS 1867-1917

Year	Faculty	Students			Degrees		Books	Bldgs.	Biennial Income
		Urbana	Total, Urbana and Chicago	Urbana	Total, Urbana and Chicago				
1867-68...	4	77	....	....	....	....	....	1	$72,753.85
1868-69...	11	128	....	....	....	1,092		1	
1869-70...	19	180	....	....	....	3,646		1	133,278.72
1870-71...	19	278	....	....	....	4,538		1	
1871-72...	24	381	....	20	....	7,307		1	193,102.47
1872-73...	25	400 '	....	14	....	8,427		2	
1873-74...	25	406	....	19	....	10,000		3	123,459.30
1874-75...	30	373	....	37	....	....		3	
1875-76...	27	386	....	28	....	....		3	183,870.11
1876-77...	36	388	....	41	....	....		3	
1877-78...	29	377	....	42	....	....		4	170,999.43
1878-79...	33	416	....	23	....	....		4	
1879-80...	30	434	....	25	....	12,550		3	133,088.89
1880-81...	28	379	....	46	....	....		3	
1881-82...	26	352	....	34	....	13,510		3	129,620.63
1882-83...	24	382	....	36	....	....		3	
1883-84...	25	330	....	42	....	14,000		3	141,032.79
1884-85...	27	362	....	45	....	....		3	
1885-86...	29	332	....	37	....	15,300		3	149,677.77
1886-87...	29	343	....	30	....	....		3	
1887-88...	29	377	....	34	....	17,288		3	180,959.97
1888-89...	30	418	....	26	....	....		3	
1889-90...	32	469	....	43	....	19,000		3	237,178.23
1890-91...	39	519	....	58(9)[1]	....	....		3	
1891-92...	43	583	....	51(9)	....	21,216		4	359,144.14
1892-93...	48	714	....	75(10)	....	....		4	
1893-94...	67	718	....	78(9)	....	....		5	491,940.55
1894-95...	80	810	....	75(1)	....	27,750		6	
1895-96...	84	855	....	82	....	28,200		9	594,938.40
1896-97...	170	878	1,059	95	137	30,100		12	
1897-98...	184	1,034	1,582	89	232	36,990		13	607,632.00
1898-99...	194	1,152	1,824	110	265	41,678		12	
1899-00...	229	1,531	2,260	154(1)	329	44,502		13	947,486.98
1900-01...	242	1,709	2,564	172	388	47,074		15	
1901-02...	279	2,020	3,016	183	484	52,717		18	1,363,716.08

[1] Honorary degrees in parenthesis included in total.

Year	Faculty	Students		Degrees		Books	Bldgs.	Biennial Income
		Urbana	Total, Urbana and Chicago	Urbana	Total, Urbana and Chicago			
1902-03...	316	2,342	3,381	229(11)	525	57,594	18	
1903-04...	351	2,674	3,594	313(9)	628	66,639	19	$1,814,863.78
1904-05...	350	2,779	3,736	270(27)	591	74,326	27	
1905-06...	408	3,225	4,107	313(2)	618	83,136	27	2,166,372.29
1906-07...	442	3,577	4,341	390(3)	608[1]	95,946	28	
1907-08...	472	3,959	4,770	411(3)	624	108,283	32	3,102,761.42
1908-09...	497	4,141	4,966	568	799	127,106	33	
1909-10...	538	4,323	5,131	584(3)	766	157,836	35	3,199,832.54
1910-11...	555	4,401	5,217	602(2)	792	180,371	36	
1911-12...	583	4,340	5,200	646(2)	861	209,529	44	4,294,952.88
1912-13...	587	4,369	5,096	682	845	233,586	46	
1913-14...	704	4,766	5,560	848	1,029	262,926	47	5,622,928.87
1914-15...	739	5,446	6,002	818	983	300,592	53	
1915-16...	762	6,298	6,437	933	1,129	330,895[2]	60[3]	6,278,590.69
1916-17...	840	6,759	6,828[4]	989	1,175	397,710	61	
Total..				10,440	14,847			

ANNALS OF THE UNIVERSITY

A complete record of all matters referring to the university from the passage of the congressional act of July 2, 1862, donating public lands to the states and territories which designed to provide colleges for the benefit of "agriculture and the mechanic arts," up to the very last event of yesterday, has been prepared by the university scribes, and arranged and published, by years, in the 1916 University of Illinois Directory. Lack of space induces the editor of this work to condense from the annals some of the most noteworthy facts, to serve as an addendum to the more connected history.

FIRST MEETING OF THE BOARD (1867)

The first meeting of the University Board of Trustees was held at Springfield, March 12, 1867. Nominations for the position of regent being called for, the names of Hon. Daniel J. Pickney of Ogle County, Dr. N. N. Wood of Morgan County, Hon. J. L. Pickard of Cook County, and Dr. John Milton Gregory of Kalamazoo, Michigan, were proposed. Dr. Gregory was elected and granted a salary of $3,000 a year. A committee of five, with the regent as chairman, was selected to prepare a

---

[1] Seven of these are honorary, being the only literary degrees ever conferred by Chicago Departments.

[2] In addition June 1, 1917, there were 102,029 pamphlets, 4,123 pieces of sheet music, 3,188 maps, and the libraries of the College of Medicine and College of Pharmacy in Chicago contain 17,572 volumes and 3,600 pamphlets.

[3] Four additional buildings in Chicago. Fifty-one of these sixty-four buildings have a valuation in excess of $5,000. Figures as that of May 1, 1916.

[4] Excluding duplicates.

course of study and to report to the board. John W. Bunn of Springfield was elected treasurer, and a finance committee was appointed to serve for one year. Willard C. Flagg of Madison County was elected corresponding secretary; O. B. Galusha of Grundy County, recording secretary. The board passed a resolution favoring the establishment of a mechanical department to be located at Chicago. March 29th—An election was held in Urbana and Champaign to decide whether the two cities should appropriate $45,000 for the university, Champaign to give $25,000; Urbana, $20,000. The vote was as follows: Champaign— For, 676; against, 4. Urbana—For, 406; against, 0.

On March 29th Dr. Gregory visited Champaign and Urbana for the first time, and on April 1st entered upon his duties.

University Open to Students (1868)

On March 2, 1868, the university "opened for the reception of students"—fifty-seven students, two professors and the head farmer the first week. Only three students registered the first day, although they had been urged to present themselves for examination on the first day. Total enrollment for first term, seventy-seven students (all men), with three professors (Thomas J. Burrill being employed later during the term as instructor in botany). Of the seventy-seven students, forty-five came from Champaign County; the rest from nineteen counties of the State. The larger number of the students were of preparatory rather than of university grade. The following departments were organized, classical as well as industrial subjects being offered: I. Science, Literature and Arts; II. Agriculture; III. Mechanical Science and Art; IV. Military Tactics and Engineering; V. Mining and Metallurgy; VI. Civil Engineering; VII. Analytical and Applied Chemistry; VIII. Natural History, Practical Geology, etc.; IX. Commercial Science and Art. The broad plan of organization of Regent Gregory has had a deep influence on the entire history of the university.

The inaugural ceremonies and formal opening of the university occurred March 10, 1868, Hon. S. W. Moulton presiding. The music was under the direction of George F. Root of Chicago, who set to music the dedication hymn, written by Dr. Gregory, as follows:

We hail thee! Great Fountain of learning and light;
There's life in thy radiance, there's hope in thy might
We greet now thy dawning, but what singer's rhyme,
Shall follow thy course down the ages of time?

O'er homes of the millions, o'er rich fields of toil,
Thy science shall shine as the sun shines on soil,
And Learning and Labor—fit head for fit hand—
Shall crown with twin glories our broad prairie land.

And as generations, in the grand march of time,
Shall fill the long ages with numbers sublime,
Thy portals shall throng with the lowly and great
Thy Science-crowned children shall bless all the State.

Then hail thee! blest fountain of labor and light,
Shine on in thy glory, rise ever in might;
We greet now thy dawning; but ages to come
Must tell of the grandeur, and shout Harvest Home.

Letters from Governor Oglesby, Senator Yates and Gen. John A. Logan were read. The principal address was delivered by Newton Bateman, state superintendent of public instruction. General Hurlbut then introduced Dr. Gregory. The exercises were followed by a banquet in the dining hall of the university.

The following extract quoted from Dr. Gregory's inaugural address gives a clear idea of the fundamental plan underlying the pioneer days of the university, which has been developed in detail into a broad present-day system of learning and training: "We shall effect the more formal and more perfect union of labor and learning. These two will be married in indissoluble bonds at our altars. The skilled hand and the thinking brain will be found compatible members of the same body. Science, leaving its seat in the clouds and coming down to work with men in shop and field, will find not only a new stimulus for its studies, but better and clearer light for its investigations and surer tests for its truths. And labor, grown scientific, will mount to richer products as well as easier processes. Thus these two, Thought and Work, which God designed to go together, will no longer remain asunder. Labor itself will be elevated to honor. Labor will be made more productive. Our national power and perpetuity will be greatly promoted. But there remains a grander and a broader triumph than all these. If we succeed, we shall demonstrate the practicability and point out the path of universal education. Let us but demonstrate that the highest culture is compatible with the active pursuit of industry, and that the richest learning will pay in a corn field or a carpenter's shop, and we have made universal education not only a possible possession, but a fated necessity of the race. Prove that education in its highest form will 'pay,' and you have made for it the market of the world."

1870

The Department of Mechanical Engineering was created in February, 1870. In the following August, by a vote of five to four of the trustees, it was decided to admit women to the university. In September, the committee appointed by the various agricultural societies of the State to investigate the rather extensively circulated criticism of the Illinois Industrial University that it was primarily a classical school reported that "it was not."

In September, 1870, student government was adopted. The legislative body consisted of a general assembly elected by a vote of the students. The judicial department was a council of five chosen from the general assembly, and the executive department consisted of a president and vice-president of the government, an adjutant for each building and hall sergeants.

1871

In February, 1871, the first building appropriation for the university was introduced into the Legislature. It provided for $100,000 a year for two years for a main building, and $12,500 a year for two years for a mechanical engineering building, besides $25,000 a year for running expenses, apparatus, etc. As passed in the following month, the bill provided $75,000 for a building to cost not more than $150,000, and $75,000 more was to be appropriated at an adjourned session. This was done and the building was completed at the expense of university funds.

On September 13, 1871, the Drill Hall and the Mechanical Shops were opened and the corner-stone of University Hall was laid. In November appeared "The Student," the first publication to be issued by the students of the university.

1872, 1873, 1874

In February, 1872, was organized the University Young Men's Christian Association; in June the Alumni Association was founded, and in July the board of trustees reaffirmed the basic plan of the university by passing a resolution declaring that agriculture and the mechanic arts were the primary studies of the institution, "all others being secondary."

PRESENT ENGINEERING GROUP OF BUILDINGS

In September, 1873, the name of "The Student" was changed to "The Illini."

University and Adelphi halls were dedicated in December, 1873, and Philomathean Hall in May, 1874.

1876, 1877

A preparatory department was established in March, 1876. In June the board of trustees passed a resolution condemning secret societies "as detrimental to the scheme of self-government attempted by the students."

In March, 1877, the School of Art and Design was established, and in September of that year the chemical laboratory was located and Major Dinwiddie, the first army commandant, took charge of the military department.

1881, 1882

In December, 1881, the regent reported to the board of trustees that the faculty had passed rules providing that no student could enter the university until he had pledged himself not to join a fraternity; and that no student should graduate until he had certified that he had not belonged to any while in the university. The adoption of these rules had disclosed the existence of four societies whose members petitioned the faculty to rescind the rules. The faculty turned the petition over to the board, which recommended that the request be refused. Like petitions presented the following spring met with the same action.

In June, 1882, it was decided to build an astronomical observatory, and in September it was opened.

1884, 1885, 1886, 1887

The Young Women's Christian Association was organized in March, 1884.

In June, 1885, the Legislature changed the name "Illinois Industrial University" to "The University of Illinois." In December of that year the attorney-general of the State sustained the faculty ruling against secret university societies, and although the students had a Chicago lawyer appear before the board of trustees in December and plead the case of the fraternities, the latter body stood behind its original ruling.

In September, 1886, the Legislature passed a bill providing for the popular election of university trustees.

One of the really noteworthy dates—April 23, 1887—the students adopted the old college yell, originated by C. P. Vangundy—"Rah Hoo Rah, Zip Boom Ah, Hip Zoo Ra Zoo, Jimmy blow your bazoo, Ip-sid-di-i-ki, U. of I., Champaign."

1891, 1892, 1893, 1894

A committee of the board of trustees recommended, June 10, 1890, that the preparatory department "be dispensed with as soon as adequate provision for doing its work is made by some public or private institution located in the vicinity of the university."

In September, 1891, the Electrical Engineering Department was established, and in March, 1892. the corner-stone of the Natural History Hall was laid. The board of trustees voted an appropriation for a woman's gymnasium in November, 1892.

The office of registrar was created in September, 1893.

Dr. A. S. Draper was elected regent in April, 1894.

1896, 1897

In August, 1896, the Chemical Laboratory was partially destroyed by fire caused by lightning, loss $40,000. In the following month the corner-stone of the Library Building was laid. In April, 1896, the Chicago College of Pharmacy was affiliated with the university, and in March, 1897, the College of Physicians and Surgeons of Chicago also became by affiliation its Medical Department. In September of the latter year the College of Law was opened.

1899, 1900

The Department of Domestic Science was established in March, 1899; the Christian Association House opened in September of that year; the Department of Pedagogy and School of Household Science was founded in September, 1900, and the Agricultural Building was completed and opened at the same time.

1901-1904

In May, 1901, the Chicago School of Dentistry was affiliated with the University of Illinois.

The University Senate was created in September, 1901. In the following month the Chicago School of Dentistry opened as a department of the university, and in March, 1902, the School of Commerce was organized. The university water works plant was also completed at the date last named.

The new Chemistry Building was opened in September, 1902.

In December, 1903, the Engineering Experiment Station was organized, and the name of the Preparatory Department was changed to the Academy of the University of Illinois.

EDMUND J. JAMES BECOMES PRESIDENT

Work was begun on the Woman's Building April 1, 1904, and on August 19th of that year occurred the election of Edmund J. James to the presidency of the university.

The Department of Forestry and Landscape Gardening was established in September, 1904.

1905-1910

December, 1905, marks the appointment of student advisers from the faculty.

On University Memorial Day, May 29, 1906, a reception was given to Gen. Nelson A. Miles. On the following day he reviewed the university regiment and gave the Decoration Day address. The corner-stone of the new Auditorium was also laid.

The board of trustees created the position of supervising architect June 4, 1907.

In September, 1907, The Illini becomes The Daily Illini. In October ground was broken for the erection of the University Club Building.

NEW AUDITORIUM DEDICATED

On November 4-5, 1907, the new Auditorium was dedicated with a series of concerts and other exercises in honor of Edward McDowell. Addresses by the architect of the building, Clarence H. Blackall, and Prof. Newton A. Wells, designer of the memorial tablet, and by President James; but the chief address was by Hamlin Garland, who was an intimate friend of McDowell. The Y. M. C. A. Building was completed in June, 1908, and in September the Christian Association House, formerly occupied by the Men's and Women's associations, was given over to the exclusive use of the Y. W. C. A.

In May, 1909, the corner-stone of Osborne Hall was laid by Bishop Edward W. Osborne.

In December, 1909, the board of trustees authorized the president to accept from the commission of the Illinois Farmers' Hall of Fame a picture of Cyrus Hall McCormick, and his name was duly enrolled therein, with appropriate ceremonies in the University Auditorium. The portrait was unveiled by Miss Muriel McCormick. granddaughter of the inventor.

The Chicago & Northwestern Railway Company presented to the university a locomotive testing plant, in June, 1910.

In August of that year was laid the corner-stone of Lincoln Hall.

1911-1916

In January, 1911, the name of James Nicholas Brown was enrolled in the Illinois Farmers' Hall of Fame, he being the second man to receive that honor.

In March of the same year was held, at the university, the second annual conference of the presidents of the smaller colleges of Illinois, the purpose of the meetings being to bring each of the colleges in closer touch with the others, and also to effect a closer relationship with the university.

On September 17, 1912, ground was broken for the new Armory, an initial legislative appropriation of $100,000 having been made. In November the Archaeological Museum was opened in Lincoln Hall, and in December the contract was awarded for the erection of a new Y. W. C. A. building.

In April, 1913, the first locomotive was installed in the new Locomotive Testing Laboratory presented by the Chicago & Northwestern Railway, and the new Commerce. Building was formally dedicated.

On April 29, 1913, word was received of the death of former president Dr. Andrew S. Draper in Albany, New York.

On November 4, 1913, a dinner was given in honor of Prof. N. C. Ricker, founder of the architectural department, and a professor who had seen forty years of faithful service with the university. In the same month the $60,000 Y. W. C. A. Building was dedicated.

The laying of the corner-stone of the addition to the Chemical Building occurred October 9, 1914.

In January, 1915, was organized Keramos, the first ceramics fraternity in the United States, with fourteen charter members.

In June, 1915, the military department was gratified to receive the announcement that the Legislature had appropriated $125,000 for the organization of a battery of 171 members.

THE UNIVERSITY AUDITORIUM

The new Administration Building was occupied in September, 1915, and the College of Commerce opened; also the corner-stone of the new Ceramics Building was laid.

In November, 1915, Battery F was organized among the faculty and students as part of the Illinois National Guard. A six years' course in dentistry was established by vote of the University Senate, in December, 1915, and in the following January a site for the Pharmacy School was purchased in Chicago.

DEATH OF DR. T. J. BURRILL

On April 14, 1916, occurred the sudden death of Dr. T. J. Burrill, who had been connected with the university since its foundation, in the Natural Science departments, as dean and regent, and during the last two years of his life as professor of Botany, emeritus. His funeral, which was largely attended, was held at the Auditorium. No member of the faculty had more or warmer friends and admirers than Professor Burrill. On June 13th, Alumni Day, a special convocation was held in his honor.

1916-1917

June 21st—Battery F goes to Mexican border.
September—Engineering College adds Department of Aeronautics.
October 21st—Laying of corner-stone of Woman's Residence Hall.
December 7th—Dedication of Ceramics Building.

1917

January 25th—Hon. W. B. McKinley gives $120,000 for erection of infirmary for students.

May 21st—School of Military Aeronautics established by United States Government at university.

ADMINISTRATION

To the foregoing historical sketch, as edited and brought up to date by Dr. Phelps, is to be added certain information gleaned from the "Annual Register" of the university for 1916-17, which is its official yearly publication. From its pages it is gathered that the government of the university is vested by law primarily in a board of trustees, consisting of twelve members.. The governor of the State, the superintendent of public instruction and the president of the State Board of

Agriculture are members ex-officio. The other nine members are elected by the people of the State for terms of six years; the terms of three members expire every second year.

The administration of the university is vested by the board of trustees in the president of the university, the vice-president, the senate, the council of administration, the faculties of the several colleges, and the deans of the colleges and directors of the schools.

The president is the administrative head of the university.

The senate is composed of the full professors and those other members of the faculty who are in charge of separate departments of the various colleges and schools. It is charged with the direction of the general educational policy of the university.

The council of administration is composed of the president, the vice-president, the dean of the Graduate School, the deans of men and women, and the deans of the several colleges. It constitutes an advisory board to the president, and has exclusive jurisdiction over all matters of discipline. The council does not determine educational policy; but when any matter arises which has not been provided for by common usage or by rule of the senate and cannot be conveniently laid over until the next meeting of the senate, the council may act upon the same according to its discretion.

The faculties of the colleges and schools of the university, composed of the members of the corps of instruction of these colleges and schools, have jurisdiction, subject to higher university authority, over all matters which pertain exclusively to these organizations.

The dean of the Graduate School, the deans of the several colleges, and the directors of the schools are responsible for the carrying out of all university regulations within their respective departments.

Departments and Courses

For the purpose of administration the university is divided into several colleges and schools. These are not educationally separate, but are interdependent and form a single unit.

The colleges and schools are as follows:

    I.   The College of Liberal Arts and Sciences.
    II. The College of Commerce and Business Administration.
    III. The College of Engineering.
    IV. The College of Agriculture.
    V.   The Graduate School.
    VI. The Library School.

VII.   The School of Music.

VIII. The School of Education.

IX.   The School of Railway Engineering and Administration.

X.   The College of Law.

XI.   The One-year Medical College.

XII.   The College of Medicine.

XIII.   The College of Dentistry.

XIV.   The School of Pharmacy.

The three institutions last named are located in Chicago.

THE COUNCIL OF ADMINISTRATION

Edmund Janes James, Ph. D., LL. D., president.

David Kinley, Ph. D., LL. D., vice-president, dean of the Graduate School, and professor of economics.

Eugene Davenport, M. Agr., LL. D., dean of the College of Agriculture, director of agricultural extension service, and professor of thremmatology.

Thomas Arkle Clark, B. L., dean of men and professor of rhetoric.

Charles Russ Richards, M. E., dean of the College of Engineering, director of the School of Railway Engineering and Administration.

Kendric Charles Babcock, B. Lit., Ph. D., LL. D., dean of the College of Liberal Arts and Sciences.

Frederick Brown Moorehead, A. B., D. D. S., M. D., dean of the College of Dentistry and professor of oral surgery and pathology.

Daniel Atkinson King Steele, M. D., LL. D., senior dean of the College of Medicine, professor of surgery and clinical surgery, and head of the department of surgery.

Albert Chauncey Eycleshymer, Ph. D., M. D., junior dean of the College of Medicine, professor of anatomy, and head of the department of anatomy.

Nathan Austin Weston, Ph. D., acting dean of the College of Commerce and Business Administration and assistant professor of economics.

Henry Winthrop Ballantine, LL. B., dean of the College of Law and professor of law.

Fanny Cook Gates, Ph. D., dean of women.

GENERAL ADMINISTRATIVE OFFICERS

OFFICE OF THE PRESIDENT

Edmund Janes James, Ph. D., LL. D., president.

Edward Joseph Filbey, Ph. D., private secretary to the president.

Vergil Vivian Phelps, B. D., Ph. D., executive secretary.

OFFICE OF THE VICE-PRESIDENT
David Kinley, Ph. D., LL. D., vice-president.

OFFICE OF THE REGISTRAR
Charles Maxwell McConn, A. M., registrar.
Harrison Edward Cunningham, A. B., assistant registrar.
Levi Augustus Boice, recorder.
Ira Melville Smith, LL. B., examiner.
George Philip Tuttle, Jr., B. S., assistant examiner.

OFFICE OF THE COMPTROLLER
Lloyd Morey, A. B., B. Mus.,.C. P. A., acting comptroller.
Marsh Everett Thompson, cashier.
Ennes Charles Rayson, A. B., auditor.

OFFICE OF THE DEAN OF MEN
Thomas Arkle Clark, B. L., dean.
Arthur Ray Warnock, A. B., assistant dean.

OFFICE OF THE DEAN OF WOMEN
Fanny Cook Gates, Ph. D., dean.

ADVISER TO FOREIGN STUDENTS
Arthur Romeyn Seymour, Ph. D., adviser.

OFFICE OF THE HIGH SCHOOL VISITOR
Horace Adelbert Hollister, A. M., high school visitor.
John Joseph Didcoct, A. M., M. S., assistant high school visitor.

INFORMATION OFFICE
Burt Eardley Powell, Ph. D., director, university historian, and editor of press bulletins.

OFFICE OF THE SUPERVISING ARCHITECT
James McLaren White, B. S., supervising architect.
Ralph Leverett Kelley, B. S., assistant to the supervising architect.
Joseph Morrow, superintendent of buildings.
Evelyn Atkinson, superintendent of grounds.

UNIVERSITY HEALTH OFFICER
Joseph Howard Beard, A. M., M. D., health officer.

DEPARTMENT OF PHYSICAL TRAINING FOR MEN
George A. Huff, director.

DEPARTMENT OF PHYSICAL TRAINING FOR WOMEN
Louise Freer, B. S., director.

DEPARTMENT OF MILITARY SCIENCE

Robert Walter Mearns, major Twelfth U. S. Infantry, professor and commandant.

Clement Augustus Trott, captain U. S. Infantry, assistant professor and assistant commandant.

William James Davis, captain U. S. Infantry, assistant professor and assistant commandant.

Joseph Howard Barnard, captain U. S. Cavalry, assistant professor and assistant commandant.

Robert Ross Welshimer, captain U. S. Coast Artillery Corps, assistant professor and assistant commandant.

Frederick William Post, first sergeant U. S. A., retired, administrative assistant.

THE UNIVERSITY LIBRARY

Phineas Lawrence Windsor, Ph. B., director.

Francis Keese Wynkoop Drury, A. M., B. L. S., assistant librarian.

CURATORS

Frank Smith, A. M., professor of systematic zoology and curator of the Museum of Natural History.

Arthur Stanley Pease, Ph. D., professor of the classics and curator of the Museum of Classical Art and Archeology.

Neil Conwell Brooks, Ph. D., assistant professor of German and curator of the Museum of European Culture.

THE COLLEGES AND SCHOOLS

THE COLLEGE OF LIBERAL ARTS AND SCIENCES

Kendric Charles Babcock, B. Lit., Ph. D., LL. D., dean.

Howard Vernon Canter, Ph. D., assistant dean.

THE COLLEGE OF COMMERCE AND BUSINESS ADMINISTRATION

Nathan Austin Weston, Ph. D., acting dean.

THE COLLEGE OF ENGINEERING

Charles Russ Richards, M. E., dean.

THE COLLEGE OF AGRICULTURE

Eugene Davenport, M. Agr., LL. D., dean.

Fred Henry Rankin, assistant to the dean.

THE COLLEGE OF LAW

Henry Winthrop Ballantine, LL. B., dean.

THE GRADUATE SCHOOL

David Kinley, Ph. D., LL. D., dean.

THE LIBRARY SCHOOL

Phineas Lawrence Windsor, Ph. B., director.
Frances Simpson, M. L., B. L. S., assistant director.

THE SCHOOL OF MUSIC

John Lawrence Erb., F. A. G. O., director.

THE SCHOOL OF EDUCATION

William Chandler Bagley, Ph. D., director.
John Alfred Stevenson, A. M., secretary.

THE SCHOOL OF RAILWAY ENGINEERING AND ADMINISTRATION

Charles Russ Richards, M. E., director.

THE ONE-YEAR MEDICAL COLLEGE

Kendric Charles Babcock, Ph. D., LL. D., dean.

THE SUMMER SESSION, 1917

Kendric Charles Babcock, Ph. D., LL. D., director.

THE COLLEGE OF MEDICINE

Daniel Atkinson King Steele, M. D., LL. D., senior dean.
Albert Chauncey Eycleshymer, B. S., Ph. D., M. D., junior dean.
William Henry Browne, secretary.

THE COLLEGE OF DENTISTRY

Frederick Brown Moorehead, A. B., D. D. S., M. D., dean.
William Henry Browne, secretary.

THE SCHOOL OF PHARMACY

William Baker Day, Ph. G., acting dean and secretary.

THE UNIVERSITY SENATE

Edmund Janes James, Ph. D., LL. D., president.
Nathan Clifford Ricker, D. Arch., professor of architecture, emeritus.
Ira Osborn Baker, C. E., D. Eng., professor of civil engineering.
Stephen Alfred Forbes, Ph. D., LL. D., professor of entomology.
Charles Wesley Rolfe, M. S., professor of geology.
Arthur Newell Talbot, C. E., professor of municipal and sanitary engineering.
Samuel Wilson Parr, M. S., professor of applied chemistry.

Herbert Jewett Barton, A. M., professor of the Latin language and literature, chairman of the department of the classics, and secretary of the senate.

Charles Melville Moss, Ph. D., professor of the Greek language and literature.

Daniel Kilham Dodge, Ph. D., professor of the English language and literature.

David Kinley, Ph. D., LL. D., professor of economics, vice-president and dean of the Graduate School.

Eugene Davenport, M. Agr., LL. D., professor of thremmatology, dean of the College of Agriculture, director of the Agricultural Experiment Station, and director of Agricultural Extension Service.

Albert Pruden Carman, A. M., D. Sc., professor of physics.

Evarts Boutell Greene, Ph. D., professor of history.

Thomas Arkle Clark, B. L., professor of rhetoric and dean of men.

Arthur Hill Daniels, Ph. D., professor of philosophy.

Newton Alonzo Wells, M. P., professor of architectural decoration.

Isabel Bevier, Ph. M., professor of household science and director of the courses in household science.

Cyril George Hopkins, M. S., Ph. D., professor of agronomy.

Morgan Brooks, Ph. B., M. E., professor of electrical engineering.

George A. Huff, director of physical training for men.

James McLaren White, B. S., professor of architectural engineering and supervising architect.

Herbert Windsor Mumford, B. S., professor of animal husbandry.

Maurice Henry Robinson, Ph. D., professor of industry and transportation.

Joseph Cullen Blair, M. S. A., professor of horticulture.

Horace Adelbert Hollister, A. M., professor of education and high school visitor.

Oliver Albert Harker, A. M., LL. D., professor of law.

Edward John Lake, B. S., assistant professor of art and design and acting head of the department of art and design.

Thomas Edward Oliver, Ph. D., professor of Romance languages.

Wilber John Fraser, M. S., professor of daily farming.

Frederick Green, A. M., LL. B., professor of law.

Harry Sands Grindley, D. Sc., professor of animal nutrition.

James Wilford Garner, Ph. D., professor of political science.

Edgar Jerome Townsend, Ph. D., professor of mathematics.

Edward Bartow, Ph. D., professor of sanitary chemistry and director of the State Water Survey. .

William Albert Noyes, Ph. D., LL. D., professor of chemistry and director of the Chemical Laboratory.

Ernest Ritson Dewsnup, A. M., professor of railway administration.

George Abram Miller, Ph. D., professor of mathematics.

Edward Cary Hayes, Ph. D., professor of sociology.

William Chandler Bagley, Ph. D., professor of education and director of the School of Education.

Julius Goebel, Ph. D., professor of German.

George Alfred Goodenough, M. E., professor of thermodynamics.

Phineas Lawrence Windsor, Ph. B., Librarian and director of the Library School.

Boyd Henry Bode, Ph. D., professor of philosophy.

Henry Baldwin Ward, Ph. D., professor of zoology.

Harry Harkness Stoek, B. S., E. M., professor of mining engineering.

Edward Charles Schmidt, M. E., professor of railway engineering.

Stuart Pratt Sherman, Ph. D., professor of English.

Charles Russ Richards, M. E., M. M. E., professor of mechanical engineering and head of the department of mechanical engineering, dean of the College of Engineering, director of the Engineering Experiment Station, and director of the school of Railway Engineering and Administration.

Charles Spencer Crandall, M. S., professor of pomology.

Edward Harris Decker, A. B., LL. B., professor of law and acting librarian of the College of Law.

John Archibald Fairlie, Ph. D., professor of political science.

John William Lloyd, M. S. A., professor of olericulture.

Jeremiah George Mosier, B. S., professor of soil physics.

John Norton Pomeroy, A. M., LL. B., professor of law.

Louie Henrie Smith, Ph. D., professor of plant breeding.

Bruce Willet Benedict, B. S., director of shop laboratories in the department of mechanical engineering.

William Edward Burge, Ph. D., assistant professor of physiology and acting head of the department of physiology.

Ernest Ludlow Bogart, Ph. D., professor of economics.

William Green Hale, B. S., LL. B., professor of law.

Madison Bentley, B. S., Ph. D., professor of psychology and director of the Psychological Laboratory.

Charles Frederick Hottes, Ph. D., professor of plant physiology.

Harry Alexis Harding, Ph. D., professor of dairy bacteriology and head of the department of dairy husbandry.

Kendric Charles Babcock, B. Lit., Ph. D., LL.D., dean of the College of Liberal Arts and Sciences and dean of the One-year Medical College.

Charles Hughes Johnston, Ph. D., professor of secondary education.

William Trelease, D. Sc., LL. D., professor of botany and acting head of the department of botany.

John Sterling Kingsley, D. Sc., professor of zoology.

Clarence Walworth Alvord, Ph. D., professor of history.

William Shirley Bayley, Ph. D., professor of geology.

Walter Costella Coffey, M. S., professor of sheep husbandry.

Laurence Marcellus Larson, Ph. D., professor of history.

Otto Eduard Lessing, Ph. D., professor of German.

Ellery Burton Paine, M. S., E. E., professor of electrical engineering and acting head of the department of electrical engineering.

Henry Lewis Rietz, Ph. D., professor of mathematical statistics.

Charles Mulford Robinson, A. M., professor of civic design.

Frank Smith, A. M., professor of systematic zoology and curator of the Museum of Natural History.

Joel Stebbins, Ph. D., professor of astronomy.

Edward Wight Washburn, Ph. D., professor of ceramic chemistry and head of the department of ceramic engineering.

Loring Harvey Provine, B. S., A. E., professor of architectural engineering and acting head of the department of architecture.

Frank Lincoln Stevens, Ph. D., professor of plant pathology.

Herbert Fisher Moore, B. S., M. M. E., research professor of engineering materials.

John Lawrence Erb, F. A. G. O., director of the School of Music and university organist.

Frederick Haynes Newell, B. S., D. Eng., professor of civil engineering and head of the department of civil engineering.

Kenneth McKenzie, Ph. D., professor of Romance languages and head of the department of Romance languages.

William Abbott Oldfather, Ph. D., professor of the classics.

John Driscoll Fitz-Gerald II, Ph. D., professor of Spanish.

Charles Alton Ellis, A. B., professor of structural engineering.

Louise Freer, B. S., director of physical training for women.

Oscar Adolph Leutwiler, M. E., professor of machine design.

Arthur Stanley Pease, Ph. D., professor of the classics and curator of the Museum of Classical Art and Archeology.

Nathan Austin Weston, Ph. D., assistant professor of economics and acting dean of the College of Commerce and Business Administration.

Guy Montrose Whipple, Ph. D., professor of education.

Charles Zeleny, Ph. D., professor of zoology.

Robert Walter Mearns, major Twelfth U. S. Infantry, professor of military science and tactics and commandant.

Eliot Blackwelder, Ph. D., professor of geology.

Barry Gilbert, A. B.. LL. B., professor of law.

Albert Howe Lybyer, Ph. D., professor of history.

Richard Chace Tolman, Ph. D., professor of physical chemistry.

Franklin William Scott, Ph. D., assistant professor of English, chairman and secretary of the department of English.

Ernest Bernbaum, Ph. D., professor of English.

Henry Winthrop Ballantine, LL. B., professor of law and dean of the College of Law.

Cullen Warner Parmelee, B. S., professor of ceramic engineering.

The officers of administration, therefore, number 155, of whom 59 are men and 46 women; the library staff comprising 7 men and 43 women.

NUMERICAL STRENGTH OF THE FACULTY

The university faculty, or officers of instruction at Urbana, is classified as follows. according to colleges, schools and departments:

Liberal Arts and Sciences—Professors, 46 men; associate professors, 9 men; assistant professors, 20 men; associates, 24 men and 1 woman; special lecturers, 3 men; instructors, 44 men and 8 women; assistants, 87 men and 15 women; graduate assistants, 22 men and 8 women; student assistants, 6 men.   Total in College of Liberal Arts and Sciences, 293; 261 men and 32 women.

One-Year Medical College—Professors, 3 men; assistant professors, 20 men; associates, 24 men and 1 woman; instructors, 3 men; assistants, 6 men and 2 women; graduate assistants, 1 man.   Total, 21; 19 men and 2 women.

College of Commerce and Business Administration—Professors, 4 men; assistant professors, 3 men; special lecturers, 1 man; instructors, 12 men; assistants, 7 men.   Total, 27 men.

College of Engineering—Professors, 21 men; associate professors, 3 men; assistant professors, 19 men; associates, 20 men; instructors, 35 men; assistants, 19 men.   Total, 117 men.

College of Agriculture—Professors, 13 men and 1 woman; associate professors, 2 men; assistant professors, 18 men and 1 woman; associates, 17 men and 6 women; instructors, 24 men and 7 women; assistants, 30 men and 7 women.   Total, 126; 104 men and 22 women.

School of Music—Professor, 1 man; assistant professor, 1 man; instructors, 6 men and 3 women. Total, 11; 8 men and 3 women.

College of Law—Professors, 7 men; assistant professor, 1 man. Total, 8 men.

Library School—Professor, 1 man; assistant professor, 1 woman; special lecturer, 1 woman; instructors, 2 women. Total, 6; 2 men and 4 women.

Department of Military Science—Professor, 1 man; assistant professors, 4 men; student assistants, 10 men. Total, 15 men.

Department of Physical Training (separate departments, 1 for men, 2 for women)—Professors, 1 man and 1 woman; assistants, 2 men and 2 women; student assistant, 1 woman. Total, 16; 9 men and 7 women.

Department of Photography—Instructor, 1 man.

Total officers of instruction at Urbana, 641, as follows: Professors, 98 men and 2 women; associate professors, 14 men; assistant professors, 69 men and 2 women; associates, 68 men and 7 women; special lecturers, 4 men and 1 woman; instructors, 128 men and 23 women; assistants, 151 men and 26 women; graduate assistants, 23 men and 8 women; student assistants, 16 men and 1 woman. Grand total, 641; 571 men and 70 women.

The officers of instruction in Chicago are divided as follows:

College of Medicine—Professors, 29 men; associate professors, 6 men and 1 woman; assistant professors, 23 men and 1 woman; associates, 8 men; special lecturers, 3 men; instructors, 59 men and 2 women; assistants, 15 men and 3 women; student assistants, 5 men. Total, 155; 148 men and 7 women.

College of Dentistry—Professors, 8 men; assistant professors, 6 men; associates, 2 men; special lecturers, 2 men; instructors, 9 men; assistants, 4 men and 1 woman; student assistants, 5 men. Total, 37; 36 men and 1 woman.

School of Pharmacy—Professor, 1 man; assistant professors, 2 men; special lecturer, 1 man; instructors, 3 men. Total, 7 men.

Total of officers of instruction in Chicago, 199.

Grand total of instructors in university, 840.

EXPERIMENT STATIONS AND SCIENTIFIC BUREAUS

As most valuable adjuncts to the university are several experiment stations and bureaus engaged in practical research work.

Agricultural Experiment Station

The most important of these institutions is the Agricultural Experiment Station, which has been in successful operation for nearly thirty years and now carries a staff of more than 100 instructors and officials. Its director is Dean Eugene Davenport and vice-director Dr. Cyril G. Hopkins.

By an act approved March 2, 1887, the National Government appropriated $15,000 a year to each State for the purpose of establishing and maintaining, in connection with the colleges founded upon the congressional act of 1862, agricultural experiment stations, "to aid in acquiring and diffusing among the people of the United States useful and practical information on subjects connected with agriculture, and to promote scientific investigation and experiment respecting the principles and applications of agricultural science." Under this provision the Agricultural Experiment Station of the University of Illinois was founded in 1888 and placed under the direction of the trustees of the university; a part of the university farm, with buildings, was assigned for its use.

The Federal grant has since been increased to $30,000 a year. This is supplemented by State appropriations which make an aggregate fund of nearly $250,000 devoted wholly to research in agriculture.

Investigations are conducted in the growing and marketing of orchard fruits, the methods of production of meats and of dairy goods, the principles of animal breeding and of nutrition, and the improvement of the economic production of crops. All the principal types of soil of the State are being studied in the laboratory under glass and in the field. A soil survey is in progress which when finished will map and describe the soil of every farm of the State down to an area of ten acres. Between forty and fifty fields and orchards are operated in various portions of the State for the study of local problems, and assistants are constantly on the road to conduct experiments or to give instruction to producer or consumer. The results of investigation are published in bulletins, which are issued in editions of 40,000, and distributed free of charge.

Much of this work is of interest to students, especially of graduate grade, and it is freely available for this purpose, so far as is consistent with the interests of the station.

Engineering Experiment Station

The Engineering Experiment Station, established by action of the board of trustees December 8, 1903, is under the immediate direction of Dean Charles R. Richards, assisted by Clarence S. Sale and ten special investigators and twelve research fellows. The purposes of this station are the stimulation and elevation of engineering education, and the study of problems of special importance to professional engineers, and to the manufacturing, railway, mining and industrial interests of the State and the country. The control of the station is vested in the heads of the several departments of the College of Engineering. These constitute the station staff and, with the director, determine the character and extent of the investigations to be undertaken.

State Laboratory of Natural History

In 1885 the General Assembly passed an act transferring the State Laboratory of Natural History from the Illinois State Normal University to the University of Illinois. This laboratory was created for the purpose of making a natural history survey of the State, the results of which should be published in a series of bulletins and reports; and for the allied purpose of furnishing specimens illustrative of the flora and fauna of the State to the public schools and to the State museum. For these purposes direct appropriations are made by the Legislature from session to session. Material of all classes has been collected in all parts of the State, field observations and experiments have been conducted, extending over many years, and fifteen volumes have been published in the form of bulletins and final reports.

The most important problem upon which the work of the survey is at present concentrated is the effect of drainage operations, sewage contaminations, and other results of industrial occupancy upon the general system of life in our principal rivers.

The State Entomologist's Office

Dr. Stephen A. Forbes is director of the laboratory. He is also the head of the State Entomologist's Office.

The work of the State Entomologist's Office has been done at the University of Illinois since January, 1885; by legislative enactment in 1899 it was permanently established at the university, the trustees of which are required by that act to provide for the entomologist and his assistants such office and laboratory rooms as may be necessary to the performance of their duties.

It is the duty of this officer to investigate all insects dangerous to any valuable property or dangerous to the public health, and to conduct experiments for the control of injury to persons or property by insects, publishing the results of his researches biennially in his official report. He is required also to inspect and certify annually all Illinois nurseries and all importations of nursery stock, and to maintain a general supervision of the horticultural property of the State with respect to its infestation by dangerous insects and its infection with contagious plant disease.

Twenty-nine reports have now been published by the entomologist, fifteen of them since the transfer of his office to the university.

State Water Survey

The director of the State Water Survey is Dr. Edward Bartow. A chemical survey of the waters of the state was begun in the latter part of September, 1895. Two years later the Legislature authorized the continuance of the work and directed the trustees of the University to establish a chemical and biological survey of the waters of the State. In 1911 the Legislature made an increased appropriation and imposed additional duties on the State Water Survey, authorizing it to employ field men to inspect water supplies and watersheds, and to make, free of charge, sanitary examinations of water for citizens of Illinois. The survey has collected data concerning the most of the water supplies and sewerage systems, and many watersheds, making chemical and bacteriological examinations to demonstrate the sanitary condition of water supplies and streams, and to determine standards of purity for drinking waters. The survey advises municipal authorities how best to obtain and conserve an adequate supply of pure water for domestic and manufacturing purposes. In 1915 a small appropriation was made for the establishment and maintenance of a sewage-experiment station.

The survey is a division of the department of chemistry of the University of Illinois. Offices and special laboratories are equipped in the Chemistry Building for conducting the work.

State Geological Survey

The Forty-fourth General Assembly passed an act—in force July 1, 1905—providing for the establishment at the University of Illinois of the State Geological Survey. It is under the control of a commission, of which the president of the University is an ex officio member and secretary. Governor Frank O. Lowden is chairman of the commission and Professor T. C. Chamberlin, vice-chairman. The director

of the staff is Frank W. DeWolf and he is assisted by fourteen chemists
and geologists, an engineering draftsman and a geographer in charge
of the topographical surveys.

The purpose of the survey is primarily the study and exploration of
the mineral resources of Illinois. Field parties are organized for the
investigation of oil, clay, coal, stone, artesian water, cement materials,
and road materials, and for general scientific investigations. The survey is charged also with the duty of making a complete topographical
and geological survey of the state. Topographical and geological surveys are now being carried on in coöperation with the United States
Geological Survey. These will lead to the publication of a series of
bulletins and maps, eventually covering the entire state.

The Forty-fifth General Assembly further charged the commission
with the duty of making surveys and studies of lands subject to over-
flow, with a view to their reclamation. Work has been carried on in
cooperation with the Rivers and Lakes Commission, the United States
Geological Survey, and the United States Department of Agriculture,
along the Sangamon, Kaskaskia, Big Muddy, Little Wabash, Embarrass,
Spoon, Pecatonica, and Saline rivers. Reports have been issued on the
Little Wabash, Kaskaskia, Spoon and Embarrass.

The laboratory work is done in connection with various department
laboratories of the University. The equipment includes a working
library, maps, and a growing collection, illustrating the geological and
the economical resources of the state. Thirty-five bulletins, a mono-
graph, and a large number of maps have been published. Many temporary assistants besides the regular corps are employed each summer.

Under an agreement between the State Geological Survey and the
Engineering Experiment Station on the one hand, and the United States
Bureau of Mines on the other, a branch station has been located at
Urbana for a cooperative investigation of the Illinois coal mining industry. The Forty-seventh General Assembly made appropriations to carry
on the work for two years, and the Forty-eighth and Forty-ninth General Assemblies repeated the appropriations for equal periods.

BOARD OF EXAMINERS IN ACCOUNTANCY

By a law passed in 1903 the State University is made an examining
board of applicants for certificates as certified public accountants. To
carry out the provisions of the law the board of trustees have appointed
a board of three examiners to prepare, conduct, and grade examinations,
and a University committee to conduct the routine work. Under the

law one examination must be held each year, in May, but examinations have been held also in November or December of each year in which there were a sufficient number of applicants. All the examinations thus far given have been held in the city of Chicago.

Applicants for the certificate of Certified Public Accountant are required to pass examinations in the theory of accounts, commercial law, auditing and practical accounting.

The Illinois Society of Certified Public Accountants offers annually a gold medal and a silver medal to be awarded to the persons passing the C. P. A. examination with the highest total marking in all subjects and with the second highest total marking in all subjects respectively.

The chairman of the board of examiners is James Hall of Chicago, and the chairman of the University committee, Dean David Kinley.

INVESTIGATION OF ILLINOIS COAL PROBLEMS

The Engineering Experiment Station, through the department of mining engineering of the University of Illinois, the State Geological Survey and the United States Bureau of Mines (of which Van H. Manning is director) are cooperating in the investigation of some of the problems connected with the mining of coal in the State of Illinois, under authority granted by the Forty-seventh General Assembly. This cooperative work is constructive as well as statistical, based upon accurate data and taking account of all existing conditions, to enable the operators and miners of the state to produce coal more safely, more cheaply and with less waste. A staff of trained mining engineers, geologists and chemists has been placed at the disposal of the coal industry of Illinois.

ACCREDITED HIGH SCHOOLS

Fifteen units of high school, or other secondary school work, are required for entrance to the University, without special examination, and the high schools of Champaign County which cover the prescribed units are these: Champaign, Fisher, Homer Township, Rantoul, Tolono and Urbana.

UNIVERSITY HONORS

The expression is not uncommon, in speaking of a university alumnus, "he graduated with honors." To the university student this means much; to the outsider it is often an undefined phrase. It is to the latter that an explanation is due, as applied to the University of Illinois, which gives public official recognition to such students as attain a high grade of scholarship in certain years and in special lines. Preliminary honors are assigned at the completion of the sophomore year on the basis of the average of the grades received during the freshman and sophomore years in all studies except military and physical training; final honors on graduation, based on the scholarship attained during the junior and senior years. Special honors are awarded at the close of the senior year on special courses, and no student is eligible for them who has received a grade of less than eighty per cent in any subject. An acceptable thesis must be prepared on the subject, or group of allied subjects in which the honors are proposed. The faculty of the College of Liberal Arts and Sciences recommends candidates for the degree of Bachelor of Arts "with honors" in a particular subject. The student must have completed the work offered for his major with an average of not less than ninety per cent, and that offered for his minor with an average of not less than eighty-five; a thesis is also required in his major subject. Candidates for the degree of Bachelor of Science in the college are eligible for final and special honors. Especially high scholarship also brings freshmen honors in the College of Liberal Arts and Sciences.

PRIZES AND MEDALS

The university engages yearly in four intercollegiate debates, the teams being chosen by competition. The I. M. I. Debating League comprises the universities of Illinois, Minnesota and Iowa; the Midwest, Illinois, Michigan and Wisconsin; the Northern Oratorical, Northwestern University, Oberlin College, and the state universities of Illinois, Iowa, Michigan, Minnesota and Wisconsin; and the Intercollegiate Peace Association offers cash prizes on the outcome of the orations delivered on some phase of the peace question. Through the generosity of William B. McKinley, a gold watch is presented to every speaker who represents the University of Illinois, either in debate or in oratory.

A medal valued at $20 and two medals of the value of $10 each are offered annually by the University to the high schools of the state for the best orations delivered in a competitive contest between their representatives. The Thacher Howland Guild Memorial prize of $25 is offered by the friends of the former instructor in English for the best one-act play produced by an undergraduate of the University; the St. Patrick's Day prize of $50 for the best essay on a subject connected with ancient Irish literature, history, or archæology; the William Jennings Bryan prize of $25 for the best essay on the science of govern-

ment, and the B'nai B'rith prizes aggregating $50 for the most meri-
forious essays on Jewish subjects.

The department of architecture, a division of the College of Engineering, offers a fellowship of $1,000 through Francis J. Plym, a Uni-
versity graduate, the holder being required to spend a year in study
and travel abroad; an annual prize of $50 is established by Joseph
C. Llewellyn of Chicago for competition in architectural engineering;
medals are also offered by the American Institute of Architects and the
Scarab Society, while the American Academy in Rome holds out its
grand prize of three years' residence and travel abroad for the study of
classic and renaissance architecture. The department of military science is awarded various medals as rewards for individual proficiency in
marksmanship and drill—bronze medals open to teams of the infantry,
artillery and signal corps which shall make the greatest number of
points and the highest scores at target practice; a gold medal for the
best drilled student, with a minimum annual grade, and the Hazelton
prize medal, also for individual excellence in drill, with and without
arms.

Scholarships and Fellowships

The scholarships with which the University is identified include the
following: Under a legislative law passed in 1905, each county of the
state is awarded a scholarship limited to a successful candidate for
entrance to the University, at least sixteen years of age, and covering
the matriculation fee of $10 and the annual incidental fee of $24; also
a scholarship carrying the same advantages and confined to each assembly district of the state; a like scholarship in ceramic engineering offered
to each county in Illinois on the nomination of the Illinois Clay Workers' Association; to each county in the state, except Cook and Lake, and
to each of the first congressional districts, one scholarship to prospective
students in the College of Agriculture, upon the recommendation of the
executive committee of the Illinois Farmers' Institute, and one for candidates for the household science department in either the College of
Agriculture or the College of Liberal Arts and Sciences, upon the recommendation of the county domestic science associations, or for counties and districts in which there are no such organizations, on the recommendation of the Illinois Farmers' Institute; four free scholarships
in music provided by Capt. Thomas J. Smith of Champaign, preferably
to candidates from that county, and covering all expenses for a musical
instruction during one year; the Joseph T. Ryerson & Son scholarships
(two) of the American Railway Master Mechanics' Association, each

providing for an annual stipend of $300 to be paid to the beneficiary during his four years' engineering course at the University of Illinois, the University of Wisconsin, or Purdue University (next examination for scholarships in June, 1919) ; students who attain the rank of commissioned officers of the University Corps of Cadets are entitled to annual military scholarships equal in value to the University incidental fees for one year; eight scholarships in the College of Law open to students of the first and second years, four of $12 each and four of $6 each; summer session scholarships exempting all teachers in the state who are qualified to matriculate as University students from the payment of the regular tuition fee, and scholarships and fellowships for graduate students who are pursuing such special research work as is pursued at the engineering experiment station and in literature. Among the latter is the research fellowship in Gaelic.

Through its president, Hon. J. P. McGoorty, the Irish Fellowship Foundation of Chicago has offered the University the sum of $1,000 as an honorarium for the fellow, whose duty it will be to pursue research in Irish language and literature at the University of Illinois. An additional sum of $200 was given for the traveling expenses of the appointee. To this fellowship the University appointed the Rev. Andrew O'Kelleher, formerly of the department of Celtic in the University of Liverpool. The fellow is now at the University and is pursuing his work. His researches will doubtless in time be gathered and published as a contribution to scholarship in the field of Celtic language and literature.

LOAN FUNDS

In 1899, Edward Snyder, professor of the German language and literature, emeritus, gave to the University $12,000 to be lent to worthy and scholarly students of the junior and senior classes and the Graduate School who need aid to complete their work. The loans range from $50 to $150 (to a junior) and $200 (to a senior, or graduate).

The fund of $100 established by the class of 1895 is open to members of the freshmen classes.

The Graduate Club, in 1907-08, founded a fund of $75 for graduate students.

In 1910, the Woman's League, of the University, gave $409.44, which is available for any woman matriculated in the University.

In September, 1912, William B. McKinley turned over to the University notes aggregating more than $12,000, to be used as a loan fund for undergraduate men, with preference to upper class men.

Gordon Strong of Chicago has offered $250, for 1916-17, to be loaned to self-supporting students of high scholastic attainments.

In 1915, President James established the Margaret Lange James Loan Fund, in memory of his wife. His original fund of $5,000 was supplemented by other gifts until the fund now amounts to $5,650. The loans are made to matriculated students, preferably women, who have resided at the University at least one year, have reached junior rank, and who have declared their intention to graduate.

UNIVERSITY EXTENSION WORK

Extension work has not been organized as a separate administrative unit in the University of Illinois. Several departments, however, have initiated activities, both on the campus and in the state at large, which serve to make some of the facilities of the University available to groups of mature persons who are engaged in various industries and professions.

AGRICULTURE

Each of the departments of the College of Agriculture does extension work and, so far as possible, provides special men for this purpose. In addition to this, a separate service known as Agricultural College Extension, offers courses in the principles and methods of extension work, conducts extension enterprises that do not deal with technical subjects, and co-operates with the other departments in projecting their work in the state.

Some of the more general college extension enterprises are:

(1)   A two weeks' course in agriculture, known as the Corn Growers' and Stockmen's Convention, held annually at the College of Agriculture since 1898. The work includes lectures, conferences and demonstrations in the subjects of stock-judging, milk-testing, farm mechanics and farm crops. (Omitted in 1915 and 1916 on account of the "foot-and-mouth disease.")

(2)   Agricultural extension schools of a week's duration.

(3)   Demonstrations held in connection with soil fertility and crop fields throughout the state.

(4)   Cooperation, by furnishing teachers and lecturers with other educational agencies for rural communities, e. g., farmers' institutes, special lecture railway trains, the Boys' State Fair School.

(5)   Educational exhibits at fairs and expositions.

(6)   School and community excursions to the University.

Part of the Main Campus Today

For the Cooperative Extension Service in agriculture and home economics conducted by the University of Illinois and the United States Department of Agriculture, under the provisions of the Federal Smith-Lever Act of May 8, 1914 (see pp. 402-403).

CERAMIC ENGINEERING

In addition to the regular four-year technical curriculum, the department of ceramic engineering cooperates with the clay and allied industries by offering annually, at Urbana, during the second and third weeks in January, a two weeks' industrial course in the principles underlying the manufacture of clay products, for those who have not the time nor the preparation required for academic studies. The work includes lectures, laboratory work, practice in firing kilns, and informal gatherings for question asking. A common school education is sufficient to enable one to do the work of this course. No charge of any kind is made.   .

Eugene Davenport, M. Agr., LL. D., is the director of the agricultural extension service, which is a cooperative arrangement between the University of Illinois and the United States Department of Agriculture. Walter Frederick Handschin, B. S., is vice-director of the service and state leader of the county advisers, of whom there are twenty-two representing DeKalb, Kankakee, Livingston, McHenry, Kane, DuPage, Tazewell, Will, Peoria, Champaign, Winnebago, Iroquois, Bureau, La-Salle, Grundy, Adams, Hancock, McLean, Mason, Woodford, Mercer and Lee. The county adviser for the Champaign County Bureau is Charles H. Oathout, B. S.

Under the provisions of the Smith-Lever Act, approved by the President of the United States on May 8, 1914, and the terms of its acceptance by the State of Illinois, the University becomes cooperatively responsible for a system of demonstration service designed to combine the results of scientific discovery with the most approved.practice on the farms and in the households of the state.

A further cooperative relation has been established by the Department of Agriculture whereby the University undertakes to become jointly responsible for certain extension work which the department is conducting out of its own funds. This cooperative work consists of the following:

1() Cooperation with county farm bureaus in the employment of agricultural advisers.

(2) Cooperation with local associations in home economics demonstrations.

(3) Employment of extension specialists in agriculture and home economics as special advisers in the field.

(4) Cooperation with the United States Department of Agriculture in its extension activities:

    a. In support of county advisory work.

    b. In farm management demonstration.

    c. In junior extension.

HOME ECONOMICS

Isabel Bevier, Ph. M., is the vice-director of Home Economics Extension and Mamie Bunch, A. B., state leader in Home Economics Demonstration, with five assistants.

The service in home economics may be classified as follows:

1. Correspondence.—Numerous requests come from individuals and clubs for help in solving some problem of preparing food, planning a house, feeding a child, or in preparing topics for club study.

2. Service for Organizations.—This includes demonstrations and addresses before farmers' institutes, federated or local clubs, parents' and teachers' associations, the State Fair School, or other groups of people.

3. The School for Housekeepers.—This is held annually, at Urbana, during the last two weeks in January. It offers instruction in food, clothing and shelter, and provides an opportunity for the discussion of some of the fundamental problems of home life and management. No fees are charged in connection with this school.

4. Movable Schools.—The department of household science will, in so far as possible, provide instruction on request for a movable school in any community which is sufficiently interested to pay the local expenses (hire of hall, etc.) and the traveling and living expenses for the week of one or two instructors.

5. Demonstration Car.—This car marks a new departure in demonstration work. Hitherto, demonstrations in Home Economics have been confined largely to the cooking of food. It is the purpose of this car to extend this method of presentation to power equipment and house furnishings; to show the machines, the kitchen utensils, and the color schemes, not just to talk about them.

In accordance with this idea, this car shows how power commonly used upon the farm may also be employed in performing a large part of the heavy labor of the home, thereby contributing to the health and comfort of the housekeeper; how to secure an adequate water supply for both the house and barn with the necessary provision for sewage disposal;

and finally how, by attention to equipment and to the principles of form and color, the essentials of comfortable living may be secured for the country home at a reasonable cost.

The car and its equipment provide sufficient material for demonstration work for a week. The University pays the salaries of the demonstrators and furnishes the exhibit. The local committee is responsible for the following details: (a) Proper advertising of the car; (b) arranging with local railroad as to the location of the car on a spur or switch where it will not be bumped and where it is readily accessible; (c) securing a suitable hall for lectures and demonstrations that cannot be held in the car; (d) providing hard coal for the heater, gasoline for the engines, and janitor service; (e) providing board, room, and comfortable living conditions for the demonstrators, whose hours of service are long and duties exacting; (f) mileage of the car.

University Finances

The report of the comptroller of the University for the year ending June 30, 1916, is a document which cannot fail to impress any citizen of Illinois with its greatness as a business and a financial institution, and as one of the most valuable material assets of the state. The statements show that the assets of the University have reached a total of $6,389,755.49, covered by the following items: Cash on hand and in bank, $125,618.92; notes, accounts, etc., receivable, $177,578.42; supplies, $166,878.48; plant and property, $6,045,298.59. The last named include land and land improvements, $1,083,649.49; buildings, furniture and equipment, $4,961,649.10.

It appears that the income of the University was derived from five sources: United States grants, state appropriations, student fees, departmental sales and interest on bank balances.

Receipts from the United States grants were divided as follows: Land Grant act of 1862, $32,450.34; Morrill act, $25,000; Nelson act, $25,000; Hatch act, $15,000; Adams act, $15,000; Smith-Lever act, $36,282.20.

State Appropriations: Land, buildings and equipment, $436,500; administrative offices, $76,145; general departments, $111,550; instruction, $1,243,055; physical plant, $218,250; research, $97,000; contingent expense, $243,370; water survey and investigation, $28,500.

Student Fees: Urbana departments, $174,264.37; Chicago departments, $72,659.97.

Departmental Sales: Agricultural College and Experiment Station, $146,524.30; Engineering College and Experiment Station, $1,041.58;

College of Liberal Arts and Sciences, $1,255.74; College of Medicine, $3,189.65; College of Dentistry, $10,041.48; School of Pharmacy, $76.18; physical plant, $5,961.22; miscellaneous (including receipts from the Smith farms, from symphony concerts, accountancy examinations, the University Directory and the summer session), $16,914.59.

The income from interest on bank balances amounted to $17,844.16.

It will be seen that as an income producer the Agricultural College and Experiment Station overtops the other departments of the University. Of these receipts, animal husbandry produced $26,089.97 and dairy husbandry, $65,293.98. The sales from the creamery amounted to $56,301.77, and from the pure bred herd $7,159.32.

The expenditures for the year on account of instruction and research reached a total of $1,870,508.94, divided as follows: Agricultural College and Experiment Station, $677,924.90; College of Liberal Arts and Sciences, $483,157.33; Engineering College and Experiment Station, $317,522.73; Colleges of Medicine and Dentistry and School of Pharmacy (Chicago), $213,301.05; Graduate School, $49,502.34; College of Commerce, $44,641.10; College of Law, $30,649.44; summer session, 1915, $23,768.63; School of Music, $19,215.13; School of Library Science, $10,006.48; summer session, 1916, $819.81.

The total expenditures for the year were: Administration and general expense, $154,525.72; instruction and research, $1,870,508.94; general departments, $178,772.53; physical plant, $212,500.69; land and buildings, $517,048.96.

The largest item of expenditure on account of the College of Liberal Arts and Sciences was in support of the department of chemistry, $105,-053.31; in the Engineering College and Experiment Station, for mechanical engineering, $63,660.54; in the Agricultural College and Experiment Station, for agronomy $176,839.80, animal husbandry $140,195.01; and dairy husbandry $132,825.11, of which $49,959.40 was applied to the creamery.

Of the $517,048.96 expended on land, buildings and general equipment, the chief item for new buildings and improvements was thus divided: Chemistry building, $202,048.58; ceramics building, $116,-192.05; vivarium, $51,744.65; administration building, $20,482.30; pharmacy buildings, $18,359.35.

TOTAL VALUATION OF UNIVERSITY PROPERTY

The inventory of land owned by the University indicated a valuation of $833,050.05 reported June 30, 1915, with additions of $78,116.88 during the following year, making a total of $911,166.93. The improve-

ments for the year ending June 30, 1916 (including tunnel and con-
duits, $94,681.69, and military drill field, $12,733.65) amounted to
$172,482.56. Total value of land and improvements, $1,083,649.49.

The buildings of the University are valued as follows:

STRUCTURAL GROUPS

	Building Value
Liberal Arts and Sciences Group—	
Astronomical Observatories	$ 11,600.00
Botany Laboratory and Greenhouse	22,150.00
Chemistry Building	77,800.00
Entomology Building	6,950.00
Lincoln Hall	220,375.00
Natural History Building	180,400.00
University Hall	23,500.00
Totals	$542,775.00
Engineering Group—	
Ceramics Laboratory	$ 13,125.00
Electrical Engineering Laboratory	20,575.00
Engineering Hall	92,000.00
Laboratory of Applied Mechanics	23,525.00
Locomotive Laboratory and Reservoir	32,900.00
Mechanical Engineering Laboratory	32,050.00
Metal Shops	11,950.00
Mining and Ceramics Laboratory	19,300.00
Physics Laboratory	187,475.00
Transportation Building	78,900.00
Wood Shops	30,675.00
Totals	$542,475.00
Agricultural Group—	
Agricultural Building	$123,300.00
Agronomy Building	14,000.00
Agronomy Greenhouse	6,450.00
Farm Mechanics Building	26,150.00
Floriculture Service Buildings and Greenhouses	83,680.00
Genetics Building	10,231.30
Horticulture Building	8,740.00
Horticulture Service Building	2,820.00
Stock Judging Pavilion	108,150.00
Horse Barn	1,320.00

Dairy Barn .... $ 3,800.00
Beef Cattle Barn 21,950.00
Dairy Farm House 2,350.00
20-Acre Dairy Barn 2,600.00
Dairy Horse Barn 1,800.00
Dairy House and Shop 2,050.00
Dairy Experiment Barn 10,340.00
Sheep Barn 2,740.00
Brood Mare Barn 2,990.00
Tool Shed 1,615.00
Work Horse Barn 1,320.00
Swine Sheds 1,290.00
Soil Bins 7,884.42

Totals $447,570.72
Law Building 23,425.00
Commerce Building 95,425.00
General University Use—
Armory $224,535.00
Auditorium 111,000.00
Library 131,400.00
Men's Gymnasium 53,270.00
Men's Gymnasium Annex 10,140.00
Woman's Building 190,000.00

Totals $720,345.00
Administration Building 145,702.13
President's House 5,915.00
Service Buildings—
Greenhouse .... $ 5,100.00
New Power Plant 42,315.00
Old Power Plant 12,935.00
Pumping Station 6,490.00
Storehouse 1,950.00

Total .... $ 68,790.00
Tenant Houses 6,450.00

Grand Total $2,598,872.85
To this total valuation of the buildings must be added the value of
the land and land improvements, $1,083,649.49; the general furniture,

$52,158.12; the departmental equipment (less library), $1,198,947.71; the library itself, $594,432.79, and the inventory of "construction in progress" to make up the total of $6,045,298.59, which represents the value of the total University plant in buildings, with their contents and real estate with all improvements. Buildings are now completed. Woman's residence hall nearly completed (ready September 1, 1917). Smith music building in process of erection.

CHAPTER IX

THE RAILROADS

PRESENT STEAM AND ELECTRIC LINES—ILLINOIS CENTRAL AND THE
FIRST GREAT WESTERN—EARLY ISOLATION OF CENTRAL COUNTIES—
VITAL QUESTION, GREAT CENTRAL HIGHWAY—ILLINOIS CENTRAL
INCORPORATED (1836)—STATE SYSTEM OF INTERNAL IMPROVEMENTS
—NARROW STATE POLICY—THE GREAT WESTERN RAILWAY (HOL-
BROOK) COMPANY—GREAT WESTERN REINCORPORATED (1849)—
WAYS OF UTILIZING LAND GRANT—ROBERT RANTOUL, CREATOR OF
THE ILLINOIS CENTRAL—RELATIONS OF THE ILLINOIS CENTRAL WITH
THE STATE—ACTUAL SURVEY AND CONSTRUCTION—WEST URBANA
(CHAMPAIGN) FOUNDED—JUST BEFORE THE RAILROAD CAME—RAIL-
ROAD LANDS DRAW SETTLERS—CONGRESS ATTEMPTS TO REGULATE
LAND PRICES—INCREASE OF POPULATION IN CHAMPAIGN COUNTY—
THE WABASH RAILROAD—THE BIG FOUR—CHICAGO & EASTERN
ILLINOIS—ILLINOIS TRACTION SYSTEM—URBANA AND CHAMPAIGN
RAILWAY, GAS & ELECTRIC COMPANY—WILLIAM B. MCKINLEY.

The railroads of Champaign County, both steam and electric, have
completed its mediums of development, originating in its great wealth
of the soil and its remarkable intellectual spirit which received such an
early and permanent impetus. Both of these agencies were the means
of drawing to the county thousands of its best men and women, and
when transportation facilities were assured to bring them closely to the
markets and the people of the neighboring counties and states, they
remained to enjoy their homes and societies and assist in the further
development of the localities in which they had settled.

PRESENT STEAM AND ELECTRIC LINES

In the '50s came the Illinois Central to give them outlets and inlets,
north and south, east and west, and the second Great Western (Wabash)
to accommodate its more southern townships; in 1872 the main line of
the Chicago & Eastern Illinois Railroad was completed as the Chicago,
Danville & Vincennes Railroad, and its branches in the county now

329

supply railway accommodations to several eastern and southeastern townships; in 1889 the Big Four (Cleveland, Cincinnati, Chicago & St. Louis Railway) entered the lists as an institution of Illinois and Champaign County, and binds together the central sections with several of its largest centers of population.

The traction system, which has been increasing in mileage and efficiency since 1890, consists of an east and west trunk paralleling the Big Four east of Urbana and the Illinois Central west of Champaign. The Illinois Traction Company already furnishes an excellent interurban service between Champaign and Urbana, connecting the twin cities with Danville and intervening points to the east. The system also extends west to Decatur, there connecting with the lines to Springfield and St. Louis and to Bloomington and Peoria. It is thus intimately linked with the traction systems of Illinois and Indiana, which are among the most prosperous of any in the country.

ILLINOIS CENTRAL AND FIRST GREAT WESTERN

But before these transportation achievements were realized, there ensued a long period of abortive and discouraging efforts. The interesting and instructive record commences with the various projects connected with the internal improvement schemes of Illinois and the gradual shaping of the Illinois Central. As far as this history is concerned, the feature of this period which requires special notice is the fierce contest for the favor of the state solons between the advocates of the original Great Western and the Illinois Central. This special phase of the subject, as well as the general conditions which prevailed in the central counties of Illinois when the pioneer railroads were broached by their authors, is so well etched by Dr. Howard G. Bronson in one of the publications of the Illinois Historical Society, that it is quoted entire, with the retention only of such footnotes as add salient facts to the body of the text.

EARLY ISOLATION OF CENTRAL COUNTIES

From the time of La Salle and the early French traders down to the present the history of Illinois, in both its political and social aspects, has been closely connected with the economical development of the state. The peculiar geographic location of the commonwealth, the growth of certain industries, the extension of commerce and trade and, above all, the creation of adequate means of inland transportation, have left a deep impress on the thought of the people, their social customs, and even their attitude towards political movements. Likewise, these conditions of thought, custom and politics have affected the growth of the community.

In this interplay of economic, social and political influences the question of internal transportation has held first place among the many problems confronting the people in the long period from 1830 to the close of the Granger agitation. A glance at the map shows that while Illinois is practically encircled by natural waterways, the interior of the state, which is by far the most fertile portion, is without means of transportation, except that provided by man. Before the introduction of the railroad, the central counties such as Coles, McLean, Macon and Champaign, were practically isolated from the remainder of the country and were entirely dependent upon the local highways for any communication with the outside world.

The condition of these early country roads was wretched to an extent almost beyond description. There were a few old corduroy roads and three or four government turnpikes, but they were short and ill kept. Elsewhere, former Indian trails or newly made section roads were the only semblances of highways that existed. In summer these roads were little better than the surrounding prairies, often worse; in winter they were mud-holes. Fortunate indeed was the traveler who was not compelled to help pry the coach out of the deep mud or wait until morning for a yoke of oxen to pull him out of some worse than ordinary slough. Mails were often delayed and, during the winter storms and spring rains, not only farmhouses but even large towns were entirely isolated. Moreover, the state had shown itself utterly unable to remedy these evils. The statute books were covered with enactments declaring certain trails or mud roads public turnpikes, but even a sovereign state cannot legislate a mud-hole into a turnpike. Charters, almost without number, were granted private corporations, but without tangible results of any importance. Local enterprise was equally fruitless, and the efforts of the counties to improve the public roads had generally failed.

This absence of good highway facilities greatly retarded the economic development of the state, and especially the central portion. The cost of carrying freight over ordinary country roads, or even on well-built highways under the most favorable circumstances, is very great.[1] On such roads as existed in Illinois prior to the Civil War the expense of moving heavy freight for any distance was practically prohibitive, and ten to twenty miles was as far as grain or other bulky goods could be hauled with any degree of profit. As nearly all the products of the interior counties consisted of articles of small value compared with their bulk, this meant that an extensive network of railroads or canals was necessary to the proper development of the state. Instead of such a system of internal transportation, Illinois had nothing but execrable country roads, supplemented to only a slight extent by the few navigable or semi-navigable streams. The farmer living in the interior of the

---

[1] The cost of carrying a ton of freight from Buffalo to New York by wagon was $100, or about 20 cents per ton per mile. This was over good roads, and the cost per ton, per mile, for carrying grain in Illinois must have averaged considerably more.

state could carry only a small part of his crop of wheat or corn to market to be exchanged for "store goods," and the total amount of grain received at Chicago, St. Louis and Peoria from the interior counties of Illinois was insignificant.

The great bulk of the population in the forties and fifties was engaged in agriculture and the inadequate system of transportation had a depressing influence on that occupation. Farmers living near the waterways found good markets for their produce, but those not so favorably situated shipped little grain or wheat outside the state. Only slight cultivation was necessary to have the rich prairie soil bring forth abundant crops, and the immediate needs of the farmer and his family were easily supplied. Labor-saving machinery was not in general use and the work of gathering the crops had to be performed by hand, with farm labor scarce and commanding high wages. As a result, there was no incentive to raise large crops, while the amount of physical work involved made it impossible for the farmer to plant or gather more than a moderate yield. Shiftless methods of farming were the natural consequence, and only a small portion of the arable land was under cultivation. Out of a total area of 35,000,000 acres, slightly over 3,000,000 were planted in the five staples: wheat, corn, oats, rye and potatoes. One-third of the entire area, or 11,500,000 acres, was still unoccupied government land, and much of the remainder had never been broken by the plough. At the same time, the yield per acre was much less than could have been expected from the almost virgin soil of the prairies.

Inadequate transportation and backward agricultural conditions greatly retarded the settlement of the commonwealth and influenced the social and political life of those within its borders. The earliest settlements were made by the French at Cahokia and Kaskaskia near the Mississippi River, and until the end of the third decade nearly all subsequent settlements were also near the banks of the Ohio, the Mississippi and Illinois rivers, especially in the southern counties. At the beginning of the fourth decade the majority of the population were immigrants from Kentucky, Tennessee, and other parts of the south, or their descendants. Then, from 1830 to 1850, there occurred a heavy immigration into the northern and central counties; most of the new settlers coming from the eastern states, or Europe. By 1850 Illinois had a population of 850,000, and three-fourths of the inhabitants were living north of Vandalia and were of northern or European stock.[1] Furthermore, despite the absence of good transportation, 375,000 people were in the thirty-six counties which possessed neither a canal, a river, nor a railroad; and the number living more than ten miles from such means of communication must have been considerably larger.[2]

---

[1] The 30 counties south of Vandalia had a population of 219,863; the 69 north of that town, 631,607. The foreign born population was as follows: England, 18,628; Scotland, 4,661; Wales, 572; Ireland, 27,786; British America, 10,699; Germany, 38,446; total (including minor nationalities), 110,593. Native born of foreign parents not given.

[2] The 36 counties, without railroads, canals or navigable rivers, had a population of 375,529 in 1850, or 44.1 per cent of the total.

In the very earliest white settlements in Illinois the lack of good highways and the economic isolation of the interior proved a serious check to the growth of the community, but as the population was small and distributed along the few navigable rivers, slight attention was given to the matter of transportation. Nor did the heavy immigration from the southern states make necessary a radical improvement.

The settlers had always been accustomed to poor roads; they were settled near the Ohio, the Mississippi and the Illinois; and the number of people of the state was still small. However, the enormous growth of population from 1830 on—the increase was from 150,000 in the former year to 800,000 in 1850—made necessary the solution of problems which before had been borne as an unavoidable accompaniment of frontier life.

This was particularly true of the central counties. In 1830 a few thousand log huts scattered over the heart of the state were the only signs of civilization. But every succeeding year witnessed an increase in the number of homestead entries, the thickening of settlements and the rapid extension of cultivated land. The settlers were no longer shiftless, easy-going trappers or their hardly less shiftless companions on the clearings; in their place were energetic and progressive newcomers from New York, New England, and even Ireland, Germany and old England. As population and wealth grew and the disadvantages of the isolated economic conditions became more burdensome, greater and greater attention was given to the question of local and through transportation which could do away with the unbearable frontier life. The demands of the interior counties for a closer economic connection with the remainder of the state found a natural expression in the political field, and for some fifteen years, from 1835 to 1851, the solution of this problem was the subject of political debate, legislative action and popular vote. The center of the field was occupied by plans for some form of a central railroad, and it is the political aspects of this project that forms the theme of the remainder of this paper.

·Vital Question, Great Central Highway

A great central highway connecting the northern and southern counties of Illinois had always been a favorite project with the legislatures and executives of the state. As early as 1830, ·Governor Colès suggested that Lake Michigan might easily be tapped and the water taken by canals, not only into Illinois, but on the dividing line between that river and the Wabash down through the center of the state. Only two years later, Lieutenant-Governor A. M. Jenkins proposed in the Senate that a survey be made for a central railroad from Cairo to Peru, and though somewhat premature, the proposal created considerable discussion, both in and out of the·Legislature. By 1835, the building of the "Central" had become one of the important issues in state politics. The project was ably advocated by such newspapers as the Sangamon Journal, and also a number of leading citizens, prominent among them being Sidney Breese, whose fifteen years of service in promoting the undertaking entitles him to be called the "Father of the Illinois Central Railroad."

ILLINOIS CENTRAL INCORPORATED (1836)

With such support it was not long before definite measures were undertaken, and on January 18, 1836, the Illinois Legislature incorporated the (Illinois) Central Railroad Company to construct a railroad from "the mouth of the Ohio" to a point on the Illinois River at or near the termination of the Illinois-Michigan canal. Darius B. Holbrook, a New York speculator and promoter who had lately come to the west, was the leading spirit in the company and with him were associated Governor Reynolds, Lieutenant-Governors A. M. Jenkins and Pierre Menard, Judge Sidney Breese and Alfred K. Snyder; besides fifty-three others of less note. These gentlemen constituted the first board of directors, and a capital of $2,500,000 was authorized. From the first this road was regarded as a peculiar state institution and, lest its policy should be dominated by a foreign monopoly, provision was made that no person could subscribe to more than five shares of stock, and that at least one-fifth of the capital should be offered for sale in the state. Provision was also made that whenever the company earned more than twelve per cent on the cost of construction for a period of ten years, the Legislature could so reduce earnings and tolls for the next ten years that the earnings would not exceed that amount; reports being made to the state to show cost of construction and gross and net receipts. In return for this restriction on the powers of the company the Legislature inserted a clause in the charter agreeing not to incorporate any competitive railroad for a period of fifty years.

While not a direct issue in state politics, the incorporation of the Central Company shows the strong hold the project had upon the minds of the people. The incorporators were leading politicians and men of affairs of the community and the company itself enjoyed many privileges not usually granted to a "foreign" company. At the same time, like most western corporations, it was without financial backing, and its incorporation is only an evidence of popular interest.

STATE SYSTEM OF INTERNAL IMPROVEMENTS

Hardly was the company organized when it was swept aside by a movement of far greater general interest. So long as canals were the only artificial means of cheap land transportation, their prohibitive cost prevented the people of the western states from making any attempt to create a general system of internal improvements. The introduction of the locomotive into England and soon after into the eastern states provided a cheap yet efficient means of inland communication. As if an accompaniment of this invention, there took place in the United States a period of unprecedented financial prosperity, while the speculative spirit among the state legislatures was fostered by the Treasury Distribution act of 1837, and other fiscal measures of the national government. Thus the financial and technical difficulties in the way of an extensive system of internal improvements were apparently removed.

Like one of her own prairie fires, the demand for state construction of an extensive system of internal improvements spread over the State of Illinois. Mass meetings, conventions, parades, etc., were held in all parts of the state; the newspapers took up the movement and their columns were filled with editorials and contributed articles; finally, the politicians seized it as a means of personal and party popularity, and the Legislature passed the celebrated Internal Improvement Act of 1837. The political "deals," log rollings and tricks adopted to secure the passage of the measure, even by such men as Douglas, Logan and Lincoln, are familiar to every reader and need not be repeated. It is interesting to note, however, that it was the influence of the central portions of the state, i. e., the portions most in need of railroads, which finally secured the passage of the measure.

The system of the internal improvements provided for by the act extended to all parts of the state, and was a worthy conception of the strongest General Assembly ever held in Illinois. The backbone of the system was a central railroad from Cairo northward via Vandalia, Shelbyville, Decatur, Bloomington and Savannah to Galena, at the time the most important city in the state. In addition, there were several cross lines extending from the main stem to the important cities on the eastern or western boundaries. The entire system amounted to about 1,200 miles, but the estimates as to cost of construction were surprisingly low. Three and a half million dollars was regarded as sufficient to build the 450 miles of the main line, while the Shelbyville and Alton branches were to cost $650,000 and $600,000, respectively, or from $7,000 to $10,000 per mile; less than one-fourth what it cost the present company fifteen years later. A loan, based on the credit of the state, was to provide the funds, while a board of seven commissioners was appointed to manage the enterprise during the construction and after completion.

NARROW STATE POLICY

From the political viewpoint the internal improvement plan is interesting as the first and fullest expression of the celebrated Illinois "state policy." With a narrow state loyalty, almost inconceivable now, the central and northern parts of the state insisted that every railroad passing through the territory of Illinois should terminate at an Illinois city. In other words, outside or "foreign" centers should not be built up at the expense of local towns with a deep-seated ambition to be the London or New York of the west. The internal improvement system was the ideal of these narrow sectionalists; and Galena, Quincy, Alton, Cairo and Carroll were made the termini of the railroads, and were established as the commercial centers of the state, in so far as the Legislature could do so by enactment.

Despite the enthusiasm of the populace; despite the reckless generosity of the Legislature—with other people's money; despite the strict adherence to the Illinois state policy, the project was doomed to failure.

Immediately after the passage of the act, the commissioners commenced work, and for a while it seemed as if this colossal undertaking might be finished. Grading was commenced at Cairo, Galena and intermediate points; tens of thousands of dollars was expended on the dikes and levees at Cairo; large quantities of rail were purchased; about forty miles of embankment north of Cairo completed; and, altogether, something like $1,000,000 was expended on the central route and branches, although certainly not in the most effectual manner. .But the task was· entirely beyond the ability of the state; financial difficulties prevented the floating of the necessary bonds, while extravagance, graft and mismanagement exhausted the money already procured, and 100 miles of grading and a few thousand tons of iron were the only tangible results of this second attempt to construct a railroad through the center of Illinois.

THE GREAT WESTERN RAILWAY (HOLBROOK) COMPANY

Even this failure did not deter the state or its citizens from endeavoring to complete the project, and on March 6, 1843, only six years after the passage of the Internal Improvement Act, the Legislature incorporated the Great Western Railway Company, better known as the Holbrook Company. To understand this act it is necessary to go back six years, to March 4, 1837.

On that date the Cairo City & Canal Company was incorporated with power to hold real estate in Alexander County, especially the tract of land now included in the corporate limits of Cairo, and to carry on general industrial enterprises. Mr. Darius P. Holbrook of New York, the promoter of the company of 1836, was elected president, and for twenty years the enterprise was dominated by his masterful personality until the two became synonymous. During the prosperous period ·just before the panic the company borrowed between $2,000,000 and $3,000,- 000, largely from English capitalists; purchased several acres of land at the mouth of the Ohio River; established industries of all kinds; laid out an extensive city at what is now Cairo; protected it by embankments and levees; carried on a general mercantile business, and enacted ordinances for the government of the citizens of Cairo. However, the resources of the company were not equal to the demands made upon it and the failure of the internal improvement ·policy in 1840, following closely after the severe panic of 1837, forced the enterprise into bankruptcy. English investors refused further financial support, and the stoppage of work on the state railroad destroyed the undeveloped industries of Cairo. The directors neglected the undertaking; the property in and near the city was abandoned, and for a time the place was occupied only by squatters and disreputable characters from the river boats.

The extreme depression existing in Illinois after the panic of 1837 and the failure of the state policy prevented Mr. Holbrook from doing anything with the Cairo City and Canal Company until 1843. Realizing the possibilities of the "Central" Railroad, he induced the Legislature to pass the Great Western Railway Act of that year. According to the charter, the president and directors of the Cairo City and Canal Company were incorporated as the Great Western Railway Company, and were given authority to construct a railway from Cairo to the Illinois-Michigan Canal. In many ways this act was quite favorable to the state. The otherwise worthless grading done in 1837 and 1840 was to be purchased at a fair valuation; twenty-five per cent of the net receipts from operation, after a twelve per cent dividend had been paid on the stock, were to go to the state; and the Legislature could alter the charter of both the Great Western and Cairo City and Canal companies after all the indebtedness of the former was paid. But for half a dozen years the Cairo Company had been known as a flagrant example of speculative and corrupt corporate management, and to turn over to such a company without reasonable compensation, or even adequate safeguards as to the completion of the work, the most important industrial enterprise within the state was, to say the least, a short-sighted policy. Moreover, a clause was inserted in the closing section of the act surrendering to the company any public lands which might come into the possession of the State of Illinois during the life of the charter. Not even a guarantee was demanded that such lands should be used for the construction of the railroad. This legislation shows the wretched financial condition the state was in in 1843, and illustrates the lack of foresight characteristic of the General Assemblies during the period.

For a time it seemed as if the company was seriously determined to proceed with the "Central" Railroad. Large sums were borrowed and expended in finishing the original state surveys and completing the grading. Numerous buildings were erected at Cairo, and an extensive system of levees was planned and partially constructed. But conditions were not favorable, and the company could not obtain capital to continue the work. Several millions had already been expended by the Cairo company without dividend-paying results; all Illinois credit, both state and private, was under suspicion on account of the partial repudiation of the state debt, and eastern and European capitalists refused to risk further investments in Illinois. Lack of funds stopped all construction within a few months after the charter was secured and the directors finally gave up in despair. On March 3, 1845, with the consent of the company, the charter was repealed by special act of the Legislature; all work done by the company reverted to the state, and the third and most promising attempt to construct the "Central" Railroad ended with heavy loss to the promoters and no profit to the state.

GREAT WESTERN REINCORPORATED (1849)

For six years after the incorporation of the Great Western no further attempt was made to build the railroad, and the energies of the supporters of the project were spent in various attempts to secure aid from the national government, but without success. However, it seemed reasonably certain that the difficulties would be removed and a definite grant of land made in some session of the Thirtieth or Thirty-first Con-

gress. Any measure would undoubtedly be of considerable value to the
State of Illinois or to private parties who might build the road, and
the Cairo City and Canal Company determined to make use of the
apparently favorable conditions. Accordingly, after the failure of the
Land Grant Bill in the first session of the Thirtieth Congress the Cairo
City and Canal Company petitioned the Legislature for a renewal of
their previous rights, which had been lost by the act of March 3, 1845.
Although the Holbrook companies were disliked throughout the state,
they represented the wealthiest aggregation of capital in Illinois, and
apparently were the best able to complete the Illinois Central Railroad.
In recognition of this fact the Legislature, on February 10, 1849, reincorporated the Great Western Railway Company, with all its former
privileges, including the obnoxious clause surrendering to the company
whatever lands the federal government should grant the state. Moreover, this was done without any restriction of importance being placed
on the disposal of these lands.

Such action by the Illinois Legislature was almost fatal to any federal land grant, and Senator Douglas at once attempted to have the
charter repealed. With the assistance of his colleagues at Washington
and prominent citizens of the state, he was able to induce the president
and the directors of the Cairo City and Canal Company to execute a
release of the Great Western charter. However, the surrender was con-
ditional upon the acceptance of the release by the Legislature at its next
session, and the incorporation of another company to carry on the
project.

At the following session of Congress the Illinois delegation secured
a grant of land to the State of Illinois to assist in the construction of
the railroad, the total amount of land thus given varying from 2,500,000
to 3,000,000 acres. The mere passage of the Federal Land Grant Act
was the least difficult of the many problems confronting the friends of
the Illinois Central. For some years the questions connected with this
railroad had been before the Legislature and the citizens of the state,
and now that success was probable, all the previous conflicts were
renewed with additional strength. The most troublesome of these conflicts involved the method of construction and the route.

Ways of Utilizing Land Grant

There were four possible ways of utilizing the land grant, each of
which had its vigorous adherents: State construction of the railroad
by means of the grant, along the line of the internal improvement plan
of 1837; surrender of the grant to the bondholders and construction
by them on terms similar to those made by the holders of canal bonds
in 1840; completion by the Great Western Railway Company under its
charter of 1849, including the retention of all state lands; creation of
an entirely new private corporation and the transfer to it of the land
grant under certain restrictions and with certain payments to the state.

To many citizens state construction was still a feasible project.
From 1831 to 1843 the various plans for the railroad depended on gov-

ernment support, and despite the collapse of the internal improvement plan of 1837, there was considerable talk of direct construction by the Legislature. The cost of building the road was underestimated, while the value of the land was overestimated. It was thought possible to build the road without recourse to bond issues, and the profit from operation would then quickly retire the old state debt. But the panic of 1840 and the depressing influence of the debt was still vivid in the minds of the citizens of Illinois and they generally condemned any fur-' ther work by the state.

Another form of semi-legislative management was contained in the so-called "bondholders" plan, which was submitted to the Legislature in January, 1851. For instance, Mr. J. S. Wright of Chicago published a pamphlet in which he took the ground that the grant, being of such immense value, the state should hold the lands and again attempt the construction of the road.

As a result of the internal improvement legislation, a debt of some $15,000,000 had been accumulated and the state was unable to meet the full interest charges. In fact, bankruptcy or repudiation had been barely escaped and the creditors supposed there would be difficulty in attracting capital for the construction of the road. Under the circumstances, certain eastern bondholders suggested an arrangement somewhat similar to the one under which the Illinois-Michigan Canal was built. A company, composed largely of bondholders, was to be chartered and given power to construct the railroad; $4 of stock or $3 of bonds entitled, "New Internal Improvement Stock," was to be given for each $1 of cash paid in. The state was to receive stock of a par value equal to the value of the land sold, and in addition pay all expenses of survey, etc. The stock belonging to the state must be set apart to retire the state debt. The stock of the new company, in addition, could be made the basis for state banking. On the whole, the terms were about as onerous as could be imposed on a bankrupt state, and are in striking contrast to the Illinois Central charter. The project never received serious attention from either the newspapers or the Legislature.

Construction by the Great Western was of much greater importance. The charter of 1849 was evidently obtained with the distinct object of securing the federal land grant and no work was done on the railroad until it was almost certain Congress would pass the act. Then construction work was started and it was stated that large quantities of rail were purchased in England. At the same time active efforts were made to defeat any bill repealing the charter. It is uncertain whether this company intended to carry on the work, or, as Senator Douglas alleged, merely sell the charter in Europe. At any rate the opposition to the Great Western, especially in the southern part of the state, was bitter and deep seated.

The last plan was to turn the grant over to a private corporation, other than the Cairo City and Canal Company, under proper restrictions. The memorial of the Boston capitalists (they later built the road) was the first direct proposition of the kind, but it is probable that the memorialists had suggested to the leading legislators of the state a plan along the lines of their memorial. In all probability, other capitalists were also deeply interested in the railroad. However, there was no definite project of the kind before the people during November and December, 1850.

Congress passed the land grant act in September, 1850, and the Legislature was elected the following November. On account of the release of the Great Western charter it was necessary to settle the matter at the first session of the General Assembly and the selection of proper representatives and senators was of vital importance. As soon as it became evident that the federal Congress would act favorably on the Illinois Central bill the advocates of state construction and the friends and opponents of the Cairo City and Canal Company commenced an active campaign to secure a majority of the members of the Legislature. Other state issues were consigned to the background and the question of the land grant and the acceptance of the Great Western release were the important factors in the election of members to the Fifteenth General Assembly. The newspapers of the state had numerous editorials and contributed articles defending or opposing the respective plants, or else emphasizing the importance of one route over another. Mass meetings and conventions were held at various points along the line of the proposed railroad and the excitement often was at fever heat. By November the controversy had become bitter and personal. Individual motives were impugned; the character of some of the leading newspaper editors, of Mr. Holbrook, Senator Douglas, Judge Breese and others, was maligned, and charges of bribery and fraud were frequent. By the time the Legislature convened in January the whole discussion had degenerated into a typical Illinois political fight. On the whole, the opponents of both state ownership and the Holbrook company had much the better of the argument. Only a few newspapers, such as the Benton Standard and the Cairo Times, and a few politicians, the most prominent of them being Sidney Breese, openly defended the Cairo City and Canal Company, or its subsidiary company, the Great Western. However, the latter company was already in possession of the desired charter and, conditionally, of the land grant. Thus, inaction on the part of the Legislature meant success for the Holbrook party and the Cairo City and Canal Company exerted every effort to block legislation and prevent the incorporation of a rival company. On account of the many minor fights it was not at such a disadvantage as indicated by newspaper editorials.

Many of the plans had been thoroughly discussed during the campaign and when the Legislature met the first day of January, 1851, its members were well acquainted with the main points at issue. In the organization of the house the Holbrook faction secured a temporary advantage by the election of Judge Breese as speaker and during the first two weeks of the session they were strong enough to prevent radical action. Bills were presented in both houses repealing the charter of the Great Western but both were strongly opposed. The Senate passed a bill in regard to the Illinois Central, though it did not accept the release; the House passed a bill accepting the release and refused to adopt the Senate measure. A large majority of the members of each body favored accepting the repeal of the Great Western charter, but so far in the session the Holbrook proposition was the only reasonable measure before the Legislature and many preferred to retain the Cairo Company rather than to be entirely without a means of building the road.

ROBERT RANTOUL, CREATOR OF THE ILLINOIS CENTRAL

At this stage of the contest affairs were entirely altered by a business-like memorial presented by Mr. Robert Rantoul of Massachusetts, acting in the interest of a group of wealthy New York and Boston capitalists. In brief the plan of the memorialists was as follows: The Legislature should create a corporation and surrender to it the federal land grant. In return the corporation agreed to build a railroad "equal in all respects to the railroad running between Boston and Albany with such improvements thereon as experience has shown to be desirable and expedient, to complete the road by July, 1854, and to pay to the state ...... per cent of the gross receipts in return for the land." The memorialists were men of considerable capital and had had experience with railroad promotion in other parts of the country. On the whole they made a more favorable offer than could have been expected.

Coincident with the transmission of this memorial Mr. Gridley introduced in the Senate a bill "for an act to incorporate the Illinois Central Railroad." On February 5th Mr. J. L. D. Morrison offered a substitute for the original bill and on the next day it passed by a vote of 23 to 3. Four days later it passed the house by an almost unanimous vote of seventy-two to two, and was immediately signed by Governor French.

The passage of the charter through both houses was not as easy as the vote indicates. Shortly after the receipt of the memorial the whole matter was referred to a committee and the members, in connection with Mr. Rantoul and Colonel Bissell, the representatives of the promoters spent considerable time in preparing the measure. As the duration of the session was limited to forty days the Holbrook interests made every effort to delay the bill and during the last week of January and the first of February it looked as if their efforts would meet with success. At last, as noticed above, the bill was passed by both houses only a few days before the close of the session. The main difficulty came in the selection of a route and the Legislature was finally forced to leave the exact location of the road to the incorporators. The other point of conflict was the percentage to be paid the state. This was finally fixed at seven per cent of the gross receipts, but at the same time, the company was freed from paying any state or local taxes.[1]

---

[1] In the original memorial the amount paid to the state was left vacant. It was proposed in the House that 10 per cent be given, but the company, through the efforts of Robert Rantoul and Representative Bissell, managed to reduce the percentage to 7. The real reasons for the action of the Legislature in this matter are not known and in his campaign for election as governor Colonel Bissell was accused of having obtained the reduction to the disadvantage of the state.

With the incorporation and construction of the Illinois Central ended the long struggle to secure railway communication for the interior of the state. The way was blazed for new railroads in all sections of Illinois and their completion opened up to settlement the hitherto unoccupied counties. The economic isolation of the interior ceased and the state became an economic whole.

Politically, the effects were equally far reaching. The construction of the "Central" and the chartering of other companies satisfied the need of good transportation and the demands of the interior counties for internal improvements carried on by the state died away as the need became less and less. The important, and at times dominating, issue of state construction of canals and railroads, which entered so deeply into the political life of the commonwealth from 1830 to 1850, ceased to be of popular interest. The construction of the railroads and the broadening influence of improved communication also eliminated from the field the celebrated question of "State policy," for twenty-five years a bone for contention between the northern and southern counties. In brief, the chartering of the Illinois Central marks the close of the political agitation for state internal improvements. After 1851 these matters which had repeatedly agitated the community disappeared and their places were taken by other questions.

To Dr. Bronson's paper a few facts should be added in elucidation of the charter requirements imposed by the state upon the Illinois Central (and which have been faithfully performed), as well as to more closely connect the great corporation with the localities of Champaign County, the interests of which were so fostered by its coming.

After a thorough discussion of all the interests involved, sections were incorporated into the charter requiring the company to pay five per cent of its gross receipts into the state treasury semi-annually; exempting railroad lands from taxation and the stock of the railroad for six years; after which an annual state tax was to be levied on the railroad properties, and should that exceed three-fourths of one per cent per annum, such excess should be deducted from the before mentioned gross receipts; provided the five per cent on the gross railroad receipts and the state taxes to be paid do not amount to seven per cent of the gross receipts of the company, in which case the difference, up to seven per cent shall be paid by the company into the state treasury.

Relations of the Illinois Central with the State

In pursuance with these charter provisions, the first four semi-annual payments made to the state treasury by the Illinois Central Company consisted of five per cent of the gross earnings; since April 30, 1857, the payments have been made on a basis of seven per cent of the gross earnings. The first semi-annual payment, made October 31, 1855, amounted to $29,751.59; this sum had been increased to $718,-705.01 on October 31, 1915. The total paid into the state treasury in the past sixty years is $36,973,294.38. In a few instances, as in 1895 and 1896, the Illinois Central Company has advanced the semi-annual payments months before they were due, and thus relieved the state from a deficit in the treasury. By an opinion of the attorney general of the state the provisions of the railroad charter apply to the Illinois Central Railroad from Cairo via Centralia to La Salle, over 300 miles; from La Salle via Galena to Dunleith, over 146 miles; from Centralia to Chicago, nearly 250 miles. The charter does not apply to any roads leased, purchased or built by the company other than the 697.5 miles referred to.

The Illinois Central Company listed its property with the auditor of public accounts from 1855 to 1859, but from that year until the spring of 1906 did not do so, claiming that the seven per cent of its gross earnings was the maximum amount which it was required to pay into the state treasury. Since 1906 the railroad company has listed its property with the auditor, and after paying five per cent of its gross earnings and the state taxes, makes up any deficit which may thereafter occur up to seven per cent of its gross receipts. The state of Illinois and the Illinois Central have, on the whole, been harmonious partners.

ACTUAL SURVEY AND CONSTRUCTION

Now, as to the actual work of survey and construction—an engineering party, organized at Chicago, May 21, 1851, began the preliminary survey of the Chicago branch and before the end of the year that line was surveyed and staked. The grading was completed in 1852. In May, 1853, the section from La Salle to Bloomington was opened to the public, and in July of the following year the first train entered West Urbana from Chicago, 128 miles. The Illinois Central depot, which had been commenced a year previous, was ready for the reception of travelers. In August following the arrival of the Illinois Central train, the old mail coach was abandoned and Postmaster A. P. Cunningham commenced to use the railroad for communication by letter and newspaper.

WEST URBANA (CHAMPAIGN) FOUNDED

Soon after the completion of the line to the central part of the county, T. R. Webber, as master in chancery and under a decree of the Circuit Court, platted and sold that portion of the Busey estate north of Springfield Avenue between First and Wright streets. This was followed by the platting of the land between Neil and First streets, by the Illinois Central Railroad, which is now the main business section of Champaign. Soon afterward, Jeffrey A. Farnam and Nathan M. Clark, two construction engineers of the newly built railroad, and John P. White, made an addition to West Urbana under the firm name of Farnam, Clark & White. In that addition fifteen acres were set apart for a public park, the first in the county and known as White Park.

If the depot be excepted, the Illinois Central erected the first building in the business part of what is now Champaign. It was the temporary building used by its corps of construction engineers at the northwest corner of First South and Market streets. This was soon followed by the first general store erected by John C. Baddeley, on North Neil Street, which the proprietor opened in October, 1854. Mr Baddeley was the postmaster also. From this time on, West Urbana grew apace.

JUST BEFORE THE RAILROAD CAME

Judge J. O. Cunningham came into the county while the workmen were grading the Illinois Central from Chicago, and thus pictures conditions during that raw period: "In 1853, twenty years after this became a county, I first saw these beautiful landscapes then almost in a state of nature, and determined to make this my future home. Except in the limited increase in population, the county has made but little advancement in twenty years. From two postoffices, Van Buren and Ludington, afterward changed to Homer, the number had increased to five only. None of the streams were bridged except the Salt Fork at Homer. The roads were little better than traces across the prairies and through timber belts, with but little improvements in the lanes in the way of grading and culverts. The settlements were confined to the groves and timber belts almost exclusively. I only remember a few farms opened a mile from the timber. The road from Urbana to Mahomet—from timber to timber—had perhaps not to exceed six farms opened upon it. Few could be found who were daring enough to assert that these prairies would ever be settled. Lands could be had at from a few cents per acre for government lands under the graduation law to $10 per acre for choice improved locations. There were, perhaps, five or six cheap church buildings, one of which was in Urbana, and not to exceed a dozen schoolhouses of all kinds. No railroad, or other public means of conveyance, touched the county, although the Illinois Central was located and partly graded. Transportation to the county was conducted entirely by private conveyance, and mostly from the Wabash towns, to which merchandise was brought from the eastern cities by canal and by river steamers."

Railroad Lands Draw Settlers

The result upon the growth of the Champaign County population which followed from the throwing upon the market of large tracts of railroad lands was most marked after the line had been fairly projected into its territory. The land thus donated to the Illinois Central by the state (given to the commonwealth by the Congressional Act of 1850) amounted to 2,595,000 acres, lying within fifteen miles of its road.

On the 12th of October, 1854, the following announcement appeared in the Urbana Union, issued by John Campbell, land agent of the Illinois Central: "The lands of the Illinois Central Railroad Company, situated upon and within fifteen miles of the Chicago branch of their road, and extending from a point in Effingham County, known as the north boundary of township six, north of the base line, to a point in Iroquois County on the north boundary of township number twenty-eight, north of the base line, are now offered for sale.

"The limits above mentioned include lands situated in the counties of Jasper, Effingham, Cumberland, Coles, Moultrie, Piatt and Champaign, and a part of Iroquois, Livingston and Shelby.

"The character of these lands is too well known to require description or comment in commending their quality. Persons having made application for any of these lands, and all others wishing to purchase or obtain information as to the quality of particular tracts and terms of sale, are requested to apply at the office of the undersigned at the Urbana Depot, where plats of the land may be seen and information in reference to these lands cheerfully given."

Congress Attempts to Regulate Land Prices

Many pamphlets had already been distributed in the more settled section of the east, assuring settlers upon the railroad lands not only a competency from the first, but a prospective fortune; it was the old story of the progressive and unchecked accumulation of eggs and chickens. Congress also took a hand in another direction, by attempting to regulate the prices of public lands, and in August, 1854, had passed what was known as the Graduation Law. By its terms the prices of all public lands remaining unsold were reduced and graded according to the periods in which they had been on the market. Those which had been opened to settlement ten years or upwards were reduced to one dollar per acre; those fifteen years or upwards, to seventy-five cents; twenty years or upwards, fifty cents; twenty-five years or upwards, twenty-five cents, thirty years or upwards, twelve and a half cents per acre. Under this statute many obtained cheap lands and made for themselves good homesteads; as, at that date, there were many tracts in the county which, owing to their remote location, had been rejected by both homeseeker and speculator. It is a fact that some of the lands which originally sold for $12\frac{1}{2}$ cents per acre are now marketable at from $100 to $125 per acre.

INCREASE OF POPULATION IN CHAMPAIGN COUNTY

The ultimate result both of this exploitation of the railroad lands, and the efforts of the national authorities to protect the interests of homeseekers in regulating the prices of public lands, was to start a rush of emigration from the eastern states to the timber lands and prairies of Illinois. Even the prairie townships of Champaign County, like Stanton, Harwood, Ayers and Crittenden, east of the Illinois Central, and Colfax, Brown and East Bend, west of the line, which up to the time of its coming had been practically without population, soon showed signs of life, while the prairie neighborhoods of the timber belts and the groves themselves received a new population in colonies. As many of the newcomers were not practical farmers, such additions were not always advantageous to the county.

In the latter class were not a few settlers on the railroad lands; and when family sickness, and frosts, and blights, the Civil War and other unforeseen hindrances appeared, many returned discouraged to the East. Many others remained and earned their homesteads and reputations in the new country. It is justice to the Illinois Central to add that it was always lenient and even generous in its dealings with those who purchased its lands at an early period, and were unable to meet the terms of the purchase.

Until the coming of the Illinois Central there was virtually no settlement in what are now Rantoul and Ludlow townships except the farm opened by Archa Campbell at Mink Grove. But the building of the railroad promptly stimulated settlement, especially in the neighborhood of what is now the village of Rantoul. A large colony from northern Ohio came in 1857, and both Rantoul and Tomasboro became stations on the Illinois Central. Further north Pera station (now Ludlow) had been established at an earlier date. Both Tolono and Pesotum were stations established in the '50s, a land office being in operation at the former place in 1855. Savoy became a station through the activities of the great Dunlap fruit farm and nursery which was established at that point in 1858.

What is now the Champaign and Havana branch of the Illinois Central, after passing through several transformations, in September, 1886, was sold under foreclosure to the Illinois Central. The stations west of Champaign are Bondville and Seymour, in Scott Township. The line extends from Champaign to Havana, Mason County.

The Rantoul division of the Central, from Leroy, McLean County, to the Indiana state line, was chartered in 1876 as the Havana, Rantoul & Eastern Railroad. It was built as a narrow-gauge line, operated as such in 1881, and afterward changed to standard. Under other names it was several times in the hands of a receiver, and in 1886 was absorbed by the Illinois Central. It crosses the main line of the Central at Rantoul and, besides Fisher, its stations are Lotus, Dewey, Gifford and Penfield.

THE WABASH RAILROAD

The Wabash Railroad in Illinois is based upon the old Northern Cross Railroad, projected as a part of the Internal Improvement scheme of 1837. The section from Springfield to the Illinois River at Meredosia, Morgan County, fifty-eight miles west, was completed in 1842. It was operated for a time by mules, but it was finally abandoned as an enterprise ahead of the times and an unprofitable undertaking. In 1847 the line was sold to Springfield capitalists, then transferred to New Yorkers, who organized the Sangamon & Morgan Railroad, reconstructed the road in part, and opened the line for business in 1849. In 1856 several Ohio and Indiana companies were consolidated as the Toledo, Wabash & Western Railroad, and two years later a reorganization was effected as the Great Western Railroad Company—not to be confused with the old corporation by that name which died a natural death just before the Illinois Central was galvanized into life by Senator Douglas.

It was at this period of its history that the line was built through southern Champaign County. Old Sidney, which had been platted in 1837 as a foreordained station on the Northern Cross Railroad finally came to its own, over twenty years later, as a station on the Great Western. Philo, midway between Sidney and Tolono, was similarly honored; as were eventually Sidney, Tolono, Sadorus and Ivesdale. A branch of the Wabash cuts through the northwest corner of the county; stations Foosland and Lotus.

The Wabash system was mainly an outgrowth of the Wabash, St. Louis & Pacific, the consolidation of its eastern and western divisions under the present name having been effected in 1889. ·

THE BIG FOUR

The Big Four came into existence in 1889-90 through the consolidation of the Cincinnati, Indianapolis, St. Louis & Chicago, the Cleveland, Columbus, Cincinnati & Indianapolis and the Indianapolis & St. Louis railway companies, with certain leased lines in Illinois. It was constructed through Champaign County as the Indianapolis, Bloomington & Western in 1869. Ten years later it was sold under foreclosure, in 1881 was consolidated with the Ohio, Indiana & Pacific Railroad, in 1887 took the name of the Ohio, Indiana & Western, and in February, 1890, was reorganized as the Peoria & Eastern Railroad and leased to the Cleveland, Cincinnati, Chicago & St. Louis Railway. It is an east and west line passing through two central tiers of townships, its stations being Ogden, St. Joseph, Urbana, Champaign and Mahomet. The large shops at Urbana were opened in April, 1871.

CHICAGO AND EASTERN ILLINOIS

The Chicago & Eastern Illinois was chartered in 1865 as the Chicago, Danville & Vincennes Railroad, its main line being completed in 1872. It was sold under foreclosure in 1877 and reorganized as the Chicago & Nashville, but later in that year took its present name. In 1894 it was consolidated with the Chicago & Indiana Coal Company. On the main line in Champaign County are the stations of Bongard, Block, Sidney, Tipton, Royal and Gerald. It crosses the Big Four about a mile east of St. Joseph. The branch which passes through the southeast corner of the county accommodates Long View and Broadlands.

ILLINOIS TRACTION SYSTEM

The Illinois Traction system passes east and west near the center of the county, south of the Big Four and Illinois Central, taking in

Ogden, St. Joseph, Mayview, Urbana, Champaign, Staley, Bonville, and Seymour, with designated local stops between these points. It is linked with Danville and the Indiana electric system on the east and is connected with Decatur and the western and southwestern lines to Springfield and St. Louis. Champaign is the headquarters of the Illinois Traction system and the home of its president and general manager, William B. McKinley. The other officers are Charles Dilley, vice-president; George M. Mattison, treasurer, and H. J. Pepper, manager.

URBANA AND CHAMPAIGN RAILWAY, GAS AND ELECTRIC COMPANY

Officially, the local system is known as the Urbana and Champaign Railway, Gas and Electric Company, and the wide scope of its corporate activities is indicated by the title. The original corporation was the Champaign and Urbana Gas Light and Coke Company, which was incorporated February 18, 1867, by John Faulds, Daniel Gardner, Thomas A. Cosgrove, C. R. Griggs, John G. Clark and C. M. Sherffy. Gas was first supplied to the people of Champaign in September, 1869.

On the 25th of the same month Edward Ater, Daniel Gardner, Clark R. Griggs and others organized the Urbana and Champaign Horse Railway Company, as incorporators, with a capital of $10,000. The first street cars were run by mules in 1863.

In March, 1889, the United Manufacturing Company was formed and authorized, under its charter, to manufacture brick and tile, steam heating apparatus and chemicals and drugs, as well as electric light machinery, and to supply power, water and light. It took over the old water works constructed under the franchise of 1884 and the plant of the Western Electric Light Company, which had been in operation since September, 1885. Both of these plants had been built and developed by Mr. McKinley, who was the moving power in the organization of the United Manufacturing Company. In 1890 he was elected president of the reorganized Urbana and Champaign Railway, Gas and Electric Company, and the electric railway at once took first place in the general scheme.

WILLIAM B. McKINLEY

Probably no man is better known in Illinois as a promoter and consolidator of public utilities than William B. McKinley. Between 1890 and 1900 he built or reconstructed electric roads in Springfield and Defiance, Ohio; Bay City, Michigan; and Joliet, La Salle, Galesburg, Quincy, Danville and Decatur, Illinois; besides the Champaign and Urbana Electric Railway. Since then, aside from his congressional work, he has given his attention largely to the development of interurban electric systems in Illinois and Indiana, one of his completed enterprises having been the joining of the system which centers at Champaign with the Danville and Decatur lines to the east and west, respectively. The Danville, Urbana and Champaign Railway Company was granted a franchise in 1901, and the line opened to Danville in 1903. In 1907 the system was extended west to Decatur. This section is said to be the only interurban line in the country operating sleeping cars.

In December, 1890, an ordinance was passed by the City Council of Champaign granting the Urbana and Champaign Railway, Gas and Electric Company the right to light the streets of that place, and a similar privilege was accorded the corporation by the municipal authorities of Urbana. The first arc lamps were used in Urbana during 1893 and in Champaign during 1896.

The water supply of the Twin Cities is controlled by the Champaign and Urbana Water Company, so that transportation interests are what remain to the great corporation which has had a continuous history of sixty years. For many years H. J. Pepper has been its active and resident manager.

For three or four years, during the '90s, B. F. Harris, now president of the First National Bank of Champaign, owned and operated the street railway, gas and electric system of the two cities. He sold out his interest to Mr. McKinley, who enlarged and improved the system and has stood at the head of the ownership ever since.

CHAPTER X

COUNTY'S MILITARY RECORD

Four Revolutionary Soldiers—The Hopkins Expedition of 1812—
Served in the Black Hawk War—"Uncle Tommy Butler"—
Mutual Excitement—The Mexican War—Civil War Officers
—John S. Wolfe Enlists and Recruits—Company A, Twen-
tieth Illinois Infantry—Colonel Wolfe of the One Hun-
dred and Thirty-fifth Regiment — The Twenty-fifth
(William N. Coler, Colonel)—Twenty-sixth Regiment
—Seventy-sixth Regiment (Col. S. T. Busey)—Ready to Obey
—Fort. Blakeley Carried by Storm—Minor Officers of the
Seventy-sixth—The One Hundred and Twenty-fifth Regi-
ment (Col. James W. Langley)—The One Hundred and
Thirty-fifth Again—Cavalry Companies—Prominent in Scat-
tered Commands—Spanish-American War Service—State University, Present Military Center.

The military record of Champaign County really commences with
its participation in the Civil War. Its connection with the National
conflicts which preceded the War of the Rebellion is an indirect one, or
is confined to the service of scattered individuals.

Four Revolutionary Soldiers

Although it would have been manifestly impossible for any settlers
on the soil of the present Champaign County to have participated in
the earlier wars of the nation, some of their soldiers who went from
the older states and afterward settled in Illinois passed their last years
in that section of the State. It is of record that at least four Revolutionary soldiers have died and been buried in Champaign County:
William Hays, the grandfather of Asa F. Hays, who died in 1852 on
the old Albright farm, near the Somers schoolhouse, a few miles northeast of Urbana; William Kirby, of the well known family which settled
on the north side of the Big Grove; Newton Shaw and Robert Brownfield, father of the well known millwright and 'Squire John Brownfield.
The father died in 1841. John, while a youth and while the family

351

was living in Harrison County, Kentucky, was a volunteer in the War of 1812 and spent several months in the Harrison campaigns in the Maumee country, for which he received a Government land warrant. The family came to Champaign County in 1832.

All the Revolutionary soldiers except Mr. Brownfield were buried in the Clements cemetery, about four miles northeast of Urbana, and Mr. Brownfield himself was buried in private grounds in that neighborhood.

The Hopkins Expedition of 1812

The county, as at present defined, had no settlers to serve in the War of 1812, and is identified with that conflict only from its territorial location. It was in the direct line of march of General Hopkins, a Revolutionary veteran in command of the Kentucky riflemen at Vincennes, who, after destroying the hostile Indian villages in the Wabash Valley, was to march across country and join General Russell at Peoria Lake, in the Illinois Valley, and finish the work of destruction among the enemy red men of the Illinois country. But the troops were undisciplined and some deserted even before they reached the Grand Prairie. Those who remained hunted game, threw off all pretentions at discipline, and on the fourth day from Fort Harrison, on the Wabash, the expedition, as a whole, lost its way. To make the confusion worse, if possible, the Indians, who had discovered the state of affairs, set fire to the prairie grass and otherwise harassed the force.

General Hopkins, in describing his ill-starred expedition, says that on the night of October 19, 1812, the soldiers encamped at a grove of timber affording water, and, in consideration of the distance and general direction marched, county historians have long claimed that the description and facts fix the locality as the Big Grove of Champaign County. Capt. Zachary Taylor was of the Hopkins party and did all he could to second the efforts of the commanding general to bring the men into some kind of subjection. All such efforts were in vain. What started from Vincennes as a little army less than a week previous had become a mob which broke into fragments and disappeared.

Served in the Black Hawk War

Quite a number of families had settled in what is now Champaign County at the outbreak of the Black Hawk War, and at least two of the men are known to have joined Captain Brown's Mounted Rangers, or United States Regulars, as they were also called. They furnished their own horses, clothes and guns, and were paid $1 a day for their services. The term of enlistment was for one year. The company of Vermilion County men naturally mustered at Danville, the county seat; in fact, most of its members were citizens of that place, perhaps half a dozen coming from the western districts. The entire regiment, under orders for the seat of war in northern Illinois, crossed the Wabash River at Terre Haute, and a northwesterly course led them through Champaign County. One night the ground near the creek on West Main Street, Urbana, near the present site of the Christian Church, was chosen as a camp, and was so occupied until the next morning. The regiment marched through the county under arms from the south to the north line.

Thomas L. Butler, Martin Rhinehart, Jacob Heator, James Johnson, Thomas Richards, Elias Stamey and Rev. Mr. Mahurin comprised the delegation from the western part of Vermilion County. The last named was a Baptist minister who resided and preached in Big Grove. He went forth as a chaplain and never returned.

Jacob Heator was also a pioneer settler of that locality, in Section 28, and in 1834, soon after his return from military service, invested his wages in a piece of land which he purchased from John Whittaker. He lived on that property until about 1854, when he sold to William N. Coler (the Civil War colonel) and migrated to Iowa, where he died.

· "UNCLE TOMMY BUTLER"

Thomas L. Butler and Martin Rhinehart, two of the oldest and most popular citizens of the county, were long noted as the only survivors of the Black Hawk War in Champaign County. Mr. Butler came to Illinois from his native Pennsylvania in the fall of 1828, at the age of twenty-two, and first settled at Danville. Before the Black Hawk War he had taken up land near the present village of Homer, one of his neighbors being Moses Thomas, the probate justice and part proprietor of the village site. Judge Thomas was his brother-in-law. "Uncle Tommy Butler," as he was familiarly called, was a small man, but wiry, active and plucky, and many of the old settlers of larger stature say he could swing a cradle with any of them. He was wont to say that the $1 a day which he received as a soldier of the Black Hawk War was a welcome addition to his income. The hard frost of 1829 killed all the corn and "times were still close" in the western part of the county, which depended so much on that crop. He was one of the Champaign County settlers who made frequent trips to Chicago with ox teams, to take his crop to market and buy groceries and other family

supplies. The round trip occupied seventeen days. "Uncle Tommy'
lived to be very old and was finally killed in a railroad accident.

A sketch of Martin Rhinehart, who, with his father, was an early
settler in the Big Grove in Somer Township, northeast of Urbana, has
already been given. He died in Wisconsin many years ago.

MUTUAL EXCITEMENT

During the Black Hawk War the inhabitants of the Sangamon Timber were especially excited over a rumored Indian raid from McLean
County. Some Kickapoo Indians had gathered at Old Town Timber,
a few miles to the west, huddling together like badly frightened sheep,
their entire object being to keep out of the war. But the few settlers in
the Sangamon Timber of what is now Champaign County got a different
idea of their intentions, gathered in a cabin and prepared boldly for
defense, if not offense. Nothing happened on either side, and the panic
died after a few days into a complete calm.

THE MEXICAN WAR

The scene of operations in the Mexican War was so far from Champaign County, and the interior of Illinois was even then so sparsely
settled, that there is little of an individual nature to record connecting
that section of the State with the conflict beyond the southern border.
William N. Coler, so prominent in the Civil War, served as a youth in
the war with Mexico.

CIVIL WAR OFFICERS

The breaking out of the Civil War, like a sudden and tremendous
storm, sent an electric shock throughout the United States, and nowhere
was it more pronounced than in eastern and central Illinois. Not only
was the response to the presidential call for troops prompt and generous
on the part of the rank and file, but several officers of prominence are
to be credited to Champaign County. Among these leaders were
Gen. Samuel T. Busey of Urbana, Cols. William N. Coler, John S.
Wolfe, Richard H. Nodine and James W. Langley of Champaign, and
Capt. Nathan M. Clark of Urbana.

JOHN S. WOLFE ENLISTS AND RECRUITS

Champaign and Urbana were the centers for recruiting. The attack
on Fort Sumter commenced on a Friday, and by Monday Champaign

County men were enrolling themselves for Union service. John S. Wolfe, a young lawyer of Champaign, had studied law with John M. Palmer, then of Macoupin County, and had been admitted to the bar in 1859. First he had opened an office at Carlinville with his fellow student, James W. Langley, and a year later had moved to Champaign, where he resided most of the time until his death in 1904.

COMPANY A, TWENTIETH ILLINOIS INFANTRY

A day or two after President Lincoln's call for 75,000 men, Attorney Wolfe made an eloquent address at a public meeting in Champaign called to enroll volunteers, and enforced his words by stepping forward and placing his name at the head of the list. Others soon followed and he was chosen captain of the company, which was organized within a week as A, Twentieth Regiment, Illinois Volunteer Infantry. The unit was placed in a camp of instruction at the fair grounds north of Urbana. The men selected as their lieutenants were Daniel Bradley and George W. Kennard, the former to be the colonel and the latter the major of the regiment. The rush for enrollment prevented the company and the regiment from being formally organized until May 14, 1861. It went into camp at Joliet, and was mustered into the service on June 13th, even then being one of the first regiments in the State to enter the three-years' service. As a result of resignations and promotions in Company A, William Archdeacon, John H. Austin and Andrew Rogerson were advanced to the grade of first lieutenant and the two last named to the captaincy. After three years of fighting and marching the Twentieth veteranized, participated in the grand review at Washington at the close of the war, and was mustered out at Louisville, Kentucky, July 16, 1865.

COLONEL WOLFE OF THE ONE HUNDRED AND THIRTY-FIFTH REGIMENT

Captain Wolfe was obliged to resign after about a year of service on account of disability, but, having recovered his health, he assisted in the organization of the 100 days regiment, the One Hundred and Thirty-fifth, which was mustered in at Mattoon, June 6, 1864. Of that he was chosen colonel, his command being on duty chiefly in Missouri guarding railways and other lines of communication between various sections of the Union armies in the Southwest. Dr. S. H. Birney of Urbana, who served as surgeon of the One Hundred and Thirty-fifth, afterward became one of the prominent members of his profession. He spent ten years in Denver, but returned to Urbana in 1898 and died there two years later.

At the conclusion of the war Colonel Wolfe returned to Champaign and resumed his practice and partnership with James W. Langley, who had himself become a colonel, and continued in active and successful professional work at Champaign until his death June 23, 1904. During the last thirty years of that period he was local attorney for the Illinois Central. Colonel Wolfe spent considerable time in travel during the last few years of his life.

THE TWENTY-FIFTH (WILLIAM N. COLER, COLONEL)

Soon after the departure of the Twentieth Regiment for its camp at Joliet, William N. Coler, a prominent lawyer, newspaper man and Democratic leader of the county and a resident of Urbana, was commissioned by President Lincoln to organize a regiment in Champaign County and adjoining territory, and by the early part of July had completed the organization, the Twenty-fifth Illinois Volunteer Infantry. It was accepted in August, 1861, and of the ten full companies, C was enlisted at Homer, I at Middletown and K at Urbana, nearly all the men being residents of the county. Colonel Coler, who had served in the Mexican War as a youth under Col. G. W. Morgan (famous in the Confederate cavalry service), continued in command of the Twenty-fifth Illinois Infantry until the fall of 1862, when he returned to the county and located at Champaign. Ten years afterward, with his sons, he moved to New York City.

Colonel Coler's successors, in command of the Twenty-fifth Regiment, were Col. Thomas D. Williams, who was killed in battle, December, 1862; Col. Caswell P. Ford, who resigned in April, 1863, and Col. Richard H. Nodine of Champaign, who was promoted from major and was mustered out with his regiment September 5, 1864. George W. Flynn of Urbana, early became adjutant of the regiment and held the office until it mustered out. In the same regiment were Dr. R. H. Brown of Mahomet and Dr. Myron S. Brown of Urbana, assistant surgeons. M. B. Thompson was sergeant major.

The successive captains of Company C were Charles A. Summers and Zebulon Hall of Homer; of Company I, Samuel Houston of Newcomb, afterward promoted to major, and Everett G. Knapp of Champaign, and of Company K, Ezekiel Boyden, James M. Tracy and Edward S. Sherman, all of Urbana.

When the term of service of the Twenty-fifth ended in September, 1864, Col. W. H. Gibson, commander of the brigade to which the regiment was attached, addressed the men, through an official order, congratulating them on their splendid record, and referring especially to their bravery at Pea Ridge, Corinth, Champion Hills, Stone River. Chickamauga, Missionary Ridge, Noonday Creek, Pinetop Mountain, Kenesaw Mountain, Chattahoochie, Peachtree Creek and Atlanta.

TWENTY-SIXTH REGIMENT

The Twenty-sixth Regiment was recruited soon after the Twenty-fifth, and Charles J. Tinkham of Homer became its first lieutenant colonel. Company F of the regiment was largely recruited from the eastern part of the county. Its captains were C. J. Tinkham and Lee M. Irwin, both of Homer. A large proportion of this company veteranized with the regiment, participated in the Sherman campaigns, and was mustered out at Louisville, July 20, 1865. It was in twenty-eight battles and numerous skirmishes and its marches covered nearly 7,000 miles.

SEVENTY-SIXTH REGIMENT (COL. S. T. BUSEY)

The Seventy-sixth Regiment was mustered into the Union service at Kankakee, August 22, 1862. Samuel T. Busey of Urbana was elected captain of Company B, and on the organization of the regiment became its lieutenant colonel. In that capacity he went south to Columbus, Kentucky, then the base of supplies for Grant's army at Corinth. The regiment garrisoned Holly Springs and performed other necessary service for the coming commander of the Union armies.

READY TO OBEY

In April, 1863, he became colonel of his regiment, and joined Grant's army in the rear of Vicksburg. His division being sent to Snyder's Bluff to guard the rear, the officers of the division circulated a petition to General Grant- requesting that their troops be sent to the front. Colonel Busey refused to sign it, stating that Grant was in command, and it was the duty of a brave soldier to take any position assigned him, and not annoy the commanding general who was responsible for results. When chided by other officers, he quietly remarked: "The Seventy-sixth is ready to go when and where it is ordered and will do the best it knows how, but I trust I have no officer willing to seek promotion by needlessly sacrificing a single man." Three days later the division was ordered to the extreme left. The first night it is said that two of the regiments whose officers had expressed themselves as unwilling to be relegated to the rear were surprised and routed and more than 100 taken prisoners. The Seventy-sixth came to the rescue, prevented what might have been a general rout, advanced the line on the river bank, and afterward took and held the most advanced position on the entire line until the surrender. Colonel Busey then led his regiment to Jackson, Mississippi, and held the post of honor, the extreme right, during the siege of Vicksburg. He is said to have been the first Union officer to enter the city after its evacuation by the Confederate army, and won the gratitude of its citizens by his efforts to subdue incendiary fires and restrain lawlessness.

Fort Blakely Carried by Storm

Colonel Busey refused promotion to brigadier general because he wished to remain in close touch with his old regiment; he also declined the command of the Natchez post for the same reason. The Seventy-sixth was then attached to the Reserve Corps of the Mississippi River, and he led several important expeditions into the surrounding country. Still in active command of his regiment, he left Memphis January 1, 1865, and was the first to report to General Canby at New Orleans of the army which afterward operated against Mobile. Fort Blakely, the last stronghold to that city, was carried by assault, after a hot siege of ten days, April 9, 1865. The Seventy-sixth was the first inside the Confederate works. and suffered a greater loss than all the remainder of the command.

Colonel Busey was the second man on the enemy's works. The private who preceded him was killed and the colonel wounded after a fight with several men. He was sent to the hospital at New Orleans, but returned to the front in June and was then mustered for discharge at Galveston, Texas. He was formally mustered out at Chicago, August 6, 1865. He was afterward commissioned as brevet brigadier general, on recommendation of General Grant and others, for special gallantry in leading his regiment in the assault on Fort Blakely.

Minor Officers of the Seventy-sixth

George J. Hodges of Champaign was mustered in as quartermaster of the Seventy-sixth, and was succeeded August 9, 1864, by John W. Somers, a brother of the well known Urbana lawyer and government official. He afterward moved to Iowa.

Companies B and G were composed almost entirely of men from Urbana and Champaign and their neighborhoods. Succeeding Colonel

Busey as captain of Company B upon his promotion to the lieutenancy were Homer W. Ayers, Ning A. Riley, John K. Miller and Robert A. Frame, all of Urbana and promoted from first lieutenant. Company G had as captains Joseph Park and Joseph Ingersoll of Urbana. Captain Park served from the muster in, August 22, 1862, until January 5, 1863, and Captain Ingersoll from that date until the muster out, June 20, 1865. James S. McCullough, who was county clerk in 1873-96, lost an arm while fighting as a youthful soldier of the Seventy-sixth at Kenesaw Mountain.

THE ONE HUNDRED AND TWENTY-FIFTH REGIMENT (COL. JAMES W. LANGLEY)

The One Hundred and Twenty-fifth Regiment was raised largely in the two counties of Champaign and Vermilion, and was mustered in at Danville, September 3, 1862, under command of Col. Oscar F. Harmon of that place, with James W. Langley, the Champaign lawyer and partner of John S. Wolfe, as lieutenant colonel. A. M. Ayers of Urbana was quartermaster. Colonel Harmon was killed in battle at Kenesaw Mountain, June 27, 1864, and Lieutenant Colonel Langley succeeded to the command, which he retained until the muster out at the end of the war. In that bloody engagement Capt. Nathan M. Clark of Company E, Champaign, lost an arm, and was succeeded in the command by George W. B. Sadorus of Sadorus. Captain Clark, who served as sheriff and county clerk after the war, died in 1869. Frederick B. Sale of Newcomb, who was captain of Company F, was succeeded by John B. Lester of the same town, who had advanced from the ranks to the head of his company. He afterward became prominent in township and county affairs.

The record of the One Hundred and Twenty-fifth Regiment embraces the battles of Perryville, Missionary Ridge, Buzzard's Roost, Kenesaw Mountain and Peachtree Creek, the siege of Atlanta, the march to the sea, the Carolina campaign and the grand review.

THE ONE HUNDRED AND THIRTY-FIFTH AGAIN

As noted in the sketch of John S. Wolfe, the One Hundred and Thirty-fifth Regiment, which he assisted to raise and of which he was colonel, was mustered into the service in June, 1864, for the 100 days service. Companies A and B were raised in Champaign County and their respective captains were Benjamin Burt of Urbana and Edward Bailey of Champaign.

Company I, Second Regiment, Illinois Cavalry, largely composed of Champaign County men, was successively commanded by Charles A. Vieregg and Henry Bartling of Champaign and Moses E. Kelley of Pesotum. Many of its members became veterans after their three years' service, and the regiment was not mustered out (at Springfield) until November 24, 1865. Its battles and skirmishes ranged up and down the Mississippi Valley.

Company I, Tenth Illinois Cavalry, also numbered many men from Champaign County. It was mustered into the service at Camp Butler in September, 1861, and its captains were James Butterfield and William H. Coffman of Champaign.

PROMINENT IN SCATTERED COMMANDS

The record of Champaign County in the Civil War would stretch out to much greater length if mention were made of all who honored their sections and themselves in official positions below captaincies, those who bore themselves faithfully and bravely in the ranks, and not a few who attained some prominence in scattered commands. In the last named class must, however, be mentioned Dr. Charles A. Hunt, the able physician and ex-mayor of Urbana, who died at Mount City Hospital, Mississippi, in August, 1863, while as bravely performing his duties as surgeon of the One Hundred and Twenty-sixth Regiment as though he were leading a charge on the field of battle; Dr. J. T. Miller, also of Urbana, surgeon of the Sixtieth Infantry; Dr. Charles A. Thompson of Urbana, first assistant surgeon of the Twenty-fifth Illinois Infantry and finally surgeon of the Ninetieth; Capt. Eugene P. Frederick of Ogden Township, a stanch German-American, who rose from a private to a captaincy in the Fifty-first Infantry. There were quite a number of Champaign County citizens in Companies B and E of that regiment, as well as in Company G of the Seventy-second.

SPANISH-AMERICAN WAR SERVICE

At the outbreak of the Spanish-American War, in the spring of 1898, Company M of the Fourth Regiment, Illinois National Guard, had been organized for a number of years. Its membership was mostly drawn from Champaign and Urbana. On April 25th, Adjutant General Reece ordered the regiment to report at Springfield and on the 20th of May, with Company M, it was mustered into the service of the United

States by Captain Roberts of the Seventeenth Infantry, the regiment being under the command of Col. Casimer Andel of Belleville.

Roster of Company M at the time of muster in: Captain, William R. Courtney of Urbana; first lieutenant, Arthur W. Smith, and second lieutenant, Fred E. Thompson, both of Urbana; first sergeant and quartermaster sergeant, George E. Doty and Sidney G. Choate of Champaign. The Fourth Regiment, as a part of the Second Brigade, arrived at Jacksonville, Florida, May 29th, and was stationed at Camp Cuba Libre under command of Gen. Fitzhugh Lee. While at that point Colonel Andel resigned and was succeeded by Col. Eben Swift of the Ninth Regiment. After remaining on provost duty until October, the Fourth was transferred to Savannah, Georgia, the men devoting their time to drill and practice marches. In January, 1899, it embarked for Havana, and during its three months' stay on the island was stationed at Camp Columbia, near Havana, performing faithfully its duties of guard and camp, and keeping in condition for any call which might come. On the 4th of April, 1899, it embarked for home on the steamers "Whitney" and "Yarmouth," and was mustered out at Camp McKenzie, Augusta, Georgia, on May 2d. There were only three death in the Champaign County company—those of Herman McFarland and George E. Turner of Urbana and Percy H. Tittle of Champaign.

Sidney Cohen is the present captain of Company M, Fourth Infantry, and is active in present-day military matters.

STATE UNIVERSITY, PRESENT MILITARY CENTER

Since the commencement of the world war military matters have been greatly stimulated in Champaign County, especially at the University of Illinois, the head-center of all such movements, which, even before the culmination of European clashes, had given more attention to such matters than any other educational institution in the country. The military instruction therein is in charge of Maj. Robert W. Mearns, a graduate of West Point, who saw twenty-four years of service in the United States army, including three years as major of Philippine scouts. Major Mearns was appointed professor of military science and tactics of the State university in 1916, and the four assistant professors have all been connected with the regular army. The teaching and administrative force under the major comprises fifteen members.

The course at the university has special reference to the duties of officers of the line, and the supply of arms and ammunition is furnished by the war department. Every male student under twenty-five

The Armory and Aviation Corps

years of age is required to drill twice a week, and also to earn a certain number of credits in study. A committee appointed by the president of the university examines candidates for nomination to the governor of the State for commissions as brevet captains in the State militia. Only seniors are eligible. Since the outbreak of hostilities against Germany student volunteers must pass their physical examinations both at the university and before the authorities of the regular recruiting offices.

The Cadet Brigade of the University of Illinois consists of two regiments of infantry, comprising two headquarters companies, two machine gun companies, two supply companies and twenty-four companies; a signal company, an engineer company and a hospital company. There are 2,127 cadets enrolled in the military department, including the band of 167 men and 113 commissioned officers.

Under the act of Congress of June 3, 1916, there have also been established at the university three units of the Reserve Officers' Training Corps. All male students of the university, except in the professional departments, who are citizens and physically able, are enrolled in the corps during their freshman and sophomore years, and are required during these two years to devote three periods a week of not less than one hour each to military science and training. At the end of the sophomore year a student, who is recommended by the president of the university and the professor of military science and tactics, may sign a form of written agreement prescribed by the secretary of war and thus enroll himself for two more years of service in the Reserve Officers' Training Corps. For such the hours devoted to study and training are materially increased. A student who thus completes the elective advanced course is eligible for appointment by the President of the United States as a reserve officer of the United States army for a period of ten years; and is also eligible for appointment as a temporary second lieutenant of the regular army in time of peace for purposes of instruction, with the allowances provided by law for that grade, and pay at the rate of $100 a month for six months. On the expiration of this period of service with the regular army, he reverts to the status of a reserve officer.

The military status of the University of Illinois has been described somewhat at length because it so far overshadows everything else of that nature in Champaign County. It is a feature in which its citizens take an excusable pride, and one which has done as much as any one thing, during the past two or three years, to bring the university into National prominence as a builder of virile and patriotic young manhood.

PIONEER RESIDENTS OF CHAMPAIGN

CHAPTER XI

TOWNSHIP AND CITY OF CHAMPAIGN

PIONEER SETTLERS AT AND NEAR CHAMPAIGN—HOME FRUIT FARM
AND THE DUNLAPS—FIRST ADDITIONS TO THE RAILROAD TOWN—
FIRST BUILDINGS ERECTED—FIRST PRESBYTERIAN CHURCH ORGAN-
IZED—THE FAMOUS "GOOSE POND" CHURCH—"LITTLE BRICK"
SCHOOLHOUSE—ADDITIONAL IMPORTANCE (1855)—BANK FOUNDED
IN WEST URBANA—VILLAGE AND CITY ORGANIZATIONS VOTED—
PROGRESS AND SETBACKS—COMMISSION FORM OF GOVERNMENT
ADOPTED—MAYORS OF CHAMPAIGN—THE CHAMPAIGN PUBLIC
SCHOOLS—HISTORICAL ACCOUNT—PERSONNEL OF THE BOARDS OF
EDUCATION—THE TEACHING FORCE—THE BURNHAM ATHAENEUM
—CITY HALL—PROTECTION AGAINST FIRE—WATER SUPPLY AND
DISTRIBUTION—SANITARY SEWERAGE SYSTEM—PARKS AND BREATH-
ING PLACES—CEMETERIES—THE FIRST PRESBYTERIAN CHURCH—
FIRST CONGREGATIONAL CHURCH—THE FIRST METHODIST EPISCO-
PAL CHURCH—EVANGELICAL LUTHERAN CHURCH—ST. PETER'S
EVANGELICAL CHURCH—ST. MARY'S ROMAN CATHOLIC CHURCH—
FATHER A. J. WAGNER—ST. JOHN'S PARISH—HOLY CROSS PARISH—
FIRST BAPTIST CHURCH—EMMANUEL EPISCOPAL CHURCH—BENEV-
OLENT AND CHARITABLE INSTITUTIONS—UNITED CHARITIES ASSOCIA-
TION OF CHAMPAIGN AND URBANA—JULIA F. BURNHAM HOSPITAL—
GARWOOD HOME FOR OLD LADIES—YOUNG WOMEN'S CHRISTIAN
LEAGUE—THE DORCAS SOCIETY—WOMEN'S CLUBS—THE ART AND
THIRTY CLUBS—SOCIAL SCIENCE CLUB OF THE TWIN CITIES—THE
CHAMPAIGN SOCIAL SCIENCE CLUB—WOMAN'S CLUB OF CHAMPAIGN
AND URBANA—CHAMPAIGN COUNTY COUNTRY CLUB—THE GRAND
ARMY POST—CHAMPAIGN CHAMBER OF COMMERCE—LOCAL BANKS
—CHAMPAIGN NEWSPAPERS—SECRET AND BENEVOLENT SOCIETIES.

The township of Champaign is southwest of the center of Champaign
County, and as it is not in the Timber Belt had to await development
until the settlers of the new country had been educated to the idea of
improving prairie lands. In the early '40s appeared a brave man, who
ventured across the range line away from the Big Grove to make his
home in Township 19, Range 8 east.

In 1843 William Phillips, a Methodist preacher, familiarly called "Billy Phillips," located on the southwest quarter of the northeast quarter of Section 12, now not far from First Street, Champaign. John S. Beasley had made some large land investments in the township, but it remained for Elder Phillips actually to plant a home on the prairie soil. He had no neighbor for about five years, but in 1848 James Myers entered forty acres in Section 1, adjoining the Phillips home to the north, and both tracts are now within the limits of the city of Champaign, as well as the pieces entered about the same time as the Myers farm by Moses Moraine, Robert Logan, Thomas Magee and Joseph Evans, in Sections 1, 12 and 13. Col. M. W. Busey's purchases of 1849 were in Sections 12 and 14, some of the latter lying without the city limits. In 1852 Barney Kelley entered the whole of Section 25, about a mile south of Champaign, which remained his homestead until his death. In the spring of that year Col. W. N. Coler entered about 1,500 acres of land in the vicinity of what is now the city. Elias Chester of Ohio, the father of E. O. and E. E. Chester, in 1854 patented lands in Sections 21 and 29, three or four miles southwest. East of the Chester tracts was the farm opened and improved by J. B. Phinney. His homestead was a model in the early days, its proprietor became an influential citizen and died at his home in Champaign Township.

HOME FRUIT FARM AND THE DUNLAPS

In 1856 Mathias L. Dunlap purchased a large tract in the southwest quarter of Section 36, just north of the Tolono Township line, and two years afterward opened the first nursery and fruit farm operated on scientific principles in the county. He protected his tree nurseries and his orchards with belts of forest trees, and finally demonstrated that such enterprises could be made profitable in what was naturally an open prairie country. Mr. Dunlap had had a business training in young Chicago; had surveyed much of Cook and DuPage counties, and for years before coming to Champaign had been prominent in the politics of Cook County and the State. For a decade he had also been engaged in the nursery business on the prairies in the Chicago neighborhood and was well known as a writer for the agricultural press. For twenty-two years he was the agricultural editor of the Chicago Tribune; was editor of the Illinois Farmer from 1860 to 1865 and declined the position of commissioner of agriculture tendered by Lincoln. The location of the

Illinois Industrial University (now the University of Illinois) was due as much to his influence and labor as to those of any other man, and he always insisted that it should remain purely an agricultural college. He was a member of the first board of trustees of the university. He raised a large family, like a wise father, and died at his home near Savoy, February 14, 1875. Rural Home Fruit Farm, his creation, since so wonderfully developed by his son, Hon. H. M. Dunlap, has become noted throughout the United States for its wonderful apples. H. J. Dunlap, another son, has become unusually prominent as an editor and promoter of horticultural interests.

SCENE IN THE DUNLAP ORCHARDS, SAVOY

About the time that M. L. Dunlap located in the township, Frederick Beiser opened the first truck farm of any importance and for years supplied the neighboring territory with vegetables.

FIRST ADDITIONS TO THE RAILROAD TOWN

With the opening of the Illinois Central Railroad from Chicago in 1854, and the building of its depot two miles west of the courthouse, the least prophetic could not but foresee that business and population were bound to gravitate to that locality. Soon afterward, as has already been stated, T. R. Webber, under a decree of the Circuit Court, platted and sold that portion of the Busey estate between First and Wright streets, north of Springfield Avenue, while the Illinois Central platted what is now the main business portion of Champaign in the vicinity of Neil and First streets, on what is now West University Avenue, known as Farnam, Clark & White's Addition.

In what is now the west side of the city, Farnam, Clark & White made an addition and donated fifteen acres for a public park, the first in the county. The addition was platted in April, 1855, in the name of John P. White, who owned a third interest in it. His partners, Jeffrey A. Farnam and Nathan M. Clark, who were owners of the other two-thirds, were Illinois Central engineers, who perhaps did not wish to be prominently known in the matter. This may also account for the fact that a monument erected in what has since been developed into the City Park, or White Park, on West University Avenue, gives the credit of the gift to Mr. White alone.

First Buildings Erected

In the early spring of 1854, shortly before the first train over the Central pulled in from Chicago, Mark Carley erected the first dwelling upon the new town site, and moved his family into it from Urbana. It is reported that he moved in something which caused more excitement than his family—a piano, grand or otherwise, but the pioneer of its kind in the county and sole possessor of the glory for some time. A rough wooden building, or shed, had been erected at First South and Market streets, and on October 10, 1854, John C. Baddeley opened the first general store on North Neil Street. He was appointed postmaster in the following year and combined his light official duties with the heavier responsibilities of business.

First Presbyterian Church Organized

The religious bodies of the young town had obtained a foothold earlier, if anything, than any other of its institutions. In the fall of 1850 Rev. John A. Steele, under authority of the Presbytery of Palestine (which then had jurisdiction over this county), organized a church, the membership of which was largely drawn from settlers in the western sections of the Sangamon Timber. Soon after the building of the Illinois Central and the founding of West Urbana, to better accommodate its scattered members, services were held in the new depot building. Sunday trains were not then running. A church building was erected in 1855 upon the present site of the Presbyterian Church.

The Famous "Goose Pond" Church

The First Congregational Church was organized mostly by those living in the town of Urbana in the fall of 1853. Rev. W. W. Blanchard was its first pastor. This church likewise changed its location to West Urbana, and was for years known and loved as the Goose Pond Church. In 1855-56 the house of worship, which was the scene of many notable meetings, was erected at the northwest corner of University Avenue and First. While Lincoln was coming into notice as a circuit lawyer and an Illinois politician, especially while he was bearding the Little Giant in the open, he often spoke in the Goose Pond Church. It is of record, for instance, that he addressed the citizens of West Urbana in June, 1856, and September, 1858. An emergency meeting was held in the little church in October, 1856, to provide for Dr. Blanchard's salary, and the proud report of the committee was that "$350 and a yoke of oxen were raised, and this, too, within the membership of the church." In the spring of 1858 meetings were held to organize the Young Men's Literary Association and the school commissioners of the township discussed the advisability of establishing public schools for "both sides of the track." In December, 1859, a largely attended gathering was held in the Goose Pond Church in memory of John Brown.

"Little Brick" Schoolhouse

Sharing the honors with the Goose Pond Church in these early days was the "Little Brick," or the public school of District No. 1, corner of Hill and Randolph, the site of the present Central School. Dr. R. W. Shoemaker and his wife had taught a private school in the little frame building just west of First Street, on University Avenue, but the Little Brick was the first public school. The site was given by J. P. White for the purpose, and the structure was completed in 1855. It was west of the Illinois Central tracks, which, for several years, constituted the base line by which every landmark was located. It was in the Little Brick that the caucus was held in May, 1858, which decided "No License" for West Urbana by a majority of forty-eight. There, also, in January, 1860, the charter members of the Urbana Street Railway met to organize. In the following month a rousing mass meeting was held in the Little Brick to decide upon the name for the proposed city. Dr. J. W. Scroggs moved the old name of the Illinois Central station, West Urbana, be retained, but Dr. J. P. Gauch's amendment that it be changed to Champaign was adopted by a vote of 36 to 21. And so it has remained to this day. Other momentous occasions connected with local history, too numerous to enumerate, had their settings in the Little Brick.

ADDITIONAL IMPORTANCE (1855)

The year. 1855 was filled with events, aside from the building of No. 1 schoolhouse. Robert B. Smith & Brother opened the first drug store, McLaurie & Leal the first stove and tin store, Dr. H. C. Howard erected a steam flouring mill at Main and Walnut streets, Mark Carley built a warehouse, L. S. and W. E. Smith established a lumber yard, Henry C. Whitney moved from Urbana as the pioneer resident lawyer, and John Mills superseded Mr. Baddeley as postmaster, who moved the office to the east side of the Illinois Central tracks. In August of that year, less than eighteen months after the building of the first residence at the station, a census was taken by the State authorities of the people occupying the platted sections and it was found that there was a population of 416 at West Urbana.

BANK FOUNDED IN WEST URBANA

For some time after West Urbana was started the east side of the track had the postoffice and business honors, as well as the Grand Prairie Bank. But in June, 1856, a branch of that concern was opened at the northeast corner of Main and Oak streets. Until the bank building was completed at University Avenue and First Street, the cash of the bank was carried daily to the main bank at Urbana. At the completion of the new building, the business at West Urbana was continued as the Cattle Bank.

VILLAGE AND CITY ORGANIZATIONS VOTED

In January, 1857, the school census indicated 357 children of school age, and a total population of 1,202, and on the following 27th of April a village organization was voted, under the name of West Urbana. The members of the first board of trustees were: E. T. McCann (president), John W. Baddeley, A. M. Whitney, J. J. Sutton and J. P. Gauch.

In April, 1860, the people of Champaign (the new name having been adopted in February) voted in favor of municipal government, and the city was organized, under a special charter, under the name of Champaign. As the postoffice and railroad station had been changed accordingly, the transformation from West Urbana was made quite secure.

Progress and Setbacks

As has been made plain in the preceding chapter, Champaign bore herself with honor during the trying times of the Civil War, being first in the county to make a practical response to the call for troops, and sending forth for more than four years the best of her men both into the ranks of the soldiery and as able and brave leaders at the very front. During that period, in the fall of 1863, a crude street car line was built between Champaign and Urbana, but it was, on the whole, no proper time for the consideration of local advantages, and such developments therefore languished. The city had barely recovered from the drain upon its best citizenship and financial resources before a destructive fire destroyed some of the most valuable property within its limits. On July 4, 1868, almost the entire square bounded by Main and Taylor streets on the north and south, and by Market and Walnut on the east and west, was burned over. As the first volunteer fire company had been organized but the year before, little was accomplished to stay the destruction.

As the years went by, however, the scars were healed, as well as those caused by destructive fires of later years, and even a better class of buildings followed. The interurban system between Champaign and Urbana was built and connections made with the sections of the Illinois Traction System to the east and to the west, as has been fully detailed in the chapter on transportation. Systems for both the drawing and distribution of water and for the sanitary drainage of the city were founded and perfected, the latter being especially indebted to Prof. A. N. Talbot, sanitary engineer of the University of Illinois.

In the development of the city of Champaign much credit is also freely given to the manifold influences emanating from the great university at its doors, and which, in turn, looks for so many necessities and pleasures to the western member of the Twin Cities.

Commission Form of Government Adopted

For a period of fifty-seven years the city of Champaign was conducted under an aldermanic form of government, but on February 20, 1917, the people took a referendum vote on the proposition to change it to the commission system. It carried by a majority of 285. The vote for the change was 719 men and 589 women, a total of 1,308; against, 786 men and 237 women, or a total of 1,023. On April 17th, the first city election was held under the changed, or commission, form of government, with the result that S. C. Tucker was chosen mayor, and H. B.

Ramey, George J. Babb, George B. Franks and J. T. Boland the first board of commissioners.

MAYORS OF CHAMPAIGN

The successive mayors of Champaign have been as follows: E. T. McCann, 1860; D. Gardner, 1861; J. S. Wright, 1862-63; E. L. Sweet, 1864-65; C. E. Larned, 1866-68; C. B. Smith, 1869-70; J. Dickerson, 1873-75, 1879; Henry Trevett, 1876-79; B. C. Beach, 1880, 1885, 1886; L. S. Wilcox, 1881, 1882, 1887, 1888; J. B. McKinley, 1883; W. A. Day, 1883, 1884; Levi Dodson, 1872; Sandford Richards, 1874; P. W. Woody, 1889, 1890; J. B. Harris, 1891-94; C. J. Sabin, 1899, 1900; E. E. Chester, 1895, 1896; C. J. Mullikin, 1901, 1902; J. R. Scott, 1897, 1898; E. S. Swigart, 1903, 1904; S. C. Tucker, 1909; William Coughlin, 1911-13; Shields A. Blain, 1905-08; O. B. Dobbins, 1914, 1915; E. S. Swigart, 1916, 1917; S. C. Tucker, 1917-.

The term of office of the newly-elected officials commenced on the 1st of May and will conclude two years from that date. While under the commission form of government the candidates are elected ordinarily for a period of four years, at Champaign the election occurred at the close of two years of a quadrennial period, leaving two years as a hold-over. The next candidates will be elected for the full term of four years.

THE CHAMPAIGN PUBLIC SCHOOLS

These are not city but district schools. School District No. 71, Champaign County, Illinois, is a corporate body independent of the city government, managed under the school laws of the State by a board of six members elected two each year for three-year terms, with a president elected annually who has the usual powers of a presiding officer and a vote in case of a tie.

The territory of the district includes parts of Townships 19-8 and 19-9, nine and seven-eighths sections, about 6,320 acres. This takes in all of the territory of the city of Champaign and considerable tracts lying outside of the city.

This Champaign school district had in operation during the school year 1916-17 a high school enrolling 690 students, with 28 high school instructors, and 58 elementary schools enrolling 2,141 pupils, housed in nine buildings, with 58 regular teachers and five teachers in charge of special work. An attendance officer, a school nurse, a superintendent of buildings and grounds, a clerk, a librarian, an engineer, a dozen janitors, a cafeteria manager, with the superintendent of schools in gen-

SOUTH AND EAST SIDES OF PRESENT HIGH SCHOOL

eral charge of all educational plans and activities, also belong to the list of employes. The schools employ a great many more workers and requires in the most of them a much higher grade of preparation and personal fitness for the work than does any other governmental agency affecting the same population. They also render direct personal service to a much larger number.

In administering this system there is never any cessation of the effort to improve in every way possible the excellence of the instructors, of the facilities for instruction, of the courses of study and of the general plans and purposes of school management. Progress is sought in every direction in which progress has been proved to be safe and beneficial, so far as the limitations imposed by revenue conditions and by the forces of tradition in the community permit. It is the purpose to make both the elementary and the high school education such as will be most useful to the pupils and to the State in their future activities as citizens. While no superlative excellence is claimed, it is the endeavor to keep the schools up to the standard proper for this educational center of Illinois. The high school is accredited to the University of Illinois, to all colleges of the North Central Association and to Smith, Wellesley and Mount Holyoke.

Every high school should, first of all, serve its own community, as well as the state at large, by giving to its pupils what they are likely really to need in life. The special plans of each high school should be shaped by its environment. The fact that the University of Illinois is so large a part of the local environment in Champaign that about two-thirds of our high school graduates enter that institution makes preparation for college of greater importance here than in most high schools; but the needs of the other third are not neglected, commercial, agricultural, domestic, mechanical and scientific courses adapted to their practical needs being maintained, as well as those in language, literature, history and government, which are also useful in a broad sense to all intelligent citizens.

The annual official reports sent back each year to all high schools give the gratifying information, in the case of the Champaign High School, that, though it is plain that graduates of this school of a general average of ability come into competition with a small percentage of chosen graduates, they not only keep their university scholarship records up to the general average of their university classes but raise it noticeably above that average. This can be the result only of greater native ability in Champaign youth or of better preparation. The reader may draw one or the other conclusion.

The schools plan, in general, to serve the needs of the children of the present generation and of the state in the near future by preparing those children for the demands of that future, so far as the foresight of instructors makes this possible and the choices of courses made by pupils and their parents are wisely made with respect to the particular abilities and purposes of the individual pupils. In the elementary schools, a general training is given in the fundamental knowledge and skills believed to be serviceable in life to all citizens. In the high school, a considerable variety of work leading to different vocational ends is offered, the various curricula providing, as already suggested, so far as time of preparation and the age of pupils makes possible, either for early entrance into occupations or for taking up higher education.

The schools of Champaign were among the early pioneers in the development of courses in manual training and household arts and science and in recent years these courses have been brought up to a rank equal with that of any other arts and sciences in the curricula by offering courses in woodworking, mechanical drawing, clothing, foods, etc., requiring an equivalent amount of time and study with other full courses.

In the nursing service, Champaign has long passed the stage at which the value and necessity of such work is questioned. In the field of the attendance officer, a highly serviceable and quite unusual system for securing the co-operation of school and home forces for the educational and moral welfare of pupils has been worked out. Special teachers of art and music lead the pupils into appreciation and power in these refining elements of education. Three special teachers are assigned to the task of assisting and directing pupils who, for any reason, need help. In this way, the individual pupils are enabled, except in extreme cases, to keep up with their regular classes with great advantage to themselves and with economy to the schools thus saved from giving two years for one grade.

The cost of the present high school building has been about $300,000 and its equipment $12,000; while the investment in the elementary school buildings totals over $350,000 and their furnishings about $10,000. The bonded indebtedness of the district being $214,000, the people thus have a paid-up investment of not far from $500,000 in their school property. Champaign has always believed the education of its children a good investment.

The increased cost of living and of building in recent years have increased the difficulty of the financial problems of the schools, especially, as assessed valuations have not increased so rapidly. Nevertheless, the elementary and a high school enrolling double the normal number for a community of the population of Champaign have both been maintained, and much paid on buildings on the 3 per cent tax rate, though most communities maintaining separate elementary schools and township high schools find it necessary to make the total rate 4 per cent, or higher.

The disbursements for the year 1916-17 were $129,644.79 and for the year 1915-16 $178,164.36, including considerable payments on the new high school building.

The number of pupils enrolled in the different schools during the year 1916-17 was as follows: Columbia, 158; Gregory, 294; Central, 247; Avenue, 266; Dr. Howard, 165; Lincoln, 283; Colonel Wolfe, 276; Marquette, 309; Lawhead, 143; High School, 690.

In the Columbia and Lawhead buildings no grades above the fourth were taught; in the Gregory and Lincoln buildings, all grades including the sixth; in the Dr. Howard, Avenue, Colonel Wolfe and Marquette buildings, all grades including the seventh; while the Central had two seventh grade schools and five eighth grade groups, instructed under the departmental plan.

By the school census finished June 30th by Mr. Charles Gooding, the total number of residents in the district was shown to be 17,427, 9,374 males and 8,053 females. Of these 16,344 were white and 1,083 colored; 16,859 within the corporate limits of the city of Champaign and 568 outside of those limits; 9,384 west of First Street and 8,043 east. The total number of school age, that is, between six and twenty-one, was 4,738, 2,709 males and 2,029 females. The enrollment in the public schools is about 60 per cent of the whole number of school age.

HISTORICAL ACCOUNT

The first school in West Urbana, now Champaign, was taught by Mrs. Shoemaker, the wife of the first physician in the village, now Mrs. Susan Jefferson, residing at 901 West Church Street with her brother, Judge C. C. Staley. In a letter from Wenatchee, Washington, where she is now (July, 1917) visiting relatives, she states that this school was taught by herself in a two-room frame building, the residence of Dr. and Mrs. Shoemaker, situated on East Main and First streets, just east of the old Doan House. The school was held in the front room. It was a private school and each pupil furnished his own seat and desk. Among the pupils she remembers were C. F. Columbia, Willis and William Jefferson, sons of H. Jefferson, afterward her second husband, and members of the Myers family.

Mrs. Jefferson is at the present time also the oldest living member of the First Presbyterian Church, with which she united at or soon after its organization.

Brink's History of Champaign County, 1878, reports that the second school was taught by Howard Pixley, on the West Side, in a house occupied by Joshua Dickerson.

Mrs. F. A. Parsons of Chanute, Kansas, a daughter of Mrs. C. G. Larned, who was county superintendent from 1877 to 1881, reports an early private school taught by Misses Mary and Anna Ayers in their home, who emphasized kindness to animals quite in the modern spirit;

FIRST SCHOOL IN CHAMPAIGN

also one taught by a Miss McAllister and another taught in a room above one of the stores between Walker's furniture store and Rugg's shoe store.

As the Illinois law on which our present state-wide system of free schools is based was passed in 1855, the first school districts were doubtless organized at that time, No. 1 west of First Street and No. 2 east of it.

The first public school building in District No. 1, long designated as the Little Brick, was built in 1855, on the corner of Randolph and Hill, the site being donated by J. P. White. It cost $4,000 and an addition afterward made cost $2,000. This was for a number of years the only school building in District No. 1.

Beginning in 1868, the second building in this district was erected at the location of the present Avenue building on a site bounded by Lynn, University and Park, this also being donated by J. P. White. It was a quite pretentious brick structure of three stories above a basement, costing about $80,000. It was occupied in 1870 and was known as the

West High School until its destruction by fire in 1893. In 1871, Lathrop's Directory of Champaign County says of this building, "One more complete in all its appointments, in rooms, finish and furniture, cannot be found in the West."

The first public school building in District No. 2 stood on the site of what afterward became the Marquette building. A frame schoolhouse was erected in 1860 at a cost of $7,200. In 1868 the schools were graded. In 1869 the building was remodeled and enlarged, bringing the cost to $15,000, and the building was destroyed by fire in 1870.

A new frame building was dedicated in August, 1871, and completely destroyed by fire December 4, 1871, and a third building erected in 1872. This was first known as the East High School building and later as the

LITTLE BRICK SCHOOL

Marquette building. It was used until 1908, was closed for a time on account of unsafe condition and was remodeled in 1910 at a cost of about $16,000 and is now one of the most serviceable buildings in the district for school purposes. In 1916 it received by vote of the district an addition of two lots to its playground at a cost of $6,000. From these three houses were removed. During the school year 1916-17, through subscriptions made by the Mothers' Club of that neighborhood, it received the best playground equipment in the district.

As early as 1858 a proposal was made to unite Districts No. 1 and
No. 2; but No. 1 was in debt for its first building and No. 2 did not
wish to assume a part of that responsibility; so resolutions were adopted
to unite the two districts when they should be on equal terms financially.
That condition was not reached until 1890; but on the 28th of April
of that year the two districts were consolidated as Union District No. 6.
This name was changed to School District No. 71, Champaign County,
in 1901, and a small change of boundary was made on the northeast in
1907.

Soon after the formation of Union District No. 6, it was decided to
place a new high school building nearer to the center of population.
Accordingly, the Little Brick was torn down and a new high school building erected on its site in 1893. This was enlarged in 1905 and important
alterations providing laboratories and shops were made in 1908, making
the total cost of the building about $36,000. Yet it was soon necessary
to lease rooms outside to accommodate the growth of the school, four
teachers being thus provided with class rooms for two or three years.
This building was last used for high school purposes in 1913-14, its
total service being only twenty-one years. It is now known as the
Central School.

In the same year, 1893, the present Avenue School building was
erected to replace the one destroyed by fire on the same site. It cost
about $15,000.

In 1894 the Lincoln School was erected as a four-room building at
a cost of about $7,000, and it was enlarged to an eight-room building in
1903 at a cost of $10,000. It stands northeast of the intersection of
Healey and State streets.

Southeast of the intersection of Church and Fifth streets the Frances
Willard building was erected in 1896 at a cost of $8,000. It is a four-
room building and has not been used since the remodeled Marquette
building added eight rooms in 1910. With comparatively inexpensive
repairs, however, it will be available to provide for the next increase of
school population in that part of the district.

The Gregory building, northwest of the intersection of Columbia
and Randolph, was erected in 1898 as a four-room schoolhouse and
doubled in capacity in 1903, at a total cost of about $20,000.

In 1905 the four-room Columbia building was erected northwest of
the intersection of Neil and Beardsley at a cost of $9,200, and the eight-
room Colonel Wolfe building, southeast of the intersection of Healey and
Fourth, at a cost of $17,696.

In 1907 the four-room Harriet Lawhead building was erected, north-

First Champaign High School (West Side)

First East Side High School

west of the intersection of Fifth and Grove, at a cost of $14,000. This building was paid for in cash, no bonds being issued.

In 1910, at the same time the Marquette building was remodeled, that of the Dr. H. C. Howard School, a four-room structure, the first approximately fireproof school building in Champaign, was built on a site east of James Street between University and Park avenues at a cost of $18,000.

In 1912 a new site for a high school was purchased north of Green Street between State and Prairie. In 1913 a structure designed to accommodate a high school of 1,000 pupils was begun on this site and it was ready for use in October of 1914. It is believed that no city of no larger population than Champaign has a larger or better high school building. Its construction is permanent. It is an architectural orna-ment to the city and its interior arrangements are convenient, sanitary and in every way well adapted to its purposes. Its auditorium, seating an audience of 1,000, its swimming pool and gymnasium, its laboratories and shops, its cafeteria and many other features place it among the best modern structures. Only about half of the cost of the building and site was paid by bonds, the remaining being paid in cash from current taxation during four or five years.

The necessity for such a building as the present one is seen from the enrollment in the high school, which was as follows: 1902, 254; 1905, 313; 1911, 387; 1912, 478; 1913, 527; 1914, 585; 1915, 645; 1916, 671; 1917, 690.

Through the generosity of Hon. W. B. McKinley, a large athletic field was in 1912 donated to the district. McKinley Field is located just within the south corporation line of the city between Pine and New streets and is used especially by the high school students, thousands of spectators sometimes gathering here for the principal athletic games.

PERSONNEL OF THE BOARDS OF EDUCATION

Among early school directors in District No. 1, Charles Baddeley, J. H. Angel, J. S. Beasley, Mrs. C. B. Smith and C. F. Columbia are mentioned as serving at some time previous to 1882. There must have been a number of others.

Beginning about 1882, records show the membership on the school board of District No. 1 as follows: H. Swannell, 1873-74 to 1885-86, inclusive; Mrs. Bacon, 1882-83 to 1885-86, incl.; M. E. Lapham, 1882-83 to 1883-86, incl.; G. F. Beardsley, 1882-83 to 1887-88, incl.; Mrs. W. S. Maxwell, 1882-83 to 1886-87, incl.; Dr. F. J. Pearman, 1882-83 to 1887-88, incl.; Mrs. H. H. Harris, 1886-87 to 1889-90 incl.; H. W.

Mahan, 1886-87 to ——; Ozias Riley, 1886-87 to 1889-90, incl.; Mrs. Gish Garwood, April, 1887, to August, 1887; P. W. Woody, 1887-88 to 1889-90, incl.; E. Snyder, 1887-88 to 1889-90, incl.; Dr. C. B. Johnson, 1888-89 to 1889-90, incl.; Mrs. A. C. Burnham, 1888-89 to 1889-90, incl.; Col. J. W. Langley, 1888-89 to 1889-90, incl.

Of presidents and members of the board of education beginning with the consolidation of districts in 1890, the list is complete, as follows:

Presidents—George F. Beardsley, 1890-91 and 1891-92; N. Butler, 1892-93; John L. Ray, 1893-94; Henry Trevett, 1894-95, 1895-96 and 1896-97; Dr. C. B. Johnson, 1897-98, 1898-99 and 1899-1900; S. P. Atkinson, 1900-01, 1901-02 and 1902-03; John N. Beers, 1903-04, 1904-05 and 1905-06; F. C. Amsbary, 1906-07, 1907-08 and 1908-09; Dr. W. L. Gray, 1909-10, 1910-11, 1911-12, 1912-13, 1913-14, 1914-15, and 1915-16; Henry W. Berks, 1916-17, 1917-18.

Membership, 1870-1917—F. Dollinger, 1890-91 to 1892-93, inclusive; Edward Snyder, 1890-91 to 1892-93, incl.; R. R. Mattis, 1890-91 to 1897-98, incl.; Mrs. Marian Healey, 1890-91 and 1891-92; Dr. C. B. Johnson, 1890-91; Mrs. Mary H. Gere, 1890-91; Henry Trevett, 1891-92 to 1893-94, incl.; Mrs. J. W. Mulliken, 1891-92 to 1893-94, incl.; Mrs. S. S. Jones, 1892-93 to 1894-95, incl.; F. U. Helbing, 1893-94 to 1907-08, incl.; William Williamson, 1893-94 to 1895-96, incl. Ozias Riley, 1894-95 to 1896-97, incl.; Mrs. H. J. Pepper, 1894-95 to 1896-97, incl.; Mrs. H. Swannell, 1895-96 to 1900-01, incl.; Dr. W. L. Gray, 1896-97 to 1907-08, incl.; G. C. Willis, 1897-98 to 1902-03, incl.; Mrs. S. A. Carnahan, 1897-98 to 1902-03, incl.; John W. Stipes, 1898-99 to 1903-04, inclusive; Sarah H. Swigart, 1901-02 to 1903-04, incl.; I. A. Jackson, 1903-04 to 1905-06, incl.; Mrs. Mary C. Lee, 1903-04 to 1908-09, incl.; Oren L. Percival, 1904-05 to 1906-07, incl.; Mrs. Lucy W. Wallace, 1904-05 to 1906-07, incl.; F. J. Akers, 1906-07 to 1908-09, incl.; H. S. Capron, 1907-08 and 1908-09; Mrs. Florence H. Miller, 1907-08 to 1909-10, incl.; C. B. Hatch, 1908-09 to 1910-11, incl.; Dr. R. E. Shurtz, 1908-09 to 1910-11, incl.; Mrs. R. D. Burnham, 1909-10 to 1914-15, incl.; John W. Armstrong, 1909-10 to 1911-12, incl.; T. E. Smith, 1909-10 to 1915-16, incl.; Mrs. F. E. Bainum, 1910-11 to ——; Dr. B. A. Smith, 1911-12 to 1913-14, incl.; Robert Dimmer, 1911-12 to ——; Ben. Long, 1912-13 to ——; Mrs. D. P. McIntyre, 1915-16 to ——; Dr. W. E. Schowengerdt, 1914-15 to ——; C. D. Brownell, 1916-17 to ——.

THE TEACHING FORCE

The first public school teacher, beginning work in the Little Brick

CHAMPAIGN HIGH SCHOOL (1893)

CHAMPAIGN HIGH SCHOOL (1913)

was probably Mrs. Mary A. Fletcher, a sister of Mark Carly, about 1855 to 1857. It is also reported in Judge Cunningham's history that Mrs. Fletcher came from a southern state and that she later began to conduct a young ladies' academy in the building vacated by the First Presbyterian Church' in 1867. Bunk's history says she was the third teacher in the village and that she taught in the First Congregational Church, her recompense coming partly from the public funds and partly from rate bills. About 1859, there were two teachers named Clark and Wallace. About 1860, Truesdell and Miss Mary Ayers were the teachers. In the year 1863-64 a teacher by the name of Havens taught a part of the year and Miss Harriett Trevett and Miss Mary Marcy, afterward. Mrs. Henry Trevett, finished the year, Miss Marcy continuing through the year 1866-67. About 1865-66 J. C. Oliver came in and Mrs. Mary Frisbie as a third teacher in charge of the infant class. Nellie Angel, Mary McKinley, now Mrs. R. R. Mattis, Alice McKinley, now Mrs. Conn, Annie Moore, Harriet Pratt, Elizabeth and Rebecca .Farson, Irene Beidler, since Mrs. Eppstein, Betty Wrisk, Miss Leonard, Anna Bradley, now Mrs. E. A. Kratz, and Alice Tuthill were also teachers in the early days.

In tracing the beginning of the high school in District No. 1, we find Miss Noyes as high school teacher in 1880, followed by Miss Jane Elliott, who resigned in December of 1882 and was replaced by Miss Andrews, who was re-elected as "teacher in the high school" in 1883, with Hattie Hall as assistant. In July of 1884, W. S. Hall was elected "teacher for the high school." In June of 1887, Hattie Hall was elected "principal of the high school" and this is the first time the term "principal" is used in the records. In this year, a second assistant in the high school was first employed.

Edward Bigelow was elected principal of the high school in 1889 and E. F. Adams in 1890. In May of 1891 it was ordered that Supt. R. S. Barton should act as principal of the high school also and teach two classes; but in 1892, Miss Lottie Switzer was elected principal of the high school, a position she has ever since held.

Of those known as superintendents of schools on the west side, J. C. Oliver was probably the first, followed by W. H. Lanning and he possibly by a Mr. Evans. More exact information concerning these is desired. Definite terms of service of the following are on record: M. Moore, 1880-81 to 1890-91, inclusive; R. S. Barton, 1891-92 and 1892-93; C. A. Bowsher, 1893-94 to 1895-96 inclusive; Joseph Carter, 1896-97 to 1905-06, inclusive; F. D. Haddock, Aug. 1, 1906, to Feb. 29, 1908; W. W. Earnest, March 1, 1908 to ———

1—25

THE BURNHAM ATHAENEUM

THE POSTOFFICE

Principals of the schools in District No. 2 (East Side High School) until the two districts were united are given as follows: Mr. Scovell, 1868-73; W. Water, 1873-74; Miss I. C. Childs, 1874-75; Eugene DeBurn, 1875-80; I. L. Betzer, 1880-83; Mr. Reed, 1883-84; P. K. McMinn, 1884-87; R. S. Kyle, 1887-90.

Of the East High School, after the union of the districts, T. A. Clark was principal 1890-91; N. A. Weston, 1891-92 and 1892-93; S. McGee, 1893-94.

The Burnham Athaeneum

The Burnham Athaeneum, or public library, of Champaign, is one of the city's most substantial and elevating institutions. From a manuscript history which has recently been completed by Dr. Edwin A. Kratz are condensed the facts which follow. He was a charter member of the original library association in 1868 and custodian of its few books; secretary, when the project was substantially revived in 1871; librarian when the collection was given to the city in 1876; director and secretary of the first municipal board; secretary when the library was moved to the city building in 1889; held the same position when possession was taken of the Burnham Athaeneum in 1896; president of the board when the children's department was established, and acting secretary when the first printed report was issued. Dr. Kratz is therefore thoroughly qualified to write on the subject of the Burnham Athaeneum.

The Champaign Library Association, the original organization, had its inception in a meeting held April 28, 1868, at the office of T. B. Sweet, in the Barrett Block. There were present, besides Mr. Sweet, Henry Beardsley, J. S. Lathrop, A. D. Eads and George M. Noble. At a more public meeting, May 7th, the association was formed by twenty-six members, who elected George Atherton, president; J. S. Jones, vice-president; J. S. Lathrop, treasurer, and Aaron Beidler, librarian. A reading room was soon opened on the second floor of No. 7 Main Street, having been secured of A. C. Burnham at a nominal rental. This venture was a failure, the few books collected were moved to Dr. Kratz's office, and the library enterprise went into a deep sleep. The association kept alive by engaging lecturers of renown to deliver addresses before the Champaign public, using the proceeds to collect a library fund. Incorporation papers were filed in August, 1871. New books purchased, the collection moved to the second floor of the Gazette building, and the library feature brought again to the front. Editor

George Scroggs acted as librarian, and the books remained in the Gazette building for four years. The Gazette people having erected a new building, the library was transferred to Peterson's book store, temporarily, and permanently to Rugg's shoe store on North Neil. At this period there were 700 volumes in the library. In September, 1876, the association conveyed its property to the city on condition that the municipality appropriate $1,000 annually toward the support of the library.

Up to this time the following had served as presidents: 1868, G. W. Atherton; 1869-70, H. Beardsley; 1871-72, J. C. Conklin; 1873, H. C. Beach; 1874-76, George W. Gere.

Secretaries: J. S. Lathrop, 1868; W. H. Kratz, 1869-70; E. A. Kratz, 1871-75; E. T. Whitcomb, 1876.

Treasurers: Aaron Beidler, 1868; E. N. McAllister, 1869-76.

Librarians: T. B. Sweet, 1868; E. V. Peterson, 1869; E. A. Kratz, 1870; George Scroggs, 1871-75; E. A. Kratz (second term), 1876.

The Champaign Public Library and Reading Room dates back to July 21, 1876. On September 8th Mayor Henry Trevett appointed its first board of directors—George W. Gere, William Bowen, S. L. Wilson, I. B. Arnold, E. A. Kratz, F. Dollinger, H. Swannell, D. A. Cheever and B. C. Beach. About a week later Mr. Gere was elected president and E. A. Kratz, secretary; in October the deed of gift was formally accepted by the city, and on November 21, 1876, the second floor of No. 24 Main Street was formally opened as Champaign's first Public Library and Reading Room. The public exercises were held in Barrett Hall, Hon. Abel Harwood presiding. The library remained at the location mentioned for thirteen years. In 1889 it was transferred to the southwest room of the new city hall, on the ground floor, and all library matters looked up. At this period the collection had increased to 3,700 volumes. After several requests, the city council, in 1894, increased the annual appropriation for the support of the library to $1,500.

In December of the year named A. C. Burnham announced his generous gift of $40,000 for a library building and $10,000 as an endowment fund. The necessary papers were drawn up and in January, 1895, they were accepted by the City Council, and the residence property on West Church Street was duly conveyed as a site for the Burnham Athaeneum and the Julia F. Burnham Endowment Fund provided for, in honor of the deceased wife. Without following all the details, it is sufficient to say that the third and permanent home of the library was publicly opened December 17, 1896. The exercises were held in the Presbyterian Church, Captain T. J. Smith acting as master of ceremonies and the building being presented by Mr. Burnham's devoted friend and legal adviser, George W. Gere.

The building, as it stands, presents a pleasing exterior of light gray brick. The entrance is between two massive fluted pillars, reaching to the eaves, with the Burnham Athaeneum engraved on the entablature. The main floor has a large vestibule, commodious reading and magazine room, reference room, offices, etc. On the second floor are a large auditorium or lecture hall, and children's, club and directors' rooms. From the annual report of the board of directors to the city council for the year ending June 1, 1896, when the library occupied the Athaeneum building, it is learned that the total number of volumes then housed was 18,356.

In 1898 the Mason library of 800 volumes was added, through the generosity of Benjamin F. Johnson, and in September of the following year, the children's department was established. A branch library was permanently founded in 1903, and in 1907 it was established in the Marquette school building.

The annual amount appropriated by the city council for the maintenance of the library has increased from $1,000 in 1876, to $1,500 in 1895, $2,400 in 1900, and $6,000 in 1916. The library now contains 21,268 volumes.

Since 1876 the Public Library and Burnham Athaeneum have had the following officers:

Presidents: George W. Gere, 1876-80; James B. Russell, 1880-89; Henry F. Aspern, 1889-93; B. C. Beache, 1893-96; Manford Savage, 1896-99; Edwin A. Kratz, 1899-1906; Henry W. Berks, 1906-10; Robert D. Burnham, 1910—

Secretaries: E. A. Kratz, 1876-93; H. S. Capron, 1893-99; W. W. Maxwell, 1899-1905; Miss Ray L. Bowman, 1905-10; Mrs. J. B. Russell, 1910-14; William F. Woods, 1915—

Treasurers of the Endowment Fund: G. N. Cunningham, 1896-98; F. H. Lloyd, 1898-1903; H. W. Berks, 1903-06; R. D. Burnham, 1906-09; Miss Ray L. Bowman, 1909-10; William M. Honn, 1910-11; E. A. Kratz, 1911-14; W. F. Woods, 1915—

The librarians during that period have been: Mrs. M. M. Frampton, 1876-83; Mrs. Annie M. Beidler, 1883-84; Mrs. M. M. Frampton, 1884-90; Mrs. W. A. Plottner, 1890; Miss Nellie C. Kellogg, 1890-93; Mrs. M. M. Frampton, 1893-96; Miss Anna LeCrone, 1896-1901; Miss Florence E. Carter, 1901-03; Miss Jeannette Roberts, 1903-15; Miss Ethel G. Kratz, 1915—

THE CITY HALL

The City Hall building housing the various departments of the municipality, and containing the old Council chamber and accommodations for the new board of commissioners, was completed in 1889. It is a brick building, with an unimposing tower, standing at Neil Street and University Avenue, and its appearance is really not commensurate with the standing of Champaign as a progressive corporation and not up to the standard of its other public buildings.

PROTECTION AGAINST FIRE

The city of Champaign is protected against fire both through a modern system of water works and a paid department of ten firemen. The fire apparatus comprises two combination chemical and hose

CHAMPAIGN AND URBANA WATER WORKS

wagons, an aerial ladder truck and a modern auto engine. John Ely is head of the department, which is housed in the City Hall building, as well as the police department, under A. U. Keller. Additional protection against fire is afforded the city through the system of close co-operation established between the municipality and the fire departments of Urbana and the University.

WATER SUPPLY AND DISTRIBUTION

The present plant of the Champaign and Urbana Water Company was located in 1884, when a shaft being sunk for coal struck so much

water at a depth of 160 feet that the shaft could be continued no
further. The plant was completed in 1885. Active in the organiza-
tion and construction of the water works were Henry Trevett and
William Day, and in its operation afterward, W. B. McKinley, H. H.
Harris, George W. Davidson, M. A. Goff, John N. Beers and J. S.
Pollard. In 1899 the present owners took charge, namely: W. L.
Prettyman, president; F. C. Amsbary, vice-president and manager, and
J. B. Prettyman, secretary and treasurer.

The plant and pumping station at Urbana comprises twenty-four
deep wells, with separate heads. The supply is pumped from the wells
into the receiving reservoir, thence through the iron removal filters
to the two clear-water basins, whence it is forced by pumps into the
eighty miles of distributing mains supplying the cities of Champaign
and Urbana with 2,000,000 gallons of water daily.

SANITARY SEWERAGE SYSTEM

Besides the natural surface drainage of Champaign and Urbana,
which is good, the Twin Cities have two complete sanitary sewerage
systems. There are about thirty miles of sewers in the Champaign
district and half as much in the Urbana district. In both cases the
sewage is disposed of by means of a septic tank located well outside
the city limits. As stated, the systems were devised by Professor A.
N. Talbot, head of the department of Municipal and Sanitary Engineering, University of Illinois.

PARKS AND BREATHING PLACES

Pleasant parks and open breathing places are active agents in the
promotion of public hygiene, as well as wisely-devised water and sewerage systems. Although not crowded or besmirched, as are so many
manufacturing centers, Champaign has its creditable parks. City
Park, as often known as White Park, which lies along West University
Avenue, contains nearly thirteen acres in the main church district and
is the largest and most finished of the public grounds. It is named
after James P. White, one of the donors of the original site and likewise a generous patron of the public schools. Its most striking deco-
rative feature is the fountain near the center, bearing a remarkable
piece of statuary, entitled "The Prayer for Rain," the descriptive verses
of Edward Kemeys being chiseled in the tablet beneath.

The fountain and concrete walks around it were the gifts of B. F.

GENERAL VIEW IN WHITE PARK

THE PRAYER FOR RAIN

THE JOHNSON FOUNTAIN

Johnson, a former citizen of Champaign. Rasmus B. Anderson, former minister to Denmark, once said of "The Prayer for Rain," and the fountain as a whole, that it was one of the most artistic productions he had seen either in the United States or Europe.

James R. Scott donated the original site of the park which bears his name, on East Springfield Avenue. It comprises about three and a half acres. Beardsley park, of less than two acres, in the northern part of the city, was donated in the raw by George F. Beardsley, in 1874.

Washington Park, comprising two acres south of the student district, was platted in 1905.

CEMETERIES

The two cemeteries maintained by Champaign are Mount Hope, on Maple Avenue south of the University, and Rose Lawn, at South Fourth and the city limits.

THE FIRST PRESBYTERIAN CHURCH

The founding of the First Presbyterian and the First Congregationalist churches of Champaign, as Urbana institutions, has already been described as a salient fact in the founding of the new railroad town itself. As the Presbyterians first moved their headquarters to West Urbana their organization is entitled to precedence.

The First Presbyterian Church was organized in September, 1850, with only eight members. It was organized under the name of the First Presbyterian Church of Urbana. At that time Champaign was unknown, and Urbana was only a village of some twenty houses. Services were held in the courthouse and in the schoolhouse in Urbana until 1854, when they began to hold them in the Illinois Central freight depot in Champaign. In that same year lots were secured and in 1855 the first church building was erected at a cost of $1,700, on the site of the present church building. On December 28, 1856, a colony of ten members were dismissed from this church and organized into the First Presbyterian Church (N. S.) of Urbana. On April 10, 1858, another colony of forty-four members were dismissed and organized into the First Presbyterian Church of Mahomet. In that same year the name of the church was changed to the First Presbyterian Church (O. S.) of West Urbana. When the name was changed to the First Presbyterian Church of Champaign is not recorded. The present church building was begun in 1867, but was not completed until 1869. On June 15,

1874, nine members were dismissed from this church, in order that they might be organized into the Prairie View Presbyterian Church. The church has, therefore, been the mother of three other Presbyterian churches.

On the first Sunday in March, 1909, the present building was seriously damaged by fire, and the pipe organ then in use almost ruined. But with commendable zeal the members of the church immediately set about, not only to replace the damaged portion of the building, but also to make the church as modern as possible. An addition to the old building was built, enlarging the kitchen and pastor's study, and providing parlors and additional rooms for Sunday school.

Between 1850 and 1858 the church was served by four ministers, viz.: H. F. Bowen, R. H. Lilly, E. K. Lynn and Joseph Platt. Only one of these, Rev. E. K. Lynn, was installed as pastor. The Rev. George McKinley became pastor in September, 1858, and continued until February, 1870, when he resigned on account of ill health. He was followed by the Rev. John S. Frame, whose pastorate was cut short by his sudden death, October 13, 1874. The Rev. A. J. Berger succeeded to this work in January, 1875, and remained as pastor until May, 1881, when he was compelled to resign on account of ill-health. Then came the long pastorate of the Rev. C. N. Wilder, D. D., from October, 1881, until November, 1902. The Rev. E. W. Clippinger began his pastorate on June 15, 1903, and resigned May 1, 1911, to accept a call to the Tabernacle Presbyterian Church in Indianapolis, Indiana. The present pastor, Rev. Chas. Ryan Adams, D.D., began his work here November 12, 1911, and the church has a membership of about 750.

First Congregational Church

On November 1, 1853, a little colony of Congregationalists residing in Urbana were called together by Rev. W. W. Blanchard and organized into the First Church at the residence of Moses P. Snelling in that city. These charter members were John T. Rankin and Mary A., his wife; Moses P. Snelling and Caroline, his wife; Tama Campbell, Jane Higgins and Alsethia Snyder. In 1856 it completed a church building at the northwest corner of University Avenue and First Street, which, from a leading feature in the immediate landscape, was long called Goose Pond Church, and, as has been recorded at some length, was the scene of many notable gatherings, outside the pale of the church.

Rev. W. W. Blanchard, who assisted in organizing the church supplied the pulpit until January 13, 1855, after which the church was without a regular pulpit supply until about a year later. During the year 1855 the first church building was erected, on a lot donated by the Illinois Central R. R. Co., at a cost of about $1,000. The site was at the corner of First Street and University Avenue, Champaign. In the year 1866 the second church building was erected, on West Park Street, at a cost of $16,000.00 and during the seven succeeding years the church was constantly increasing in members and influence in the community. On the evening of September 12, 1873, the church building on West Park Street was burned, and the Sunday service and Sunday school was held in Barrett Hall for about a year following.

During the next year (1874) the present church building was built (corner Church and State streets) at a cost of $22,000.00 and was dedicated free of debt. In 1883 a pipe organ was purchased through the efforts of the Young People's Society at a cost of $2,000. In 1895 a parsonage costing $4,600 was secured. In 1910 a branch church building, at a cost of $3,600, was erected at the corner of Fifth and Grove streets. During the more than sixty-four years of its history the church has had but eight ministers or pastors. The names of these are as follows, with the years of service: 1856-7, Rev. W. H. Halliwell; 1857-1868, Rev. S. A. Vandyke; 1869—, Rev. E. N. Andrews; 1870-1872, Rev. T. J. Valentine; 1872-1887, Rev. W. G. Pierce; 1888-1892, Rev. John Allender; 1892-1907, Rev. Franklin L. Graff; 1908 (and at present), Rev. John Andrew Holmes. Dr. Holmes has accepted a call to the First Congregational Church of Lincoln, Neb., and will leave in September. Of the present list of 550 members, 414 have been received by him.

On June 24, 1917, the church voted informally to dispose of its present property and build a hundred thousand dollar church on the east side of the city.

The First Methodist Episcopal Church

In April, 1855, John Walkington came from Brown County, Ohio, and located on a farm about three miles south of the present city of Champaign. He united with the Methodist Church at Urbana, and in the fall of that year Rev. W. F. T. Spruill, pastor of that organization, appointed him a class leader for a few of his faith who gathered for services at the Illinois Central depot at the new station, West Urbana. Mr. Walkington organized a class consisting of John Walkington, A. J. Stewart and Ann R. Stewart; which was the beginning of the First

M. E. Church of Champaign. Rev. Richard Holding, Rev. Lester Janes and Rev. William Munhall preached occasionally. The conference sent Rev. P. N. Minnear to the charge as its first resident minister. He was succeeded by Revs. A. C. Armentrout, G. R. McElfresh, E. D. Wilkins, and W. H. Webster. In September, 1863, during Mr. Webster's pastorate, the first church building was dedicated, the congregation having previously worshipped in such halls at Clark's and Bailey's. An addition was made to the house of worship during the pastorate of Rev. G. H. Adams, who served in 1865-67. He was followed by Rev. J. H. Noble, who occupied the pulpit for two years. The membership so increased during his pastorate that it was decided to form another church across the tracks. Accordingly, a building for the new society was erected at East University Avenue and Sixth Street, its pastor being appointed in the fall of 1868. The successors of Mr. Noble until 1887 were Revs. W. R. Goodwin, W. N. McElroy, Horace Reed, J. H. Noble (second term), W. N. McElroy (second term), J. G. Little, N. P. Heath (died in 1879), T. A. Parker, E. D. Wilkins, M. W. Everhart, J. Villars and W. D. Best. In 1887 Rev. J. B. Wolfe assumed the pastorate, and in 1889, during his incumbency, was dedicated the first brick church located on West Church Street. In the succeeding seventeen years Revs. T. M. House, R. G. Hobbs, W. H. O'Neal, G. E. Scrimger, W. A. Smith and C. Galeener served the First M. E. Church with such effect that a larger house of worship was required. One was therefore erected in 1906, and is still occupied. Since the year named the pastors have been Rev. J. W. VanCleve, Rev. Joseph Nate and Rev. R. H. Schuett, the last named having been in service since 1912. The church has a present membership of 1,400.

Besides the Fifth Street branch, the Methodists of Champaign have missions on North Fifth and East Tremont. The Bethel African M. E. Church is on East Park, Rev. E. G. Jackson, pastor.

EVANGELICAL LUTHERAN CHURCH

The Evangelical Lutheran Church at Champaign was organized in 1855 by Rev. C. A. F. Selle. Its pastors, in chronological order, have been Revs. Selle, M. Zucker, Theodore Mertens, T. Buszin, H. Ginpe, F. Lindemann, C. Brauer, L. Frese, C. Mueller, C. Frappe, W. Roecker, and G. Stiegmeyer. The present strength of the church is sixty-five voting members. The house in which they worship was originally built in 1899 and remodeled in 1915.

St. Peter's Evangelical Church

St. Peter's Evangelical Church of Champaign originated in the attempt of the German Synod of the Northwest to establish an organization of that faith in 1859. Although the attempt was unsuccessful at the time, it was renewed by Rev. J. M. Hartmann in 1863. In the spring of 1864, after six months of preaching and labor, he succeeded in organizing a congregation of twenty-one members, who decided to appoint and support a pastor. Rev. Julius Schumm, of Lancaster, Wisconsin, was finally appointed by the synod as pastor of the new church, and Mr. Hartmann presented him to the congregation in October, 1864. Sites for a church and school were immediately purchased, and the buildings completed on December 31, 1865. At the General Conference held in September, 1866, the congregation was taken into the Synodical Bond, under the name "German Evangelical St. Peter's Church of Champaign." In July, 1869, Mr. Schumm preached his farewell sermon; and was succeeded during the following four years by Revs. Kammerer, Buehlow and Andreas, and in 1873 by Rev. H. Strehlow, who served the church with rare efficiency and faithfulness until 1896. The church membership had greatly increased, but the congregation was poor; yet Mr. Werhahn, Mr. Strehlow's successor, accomplished the task of raising funds for the building of an ample house of worship, which was dedicated in December, 1896. He was succeeded by Rev. W. Sussmuth in 1899, and the latter by the present pastor, Rev. H. F. Mueller, in 1906. St. Peter's Church now numbers 170 families, or about 500 members.

Grace English Lutheran Church is located on West Springfield Avenue.

St. Mary's Roman Catholic Church

St. Mary's is the mother parish of Champaign County, and originally included not only the territory now within the jurisdiction of St. Patrick's (of Urbana) and St. John's and Holy Cross (Champaign), as well as its own, but its priests ministered to the spiritual needs of the Catholics of Ivesdale, Tolono, Bement, Rantoul, DeLand, Mahomet and several other outlying vicinities. It is also recorded that these pioneer priests occasionally celebrated mass in Danville before the establishment of a Catholic Church there. In 1854 the Illinois Central was being built through Champaign County, and there, as in Illinois generally, a great portion of the work was done by Irish laborers. To care for the spiritual needs of the Catholics of central Illinois, Rev. Thomas Ryan was appointed a missionary priest, and it was in 1854 that he founded St. Mary's parish, the membership of which was at first largely composed of Irish railroad men. The little brick church which he undertook to erect shortly after his appointment was wrecked by a prairie wind storm, which left the Catholics of both Urbana and West Urbana without a house of worship for about four years. Then a small frame building was erected on the present property on East Park. This little house of worship was not entirely completed until 1861. Father Lambert, a priest from Indiana, succeeded Father Ryan in 1858, shortly after the second church was commenced, but resigned the following year, and was followed by Rev. A. Vogt. Rev. Thomas Scanlon assumed charge of the parish in 1860, and after his death came a second Father Thomas Ryan, who remained two years, made the little frame church more comfortable and complete, and founded the parish house. Afterward he bought the land which was consecrated as St. Mary's cemetery and died in Paxton several years later. Rev. Patrick Noone succeeded the second Father Ryan; after him came Rev. M. Prendergast, who had charge of the parish in 1865-66, and his successor, Rev. Patrick Toner, served the parish for thirteen years. In the year following his appointment he enlarged the church and the frame structure continued to do service until the present brick edifice was erected in 1888. Between the years 1872 and 1874 he built a new parochial residence, which, in turn, gave way to the present handsome brick dwelling in 1895.

In 1876 Father Toner commenced the erection of a brick schoolhouse, which was opened in September, 1878, and placed in charge of the Sisters of Notre Dame, Milwaukee. For thirty-eight years or until June, 1916, they conducted the school, when it was transferred to the Benedictine Sisters of Nauvoo, Illinois. The old brick schoolhouse, which had done service during nearly the entire period, was razed in the spring of 1915 to make room for the elegant St. Mary's school now occupied.

Besides performing this energetic and effective work at Champaign, Father Toner erected churches at Tolono and Ivesdale in 1870 and one at Rantoul in 1871. In May, 1879, the strain undermined his health and he was compelled to retire from the active work of the church. Subsequently he lived in retirement in Ireland, where he died.

At the time of the retirement of Father Toner from St. Mary's parish, in 1879, Tolono was made a separate parish and placed in charge of Rev. A. J. Wagner, formerly Father Toner's assistant at Champaign.

Father McDermott was pastor of the parish for a short time after the retirement of Father Toner, and early in 1880 Rev. Father Keating commenced his pastorate of eight years. During that period a new convent was erected for the Sisters.

FATHER A. J. WAGNER

At the retirement of Father Keating, Father Wagner was transferred from Tolono to St. Mary's parish; he finished the brick church commenced by his predecessor and also enlarged the schoolhouse. The beloved and honored Father Wagner served St. Mary's for twenty-five years and six months, or until his death, October 28, 1913. The building of the present church edifice was well under way when he assumed his duties as head of the parish. He energetically pushed the venture to a conclusion, and the church was dedicated by Rt. Rev. J. L. Spalding, D. D., on October 28, 1888. In 1895 he built a new rectory, enlarged the school and improved the cemetery. When Father Wagner became priest, St. Mary's property was valued at about $10,000; when he died it was worth more than $125,000. In truth, Father Wagner was a man of rare executive ability, as well as of charity, spirituality and real benevolence.

Rev. J. F. Lockney, D. D., succeeded him, but after about a year retired to Boston, Massachusetts, where he died in February, 1917. Rev. R. F. Flynn, the present pastor, assumed his duties in September, 1914. Under his pastorate the elegant two story brick school building was completed, being dedicated November 14, 1915, greatly adding to the value and fine appearance of the church property. This now covers the entire block bounded by Wright, Sixth and Church streets, and Park Avenue. It includes the school, church, rectory and convent, and is conservatively estimated at $150,000. The congregation also purchased the land for St. Mary's cemetery, but this burial ground serves other congregations as well, and is not included in the estimate of St. Mary's property. At present there are over 160 families in the parish and the school which is accredited to the University of Illinois, has an attendance of 200.

ST. JOHN'S PARISH

This was organized for the benefit of the German-speaking portion of old St. Mary's. Services were first held by missionary priests and by the Catholic pastor of the Danville Church. The first resident priest was Rev. Charles Steurer, who assumed charge about 1894. He served five years, during which he built the present rectory, a two-story frame residence at the northwest corner of Locust and Logan streets. Father A. A. Geyer succeeded him and under his pastorate a substantial addition was built to the church, which was the old frame building erected by St. Mary's parish and replaced by the brick house of worship in 1888. The new addition was about to be occupied when, on the night of June 11, 1902, it was completely demolished by a cyclone. It was restored within the coming year.

In 1904 Father Geyer accepted the pastorate of St. Mary's Church, Rock Island; was succeeded by Fathers Edward A. Jakob, William E. Frawley and others; but returned to St. John's parish in 1915 and is still at its head.

Holy Cross Parish

The remarkable growth of Champaign westward necessitated the formation of another Catholic parish in January, 1912. Father W. E. Frawley, who had been attached to St. Mary's Catholic Church at Peoria, serving as chancellor of the diocese, was appointed rector of St. John's Church, Champaign, in December, 1911. Soon afterward he completed a religious census of the Catholic families residing west of the Illinois Central Railroad, and ascertained that 140 families resided in that territory; therefore, the authorization of the foundation of Holy Cross Parish covering that territory was given January 12, 1912. In April the property for a church site was purchased at the southeast corner of Clark and Elm streets. The corner-stone of the church building was laid in July, and Father Frawley, having been appointed rector of the new parish, the first mass in the new church was celebrated on December 22, 1912. The church, a two story brick structure, faces north on Clark Street, and has also been occupied since September, 1913, by a parochial school. Adjoining the house of worship on the east is the rectory. In July, 1916, the balance of the half block to Prairie Street was purchased by the parish, the plan being to erect a convent upon at least a portion of the land.

First Baptist Church

The First Baptist Church of Champaign occupies a massive and ornate structure at University Avenue and Randolph Street. The first house of worship was a small frame building with a tiny cupola perched on the front of the roof and was built in 1868. The organization was effected in 1865 under the pastorate of Rev. William Remington, and his successors were: Rev. G. W. Riley, 1867-70; Rev. A. L. Farr,

1870-74; Rev. A. Cleghorn, 1874-78; Rev. I. N. Carman, 1878-81; Rev. F. M. Williams, 1882-83; Rev. O. B. Read, 1883-85; Rev. H. H. Bawden, 1886-90; Rev. E. A. Stone, 1890-94; Rev. W. H. Stedman, 1894-1903; Rev. George C. Moor, 1903-09; Rev. E. B. Rogers, 1909-11; Rev. D. O. Hopkins, since 1911. The First Baptist has a membership of over three hundred.

The Salem Baptist Church on North Fifth Street was erected in 1908. Rev. S. W. Batchlor is the present pastor.

EMMANUEL EPISCOPAL CHURCH

Up to December, 1870, there were no established services of the Episcopal Church in Champaign. About the beginning of the Civil

VIEW ON WEST CHURCH STREET

War the town was visited by Rev. John Wesley Osborne, of Chicago, who, as diocesan missionary, seems to have had jurisdiction along the Illinois Central Railroad from Chicago to Cairo. Mr. Osborne probably held services at Champaign, but there is no record of any official acts. Regular services were established when Rev. Albert E. Wells located in the city during December, 1870, as a missionary of the Illinois diocese. At that time the congregation met in Bailey's Hall on Neil Street. Mr. Wells continued to reside in Champaign and hold services until November, 1871, when he took charge of St. Peter's Church, at Mound City, Illinois. Periodically, renewed efforts were

1—26

made to establish the Episcopal Church service at Champaign, and finally Rev. Daniel F. Smith opened the Little Brick schoolhouse, on the corner of Randolph and Hill streets to an Episcopal congregation, December 8, 1875. In August, 1878, he severed his connection with the work and in the following month Rev. William C. Hopkins accepted charge of the mission, and continued in that capacity for about four years. In July, 1882, Mr. Hopkins was succeeded by Rev. Jesse Higgins and Rev. Arthur Q. Davis, associate priests, residing at Champaign and holding services there, as well as at Urbana, Tuscola and other missionary points. During that year the congregation was incorporated as Emmanuel Church under state laws, a church building contracted for and Rev. D. W. Dresser installed as the new rector. The building was opened for service in April, 1883, being consecrated by Rt. Rev. George F. Seymour, bishop of Springfield. The original rectory was first occupied by Dr. and Mrs. Dresser in July, 1886, and in 1902 a large and more modern residence was provided. The church building was continually improved and many handsome and impressive memorials were added to its interior. A large memorial window was inserted in memory of Dr. D. W. Dresser, who died November 18, 1900. In 1901 the Emmanuel mission became a parish, Dr. James E. Wilkinson serving from that year until his resignation; on account of ill health in April, 1906. In September of that year Rev. Harry T. Moore took charge of the parish, was succeeded by Rev. L. S. Sherman in April, 1907, and he, in turn, was followed by Rev. H. C. Goodman in November, 1910. The fire of the preceding February had made it necessary for services to be held in the University chapel for some time. In June, 1914, Mr. Goodman resigned and in September Rev. George P. Hoster, to whom a call to the rectorship had been extended several years previously, commenced his work.

In August, 1916, occurred the death, by accident, of John Luther Polk, Jr., a member of the vestry. At the October meeting of that body Dr. Hoster, acting in behalf of Dr. and Mrs. John L. Polk, presented the following: "Dr. and Mrs. Polk will build a church costing not less than $25,000, nor more than $30,000, to be a memorial to their sons, John Luther, Robert Collins and Justice Cicero Polk," and requesting that the name be changed to read "Emmanuel Memorial Church." On May 1, 1917, the contract was signed with A. W. Stoolman for the erection of the church, parish house and rectory, the work to be completed in the fall of 1917.

In addition to the foregoing, there are a number of churches within the city limits worthy even of more specific mention than can be given them, but the information urgently requested was not supplied. The University Place Christian and the Christian Science churches are in that list. It is known that the First Church of Christ Scientist has been organized since 1908, has a beautiful edifice for worship, the usual rest and reading room down town, and is growing steadily.

BENEVOLENT AND CHARITABLE INSTITUTIONS

There are a number of institutions and organizations of a benevolent and charitable nature which are nobly co-operating with the churches in various lines of practical work designed to relieve the physical ailments and material embarrassments of life from which none are positively exempt. Both the Y. M. C. A. and the Y. W. C. A. have large and growing organizations, the work being largely centered at the University of Illinois; the Salvation army is doing the usual work of proselyting and regeneration; there are the Julia F. Burnham Hospital, the Garwood Home for Old Ladies, the Young Women's Christian League, the Dorcas Society, and other institutions, tried and true, and, as an organization, through which all can work and to which many contribute, the United Charities Association of Champaign and Urbana.

UNITED CHARITIES ASSOCIATION OF CHAMPAIGN AND URBANA

In the fall of 1911 the State Conference of Charities and Corrections met in the Twin Cities, Dr. E. C. Hayes of the University of Illinois being largely responsible that this organization was asked to meet here. As a result of the interest aroused through this state conference a meeting was held shortly afterwards at the Y. M. C. A. at which all the various organizations interested in problems of poverty were represented, and it was there decided to organize the United Charities Association of Champaign and Urbana. It had already seemed to many who had come in contact with the problems of the two towns that some central organization should be formed as the towns were too large for individual work to be effective. Knowledge gained by one person was not passed on to the next working with a family. There was much overlapping, several individuals helping the same family, each thinking they were the only ones assisting.

The first regular meeting of the Association was held December 28, 1911. At that time a constitution and by-laws were adopted and the following officers were elected: Dr. E. C. Hayes, president; Mr. F. H. Boggs, vice-president; Mr. J. M. Kaufman, treasurer; Mrs.

S. P. Sherman, secretary pro tem. Later Miss Florence W. Clark was employed as secretary to give all her time to the work and she took up her duties on February 20, 1912. In May, 1912, the organization was incorporated.

When the first annual meeting was held in December, 1912, the organization had worked with 119 resident families including .486 individuals. The volume of work has increased as those in need have come to know of the organization and those wishing to help have come more and more to realize the effectiveness of associated charities methods to lift a family out of dependency and help them to again be self-supporting.

During the winters of 1913-14 and 1914-15 when industrial conditions all over the country were bad, the number of families assisted reached as high as 350 a year, comprising about 1,500 individuals, and

JULIA F. BURNHAM HOSPITAL

this past year 306 families came to the attention of the organization, these families comprising about 1,100 individuals.

At present the organization has 210 contributing members, and the officers are president, Mr. E. S. Swigert; vice-president, Mr. M. W. Busey; treasurer, Mr. J. H. Thornburn; secretary, Miss Gertrude Longden.

JULIA F. BURNHAM HOSPITAL

The Julia F. Burnham Hospital on East Springfield Avenue is a practical memorial to the energetic and faithful labors of Mrs. Burnham, for nearly thirty years a sister, and a mother of mercy and charity, in Champaign and Urbana, and at the time of her death, October 28, 1894, and for some years prior thereto, she was a prominent worker in the State Board of Charities. Her husband, Albert C. Burnham, located in Champaign in 1861, then in his twenty-third year, read law with James B. McKinley, and after his admission to the bar was associated with his preceptor in the banking and investment firm of McKinley & Burnham. After his marriage in 1866 he became the senior member of such banking concerns as Burnham, McKinley & Company and Burnham, Trevett & Mattis, and at his death, September 13, 1897, he left a large estate. In the late years of his life, in happy harmony with the wishes of his wife, his time, attention and money had been largely devoted to charitable work, and through his gift of $10,000 (afterward increased to $25,000) the Julia F. Burnham Hospital was opened on March 5, 1895. Mrs. Burnham's death occurred in the previous October.

Mr. Burnham's original gift was intrusted to the Social Science Club, in which Mrs. Burnham had been deeply interested, and the membership of which was identical with that of the Julia F. Burnham Hospital Association. H. H. Harris, husband of another prominent member of the club, tendered a site of eight lots for the hospital grounds. It was later deemed expedient to decline this offer, and the present location was purchased through an additional donation made by Mr. Burnham. In case the club, to which the foundation was consigned, should disband, ample provision was made for the permanent management of the hospital. An endowment fund was also placed at the disposal of the Hospital Board. The hospital is well managed.

GARWOOD HOME FOR OLD LADIES

The Garwood Home for Old Ladies is a comfortable house at North Market Street and the city limits. Although the late L. C. Garwood left the greater part of his estate to found and maintain the Home, complications followed in the settlement and investment of various interests so that all has not been accomplished that was designed. Under the terms of his will none are admitted who have not resided in Champaign County for at least five years, and many old ladies of fine character have been made comfortable in the delining years of their lives. Mrs. Arthur Spalding, closely identified with Mr. Garwood's interests during his life and with the estate afterward, has been a mainstay of the institution from the first. Walter H. Johnson is the superintendent.

Young Women's Christian League

The Young Women's Christian League provides a home for working women on West Church Street, at a small cost. It has a matron and accommodations are furnished to fourteen girls and women. The board of management comprises two members from each religious denomination in the city. The Home was opened in January, 1917, and the following have served since as its officers: Mrs. B. F. Harris, president; Miss Sara Monier, treasurer, and Mrs. T. J. Paisley, secretary.

The Dorcas Society

The oldest charitable organization in Champaign is the Dorcas Society. It has always done useful service in the community, and Mrs. John W. Stipes is its president. For many years its chief spirit was Mrs. Harriet Lawhead, who devoted her life to charitable work and came to be known as the unfailing friend of all the poor and needy. One of the public school buildings of the city is named in her honor, the Lawhead School.

Women's Clubs

The Twin Cities are both strong in the field of women's clubs and, in not a few cases, the activities of the same organization cover both cities. Among the ladies who are leaders in the uplifting work promulgated by such clubs are included many of the foremost women of both Champaign and Urbana, and the work of these clubs has had a markedly beneficial influence on the social and intellectual atmosphere of both cities.

The Art Club

One notable feature runs through the history of these fine bodies of womanhood, and that is the strong influence exerted by the University of Illinois in the establishment and development of the women's clubs of both Champaign and Urbana. The Champaign Art Club, the mother of them all, organized in 1876, was an offspring of the University department of art, of which Professor Kennis was the head. In her paper read before the Art Club and its friends during a meeting commemorative of its twenty-first anniversary, Mrs. W. S. Maxwell said that Professor Kennis delivered a lecture before the club at its first formal meeting, advancing many ideas which were subsequently adopted in its founding and plan of study and investigation. Again says Mrs. Maxwell: "In those early days, when our city libraries were less equipped than now, the college professors used to furnish us with books, as well as talks and lectures upon subjects connected with our studies."

The initial inspiration which finally led to its organization was the collection of sculpture and engravings of masters, both ancient and modern, purchased and installed by the University and the citizens of the Twin Cities in 1874. Credit for the selection of the collection was also largely due to Dr. Gregory, who visited Europe at his own expense to perform that work. The original membership of the club was twelve—Mesdames J. M. Healey, Jonathan Bacon, Don Carlos Taft, E. V. Peterson, A. E. Harmon, Phoncene W. Frisbee, of Champaign, and Mesdames Alexander, J. W. Porter, J. E. Hunt, T. J. Burrill, C. D. Webster and W. H. Smith, of Urbana. The first constitution of the Art Club was adopted December 18, 1890, having been drafted mainly by Mrs. J. B. Russell, Mrs. George W. Gere and Mrs. G. C. Willis. For many years the study of the Art Club was devoted exclusively to art and art history, on the lines laid down by its originators, but there has been a continual broadening of its scope of late years. Among its best known presidents have been Mrs. Anna S. Clark, Mrs. E. A. Kimball, Mrs. A. C. Burnham, Mrs. Jonathan Bacon, Mrs. Henry Swannell, Mrs. W. H. Smith, Mrs. J. B. Russell, Mrs. W. K. D. Townsend, Mrs. G. C. Willis, Mrs. J. B. Harris, Mrs. G. W. Gere, Mrs. R. R. Mattis, Mrs. J. W. Porter, Mrs. J. L. Ray, Mrs. C. B. Hatch, Mrs. H. H. Harris, Mrs. H. E. Cushing, Mrs. J. B. McKinley, Mrs. C. N. Wilder, Mrs. D. F. Carnahan, Mrs. T. J. Burrill, Mrs. J. R. Stewart, Mrs. T. A. Naughton.

THE THIRTY CLUB

The Thirty Club was organized by the ladies of Champaign and Urbana, in 1885, chiefly under the leadership of Prof. J. C. Pickard, instructor in English and literature at the university, and Prof. Nathaniel Butler, at the head of that department and for many years past identified with the University of Chicago. For the first five years of its existence the organization was known as the Shakespeare Club, the name defining its scope of study. Since then its curriculum has included other branches of literary study, both classical and current. Its present officers are: Mrs. H. H. Stoech, president; Mrs. H. S. Capron, vice-president; Mrs. A. P. Carman, secretary.

SOCIAL SCIENCE CLUB OF THE TWIN CITIES

The Social Science Club of Champaign and Urbana originated in a visit of Mrs. J. L. Ray and Mrs. H. H. Harris to Washington, in attendance at the National Council of Women, during the year 1888. Largely through their enthusiasm and initiative an organization was effected among the women of the Twin Cities known as the Social and Political Science Club. In 1892 the word Political was eliminated, although the activities of the club and its studies were in no wise curtailed, social science logically covering not only the political phases of the subjects of special interest to women, but the sociological and all others.

From the beginning of the original club's history the presidents have been Mrs. J. L. Ray, Mrs. H. H. Harris, Mrs. S. A. Forbes, Mrs. G. W. Gere, Mrs. Edward Snyder, Mrs. J. R. Sewart, Mrs. S. T. Busey, Mrs. B. F. Harris (died in January, 1896), Mrs. I. N. Wade, Mrs. F. M. Wright, Mrs. H. M. Dunlap, Mrs. A. N. Talbot, Mrs. George A. Turrell, Mrs. J. T. Davidson, Mrs. John A. Glover.

During the administration of the following club board, Mrs. J. R. Stewart, Mrs. F. M. Wright, Mrs. I. O. Baker and Mrs. J. T. Davidson, in 1893, this club procured a charter from the State, the signatures of the entire membership of thirty-five being appended to the application for an incorporation, whose purpose should be the maintenance of the Julia F. Burnham Hospital. A short time later one-half of the members withdrew from the parent club and founded. with an equipment of new officers, the Champaign Social Science Club, whose purpose was to continue its literary studies and to spend its energies on the maintenance of the new hospital. The original club under its then existing administration relinquished all its rights and interests in that organization and has since followed its social and literary pursuits.

THE CHAMPAIGN SOCIAL SCIENCE CLUB

The Champaign Social Science Club was founded in the fall of 1893 for the special purpose of helping to maintain a hospital convenient to the people of Champaign which had been made possible through the donation of $10,000 by A. C. Burnham to found a memorial hospital in honor of his late wife, Julia F. Burnham. Aside from the careful consideration of literary and civic studies, this club, its membership limit having been increased to forty, has succeeded by the faithful efforts of years in bringing the hospital through the trying vicissitudes attendant on the establishment of so important an institution and fixing it on a footing which makes it a reliance for valuable public service and a source of pride to those who stood by it during the days of its infancy. The meetings of the clubs have always been conducted in the Burnham Athenaeum, the city public library building.

WOMAN'S CLUB OF CHAMPAIGN AND URBANA

An organization of much influence and energy is the Champaign and Urbana Woman's Club. It was organized at the home of Mrs. G. C. Willis in Champaign in 1897, and a full list of working departments was soon provided for the club. It is intellectually and numerically strong and is a member of the State organization. Its first officers were as follows: President, Mrs. Joseph Carter, who held three terms; secretary, Mrs. H. S. Piatt; treasurer, Mrs. F. L. Bills. Succeeding Mrs. Joseph Carter as president were Mrs. S. A. Forbes (two terms), Mrs. M. W. Busey and Mrs. Mary C. Lee.

CHAMPAIGN COUNTY COUNTRY CLUB

The Champaign County Country Club is one of the prosperous organizations which have given the Twin Cities a high standing among people who still believe in the necessity for outdoor exercise and recreation. It was organized in 1904, and as a corporation leased for ten years the beautiful forty-acre homestead of E. O. Chester adjoining the city limits of Champaign on the southwest. At the expiration of the lease, in 1910, the club purchased the grounds. A handsome clubhouse has been constructed, with wide porches and roof garden, offering charming views of the adjoining country. A nine-hole golf course was also laid out, tennis courts built, bowling alleys installed, croquet grounds completed and playgrounds for children platted in a wooded stretch. Tournaments and entertainments of all kinds add to the enjoyment and membership of the club, which is divided into various classes. Honorary members may be received from localities outside of Champaign County. The total membership is considerably in excess of 200. Since the organization of the Country Club in 1904 the following gentlemen have served as presidents: B. F. Harris, M. W. Busey, N. M. Harris, W. L. Gray, R. R. Mattis, E. S. Swigart, F. W. Woody, D. P. McIntyre, J. B. Prettyman, R. D. Burnham, John A. Glover and George A. Huff.

THE GRAND ARMY POST

Colonel Nodine Post No. 140, G. A. R., was mustered in June 17,

1882, and the names of its successive commanders have been: J. W. Langley, dead; George W. Harwood and E. A. Kratz; S. E. Weeks, H. T. Sperry, A. P. Cunningham and Jacob Buch, all of whom are deceased; Walter E. Price and John B. Weeks; Edward Bigelow, dead; W. H. Coffman; George K. Sheffer and Ben. J. Craven, both dead; A. T. Hall; W. G. Abbott and J. B. Russell, deceased; J. N. Beck; George F. Beardsley and Arthur C. Price, dead; Joseph Jutton; M. Bongart, deceased; S. P. Atkinson, Charles M. Miller, A. K. Hefflefinger, J. H. Bainum, William Myers and C. B. Johnson; P. T. Platt, dead, and A. J. Houston. The elective officers for 1917: Commander, L. C. Pittman; S. V. C., M. M. Myers; J. V. C., J. M. Campbell (dead);

COUNTRY CLUB HOUSE AND GROUNDS

O. D., H. A. Glascock; chaplain, W. H. Coffman; surgeon, S. Van Brunt; Q. M., Adam Frison; Adj., Walter E. Price; O. G., Chris Grein; P. I., C. B. Johnson; Q. M. S., Charles Miller. In April, 1917, the post had a membership of seventy-nine; five had died during the year.

CHAMPAIGN CHAMBER OF COMMERCE

An agency which has done much toward the development of Champaign County is the Chamber of Commerce of Champaign. It was incorporated April 30, 1904, as The Retail Merchants' Association of Champaign, Illinois, with Seeley C. Gulick, W. I. Ferguson, D. E. Harris, F. K. Robeson, M. A. Nelson, M. E. Smith and F. D. Kirkpatrick as the first board of directors. Mr. Robeson was elected president. The work of the organization was directed almost wholly to the correction of trade abuses which caused heavy losses to business firms and increased cost of goods to patrons who paid their bills and asked only a square deal.

On May 5, 1905, following discussions of plans for broadening the work of the organization, the name was changed to "Chamber of Commerce of Champaign, Illinois," and the new activities were conducted that year under direction of J. R. Trevett, president, and J. M. Kaufman, W. I. Ferguson, M. A. Nelson, W. R. Bradley, C. H. Baddeley and G. C. Willis as directors. Under the new plan the association took up a variety of subjects for consideration, keeping the commercial department almost entirely separate from the general work. A public rest room was one of the early undertakings and is still in operation with attendance on the part of shoppers and strangers in the city, which more than justifies the expense incurred. Free parcel checking, free local telephone service, toilet facilities are offered the general public without formality. Another feature which has been strengthened during the last five years is the information bureau, free, as are other services, and a reality in all the name implies.

Among the accomplishments of the association are the change from a blacklist for the protection of merchants to a credit rating system designed to be of use to all citizens and fair to all, the ratings being based wholly on the custom of handling accounts and systematized to follow any changes readily. The association was responsible for the lighting of the business section of the city, and after investing over $3,000 gave the distributing plant to the city.

It promoted the high school bond issue, the installation of city lighting system, and bond issue for motorizing the fire department; initiated and perfected the organization of the county farm bureau and established the county office in Champaign; also assisted the City Council in the preparation of building ordinance, and has done much work to procure for the city adequate surface water and sanitary sewer system.

Industrially, the association has not been active during the last five years. Prior to that time a "factory fund" had been created by the sale of an 80-acre tract of land divided into 342 lots. Much of this money was spent as factory bonus and lost on the factories so procured, but the net result has worked out to about balance the account. The disposition now is to not bid for factories; however, manufacturing concerns are not discouraged if they find upon investigation that they can do well in Champaign.

Co-operation with the University of Illinois is active, friendly and helpful, because Champaign realizes that that great educational institution is one of its most valuable assets.

Until a few years ago the shops of the Illinois Central Railroad were located in the business section of the city. Through efforts of this association directed by a friendly spirit, the shops have been moved about two miles north of the city where the company has spent over $1,000,000 on new buildings and equipment, making this division one of the best along the main line.

Looking back over the years which have passed, we find the following men have served as president: F. K. Robeson, 1903-04; J. R. Trevett, 1904-06; E. M. Burr, 1906-07; B. F. Harris, 1907-10; C. A. Kiler 1910-11; S. K. Hughes, 1911-12; F. C. Amsbary, 1912-13; J. M. Kaufman, 1913-15; D. G. Swannell, 1915-16; A. E. Huckins, 1916-17.

C. D. Brownell, now serving as president, is an active business man, and has been called upon to serve the community as a member of the city council, the board of education, and by special duties as member of various committees for investigation. In his new place he is giving the same thought and time to the work in hand which had made his service valuable in other capacities. C. W. Murphy is the efficient managing secretary.

Of the men named, all are still actively engaged in business in Champaign and reaping their part of the benefits which the whole community enjoys as a result of the unselfish and often unpraised work of the people organized as The Chamber of Commerce of Champaign, Illinois.

Hardly an undertaking in the city is completed without this organization in some way having a part in its performance. It is commonly regarded as the central association to which all look for assistance in community work, and it has never been found unwilling.

Local Banks

The banks of Champaign are commensurate with the large needs and pronounced progress of the city.

The oldest of its financial institutions is the Trevett-Mattis Banking Company. The original concern was founded by the late Albert C. Burnham, in 1861. He was then a young man of twenty-three, who had recently been admitted to the bar as a student under James B. McKinley, and became associated with that gentleman both as a law and a farm investment partner. Within a few years the legal portion of the partnership was almost obliterated by the growth of the business conducted for eastern capitalists in farm securities. In 1871, the business was assumed by Burnham, McKinley & Company, and a few years later William B. McKinley, nephew of James B., was installed as a clerk in the office. The two McKinleys became partners in 1877, Mr. Burnham having reorganized the original business in 1876 under the name of Burnham, Trevett (J. R.) & Mattis (R. R.). The firm so continued until 1897, when the death of Mr. Burnham necessitated a change to Trevett & Mattis. In 1903, the business was incorporated under the state banking law of Illinois as the Trevett-Mattis Banking Company, under which name its affairs have since been conducted. Its specialty is still farm loans, although it transacts a large general banking business. Its capital and surplus amount to $200,000. Following are its officers: Ross R. Mattis, president; John R. Trevett, vice-president; Henry W. Berks, second vice-president; Wallace P. Spalding, cashier; John H. Trevett, secretary.

The First National Bank of Champaign was chartered under the

THE OLD ANGLE BLOCK (1858)

National Banking Act January 30, 1865. It was founded by B. F. Harris, and at the head of its affairs have successively been his son, Henry H. Harris, and his grandson also, B. F. Harris. The bank building was originally a frame structure located on the site of the present Kuhn building. In 1872, a new building was erected at the present location on Main Street, and in 1900 the fine, large five-story structure now occupied as its headquarters and by various office firms was completed. Newton M. Harris, brother of the president, is vice-president of the First National Bank, and Hazen S. Capron, who succeeded the late G. A. Turell, cashier. A striking idea of the growth of its business may be gained from the statement that the average deposits during its first year, 1865, amounted to $7,359.65, and fifty years afterward, 1915, to $1,626,274.38. A record of the First National and its founders and promoters is given in detail elsewhere.

The Baileys are, like the Harrises of Champaign, bankers, both by training and inheritance. David Bailey, one of the founders of the First National, in 1865, disposed of his interest therein during the '70s, and in 1882 joined his son, Captain Edward Bailey, in founding the Champaign National Bank. In the fall of 1879 the latter had associated himself with W. S. Maxwell and James C. Miller in establishing the private bank of Bailey, Maxwell & Miller. In 1882 the business was chartered as the Champaign National Bank with a capital of $50,000. Edward Bailey has been president ever since, its transactions having expanded commensurate with the splendid growth of the city. P. L. McPheters is the present cashier. The details of the development of the bank and the facts regarding the careers of David and Edward Bailey, father and son, are to be found in other pages of this work.

The Commercial Bank is the creation of M. W. Busey, son of Simeon H. Busey of Urbana, who also assisted in founding the First National Bank of Champaign. He is its president; George W. Busey, a brother, vice-president, and J. C. Somers, cashier. Its location is on East University Avenue.

The Citizens State Bank was organized in 1895 and incorporated in 1908. Its building is on North Neil Street, and its officers: A. M. Burke, president; E. I. Burke, vice-president; C. L. Maxwell, cashier.

The predecessor of the Illinois Trust and Savings Bank of Champaign was the Illinois Title and Trust Company, which was incorporated in September, 1902, with the following officers: F. B. Vennum, president; V. W. Johnston, vice-president; Shields A. Blaine, cashier. It then had a capital stock of $100,000. The Illinois Trust and Savings Bank was incorporated as a state institution in August, 1912, with a capital stock of $150,000, and the following officers: V. W. Johnston, president; Fred Collison, vice-president; Walter W. Stern, second vice-president; E. M. Vennum, cashier; George R. Shawhan, manager of the savings department. There has been no change in the first or last office; the present vice-president, however, is Walter W. Stern; cashier, F. Way Woody. The surplus and undivided profits of the bank are $25,000; average deposits, $625,000.

CHAMPAIGN NEWSPAPERS

The press of Champaign is represented by the Gazette and the News. As early as May, 1857, L. G. Chase and Albert Gore issued the "Spirit of the Agricultural Press," a handsome quarto, the objects of which were pithily defined by its name. But the venture evidently was not fathered by the right partnership and survived less than a year.

With the material left by the Press, Dr. John W. Scroggs, on March 10, 1858, issued the first number of the Central Illinois Gazette, a Republican newspaper. In its editorial management he was associated with William O. Stoddard, and for a short time Messrs. Cunningham and Flynn, of the Urbana Union, appeared to have had a silent financial interest in the newspaper venture at West Urbana. The Gazette had attained a fair circulation and influence by 1860, and upon Lincoln's election Mr. Stoddard was appointed to a secretaryship in the executive office and retired from newspaper work. Dr. Scroggs sold the paper to John Carrothers of the Union, in the winter of 1862-63, and the two publications were consolidated for about a year under the name of the Champaign County Union and Gazette. Then the material was separated and the Gazette office turned over to John W. Summers, a practical printer, by whom the newspaper venture was continued. In the summer of 1864 Mr. Summers sold to another printer, John Robbins who, within a few months, turned the enterprise over to George W. Flynn, George N. Richards and J. O. Cunningham. On October 14, 1864, they again commenced the publication of the Gazette at Urbana; in April, 1866, Judge Cunningham retired from the editorship, and in September of that year Mr. Richards withdrew from the partnership, leaving Mr. Flynn alone until the spring of 1868. Then George Scroggs purchased a half interest in it. The business of bookbinding was added, and in 1871 Judge Cunningham became an equal partner. The binding and job printing department was moved to Urbana, and in 1872 the firm was dissolved, Mr. Scroggs becoming sole proprietor of the Gazette and Flynn & Cunningham of the bookbinding and job plant at Urbana.

Mr. Scroggs was a strong writer and an able man and brought great influence to the Gazette. In 1878 he was elected to the lower house of the Illinois Legislature, and was afterward appointed consul to Hamburg, Germany, whence he returned to his home in Champaign and died on October 9, 1879, as the ultimate result of injuries received during the last year of the Civil War.

Under the provisions of Mr. Scrogg's will, the publication of the Gazette was continued by his executor, H. J. Dunlap, for several years.

It had commenced the issue of a daily edition in 1883, and in 1890 it was sold to H. H. Harris of Champaign. It continued under the financial control of Mr. Harris and under the editorship of J. R. Stewart. In 1900 the plant was sold to Messrs. Stewart, Davis & Flanigan. Subsequently, the business was incorporated and in 1911 Mr. Stewart retired from active participation in its editorial and business management. The Gazette publishes a daily evening edition and is Republican in politics.

On February 21, 1891, E. B. Chapin, formerly of the Tolono Herald, issued the first number of the semi-weekly Champaign County News. In 1895, an evening edition was added, and in 1903 a morning edition. In 1915 Mr. Chapin sold the News to E. R. Mickelberry and D. W. Stevick, who have since conducted its editorial and business affairs.

SECRET AND BENEVOLENT SOCIETIES

The secret and benevolent organizations of Champaign are in keeping with the standing and growth of the communities which constitute the city as a whole. The Masons, the Odd Fellows, the Knights of Pythias and the Pythian Sisters; the Elks, the Moose, the Eagles, the Knights of Columbus and the G. A. R., with others of undoubted worth, have established a firm foothold and each contributes its share to the general fund of sociability, morality and charity.

As is the rule, the Masons, that old standard order, were the first to effect a stable organization. Dr. Edwin A. Kratz, with his usual thoroughness and correctness, wrote a history of the Western Star Lodge No. 240, A. F. & A. M., the original body, in June, 1916. The facts which follow are taken from that account, with additions made by the doctor to bring the record up to the summer of 1917:

Friday, March 27, 1857, the petition for a Lodge U. D., in West Urbana was forwarded to the Grand Master by Worshipful Brother Alfred M. Whitney, together with the fee therefor, $25.

M. W. Bro. James H. Hibbard, the G. M., issued his dispensation giving life to Masonry in the little village some time in April, doubtless the latter part of the month. (These two papers have been lost by fire in the Grand Secretary's office, and the date and names thereon cannot be verified.)

Monday, May 11, 1857, the brethren named in the dispensation assembled in Whitney's Hall, southwest corner Main and Market streets, and opened the first meeting of the lodge. There does not appear to have been a formal institution of the lodge, and it is not known who was present at this meeting, or what business was transacted, since our first record was also destroyed by fire; but it is understood that the officers were: A. M. Whitney, Master; J. Dallenbach, S. W.; A. P. Hensley, J. W.; M. L. Dunlap, Treas.; W. B. Fowler, Secy., and that Dr. H. C. Howard petitioned for the degree; also that the first Monday in the month was designated for stated meetings, and the minimum fee of $20 adopted for the degrees.

The report to the Grand Lodge for four months' work showed that two petitioners were rejected, four initiated, three passed, one raised and four affiliated, making twelve members, and the trestle board showing ample work outlined.

Wednesday, October 7, 1857, the Grand Lodge, then in annual assembly, upon the inspection and approval of the work of this Lodge, U. D., granted a charter therefor under the name, number and style of Western Star Lodge No. 240, A. F. & A. M., located in West Urbana, now Champaign City. The names inscribed on the charter are: Alfred M. Whitney, John Dallenbach, Archibald P. Hensley, Mathias L. Dunlap, William B. Fowler, Henry C. Whitney and Nathaniel C. Beasley, and the first three were named as the principal officers. (These brethren were no doubt the original petitioners, for it was the custom at that time not to add other names to the charter.)

What seems strange is, that they kept on working during the interim supposed to be dormant; for the old ledger shows three raised and two affiliated prior to the lodge being constituted. .

Tuesday, January 12, 1858, the lodge was duly constituted and set to work by Worshipful Brother Washington C. Cassell of Urbana Lodge No. 157, as the proxy of the M. W. Grand Master, with eighteen members.

"We take especial pride in our name because it is of great historical importance to the Masons of this grand jurisdiction—being, the name of the first Masonic lodge located on Illinois soil, which was then the outskirts of civilization, namely, of 'Western Star Lodge No. 107,' instituted at Kaskaskia, December 14, 1805, by virtue of a dispensation issued from the Grand Lodge of Free and Accepted Masons, of the State of Pennsylvania. 'Western Star Lodge No. 107' materially assisted, with several others in 1822, in the formation of the first Grand Lodge of Masons in Illinois, and taking a charter from it as 'Western Star Lodge' No. 1, A. F. & A. M. It furnished the first Grand Master, as well as the first governor of the state, in the person of Shadrach Bond. This Grand Lodge, together with its constituent bodies, ceased to exist in the year 1829, being swept away by the anti-Masonic political disturbances of that period, but 'Western Star Lodge' No. 240, A. F. &

A. M., lives to perpetuate the name and memory of that pioneer lodge to the end of recorded time."

This lodge has never been what is known Masonically as a "Moon Lodge," which meets on a certain day of the week on or before the full moon.

The lodge met regularly on the first Monday evening of every month until January, 1859, when two meetings were deemed necessary, and the first and third Mondays were designated for stated meetings. This arrangement held good until June, 1867, when a change was made to the second and fourth Mondays in the month, which still prevails, and it has never yet failed of a quorum.

The lodge prospered from the start, each succeeding report showing more members until 1871, when its maximum of 135 was reached, then occurred a gradual decrease to 104 in 1882, since which time the upward tendency has been steady and permanent. The present membership (1917) is about 460.

"During the War of the Rebellion, now known as the Civil War, many of our members enlisted in defense of country and fought to maintain our flag unsullied, quite a number of whom were honored with commissions ranking from lieutenant to brevet brigadier-general, with a sprinkling of 'high privates,' besides the numerous men in the ranks. At the close of hostilities in our national family, the seekers after 'light' were a host, and the closest scrutiny in the history of the lodge was had during the eighteen months of the years 1865-66, when thirty for initiation, eleven for advancement, and two for affiliation were thrown aside as imperfect ashlar for our symbolic structure."

The lodge has been "at home" in the following places, all being on the third floor of substantial brick buildings:

1.   Whitney's building, southwest corner Main and Market streets, 1857-1865.

2.   Gardner's Building, No. 5 Main Street, 1866-1869.

3.   Mather Block, Nos. 65-67 Market Street, 1869-1871.

4.   Bailey's Block, Nos. 47-49 Neil Street, 1872-1898.

5.   Masonic Block, Nos. 20-22 Main Street, 1899-1913.

6.   Masonic Temple, Nos. 202-04 West Hill Street, 1914——.

The lodge became a freeholder, mainly through the efforts of Worshipful Brothers J. P. Gulick, L. W. Faulkner, J. B. A. Collan and E. A. Kratz on Monday, March 28, 1898, by a majority vote accepting a contract for the Eichberg Building, Nos. 20-22 Main Street. The conveyance for this income property was made Friday, May 13, 1898, and the lodge became domiciled therein December 21, 1898.

The purchase price was $18,000. There was a mortgage of $8,000 and the lodge issued notes for nearly $6,000, showing that 7-9 or about seventy-five per cent holding represented debt, with only 150 members to shoulder the burden; but in ten years the entire incumbrance was liquidated without increasing the fees or dues. September 13, 1909, by a vote of ninety-eight for to ten against, out of 310 members, this income property was sold for double the purchase price, the chapter, having one-third interest, agreeing thereto, and the lodge became a renter once more.

September 27, 1909, the first step towards a magnificent temple was the appointment of a committee to investigate a site, to wit: H. W. Berks, J. N. Beers, C. H. Baddeley, B. F. Harris, J. W. Davidson, H. Roberts, Isaac Kuhn, J. J. Dallenbach and D. P. McIntyre.

April 25, 1910, the lodge selected the Kuhn site, 132 feet square, at the northwest corner Hill and Randolph streets, for $15,800, and the committee was made a permanent building committee with full power and authority to select plans and erect a building thereon. Western Star Lodge No. 240, A. F. & A. M., Champaign Chapter No. 50, R. A. M., Champaign Commandery No. 68, K. T., each took one-third interest in said grounds, and agreed to share equally in the building. January 22, 1912, the building committee reported that the general contract had been let to A. W. Stoolman, who commenced operations without delay.

Wednesday, September 4, 1912, the cornerstone of this magnificent building was laid by the Grand Lodge, A. F. & A. M., Delmar D. Darrah, G. M.

November 24, 1913, the three Masonic bodies created the Masonic board of control and invested it with the full supervision and management of the temple.

January 2, 1914, said board of control accepted the custody of the temple and found an indebtedness of $74,556. The building committee was subsequently relieved and discharged.

Thursday, January 8, 1914, this magnificent Masonic home was dedicated by the Grand Lodge, A. F. & A. M., Henry T. Burnap, G. M., and the first meeting of our lodge held therein immediately afterwards.

On March 23, 1914, the Commandery sold one-half of its interest to the lodge, thus making the relative proportions of ownership one-half, one-third and one-sixth, and the appointment of the board of control to be 4, 3, 2, respectively.

The worshipful masters of the lodge have been (under dispensation): 1858, A. M. Whitney; 1859-60-61-62-63, Nat C. Beasley; 1864, C. F.

Columbia; 1865, Nat C. Beasley; 1866-67-68-69, L. W. Faulkner; 1870-71-72, Isaiah H, Hess; 1873, Charles E. Baker; 1874-75-76-77, George Scroggs; 1878, H. J. Dunlap; 1879-80-81-82-83-84-85-86-87, Edwin A. Kratz; 1888, H. J. Dunlap; 1889-90-91-92, Joseph O'Brien; 1893, J. B. A. Collan; 1894-95-96, John S. Wolfe; 1897, T. J. Baddeley; 1898-99-00-01-02, Joseph P. Gulick; 1903-04-05, Henry W. Berks; 1906-07, Boyd S. Blaine; 1908, A. D. Mulliken; 1909-10, F. M. Brown; 1911, Henry W. Berks; 1912, D. G. Swannell; 1913, Alonzo P. Kratz; 1914, M. J. A. Fluck; 1915, J. E. Filson; 1916, F. R. Smedley.

Prior to 1898 the elections were held in December. Since that time they have been held in June. F. I. Fleming is the present senior warden; Edwin V. Kratz, junior warden; T. J. Baddeley, treasurer, and O. F. Miller, secretary.

Champaign Chapter No. 50, R. A. M., was organized under dispensation March 3, 1859, with the following elective officers: High priest, Jacob P. Gauch; king, William Munhall; scribe, Lavius Fillmore; secretary, John B. Thomas; treasurer, William Stewart. The following have since served as heads of the chapter: Nat C. Beasley, 1863-67; A. W. Beasley, 1868; James M. Healey, 1869; H. J. Dunlap, 1870-78; E. N. McAllister, 1879-88; Edwin A. Kratz, 1889-94; L. W. Faulkner, 1895-99; Seely Brown, 1900-05; Henry W. Berks, 1906-07; Edward C. Ireland, 1908; George E. Cogswell, 1909-10; D. B. Wright, 1911-12; E. A. Gardner, 1913-14; F. S. Coogler, 1915; S. L. Fleming, 1916; J. G. Gulick, 1917. The present officers, besides Mr. Gulick, high priest, are: B. L. Kirk, scribe; J. J. Dallenbach, treasurer; A. C. Singbusch, secretary. The chapter has a membership of about 270.

The Masons also number as their active bodies at Champaign: Commandery No. 68, K. T., and Vesper Chapter No. 128, O. E. S. There is also what is called Saxa Rubra Conclave No. 2, Red Cross of Constantine, organized in 1893, with J. B. A. Collins as first commander. J. P. Gulick is the present head of the conclave, which seems to be more a social body made up of Masons than an organization identified with the rites of the Order.

The Independent Order of Odd Fellows organized Champaign Lodge No. 333, October 9, 1866, with the following officers: James A. Bowermaster, N. G.; Valentine Baker, V. G.; G. N. Richards, R. S.; E. B. Smith, C. S.; C. B. Whitmore, treasurer. At present its elective officers are: William Walkington, N. G.; J. R. Cooper, V. G.; Harry King, R. S.; H. L. Babb, F. S.; W. H. Hamersmith, treasurer. The present membership of the lodge is about 260. The Order is also represented by the following: Kaulback Lodge No. 549, composed of German members; Champaign Encampment No. 68; Canton Zonar No. 17, and Triumph Lodge No. 410, Rebekahs.

The Knights of Pythias have Valliant Lodge No. 130, and Unity Company No. 33 (uniformed rank), and the Pythian Sisters, Champaign Temple No. 129.

The Champaign Lodge of Elks, No. 398, have a house and auditorium on West Hill Street; the hall of the Fraternal Order of Eagles, Aerie No. 563, is on North Neil Street; the Knights of Columbus meet at St. Mary's School on East Park Avenue; the Foresters' Court, Watago No. 3251, assembles in Carpenter's Hall; the Moose lodge on the third floor of the Imperial building; the Modern Woodmen of America at Nelson's Hall on Main Street, and Colonel Nodine Post No. 140, G. A. R., at its hall on North Walnut Street. There are also several lodges composed of colored men and women, such as the Grand United Order of Odd Fellows, the Household of Ruth, the Sisters of the Holy Cross, and the Pilgrim Knights of the World.

The Twin Cities Federation of Labor, with headquarters in Urbana, is represented by eighteen labor organizations, the membership of which is drawn from Champaign and Urbana.

CHAPTER XII

URBANA TOWNSHIP AND CITY

Male and Female Seminary—Absorbed by the Public School System—Another Seminary Project—Civil War Bars Progress—The Institute as the Forerunner of the University—Period of Ups and Downs—Leading Up to the City of Urbana—Original Corporate Limits and First Election—Urbana's Mayors—The City Hall and Departments—Crystal Lake Park—Leal and Carle Parks—Public Schools of Urbana—The High School—The Urbana Free Library—The Local Press—Early Preachers in the Urbana Neighborhood—Rev. James Holmes, Pioneer Methodist—Coming of Rev. S. W. D. Chase—First M. E. Class and Church—Dr. McElroy's Statement—Present First M. E. Church—Rev. William Munhall—First Baptist Church — First Presbyterian Church — The Universalist Church—First Christian Church—Trinity M. E. (University) Church—St. Patrick's Church—The Unitarian Church—University Baptist Church—McKinley Memorial Church—Cunningham Children's Home—Early Sunday Schools of Urbana—Banks and Industries—Urbana Societies.

Urbana was located and platted as the county seat when railroads were weird and untried "contraptions," viewed with dread by the average farmer and countryman as an amorphous vampire which drew the lifeblood from a given territory and left nothing but paper towns and ruined hopes behind. Its future was based upon its accessibility to the settlements—actual and potential—within the country designated as Champaign County; such accessibility to be determined by condition of the average turnpike and country road of the '30s, and by a conservative forecast of the extension of the facilities for outside communication. Urbana was nearly in the territorial center of the county, and seemed the most convenient point to reach from the groves and timber lands which were the early sensible areas of settlement. Consequently, Urbana was founded where it is, and was not brought to a sense of its original near-sightedness until the place had jogged along for twenty years.

In the meantime, the locality had acquired a sort of political and intellectual aristocracy, which it retains largely to this day, because of the fact that so many able men collected at the county seat of justice and became also prominent, at a later day, in founding the University of Illinois within its corporate limits.

MALE AND FEMALE SEMINARY

In the early '50s, when it became evident that the Illinois Central was to have a station to the west of Urbana proper, the citizens of the old town bestirred themselves to consolidate the already material gains of their place as an educational center. Danville, Paris, Marshall and Shelbyville, county seats to the near south and east, had seminaries of learning, and why should not Urbana? As early as 1852, the Urbana Male and Female Seminary was established under the nominal patronage of the Methodist Church, although it was liberally encouraged by citizens of all sects and of none. James S. Busey gave a block as a building site—the same ground now occupied by the Oregon Street public school, and in the fall of 1855, while the foundations of the Free School law were being laid, the handsome two-story seminary building was completed. In the upper part of the structure was a large assembly hall, and in the lower part the recitation rooms. Rev. John M. Miller, an able educator, was brought from Kentucky to take charge of the enterprise, but died within the succeeding six months.

ABSORBED BY THE PUBLIC SCHOOL SYSTEM

Within the following two years Prof. A. M. Wheeler and Rev. L. Janes, both successful teachers, became its principals; but when Thomas R. Leal, who was chosen county superintendent of schools in 1857, commenced his reorganization of the county schools under the new law, the seminary went by the board, and in May, 1858, the citizens of Urbana voted in favor of purchasing the Urbana Male and Female Seminary for a free public school. For that purpose it was voted to tax the school district $5,000. The seminary at Homer went the same way; went to strengthen the system of the public schools.

ANOTHER SEMINARY PROJECT

Early in 1859, soon after the absorption of the Urbana Male and Female Seminary into the public school · system, Rev. Jonathan C.

First School House in West Urbana (1854)

The Perkins School House

Stoughton of Freeport, Illinois, and two capitalistic associates planned to plat a town addition west of Urbana, sell off some of its lots and from the proceeds erect a seminary or college building within the tract thus exploited. Enthusiastic meetings were held both in Urbana and West Urbana—Dr. C. A. Hunt of the former and Dr. J. W. Scroggs of the railroad town, being especially prominent. By July, 1860, the Urbana Clarion was able to announce that "the construction of an educational building 180 feet front by 80 feet deep, five stories high above the basement, between Urbana and the depot, is now a fixed fact." Further: "The building is to be located on the open space between the towns, twenty or thirty rods from the Urbana Railroad, which will render it easy of access to students in either place; and if but one-half the benefits anticipated are realized, it will do very much to render our town and county a desirable place of residence. A school of a high order is very much needed in this part of the state, it being almost entirely destitute of any but common school facilities."

Civil War Bars Progress

In 1859, the Urbana Railroad had been chartered to build a line between the two towns and eastward, but the work of grading the line between Urbana and Champaign had been only partially completed when the Civil War blocked the project until 1863. The war also stopped the erection of the building of the Urbana and Champaign Institute. While the enterprise was thus hovering in the balance, Dr. Hunt (in July, 1862) suggested that the partially completed building could be turned over to the proposed Agricultural College under the Morrill act and adapted to its uses. The idea grew in favor, so that by the fall of 1865 a committee of investigation from the General Assembly reported in its favor.

The Institute as the Forerunner of the University

As the seminary building eventually became the mother of the large and imposing progeny of university buildings, its description, while still unfinished, is interesting. "The Urbana and Champaign Institute," says the account of a local paper, "is a substantial brick building with stone foundation, standing on a beautiful elevation about one-half mile from the Illinois Central Railroad at Champaign City, and about an equal distance from Urbana, the county seat of Champaign County.

The whole structure is beautiful in its architectural proportions and very imposing in its appearance. The main building is 125 feet front by 40 feet in depth, and five stories high. From the center a wing projects forty-four by seventy feet four stories high. The front wall has a projection, eight feet by forty, with pilasters and towers ornamenting the corners. The inside of the building is unfinished, and may be somewhat modified from the original plan. The walls are without a crack or blemish. The building is under contract to be wholly finished at the expense of the county in the early part of the coming summer."

The fight for the location at Urbana was a long one, but virtually decided by the election of C. R. Griggs, of that place, as a representative in the lower house of the Legislature and an enthusiastic champion of the Champaign County location. After passing both houses, the bill fixing the site of the Industrial University was approved by Governor Oglesby in February, 1867.

PERIOD OF UPS AND DOWNS

Although the Urbana Railroad was opened to Champaign in August, 1863, its stock was rolled by mules. But in 1870 the town at last secured steam railway connections by the completion of the Danville, Urbana, Bloomington & Pekin Railroad. Then, with the coming of the railroad and the firm establishment of the Industrial University at its very doorway, when things seemed really to be looking up, came the destructive fire of October 9, 1871. While the great conflagration at Chicago raged, in proportion to the area of the place the fire at Urbana seemed, at the time, equally disastrous. From the Whitcomb residence, at the corner of Market and High streets, it was driven northward to the railroad track, only two houses escaping destruction. Within a few months, however, better buildings arose to replace those burned; so that, on the whole, the early '70s mark the commencement of Urbana's continuous growth. Its development has been steady, chiefly as a clean, healthful, orderly residence city, possessing social and educational advantages of a high order, not crowded by a miscellaneous industrial populace, or besmirched by belching and unsightly factories. Its stores furnish the necessities, comforts and luxuries desired by the community, and its banks every financial facility required.

Churches and societies are numerous and well supported.

Leading Up to the City of Urbana

As has been repeatedly noted, the late Judge J. O. Cunningham was for so many years identified with Urbana and the State University that it was particularly fitting that he should contribute "Early Historical Sketches of the City of Urbana" to the official publication of the corporation in 1916, and that C. B. Holmes, its city clerk since May 1, 1877, should complete its political history to that year. From these reliable sources is extracted the running sketch which follows.

In the beginning there was nothing to be seen or encountered other than the vast expanse of prairie, unbroken and untrodden except by the wild Indian. Across this prairie in different direction and from groves of timber to other groves lay single trails, the only roads or other evidences of occupation in existence. Wild Indians, no less wild than the

VIEW ON WEST MAIN STREET

scenery above described, were the only occupants, and they changing locations with the results of wars, were for untold ages, before History took cognizance of the location, its only occupants.

These people made no improvements in any country they occupied other than the trails, and for these were indebted to the wild buffalo, their joint occupant, who in search of pasture and saline springs, made regular tours across the country, which in time were the Indian trails and the white man's early roads.

These few words tell the history of Urbana and of Champaign County until the coming of the United States surveying corps, which during the summer of 1822, under the direction of the deputy surveyor general, Elias Rector, surveyed the thirty-six square miles which constitute the township of Urbana, and were probably the first of our race who saw and closely observed these scenes; unless we except some possible white squatter, who had ventured unauthorized, to set up his home hereon. This however was quite improbable, for not until the year 1819 was the Indian title to this country extinguished and white occupancy possible.

In the year 1822, probably contemporaneously with the survey, came the first white inhabitant of the township, Runnel Fielder, who set up his home in Section 12, about two miles east of the city of Urbana, During the same year, but it is believed a little later in the season, came also William Tompkins, who is believed to have been the first permanent inhabitant of the ground now bearing the name "The City of Urbana!" The latter was at first a "squatter," for not until February 4, 1830, nearly eight years after his settlement thereon, did he become the owner of his home lot, which was the west half of the southeast quarter of Section 8, of the township. His cabin, the first permanent structure erected within the city, was located closely to the southwest corner of the tract, about where the rear end of the Courier building now stands.

Other than the standing timber the tract had little to invite its selection as a home and the reason therefor must have been its nearness to a spring of water a few rods to the southwest, near the front of the Flat Iron building, but upon another section of land. This spring, from which gushed a copious flow of water, had long been the center of an Indian encampment or village, which extended many rods to the east and to the southwest. Here, when Tompkins came, were abundant evidences of Indian occupancy in the numerous bones along the creek and of old corn hills on the adjacent prairie. Hence the name of the creek,—"Bone-Yard Branch."

Tompkins, soon after becoming the owner of his home, sold the same to Isaac Busey, an incoming emigrant from Kentucky, who was not long the only citizen of the site of the future city, for in 1832 came Thomson R. Webber, also from Kentucky, who built a cabin upon the site of the Webber home in the east part of Urbana.

The General Assembly of Illinois, at its session of 1833, established by law the county of Champaign, as it now exists, with the provision that commissioners, who were therein named, should locate the county seat of the new county and that the same should be called "Urbana."

This commission met in the June following and among several proposed locations selected the lands a short distance east of the then Busey home, where the courthouse now stands and there drove the stake which was to be the county seat and gave it the legal name of "Urbana." This event marks the first location of that name within this territory.

Lands given to the county to induce the location of the county seat by Isaac Busey, William T. Webber and Col. M. W. Busey were soon thereafter platted around the courthouse square, received the legal name, and a sale of the same, at auction, was advertised for an early day.

Thomson R. Webber, who was at the first appointed to the clerkship of the Circuit Court and also as clerk of the Board of County Commissioners, built a cabin across the street west of the square and lived upon that lot until driven therefrom by the great fire of October 9, 1871.

The population of the new county at its inception did not exceed 1,000 and was probably much less, for the official census of 1835, over two years later showed but 1,038 inhabitants.

At this date there were but two postoffices in the county, one, Van Buren, four miles to the northeast of Urbana, and one, Luddington, two miles north of Homer. Urbana postoffice was established September 2, 1836, with Thomson R. Webber as postmaster, who held that position for over fourteen years.

The first term of the Circuit Court was held on April 6, 1835. Nothing was done save the appointment of Mr. Webber as clerk, the approval of official bonds and the continuance of the only two cases for want of service. Mr. Webber held this office until succeeded by W. H. Somers in 1857. Hon. James Harlan was presiding judge.

The General Assembly, at its session of 1855, passed an act chartering the City and an election held on June 2, 1855, chose Hon. Archa Campbell, Mayor, and set the municipal government in action.

Original Corporate Limits and First Election

By an act of the General Assembly of the State of Illinois, approved on the 14th day of February, 1855, the City of Urbana, Illinois, was chartered.

The limits of said city at that time were fixed as follows: Beginning at a point in center of section 9, thence west two miles, thence south one mile, thence east two miles and thence north one mile to beginning.

An election was held at the courthouse on the first Monday in April, 1885, "when and where a majority of the legal voters, residing within said limits, voted 'for incorporation.'"

Section 3 of the chapter of said city provides that "if a majority of the citizens shall vote for incorporation the following named persons, to-wit: William Park, J. W. Jaquith, W. N. Coler, A. G. Carle, Alonzo Lyons, A. M. Whitney, Moses Snelling, or a majority of them, shall meet at the courthouse on the first Saturday in May and divide said city into wards, appoint three judges of election in each ward and appoint a day of election."

On the 5th day of May, 1855, J. W. Jaquith, W. N. Coler, William Park and A. G. Carle met in the courthouse and divided the city into three wards, and called an election to be held in said city on the first Saturday in June, 1855, for the election of one mayor and also two aldermen for each of said wards.

At said election Archa Campbell was elected mayor, and for aldermen of the first ward William C. Beck; second ward, John Gere and Daniel Jarvis; third ward, E. Harkness and Jesse D. Jaquith; who were installed "at a meeting of the citizens held at the courthouse on July 14, 1855," and at a meeting of the council held on said date, the council decided a contest between Mr. Harvey and Mr. F. B. Sale for alderman of the first ward and declared Mr. F. B. Sale elected to said office, and he was duly installed. Said council appointed Mr. S. J. Toy as city clerk.

At a special election duly called and held at the Pennsylvania House in the city of Urbana on the 19th day of April, 1873, for the purpose of voting upon the proposition of the adoption by the city of an act entitled, "An Act to Provide for the Incorporation of Cities and Villages, passed by the General Assembly of the State of Illinois, and Approved April 10, 1872."

The vote for adoption of said act at said election was 350 votes, and against the adoption of said act, 136 votes.

The City Council of the city of Urbana, Illinois, at a regular meeting thereof, held on the 21st day of April, 1873, upon the canvass and declaring the result of said election, adopted the following resolution:

"Be it resolved by the City Council of the City of Urbana, That we hereby declare said City, from and after this date, April 21, 1873, organized under the General Law of the State of Illinois, for its charter, and the question of minority representation in the City Council, we declare defeated."

Signed—   E. HALBERSTADT, Mayor.

                                     F. M. ALLEN, City Clerk.

D. McKinzie, L. A. McLean, S. H. Busey, J. A. Myers, J. H. Shuck, Jas. Somers, Aldermen.

Urbana's Mayors

Following is a list of the mayors of the city: Archa Campbell, July 14, 1855—June 10, 1856; Ezekiel Boyden, June 10, 1856—June 22, 1857; Jesse W. Jaquith, June 22, 1857—June 28, 1858; E. Boyden, June 28, 1858—June 11, 1859; C. A. Hunt, June 11, 1859—June 28, 1861; Edward Ater, June 28, 1861—June 22, 1864; Jos. W. Sim, June 22, 1864—June 4, 1866; Clark R. Griggs, June 4, 1866—June 8, 1867; Eli Halberstadt, June 8, 1867—July 6, 1868; J. M. Davies, July 6, 1868—June 23, 1869; Myron S. Brown, June 23, 1869—June 20, 1870; W. J. Ermentrout, June 20, 1870—June 12, 1871; Eli Halberstadt, June 12, 1871—April 28, 1874; Royal A. Sutton, April 28, 1874—May 3, 1875; J. T. Miller, May 3, 1875—May 7, 1877; A. P. Cunningham, May 7, 1877—April 26, 1880; S. T. Busey, May 25, 1880—May 15, 1889; C. A. Besore, May 15, 1889—May 15, 1891; Jas. H. Brownlee, May 15, 1891—May 15, 1893; Wm. B. Webber, May 15, 1893—May 15, 1895; Geo. W. Hubbard, May 15, 1895—May 15, 1899; Samuel C. Fox, May 15, 1899—May 15, 1901; John A. Glover, May 15, 1901—May 15, 1903; John A. Glover, May 15, 1903—May 15, 1905; Samuel C. Fox, May 15, 1905—May 15, 1907; Samuel W. Love, May 15, 1907—May 15, 1909; George W. Hubbard, May 15, 1909—May 1, 1911; Franklin H. Boggs, May 1, 1911—May 1, 1913; Olin L. Browder, May 1, 1913—May 1, 1915; Olin L. Browder, May 1, 1915—May 1, 1917.

At the election held May 1, 1917, the following were elected: Chester W. Richards, mayor; C. B. Holmes, city clerk; Theodore Bercher, treasurer; W. C. Maguire, city attorney; U. G. Martin, police magistrate; Rodger Tyrell, alderman from the First Ward; Thomas Bishop, Second; Jacob White, Third; Fred Kirkpatrick, Fourth; George W. Exton, Fifth.

The City Hall and Departments

The City Hall, which is a plain brick building two stories in height, houses the municipal offices and the Council Chamber, and adjoining it is a small building for the accommodation of the fire department. The apparatus comprises a chemical hose and truck, a horse truck and a motor truck. The department is in close touch with the organizations of the State University and the City of Champaign, and has also the advantage of fire protection through the facilities of the water works. Urbana and Champaign cooperate further in the operation of a complete sanitary system of sewerage, originally devised by Professor A. N. Talbot, of the University of Illinois.

CRYSTAL LAKE PARK

In the summer of 1907 a Park Board was formed to take over, improve and manage the various public grounds within the city limits of Urbana. The present members are Justin S. Hall (president), Joseph C. Blair, David C. Busey, Albert Shaff and Charles Fleck; W. E. Atkinson, secretary.

Crystal Lake Park is the largest and most beautifully improved recreation ground in Urbana. It comprises sixty-three acres of landscape and waterways in the northeastern part of the city, the main entrance to the park being at Lake and West Park streets. The tract lies partly on a hillside and partly in a lower valley of broken surface,

IN CRYSTAL LAKE PARK

the original creek .having been deepened and molded into a pretty winding lake. The higher land is a beautiful grove, containing a pavilion and amusement hall, with many conveniences for amusement and rest. The annual sessions of the Twin City Chatauqua Association are held at this park, which is one of the most picturesque places of the kind in Eastern Illinois. Thirty-nine acres of the tract originally consisted of a private park owned by B. F. Swartz, about fifteen acres in the northeastern part were donated by Judge J. O. Cunningham and his wife, and the balance was bought from the judge and from the Champaign County Fair and Driving Association. The buildings and speed-course of that association, covering some seventy-five acres, adjoin Crystal Lake Park to the north.

Leal and Carle Parks

Leal Park, of three acres, a block west of Crystal Park, was laid out in November, 1907. Pretty walks, lined with shrubbery and a pagoda, or rest house, are features of that attractive breathing spot.

Carle park of ten acres in the southern part of the city, is only partially improved. It was donated to the city by Margaret B. Morris (Mrs. Carle), in October, 1911.

Public Schools of Urbana

The Urbana schools were organized in the early '50s by the pioneers of this county and have gradually grown from the one room school on Elm Street to the present system with seven buildings and seating capacity for 2,200 pupils.

The late Dr. Thomas J. Burrill was at the head of the Urbana school system for a short time preceding his enrollment as a member of the faculty of the University of Illinois. J. W. Hays served as superintendent from 1871 to 1906, and Mr. A. P. Johnson from 1906 to the present date, 1917.

On the present site of the Leal school was a seminary which was used in the early '70s as the public school of Urbana. This building burned in 1872 and was replaced by the old part of the present Leal building in 1873. The east and west wings of this building were added later. At present the Leal building contains twelve school rooms.

The Lincoln school building of eight rooms was finished and occupied in 1902, replacing the old West ward four-room building.

The Webber school building of eleven rooms was completed and occupied in April, 1906, taking the place of the old East ward building which is now used as a dwelling.

The present Number Four school building was erected in the fall and winter of 1906 and 1907 and was occupied for school purposes in the winter of 1907. This building is located a mile east of the city limits, on a half acre of ground donated to the school district for school purposes by Mr. Smith.

The J. W. Hays school building of four rooms was occupied on March 4, 1909, and is located upon eight lots of the Busey farm in the northwest part of the city.

The above grade buildings are modern and have in addition to the usual cloak rooms, play rooms in the basement suitable for games by the children in bad weather.

1—28

The New Urbana High School (1916)

The Thornburn school building was erected in 1897 on some lots at Railroad and North streets, donated by the late John Thornburn in 1897 and was used for high school purposes until December, 1914; when the high school was moved to its new quarters in the present High School building. The Thornburn building now houses the departmental grammar school composed of seventh and eighth grades, about 320 pupils.

The school buildings, equipments and sites are valued at $337,200.

The cost of maintaining the schools for the year 1916-1917 was about $80,000. There was a total enrollment of about 2,200 pupils of which 512 were enrolled in high school. These were taught and supervised by 67 teachers.

In addition to the usual academic subjects the following are offered in the Urbana schools: Manual Training, seventh and eighth grade and high school; Domestic Science, seventh and eighth grade and high school; a complete Commercial course and Cafeteria in connection with the high school.

In the fall of 1914 all of the seventh and eighth grades were brought to the Thornburn school and the departmental plan has since been used in this school. The pupils are classed into sections of nearly equal working ability and each section does as much work as it is able. Some sections completing two years' work in a year and a half while other sections require two and a half years for the same amount of work.

In the spring of 1917 Home Gardening Clubs were organized in each grade school and as a result about 120 pupils are engaged in this project. Each pupil must have at least 100 square feet in his garden and may have as much more as he can work. Three-fourths of the pupils have more than 250 square feet in garden.

THE HIGH SCHOOL

The most recent addition to Urbana's public schools, the High School, represents a departure from the accepted "cut and dried" style and plan which has been in vogue for so many years and give a building embodying recent ideas both in arrangement of plan and style of design.

In place of the former study rooms where all pupils were assembled during study hours, we find the pupil left independent to work out his own schedule. Lockers are provided in locker rooms on the ground floor for books, wraps, etc., and study rooms or libraries are located between the recitation rooms for each subject. For example, between the two recitation rooms, for and separated from them by plate glass partitions, thus affording supervision from the recitation rooms in a history, library or study room where the pupil goes to study that subject. All reference books for this course are kept in this room. The assembly room is used for opening exercises and for mass meetings only. So much for the plan of organization.

The building, a three-story fireproof structure, faces its main facade, about 200 feet long to the west. It is designed in the Gothic style of architecture, which is at once the most dignified and appropriate style for buildings of this character requiring special lighting features. The exterior is of dark red brick with Bedford stone trimmings. Entrance is gained at the center of the principal facade and at either end of the main-corridor. The central entrance leads to the main or first floor while those at the ends lead to the ground story.

The ground story houses the Domestic and Manual Arts departments and mechanical equipment. Besides the cooking laboratory, model dining room, pantry, and sewing room, and a modern cafeteria are accommodated on this floor. Lunches are served each day to about 100 pupils at an average cost per pupil per meal of 18 cents.

The manual training rooms, boiler room and fan rooms are located under the auditorium and stage.

At either side of the stairways leading from the main entrance to this floor are the boys' and girls' locker rooms fitted with lockers which are ventilated directly into the ventilating system of the building.

Toilet rooms for both sexes are located at opposite ends of the corridor. Directly across the corridor opposite the main entrance on the first floor is the auditorium, seating 600 on the main floor and 200 in the balcony and is equipped with large stage and dressing rooms. At either side of the main entrance are the principal's office and Superintendent's office, the latter opening directly into the board meeting room. The remainder of the first floor is given over to the biological laboratory with demonstration and storage rooms, two recitation rooms, five class rooms, emergency room and boys' and girls' toilet rooms.

The second floor contains the commercial group, physical and chemical laboratories, demonstration rooms, three class rooms, two recitation rooms, study rooms, library, and men and women teachers' toilet rooms. The third floor occupies the tower over the central portion and is given over to the music and art departments.

All the walls of toilet rooms and cooking department are of white enameled brick, walls of locker rooms and laboratories are of brown glazed brick, and walls of gymnasium are of buff brick. Corridors are of promenade tile laid in pattern. The mechanical equipment is complete in every respect.   Heating and ventilation are supplied by heated fresh air driven to all parts of the building by means of a fan blower. Each room is equipped with thermostats which automatically control the heat supplied to the room and keep the temperature constant.

A complete vacuum cleaning system is installed in this building so that all rooms and corridors may be thus cleaned without raising the usual dust by sweeping.

.The gymnasium wing, under construction at the present time, is of similar construction and will accommodate swimming pool with proper means of water purification, gymnasium with running track, locker and shower rooms, laundry, team rooms and physical director's office and in addition will provide two regular classrooms.

The Urbana Free Library

The parent body of the Library Board was a Library Association organized in December, 1872, and on February 17 following, a reading room was opened in charge of James Williams.   In June, 1874, the property was transferred to the city of Urbana, its Council agreeing to maintain, the library, and in the following month the first Board of Directors was elected, viz: William Sim, J. M. McConney, Frank G. Jaques, C. D. Webster, J. W. Hays, S. M. Morton, H. M. Russell, A. Van Tuyl and J. W. Porter.   At this meeting S. H. Hook was chosen librarian and the institution was christened the Urbana Free Library. On November 1, 1874, Ida B. Hanes was elected librarian to succeed Mr. Hook, and is still holding the position.   At present there are over 23,000 volumes in the library.

In February, 1917, Mrs. S. T. Busey offered the Board $35,000 for a new library building.   The gift was gratefully accepted and action at once taken to secure plans.   Ground was broken early in the summer of 1917.   The site for the new building cost over $12,000; cost of building and furnishings estimated at $55,000.

The plans of the Busey Memorial Library show the main front of the building on Race Street as both elegant and massive.   The entrance is colonnaded, with fifteen-foot stone columns standing on either side and the doors are of massive bronze.   The main floor will be several feet above the street level and the lower floor a few feet below.   On the lower floor, at the southeast corner, is to be a room twenty-eight feet by thirty feet, called the English room, to be devoted to the Champaign County Historical Society.   On the north side of the building will be a lecture room, seating 200 people, with stage, and equipment for giving illustrated lectures, or plays. In the west end of this floor there is a room for book stacks, and an unpacking room, storage room, etc.

The central feature of the upper floor as one may enter by the eastern entrance, is a large memorial room, finished with pink Tennessee marble floors and walls, with dome ceiling. Opening from this main room to the south will be a magazine room, children's reading room, and cataloging room. To the north will be general reading room, reference room, and reference library.

At the west end of the Memorial room is the entrance to and exit from the book stacks. The stack room is estimated to accommodate 80,000 volumes. The library at present numbers over 25,000 volumes.

The building is to be made as nearly fire proof as is possible. Around the outside on the east and north will be a concrete and Bedford stone terrace, with stone ballustrade. The dimensions of the building over all, will be 103 feet 6 inches north and south, by 97 feet east and west.

The Local Press

A county seat, wherever fixed, is usually prolific of newspapers; and Urbana verified the rule. When the Illinois Central was projected through the county, and before the grading had even commenced, Champaign County was viewed as a legitimate, if not promising, experimental territory for the venturesome journalist. Colonel William N. Coler, a budding lawyer and Democrat, determined to blossom as the pioneer editor of the county, and formed a union with Henry K. Davis, a practical printer and newspaper man. They purchased a small stock of type in Cincinnati, with a little hand press, which was hauled from the Wabash Canal on one wagon to the courthouse and there temporarily planted. From that plant, on September 25, 1852, was sent forth the first number of the Urbana Union, in support of Franklin Pierce, Democratic candidate for president, by Coler and Davis, editors and proprietors. In two months less two days the firm was dissolved and Mr. Davis went on to Washington to accept office under the new administration, leaving Colonel Coler to continue the Union through its thirty-sixth number, when he retired from editorial life. In July, 1853, Benjamin A. Roney, a practical printer, but inexperienced as an editor, assumed the proprietorship, but left suddenly in March of the following year. George N. Richards, George W. Flynn and J. O. Cunningham then entered the field. Messrs. Flynn and Cunningham established a branch office at West Urbana in October, 1857, and in August, 1858, severed their connection with the Union. David S. Crandall and his son, Charles E., talented newspaper men of Lockport, New York, bought the paper and continued its publication until early in 1861, when they sold to John Carrothers, of Urbana. The various shiftings back and forth between Urbana and Champaign have already been described. Mr. Carrothers failed in 1863, the Union returned to the unwilling hands of the Crandalls, was turned over to Nicolet & Schoff, who made it a strong paper, and in 1882 was moved to another county.

"Our Constitution" was published from July, 1856, until the fall of 1859, when the office was moved from Urbana to Champaign; the Urbana Clarion, from October, 1859, to the spring of 1861, when it suspended, and in 1877 appeared the Champaign County Herald, the forerunner of the Courier-Herald of today. S. C. Harris and Company were its first publishers. Andrew Lewis then became the sole owner of the plant, selling in May, 1879, to M. W. Mathews and C. B. Taylor. Two years later, Mr. Mathews, one of the able lawyers and legislators of the state, became the sole proprietor and editor of the Herald and thus continued until his death in 1892. With L. A. McLean, an able financial manager, as well as a forceful writer, he made the publication a successful newspaper in every sense of the word. Under one of the provisions of Mr. Mathews' will Mr. McLean continued the publication of the Herald in behalf of the estate, but after three years he retired, leaving it in charge of John Gray.

The Courier was established in July, 1894, by T. M. Morgan, as a morning daily and weekly newspaper. Soon afterward S. W. Love bought the plant and added to its mechanical facilities, and in September, 1901, sold the establishment to Joseph Ogden and Howe Brown. E. L. and John Wait and J. K. Groom became successively identified with it, the last named incorporating the business as the Urbana Courier Company. C. O. Carter then purchased an interest in the office, and the daily edition was changed from morning to evening. In 1904 F. E. Pinkerton, of Rantoul, became owner of the Courier, and in September, 1905, sold a half interest in it to George W. Martin, who, in 1908, disposed of his share to Frank C. McElvain. Mr. Pinkerton disposed of his interest to A. T. Burrows in December, 1909, and in October, 1913, Mr. McElvain also sold to Mr. Burrows. Since that time the consolidated Courier-Herald has been a corporation controlled by the Burrows family.

EARLY PREACHERS IN THE URBANA NEIGHBORHOOD

From 1831 to 1839 preachers of various denominations held forth in the neighborhood of the Big Grove, but it was not until the latter year that any part of what is now Champaign County had a regular standing in the religious field. At that time it appears in the Conference minutes of the Methodist Episcopal Church as the Urbana Mission.

Probably the first sermon ever delivered in the county was by John Dunham, a United Brethren missionary, who, some time in 1831, preached at the house of Matthias Rhinehart in the Grove. He is said to have ridden an ox on his circuit, and it is further intimated that both were very noisy. Rev. William Peters, "Uncle Billy," lived in Salt Fork Timber, traveled his religious beat not long after Mr. Dunham, and as he had no land upon which to farm and help both ends meet, is reported to have helped pay his traveling expenses by buying whiskey on the Wabash at 20 cents a gallon and retailing it on his rounds at 50 cents. John G. Robertson was an early Baptist immigrant preacher from Kentucky and held meetings in the Big Grove and the Sangamon Timber.

The labors of Mr. Robertson resulted in the organization of the Baptist church, at the Brumley schoolhouse two miles east of Urbana, in September, 1838, and of the Mahomet church in March, 1839. Rev. J. D. Newell, then residing at Waynesville, DeWitt County, was the organizer of both churches.

REV. JAMES HOLMES, PIONEER METHODIST

Rev. James Holmes, who, in 1835, came to the Big Grove region to build a sawmill for John Brownfield, remained to organize a class in Methodism, probably in the winter of 1836. While not in Urbana, the class became the germ of the subsequently formed Urbana Mission, Urbana Circuit, Urbana Station, and the First Methodist ·Church of Urbana. Among its members were Walter Rhodes (leader), and Mary Ann, his wife; Lewis Adkins and his wife Nancy; Susan Trickle, subsequently the wife of James Kirby; Sarah and Ann Brownfield; Alexander Holbrook, and the preacher and his wife. A campmeeting held at Haptonstall's mill, a mile below Urbana, in 1839, under charge of Elder S. W. D. Chase, of the Bloomington district, so brought the locality into notice that from that time on, it was known officially to the Methodist Conference as the Urbana Mission. Its territory embraced the settlements in the Big Grove upon the Okaw, the Ambraw and the Salt Fork, nearly to Danville. Elder Chase moved from the Wabash country to Urbana in the autumn of 1839 and thus became its first settled pastor.

Coming of Rev. S. W. D. Chase

Many years afterward Mr. Chase tells the story of his coming: "My next appointment (1839) was Urbana Mission. This caused a move of one hundred and fifty miles. We were compelled to move in an ox-wagon, camp out about half the nights and take the weather as it came; so we had rain, mud and storm. When we arrived in Urbana our goods were all wet, a fierce wind blowing from the northwest and no empty house in town. We took up lodging for a few days with Simon Motes, in his cabin in the north part of the village. The little society and friends had put up the body of a hewed log cabin with rafters, but no roof, floor or chimney.

"I organized a society four miles north of Urbana at Esquire Rhodes'; another east of Rhodes' three miles at the house of John Gilliland; another, down east of Urbana ten miles, at Widow Bartley's; and still another east of that on the main road leading to Danville at Pogue's. Then to old Homer.

"My first visit to Homer was on Sabbath morning, hunting a place to preach, but there was neither hall, schoolhouse, church nor empty house; so the prospect was gloomy. At last a gentleman remarked: 'Do you see that little white house in the north part of the village?' I said, 'Yes.' 'Well,' said he, they have dances there; maybe you might get in there.' So I went and stated my business. 'Well,' said the doctor (Dr. Harmon Stevens), 'we have dances twice a week here. I don't know how that would work. What do you think of it, wife?' 'Well,' said she, 'I don't know.' I said, 'You don't dance on the Sabbath.' 'No,' said the doctor. 'Well, then,' I said, 'let me preach on Sunday; we'll have no friction.' So they consented. Before the year was out the doctor and his wife professed religion and joined the Methodist Episcopal Church, and we organized a society. I never knew what became of those dancers.

"I then organized a church in Sidney. I went from Urbana to Sadorus Grove, fifteen miles, without a house to stop at, making it a cold ride in bad weather. Nine miles below, or south of, Sadorus, at John Haines', we had a small society. Five miles below on the Okaw was where William Brian lived in a small cabin. Here we organized a society. Continuing down the river five miles, we came to Old Father West's. Here we organized another society. Still continuing south we came to Flat Branch, where we organized another society in the cabin of John and Sarah Poorman. We are now forty miles south of Urbana. This entire round was made every three weeks.

"In 1840 we put up the frame of a small church, thirty by forty feet, in Urbana and inclosed it; and in the fall, as I was leaving for my next appointment, I was sued for the shingles that went on the church.

"It was at a campmeeting, one and one-half miles east of Urbana (at Haptonstall's), that Jake Heater, said to be the bully of the county, got under strong convictions. He was told to go to the altar and pray and he'd feel better. So Jake went and kneeled down, and his prayer was: 'Oh, Lord God, rim-rack and center shake the divil's kingdom.'"

It was in this manner, and with such a field and the material furnished by the rough pioneers, that this pioneer preacher laid the foundations for the Christian civilization we now enjoy.

First Methodist Class and Church

Among the names of those who joined the first class organized at Urbana are Jacob W. Slater and Rebecca, his wife; Samuel Motz and Sarah, his wife; Mrs. Benedict and Simeon Motz. The parsonage occupied by the new pastor and his family, already partly prepared, was finished with split-board roof and floors, mud and stick chimney, and not long afterward a little house of worship was commenced on the lot donated by the county commissioners, on the south side of Elm Street, between Market and Race.

Judge Cunningham continues: "So far as known no subscription paper figured in the transaction, perhaps for the reason that there was little money in those days with which to meet obligations. In Mrs. Nancy Webber's timber was plenty of material and the muscle necessary to transform it into a building was at hand. So pastor and people, alike muscular and zealous, turned out and, with axes, went to the woods, cut, scored and hewed out the timbers, studding and rafters from the standing trees. Logs for lumber for siding were likewise cut and hauled to Colonel Busey's saw-mill, then doing business upon the creek just above Crystal Lake Park, from the water power there furnished. The shingles were bought upon a promise to pay from a manufacturer near by, and in a few weeks the structure was reared and enclosed, but neither floored nor plastered, except that the pulpit space and the "Amen corners" were floored.

"In this condition, with neither windows nor doors and with no other seats than those afforded by the uncovered sleepers of joists, hewn upon the upper side, was the structure occupied by a worshipping congregation for the first summer and perhaps for a longer period when the weather permitted. It was not until 1843 that the building was finally completed according to the original plan, being floored, plastered and seated with rude slab benches. This final work had been done by free contributions of labor and materials. It is said that Colonel Busey gave the flooring, Archa Campbell the glass and Matthias Carson, a skilled mechanic, the window sash and door. In its finished condition it was unpainted, both inside and outside, until two zealous sisters, Harriet Harvey and Susan Cantner, with discriminating zeal for outside appearance, unassisted by anyone, whitewashed the entire outside of the house as well as the rough plastering on the inside, using a preparation of lime and other ingredients, including among them salt. The building looked well in its coat of whitewash, but the town cows, then quite numerous, lost to all reverence for the sacred character of the structure, were tempted by the salt to lick the clapboards, which they persisted in doing so long as the saline taste remained. At times, owing to this practice of the cows, a worshipping congregation was disturbed and, to secure their legal rights, it became necessary to station a guard of boys upon the outside during service.

"This building, in the condition above described, was alternately used as a place of worship, as a schoolhouse and, in cases of great necessity, it housed homeless and destitute families until the stress of circumstance passed, and they could be housed elsewhere. Mr. James Kerr, of Urbana, relates that when, in the autumn of 1851, he, with his father, A. M. Kerr (for a term of years coroner of Champaign County) came with a family of ten persons, immigrants from Tennessee to Urbana, they found no friendly door opened to them, and in their distressed condition—most of them being sick—were very glad to avail themselves of the permission given by those having this building in charge, to spread their beds upon its floor and remain until, somewhat recovered from their weariness and chills, they were enabled to find other accommodations.

"It is said that the first minister who occupied this, the first church building erected in the county, after its completion, was Rev. W. D. Gage, who was appointed to the Urbana circuit in 1843. This building continued the one church house of the county for some years, open, as occasion demanded, to the use of such other denominations as desired its use, until the year 1856, when a new building was erected and the old one was converted into a livery barn.

"The class formed in the neighborhood north of Urbana by 'Rev. James Holmes, subsequently built a small church building for their use which was erected near the center of Section 27, in Somer Township, and was the first of the many country churches erected in the rural districts of the county.

"Rev. Arthur Bradshaw was followed at Urbana by others of the pioneer pastors. The theology and church discipline enforced by these early preachers were of the most stalwart character, and tolerated no failures to attend the 'means of grace' or other lapses from Wesley's rules."

DR. McELROY'S STATEMENT

Following is the copy of a letter written to Judge Cunningham by Dr. W. M. McElroy:

"My Dear Bro. Cunningham: I think I can now clear up the story of Urbana Methodism. James McKean, then on the Eugene Circuit (later Danville Ct.), had an appointment and preached in Big Grove in 1829 and 1830. The conference year beginning in the autumn of 1829. Probably on the east side of the Grove. In the conference year beginning in the fall of 1836, Mr. Holmes organized the class four miles north of Urbana, as stated in my previous letter. During the conference year beginning in 1838, S. W. D. Chase held camp meeting at Haptonstall's Mill. The class you mention of which Simon Motz was leader, was organized before Bradshaw came, probably after the camp meeting,—maybe before. There was a class at John Gilliland's, seven miles northeast of Urbana, another ten miles east, at Widow Bartley's, another at Pogue's, ten miles east on the Danville road. These classes were in existence before Bradshaw's term, in all probability, and were not organized by him."

LATER PROGRESS OF THE METHODIST EPISCOPAL CHURCH

Early in the '50s, because of the continuous growth of the society, a movement was set on foot to provide a larger church building, and on July 27, 1855, the cornerstone of the new structure was laid. The following year it was inclosed and finally completed and dedicated in 1859, Rev. Peter Cartwright officiating.

About 1890 a movement was started to meet the growing demands of the society for better church facilities, which languished for many months, or until December 17, 1892, when J. C. Sheldon, president of the Board of Trustees, came to the rescue with an offer, which was gratefully accepted, to erect and enclose the walls, leaving the society and its friends to complete the building. Subscriptions were by this generous offer greatly stimulated, and the old building was turned over to the demolishers March 4, 1893, the last service being held there

March 3d. The present structure was dedicated March 25, 1894, free from debt of any kind. It cost $21,150 exclusive of the pipe organ, which cost $3,500.

Successive pastors: 1839, A. Bradshaw; 1840, J. W. Parsons; 1841, A. Bradshaw (second term) ; 1842, L. Oliver; 1843, W. D. Gage; 1844, A. S. Goddard; 1845, J. Fox; 1846, W. Pitner; 1847, C. J. T. Tolle; 1848, W. G. Moore; 1849, J. C. Long; 1853-4, W. E. Johnson; 1855, W. F. T. Spruill; 1856-7, W. H. H. Moore; 1858, M. Butler; 1859, A. Semple; 1860-1, A. S. McCoy; 1862-3, W. B. Anderson; 1864, B. Hungerford; 1865, W. H. Webster; 1866, A. S. McCoy (second term); 1867-8, J. G. Little; 1869, J. Shaw; 1870, W. H. H. Moore (second term) ; 1871-2-3, D. Gay; 1874-5-6, W. F. T. Spruill (second term) ; 1877, D. Gay (second term) ; 1878, P. C. Carroll; 1879, M. A. Hewes; 1880-1-2, J. Miller; 1883-4-5, A. C. Byerly; 1886-7, R. McIntyre; 1888, R. G. Hobbs; 1889, F. Crane; 1890, F. C. Bruner; 1891-2, M. D. Hornbeck; 1893-4, U. Z. Gilmer; 1894-8, J. F. Wohlfarth; 1898-1904, J. W. Miller; 1904-1908, A. S. Flannigan; 1908-1909, H. C. Gibbs; 1909-1915, R. F. McDaniel; 1915-1916, A. C. Piersel; 1916-17, W. F. Pitner.

Rev. William Munhall

Among those identified with Methodism in the earlier days of the county was Rev. William Munhall, an eloquent and classical preacher, who often filled the pulpit of the Urbana church and others in the county. But he seems to have been too much a man of affairs to confine his activities to church matters alone. He served as county treasurer and assessor in the late '50s, and was editor and publisher of the Urbana Clarion and Champaign County Democrat during a portion of the Civil War period. He was intensely loyal, a stalwart Union man and, in every respect, a good citizen and Christian man. He died while visiting a sister in Cleveland, March 9, 1864, his remains being brought for interment to Mount Hope Cemetery, Urbana. William H. Munhall, a son, moved to Champaign in 1865, having mastered the printer's trade in Cleveland. He was identified with the Gazette printing office for twenty-eight years, afterward was the head of the Munhall Printing House, and died May 23, 1917.

The First Baptist Church

The Baptist society which was organized at Brumley's schoolhouse, two miles east of Urbana, held its meeting therein for more than a decade, when its headquarters were changed to the county seat and it became the First Baptist Church of Urbana. In 1856 the church erected a house of worship on Cunningham Avenue, the second building of the kind in the county, and the first in the county to have a bell. The "Urbana Union," of September 27, 1855, has the following real news item: "The bell for the new Baptist church has arrived, and will soon send forth its mellow peals to vibrate over the prairies as often reminding us of the persevering and noble-hearted efforts of the ladies of Urbana, through whose efforts alone the purchase has been made. The bell is one of beautiful tone and will tend much to enliven our place, especially on Sabbath mornings when we shall, henceforth, be greeted by the welcome sounds of the 'church going bell.'" The edifice now occupied was erected in 1895 and stands upon the site of the little church of 1856. It has a present membership of more than 700.

First Presbyterian Church

The First Presbyterian Church of Urbana was organized in September, 1850, by Rev. John A. Steele, under authority of the Presbytery of Palestine, Crawford County. Its original members were Mr. and Mrs. Robert Dean, Mr. and Mrs. Solomon Campbell, Mr. and Mrs. Adam Karr and Mr. and Mrs. John J. Rea. The house of worship in use on West Green Street was erected in 1900. Rev. John J. Wilson is the pastor in charge.

University Baptist Church

The University Baptist Church of Urbana was organized in the fall of 1912 by the Illinois Baptist State Conference. Its membership of 300 is drawn entirely from the students of the University. Rev. Martin S. Bryant is pastor. For four years services were held in the Y. M. C. A. auditorium, but in November, 1916, a church building was erected, at a cost of $33,000, on South Fourth Street.

The McKinley Memorial church was erected by Hon. W. B. McKinley in memory of his father, Rev. George McKinley, and is an elegant and impressive house of worship.

The Universalist Church

Universalist ministers held services in the courthouse and various residences for many years previous to 1859, when a church was formally organized. Meetings continued to be held in the courthouse until 1871,

when a brick house of worship was erected on Green Street. Among
the early ministers of the church were Rev. E. Manford, Rev. T. C.
Eaton, Rev. Josiah Davis and Rev. D. P. Bunn. The handsome and
convenient edifice now occupied was completed in 1913. Rev. E. V.
Stevens is the pastor.

First Christian Church

The First Christian (not Disciple) Church of Urbana is the only
society of that denomination in the Twin Cities. It was organized in
1885 by Rev. Robert Harris, then secretary of the Central Illinois
Christian Conference. Mr. Harris had charge of the church from
1885 to 1892. Services were held in a hall over one of the stores until
1889, when the first church edifice was erected on West Main Street
near the site of the present house of worship, at a cost of $2,500. Other
pastors who have served the church: Rev. W. G. Voliva, Rev. J. J. Patterson, Rev. Mrs. A. A. Draper, Rev. G. D. Lawrence, who was pastor
from 1896 until 1904. Up until 1900 the church had preaching only
every other Sunday. In 1900 the church engaged Rev. Mr. Lawrence
for full time, and has maintained "full-time" preaching ever since.

Rev. W. H. Sando was pastor from 1904 until 1907; Rev. D. A.
Boatwright from 1907 until 1908; Rev. W. O. Hornbaker from 1908
until 1912. During Rev. Mr. Hornbaker's pastorate a commodious
new church building was erected at a cost of $25,000. Rev. Clarence
Defur was pastor from 1912 until 1914. Rev. R. C. Helfenstein, the
present pastor, was called September 1, 1914. The membership of the
church is 300, of which number 208 are active members.

Trinity M. E. (University) Church

Trinity, the Methodist University Church, was organized in 1892
and was first known as Park's Chapel. The names of its pastors: Rev.
E. K. Towl, Rev. Clarence Reed, Rev. W. W. Henry, Rev. Willard N.
Tobie (1899-1907) and Rev. James C. Baker, since the latter year.
The first church building was erected in 1893 and destroyed by fire in
the following year. A second church was at once built and replaced
by the present structure, which was dedicated in November, 1906. The
work of Trinity Church is now being merged in the Wesley Foundation
and another edifice, to cost about $200,000, will soon replace the present
building, being located two blocks farther south, at the corner of Green
Street and Mathews Avenue. The present number of members is 825.

Other churches of this denomination in Urbana are the Free Will and Grace Methodist.

St. Patrick's Church

St. Patrick's Catholic parish in Urbana was founded in July, 1901, by Rev. J. H. Cannon. It was an offshoot of old St. Mary's parish, at Champaign. Within the first few years of its history the Urbana congregation acquired property at the corner of West Main and Busey streets, and erected a substantial church and rectory, at a cost of $56,000. Father Cannon remained in charge of the parish for about nine years, and has been succeeded by Rev. Stephen N. Moore and Rev. J. W. Cummings, the present incumbent. About twenty years ago Father Cummings was assistant to Father Wagner, at St. Mary's parish, Champaign. St. Patrick's parish embraces some sixty families.

The Unitarian Church

The Unitarian Church of Urbana was organized in April, 1907, by Rev. Albert R. Vail, who is still its minister. Its house of worship was completed in the fall of 1909. The present membership of the society is 185.

Cunningham Children's Home

In 1894 Judge J. O. Cunningham and his wife presented their old home, with fifteen acres of land, one mile north of the courthouse to the Illinois Conference of the Woman's Home Missionary Society of the Methodist Episcopal Church to found an orphanage for children. Its official title is the Cunningham Deaconess' Home and Orphanage, but the institution is popularly and gratefully known as the Cunningham Children's Home. The deed of gift declared that "neither nationality nor creed shall be considered—simply the need of the child." The Board of Management and the superintendents have faithfully conformed to this pronouncement, and for some years about seventy children, the offspring of various nationalities and creeds, have been protected physically and morally, amid pleasant and comfortable surroundings, and afterward placed in the way of becoming intelligent and good members of society. Its mainstay of support is the Woman's Home Missionary Society, although it has received numerous outside donations and has a small endowment fund. The buildings of the Home comprise two comfortable and attractive buildings.

The original building was completed in 1895, and the institution was opened, on October 25 of that year, with a matron in charge and four homeless little children as inmates. Additions to that structure were subsequently made of a playroom, schoolroom, nursery, two dormitories and other accommodations. In 1911 another building known as Sheldon Hall was erected, containing play and school rooms, boys' dormitory, industrial room and laundry.

The successive superintendents and matrons who have served since the opening of the Home in 1895 are as follows: Mrs. F. C. Woodruff, 1895-99; Miss Matilda Reeves, 1899-1903; Miss Jones, 1903-04; Miss Eva Schell, 1904-06; W. A. Davis and wife, 1906-12; Rev. Xenophon M. Fowler and wife, superintendent and assistant superintendent, respectively, 1912-17.

THE CUNNINGHAM CHILDREN'S HOME

At the coming of Rev. and Mrs. Fowler the authority to administer corporal punishment was taken from the workers and given only to the superintendent and wife. Since 1915 all corporal punishment has been banished from the Home. A credit system is now used, placing each child on its own merits. Those getting an average of eighty percent are eligible to a picnic, those who average ninety percent are entitled to a hike, and those whose average is ninety-eight per cent are treated to a special chicken dinner.

Since 1914 provisions have been made to keep boys until they are twelve years of age and girls until they are eighteen. Two grades, seventh and eighth, were added to the courses of study, which necessitated the hiring of an extra teacher.

Finally, the following ingenious and informing acrostic, prepared by Superintendent Fowler, cannot but answer all pertinent questions which may arise in the minds of those who are not already posted on the merits of the Cunningham Children's Home:

C unningham slogan is "Be good; do good; make good."

U niversity of Illinois Sociology class rated Cunningham Children's Home as a model small institution.

N. umber of children cared for during the year, 87.

N ursery has been closed, renovated and opened again.

I tems for one dinner: 8 chickens, 1 bu. potatoes, ½ bu. onions, 10 loaves bread, 1½ pound butter, 8 quarts preserves.

N o boys are received over six; our oldest is now twelve.

G irls are taken under twelve and kept until they are eighteen.

H eat, lights and repairs in the 48 rooms, 6 bath rooms and halls cost over $1,000 annually.

A ll our physical, industrial, educational, and spiritual training aims toward Christian citizenship.

M embers of Catholic, Protestant, and atheistic families are alike accepted.

C hildren came from Pennsylvania, Indiana, Missouri, Kansas, Arkansas, and 13 counties of Illinois.

H alf-orphans constituted the majority of our membership; 11 were children of insane mothers.

I ndustrial classes in cooking, sewing, darning, and basketry were held weekly.

L ithuanian, Norwegian, Swedish, Polish, Scotch, Irish, German, French and American children were here.

D octor's calls were made on only 2 children; 6 visits on one boy, one on another; cost, $14.

R epairs on shoes average over $15 per month in winter.

E ndowment has been started; amounts now to nearly $3,000.

N ational W. H. M. S. sent for salaries, $785.50; other Conferences, $740.32.

S cholarships cost $60 per year; kindergarten scholarships, $15.

H ome employs Superintendent, Asst. Supt., 6 Dept. Matrons, 3 Teachers, Cook, Laundress and Farmer.

O ur pay roll for all fourteen workers averaged only $275 per month.

M any children were turned away for lack of scholarships.

E ven the smallest donation from You will be thankfully received.

EARLY SUNDAY SCHOOLS OF URBANA

By A. O. Howell

Myself and family removed to this township in October, 1853, and purchased the farm on which we now reside. I organized a Union Sunday school in the old brick courthouse, April 19, 1854. The officers were: A. O. Howell, superintendent, and M. A. Barnes, secretary. Rev. W. W. Blanchard was pastor of the Congregational Church at that time and had many doubts about the success of the enterprise. The first Sunday there were 30 members in attendance; the second, 53; May 3d, 123. The Methodists and Baptists were cordial, in good feeling and co-operated with the new school. Many of our members were preparing to build and remove to "the depot," afterwards called "West Urbana," now Champaign City. Sunday school, with its officers, library, &c., was removed to an unfinished building of Deacon Moses Snelling, on University Avenue, now the residence of Mr. James Wright. We had rough boards for seats and a goods box for a pulpit. Here we reopened and reorganized the first Sunday school ever held in Champaign, on the 4th day of March, 1855. We changed our name from "First Union Sunday School of Urbana, Ill.," to "First Congregational Sunday School of Champaign.' We built the first Congregational Church on the corner of University Avenue and Sixth Street, (sometimes called the Duck Pond Church) where our Sunday school numbered, on one Sabbath, 202. Thus I supposed for many years, that I had the honor of arranging and superintending the first Sunday school with a library and regular organization in this county for four years, but many years after I learned from B. F. Harris that he had antedated me two years. His Sunday school was held in a little church on his farm on the Sangamon. He carried his library to his Sunday school every Sabbath in a red handkerchief and back to his house at night. I carried my library to the courthouse in a candle box, in my then new rockaway buggy, and back at night. The four years war killed off and scattered our thorough members, and since then, oh, how sadly changed is our once humble and thorough church and Sunday school. I wish to say here that this was not the beginning of all the good church and Sunday school work done in this county. It would be difficult to overestimate the noble work done by our venerable Father Bradshaw for many years previous to this, but in consequence of his immensely large circuit, the meetings and sessions of church and Sunday school work were necessarily quite semi-occasionally.

I find from the old minutes of Illinois Conference of Methodist Episcopal Church that in 1839, in the month of September, I was appointed to Urbana Mission. In October I landed in Urbana with my family. I do not know what had been done about a Sabbath school prior to that time, but the spring following we organized a Sabbath school, in which Baptists and Presbyterians took part, especially Milton Vance, a dry goods merchant, but the Sabbath school was under the auspices of the Methodist Episcopal Church. It was in the spring of 1840 I made the purchase of a church lot from the county for $3, and the summer following we erected a church building 30x40 feet, enclosing it, but did not finish it for some time. The Baptists had no church organization in Urbana, but I think they had in the Brumley neighborhood. But from the spring and summer of 1840 the Methodist Episcopal Church had a small Sabbath school organized in Urbana. I can not give particulars, nor can I say at what date the Baptist Church organized a Sabbath school in Urbana or organized a church in Urbana, or built a church, etc. I know the little church house we put up in 1840 was the first in the county. From 1840 to 1850 the Sabbath schools in Urbana were no big thing.

BANKS AND INDUSTRIES

There are five banks in Urbana—Busey's State, the First National, Urbana Banking Company, the First State Trust and Savings and the First University.

Busey's Bank, subsequently Busey's State Bank, is the name of one of the solid financial institutions and the second oldest bank in Champaign County. The name has become a household word throughout that part of the state, and is recognized as standing for financial integrity, square dealing, and all that pertains to a careful management of the property of other people and conservative banking methods.

This institution, under the name of Busey Brothers & Company, was organized in the fall of 1868, by the Hon. S. H. Busey, Col. S. T. Busey, and Dr. W. R. Earhart. In about a year Dr. Earhart sold out his interest to his partners, who now styled the firm Busey Brothers, under which name the business was conducted for several years, or until the interest of Hon. S. H. Busey was purchased by his son, Matthew W. The new firm of S. T. and M. W. Busey carried on the business under the title of Busey's Bank.

In 1888, after twenty years of continuous service, Col. S. T. Busey sold his interest, and the bank was reorganized, with Hon. Simeon H. Busey as president, Matthew W. Busey as vice-president, and George

(a) First Brick House in Urbana (1841)

(b) Present Postoffice

THE OLD AND THE NEW

W. Busey as cashier. This partnership continued until the death of Hon. S. H. Busey, which occurred June 3, 1901, after which the bank was again reorganized with Matthew W. Busey as president, George W. Busey as cashier, Garrett H. Baker and Paul G. Busey as assistant cashiers.

In 1907, George W. Busey retired, his position being taken by Garrett H. Baker as cashier, and Paul G. Busey advancing to the position of vice-president. The ownership of the bank from that time until the present has been in the hands of M. W. Busey, Paul G. Busey and G. H. Baker. Other members of the force at present are Charles A. Bongart, teller; Bowen Busey and Glenn Ross, assistant cashiers.

In 1913 the owners incorporated the bank under the name of Busey's State Bank, with a capital stock of $100,000 and a board of directors composed of M. W. Busey, Paul G. Busey and Garrett H. Baker. A short time prior to the incorporation the bank had the honor of being the depository of the treasurer of the University of Illinois.

Within the last year the bank has enlarged its quarters on Main Street, of Urbana, to twice its former size in order to keep up with the growth of its business, and has at the present time one of the finest banking homes in Champaign County. This bank is a charter member of the Illinois Bankers' Association, its officers having served on its executive committee for a great many years, and is also a member of the American Bankers' Association.

The First National was chartered April 6, 1883, with Charles L. Burbee as president; George W. Curtis, vice-president, and P. Richards, cashier. Mr. Burbee served as president for a few years and was succeeded by Mr. Richards, who served a few years, or until his death, January 1, 1899. Judge Francis M. Wright then became president and continued as such until January 1, 1906. Since that date A. F. Fay has been at the head of its affairs. C. W. Richards is vice-president. G. W. Webber has acted as cashier since 1907. The capital of the First National is $50,000; surplus and undivided profits, $60,000; average deposits, $500,000.

The Urbana Banking Company was organized May 18, 1903, with a capital of $100,000. Its officers have remained unchanged, viz: John H. Savage, president; J. W. Shuck, vice-president; Thomas A. Burt, second vice-president; John H. Thornburn, cashier; Minnie Jaques, assistant cashier. The capital stock is still $100,000; surplus and undivided profits, $20,000; average deposits, $650,000.

The First State Trust and Savings Bank is officered as follows: S. E. Huff, president; Harry Gardner and C. H. Wallace, vice-presidents; Abner Silkey, cashier.

First University Bank: David H. Lloyde, president; C. L. Lloyde, vice-president; H. R. Dow, cashier. This institution was organized in September, 1915.

The manufactures of Urbana are of modest proportions, but include brick and tile making, a foundry and machine shop and a planing mill. S. E. Huff & Company and Hunter, Rourke & Company are the workers in wood, and also operate large lumber and coal yards. The Leavitt Foundry and Machine Shop is the iron-working plant, and Alvin E. Huckins owns and conducts the brick and tile works, which he purchased of the Sheldon Brick Company in 1912. Bissell & Sherrill were manufacturing brick at Urbana as early as 1853, their kilns being on the ground now occupied by the Huckins yards. O. C. Wysons, W. J. Foots and Royal A. Sutton conducted the enterprise after Bissell & Sherrill and the Sheldon Brick Company, with which George and C. C. Sheldon were identified (uncle and nephew), as well as John W. Stipes, as manager, immediately preceded Mr. Huckins. It is therefore the oldest industry in Urbana.

URBANA SOCIETIES

The county seat has numerous lodges and societies, the histories of which, as a rule, are not accessible, and perhaps would be of more special interest to those who are closely identified with them. The Masons have a temple on West Main Street, and their lodge (Urbana No. 157) is the oldest of that order in the county. Urbana Chapter No. 80, R. A. M., Urbana Council No. 19, R. & S. M., Urbana Commandery No. 16, K. T., and Hope Chapter No. 104, O. E. S., are other strong Masonic bodies.

The I. O. O. F. Hall is corner of Main and Race streets, and the local order embraces Urbana Subordinate Lodge No. 39, Urbana Encampment No. 98 and Olive Lodge No. 57 of the Rebekahs.

The Knights of Pythias and the Pythian Sisters meet on West Main Street, and the Ben Hurs, Elks, Red Men and Woodmen are also represented by organizations. The club rooms of the B. P. O. E. are in the Flatiron building, and the lodge (No. 991) has a membership of over 250.

The women's clubs of the Twin Cities co-operate so intimately that most of the strongest of them have no distinct dividing lines. Sketches of the Art, Thirty, Social Science and Woman's clubs, which embrace both cities, have already been given. The Urbana Fortnightly Club has, from the first, been a distinctive organization of the county seat.

It was organized prior to 1885, as an informal reading club; was formally organized, with officers, in 1895, with Mrs. S. T. Busey as its president; was admitted to membership in the Illinois Federation of Women's Clubs in 1896, and has so extended its studies and prescribed membership as to embrace literature and domestic science and admit thirty women into its life. It also has a list of honorary members who are non-residents. At Urbana is also a strong Chautauqua Circle.

CHAPTER XIII

RANTOUL TOWNSHIP AND VILLAGE

NATURAL ADVANTAGES—ARCHA CAMPBELL—JOHN W. DODGE, LEADER
OF OHIO COLONY—JOHN ROUGHTON—THE PREEMPTORS' FIGHT—
RANTOUL PLATTED—PRESENT VILLAGE—THE LOCAL NEWSPAPERS
—CHURCHES AND LODGE—THE FIRE OF 1901 AND ITS RESULTS—
THE CHANUTE AVIATION FIELD—THOMASBORO.

Rantoul Township, north of the central part of the county, is one of
the most prosperous sections to be described in this work. It contains
perhaps the most important part of the village of Rantoul, and Thomasboro as a whole. The country is well watered by the Salt Fork, and
the farmers of the township have always constituted a substantial
element of the county's population.

Much of the territory now covered by Rantoul Township was
included in what was formerly known as Mink Grove. It was a favorite
camping place both of the Indians and the pioneers traveling back and
forth between the Chicago region and Champaign County.

NATURAL ADVANTAGES

Rantoul is one of the largest townships in the county, having an
area of forty-eight and a half sections of land. Mink Grove lies mostly
in the northern part of the township, extending into Ludlow township.
Otherwise, the country was practically prairie land, very fertile, as the
settlers eventually discovered, and well watered by the tributaries of
Salt Fork. The natural drainage is toward the south and west, and
this has been supplemented by expensive ditches dug along the courses
of the waterways; so that no better lands are to be found in the county
than those included in Rantoul Township.

The township was, of course, named in honor of Hon. Robert Rantoul, of Massachusetts, who may be justly called the savior of the
Illinois Central Railroad, to which the township and the county owe so
large a share of their development.

Modern Concrete Fireproof Silos

ARCHA CAMPBELL

The first white settler in what is now Rantoul Township was Archa Campbell, who afterward became a probate justice, county commissioner, Urbana's first mayor and a prominent citizen generally. As a matter of fact, he did little more than open up farms on the present site of the village and on the ridge in what is now Hensley Township, about midway between Thomasboro and Mahomet. In the fall of 1848 Mr. Campbell built a log cabin fourteen feet square on his Rantoul place. It was roofed with rough boards twelve or fourteen feet long, but fully answered the purpose of holding down his title to his claim.

Mr. Campbell's nearest neighbors were Franklin Dobson, on the Sangamon River, nine miles west, and Lewis Adkins, at the north end of Big Grove, eight miles south. Largely through the influence of Mr. Campbell the Illinois Central Railroad located the station of Rantoul, from which the township afterward derived its name. He built the first dwelling there, which was subsequently occupied by George W. Terry and wife, and his entire property at Rantoul passed out of his hands in 1858, Guy B. Chandler purchasing the farm.

In 1852 Lewis L. Hicks entered a section of land two miles northeast of the present site of the village, and the following year was joined by his brother-in-law and sister, Mr. and Mrs. Gilbert Martin.

JOHN W. DODGE, LEADER OF OHIO COLONY

Until the building of the Illinois Central in 1855, Rantoul township virtually remained unoccupied as far as permanent habitations were concerned. But the completion of that enterprise opened a new and brighter prospect for the northern and central parts of the county, and Rantoul shared in the general awakening and flow of immigration. They came from the East and from the South—John W. Dodge, John Penfield, John Roughton, James T. Herrick and others who preceded the large Ohio colony the members of which located at and near the station in 1857.

John W. Dodge, the advance agent of the settlers from Northern Ohio, arrived in 1855 from Twinsburg, for the purpose of pre-empting land for his friends and associates, several of whom accompanied him. He was well qualified for that leadership, having spent years in opening small farms from the dense timber lands of Northern Ohio. Such strenuous labors had weakened his constitution, and when he came to the Rantoul region he was not in stalwart health. He and his associates of the Ohio colony pre-empted several sections of land in what are now Rantoul and Ludlow townships and built eighteen pre-emption shanties. At the land sale in Danville during the following winter they paid the government for about three thousand acres of land at an average price of $3 an acre, including incidental expenses of pre-empting.

A year later Mr. Dodge commenced making improvements, sleeping at first in a pre-emption shanty without floor, door or window. He afterward moved three others together, and occupied them with his family and other newcomers, numbering from fifteen to twenty persons, during a whole summer, while a better house was being built. Groceries and provisions, lumber and hardware, were brought from Chicago. In those days wild game of different kinds was plentiful. Prairie chickens, ducks, geese and sand-hill cranes were out in force, during the season. The cranes would gather together in an open space and perform a dance, keeping time with their leader. Prairie wolves were also everywhere, and during the first year's stay of the pioneer members of the colony deer were seen in herds, passing from Buck Grove to the Sangamon timber in a regular procession. At one time sixty were counted in line.

After directing most of the Ohio colony well along toward permanent settlement, Mr. Dodge farmed some of his land with indifferent success, then started a drug store in the village, and early in the period of Illinois Central land sales "got into the game" and within five years had sold some 50,000 acres to settlers and investors, all in the vicinity of Rantoul. Finally he retired, as he should, to an honorable rest.

John Roughton

In 1854 John Roughton, also an Ohio man of Pike County, settled at Urbana as a blacksmith, afterward engaged in the grocery business, and in November, 1855, pre-empted the northeast quarter of Section 27, in what is now Ludlow Township, just north of the railroad station, and started a blacksmith shop at the railroad station. In 1861 he moved to the Big Grove, but after serving in the Civil War returned to improve his old pre-emption, and eventually became prominent in the village affairs of Rantoul.

The Pre-emptors' Fight

Mr. Roughton had much to do with protecting the interests of those who pre-empted land in Rantoul and Ludlow townships in the late '50s, and more than thirty years afterward told the story in these words:

"The grant of lands made by Congress to the Illinois Central Railroad Co., designed to aid in the construction of their road, included every alternate or even numbered section on either side of the entire length. All lands still in possession of the government and lying within fifteen miles of the road were reserved to the United States (taken out of market) so that the company might select other lands in lieu of even numbered sections on its immediate line which had previously been taken up for settlement. In 1855, the railroad company having made their selections, those still remaining were again brought into market by the proclamation of the President, Franklin Pierce. Previous to the time appointed for public sale a large majority of said lands were entered under the then existing Pre-emption Act. At said sale, which soon followed, all the lands in the then Danville district, those which were as well as those which were not pre-empted were sold, provided that should the pre-emptor make satisfactory proof to the governor the purchaser would receive back his money without interest. The speculators, who in those days were dubbed land sharks, taxed their ingenuity in devising methods by which to entice, or if need be, to drive away the poor man from his home and fireside. With some who cared not to become actual tillers of the soil they easily effected a compromise. Others, affrighted by threats of litigation, accepted a small bonus and left their lands. Those remaining in Champaign County, occupying as they then did nearly four thousand acres, being more resolute, could not be intimidated. Then came the tug of war and in dead earnest did Greek meet Greek, each determined to fight it out to the bitter end. Were those lands subject to pre-emption was the only issue. The speculator set up the plea that they were reserved to the United States, and therefore exempt by the act under which the pre-emptions were made. On the other hand it was claimed that, while it was true that these lands had been reserved for the purpose above set forth, it was equally true that the President by his proclamation put an end to the reservation and by his declaration that they were now subject to private entry he announced the fact that they were also subject to pre-emption.

"Litigation commenced. The Supreme Court of the State was appealed to for its decision. In that court the speculator obtained a victory. It was, however, currently believed that the victory was obtained by collusion with the pre-emptor who was defendant in the case. A number of suits in ejectment followed in the inferior courts and as a matter of course the same decision rendered. The pre-emptors of the county met together in council, at Champaign, organized a pre-emptors' protective association, appointed a convention to be held at Onarga and elected delegates to the same. Notices were scattered abroad and every one interested was invited to be present and participate in its proceedings. John Roughton and N. L. Seaver, of Rantoul, and Luther Eads, of Champaign attended the convention from Champaign County as delegates. Quite a number also attended from counties on the main line of the Illinois Central Railroad. The convention passed a series of resolutions expressive of its indignation against its oppressors, levied a tax of 20 cents per acre upon every pre-emptor with a view of raising a defense fund and appointed John Roughton to wait upon them and take their note for that amount payable in one year after date to the order of N. L. Seaver, who had been elected treasurer of the association. It also appointed an executive committee and instructed that committee to select a suitable case for appeal to the Supreme Court of the United States and to employ a competent attorney to prosecute the same. It also listened to an address delivered by an attorney from Danville, who came there for the purpose of submitting to the convention a proposition to carry up to the Supreme Court any case that might be selected for that purpose. He asked that a committee be appointed to confer with him. John Roughton, N. L. Seaver and a gentleman from Woodford County were appointed as that committee. They retired to a private room, received his proposition and reported to the convention. It was as follows: For taking up a case from the Circuit Court and carrying it on to its completion, if successful, eight thousand dollars; if unsuccessful, five thousand. The proposition was rejected by nearly a unanimous vote and the executive committee urged to prosecute its mission as speedily as possible. A few weeks afterward Mr. A. B. Ives, an attorney who resided at Bloomington and who had been employed in defending some of the cases which had been tried, reported to N. L. Seaver and John Roughton, one of them at the same time expressing it as his opinion that it was the best that could be found. He also expressed a desire to meet the committee with a view of being employed by them as their attorney. Luther T. Eads, who had been appointed chairman of the committee was therefore urged to call its members together. He, however, having become somewhat disappointed in consequence of the rejection of Mr. Drake's proposition at the convention refused to do so. Mr. Ives being advised as to the condition of affairs came to Rantoul where he entered into an agreement with Messrs. Roughton and Seaver to carry up the case he recommended and continue the same until a decision was obtained. In consideration for which, Mr. Roughton was to collect the tax levied by the convention and turn the notes over to him at their face value. Afterward the gentleman in Woodford County agreed to do the same. Mr. Ives went to Washington and Mr. Roughton visited every pre-emptor in Champaign County, from whom he collected notes amounting to between seven and eight hundred dollars and turned them over to him. The first and second winter sessions of the Supreme Court dragged along their weary length and no decision was obtained.

> " 'Uncertainty!
> Fell demon of our fears! the human soul,
> That can support despair, supports not thee'."

"When the third came the yearnings of every heart were those expressed by Froude in his 'Fall of Saguntum':

> " 'But be not long, for in the tedious minutes,
> Exquisite interval, I'm on the rack;
> For sure the greatest evil man can know,
> Bears no proportion to the dread suspense.' "

"However, before the expiration of this term victory perched upon the pre-emptor's banner—for in the month of September of the year 1860, Mr. Ives communicated the intelligence from Washington City, that the Supreme Court of the United States had given their decision reversing the decision of the Supreme Court of the State of Illinois.

"How many of the old pre-emptors of 1855 now remain on their lands it would be difficult to determine. Suffice it, however, to say by way of conclusion, that this writer, aided by his only son, Reuben Roughton, has succeeded in rearing upon his a pleasant home where he now lives and where during the remainder of his earth life he expects to

> " 'So live, that when his summons come to join
> The innumerable caravan, that moves
> To that mysterious realm, where each shall take
> His chamber in the silent halls of death,
> And go not, like the quarry slave at night,
> Scourged to his dungeon; but sustained and sooth'd
> By an unfaltering trust, approach his grave,
> Like one that draws the drapery of his couch
> About him and lies down to pleasant dreams.' "

The record shows that Mr. Dodge permanently located at Rantoul May 9, 1856, and that, soon afterward, came James T. Herrick, his brother-in-law, James Smithers, C. F. Post, John B. Perry, Columbus Carnes, Frank Eads, Anderson Brown and Benjamin Bradley.

RANTOUL PLATTED

John and Guy D. Penfield also came to Rantoul from Michigan, in 1856, being accompanied by a number of neighbors and residents of their home town. The Penfields platted the town in 1856 and afterward did much to improve it.

In that year G. W. Carter, Abraham Cross and John A. Benedict also arrived.

J. J. Bois was appointed agent of the Illinois Central Railroad in May, 1857, and held that position for more than thirty years.

PRESENT VILLAGE

The village of Rantoul has had a steady growth from the first, even the fire of 1901, which swept away its business section, being only a tem-

RANTOUL BUSINESS STREET

porary set-back. It is the natural commercial center of a rich country, and its thorough transportation facilities at the crossing of the main Illinois Central line, the Rantoul branch, and the interurban have solidified its standing. In population, progressiveness and promise it is third in the county, after Champaign and Urbana. Rantoul is the owner of a modern water and light plant, has two solid banks—the First National and Commercial—and two large elevators, controlled respectively by J. W. McCullough & Son and the Farmers' Elevator Company. W. H. Justice is superintendent of the village schools, the condition of which is told in the report of the county superintendent, published elsewhere.

THE LOCAL NEWSPAPERS

Rantoul first became a village in 1870, having been incorporated, under the state laws, in 1890. Its progress, from first to last, is largely due to wide-awake local newspapers, represented by the Press and the News. In 1873, H. E. Bullock and Abraham Cross commenced the publication of the Rantoul News, the outfit being moved from Paxton, the county seat of Ford County, on the north. The narrow-gauge railroad, now the Paxton branch of the Illinois Central, was then in course of construction, and the News upheld the enterprise through all its early difficulties. C. W. Gulick began the publication of the Rantoul Journal in October, 1875, its active manager being F. E. Pinkerton, afterward of the Urbana Courier. After about two years they were consolidated as the Rantoulian. After some changes Mr. Pinkerton again secured control and the sole ownership. About 1879 he changed the name of the publication to the Rantoul Press, which he published almost continuously until 1895, when the Press was sold to F. R. Cross and C. B. E. Pinkerton. Their successor was the present editor and proprietor, F. E. Riker.

The Rantoul News was started by F. R. Cross about 1889, and, after being several times sold, came into the possession of E. J. Udell, who continued its publication and editorial management until the time of his death in 1903. C. A. and W. Gray afterward became editors and proprietors, under the corporate name of the News Printing Company. The Press and the News are lively promoters of the best interests of Rantoul.

CHURCHES AND LODGES

The village, like other moral and intelligent communities of its size, is favored with a number of strong churches and lodges. The religious bodies are the Methodist, Rev. M. M. Want, pastor; the Baptist, Rev. E. C. Poole; the Christian (Campbellites), Rev. A. F. Hensaker; the Congregational, Rev. J. R. Cullen; the Catholic, Rev. W. J. Drummy; the Free Methodist, Rev. O. W. Haynes, and the Christian Scientists, Mrs. H. M. Morris, first reader. The Episcopal Church of Rantoul is the oldest of the local religious organizations. Its first services were held in the depot of the Illinois Central Railroad in May, 1857, by Rev. John W. Osborne, a missionary of the Episcopal Church. Later services were held by Mr. Osborne in the schoolhouse until 1870, when the society was organized as a parish by Rev. W. M. Steel. The schoolhouse was purchased and rebuilt as a church, which was consecrated in

1876. The Episcopal rectors of longest service have been Rev. W. M. Steel, Rev. W. H. Tomlins, Rev. F. W. Burrell, Rev. John C. White, Rev. Joseph A. Antrim and Rev. John M. Page, the present pastor.

As to the societies, the Masons, including the Order of the Eastern Star; the Odd Fellows and the Rebekahs; the Modern Woodmen of America, and the Grand Army of the Republic, with the Women's Relief Corps, all have organizations of more or less stability.

The Fire of 1901 and Its Results

The most destructive fire in the history of Rantoul was that of August 9, 1901. The flames burst forth at 11:40 A. M. of that day,

THE HIGH SCHOOL

from the Goff-Yates elevator, near the Illinois Central tracks, west of the south division of the business section of the village. Within thirty minutes, so strong was the wind and dry the material fed to the fire, that the section was all in flames, and within less than three hours the business district was virtually swept clean, and many of the best residences had also dissolved before the conflagration. The general course of the fire may be described as from the elevator to W. S. Snyder & Sons' implement house and Steel's blacksmith shop to Bailey's livery; thence south through the business section along the rear of various structures to the City Hall, the First National Bank, Steffer & Leonard's store, Miller & Hamilton's hardware store, to the offices of the News and the Press; thence to the Masonic Hall and Opera House. When the flames had subsided it was found that the only business houses or industries left were Coon Brothers' old telephone office, Clark & Rusk's elevator, Sweedburg's blacksmith and machine shop and Durbin's mill. The only hotel left was the Martin House. Rebuilding commenced promptly after matters with the insurance companies could be adjusted, and the citizens of Rantoul get their bearings, and the new village which soon arose was a great improvement over the old.

The general result is seen in the clean, substantial and modern appearance of the business houses, and the corresponding appearance of the village streets. Coupled with its advantages of moral, intellectual and social growth, Rantoul has all the necessary qualifications of a desirable residence town numbering fifteen hundred people.

THE CHANUTE AVIATION FIELD

A mile southeast of Rantoul is Chanute Field, the largest aviation field in the United States with the exception of the Wright grounds near Dayton, Ohio. The school, the headquarters of which are at this point, was established in July, 1917, and two thousand workmen were employed in preparing the necessary buildings and getting the grounds in proper shape. Something like a million dollars were expended in a few weeks on the site of the field which covers about a section and a half of land. The flying field proper is a level prairie of 640 acres. Captain C. C. Edgar of Washington, D. C., was in charge of the construction work; Major J. L. Dunsworth, commandant, and Captain Roy S. Brown in active charge of the flying. Captain Brown's chief assistants were Captain T. J. Hanley and Captain John C. McDonnell. The two original squadrons, each in charge of a captain, were reinforced by others as the number of student aviators increased. The majority of them had studied aviation, theoretically, at the ground schools at Princeton, Cornell, Illinois, Texas, Ohio and other universities, and at the Massachusetts Institute of Technology. Their curriculum had included the construction of aeroplanes, theory of flying, and applied mathematics, physics, photography and map making. If they had not received this course of instruction, it was given to them at Chanute Field. But the prime purpose of the training there is to get them a thousand feet above the earth and, with nothing around them but air, teach them to coolly deal with "balky" engines and treacherous winds and pockets, to train machine guns, drop bombs and all else required by their calling. At first they mount with capable instructors; soon they are required to try their wings alone, and after two months, if they pass the required tests, they receive their diploma of R. M. A. (Reserve Military Aviator) and are ready for duty either with the army or navy.

THOMASBORO

Thomasboro, in the southwestern part of Rantoul Township, is an Illinois Central Station, is quite a shipping point for grain and produce and has banking facilities (through the First National) which meets all demands of the townsmen and neighboring residents. Its school and church advantages are also adequate. Its population is numbered at about three hundred.

CHAPTER XIV

HOMER VILLAGE AND SOUTH HOMER TOWNSHIP

South Homer Township—The Wrights—M. D. Coffeen & Company—Moses Thomas and the Old Mill—Old Homer Platted—Exodus to New Homer—Homer in October, 1855—The Churches—The Corporation—Village of Today—Newspapers of Homer—The Woman's Club—Lodges.

Less than a mile from the Vermilion County line, the village of Homer lies in the southeastern part of Champaign County on the Wabash line. It is a neat, growing corporation, having within its limits some twelve hundred people, with concrete walks and streets, substantial looking stores, two grain elevators, a public library, newspaper, two banks, a pretty public park, a good graded school, churches, lodges and societies. It is the trading and banking center of a prosperous agricultural district, the advantages of such a situation being mutual.

South Homer Township

As to the township of South Homer, outside of the village, it is eight and a half miles from north to south and three and three-quarters from east to west. In its northern and central portions it is drained by the Salt Fork of the Vermilion River and in the south by the headwaters of the Little Vermilion River. These streams afford good natural drainage, and this advantage is supplemented by artificial drainage, especially along the Little Vermilion. Except immediately adjacent to the Salt Fork the lands of the township are of the best quality; in places, these consist of abrupt bluffs and, in other localities, of bottom lands so low that they are subject to overflows of long duration.

The Wrights

That part of the county long known as the Salt Fork Timber extended eastward into Vermilion County, with Danville as its metropolis. At an early day the Wrights settled in that region on both sides

469

of the line. Among them was John B. Wright, a Virginian, who had become prominent in Indiana before he brought his family to Champaign County and located on a farm about a mile north of the present village of Homer. That was in September, 1830.

M. D. COFFEEN & COMPANY

James S. Wright was one of his sons, who, in 1837, broke away from the farm and the malaria-ridden country and went to work on the Illinois & Michigan Canal, then being dug between Chicago and the Illinois River. Soon afterward he returned to the locality of Homer, however, with enough money to buy some land and become an independent farmer. He secured his first real start in life through his association with M. D. Coffeen, a young, intelligent and enterprising merchant, who was aiming to establish a trading center near the Wright place, the Moses Thomas mill and a section of the county generally, the settlers of which were coming to demand such accommodations nearer than Danville.

MOSES THOMAS AND THE OLD MILL

Moses Thomas came about 1829 and entered land not far from the village of Homer. He erected and operated the first mill with other than manual or horse power, near the southwest corner of Section 33, in the northeast corner of the township, and was one of the proprietors of Old Homer laid out upon lands near by. Both by appointment and election he served as probate justice in 1833-37, when he was succeeded by his son, John B. Thomas.

OLD HOMER PLATTED

In 1837 M. D. Coffeen formed a partnership with Samuel Groenendyke, of Eugene, Ind., and, under the name of M. D. Coffeen & Company, they decided to plat a town at the intersection of Sections 4 and 5, Town 18, and Sections 32 and 33, Town 19, a mile north of the present village. There are several explanations as to the naming of the place, but the one which seems to have come most directly from Mr. Coffeen himself is to this effect: One day in 1837, after the proprietors had located their general store, they commenced to talk about putting up a blacksmith shop (Wright was a blacksmith) and possibly a hotel, as well as about platting a little town. Mr. Groenendyke remarked "Yes, that plan would be more homer to me" (meaning more homelike to Mr. Coffeen) than to have it as it was then, with no place at which to stop.

At this Mr. Coffeen, who is also said to have been somewhat of a scholar and a great admirer of the Greek philosopher, replied, "Well, then, Homer it shall be." It is of record that at a meeting of the county commissioners held in April, 1837, a license was granted to Green Atwood to keep a tavern in the town of Homer. The Coffeen store was a great success and drew a large trade from the Sangamon, Okaw and Ambraw settlements, and the partnership continued until the death of Mr. Groenendyke, the non-resident partner, in 1860.

EXODUS TO NEW HOMER

Thus Old Homer reached the dignity of a bustling little village of several hundred people, notwithstanding its rather low and unhealthful

HIGH SCHOOL AT HOMER

site. But when the Great Western (now the Wabash) Railroad was put through the southern part of the county in 1855 and its course lay a mile and a quarter south of Homer, Mr. Coffeen who had acquired land at that locality, platted a town of the same name there, with the railroad station as its nucleus. He invited all his townsmen to move to the new town of Homer and offered to exchange lot for lot for the benefit of those who owned real estate in the old village. The proposition was generally accepted and the business men agreed to close their stores permanently after April 1, 1855, and move their goods, and such of their buildings as were presentable, to the new town of Homer. It is stated that "everything went to the new town except the Salt Fork and the pioneer mill of Moses Thomas," which, from necessity, were left behind. A general housemoving, with Mr. Coffeen in the lead, was begun, and continued until the former thrifty town became a waste of abandoned streets, alleys and lots, covered with the debris of its former greatness. The Homer & Ogden Electric Railroad now crosses the Salt Fork a few rods above the mill erected by Moses Thomas and, crossing the town plat of Old Homer, connects, by business and social ties, thriving towns which have grown up on the prairie in places unthought of by the men of that day as needing such facilities.

When Old Homer became a deserted village and New Homer a thing of life, James S. Wright, who had been an independent merchant for ten years, graduated to the larger financial and political field which centered in Champaign and Urbana. He had in the meantime been county surveyor for many years and served in the Legislature as a Whig.

Homer in October, 1855

How the second village of Homer looked when it was very young is thus described by the editor of the Urbana Union in his issue of October 25, 1855: "On Tuesday of this week we visited this town for the first time since its location on the prairie. The present site, on a high and commanding point on the Great Western Railroad, is considered much healthier than the old town. We were informed by the physicians that amidst the great amount of sickness the present year the town has been comparatively free from it. It is expected that the cars will soon pay the town a visit, and that the whistle of the locomotive will wake to new life the business of the town and surrounding country, which is already good. Several new houses are already being built, and many more will be commenced when facilities for getting lumber are better.

"Our friend, M. D. Coffeen, Esq., has just finished a new and commodious building for the accommodation of his extensive business, which we admire very much on account of the convenience of its arrangement and the superior beauty of the workmanship. The carpenter work was done by Mr. Cyrus Hays and the painting, which is really elegant, by John Towner. Besides Mr. Coffeen's drygoods store, there are several others, and a drugstore by Judge John B. Thomas, all doing a fine business. A steam sawmill has, during the summer, been put in operation, which is turning out a vast amount of ties for the Great Western Railroad."

The Churches

The locality of Old Homer, even before the village was platted, was visited by various missionaries or preachers, such as Rev. William I. Peters and Rev. Cyrus Strong, already mentioned, who probably conformed to the tenets of the United Brethren and the Disciples of Christ. A little later Rev. James Homes formed a class in Methodism at Urbana, and in 1839 Urbana Mission was formed, with Rev. Arthur Bradshaw as its pastor in charge. In that year, as previously told in his own words, he organized a society at Old Homer, which was then very young. The locality was included in what afterward became the Urbana Circuit until 1853, when it was set off as a station.

The Methodist Church moved with everything else from Old Homer to the new town in 1855. Its early preachers, after the village was made a Methodist station, were Rev. William Sim, Rev. J. Cavett, Rev. J. C. Long, Rev. J. Shinn, Rev. Peter Wallace, Rev. Isaac Groves and Rev. G. W. Fairbanks. The present pastor is Rev. J. P. Edgar.

The Presbyterians of Homer organized in 1859 and have had as pastors Revs. McNaire, Jinkens, Knox, West, Hunter, McNutt, Steele, Shedd, Clymer, Briar, Williamson, Gherette, Barrows, Zeimer, Baker and McEwen (John A.). The original house of worship was erected in 1873; was remodeled in 1898 and rebuilt in 1909. The church membership is now 225.

THE CORPORATION

The records of the village of Homer do not extend farther back than 1880 and, through the courtesy of E. L. Bowen, who has held the position of village clerk from September 4, 1905 (his present term expires May 1, 1918) the following are given as the successive presidents of the Board of Trustees and the village clerks:

Presidents: Joseph Thomas, 1880-85; A. C. Woody, 1885-90; W. W. Mudge, 1890-94; J. W. Wallace, 1894-95; J. N. Gunder, 1895-96; W. W. Mudge, 1896-97; R. C. Wright, 1897-98; J. Bennett, 1898-99; W. A. Conkey, 1899-1900; J. Bennett, 1900-01; F. M. Smith, 1901-02; Hugh O'Neil, 1902-05; H. J. Wiggins, 1905-07; H. M. Smoot, 1907-11; R. A. Roloff, 1911-14; Fay R. Current, 1914-17.

Village Clerks: W. V. Zorns, 1880-84; J. E. Spraker, 1884-94; C. A. Conkey, 1894-95; C. J. Upp, 1895-96; L. L. Hamill, 1896-97; W. H. Brown, 1897, resigned; J. T. Palmer, 1897, resigned; J. E. Spraker, 1897-1901; F. O. Elliott, 1901-03; J. E. Spraker, 1903-05; Geo. W. Clark, 1905, resigned; E. L. Bowen, 1905—

VILLAGE OF TODAY

Homer has a good township and village hall, a substantial public schoolhouse (completed in 1892 and accommodating 270 pupils), and its electric light is furnished by a private plant, operated as the Homer Light and Power Company. Its police and fire protection are all that are necessary, and its two principal streets are well paved with brick. Through the persistent work and good management of the Community Club, of which H. M. Smoot is president, the township has fully twelve miles of substantial concrete roads, and is well advanced in the Good Roads Movement. Homer Park, one mile north of the village, is an attractive recreation ground owned by W. B. McKinley and managed by Mr. and Mrs. C. B. Burkhardt.

Besides a number of handsome stores, the village has two banks— the Citizens and that of Raynor & Babb—and two grain elevators, owned

HOMER'S MAIN STREET

and operated by Frederick Rose and J. M. Current. The Rose elevator was erected in 1908 and has a capacity of 100,000 bushels.

NEWSPAPERS OF HOMER

Homer has had a newspaper for nearly sixty years, the local press having a present-day representative in the Enterprise. The Homer Journal was the first newspaper, and was established in 1859 by George Knapp. Its editor went to the front at the outbreak of the Civil War and left the Journal to its fate. In November, 1865, it was revived under John W. Summers, but in 1870 was moved to Sidney. In February, 1897, J. M. Gray, who had previously published a paper at Gifford, issued the first number of the Pilot. Two years afterward it was moved to Allerton, Vermilion County.

The successful venture in local journalism is the Enterprise, founded in 1877 by John C. Cromer, and succeeded by I. A. Baker in 1880, Willard L. Sampson in 1885, J. B. Morgan in 1889, J. G. White in 1911 and Borgan F. Morgan in 1912.

THE WOMAN'S CLUB

In considering the elevating influences which have given Homer cultural standing in the county, both the public library under the direct supervision of Mrs. P. E. Wiggins and the Woman's Club—the latter organized and sustained by most of the intelligent ladies of the village—are entitled to special mention. The data for a complete notice of the latter organization has been courteously furnished.

The Homer Woman's Club is an outgrowth of the Tuesday Club, which was organized December 13, 1897, with the following officers: Mrs. E. T. Mudge, president; Mrs. J. G. White, vice president; Mrs. W. J. Elliott, secretary-treasurer. In the following January a constitution was adopted. The club opened with twenty-eight active members, the membership being limited to thirty. American history occupied the attention of the club during the first two years of its existence. Various literary features have since been added. The object of the club was also social, as well as literary culture, and it was therefore the custom to hold several open meetings each year, which included auction sales, guessing contests, ghost parties, valentine parties, musicales, six o'clock dinners, house picnics, railroad journeys, gypsy camps, negro weddings and lectures by University of Illinois professors. The history of the club would be incomplete without mention of the banquet which the husbands of the members gave on Thanksgiving evening of 1899. Parliamentary drills, in connection with literary and historic studies, and various socials at the houses of the members, preceded a visit of Mrs. C. B. Butler, Mrs. Stengle and Mrs. Lawson to the Decatur Woman's Club, and the consequent decision on the part of the Tuesday Club to join the Federation. In 1903 the name was therefore changed to the Woman's Club. Up to that time the successive presidents of the club had been Mesdames E. T. Mudge, A. L. Lyons, W. Lawson and J. G. White. The present officers of the Woman's Club are as follows: president, Mrs. F. Sickel; vice-president, Miss Lillian Conkey; secretary, Mrs. H. P. Morrison; treasurer, Mrs. A. L. Vollborn; historian, Mrs.

W. S. Hess. It has a total membership of 60, divided thus: literary and travel section, 28; domestic science section, 32.

Homer has also a Chautauqua Circle of some strength.

LODGES

The leading lodges in the village are those of the Masonic order, Woodmen of America, Knights of Pythias and Independent Order of Odd Fellows.

The Odd Fellows of Homer were organized in February, 1858, with Albert Norton as Noble Grand; William M. Lummies, Vice Grand; John B. Thomas, secretary; John K. Leonard, treasurer. The local lodge has a present membership of 112, with the following in office: W. F. Barton, N. G.; Ralph O'Neil, V. G.; H. E. Hoffman, secretary; R. A. Rolloff, treasurer.

The first elective officers of the Modern Woodmen of America lodge at Homer were: N. O. Barnes, V. C.; J. B. Hendrickson, W. A.; W. H. Brown, clerk; J. G. White, banker. The membership is 175 and the officers as follows: A. J. Conkey, V. C.; W. T. Davis, W. A.; O. P. Dickson, clerk; C. A. Fry, banker.

Brilliant Lodge No. 232, Knights of Pythias, was organized January 3, 1890, with the following chief elective officers: C. C., J. M. Ocheltree; V. C., W. Q. Wallace; Prelate, J. A. Allison; K. of R. S., H. B. Johnson. The present number of members is 41, and the following are serving: C. C., Fay R. Current; V. C., Frank L. Sharp; Prelate, Newton G. Foreman; M. of W., Florin Sanks; K. of R. S., Carl A. Conkey.

CHAPTER XV

BROWN TOWNSHIP AND FISHER

EARLY SETTLERS IN THE TOWNSHIP—FOOSLAND PLATTED—VILLAGE OF
FISHER—THE NEWSPAPERS—FISHER'S CHURCHES AND SOCIETIES.

The extreme southeastern part of Brown Township, in the northwest corner of the county, lies in the edge of the main Sangamon Timber; otherwise, the country stretches away toward the northwest, into Ford and McLean counties, somewhat broken by the Sangamon, as a beautiful rolling prairie, fertile as well as charming. In the Sangamon Timber of the southeast skirting the river, and on the Rantoul branch of the Illinois Central, is the neat and growing village of Fisher, already verging toward its thousand people, while in the midst of the northwestern prairie lands is the pretty little hamlet of Foosland, on the Wabash line.

EARLY SETTLERS IN THE TOWNSHIP

The first settler in Brown Township was William B. King who, in 1834, settled on the southeast quarter of Section 5, in the northwest corner of the township south of the Sangamon. He entered his claim in the following year, which was the first entry in the township. King located upon the old Danville and Fort Clark road, and for a number of years he squatted there alone, as far as permanent neighbors were concerned. But his place soon became a quite popular resort for travelers along that highway, like Prather's on the Salt Fork and Newcomb's at the ford of the Sangamon. Only two other entries of land, other than King's, were made in the township previous to 1840 and they did not become homesteads for some time. It was William Brown, an early settler on Section 3, in the northern timber belt, after whom the township was named; which was not, however, set off from East Bend until 1869.

Thomas Stevens, a wealthy cattle dealer, settled in the north part of the township in 1855, and afterward moved to Gibson City, Ford County. About the same time Ithaman Maroney located in the extreme northwest corner, but in 1862 enlisted in the Union army and did not return to the county. William H. Groves came in 1854 and located on Section 34, about two miles west of the present village of Fisher; when he died there, some forty years afterward, he had long held the record as the oldest living settler of the township. Among other pioneers were Carl Dobson, C. C. Harris, William Peabody, David Cooter, John Strauss. Lyman Smith and Steven Brown and William Foos.

FOOSLAND PLATTED

Various members of the Foos family acquired large tracts of land in the northwestern portion of the township, and upon a portion of one of the farms was platted the station of Foosland on the Wabash Railroad. The largest of the farms at that point was owned by F. W. Foos, a resident of New York City. At a comparatively late day it was thus described by the Champaign Times: "The Foos farm, at Foosland, consists of 3,800 acres. The owner, F. W. Foos, resides in New York City, but often comes to Foosland and is well known there. His resident manager is R. G. Ball, a good farmer and most competent man in every way. For the past fifteen years Mr. Ball has had the management of this big farm and seems to have given entire satisfaction, both to tenants and owner. The farm rents to tenants for $4 per acre, cash, for either grain or grass land, except that when as much as one hundred acres of grass are rented to one man, the price is but $3.75. This is much lower than neighboring land can be rented for and therefore it is much in demand. There are thirteen tenants in all. Of the 3,800 acres, there are 1,500 in grass, 700 in oats and 2,100 in corn—at least, that was the proportion last season, but the proportions differ yearly. An effort is made to keep changing from grain to grass, thus keeping the fertility of the soil. The farm is moderately well tiled, has fairly good fences around it, but the buildings are not very new or up to date. Last year there were raised on this farm—not including the 1,500 acres of grass— 105,000 bushels of corn and 2,100 bushels of oats."

The Foos farm has always been considered the best example of agricultural operations conducted on a large scale in Brown Township.

Howard, or Lotus, is a station on the Wabash, in the southwestern corner of the township.

VILLAGE OF FISHER

Fisher is the banking and trading center of a large area of country, which is primarily agricultural. It is a fine grain region and its two large elevators are controlled by the Farmers Grain and Coal Company and Vennum & Gilmore, and its two banks, the First State and the Farmers Exchange, furnish financial accommodations equal to any call of the farmers or business men.

Fisher is a good place in which to reside, being provided with good water, electric light, a well-managed graded school, churches and societies, and, as a climax two newspapers, not only to advertise such advantages, but to call attention, in behalf of its citizens, to the pressing needs of the community.

The Fisher Electric Light plant, owned and operated by the village corporation, was built in 1905-06. It became village property in 1908.

The number of pupils enrolled in the public school system of Fisher

THIRD STREET LOOKING NORTH

is 172, and the handsome building now occupied was erected in the fall of 1914 at a cost of $25,000. F. L. Lowman is the superintendent.

THE NEWSPAPERS

In December, 1889, William Rodman commenced the publication of the Fisher Times, which he continued for about two years, when the office was sold to Naylor & Bill, who changed the name to the Fisher Reporter. A. J. Bill then became sole proprietor and thus remained for about a year, and was successively followed by R. M. Hall and George E. Hass. The latter, who was both a practical printer and a versatile editor, continued to manage it for six years, or until August,

1902, when he sold the newspaper to Alva Gilmore, the present editor and proprietor.

The Fisher News was founded by Pearl M. Hollingsworth in May, 1913. He still owns and edits it.

Fisher's Churches and Societies

The religious needs of Fisher are supplied by three churches—the United Brethren, the Methodist Episcopal and the Christian, mentioned and described in the order of their founding. The United Brethren Church was organized at the residence of Rev. David Naylor, two miles west of Fisher, in 1867, by Rev. William Ferguson, of the Central

PUBLIC SCHOOL, FISHER

Illinois Conference. In the year following a schoolhouse was built in the neighborhood and regular services were held in it until 1875, when the first house of worship was erected and dedicated by Lyman Chittendon, of Westfield, Illinois. On the site of Naylor cemetery services were held in the church named until the organization of a special society at Fisher. About 1890 both societies were merged, the town church building was sold, and the country meeting-house was moved into the village and repaired. It was then dedicated by Bishop Castle, and occupied by the society until 1914, when a modern structure was erected on the site of the old church. It was dedicated by Bishop H. H. Fout under the pastorate of T. H. Decker. Following Rev. William Ferguson, organizer of the Fisher Church, were these pastors: Revs. Blake, J. Robeson, J. Crowley, B. F. Rinehart, Yeagle, Samuel, Foulk,

(Sister) Nella Niswanger, Luke, Welch, G. N. Arnold, W. G. Metsker, A. F. Brandenburg, Wilstead, J. G. Breeden, W. R. Muncie, (Sister) R. J. Nash, M. L. Watson, H. D. Hudson, T. H. Decker and C. O. Myers. The church society now has a membership of about seventy.

The Methodist Episcopal Church of Fisher was organized in 1870 and a building for worship completed the same year. Its successive pastors have been Rev. J. T. Orr, Rev. Melchoir Auer, Rev. T. I. Coultas, Rev. C. E. McClintock, Rev. D. P. Lyon, Rev. J. H. Austin, Rev. J. D. Botkin, Rev. Sampson Shinn, Rev. E. S. Wamsley, Rev. E. C. Harper, Rev. J. F. Horney, Rev. J. T. Pender, Rev. W. H. Schwartz, Rev. William Gooding, Rev. J. R. Reasoner, Rev. D. G. DuBoise, Rev. T. O. Baty, Rev. J. C. Eninger, Rev. E. K. Crews, Rev. J. F. Clearwaters, Rev. S. A. Maxey, Rev. D. H. Hartley, Rev. William Carter and Rev. J. W. Dundas. A second house of worship was built in 1874 and, with the continued growth of the society, a third, and a far more commodious building was erected in 1912. It is designed not only to accommodate a present membership of 225, but provision is even made for the future. The building, which is located on the first block south of the central part of town, is forty-six by sixty feet in dimensions, of the colonial style of architecture, brick veneered and slate roof; the auditorium, with domed ceiling, is finished in mission oak and is beautifully frescoed. The entire building is heated with steam, lighted with electricity, and modern in every way. It was completed at a cost of $11,000.

The Christian Church of Fisher was organized in October, 1885, and has also built and occupied three houses of worship—in 1886, 1903 and 1917. Its present home is an up-to-date handsome edifice, completed under the pastorate of Rev. Andrew Scott, who ministers to the spiritual needs of more than 200 church members. The regular pastors of the Christian Church, besides Mr. Scott, have been Rev. H. C. Cassell, Rev. A. B. Hubbard, Rev. H. L. Stipp, Rev. J. W. Kilborn, Rev. S. E. Fisher, Rev. J. Frank Hollingsworth and Rev. A. L. West.

The standard orders represented by lodges in Fisher are the Masonic, with a chapter of the Eastern Star; the Odd Fellows, with the Rebekahs, and the Modern Woodmen of America. One of the oldest of these bodies is Fisher Lodge No. 704, I. O. O. F., which was instituted in March, 1882. W. H. Allison was its first Noble Grand, and Ed. Waddington is at present in office. The membership of the lodge is about sixty. The Masonic lodge (Sangamon, No. 801) was organized in December, 1891, with John Odell as Master. Oscar Zook is now in the chair and presides over a lodge of about sixty members.

1—31

CHAPTER XVI

ST. JOSEPH TOWNSHIP AND VILLAGE

OLD ST. JOSEPH—PIONEER SETTLERS—THE BARTLEY AND STAYTON
FAMILIES—HIRAM RANKIN AND THOMAS RICHARDS—DEVELOPMENT
OF THE VILLAGE—ST. JOSEPH OF THE PRESENT.

St. Joseph is one of the thriving townships, comprising six square miles, southeast of the central part of the county, and lying in the western edge of the Salt Fork Timber region which stretches eastward into Vermilion County. With the denuding of much of the timber lands the old-time name has long since lost much of its former significance, although the second and third growths still make a fine showing in some localities. In St. Joseph Township the main body of timber is still on the east side of the main stream of Salt Fork, which runs from north to south through the central sections; still, the wooded lands in that belt are small in proportion to their extent in the early times. The West Branch, or Saline Creek, which unites with the main stream in Section 10, north of the central part of the township, was never thickly timbered. Thus drained and watered, St. Joseph Township is well adapted to agricultural pursuits and stock raising.

This borderland between the Salt Fork Timber and the prairie lands farther westward received an accession of substantial residents at an early day, and was settled quite rapidly when the old-time prejudice against the comparatively unwooded tracts was dissipated. At a still later date, about 1866, came the railroad, now known as the Big Four, to add to the advantages of the township as a section in which to earn a livelihood and enjoy life.

OLD ST. JOSEPH

The flourishing village of St. Jospeh, near the crossing of the Cleveland, Cincinnati, Chicago & St. Louis and the Chicago & Eastern Illinois railroads—directly on the line of the Big Four, as well as on the Danville, Urbana & Champaign electric—is known to have been the site of a favorite Indian camp, as well as a burial place for the red people; and, like the whites, they honored their dead by selecting beautiful locations for their last resting places. Several of their burial mounds were long traceable at and near Old St. Joe, which preceded the present village.

PIONEER SETTLERS

The original survey of St. Joseph Township was made in 1821 by Jacob Judy, then deputy surveyor general, and, although several entries of land were made in 1829, no permanent settlement is recorded before 1830. Nicholas Yount squatted on Section 26, about two miles south of the present village of St. Joseph, sometime during 1828, and two years afterward entered land in a regular way. He afterward resided in that locality for many years, and his children and their families after him.

The founders of the prolific Swearingen family, Bartley and John, made the first land entries in 1829 and 1830, their selections being in Sections 36 and 24, in the southeastern part of the township. In the latter year John Salisbury, the county's first sheriff, also entered land in Section 24; and the Peterses—William, Elisha, Samuel, Joseph, Robert and another William, the three last named sons of the first—in Sections 25 and 26, not far from the present station of Tipton, on the Eastern Illinois, in the southeastern part of the township. William I. Peters came in 1833 and entered lands in Sections 22 and 23, a mile south of the village. David Swearingen came in 1831, and two years later entered a tract in Section 35, in the far southern part of the township, where he spent the rest of his life. The old homestead remained in his family until a comparatively recent date. As stated by Judge Cunningham: "The name of this family, so numerous in the eastern part of the county, appears in the abstracts of titles to the real estate of that section more frequently than that of any other family. Its holdings since 1830 have been very large."

THE BARTLEY AND STAYTON FAMILIES

Joseph Stayton came here from Kentucky October 10, 1830, and in the following year settled upon land in Section 26, where he raised a family of sons and daughters, who became prominent in the township.

George, Benjamin and Jacob Bartley arrived about 1831, and within the following two or three years entered lands in Sections 22 and 23. In 1833 Jacob Bartley was elected a member of the first Board of County Commissioners.

The first person buried in St. Joseph Township was the mother of Nicholas Yount, and the first native child was that of Joseph Stayton, which died in infancy. John Ford taught the first school in 1833, the schoolhouse being Squire Peters' kitchen.

The Bartley and Stayton families were united in marriage, many years after they had settled in the township, by David B. Stayton, the son of Joseph, and Sarah Bartley, daughter of Jacob. Mr. Stayton was a lad of twelve when his father located on Section 26. His first playmates were Indians, who used to camp during the winter on the east bank of Salt Fork, some five hundred strong, a short distance below Prather's ford. For many years after the organization of the township, in 1861, Mr. Stayton was supervisor and collector, and he was always consulted about township matters as long as he lived. He also became one of the most prosperous farmers of the county, his estate of six hundred acres being a permanent exhibit of intelligent and successful farming and stock-raising. For years before his death he was the undisputed "oldest settler of St. Joseph Township."

About the time that the Bartleys located, Cyrus Strong and his sons, Orange and Ambrose, also entered lands in Sections 22 and 23, as well as in Sections 13 and 15, farther north and near the present limits of the village of St. Joseph. Their property in the latter section lay along the Salt Fork and embraced a famous ford, first called Strong's ford and later, Kelley's. Joseph T. Kelley maintained a ferry at that crossing place. Cyrus Strong, the head of the original family, was elected a county commissioner in 1836, and, as the saying is, was "quite a man."

Samuel Mapes took up land in Section 13, as neighbors of the Strong family, and the homestead was inherited by his son, Daniel.

HIRAM RANKIN AND THOMAS RICHARDS

Hiram Rankin and Thomas Richards, friends, came in 1832, and jointly entered lands in Sections 18 and 24, in the western and eastern parts of the township, respectively. While a bachelor Mr. Rankin lived with the Richards family at Hickory Grove, Section 18, but after he married the daughter of Thomas Patterson established a home of his own in Section 24, on the State road, where he spent the remainder of his life. Mr. Richards and his descendants clung to the farm in Section 18.

In 1835 James Cowden entered a homestead in Section 33, on the west side of the Fork, where he lived with his family until his death in 1860. In the same year the Argo family, comprising Benjamin,

Alexander, Moses and Isaac, established homesteads in Sections 2, 3, 10, 22 and 24, and evidently made their choice of lands with a view to permanent settlement, as they all spent their lives where they located at the time mentioned. Section 10 adjoins the present site of the village to the northwest.

DEVELOPMENT OF THE VILLAGE

In 1835 Robert Prather entered lands in Section 11, near the crossing of the Salt Fork by the Danville & Fort Clark road, and Prather's Ford at the site of Old St. Joe became even more famous than Strong's Ford, a short distance to the south. "At the height of its

ST. JOSEPH'S MAIN STREET

glory," says C. H. Gallion in his paper read at the Old Settlers reunion of July, 1886, "the village could boast only of three stores, a postoffice, a tavern, a blacksmith shop and several dwellings. The naming of St. Joseph is described by the following circumstance: It is related that at one time, when Joseph Kelley kept the tavern stand, a stranger came along and stopped with Mr. Kelley, and the two became quite agreeable friends and for several days had a jovial time together. When the stranger departed, Kelley, out of consideration for the good time they had had in company, refused to charge him anything, where- upon the mysterious stranger told the landlord that he would 'do some- thing for him' for his kindness. Soon afterward, the stranger, whom it seems was some politician of more than ordinary influence, and in some way connected with the administration at Washington, secured the establishment of a postoffice, the need of which he had perhaps learned during his stay at Kelley's. Kelley was appointed postmaster, and in his honor it was called St. Joseph, from Kelley's first name."

(Kelley's tavern, here referred to, was a famous caravansary in its time. Abraham Lincoln frequently dined or lodged there on his way from Bloomington to Urbana and Danville, while riding the circuit of the courts with Judge David Davis.)

"The present thriving village of St. Joseph dated its existence from the building of the Indiana, Bloomington and Western Railway in 1866. The earliest settler on the site of the town was Catharine Hoss, who entered forty acres of land in 1839. The first business house was opened in 1870, in the west part of town by Wm. O. Shreve and Van B. Swearingen. These gentlemen have since been actively identified with the business interests of the place, and have contributed not a little to its prosperity.

"Shortly after, A. D. Ralph moved up a store building from the old town, and opened the first business house in the east part of the village.

"In the early part of 1880, the village was incorporated under the laws of the state, and at present comprises some twenty-five business firms, two public halls, two handsome churches and a large and well conducted graded school.

"On the construction of the I., B. and W. Ry., a station called Mayview was established in St. Joseph Township about four miles west of the village, and now consists of a store, postoffice, blacksmith shop, grain elevator and a handsome Methodist Church.

"St. Joseph Township has held its place among the foremost townships, and in an early day, had much to do in the civil government of the county. The law establishing this county provided for the election of three commissioners, to be the highest in authority in the county. Jacob Bartley, of St. Joseph, was a member of the first board. Six of the members of the first grand jury, and three of the first petit jury were from St. Joseph. The first poorfarm in the county was in St. Joseph Township, the one now owned by Abe Hoy. The first bridge in the county spanned the Salt Fork where it is crossed by the State road in St. Joseph, and the first regular preacher in the county made St. Joseph one of his appointments. The first organized drainage district in the state under the new law, was in St. Joseph, and under the head of public improvements, St. Joseph Township donated $25,000 for the construction of the I., B. and W. Ry. The first supervisor was S. S. Rankin, and the subsequent representatives in the county board have been Mahlon Glascock, V. B. Swearingen, H. W. Drullinger, G. W.

Doyle, Jno. L. Smith, David B. Slayton, Abe Thompson, W. O. Shreve and the present incumbent, V. J. Gallion."

St. Joseph of the Present

The St. Joseph village of today is a progressive little community of some eight hundred people, provided with thorough facilities of transportation and communication; good drinking water and electric light service (through the Central Illinois Company); a modern public school (superintendent, A. A. Allen); two banks (the Exchange and St. Joseph); two elevators, owned and operated by Swearingen & Walker and J. A. Gillis; two implement depots; a substantial newspaper, and

The Public School

churches and societies for the religious and social gratification of both men and women.

The forerunner of the St. Joseph Record was the St. Joseph Eagle, established by Mr. Wyninger in 1890. In December, 1893, it was sold to J. H. Noble, who changed its name to the Record and continued its publication until September, 1897. Mr. Noble then sold to F. L. Dale and Charles W. Dale. Since 1904 the latter has been the sole proprietor, being assisted in its conduct by his wife in the making of a most useful local newspaper.

The Methodist Church and the First Church of Christ have well-supported organizations in St. Joseph. The former, now under the pastorate of Rev. E. B. Houck, has occupied two houses of worship—the first erected in 1877 and the present edifice, completed in 1915. The

Church of Christ, of which the pastor is Rev. Guy L. Zerby, completed its present meetinghouse in 1908.

That St. Joseph is well supplied with secret and benevolent lodges or societies is evident from the fact that these local organizations are in the list: Masonic, Knights of Pythias, Modern Woodmen of America, Ben Hur, Order of the Eastern Star, Pythian Sisters and Royal Neighbors.

CHAPTER XVII

MAHOMET TOWNSHIP AND VILLAGE

EARLY LAND ENTRIES—MIDDLETOWN PLATTED—ISAAC V. WILLIAMS
AND BENJAMIN F. HARRIS—MAHOMET INCORPORATED AS A VILLAGE
—HISTORY OF THE SCHOOLS—THE LOCAL NEWSPAPER—MAHOMET
CHURCHES—SECRET AND BENEVOLENT SOCIETIES.

In comparison with the settlements of the timber tracts along the
Salt Fork, the Okaw and the Ambraw, in the southeastern, southern
and central parts of the county, those established along the Sangamon
River, in the western and northwestern sections, were of a rather late
date.

EARLY LAND ENTRIES

The first entries in Mahomet Township were made by Isaac Busey,
of Urbana at the Vandalia land office, on October 22, 1832. They
covered 120 acres in Section 14, 80 acres in Section 15, and 160 acres
in Section 23, which included the southeastern corner of the present site
of Mahomet Village with considerable tracts to the east and southeast.
Later in the same year he entered other lands in Sections 22 and 23, and
on October 27, a few days later, Jonathan Maxwell filed on 40 acres in
Section 22.

On October 29, 1832, Henry Osborn took up lands in Sections 11
and 12, to the northeast. All the lands thus entered were east of the
river in the timber belt.

On August 10, 1833, John Bryan, who had recently become Isaac
Busey's son-in-law, entered a forty-acre tract in Section 14 adjoining the
first Busey entry. Thereon the Bryan family was established for several
generations. In 1833 John Meade also filed a homestead claim in Section 15. From which it is evident that most of the entries and settlements were made on lands at and near the present site of Mahomet
Village.

The years 1834, 1835 and 1836 saw numerous entries made in the
northern half of Mahomet Township. In the former year various tracts
in Sections 9, 10, 11, 12, 14, 15, 16 and 17, were taken up by Henry,

489

David, Solomon and James Osborn, John Bryan, Samuel Hanna, William Phillips, John G. Robertson, Lackland Howard, Charles Parker, Noah Bixler, Jeremiah Hollingsworth and John Meade. In 1835 Noah Bixler, Martha A. Robertson, Joseph Brian, Joel Hormel, Jacob Hammer, Daniel Henness, Fielding L. Scott, Joseph Henness, Joseph Hammer, John G. Robertson and Joseph Lindsey entered lands in Sections 3, 9, 10, 11, 12, 14, 15 and 17, and in 1836 Jacob Hammer, Noah Bixler, James Bevans, William Justice, John J. Rea, John Webb, George Ritter, Martha A. Robertson, James Parmes, Jonathan Maxwell, Jonathan Scott, Jeremiah Hollingsworth, Robert M. Patterson, John Lindsey and Daniel T. Porter became landholders in Sections 1, 2, 3, 4, 8, 9, 10, 13, 15 and 17.

MIDDLETOWN PLATTED

On March 15, 1836, Mr. Porter entered the southeast quarter of the northwest quarter of Section 15, and on the 10th of the month placed on record a town plat covering thirty-eight lots of that entry which he named Middletown. The plat conformed to the present Bloomington road and was the original of the village of Mahomet. Additions to the original town were mainly made to the south, west and north.

ISAAC V. WILLIAMS AND BENJAMIN F. HARRIS

About the time that Middletown was platted the stock-raising industry obtained the solid foothold in Mahomet Township to which its natural advantages pointed. Isaac V. Williams brought in the first improved stock from Piatt County, his residence being just over the Champaign County line. Benjamin F. Harris also laid the basis of his fortune, which he later invested at Champaign City, in the increase and improvement of his wonderful herds which grazed over the grassy stretches of Mahomet Township. His activities in that field covered the twenty years previous to 1856. Before the railroads came, when the most profitable markets for his live stock products were Boston, New York and Philadelphia—centers reached only on foot—"Uncle Frank," as Mr. Harris was affectionately called, was the hardest worker in the county.

Not only the township as a whole, but the village of Mahomet, was greatly benefited by such broad-gauge operations. Among others who cooperated in this early development may also be mentioned Fielding L. Scott, John Bryan, Thomas A. Davidson and sons, Wiley Davis, Rezin Bolton, John J. Rea, John Carter, George Boyer, William Stearns,

William Herriott, James C. Ware, John G. Rayburn, Joshua Smith, J. V. Pittman, James C. Kilgore, John W. Park, J. D. Webb and J. Q. Thomas.

Mahomet Incorporated as a Village

When the Indianapolis, Bloomington & Western Railroad was built diagonally through the township, in 1866, the village of Mahomet received such an impetus that it was incorporated seven years later. Within the intervening period it has become one of the best points in the western part of the county.

History of the Schools

From the first the township and the village have taken much pride in the quality of their schools and teachers, and S. C. Abbott, one of the oldest and most honored citizens of the town, has prepared the following sketch covering a period of seventy-two years, or from the time of the building of the first schoolhouse in 1832 to that of the completion of the fine structure of 1904, which, in turn, was burned two years later.

"The first schoolhouse within the bounds of what is known as district No. 29 was a log house fourteen by 16 feet built by subscription and labor donations, in 1832, about forty rods from the sand bank now owned by Jonas Lester. It was occupied in 1833 by George Cooper, first public school teacher in the township, at a salary of $15.00 per month and board among the scholars.

"The next was a log house near where Philip Cherry's old house now stands.

"In 1847 a frame house was built near where William Lindsey now lives, and in 1851 a two-story frame house near where the present brick one stands. This one was sold and is now the residence of Mr. Blanchet. In 1864 was built the brick house just torn down.

"In 1836 a school commissioner for this township, John Mead, was appointed, and in 1838 the first school trustees were chosen as follows: Jonathan Maxwell, James Osborn and Fielding Scott. On July 22, 1836, the school section (16) was sold at auction and brought $3,337.50 cash and the money was loaned by the trustees. The interest only was to be used forever for school purposes, and for 68 years that sum has been loaned and interest applied and the principal is as yet intact. The names of those who bought the land were James Yapp, John Robertson, Fielding Scott, Jno. J. Rea, Alvin Barnet, Thos. Crabbe, James Meator, Zack Osborn, John Mead and Michael Jess. The first school treasurer was Joseph Lindsey, appointed in 1838. Until 1840 the township was but one district. That year Dr. Noble Adams was the teacher for the whole township; his salary was $20.00 per month and 'board himself.' In 1841 the township was divided and made into three districts. Middletown was district No. 3. Some years later it was divided again and then was made No. 2; and fifty years later, No. 29. In 1841 Isaac Parmeter was the teacher; then followed Dr. Noble Adams, Joseph Lindsey, Jas. Brown, Wm. Danner, Jas. Brown, Jas. H. Brown, Geo. McClure, W. Stewart, R. P. Carson, A. W. Somers, W. Ingrain, Geo. Boyer, Jas. Crane, H. Phillipps, E. Harwood, D. Cheney, J. Tinkham, M. Kelsey, Wm. Whitney, Rev. S. F. Gleason, J. V. Stone, Wm. Crayne, W. Howard, W. Lindsey, L. Stewart, Rev. E. French, Chas. Baker, A. D.

BURNING OF THE HIGH SCHOOL, MAHOMET

Sizer, who for fourteen years ending in May, 1884, occupied the place as principal. The above are names of teachers from 1833 to 1884, fifty-one years. Since 1865 it has been a graded school and several teachers employed as at present. The names above are principals.

"The names of all the teachers since 1884 are known by all the adult people of the district. If we omit the names of Rev. S. F. Gleason and C. J. Tinkham of Homer, all the persons above named prominent in this community in their day have passed away.

"The new house is a handsome substantial building, concrete foundation, deep and broad with granite trimmings and a slate roof, size 70x60, six rooms and same number of large cloak rooms, principal's room, and spacious halls all furnished in latest styles. As a whole it reflects great credit on the school board, Messrs. J. O. Rayburn, C. L. Lindsey and C. B. Hoit; also on the architects and the contractor (Lon Spurgin). While the old one lasted forty years, we predict eighty years for this one. The cost of building and furnishing the building throughout with up-to-date apparatus and decorations with grading and tree planting and other outdoor improvements will be about $13,000. We are proud of the house and proud of the bevy of rosy-cheeked children that are being educated within its walls and think nothing is too good for them."

The handsome schoolhouse described was destroyed by fire on May 10, 1906, and was rebuilt on its former lines, being completed in 1908. C. P. Bauman is the present superintendent and reports an enrollment of nearly ninety, over fifty in the high school. There are four teachers in the grades and three in the high school, the school property being valued at $18,000. Throughout the township, there is an enrollment of 350 pupils.

Mahomet has a number of substantial stores; two banks, the Mahomet and Home; two elevators, the Farmers and Wykle; a newspaper, and several churches and societies.

The Local Newspaper

The Mahomet Sucker State, as the local newspaper is called, issued its first number on October 13, 1879, a few issues having been put out as the "Magnet." As the "Magnet" did not seem to draw, "Sucker State" was substituted. For the past fifteen or sixteen years the paper has been owned and edited by Charles D. Warner, C. W. Murphy, C. M. Pearson, O. D. Stiles and C. W. Pugh. During the bulk of that period it has been in charge of Messrs. Pearson and Pugh.

Mahomet Churches

The Mahomet Baptist Church was among the first of the religious organizations to take substantial shape in the Sangamon region of Champaign County. From all available sources of information it would seem that John G. Robertson, a Kentucky immigrant to the Big Grove and a zealous missionary of the country round-about, furnished the initial inspiration in the formation of Baptist societies at the Brumley schoolhouse, two miles east of Urbana, and at Mount Pleasant, now Farmer City, DeWitt County, in 1839. Rev. J. D. Newell, then residing at Waynesville, that county, was the actual organizer of both churches. Bethel church, as organized at Mount Pleasant by Mr. Newell, had a membership extending from Salt Creek to Urbana, a distance of thirty miles. Its original members were J. G. Robertson and wife, Martha A.; Fielding L. Scott and wife; Preston Webb and wife, Ulila; James Webb and sisters; Mrs. Dr. Adams and Sarah Blunt. During the summer the church moved to Mahomet as a more central field of labor, and held its meetings at the houses of various members. In the fall the society united with the McLean Association and held its meetings at the Methodist camp ground, Randolph's Grove. Mr. Robertson had been elected deacon of the church and settled at Mahomet.

Elder Newell had arranged to preach to the Baptist congregation at Mahomet once a month, and at the close of his labors, which covered more than a year, Elder William McPherson succeeded him. He also preached monthly for about a year, after which there was a short interim, although regular meetings were maintained by the church members. In 1845 F. L. Scott was elected deacon, who, with Father Robertson, served in that capacity for some sixty years. Elder Sylvester Pasley commenced his ministry of a year in 1846, and was followed by Elder Mason. In 1851 Elder Pasley was again called to the pastorate and a house of worship was completed in the following year. Then successively came Elder Justus Taylor, Elder McPherson (a second term); Elder W. R. Combs (who remained from June, 1855, to April, 1864), during whose pastorate the church united with the Bloomfield Association; Elder D. S. French; Rev. S. F. Gleason, who served the church for more than twenty-five years; Rev. S. G. Anderson and Rev. Thomas F. Chilton. The Baptist Church bought a parsonage in 1854, two years after the completion of its first house of worship, which stood north of the present public school. The building now occupied was erected in 1867. The church numbers 230 members.

The Methodists of Middletown organized a class at an early date, and from 1843 to 1855 belonged to the Monticello circuit. In the latter year the Middletown circuit was organized, and embraced all of the Sangamon settlements within the county. A house of worship was completed in 1856. Among the earliest members of the Methodist Church of Middletown were James W. Fisher, B. F. Harris, James C. Kilgore, Hezekiah Phillippe, and F. B. Sale with their families. Mr. Sale subsequently became a local preacher of Methodism, and was influential in the establishment of other circuits and stations higher up the Sangamon. Among the early pastors of this church may be named Rev. A. S. Goddard, Rev. J. A. Brittingham, Rev. L. C. Pitner, Rev.

J. C. Rucker, Rev. A. R. Garner, Rev. C. F. Hecox and Rev. Arthur Bradshaw. Rev. Grant Johnson is the present pastor in charge.

In 1858 the Presbyterians residing along the Sangamon Timber, who were affiliated with the West Urbana Church, were dismissed from that organization to form a church at Middletown. This was accomplished, a church building was subsequently erected and an organization maintained, with more or less permanence, for many years. The Presbyterians of Mahomet are at present without a pastor.

Secret and Benevolent Societies

The Odd Fellows, Masons, Modern Woodmen of America and Court of Honor all have societies in the village. The I. O. O. F. is represented by a lodge of more than 100 members organized in November, 1892. Its first elective officers were James Young, N. G.; George Warner, V. G.; William Wiles, R. S.; Peter Williamson, treasurer. Present officers: J. W. Hicks, N. G.; F. C. Daniel, V. G.; M. E. Smith, R. S.; J. J. Hayward, treasurer.

The Rebekahs were organized in November, 1895, and are of equal strength. Their first officers were: Mrs. Sarah Lott, N. G.; Miss Florence Pinkston, V. G.; Mrs. Jennie Johnston Keene, R. S.; Mrs. Vina Cummings Cooper, F. S.; Mrs. A. V. Purnell, treasurer. Present officers: Mrs. Nora Reed, N. G.; Mrs. Lizzie Ruhl, V. G.; Mrs. Fannie Wiles Johnston, R. and F. S.; Miss Lilah Clapper, treasurer.

CHAPTER XVIII

TOLONO AND SIDNEY TOWNSHIPS

VILLAGE OF TOLONO—PIONEER BUSINESS MEN—BANK OF TOLONO—
THE TOLONO HERALD—LIGHT AND WATER—CHURCHES AND SECRET
SOCIETIES—SIDNEY TOWNSHIP—FIRST LAND ENTRIES IN COUNTY—
NOX'S POINT—TOWN OF SIDNEY LAID OUT—THE VILLAGE IN 1854
—THE VILLAGE IN 1917—BANKS—THE SIDNEY TIMES—CHURCHES
AND LODGES.

Tolono, one of the southwestern townships of the county, is six miles
square, or covers an area of thirty-six sections, and with the exception
of the ridge which divides the waters of the Okaw from those of the
Ambraw is substantially a flat prairie. This physical fact has made
necessary drainage operations of quite an extensive nature, especially in
the western portion of the township. These improvements have greatly
extended the area of fertility, which was formerly largely confined to
the valleys of the streams.

VILLAGE OF TOLONO

The village of Tolono, in the southeastern part of the township at
the crossing of the Illinois Central and Wabash lines, is one of the
best trading centers and shipping points in the county. It has a population of about nine hundred people, but was virtually non-existent until
the railroads came in 1855-57. Until that time about the only settlers
were a few families along the main branch of the Okaw—John P. Tenbrook, Isaac J. Miller, John Cook and John Hamilton and their households. About 1855 Captain J. R. Swift was appointed agent for the
sale of Illinois Central Railroad lands in the neighborhood. He opened
a land office at the new station, built a comfortable residence and
erected an office building and while he remained at Tolono ran true to
his name. Captain Swift did not see the completion of the Wabash line,
although he projected a southwestern line from Tolono to St. Louis
himself. He organized a company, became president of it and managed
to have a track graded several miles toward Shelbyville across the Okaw.
But his funds gave out, and the clamoring laborers frightened him out
of the country.

Pioneer Business Men

The completion of the Wabash in the late '50s made it evident that Tolono would be a desirable place for business and residence. In 1857 T. Purrington, who had long been in government service at Washington, opened a land office at Tolono. At an early period also came such professional men as D. H. Chaffee and the lawyers A. M. Christian and Neil McDonald. Quite a large hotel, the Marion House, was also erected at the crossing of the two railroads. William Redhed, an English merchant who had been engaged in business at Chicago for several years, located at Tolono in April, 1857, as the town's first grocer. There he

BUSY SECTION OF TOLONO

continued in active business for more than thirty years. In the following year Alonzo Lyons, who had been an Urbana merchant, opened a general store at the railroad crossing, and continued in business at Tolono until his death in August, 1878. He was one of the most enterprising and honored citizens in the county. Henry C. Smith was another of the founders of the town, locating in 1857 as a carpenter and contractor, later engaging in the lumber and coal business and, when his sons matured, branching out with them into other lines of business.

Bank of Tolono

In 1865 Robert A. Bower came to Tolono from Ohio and established himself as an attorney-at-law, but in 1869 established the Bank of

1—32

Tolono, of which he has ever since been the president. William Redhed was also identified with the management of the bank in its earlier years. Its first cashier was T. M. Salisbury, and his successors have been William T. Bower, H. S. Bower, Alexander Campbell, E. B. Rogers, S. M. Bower and R. A. Bower, Jr. The assistant cashier is W. S. Redhed, of the well known pioneer family. The average deposits of the Bank of Tolono are now $100,000; paid-in capital, $25,000.

The Citizens' Bank was established by Lawrence Sandwell in 1904, with J. A. Corbett as vice-president and A. B. Campbell as cashier. In 1915 Isaac Raymond became president, and was succeeded by Mr. Corbett, Eli Trost assuming the vice presidency. Mr. Campbell continues as cashier.

TOLONO HIGH SCHOOL   .

A. B. Campbell has also published and edited the Tolono Herald since 1891. He bought the newspaper of E. B. Chapin, whose father, E. J. Chapin, a business man of Tolono, had founded it in April, 1875. Its editorial control was conferred upon the son, who, in the year mentioned, sold the plant to Mr. Campbell and moved to Champaign to enter upon the publication of the News, of that city.

The importance of Tolono as a grain center and shipping point is emphasized by its three elevators owned and operated by J. A. Creamer, Horton Brothers & Company and William Murray. The Creamer elevator was built in 1898 by Carrington & Hannah. An abundant supply of pure water has been guaranteed its people since 1895, when its water works were put in operation, and its buildings and streets are lighted by electricity, supplied by the Central Illinois Public Service Company. Its school facilities are excellent, as indicated by the report of the county superintendent, and four churches meet all the requirements of the religious elements. These organizations are the M. E. Church, Rev. Lewis Campbell, pastor; Presbyterian, Rev. W. W. Wilson; the Baptist, Rev. F. A. Morrow (Sadorus) and St. Joseph Catholic, Rev. Joseph Flannigan. A number of secret and benevolent bodies are also active, the ladies especially having become quite prominent in that regard. In this list are the Royal Neighbors of America and the Order of the Eastern Star. The former, although organized as late as December, 1900, number 130. The first Eastern Star Chapter at Tolono (No. 111) was organized in 1872, but surrendered its charter in 1883, and the present organization was effected in 1889. It is known as Tolono Chapter No. 45 and has a membership of about forty-five.

In a word, there is no excuse for either men or women to get lonesome or stagnate in the little village of Tolono.

SIDNEY TOWNSHIP

The township of Sidney in the southeastern part of the county is mainly watered and drained by the Salt Fork, which, in the early days, was quite heavily timbered on both sides. It also contains the beautiful Linn Grove, in the extreme southwest corner four miles from the present village of Sidney. The Salt Creek Timber and Linn Grove received some of the first pioneers of the county who immigrated from Vermilion County, Indiana. The land office in which the earliest entries of lands in Sidney Township were made was at Palestine, Crawford County, and those who made them were often called "Salt Forkers."

FIRST LAND ENTRIES IN COUNTY

The first entry of lands not only in the township, but in the entire county, was recorded by Jesse Williams on February 7, 1827, and was located on the east half of the northeast quarter of Section 12, on the south side of the Salt Fork. It is not known whether he actually occupied his claim, but it is a fact that Thomas L. Butler became its owner and made it his homestead for many years. In 1833 Mr. Butler also entered lands in the same section.

In October, 1827, John Hendricks made the second entry, covering the other half of the quarter in Section 12 which had been claimed by

Williams. In November of the same year Josiah Conger entered a tract as the northwest quarter of Section 5, and others in the Salt Fork Timber followed in 1828. Not long afterward William Nox, Sr., Adam Thomas and others took up claims and settled south of Salt Fork, near the present village of Sidney.

Nox's Point

Before there was a village the locality was generally known as Nox's Point, and sometimes as Williams' Point, the names being derived, of course, from Jesse Williams and William Nox.

Town of Sidney Laid Out

As has been stated, Dr. James H. Lyon came to the locality of Nox's Point about 1835, invested in lands there and on November 9, 1836,

The Town Hall, Sidney

placed upon record the plat of the town of Sidney. The place was named for the daughter of Joseph Davis, who was associated with Dr. Lyon in the founding of the town which had been designated as a station on the Northern Cross Railroad. The plat of Sidney shows twenty-eight blocks of twelve lots each, with a public square, wide streets and convenient alleys. But the Northern Cross project failed to materialize as far east as Champaign County, and Sidney had to wait for its growing days. Until the Wabash line appeared twenty years afterward not to exceed a dozen buildings were expected on that impressive plat. It is said that Lyon & Davis introduced the first fine live stock into the township and, being natives of Kentucky and typical southern gentlemen, also laid out a race track.

THE VILLAGE IN 1854

The summer and fall of 1854 witnessed a revival of confidence in the fair future of Sidney, as it was then fairly certain that the Toledo, Wabash & Western Railroad (Great Western) would make Sidney one of its stations. In June a tri-weekly mail was established between Urbana and Vincennes, the stage passing through Sidney, Bloomfield and Paris, and in July a postoffice was opened in town, with J. S. Cunningham as postmaster.

In September, 1854, this picture of Sidney was drawn by the editor of the Urbana Union: "One day last week we managed to escape the thralldom of office duties and struck out across the prairie, in a southeasterly direction. Two hours' ride brought us to the village of Sidney. This place was laid out about 1836 by Joseph Thomas, during the operations on the Northern Cross Railroad, with a fine prospect for future success. But, at the abandonment of the system of internal improvements adopted by the State, its prospects lapsed. The prospect now of its being a point on the Great Western Railroad causes the people to feel encouraged. Three lines have been run near the village—two within one hundred yards and one about a quarter of a mile away. It will make no difference which of the lines is selected, either will be sufficiently near. Messrs. Thomas & Jones have laid off a new plat to supersede the old one, and lots are now in the market.

"Sidney possesses many favorable qualities as a location. Its site is no doubt the best in the county, being high and rolling. It is situated in the edge of the southern extremity of the timber, on the Salt Fork of the Vermilion River, and surrounded by prairie that is unsurpassed by any in the county. About four miles to the southwest, at an elevation of ninety feet above the creek, is the Linn Grove, which is regarded by all who have seen it as the most beautiful location in Illinois. It is now the property of Enoch Johnson, and is frequently made the place of resort of the pleasure seekers from this place, although twelve miles distant.

"There are now two dry-goods stores in Sidney, one owned by J. S. Cunningham and the other by Messrs. Upp & Casey, both doing good business.

"Leaving Sidney in the afternoon we went north along the edge of the timber for about three miles, when we struck out on the prairie to the westward, and were soon coming over its trackless sod.

"Before leaving the settlements we passed many fine farms, among which we took particular notice of that of Lewis Jones, Esq., which lies wholly on the prairie and embraces many acres of unsurpassed fertility. The corn is above the medium crop and will surprise its owners, we think."

THE VILLAGE OF 1917

The present village of Sidney contains over 500 people and is situated in a productive grain country at the juncture of two lines of the Wabash road, with the Chicago & Eastern Illinois only a mile to the east. The

SIDNEY'S MAIN STREET

Sidney Grain Company owns three elevators, which handle a large bulk of corn, and two banks furnish the financial medium by which their operations, as well as the transactions of the merchants and house-holders, are carried on from day to day.

BANKS

On the 1st of January, 1885, Miller Winston founded a bank with a capital of $12,000. The founder is still at the head of it. There has been no change in capital, although the average deposits now amount to $200,000; individual responsibility, $350,000; individual profits, $5,300.

The State Bank of Sidney was founded in April, 1911, with the following officers, who still serve: president, George Cole; vice-president, Luther Fisher; cashier, J. F. Rankin. The capital stock of the bank is $25,000; surplus and undivided profits, $2,000; average deposits, $100,000.

Sidney offers such inducements as a desirable place of residence as a good school, a newspaper, churches and societies. There are 168 pupils enrolled in the Union school, which is under the superintendency of George H. Primer; the building, which was erected in 1900, cost $12,000.

The Town Hall at Sidney was completed in 1907.

The Sidney Times

The Sidney Times was founded in 1885, under the name of the Sidney Derrick, by J. C. Carpenter. Two years afterward he sold it to T. D. Jerauld. After about a year it came into possession of Mont Robinson and his daughter, Mrs. Ida Davison, who changed the name to the Sidney By-Way. Later, another daughter, Miss Eva Robinson, became its sole proprietor and editor, and as she was a practical printer, with her other qualifications, conducted the paper successfully for several years. It was then sold to George Clinkenbeard, his successors, previous to the adoption of the present name, being John A. Noble and F. D. Denton. About January 1, 1905, Mr. Denton changed the paper to the Sidney Times, the present proprietor, Fred H. Wood, assuming charge of it in 1913.

Churches and Lodges

There are four churches at Sidney: the Methodist, Presbyterian, Christian and Nazarene. The Methodist Episcopal Church was organized in 1857, and, although the first house of worship was commenced ·in the following year, it was not completed until 1864. Its pastors have been Revs. George Fairbanks, Peter Wallace, John Long, William McVey, Isaac Grover, Benjamin Newman, J. C. Rucker, H. H. Keith, C. Y. Hickox, W. C. Avey, B. F. Hyde, J. C. Rucker (second term), George Alexander, Abner Clark, J. Frank Poorman, H. G. Wass, D. G. Murray, J. A. Lucas, J. W. Eckman, J. Seymour, Otho Bartholow, M. G. Coleman, Joseph Long, W. E. Means, W. P. Bowman, E. E. Bean, Gilmore Cunningham, E. L. Pletcher, W. A. Poe, William L. Cunningham, R. E. Mathias, O. B. Hess, J. M. Judy and Alfred Wicks. The church now has a membership of 200. The house of worship of the present was erected in 1899.

The Presbyterian Church was organized March 4, 1884, as Vaile Chapel, and an exclusive house of worship was completed in July, 1886. Under the name of First Presbyterian Church the meeting house of the present was erected in 1899. The successive pastors have been Revs. R. V. Hunter, W. P. Jaques, B. B. Brier, W. N. Steele, J. E. Williamson, W. R. More, E. P. Gilchrist, Henry Love, Guy E. Smock, James E. Foster, E. M. Snook and George A. Hartman. The church has a present membership of about 100.

The Nazarene church was organized in April, 1915, has a membership of about forty, and has been served by Revs. B. B. Sapp, R. J. Kunze and (Miss) C. M. Ryan.

The Masons, Knights of Pythias and Odd Fellows have lodges at Sidney. Sidney Lodge, No. 347, A. F. & A. M., was chartered April 10, 1860, and the first meeting under dispensation held on the following 3d of May. The Worshipful Masters have been W. A. Smith, G. W. Hartman (four terms), William Freeman (four terms), W. A. Robinson, S. G. Boyd, W. H. Robinson, Frank Thompson, William Hays, W. M. Hanson (two terms), G. E. Raymond, C. L. Golden, J. H. Smith and J. F. Rankin. The lodge has a membership of about sixty. Besides J. F. Rankin, W. M., are the following elective officers: J. W. Cole, S. W.; V. I. Johnston, J. W.; G. C. Allen, secretary, and Luther Fisher, treasurer.

Model Lodge No. 360, Knights of Pythias, was organized May 16, 1892, with the following officers: Miller Winston, C. C.; W. F. Temple, V. C.; G. D. Boone, P.; C. W. Witt, M. at A.; Sam Sholts, M. of W.; H. L. Rud, M. at A.; M. Hess, I. G.; D. D. Rudicil, O. G. These gentlemen served as the early heads of the lodge, which has increased in membership from 22 to 78. Present officers: W. G. Francis, C. C.; G. C. Griffin, V. C.; W. D. Wood, P.; E. J. Lehman, M. at A.; William Swinney, M. of W.; J. W. Mumm, I. G.; H. B. Swarts, O. G.; F. H. Swarts, K. of R. & S.

CHAPTER XIX

AYERS AND RAYMOND TOWNSHIPS

In the southeastern corner of Champaign County is the small town-ship of Ayers, comprising less than twenty-four square miles, six sections from north to south and three and three-quarters from east to west. It is mostly watered by the Ambraw and the Little Vermilion rivers, and contains some of the choicest farm lands in the county. They were not taken up as early as those in other parts, such as the sections along Salt Fork to the north, which were more heavily timbered.

Broadlands, the only village in the township, contains some five hundred people, and rightly suggests some agricultural enterprise, or land holdings, of unusual magnitude. In the early '50s, in fact, its site was the headquarters of the largest landed estate in the county, and one of the most noted in the state.

FIRST PREEMPTION IN AYERS TOWNSHIP

The first preemption was made by a man named West, who built a shanty near the north line of the township, in what was known as Lost Grove, as early as 1850. Three years afterward he sold his right and small improvements to John F. Thompson, who brought his family there in 1855, and developed his holding into a substantial homestead which he occupied until his death.

THE GREAT SULLIVANT ESTATE

In the meantime Michael L. Sullivant, a leading and wealthy citizen of Columbus, Ohio, had been consolidating his holdings on the Ambraw, both in what is now Ayers Township and adjoining territory. He had commenced to buy direct from the government in 1852, and when the railroad lands of the Illinois Central came into the market he purchased

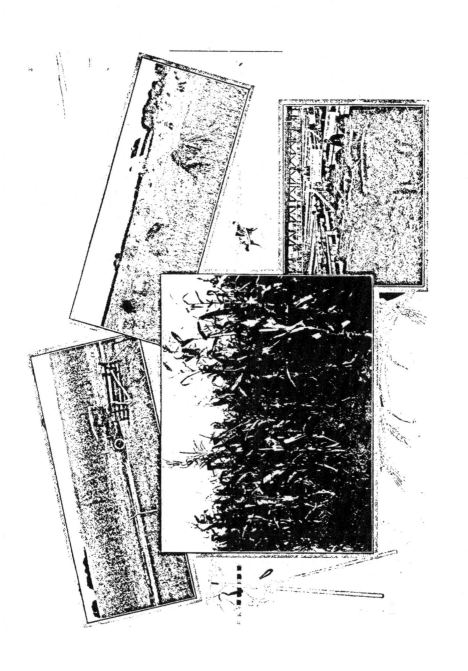

many of its alternate sections until he became the owner of 27,000 acres.
At one time he was the owner of nearly every desirable tract in the
township of Ayers. Having gathered his land Mr. Sullivant commenced to improve it on a grand scale. In February, 1855, the Ohio
Statesman, of Columbus, thus noted the departure of his first expedition:' "The outfit was an admirable one. The wagons were constructed
in such a manner as to answer the purpose of tents, and will be used as
such until suitable buildings can be erected by the mechanics of the
company for their accommodation. The Messrs. Sullivant have
purchased vast tracts of land in Central and Northern Illinois, and
are preparing for cultivation several thousand acres of land during
the present season. The party that left today intend to prepare the
land for ploughing, hedging and planting, and to erect the necessary
buildings for the tenants. They take along several bushels of locust
seed, walnuts, hickory nuts, chestnuts, red cedar berries, and a considerable quantity of Osage Orange seed for the purpose of hedging.
Another party will leave here in about a month, destined to the same
place, and still another, about the same time, will open another farm
of several thousand acres in Northern Illinois for Mr. Sullivant."

THE HEADQUARTERS, BROADLANDS

At a high and central point of his principal holdings Mr. Sullivant
erected a boarding house, with numerous barns and outbuildings, which
he called Headquarters. Near by he erected a large residence, and
commenced to improve his lands methodically and scientifically (as he
thought). At one time he also rented large tracts of his land in Ayers
Township to Alexander, the Western cattle king, who afterward became
so prominent in live stock transactions in Chicago. Mr. Sullivant called
the headquarters of his great estate Broadlands, but his attempt to farm
upon such a stupendous scale was ahead of the times and resulted in
financial failure. His holdings passed to other hands, were divided,
and sub-divided, and the community, as a whole, greatly benefitted thereby. But the memory of the grand enterprise remains in the name of
the village and the station on the Chicago & Eastern Illinois Railroad.

BROADLANDS OF THE PRESENT

Broadlands is a leading center for the handling and shipping of grain,
its three elevators being owned by Paul Kuhn & Company, of Terre
Haute and the Broadlands Grain and Coal Company and Henry Allen,

local proprietors. The last named was built in 1904 and has a capacity of 35,000 bushels.

The Bank of Broadlands was established in November, 1892, with A. M. Kenney as president and D. P. McIntyre as cashier. Mr. Kenney retained that office until 1908, when Mr. McIntyre succeeded him, Will A. Coolley assuming the cashiership. Since January, 1917, Mr. Coolley has been president of the bank, which has a capital of $25,000 and average deposits of $100,000.

There are four churches at Broadlands: The Methodist, Rev. J. R. Warlick, St. John's German Lutheran, Rev. D. Blasberg, the Evangelical Lutheran, Rev. R. Krenzien and the United Brethren, Rev. C. T. Shortridge.

The Evangelical Lutheran Immanuel Church was organized in 1875, its first house of worship having been erected in the following year. The present church building was completed in 1895. There are about fifty voting members and some 130 communicants. The schoolhouse the lecture hall were remodeled in 1913. The successive pastors of the Evangelical Lutheran Immanuel Church have been Revs. E. Martens, C. Baumann, C. H. Mueller, J. B. Graupner, C. F. J. Johanning, H. Hafner, C. Boevers and R. Krenzien.

The United Brethren Church of Broadlands was organized by Rev. J. H. Penney, its first pastor, in the fall of 1893. The list of successive pastors is as follows: Revs. J. H. Penney, McBride, A. J. Nugent, B. B. Phelps, Duger, Rosenbarger, Jinkins, O. McHargue, Dunseth, Sherril, White, Watson, Hall, McBride (second term), L. H. Coolley, G. W. Padrick, G. W. Ball and C. Tuttle Shortridge. The church has a present membership of about ninety.

Besides these religious organizations, three secret and benevolent lodges are established at Broadlands, representatives of the Masons, the Odd Fellows and the Modern Woodmen of America.

Broadlands is an incorporated village, and is a pleasant little place with unusually good pavements and well lighted streets, through the accommodations of the Central Illinois Public Service Company.

LONG VIEW

Long View is a station and little settlement on the Chicago & Eastern Illinois Railroad about five miles southwest of Broadlands, in the southern part of Raymond township. It is a brisk grain center, with two elevators; has a good bank, a high school and two churches. A number of stores add to its standing.

The Long View Bank was established in 1899 by Michael H. Keefe, Arthur C. Amsler, Clyde C. Amsler, Emil L. Wiese and Samuel A. Howard, with a capital of $5,000 which was increased to $10,000. Later Mr. Howard sold his interest, the capital was decreased to $8,000, and all the bank interests were centered in the hands of Messrs. Wiese and A. G. Anderson, of Broadlands. In 1912 Mr. Keefe and E. Clarence Churchill bought a one-half interest in the bank. The present officers are: Emil L. Wiese, president; E. C. Churchill, vice-president; A. G. Anderson, second vice-president; M. H. Keefe, cashier. The capital stock is $10,000, and the firm owns and occupies a substantial brick building. Its responsibility is $250,000. The bank owns some 1,300 acres of good land and stock in the Ogden Avenue State Bank of Chicago.

Settlement of Raymond Township

Raymond township itself was not settled at an early date, as it consists almost entirely of prairie lands lying within the valley of the Ambraw River. Much of the eastern part of the town in the '50s was embraced in the great Sullivant estate, the headquarters of which were at Broadlands. Permanent settlers were not numerous until many years afterward, when the land holdings became small and the Chicago & Eastern Illinois Railroad was built across the southeastern corner of the township in the '70s. That period also marked the establishment of Long View as a station and a village.

William M. Shawhan

The first permanent settler, William M. Shawhan, did not arrive from Indiana until 1855, and he bought the improvements of a squatter near Linn Grove and the Ambraw Timber. Mr. Shawhan had already acquired a comfortable competency and was also deeply interested in church and school work before he came to Raymond Township. Although he had been engaged in the cattle trade for some years, when he settled, with his large family, on Section 19, he did not enter actively into such pursuits, but rather devoted his energies to the work of the Disciples Church. He preached in the cabins of the settlers and was a true missionary of the Gospel. His influence was far-reaching and of the best, and his descendants have profited by it to the present.

CHAPTER XX

SADORUS AND PESOTUM TOWNSHIPS

Sadorus Township, in the extreme southwest corner of the county, contains two villages, the one which gave the township its name being the nucleus of some of the most interesting ancient history of the region. Sadorus Grove, embraced by the upper branches of the Kaskaskia, was the estate of Henry Sadorus and his family in 1824, as has been already fully described. After fifty-four years of residence and useful work the patriarch passed away, looking with pride, like those of the biblical days, upon many descendants of several generations to continue the family line.

"Stayers" of Sadorus Township

Henry Ewing and family, also Hoosiers, built a cabin in the grove just north of the present village of Sadorus, two years after Mr. Sadorus settled therein. The Ewings, William Marquis and Aikens Wright, who settled in the neighborhood during the next few years, were floaters, but William Rock, Walter Beavers, the Millers and others were stayers, and left families. Ezra Fay settled in Section 35, southeastern part of the township, in 1835, and was one of the first ministers of the sect known as Christians (New Light).

At a somewhat later date John Cook, Zephania Yeates, the Hixon brothers and others settled in the Grove region, and in the '50s, the Rice and Craw families, William Harrison, William Ellers, F. Laughlin and others.

Sadorus Village

Sadorus village commenced to take shape with the establishment of the railroad station on the line of the Great Western in 1858. Its three grain elevators, which forcibly speak of the cereal productiveness of the surrounding country, are operated under the ownership of R. E. Chambers & Foote, DeLong Brothers & Company and Baldwin & Company.

The Bank of Sadorus and the Farmers First State Bank are also institutions which make the village a reliable financial center for the village and adjacent farming communities. In the matter of schools, social and religious organizations, and other advantages of a higher nature, Sadorus is fully equal to other villages of its population.

IVESDALE

Ivesdale, a village of about five hundred people, is on the northwestern border-line of the township, on the Wabash Railroad. It was incorporated as such June 12, 1871. Although it has a twelve-hour

FIRST HENRY SADORUS HOME (1824)

service of electric light from the Bement Light and Power Company, it has no water works. Its supply of water, however, is good and abundant from private sources. Ivesdale has a modern brick village hall, where the corporate business is transacted and which is open to lectures and meetings called for public improvements.

Two institutions, mention of which should in no wise be omitted, are the First National Bank and the Ivesdale News. Both are a part of its substantial life.

The Ivesdale News was established in September, 1897, by John H. Ryan, and continued under his management until January, 1909, when it was purchased by Theodore A. Thoma. It continued under his management until December, 1912, when it was disposed of at a sheriff's sale to C. S. Coe. It was leased by Miss Elsie B. Sutton in January, 1913, and continues under her management.

The places of worship in the village comprise three churches, as follows: Methodist Episcopal, Rev. H. L. Thrall, pastor, Sadorus; St. Joseph's Catholic Church, Rev. C. C. O'Brien; German Lutheran, with no regular pastor. The following lodges have halls at Ivesdale: Modern Woodmen of America, Court of Honor, Knights of Columbus, Ancient Order of Hibernians and Catholic Order of Foresters. The Ancient Order of Hibernians in Ivesdale was organized in September, 1887, the Modern Woodmen lodge in December, 1895, and the Court of Honor in April, 1897.

PESOTUM TOWNSHIP

Pesotum Township embraces only thirty-five sections in the southern part of the county, what would have been Section 6 being occupied by the village of Sadorus and the balance of that section which is attached to the town of Sadorus. Pesotum is the name of a treacherous and bloodthirsty Pottawattamie chief, who participated in the Fort Dearborn massacre of 1812, and it is somewhat a matter of conjecture why it should have been applied to the Illinois Central station of 1854, and thus descended to the township. The watershed between the Okaw and Ambraw rivers runs nearly parallel with that railroad through the township. The surface of the country is nearly level, and much of the town, especially that lying in the valley of the Okaw to the west, has been artificially drained. The largest and most important ditch in that region is the Two Mile Slough. That locality was the scene of the first settlement—that is, the timber belt of the main branch of the Okaw— the German element having been, from the first, especially strong there. Among the early settlers may be mentioned, Squire Lee, Henry and William Nelson, Paul Holliday, S. L. Baldwin, John Meikle, Josiah Merritt, Charles Johnson, C. L. Batterman, S. D. Kelley and Benjamin F. Boggs.

PESOTUM VILLAGE

With the construction of the Illinois Central through the town from north to south, and the establishment of the station of Pesotum, the tide of settlement commenced to shift toward the east and the Ambraw valley. Within a few years after the Civil War every tract within the town had been taken up and most of them put in a state of cultivation. Year by year the village has steadily been affected by this general development, and has become the center of quite an extensive trade. It has the proper facilities for handling grain, two banks (the Bank of Pesotum and the Farmers Bank), a modern school, churches and societies, and a newspaper—the Chief, founded in 1914, and published and edited by A. F. Alblinger & Company.

CHAPTER XXI

PHILO AND OGDEN TOWNSHIPS AND VILLAGES

YANKEE RIDGE SETTLERS—CLARK R. GRIGGS—VILLAGE OF PHILO A
RAILROAD STATION—THE PRESENT VILLAGE—OGDEN TOWNSHIP—
PIONEER SETTLERS—OGDEN VILLAGE.

Philo, the only village in the township of that name, is on the line of the Wabash Railroad. It has a population of about six hundred people and its site is on one of the highest and most healthful points in the southern part of the county. One of the branches of the Ambraw rises about half a mile to the west, flowing from a pronounced ridge, which enters the town from the north and runs across it to the southeast and upon which the village is built.

YANKEE RIDGE SETTLERS

The first settlers of the neighborhood were from New England, the majority of them coming in 1856. Among them were David and Lucius Eaton, with their families; George and E. W. Parker, Asa Gooding, Dennis Chapin and J. P. Whitmore. Because of the personnel of this New England colony and their place of settlement, the locality was called Yankee Ridge, and the village and, to a large extent, the entire township, assumed a distinctive character, as if a small section of New England had been set down in that part of the West.

The location of the village was doubtless influenced also by the fact that the only grove in this portion of the Ambraw valley was in the northeast quarter of Section 15. It was called Towhead and was particularly noticeable because of the absence of trees in the surrounding country. It was entered as early as 1837 by Philo Hale who figured that the Northern Cross Railroad would strike that landmark which could be plainly seen for many miles.

CLARK R. GRIGGS

Among the Yankees who came at a later date than the bulk of the New England colony was Clark R. Griggs, a Massachusetts boot and shoe manufacturer. In the spring of 1859 he purchased a farm on Yankee Ridge, a short distance north of Philo, but because of an accident by which his right hand was crushed in a corn sheller, he abandoned farming and moved to Urbana. He there became a merchant and land dealer, was elected to the Legislature in the late '60s, and, as told elsewhere, was influential in having the State University located at Urbana and in the projection of the Danville, Urbana, Bloomington & Pekin Railroad, now a portion of the Big Four system.

Village of Philo a Railroad Station

In 1858 the village of Philo was established as a station on the recently reorganized Great Western Railroad, which, after various changes, became a part of the eastern division of the Wabash, St. Louis & Pacific system, and in 1889 of the Wabash Railroad. Previous to the establishment of the Philo station, there had been no stopping place for trains between Sidney and Tolono, and the promoters of the village, who were the heirs of Philo Hale and named it accordingly, laid out a handsome park which became quite a feature of the place.

The Present Village

The present village has two grain elevators, of which the proprietors are J. C. Trost & Company and O'Neill & Plotner. It has also two substantial banks. The older of these, the Philo Exchange Bank, was established by the late E. B. Hazen, who continued at its head till his death. The other, the Commercial Bank, was established in 1902, with the late Isaac S. Raymond as president. It began business as a national bank, but surrendered its charter in 1910, and continues as a private bank. Its president is C. A. Daly.

Philo has four churches, as follows: The Methodist, Rev. D. L. Jeffers, pastor; Presbyterian, Rev. L. F. Cooper; Lutheran, Rev. A. J. Klindworth, and Catholic, Rev. D. K. Harrington. It has also lodges of the Masonic and Odd Fellows orders, and an auxiliary council of the Knights of Columbus.

Philo has also a well organized system of public schools, so that in respect to its agricultural surroundings and to its internal financial and commercial equipment, its educational, religious and social advantages, it enjoys exceptional attraction for lovers of a well-ordered and quiet community.

Ogden Township

Ogden is a narrow township, ten and a half miles from north to south and three and three-quarters, from east to west. Its surface is very level. The southern and central sections are watered by tributaries of the Salt Fork and Stoney creek, and the northwestern portion of the township lies in the valley of the Spoon River. The only natural timber lands were known as Bur Oak Grove toward the north end of the town, and Hickory Grove, a part of which lies on the western line.

Pioneer Settlers

The first settler was Hiram Rankin, who, about 1830, built a cabin in Hickory Grove, near the north side of the northeast quarter of Section 18. Mr. Rankin soon moved into St. Joseph Township and turned his crude improvements over to his friend, Thomas Richards, who established a pleasant and comfortable homestead for his large family, various members of which developed into leading men and women of the neighborhood.

Garrett Moore, the first surveyor of the county, improved a quarter section in Section 30, also along the western border, his property subsequently passing to John Chester. John Bailey, kept a hotel on the Danville road, and William G. Clark took up a farm in the southern part of the township, at a very early day, and Samuel McClugen and William Paris settled in the Bur Oak Grove, in the northern part. Milton Babb, Eugene P. Frederick, the Miles brothers and William Cherry also settled in the northern half of the town, and in more recent years a large German population occupied the Spoon River flats in the northwest corner. They are Lutherans and, as is customary, stanchly support their church and school.

Ogden Village

The station and village of Ogden owes its existence to the Indiana, Bloomington & Western Railroad, now a portion of the Big Four system, which was constructed through Champaign County in 1866. In 1905 the Chicago & Eastern Illinois cut across the western and northwestern sections of the township, and in Section 17, about a mile east of the German Lutheran settlement on the Spoon River flats, the railroad station of Royal was established. A grain elevator was built and other accommodations provided for the shipping of the produce raised in that section of the township.

The village of Ogden, with its population of over four hundred people, is also a convenient banking center for a large area of the country around. The Ogden Bank and the First National provide such conveniences. The latter was founded in April, 1900, with C. L. Van Doren as its president. A. H. Freese is now at its head. The capital of the First National is $30,000; surplus and undivided profits, $13,000; deposits, $170,000.

Ogden has Methodist and Christian churches, of which Rev. J. B. Martin and Rev. Cummins are the pastors respectively, and Masonic and Knights of Pythias lodges.

The village has had a newspaper almost continuously since 1885, when the Ogden Sun arose. J. B. Klegg soon changed its name to the Journal, and continued its publication until his death. It then passed to William Wampler, who conducted it until 1892, when he was succeeded by Frank Osborn, who published and edited it for about a year, or until the destruction of the office by fire.

In December, 1894, J. R. Watkins started the paper which now represents the interests of Ogden and the neighborhood, the Courier. In December, 1902, he sold to J. C. Kirby, who, in May of the following year disposed of the Courier to Dale Brothers, of the St. Joseph Record. It is owned and edited at present by Mrs. Della McPherren.

CHAPTER XXII

OTHER TOWNSHIPS, VILLAGES AND STATIONS

LUDLOW VILLAGE AND TOWNSHIP—ORIGINALLY, PERA—ABEL HARWOOD
AND THE TOWN—DILLSBURG—LEVERETT—SEYMOUR AND BOND-
VILLE—COMPROMISE TOWNSHIP—PENFIELD AND GIFFORD—FLAT-
VILLE—EAST BEND TOWNSHIP—ETHAN NEWCOM AND OTHER
SETTLERS—DEWEY.

Ludlow, on the main line of the Illinois Central in the northeastern
corner of the township by that name, is a village of about three hundred people, and is the largest center of population in the prosperous
township by that name. Both the village and the township occupy some
of the highest lands in Champaign County. The country is further noteworthy as being the watershed for the headwaters of various branches of
the Sangamon and the Salt and Middle forks of the Vermillion River.

ORIGINALLY PERA

Little land was entered within the township and virtually no
improvements had been made on the lands until after the building of
the Illinois Central in 1854. Pera station was then established as the
only stopping place on the line between Urbana to the south and Loda,
Iroquois County, to the north. For a time it was simply a railroad
station, but the town plat, after a few years, was sprinkled with a
number of residences, stores and other evidences of growth, and at one
time threatened to overreach Rantoul. It now has a good graded school,
a bank, elevator, several churches at or near the village, and is destined
for future growth. The township was originally called Pera, but when
Harwood was taken away from the original territory, both town and
village assumed the name by which they are now known.

The Illinois Central was completed to Pera in 1853, and a turntable
built at that point, which was moved to Urbana in 1854. The first
railroad agent was John Lucas, who died at Ludlow in 1870. The
first school was taught in the railroad freight house by Miss Mary
Wood in 1858. The first settlers, aside from the railroad men, were
Dr. Emmons, James D. Ludlow, B. F. Dye, Isaiah Estep, L. L. Hicks,

R. W. Claypool, A. Hunt and Seth Parsons. John W. Dodge, who afterward moved to Rantoul, and others who composed the Ohio Settlement, located in 1855-57. About the same time the Lewises, Walkers and other permanent settlers arrived. John Springsteen is recorded as the first blacksmith, John P. and Samuel Middlecoff as the pioneer merchants and M. Huffman as the first postmaster.

ABEL HARWOOD AND THE TOWN

The town of of Harwood to the east of Ludlow was named in honor

OLD-TIME RAIL FENCE

of Abel Harwood, one of the largest land owners in Champaign County, and a moneyed man who had foresight to improve all the land he purchased. His fine improvements in what is now the township of Newcomb, near the Mahomet line, which included the clearing of hundreds of acres of land, its scientific cultivation and the growing of eleven miles of hedges to replace unsightly and falling fences—such developments carried along by Mr. Harwood in the northwestern part of the county, aside from his standing as a legislator and a man, fully entitle him to the honor of naming a prosperous township.

Harwood, in its essential physical features, much resembles Ludlow. Settlers came slowly to its prairies and even after the building of the Illinois Central the people of the eastern part of Pera Township were not greatly accommodated, as they had to depend entirely upon either Rantoul or Pera station for the marketing of their products or transportation.

In the general order of their coming the following settled in Harwood Township: Jeremiah Day, on Section 30, in 1852; Jacob Huffman, Section 1, 1852; Michael Huffman, 1853, Section 3; he being the first justice of the peace in Pera Township; James Custer, Section 1, 1854; A. N. and William Leneve, Section 12, 1855; J. D. Ludlow, Section 7, about the same year, and the Crawfords, the Sopers, Dr. J. C. Maxwell, James Marlatt and the Claypools, 1855-56, in various sections. The first school was taught on Section 11 in a log hut which had previously served as a pre-emption shanty, in the year 1860, by Augustus S. Crawford.

DILLSBURG

The settlement of the township was very slow until 1865, when immigration was rapid for a time, but the development was not considered permanent until the Rantoul branch of the Illinois Central was pushed through four of its southern sections, in 1881, and Dillsburg was established as a station, as well as Gifford, just over the line in Compromise Township.

LEVERETT

Leverett is a station on the main line of the Illinois Central railroad, a few miles north of Champaign, which has become quite a grain center. A. J. Flatt, who owns and operates an elevator and a store at that point, has been at the head of its development for a number of years past. In 1894 he purchased the elevator business of B. C. Beach, replaced the former building with a large one in 1897, which, in turn, gave way to the elevator now operated, which cost $15,000 and has a capacity of 50,000 bushels. In 1910 Mr. Flatt received his son, Ross A. Flatt, into partnership.

Seymour and Bondville

Seymour and Bondville are stations and grain centers on the Illinois Central in Scott Township, in the western part of the county. There are elevators in both places, and Bondville has a good bank; so that the farmers and residents of quite a section of the country look upon them as their most convenient trading, shipping and banking centers.

Compromise Township

Compromise Township, in the northeastern part of the county, is, with Rantoul, its largest territorial division, comprising forty-eight sections or square miles. With the exception of a small wooded tract in the northeast corner known as Buck Grove, most of the lands are of the flat prairie variety. That section of the township is watered by Buck Creek of the Middle Fork. The exceptions to the general rule as to surface features of the township are in the extreme north and southeast, where there are several stretches of high and undulating lands.

As the lands of Compromise Township have been thoroughly drained, they are now admirably adapted to farming purposes, and the result is that there are few portions of the county where the homesteads present a more prosperous appearance, which are more generally rural and yet which are favored with better facilities for getting its products to market.

Penfield and Gifford

Penfield and Gifford, stations on the Illinois Central in the northern part of the township, have banking and elevator facilities. The Morse State Bank at Gifford was established in 1885 and incorporated in 1912. It has a capital of $25,000 and J. D. Morse is its active head. It may be added that they are also the centers of considerable religious activity. There are Methodist organizations at both places, under the pastorate of Rev. E. B. Williams, who resides at Gifford. Rev. William O'Brien is in charge of St. Lawrence's Catholic Church at Penfield, and Rev. Blackwell, of the United Brethren Church at the same place. Besides the Methodist Church at Gifford, are the Baptist Church, Rev. E. B. Williams, pastor, and the German Lutheran, Rev. F. Mutschwann. It is needless to say that the young people of Gifford and Penfield are provided with good schools, as well as religious and moral instruction.

33½

Flatville

Although entries of land and actual settlements in the vicinity of Buck Grove and Penfield were made seventy or eighty years ago, the northern part of the town did not develop until the Rantoul branch of the Central provided an outlet for the products of the farm, in 1881. Its building caused an increase of settlement throughout the township, and was especially encouraging to the large German colony in the southwestern sections. The lands there were noticeably low and flat, but fertile, and the industrious German farmers, with thorough cultivation and persistent drainage, made the country a garden spot. They also

TYPICAL WHEAT FIELD

secured the post-office of Flatville, which, although on no railroad line, is in a rural route and a great accommodation. A number of Lutheran churches and several good schools, both parochial and district, have been established, which add to the advantages of this prosperous section of Compromise Township. Rev. Ernest Moehl has been pastor of the German Evangelical Church since 1895, and is widely known and honored. The fine edifice of the society was dedicated in January, 1915.

East Bend Township

East Bend Township, in the northern part of the county, derives its name from the abrupt bend in the Sangamon River near the center of the town, which there assumes the shape of a partial parallelogram and is sharply deflected from a southeasterly to a southwesterly direction. Not far south of this remarkable bend of the river was the famous Newcom's Ford, at the crossing of the Sangamon by the old Danville and Fort Clark road.

ETHAN NEWCOM AND OTHER SETTLERS

It was named after Ethan Newcom, who came to the neighborhood in the early '30s and gave his name not only to the ford but to the township (plus the "b"). Newcom's Ford, which was also a favorite camping place for the old-time knights of the road, was almost midway between Fisher, which abuts into East Bend Township, and the station and settlement of Dewey.

It was in this neighborhood, in the timber fringe of the Sangamon, that Mr. Newcom, Franklin Dobson, the Devores and others first settled in 1837-40. Fifteen or twenty years afterward came such as Harmon Hilberry, Alfred Houston, Richard Chism, Benjamin Dolph, C. M. Knapp, Gardiner Sweet, Harvey Taylor and others, and, with the coming of the railroad, in the early '80s, the immigration was so large as to discourage the mention of individuals.

DEWEY

Dewey provides a large section of the eastern part of East Bend Township and of the western portion of Ludlow with elevator and bank accommodations, although Fisher to the west and Rantoul to the east are much larger centers and tend to circumscribe its activities. The two grain elevators at Dewey are owned by J. M. Jones Company and Hazen & Reuter. The Dewey Bank was founded in 1902. There is a good school, two churches—German Lutheran and Methodist—and quite a flourishing Odd Fellows Lodge.

CPSIA information can be obtained
at www.ICGtesting.com
Printed in the USA
LVOW13s1131260817

546464LV00009B/50/P